3/93

D0757617

Bronson M. Cutting

Senator Bronson M. Cutting, Santa Fe, New Mexico, ca. 1934. (Photograph by T. Harmon Parkhurst, Courtesy, Museum of New Mexico, Santa Fe, Neg. No. 51501.)

Richard Lowitt

—

BRONSON M. CUTTING

—

Progressive Politician

University of New Mexico Press   *Albuquerque*

Library of Congress Cataloging-in-Publication Data

Lowitt, Richard, 1922–
   Bronson M. Cutting : progressive politician / Richard Lowitt.
     p. cm.
   Includes bibliographical references and index.
   ISBN 0–8263–1347–7
    1. Cutting, Bronson M., 1888–1935   2. Legislators—United States—
Biography.   3. United States, Congress. Senate—Biography.
4. Progressivism (United States politics)   5. New Mexico—Politics
and government—1848–1950   I. Title.
E748.C983L68   1992
978.9'052'092—dc20
[B]
92–15345
CIP

For Peter, Marilyn, and Nicholas Lowitt
and Matthew Bannister

CONTENTS

CONTENTS

PREFACE

I was a graduate student at Columbia University when I first heard of Bronson Cutting. Henry Steele Commager, it was reputed, was contemplating a biography. At that time I thought that the prestigious Cutting Fellowships awarded graduate students honored his memory. It was only in the course of preparing this biography that I learned that his father, William Bayard Cutting, was the person in whose memory the fellowships were endowed. He next came to my attention in the course of preparing my biography of George W. Norris. The venerable Nebraska senator was attracted to his junior colleague by Cutting's courage and ability in presenting and fighting for causes and issues he deemed important. In most instances Norris and other progressive senators agreed. Norris and three other senators walked out of the chamber when Cutting's successor, the man who contested his election victory with the backing of the Roosevelt administration, was sworn in following his tragic death in 1935. Cutting's mother presented Norris with his watch as a token of her son's esteem, and Norris delivered a lecture in a series designed to honor his memory.

I now stored in my mind the name of Bronson Cutting as a person whose career might well be worth examining as a progressive Republican who deserted his party, along with Norris, Hiram Johnson, and Robert M. La Follette, to support Franklin Roosevelt in 1932 and his New Deal. At that time I had no insight into Cutting's opposition to the New Deal and the reasons for the administration's support of his opponent in 1934.

After completing *The New Deal in the West* in 1984, I began to give serious consideration to preparing a biography of Bronson Cutting. I had dipped into his papers in the course of examining material pertaining to the impact of New Deal programs in New Mexico and my interest was aroused. As I immersed myself in researching his career, the more excited I became. I thought that Cutting's significance resided in his career as a United States senator, as a progressive Republican, at a critical period in twentieth-century American history at the depth of the Great Depression and at the onset of the New Deal.

A wealthy New Yorker, an outstanding student at Groton and Harvard, Cutting went to New Mexico to regain his health and stayed on. He became the publisher of the oldest newspaper in the state, served in the war, and

PREFACE

returned to New Mexico where he became involved in politics, usually in opposition, and in December 1927 was appointed to fill the unexpired term of the recently deceased senior United States senator. I assumed, as I began my research, that all of this would be the necessary and brief background to the significant portion of the biography.

Once I became involved with my research my perception quickly changed. New Mexico during its first two decades as a state has not been well re-searched. Admirable studies exist on the territorial period of its history and as a part of the Spanish and Mexican empires as well. But I could find only a handful of studies to guide me through the political thickets abounding during these decades. Nevertheless, I quickly discerned that New Mexico was just as important and possibly even more important to my biography than his service in the Congress. What made it so? The presence of a large Hispanic population, a majority during these decades, whose plight in many ways was comparable to that of sharecroppers in the South. Peonage was not unknown in both the state and the region. In the period prior to the New Deal, Cutting was if not the lone then certainly the most prominent Anglo seeking to bring Hispanic voters into the mainstream of the political process as independent citizens without ties to either a patron or a political boss. In the fluid and tempestuous New Mexico political climate characterized by intense factionalism, Cutting was able to steer a course through the political thickets with an informal machine of his own based on the support he received from Hispanic voters and veterans organized in the American Legion. Later he won the support of labor in New Mexico as well.

Cutting's fight in New Mexico was essentially for good government. Though as a United States senator he moved beyond this concern and began to probe economic reform issues, he recognized that a modicum of efficiency, honesty and integrity was necessary before anything else could be accom-plished in a state, rich in natural resources, that exported the products of its soils, where speculation and defining complex land titles was an unending process and where a community oriented way of life was being continually impaired by an intruding market economy dominated by Anglos little con-cerned with the plight of the Hispanic majority, the primary victim of this process. Cutting, like Edmund Burke before him, recognized that good government was the necessary first step in achieving any sort of reform or structural change. His model, however, was not Burke. His family had long been engaged in battling for good government in New York City. In addi-tion, on a more limited scale, his father and his uncle promoted the cause of low-cost housing. They served as Cutting's model during his early years in

New Mexico, as did Theodore Roosevelt, a close family friend. And as it turned out, the situation in New Mexico, a truly exceptional one, receives more space in my biography than does his service in the United States Senate.

In Washington, too, the issues that attracted Cutting's attention were primarily ones to improve government. His successful battle to stop customs officials from arbitrarily deciding what books and objets d'art could or could not enter the country, his fight to preserve pensions for veterans, particularly disabled ones, his co-sponsoring a bill calling for Philippine independence all fall within the scope of a traditional concern for an efficient government that fulfills its commitments with care and integrity.

It was the depression crisis that broadened his perceptions and led to his disillusionment with both Herbert Hoover and Franklin Roosevelt. The plight of desperate people became his primary concern.

As Cutting saw it, the road to recovery necessitated a shift in emphasis away from production toward consumption. If purchasing power could be broadly extended to all sectors of the population, then it would be possible to achieve a balance between supply and demand and restore the American economy to a viable base. In the triad of relief, recovery, and reform, Cutting emphasized recovery. Reform was to be considered to the extent that it facilitated a broad extension of purchasing power. This concern was basic to his criticism of both Hoover and Roosevelt: Hoover because of his inaction and his view that if production could be stimulated, jobs would follow; Roosevelt because he seemingly prized economy in the First Hundred Days and did not focus on the real problem as Cutting defined it. Cutting died in 1935 before Congress considered major banking legislation in which he was vitally interested. He favored, but never fully developed, a proposal for governmental operation of the banking system. In short, Cutting's progressivism, as expressed in the causes that concerned him, did not venture very far from the traditional mold.

The issue that posed the greatest challenge to me, one that I could not ignore and yet do not believe worthy of undue attention, is the question of Cutting's purported homosexuality. Human sexuality is a topic to which, as a historian, I have devoted little scholarly attention. Conversation and the scholarly reading I engaged in yielded no insights that I could apply to Cutting. Besides, I am still not clear in my own mind how Cutting's sexuality could provide an explanation for the way he voted or the causes he espoused. Other more reasonable explanations can be provided. The one book, a series of letters that gave me some insight into the question, I discovered on my own and it helped me to lean toward the view that Cutting was not gay. *Rat &*

PREFACE

The Devil: Journal Letters of F.O. Matthiessen and Russell Cheney, edited by Louis Hyde, delineates a meaningful, tender and lasting relationship between two mature individuals with whom Cutting was acquainted.

I decided to offer my own observations based on what my research notes yielded. Cutting, of course, knew many gay people. In Santa Fe during the 1920s it was almost impossible not to know some such individuals. Yet, as I try to suggest, I have found no direct evidence to conclude that Cutting was a homosexual and can suggest some reasons why he was not. I recognize, of course, that the issue is one of considerable public interest and that I can provide only an impression, given the limited information available in the Cutting and other papers.

ACKNOWLEDGMENTS

In the course of preparing this biography I examined manuscript collections in several repositories, and I have incurred numerous obligations to the many thoughtful and courteous librarians and archivists who assisted my efforts. First, however, I should mention two scholars who most graciously turned over to me their notes on Bronson Cutting. Both Harry Jeffery at California State University, Fullerton, and the late David Shannon at the University of Virginia intended to pursue their initial probing into Cutting's career upon completion of their current projects. I am pleased to thank them here and to note that such generosity and cooperation among scholars, while not unknown, is increasingly rare.

At the Library of Congress, David Wigdor, now assistant chief of the Manuscript Division and previously in charge of twentieth century collections, provided suggestions as to collections that I might examine along with friendship and hospitality that makes visiting the Manuscript Division a continual pleasure. The staff of the division, the people behind the desk who handle requests and offer suggestions to facilitate research, help to make their division one of the most satisfactory places I have engaged in research.

The other repository that for me rivals the Manuscript Division is located in the Coronado Room, housing Special Collections, in the library at the University of New Mexico. Dr. William Tydeman and his staff, most notably Terry Gugliotta, besides meeting all my requests, enhanced my research by suggesting numerous collections that yielded nuggets of information I otherwise would never have retrieved. I came to the Coronado Room a total stranger; I left with feelings of warm friendship for the entire staff. Upon leaving I was presented with an outstanding reader award, a University of New Mexico coffee mug that I cherish and still use.

While I do not recall the names of all the librarians and archivists at other repositories who provided assistance, several do stand out and should be mentioned: Frances M. Seeber at the Franklin D. Roosevelt Library, Dwight Miller at the Herbert Hoover Presidential Library, Peter Blodgett at the Henry E. Huntington Library, and Orlando Romero at the Museum of New Mexico. To these and all the others I extend my thanks. I am most grateful.

There are others who through their hospitality, assistance, and friendship eased my way while researching in what for me were new repositories. In

ACKNOWLEDGMENTS

Albuquerque I can mention Howard Rabinowitz, Ferenc and Margaret Connell Szasz and Paul Hutton. Here too I met Sandra Schakel, Michael and Cindy Secor Welsh, all engaged in research on New Mexico topics that related to my project. Through extensive conversations they helped broaden my understanding. At the Huntington Library both Martin Ridge and Robert L. Middlekauf, then the director, helped make my stay a most pleasant one.

Grants from the National Endowment for the Humanities, the American Philosophical Society, the Franklin and Eleanor Roosevelt Foundation, the Huntington Library, the Research Council at Iowa State University, and a Faculty Improvement Leave from Iowa State University provided some of the wherewithal necessary to research this biography. At Iowa State University Carole Kennedy, the History Department secretary, provided assistance that allowed me more time for scholarly endeavors. Audrey Burton, the department manuscript typist at Iowa State University, typed the initial version of the manuscript from my pencilled draft. Amy Forwoodson at the University of Oklahoma prepared the final version.

This volume is dedicated once again to my wife, Suzanne, my most ardent supporter and severest critic, and to our grandchildren Matthew Bannister and Nicholas Lowitt.

IMAGES AND SHADOWS

Bronson Cutting, born in 1888, was enveloped in the cocoon of a warm, loving and richly endowed family life. He was of the very rich and therefore very different in his upbringing from that of most Americans at that or any other time. His father, William Bayard Cutting, tall and well-favored, endowed with a natural, gracious and spontaneous charm, was a great lover of the country and of country sports, although his lot was cast in the city. Consequently, as his young family grew up, it enjoyed the best of both city and country life.

There were four children. William Bayard, the oldest, was born in New York City on June 13, 1878. He was followed by Justine Bayard whose birth was in Morristown, New Jersey on August 7, 1879. From an early age, she exhibited a great interest in music, eventually becoming a leading authority on liturgical Gregorian chants. Almost a decade later, on June 23, 1888, came Bronson Murray, born at Westbrook, the family home at Oakdale, Long Island. Olivia Bayard was born four years later on September 5, 1892, also at the family estate. Besides Westbrook, the Cuttings resided in a brownstone mansion on Seventy-second Street off Madison Avenue.

Home to the Cuttings was their country house, Westbrook, constructed in 1886. William Bayard Cutting had purchased the 931-acre estate from George Loralliard two years before. Facing the Connetquot River, the family property boasted spacious grounds, winding paths, stately trees and a small farm. Located just northeast of the estate was the South Side Sportsmen's Club, which William Cutting frequented as a member to fish with his friends and which undoubtedly attracted him to the area. Boating and hunting were his favorite recreational activities, and he was able to indulge in both while at Westbrook.

The family mansion was spacious and comfortable. Charles C. Haight, the architect, drew up elaborate plans that included wood paneling, tall ceilings, the main stairway and carved wood decorations. Many of the ornamental fittings were imported from England. Numerous other antique items, such as the dining-room fireplace, were acquired in Europe. The large rooms were warm in the winter and cool in the summer. The paneled "gentleman's library" was fully stocked with classics in stately calf bindings but also with more up-to-date English authors.

Additional buildings graced the Cutting estate. An annex to house guests and to provide play room for the children was finished in the early 1890s. A gatehouse, a log cabin or hunting lodge, a greenhouse, a workmen's cottage, and several maintenance buildings helped to finish the property. Two other structures were a boathouse and carriage house. When the Cuttings bought automobiles, they converted the latter into a garage.

A secure, somewhat complacent, *haute bourgeoisie* society engulfed the Cutting children, emphasizing good manners and a reverence for the best tradition of spoken English. But, thanks to Westbrook, the environment was not confining. Here, they could roam on foot, on pony, or by carriage the vast estate, which is now an arboretum dedicated in trust to the people of New York State and maintained by the Long Island State Park and Recreation Commission. The estate was partially developed in accordance with plans suggested by Frederick Law Olmsted. There was a notable pinetum for conifers native to other regions throughout the world and ponds and open spaces for picnics, croquet and tennis. With the Connetquot River emptying into Great South Bay fronting the estate, there was ample opportunity for canoeing, fishing and sailing. In 1892 a boat, the *Justine,* was built for the family to enjoy sailing among the bays of Long Island's South Shore, and the following year, William Bayard Cutting ordered a smaller boat for his children.

The Cuttings entertained extensively at Westbrook. The children mingled with the guests and participated in many of the activities. Their domestic needs were attended by a fourteen-person staff that included a coachman and several grooms who serviced the stables. Another group of employees with whom the children became acquainted was the gardens and grounds crew. With the dairymen and a superintendent of the entire estate, it totaled eighteen men. The staff moved with the family to the townhouse, where in addition, an outdoor night watchman, shared by several families on the block, patrolled the neighborhood and checked the houses from ten in the evening until early the following day.

The family was part of what Louis Auchincloss called the Brownstone Aristocracy in his study of Edith Wharton, a friend of the Cuttings. All the advantages afforded by birth—education, money, environment and family connections—would be available to the Cutting children with the understanding that wealth entailed responsibility. Bronson Cutting's ancestry offers an insight into the components leading to membership in the Brownstone Aristocracy.

He came from a distinguished lineage. The first Cutting came to America in 1718 as an indentured servant, a redemptioner who bound himself to a sea captain for service to a Virginia planter. Leonard Cutting (1724–1794) of Great Yarmouth in Norfolk was twenty-three when he embarked for the New World. He was a graduate of Eton and Pembroke College, Cambridge, with limited prospects. Six years later, he became a tutor of Greek and Latin at King's College in the Province of New York. He was awarded the honorary degree, master of arts, in 1758. While at King's College, he pursued a course of religious studies. In 1763, he returned to England and was ordained in the Anglican church.

The following year, the Reverend Leonard Cutting returned to America and served churches in New Jersey until 1766 when he left to become Rector of St. George's Church at Hempstead, Long Island. To supplement his income, he continued the classical school his predecessor had begun. In Hempstead, he met and married Ann Frances Pintard, the daughter of a New York merchant of Huguenot descent.

During the Revolutionary War, Cutting remained loyal to the Crown. After the war, he left Hempstead for churches first in Maryland and then in North Carolina. Returning to New York in 1792, he was appointed to the House of Bishops following the first convention of the Episcopal Church in America. He died two years later.

His elder son, William Cutting (1773–1820), became a prominent New York lawyer and was one of the earliest graduates of Columbia College in the class of 1793. He married Gertrude, one of the three daughters of Walter Livingston and Cornelia Schuyler. Another daughter, Harriet, married Robert Fulton. The two brothers-in-law worked together in the early development of steam navigation and the establishment of a ferry between Brooklyn and New York. After Fulton's death in 1815, Cutting became an executor and trustee of his estate. In 1849 one of his and Gertrude's sons named Fulton (1814–1875) married Elise Justine, a daughter of Robert Bayard, also of Huguenot extraction, and Elizabeth McEvers, his wife. Following his wife's death in 1852, Fulton Cutting moved to France, leaving his two sons to be raised in Edgewater, New Jersey, by their maternal grandparents Robert and Elizabeth Bayard.

His elder son, born in New York City on January 12, 1850, was Bronson's father. William Bayard Cutting, like his father and grandfather before him, graduated from Columbia College, a member of the class of 1869, at little more than nineteen years of age. He then entered Columbia Law School, receiving a bachelor of laws (LL.B.) two years later, in 1871, and a master of arts from the college the following year. In 1880, he became a trustee of Columbia College, a post he held for the rest of his life.

CHAPTER 1

Bronson's mother, Olivia Peyton Murray, was born in LaSalle County, Illinois, on September 19, 1855, the second daughter of Bronson and Ann Eliza (Peyton) Murray. Her great-grandfather arrived from England in 1770. He first settled in New England but later moved to New York City. Her father, a rigid Presbyterian reared in Jamaica, Long Island, was an engineer who by the time Olivia was of school age, had settled in Westchester County. She attended private schools in New York City. Spending the summer of 1867 in North Conway, New Hampshire, eleven-year-old Olivia had the good fortune to join two Harvard undergraduates, John Chipman Gray and Oliver Wendell Holmes, as well as Henry James and a young lady in climbing Mount Kearsarge. Olivia was captivated by the captain who acted as her guide and regaled her with stories.[1] She had her first glimpse of her future husband two years later when he delivered the valedictorian address at his commencement exercises in 1869. Shortly thereafter, he came to visit her older sister and was captivated by Olivia. He waited seven years until she came of age before marrying her on April 26, 1877.

At the time of his marriage, William Bayard Cutting was still living with his maternal grandparents in Edgewater, New Jersey. The young couple remained with them in Edgewater until they found and rented a modest house of their own in the city on Twenty-fourth Street. Cutting never practiced law. In 1871, he gave up his idea of a legal career to assist his grandfather in the reorganization and development of the St. Louis, Alton, and Terre Haute Railroad. Robert Bayard yielded the presidency to his grandson, William Bayard Cutting, and retired in 1878. Cutting, age twenty-eight, was president until 1885 when he sold the road, which then became part of the Illinois Central system, for which he had served as a director prior to the sale. He later served as a director of the Southern Pacific, Norfolk and Southern, and Santa Fe railroads, and became interested in railroad development in Florida. After 1885, however, he principally invested on his own behalf and with his brother, R. Fulton Cutting, in various enterprises, profitable and philanthropic, in New York City and throughout the nation.

He played a role in enhancing the mercantile development of the port of New York. In conjunction with others, he helped to secure and develop a large tract of land in south Brooklyn. Following in the footsteps of his paternal grandfather, Cutting established a ferry route to Brooklyn and connected the area by railroad with other lines on Long Island. Finally, he lobbied the Corps of Engineers to improve the Bay Ridge Channel leading from deep water along the south Brooklyn pier-head lines, thereby making possible the growth of the south Brooklyn waterfront.

Along with one of his associates, John W. Ambrose, Cutting lobbied Congress to secure the dredging of a new channel to the Atlantic through the shoals extending from Coney Island to Sandy Hook. This new channel, the Ambrose Channel, proved of inestimable value to the port of New York. His role in further developing the port was recognized with his election by fellow merchants as a vice-president of the New York Chamber of Commerce. In addition he served as a director of banks and insurance and trust companies, as well as other corporations. In 1899, with his brother, he helped form the American Beet Sugar Company, which became an important segment of the American sugar industry.

Business, however, was not William Bayard Cutting's real passion. He devoted considerable energies to philanthropy, cultural progress and civic betterment. Among others, he served as a trustee of the Children's Aid Society and a director of the New York Botanical Garden, the Metropolitan Opera Company, the American Museum of Natural History and the Metropolitan Museum of Art. He was also a member of the Board of Domestic and Foreign Missions of the Protestant Episcopal Church and a trustee of its General Theological Seminary. From 1883 until his death, he was sent as a lay deputy from New York to every General Convention of the church. Shortly before his death, he made a generous contribution toward the building of a synod hall in connection with the Cathedral of St. John the Divine.

As a moral reformer, along with his brother, R. Fulton Cutting, he tried to improve the quality of life among the poor of his native city through better housing. In 1879, William Bayard Cutting, his brother and another associate purchased Gotham Court, an area of run-down tenements. They upgraded them through extensive renovation and provided efficient management.[2] The following year, Cutting organized the Improved Dwellings Association, the forerunner of several similar organizations, to provide housing facilities for wage earners and to demonstrate that such ventures could be profitable.[3] He was its president until 1895, when he became a trustee for its successor, the City and Suburban Homes Company, presided over by his brother.

One group of buildings constructed by the Improved Dwellings Association in lower Manhattan, on Fourteenth Street and Avenue A, was known as the Cutting Buildings. A model apartment house, still standing on East Seventy-ninth Street, contains a plaque near the entrance dedicated to the memory of William Bayard Cutting. Throughout his life, he actively sought to improve housing conditions.

His wife, Olivia, reared a family, oversaw two homes and still found time for philanthropic and civic work. In 1872, before her marriage, she was a founder of the Monday Sewing Class in the city. She helped organize in 1881 the first women's auxiliary of the Protestant Episcopal Church in New York City. She was also an active member of a Thursday Evening Club, a literary club.

William Bayard Cutting was a devout admirer of Abraham Lincoln and stood in the reform wing of the Republican party. He found little to adulate in the "Easy Boss," Thomas C. Platt, who dominated Republican politics in both New York state and city at the end of the century, until Theodore Roosevelt became governor in 1898. Cutting strongly endorsed the fusion candidacy of William L. Strong, nominally a Republican, for mayor in 1895. Upon his election, Strong reciprocated and appointed Cutting to the municipal civil service commission. He made Theodore Roosevelt police commissioner.

Fusion politics made sense to William Bayard Cutting and even more so to his brother. R. Fulton Cutting became the leading figure in the Citizens Union created in 1897, a nonpartisan organization seeking to promote both good government and municipal reform in New York City. As Yankee Protestants, the Cutting brothers and others like them sought disinterested public service, thereby making them hostile to government by partisan political organizations. Appointments to municipal posts, they believed, should be based on fitness and character and not on service to a political party. Government, in their view, should be accountable to the electorate and not to a political organization directed by a boss wielding patronage.

The Cutting brothers and others involved in reforming New York City's government recognized that Tammany Hall could be set aside by a coalition of Republicans, independent Democrats, and dissatisfied Tammany regulars, if it held together. These fusion efforts were essentially the creations of men of wealth and standing. Their focus was on civic virtue and only to a limited extent on social melioration. They exhibited an almost negligible concern for economic reform. However, these men of the upper class recognized the necessity of seeking support from as broad a constituency as possible. The Citizens Union made considerable efforts to develop support in the major ethnic communities in greater New York and published pamphlets in German, Italian and Yiddish.

Although nominally Republicans, the Cutting brothers were more progressive than their party was. As fusionists, they sought to separate municipal from state and national politics. They endorsed a wide range of municipal reforms that would respond to the needs and reflect the aspirations of more than the highly educated and wealthy segments of the population. They recognized the necessity of employing government as an instrument for reform, and they never wavered in their self-confident belief in the necessity and legitimacy of rule by a cultivated, moral, social and economic elite. Almost two decades later, their views were reflected in the emerging career of their son and nephew, Bronson Cutting, as he began to participate in the public affairs of his adopted state, New Mexico.

The first mention of Bronson in available documents occurred when he was less than two years old. His brother, age eleven, wrote to his mother in Florida, exclaiming, "I must tell you about Bronson. Yesterday afternoon he began to walk." William Bayard, Jr. then related all the details of his brother's accomplishment. Bronson also wanted to write a letter to "Dear Mamma" and to "Sunbeams," a term his brother said Bronson was "in the habit of saying as soon as Papa enters the room." Apparently, he was a very happy and affectionate child. His brother observed him singing to and hugging one of the maids, staring at a picture of his father and muttering, "Papa picture," carrying a stool around a room, requesting that the letters his mother sent be read to him again and again and applauding various constructions he had made with his blocks while singing to himself. When asked why his parents did not come to play with him, he replied, "Bronson go to see them." These comments of an older brother point to a warm, loving and caring family environment and also suggest a precocious child.[4]

Olivia Cutting kept a diary on her own and her family's activities, but in the typescript on deposit in her son's papers, there are few entries pertaining to Bronson prior to his entering Groton in 1901. Presumably he accompanied his parents to Europe to spend the winter of 1889–1890 in Cannes. He returned as a thirteen-year-old boy in 1901. He attended the wedding of his brother serving as a private secretary to the American ambassador to Great Britain, Joseph Hodges Choate, and then that of his sister later in the same year. William Bayard Cutting, Jr. married Lady Sybil Cuffe on April 19, 1901, in a wedding that undoubtedly was a high point of the social season in London. His bride was a member of the Anglo-Irish nobility.[5] Much less is known about Justine's marriage to George Cabot Ward. It was an unhappy one and soon became a marriage in name only, for they spent most of their lives apart from one another.

Possibly more exciting to the young Bronson than his European travels was the return in 1898 of the Rough Riders from their triumphs in Cuba to Montauk Point on Long Island. The hospitality at Westbrook was extended to some of the officers. The visit of the Rough Riders provided Bronson with his first exposure to military life. No direct evidence suggests that he was aware of the pitiful condition of some of the returning soldiers. If so, their plight must have made a deep impression on him, because as an adult, the rights of war veterans became an abiding concern. While his father had some doubts about American expansionism, William Bayard Cutting and later Bronson never lost their regard for Theodore Roosevelt.[6]

But there was a dark side to his seemingly idyllic existence. Although these were joyous times for the children both at Westbrook and in the city, there was also an increasingly oppressive air about their homes as they grew older. For one thing, William Bayard Cutting suffered from gout and heart disease and was continually concerned about his health. This preoccupation with physical condition and comfort soon affected the ordering of the children's lives. Morning walks, glasses of creamy milk from the prize herd of Jerseys at Westbrook, afternoon naps, proper light for reading—all were outward signs of inner apprehensions. Gradually as the children, except possibly Olivia, the youngest, matured, they all sooner or later came to feel repressed. Despite, or more likely because of their luxurious surroundings, they became so suffocated by the unrelenting and ever-intruding care and solicitation for their daily needs that three of the four Cutting children strove as the opportunities presented themselves to carve out independent careers that would free them of the cloying atmosphere of the Madison Avenue brownstone and the Westbrook country estate.[7]

Bronson began his formal education at private schools in New York City. In 1899 his parents enrolled him in a private academy, Miss Vinton's School, at Pomfret Centre, Connecticut. In early October, after depositing Bronson at school, his father confessed to Bayard that it was "pretty tough" on Bronson who did not readily make friends and that he especially disliked the two or three boys he knew. Bronson, he said, was "almost repellent of social advances" because, his father suggested, "of a lack of confidence in his own qualities, particularly on the physical side, and of a constitutional retentiveness which makes it impossible for him to open himself freely to anyone—not even his father and mother." His father understood that some of these traits, evident to close observers in later years, would handicap a homesick eleven-year-old boy when they were added to "a sensitiveness of an unusual kind."

Bronson, however, was determined to "stick it out" at Pomfret, believing the experience would make him stronger. Moreover, he developed an avid interest in football. His brother strongly advised him to try out for the team. Bronson thought "it part of his duty to do so." The fact that he had so few boys to play with when he was at home, his father thought, "might bring him around all right," provided he could make friends and participate in the various school activities. William Bayard Cutting cautioned his older son about writing Bronson. He wrote, "Anything you say to him takes deep hold and is not treated by him as casual." Young Bronson was "conscientious to a fault in following directions."

While his father considered Bronson's character very beautiful, he recognized in it "undeniable possibilities of unhappiness." He was convinced that Bronson was determined to remain at the school "even under circumstances that would justify his coming home." Only his brother could convey to him the impression that leaving the school would be no disgrace. Stressing this last point, William Bayard Cutting noted that Bronson had "shown some signs of nervousness lately by slight facial twitchings," and should they increase, "the doctor will insist on his removal from school."[8] Whether Bronson finished the term at Miss Vinton's School in Pomfret Centre is unknown. An inherent modesty verging on shyness, a natural reticence, difficulty in forming class friendships and concern about pleasing his parents by respecting their views and especially those of his brother, helped develop in Bronson a tolerance and respect for the views of others and a reluctance to express his own. He was a private, self-contained eleven year old, and as such he always formed close personal attachments with difficulty. Groton and Harvard would help mask in Bronson what William Bayard Cutting so clearly perceived. Both would also allow Bronson opportunities to grow intellectually and to indicate his inherent brilliance. But here, too, he would have difficulty. He would be following the path trod by an equally brilliant brother who possessed an equally attractive but better balanced identity.

CHAPTER 2

GROTON AND HARVARD

The school that thirteen-year-old Bronson Cutting entered in September of 1901 was located on an attractive ninety acres near the town of Groton, Massachusetts, thirty-four miles from Boston. The institution opened its doors on October 15, 1884, with an entering class of twenty-seven boys. Parents or guardians were annually charged five hundred dollars for the tuition and board of their sons. Groton was not a church school, nor was it governed by a religious body. Students nevertheless were required to attend chapel and were exposed to the inspired principles of the Protestant Episcopal Church under the ever watchful eye and guidance of the headmaster, Endicott Peabody, an Episcopal clergyman and one of the more influential schoolmen in American history. While John Dewey was seeking to make education meaningful to youngsters in a modernizing urban democracy, Peabody was striving to educate the children both of the "new rich" and of established wealth and social prominence for leadership in the emerging gigantic corporations, in financial institutions, and in the dominant professions of the public and private sectors.

Franklin Roosevelt had entered Groton in 1896. While Roosevelt's attendance would mean much to Bronson Cutting in later years, far more meaningful at the time was the record that his brother, Bayard, established several years earlier. An outstanding scholar, Bayard edited the school paper, served as vice-president of the debating society, and played both baseball and the bass violin. His successful career at Groton helped pave the way for Bronson, but it also provided a terrible burden, for he could never rival or emulate Bayard's success in the arena that would assure both respect and popularity, namely, the athletic field. Whatever success Bronson gained at Groton, and it was considerable, would be won as a scholar and not as an athlete.

Groton was committed to a society governed by an aristocratic elite and enforced a rigorous, ordered curriculum cast in a Victorian or neo-Anglican mode. The goal of the school was to mold future leaders, who would be friendly, frank, controlled and, above all, polite and forgiving. Rector Peabody incessantly preached to Groton teenagers service to church, fellow men and country for more than half a century. At the same time, he declared that each boy must live his own life. He was unsympathetic toward any student who felt sorry for himself. Groton was a little world created and dominated by the rector who had an absolute certainty of right and wrong in the order of the universe.

To mold a well-rounded young gentleman, Groton emphasized more than the heavily classical curriculum, which was rooted in the Middle Ages. The school program stressed extensive relations between students and faculty, including the headmaster. Students were required to attend religious services at the chapel and supper and dinner at the dining hall. They were expected to participate in the gymnasium and to compete on the athletic field. All of these compulsory activities were critical to bonding. Late afternoons were devoted to the athletic program, the main travelled road to personal prestige and glory among students and masters at Groton. Bayard Cutting had excelled in Groton sports. Bronson is remarkable for achieving respect and popularity at Groton and Harvard and later in New Mexico in spite of his average athletic ability. Dressing in a stiff collar and patent leather dress shoes, all students attended supper, evening chapel and a study period. The day ended with the ritual good-night visit to the home of Rector and Mrs. Peabody where each boy filed past to shake hands and be recognized.[1]

Such was the regimen pursued by Bronson Cutting, who entered Groton in the second form and graduated five years later in June 1906. How he took to the daily routine and Spartan existence is unknown, but that he was an outstanding student is well documented from available sources. During his years at the school, Cutting continually ranked first in his form, winning in addition the Latin prize while in both the fourth and fifth forms. He was the first fourth form boy to achieve that distinction.

Thirty years later, his fellow students would remember his distinguished scholastic record. One recalled it as the highest achieved by any boy who had been at Groton up to that time. "Whenever there was a difficult question to be decided by the prefects," his classmate said, "everyone always wanted to know what Bronson's point of view was, and his judgment was always excellent." When a master was called from the room, Cutting would conduct the class in his absence, "and things would go along as smoothly as if the Master was in charge." He was liked and respected by his classmates in part, his classmate recalled, because "he did not look down intellectually upon any of his contemporaries but was ready with his friendship to all who gave him any chance."

That he had a frail physique, was shy and reserved and was not good at athletics of any kind was recalled by two of his Groton peers. By the time he entered the fifth form, Cutting was known as "Twig" to his classmates. How he earned the nickname or what it signified is not known. In the sixth form, his last year at the institution, Cutting became a prefect, one of eight or ten boys whom the rector relied on to enforce discipline. His new authority possibly impaired his popularity. Cutting was a reticent, studious boy, and in no way could he compete with the record of his brother, "who was very much more gregarious and a much better athlete," recalled a classmate in 1937. Against those odds, however, Bronson did make his own way and established his own niche at Groton.

Brief entries in Kermit Roosevelt's diary indicate that Cutting did not devote all of his time to his studies and that he was involved in most aspects of life at Groton. In January 1906, while on an extended canoe trip involving two portages, Kermit and three of his friends—all Groton students—met Cutting and a friend hiking in the woods. To help them make a fire, Roosevelt stepped out of the canoe and got soaked. Five days later, "Dickson, Morgan and I debated against Cutting, Whitridge and Morgan on whether there should be a sea level lock canal at Panama." Kermit's team, following in the footsteps of his father's success in "taking Panama" in 1903, won the debate. In February, after viewing "Mr. Baxter's Wonderful Invention," a play staged by the sixth form, Kermit noted that "Bronson Cutting, George Martin, and Morton Prince were very good." In March, he mentioned Cutting among a host of students confirmed by Bishop William Lawrence.[2]

When Cutting was fourteen-years-old and in the third form, he read a twelve-volume edition of Henry Hart Milman's *History of Latin Christianity* for fun. His feat generated much interest at the time and was recalled decades later by former students. Earlier in the previous year, his first at Groton, when the rector at chapel read out Cutting's first month's marks, they were so close to perfection that students emitted gasps and whispered exclamations. George Biddle, present at the time, recalled that "all eyes turned on the new boy" who was huddled among his classmates. He was "gray-faced, spotted, sparrow boned, a mere shell of a human being."

In the sixth form, his last year at Groton, he became editor-in-chief of the school paper and manager of the football team, gaining satisfaction and approbation he had never previously experienced. Years later, his mother told George Biddle that Bronson was "so delicate that he gave the impression of a cripple." When he became editor of the *Grotonian,* he wrote her, "You may not know it, but I believe today that I am the happiest human being in America."[3]

On the last report his parents received of his academic progress at Groton, Bronson still ranked first in his class. The rector remarked, "I hope and believe that he will win even greater laurels at college than he has won at the school."[4] Bronson's accomplishments were noted in the *New York Herald*. In award ceremonies, he took six prizes and received a *magna cum laude* diploma. As in the past, he was awarded the form prize. Two others were for outstanding marks in English, and two more were for debating. A final one was for reading aloud, indicating that by his final year he was no longer the timid soul, awed by his surroundings, whom George Biddle recalled. Further evidence to this effect was his participation in the sixth form play. Cutting played the part of a leading lady "with great intelligence and effect." In addition, during his last year at Groton, he also taught Sunday school in a nearby mission on the Boston road.[5]

Following his triumphant graduation from Groton, Bronson sailed with his mother and younger sister, Olivia, on the *St. Louis* for a European vacation. His father, who did not attend class day, had sailed earlier for the cure at Aix-en-Provence and would later join the family at St. Moritz, Switzerland. In France, among other things, Bronson visited the Louvre and toured the chateaux country. The end of July found the family at St. Moritz where Bronson and his brother, with the help of an accomplished guide, went mountain climbing. They spent a week in the Swiss and Austrian Alps. Then on August 22, Bronson and his father started in a carriage for a brief tour of Lombardy, Italy.

For the rest of the stay in Switzerland, eighteen-year-old Bronson devoted himself to mountain climbing instead of playing tennis and attending afternoon teas and formal evening dinners. On the first of September, Bronson and the ladies in his family boarded the night train for Paris. In the French capital, Bronson spent most of his time sight-seeing. From France, they departed for London where they visited and lunched with Ambassador and Mrs. Whitelaw Reid at Dorchester House and dined with Sybil's father, Hamilton Cuffe, the earl of Desart, before leaving for home. They arrived in New York on September 22.[6]

Two days later, accompanied by his parents, Bronson departed for Harvard. His parents helped him prepare his room, 58 Randolph Hall, unpacking clothing and sorting furniture. On September 26, refreshed and excited, Bronson Cutting, like several of his Groton classmates, began his career at Harvard. His confidence, prestige and popularity, given the recognition he received on Class Day, were at their highest point. At Harvard, he would be free from the tensions generated by the Groton regimen and the all-encompassing presence of the Rector Peabody, and more recently from his loving but all-embracing family. At Harvard, he could be his own person, as he explored its heady academic atmosphere. And he need not be concerned by his lack of athletic prowess.

He had good reason to be excited. The Committee on Academic Admission doubted whether his admission record had ever been surpassed, let alone equalled. On the entrance examinations, he received 3 As (in Elementary French, Algebra and Physics), 8 Bs (in Elementary Greek, Latin, History, Plane Geometry, Advanced Greek, Latin, French and Algebra), 2 B⁻s (in both Elementary and Advanced German, and English B). These grades meant that he would receive 33 points toward a degree and would not be required to take the prescribed course in English for the freshman year. His brother was told that during one long meeting of the admissions board, "Bronson's card stood before us that we might be cheered by its sight."[7]

At Harvard, where academic ability gained recognition, Bronson Cutting immediately felt at home both in his comfortable quarters and in the classrooms. Addressing the 605 entering freshmen of Cutting's class, Harvard president Charles W. Eliot remarked that one of the purposes of a Harvard education was "to allow each man to think and do as he pleases."

Cutting, freed at last from the strict regimen of Groton, did both. In his freshman year, out of seven courses, he received 2 Bs, 2 B+s, 1 A⁻ and 2 As. His professors were some of the great minds on the Harvard faculty: William James (General Problems of Philosophy), Hugo Munsterberg (Psychology), William Allan Nielson (English Literature 1745–1798), and Frank W. Taussig and Charles Jesse Bullock (Principles of Economics). In addition, Cutting registered for courses in Greek and Latin literature and mathematics. These courses, Samuel Eliot Morison informs us, were regarded by most undergraduates as basically cultural, fit for "greasy grinds" and for students headed toward professional training upon graduation.[8]

But Cutting was no "greasy grind" in his freshman year. Early in his first semester, he informed his mother, "I feel as if I'd lived here all my life. I find it great fun and of course for sheer enjoyment it leaves Groton nowhere." Although Harvard lacked charm for Cutting, it was "genial and, up to a certain rather low point, very pleasant." He had plenty of friends and new acquaintances, and was rarely by himself "except for the hours of sleep."[9]

He also found time in his freshman year to cut Friday afternoon lectures and take the train to New York, where he attended the opera and visited his family. Harvard, in short, was a liberating factor in Cutting's life, as it was for other members of the class of 1910, one of the most distinguished in the history of the college. Among his peers were Walter Lippmann, T.S. Eliot,

CHAPTER 2

John Reed, Stuart Chase, Alan Seager, Hamilton Fish, Jr., and Heywood
Broun. But Cutting knew very few members of this or any other class,
except for the Groton boys in Cambridge.[10]

Unable to attend school during his sophomore year because of ill health, he
spent it mostly in Europe to improve his health through rest and travel. At the
outset, he considered examining archaeological work in Crete and Greece and
possibly in Egypt. Bayard Cutting, seriously ill with tuberculosis, was already in Switzerland at St. Moritz with his family, as were his mother and his
younger sister, Olivia. Bronson joined the family there. While the others
traveled, Bronson entered a sanatorium to rest and recoup his health. Occasionally, he climbed mountains in the clear, crisp air of the Swiss Alps. How
long he remained at the health facility is not known, but he did spend part of
his time in travel, pursuing his plan of viewing archaeological remains in
Egypt, Greece and Italy, some of the time with his brother and his family.
During his stay at the sanatorium in Switzerland and on his travels, Bronson
was accompanied by a dilettante friend of his brother, also possibly in search
of improved health, Gordon Gardiner. Although their ages were farther apart
than was usual with friends, Gardiner was impressed with his companion's
geniality and his "never failing thoughtfulness and kindliness." They "had the
good fortune to see together, and in circumstances of every comfort, some of
the most fascinating places in the world." Gardiner remained in Italy, while
Cutting returned to St. Moritz to join his parents.[11]

Before Bronson departed for Europe, his father had ascertained that Harvard would allow him to return as a junior at the beginning of the 1908–1909
academic year. So high were his admission grades and so good were his
freshman marks, the Administrative Board stated that he could enter "the
Junior class without any deficiency whatever." In effect, Bronson Cutting
spent his sophomore year abroad. When he returned he was awarded a John
Harvard scholarship for his junior year.[12] In August, Bronson was looking
forward to returning to Cambridge, starting his junior year at Harvard and
seeing his Groton friends, some of whom were concerned about his health
and anxious to see him again.

Cutting's academic record in his junior year at Harvard was remarkable.
He received an A in each of the six courses he entered. Every paper he wrote
received a similar grade. In History 37, which examined the spread of Hellenistic culture, Cutting wrote a term paper on "Greek and Egyptian Religions
in Hellenistic Egypt." The bibliography included works in German, French
and Italian. Professor George Santayana, many years later, recalled him as a
shy pupil in his course on Greek philosophy. He took notice of him as the

16

younger brother of one of his best pupils and saw in him "the same clear intelligence, perhaps less full and enthusiastic" than Bayard displayed. Santayana remembered that although Bronson's comments in class "were inclined to be meager; he went at once to the essence of things, not always to their advantage." In addition, the young scholar took three courses in classical philosophy and one in comparative literature. During the year, he was elected to Phi Beta Kappa and was awarded another John Harvard scholarship and a Deturs, all indicating high academic distinction.[13]

However, Bronson did not ignore his social obligations. In February 1909, he enjoyed "a round of Boston gaiety—a dance every night." One host called him the "life of the party" at a dinner he gave. Gordon Gardiner's family thought "he was one of the most delightful, interesting young men that they had met for many years." A young lady in New York was glad that he "came down here last Sunday," adding that "you have a certain way of understanding things which makes it very nice to have you around."[14]

Yet by June at the end of the academic year, Bronson was again concerned about his health and planned to spend the summer seeking to regain it. He departed for Europe to join his parents and older brother at Cortina, the leading resort city in the Italian Alps. William Bayard Cutting, Jr., seriously ill with tuberculosis since 1901, was planning to return to the United States in the spring, after a winter spent in Egypt and possibly in another British or French colony in the Mediterranean. While no extant correspondence states specifically that Bronson had tuberculosis, it is clear, given his concern for rest in crisp mountain and arid desert air, that he, too, at a less advanced stage than his brother, was a victim of tuberculosis. The time they spent together in the Italian Alps was the last time they saw one another.[15]

In September, Bronson was back in Cambridge for the start of his senior year. Shortly after the academic session got underway, he started hemorrhaging from tuberculosis and had to enter a hospital until the bleeding was controlled. He then returned to New York to rest and recuperate at Westbrook and at the family residence in the city. He stopped attending classes the day he entered the hospital on November 11, 1909, and officially withdrew from Harvard on account of illness on February 8, 1910.

His brother, upon learning of Bronson's condition, explained what he would have to look forward to based upon his own experience. "Nothing," he said, "can make it anything but desperately hard to bear. For years you are going to see other fellows go ahead of you all along the line, and must learn not to mind. You'll have to think about fiddling matters of health which seem at first a destruction of manhood." Although William Bayard Cutting, Jr. did not have many months to live when he wrote to his brother, he believed that Bronson would recover and have a public career that had already been partially closed to him. Politics, he thought, would be an ideal career for his younger brother. Bayard was "ashamed of the figure we cut as a nation—possessing as I think we do the best individuals, the best raw material, to be found anywhere—to take even a moderate interest in other aspects of American life, compared to the political. [sic]" Whether or not William Bayard Cutting's suggestion was taken to heart by his brother, politics was the realm in which Bronson Cutting would fulfill his career.[16]

Although Harvard was willing to accommodate him, Bronson neither completed his course work nor received his degree. William Scott Ferguson, under whom Bronson had finished one history course and registered for another, was most sympathetic to his plight. He exclaimed, "Cutting stands in a class by himself among the undergraduates with whom I have dealt since coming to Cambridge; hence to aid such a man is like teaching a hundred." Professors and administrators were considerate and willing to assist Bronson in any possible way, and Mrs. Cutting was concerned about his education, but Bronson apparently was too ill to give the matter much thought. He never contemplated returning to Cambridge to complete his studies.[17]

To find a more suitable climate that would assist in Bronson's recovery, his father secured a private railroad car, and the family in February departed for Redlands, California. The following month, William Bayard Cutting, Jr. died in a houseboat on the River Nile near Aswan in Egypt, further accentuating the concern for Bronson's health. The Cuttings remained in Redlands through March and April and then returned by private car to New York. Enroute home, they followed the Santa Fe route, stopped briefly in Santa Fe and found the city and the region most attractive. At the end of June, Bronson and his sister, Justine, left New York for Santa Fe to establish a residence there.

In later years Bronson Cutting said he went to New Mexico to die. Instead, like many others, he found a new life. In Cutting's case, he also launched a career that would gain him state and national recognition. Granted every virtue of high culture—privilege, education and connections—Bronson Cutting established himself in New Mexico and allowed his carefully nurtured family background to take root and flower in an alien soil.

CHAPTER 3

STARTING ANEW IN
NEW MEXICO

On June 30, 1910 Bronson Cutting and his sister, Justine Ward, departed New York City in a private railroad car. In Santa Fe, a rented house awaited them. What was expected to be a brief residence, perhaps a year or two at best, turned out to be a stay of twenty-five years. About seven thousand feet above sea level, Santa Fe, a city of 5,072 people in 1910, lay in a plain rimmed on all points by mountains. Once there, new arrivals were pleased to observe that the city was also an outpost of culture and civilization. Santa Fe boasted a cathedral, historic churches, adobe buildings, a governor's palace and urbane citizens. When Cutting arrived, a small group of scholarly inclined individuals associated with the School of American Research, were exploring New Mexico's past in Spanish archives and in its abundant archaeological heritage.[1] In addition, Santa Fe was already a vast sanatorium where victims of tuberculosis, asthma, and bronchitis hoped to find relief from the damp, polluted air of the congested, urban East. Cutting's arrival predated by a few years that of large numbers of artists who would also find creative stimulation in the intermingling of Indian, Hispanic and Anglo cultures.

Although still a territory in 1910, New Mexico was at once the oldest and newest portion of the United States. Something about the grandeur of its vistas, rugged mountains and barren mesas, along with the seeming gentility, inherent courtesy and hospitality of the natives, captivated Cutting and most urbane visitors and new residents. Since 1598, however, New Mexico had been administered by governors approved first in Madrid and after 1821 in Mexico City when Mexico achieved its independence from Spain. The English-speaking Anglo came from the East, or the United States. He was an intruder, initially a trader and in 1846 a military conqueror of a land that officially became a territory of the United States in 1850.

In July 1910, the only thing Cutting and Justine appreciated in Santa Fe was the opportunity to settle into the house they had rented from a local doctor. Mary Catherine Prince, the wife of former governor L. Bradford Prince, met them at the station and took them to their new residence, "rather far from the town." At the house, besides the doctor and his wife, they met ex-governor Miguel Antonio Otero, Sr., who, Mrs. Prince informed them, "doesn't amount to a row of pins." Although the house was not as spacious as it appeared in the plans, it had a "splendid view of the mountains." What dismayed them, however, was its position on a low piece of land bounded on one side by railroad tracks and by the penitentiary on the other.[2]

Mrs. Prince invited them to "an entertainment" that celebrated the Fourth of July. While she was "exceedingly kind and in many ways very helpful," Bronson found it "impossible to get away from her," and he added, "Her conversation gets more fluent every day." Nevertheless, at the Princes's reception, they met several former governors of the territory and "a number of ladies of great culture." Dr. James A. Massie, associated with the Sunmount Sanitorium, as well as his sisters were attractive people whom they hoped to see again.[3]

From their very first days in Santa Fe, two things quickly became evident to Bronson and Justine. First, he explained to his father, "We are regarded as multimillionaires, and are charged quadruple prices for everything." Second, many of the things they desired or needed were unavailable in Santa Fe and had to be requested through their parents in New York. Bronson did not regard these matters as troublesome.[4] Purchasing a house or locating a satisfactory site upon which to build one was the primary task to be accomplished and the chief reason Justine accompanied him to Santa Fe. The arrival of an automobile, shipped from the East, eased their travel to and from town. On July 12, Bronson drove to the Tesuque Valley with Liberado Baca, "a pleasant little man though evidently the worst kind of politician." Through Baca, he hoped to meet "some other Mexicans" who could assist him in purchasing a homesite. Politics, while not his most immediate concern, was the primary one of Santa Fe, the territorial capital.[5]

The politics of the territory and of the state for most of Cutting's lifetime was one of ever-changing alliances and seemingly endless intrigue. It involved what one historian, Kenneth Owens, has called chaotic factionalism and another, Howard Lamar, the politics of disharmony. The Republican party, dominant in the nation during the post–Civil War years, also controlled the territory, although it was never a cohesive organization. The source of the political flux was conflicting claims to water rights and land grants involving huge segments of the public domain, some going back to the seventeenth century. Lawyers, of whom there were a large number in the territory, allied themselves with various politicians, ranchers, mine operators, speculators, railroad corporations and other clients to promote their claims. The over-all operation was more or less managed by the "Santa Fe ring," which for the most part successfully sought to dictate political appointments and influence legislation. The ring, nominally Republican, was in eclipse by 1910 but was still powerful enough to play a role in New Mexico's transition to statehood. For instance, it selected its most prominent leader, Thomas Benton Catron, as the first United States senator from the new state.

Throughout its existence, leaders of the Santa Fe Ring made a point to include in their schemes Hispanic leaders, or *patrones*, regardless of their party preference, by supporting their title to Spanish and Mexican land grants. Because Hispanics comprised the majority of the population, about sixty percent in 1910, the ring literally depended upon the electoral support of the patrones and their Hispanic followers.

The *patrón* system usually kept the poor Hispanic in a form of peonage but nevertheless supported a way of life that was meaningful. Tenants would farm the land of a Hispanic patrón, or "don," and would receive from him their rations of beans and chili. Although they saw very little actual money, they turned to the patrón for guidance in troubled times. By controlling the access to credit and capital, the patrón, whether Hispanic or Anglo, could sway the life of the community and participate prominently in the public life of the county and territory. The patrón generally profered advice in temporal matters, including politics, while the padre tended to spiritual concerns. In Hispanic communities, the harshness of the system would be tempered by a sympathetic patrón and by the faith and familial values of the tenants and others caught in its web.

The Spanish-speaking citizens of New Mexico were largely concentrated in the northern third of the state along the upper Rio Grande and its tributaries. For over two centuries, they had lived in virtual isolation, pursuing a primitive farming and grazing (chiefly sheep) economy. In the twentieth century, they increasingly found the basis of their way of life disintegrating. The vast majority, the poor Hispanics or *pobres,* by their customs and their culture were poorly equipped to meet changing conditions and would be required to make enormous readjustments with little or no outside aid. The culture of these native Hispanics was still dominant in the territory when Cutting arrived in 1910. Their way of life was shaped by Spanish culture, the environment, and the Pueblo Indians. Deeply embedded in their way of life were intimate ties to family, land, church, and neighbors. However, with the acquisition of New Mexico as an American territory, the pobres became a marginalized ethnic group. And the fact that political and economic power rested primarily in the hands of Anglos only accentuated this situation.

Within a month of their arrival in Santa Fe, Bronson and his sister were engaged in "a gay social whirl," and to his great delight, his health seemed in no way to be impaired.[6] One afternoon a week, they attended a Spanish class at Mrs. Prince's. Justine claimed that Bronson "knows quite a little." Another member of the class was Brian Boru Dunne, who quickly became a friend. One evening, he took them "to see the moving pictures." Dunne, the city editor of the Santa Fe *New Mexican,* was mounted on a pony and wore a large sombrero hat when he rode out to interview Bronson and Justine. She quickly and correctly surmised that he "was altogether too 'Western' to be anything but an Easterner." She also claimed that the climate seemed perfect for both of them but that Bronson could not be "perfectly sure" until he began to exercise, something he had not yet done on the advice of Dr. Massie.[7]

Meanwhile, Justine was preparing to leave Santa Fe. Frederic Bishop, an English doctor who had been his brother's medical advisor and friend, soon assumed a similar role in Santa Fe with Bronson. Before departing, she had her portrait painted by Carl Lotave, a local artist associated with Edgar L. Hewett. Cutting was infuriated when he learned of rumors spread by Hewett about Justine and Lotave. To Cutting, Hewett was "the most loathsome person I ever ran across, as well as a total ignoramus." However, the matter was quickly resolved when Justine and Bronson called on Hewett at his office in the Governor's Palace. Hewett, Bronson said, "became servile and cringing" and exhibited great embarrassment and discomfort.[8]

Justine was concerned that Bronson, then twenty-two, had almost no opportunity to mingle with people his own age. She was delighted when in late August, two of his friends arrived in town "to see the sights." Bronson introduced them to two girls he liked and the sisters-in-law of the territorial chief justice, who at times invited him to supper. While Justine was sorry to see his friends depart, she was pleased that Bronson was becoming more animated and more expansive in the company of people he felt at ease with. Among them were Francis Wilson, an attorney and "a Harvard '98 man," and H. H. Dorman, a realtor, both of whom with their spouses were dinner guests.[9]

But as Bronson became more animated, his temperature would rise, driving him to bed on the sleeping porch for several days at a time. By mid-September, he had assumed a semi-invalid status. Although bedridden for days at a time, he plunged into the social whirl of Santa Fe, having, for example, ten guests in to dine on a Saturday evening that was damp and windy. Bronson, taking no chances, greeted only his male guests from his bed on the sleeping porch, while ex-governor Miguel Antonio Otero along with Justine hosted the dinner.

Dr. Bishop, the *Dotorre,* recently arrived from England, now actively supervised Bronson's activities. He moved Cutting indoors near the fireplace. Justine, Brian Boru Dunne, and H. H. Dorman, the latter two already devoted friends, sought to keep him amused and interested with their company and by bringing others to see him. Justine, meanwhile, cancelled her plans to return East until his health improved. She also advised her parents not to come to Santa Fe at this time. Their presence could indicate to Bronson that his condition was considered more severe than what he had been told. She was relieved that most of the servants who had come from New York with them were willing to stay on, as she thought it might be difficult to recruit in the East domestic help who would be willing to come to Santa Fe.

An emerging problem was their rented house. Their lease would expire in late November, and construction on the new house on a four-acre desert tract about two miles south of town was not yet under way. Of more immediate concern was a law suit. An agent employed to secure a piano in Denver instead sent to New York for what Justine, already a talented music teacher, called "a perfectly absurd piano." They refused to accept the instrument. The agent thereafter sold it to someone else but kept Cutting's $150 advance. Bronson put the matter into the hands of his friend, Francis Wilson, who turned it over to the territorial district attorney. The piano agent was indicted by the grand jury for embezzlement.

Bronson appeared before the grand jury on Tuesday morning, September 10. He returned home at noon and informed Justine that she too would have to testify. After hurriedly dressing, she appeared entirely alone before twenty-one male Hispanic jurors. She spoke to them in Spanish and noted that Bronson "also made a hit by presenting them with a box of cigars at their own suggestion." Cutting eventually won the suit, but the agent's lawyer, A. B. Renehan, "the most unscrupulous lawyer in town" according to Justine, secured a retrial on the grounds that "Mrs. Ward smiled at the jury" and spoke Spanish to its members.[10]

The retrial was set for September 24 before Judge John R. McFie in the district court and before what Bronson called "a bribed jury." After three days of examinations, cross examinations and arguments, the case was given to the jury on the afternoon of September 27. That evening, much to Cutting's surprise, the jury upheld the earlier conviction of the piano dealer for embezzlement. Although the case seemed obvious, Renehan succeeded in prolonging it and in confusing the jury. During his two-hour appeal to the all-Hispanic jury, he referred to "certain witnesses," meaning the Cuttings, as "'despicable exotics'" and said something about "'signs of a degenerate race.'" The one positive outcome was that Bronson's health improved during the course of the litigation, although he still coughed some and had to continue with periods of bed rest, looking "very pale for several days after the trial."[11]

In October, construction began on Bronson's residence. He purchased land from Judge H. Knaebel on Buena Vista Heights, a short distance from town along the Lamy road, which commanded a beautiful view of the valley and mountains. Thomas MacLaren, a British architect residing in Colorado Springs, drew the plans for a Spanish-style home. Justine provided MacLaren with a sketch from which the architect then developed his plan. Since time was a factor, adobe, the usual building material, was not used. Instead wood, heavily plastered both outside and inside, was utilized. Stained pink on the outside, the house was built around a central open patio. The plans also called for an open loggia at one corner of the house as well as two sleeping porches. Inside there would be a long sitting room, a small office, a dining area, servants quarters and guest rooms. Unfortunately the construction would take almost a year to complete. Meanwhile, Bronson moved into a more convenient new house, provided by Francis Wilson, with bedrooms rather than sleeping porches.[12]

From the trial and Renehan's label, "despicable exotics," came the informal Exotic Club. Cutting's friends congregated for card playing, convivial conversation, and fellowship at his residence. At times, they referred to one another in exotic terms. Among its members were Brian Boru Dunne, H. H. Dorman, Miguel Antonio Otero, known as the "Little Governor," artist Carl Lotave, known as the "King of Sweden," and Francis Wilson. Dunne, Otero and Lotave dubbed themselves the "Drei-bund." Over time, the membership changed, but among the group were always some of the closest personal friends Cutting made in New Mexico. The gatherings were essentially recreational. All could escape the gossip and glare of social life in Santa Fe, where delegates were gathering to draft a constitution in accord with the Enabling Act recently approved by the United States Congress.

Bronson thought the convention would be "great fun," partly because Justine was secretly commissioned to write the opening prayer. The proceedings also gave him an opportunity to indulge in political watching in New Mexico. Indicating latent prejudice in his family correspondence, he called Charles A. Spiess, elected to preside over the convention, "the craftiest villain in the territory"—"half Jew and half nigger." He started to compile a list of delegates by districts, adding comments like the following: "able lawyer and unscrupulous politician"; "worst kind of scoundrel"; "upright judge and very good fellow, but poor lawyer"; "excellent judge in every way"; and others.

What Cutting was commenting upon was the chaotic factionalism and the political disharmony that characterized territorial politics throughout the West. He brought to New Mexico the politics of his father and his uncle. He was deeply influenced by their fusion efforts to battle graft and corruption and to further honesty and efficiency in both local and national affairs.[13]

The great fun of the convention soon gave way to an increasing deterioration of his fragile health. The social whirl, the court cases, the anxiety over house construction, and trips to nearby canyons, Indian festivals, and Durango and Roswell took their toll on Bronson and his family. As a result, he was soon spending most of his time in bed, chiefly on a sleeping porch. From the end of October to the end of the year, he was attended in bed by doctors, family and servants. Friends continually dropped by to visit, gossip and keep him abreast of local matters.

Justine masterfully attended Bronson's needs, purchased necessary items for their temporary residence, requested that others be sent from New York, and served as a hostess. All the while, she exhibited a nonintrusive, gentle but persistent concern for her brother's health. At the same time, she sacrificed her developing career in music and her marriage. Her husband, who appeared briefly in Santa Fe, quickly returned to New York, unenthused about New Mexico after his service as a colonial administrator in Puerto Rico. Their marriage was merely nominal by this time. They lived apart more than together. Justine's conversion to Catholicism made divorce an unavailable option.[14]

As for Bronson, his spirit, outwardly at least, was still cheerful and optimistic. Justine was delighted that he showed a keen interest in several young ladies in Santa Fe. Among them were two "not very pretty but rather attractive Georgia girls, nieces of Hoke Smith."[15] In early November, his parents and younger sister, Olivia, arrived in Santa Fe. They did not stay long, and each followed a different schedule, but from this time to the end of the year, one or another member of his family stayed with him. His father, however, remained the full two months. The entire family was together for Christmas. Although Bronson's health was still a matter of grave concern as 1910 came to an end, he had made a new beginning and had started a new residence. For better or worse, Bronson Cutting was settled in New Mexico.[16]

In a memoir drafted in 1939, Justine made penetrating insights into the effects of her brother's physical condition on his character and personality. During his illness, he spent much of his time playing the piano. In addition, he was an omnivorous reader, a trait evident from his early childhood. Dr. Bishop recalled that Cutting never stopped consuming books, "even in the midst of a hemorrhage." Most striking was that he retained nearly everything he read, that the information was ordered and accessible and that he could promptly recall facts and statistics.

Unsettling to friends and family were the long silences that illness imposed upon him. His parents, still grief-stricken over the death of Bayard, became even more anxious about their remaining son now enduring the same struggle with tuberculosis. Their solicitude for his health, their fright over his every cough, over every breeze or draft, pushed Bronson into ever deeper silence as he grew ever more pale. A further complication was that his father, besides suffering from severe gout, had a weak heart, which the higher altitudes, considered beneficial for tubercular patients, worked a hardship on him.

Justine became increasingly aware of the heavy silence between them on the trip to Santa Fe and during her stay there. She also observed that Bronson's silence was one "of mystery and discomfort." It was not the confident, shared silence of intimacy. To be sure, Bronson would respond both promptly and pleasantly to any query, and he maintained a sense of humor. Although he listened patiently, he did not actively participate in conversations, and he rarely advocated a point of view. Very few details escaped his observation; most remained etched in his memory. He seemed amused by most everything that was affected or pretentious, yet he rarely expressed an unkind judgment. As others came to notice when Cutting became a public figure, he had a keen "appreciation of everyman's liberty and right to be just as he was" so long as his point of view was sincere. Although Cutting held strong opinions about politicians, he took the variety of people he encountered and met in New Mexico and elsewhere on their own terms and never for a moment thought they ought to conform to his standards. Despite being given to introversion and deep silences, he could also exude considerable charm, and when his health permitted, he could actively participate in his new home community.[17]

In an undated horoscope drafted in pencil, he examined himself and projected his career in New Mexico. So revealing a document deserves full quotation:

Born under the planet of Venus, sign of Leo, you are jolly and good natured, you are free-hearted, you are an excellent manager, a clear observer. You love to do good—you are able to do so too. But you do so in a practical way, not for fame. You are modest about your good works. You are a bachelor, not but what you could have married but you have never loved any woman and you are happy in your bachelor home with a sister for a housekeeper. You will never marry but you will have lots of good friends among the ladies. You will travel extensively all over the United States and to foreign countries. You will own land—city property and mines and oil wells—some of them in New Mexico and some in other states. You will live to be over 80. You will always make your home in New Mexico and take an active interest in the development of the State in every way. You will hold office several times and will do lots of good in office. You will represent New Mexico in Washington, D.C., from 1932 to 1940. You will do best not to be governor of New Mexico. You have no enemies now and don't want any.[18]

Although worried about his precarious health, Bronson was gaining some insights into New Mexico. He met most of the territorial political leaders. Immediately critical of them, he measured them through the fusion criteria for good government and social morality, perceptions that would always be with him, but he had only an inkling of how society, economy, and hence political life truly meshed and functioned. As he regained his health and found a meaningful role to play, his understanding would grow immeasurably. Since he had no overwhelming need to pursue wealth for its own sake, he would garner opportunities to play a role in the life of his community when New Mexico entered the Union as the forty-seventh state in January 1912.

FINDING A PLACE
1911–1913

Settling in Santa Fe, participating in its society, and observing political behavior in the capital city was fine if one were a mere dilettante. Neither Bronson nor members of his family, however, were casual onlookers. The question in their minds was just what Bronson would do with his life as he slowly regained his health. By 1913 he had found a place for himself, a meaningful and challenging career that catapulted him from an observer to a participant in the public life of his adopted city and state.

As 1911 got underway, Bronson was still convalescing, with his family on hand. Friends from town visited daily for lunch, tea, and an occasional dinner. By early February, the family had departed. His father, who celebrated his sixty-first birthday on January 12, was first to leave. In the absence of his family, Bronson was cared for by Doctors Bishop and Massie. Brian Boru Dunne and the Little Governor, Miguel Antonio Otero shared bachelor quarters with Cutting. Although he was feeling better and was able to take walks, he tired easily.[1]

That he fatigued with little exertion and feared future hemorrhaging only reinforced the premise, noted in his self-cast horoscope, that he would never marry. Certainly, he never seriously pursued Callie Hull, whose sister wrote him, "There is not a day that passes in which she does not long to get back to New Mexico and to see her particular friend in Santa Fe." She added, "It's not good taste to give compliments to your face, as I won't tell you what I've heard her say about you." Whether Callie confided those thoughts directly to Bronson is unknown. None of her letters appear in his papers, having been removed and destroyed by his mother after his death.[2]

The political scene, his new house and his own well-being more directly concerned him. In the area of politics, the primary issue was the agonizing delay of the New Mexico legislature in approving statehood, selecting two United States senators and formally entering the Union. Looking after their son, Mr. and Mrs. Cutting forwarded from New York fixtures and other items for the house, which was nearing completion. They also included sheet music, including opera scores, to enhance his enjoyment of the piano. Episcopal church affairs, never placid or dull, also interested him. At one meeting, everybody was "shouting, stamping and pounding the table at once." The issues that divided the congregation revolved around the minister, James G.

Mythen. The vast majority of the congregation desired to become an established parish rather than remaining a mission, a change that needed the approval of the bishop. Opposed to Mythen, the majority and the change was former territorial governor L. Bradford Prince, who quickly alienated most of the congregation with his belligerency and his tactics. Prince succeeded to the extent that the Reverend Mythen, about to depart on vacation, received from the bishop a letter of dismissal.[3]

The first indication that Cutting was considering a possible career option was in late winter 1910 and early spring 1911. He noted that the *Tribune-Citizen* had been bought by Holm O. Bursum and others associated with the Santa Fe Ring. Cutting thought this development "finished the Santa Fe newspaper scheme" in which he was involved with another former territorial governor, Herbert J. Hagerman, a bitter Bursum enemy. Cutting was involved because his father wanted to launch him on a rewarding career. One option was starting a daily newspaper in Santa Fe, provided prominent, independent-minded citizens would identify themselves with it. Hagerman, Richard Hanna, Francis Wilson and Levi Hughes—all progressive Republicans—wanted Cutting and his father to invest heavily in the endeavor in return for a management voice. Cutting observed that "advices from Washington are that the Democrats and insurgent Republicans are firm not to admit New Mexico until the present Republican ring are [sic] out of power." Hagerman's hope, shared by Cutting, was that the paper would help to accomplish that purpose. The *Tribune-Citizen* and the *New Mexican* were already being published in Santa Fe. The expense of launching a new paper, constructing a well-equipped printing plant, hiring a competent staff and having on hand "from 10 to 15 thousand for working capital" did not seem feasible to either Bronson or his father, although their subscribing would insure them "a pretty fine hand in the running of the paper." Nothing came of this venture, the first written indication of a possible career for Bronson Cutting in New Mexico.[4]

For his part, Bronson was worried that having "primary or heavy responsibility" in running a newspaper would impose undue stress on his weak constitution. His father quickly reassured him that his only object in suggesting this enterprise was to provide him with "a real interest in a good and valuable project." He added that the term *valuable* was to be interpreted "as an influence and not as a dividend payer." The job, if a future arrangement developed, should "occupy just as much of your time and work as it would be beneficial to give." Although his father was willing to invest heavily in a suitable newspaper project and to act as Bronson's banker, he preferred to maintain his anonymity. He wanted the major portion of the stock to be issued in other names, with the certificates endorsed over to Bronson. He was insistent, however, that New Mexicans own a good share of the stock, as close to half as possible, and thereby insure local interest in the stability and success of the newspaper. For the journal to succeed as a "reforming agent," the senior Cutting believed, the paper must not become "an organ of any man." In sum, Bronson must not be the central figure, a stranger "butting in to teach his elders." Instead, the venture should be "a New Mexican effort for better things," an arrangement that would give the newspaper a broader base of public appeal.

His father's only admonition was that Bronson should do nothing to alienate friends such as Brian Boru Dunne, the city editor of the *New Mexican*. Neither should he anger ex-governor Otero, with whom his father was considering a possible business deal and who was courting the widow of a former editor of the same paper at the time. William Bayard Cutting was in part reflecting his distaste, as a progressive-minded citizen, for some of the journalistic enterprises evident in New York City, where Tammany Hall dominated municipal affairs.[5] However, the newspaper scheme was not feasible. A year would pass before another prime opportunity arose.

Meanwhile Bronson wrote enthusiastically about his life in Santa Fe, enjoying it, as his sister said, "more and more." Indeed, he was becoming part of the community. He was elected a warden in the Episcopal church and thus became directly involved in the controversy engulfing the parish. He was exposed to the wrath of Mrs. Prince who vigorously defended her husband against those "vulgar people" unable to appreciate him. The central argument was Prince's opposition, despite the approval of a large majority of the congregation, to removing the church from the supervision of the Board of Missions and raising it to a parish. The issue flamed out of control primarily because the bishop, J. M. Kendrick, agreed with Prince. The rector, James G. Mythen, who had sided with the congregation, became a victim of Prince's wrath. Sympathetic to Mythen's plight, Cutting believed that to continue receiving funds from the Mission Board when the congregation was capable of supporting itself as an independent parish was of dubious honesty. His interest in the Santa Fe Episcopal Church was as keen as that of his father in church affairs in New York City. He was concerned with promoting its utility, in part because the church provided him with his first opportunity to participate in the public life of his adopted community.[6]

On August 19, Bronson moved into his new home, soon dubbed "Los Siete Burros," but initially called Buena Vista Palace. The name was taken from an amusing tale, related by Brian Boru Dunne, about an old priest

CHAPTER 4

trying to teach some Hispanic children the catechism by asking how many sacraments there were. Once the name was agreed upon, five members of his intimate circle of friends became burros: Justine; Brian Boru Dunne; H. H. Dorman; and two younger members attending the New Mexico Military Institute in Roswell, Tony Luna and Miguel Antonio Otero, Jr., known as Mike. With Cutting, they made the six burros and collectively agreed upon "Los Siete Burros" as an appropriate name for the residence.[7]

As Cutting settled into Los Siete Burros and entertained guests at tea, dinner or bridge, the long quest of New Mexico for statehood was coming to an end. On August 19, 1911, the United States House of Representatives followed the Senate in admitting both Arizona and New Mexico to the Union. Two days later, President Taft signed the joint resolution. To the assembled delegation on hand to witness the signing, he remarked, "Well, gentlemen, it's done."

However, the politics of statehood was only beginning. The territorial governor of New Mexico, William J. Mills, immediately set the first state election for November 7, 1911. Selected on that date would be the governor, two congressmen, members of the first state legislature, and numerous county and state officers. In addition, if voters wished to make the state constitution easier to amend, they could ask for a blue-tinted ballot instead of the usual white ballot provided at polling places.[8]

In New Mexico, the president's approval of statehood prompted widespread celebration. In Santa Fe, Bronson and family members drove his motorcar bedecked with forty-eight–star American flags through the narrow streets. There was great rejoicing. At Los Siete Burros, the conversation among the guests inevitably turned to politics. Enjoying Cutting's hospitality were leading political figures. The views of some, such as Thomas Benton Catron, L. Bradford Prince and Mrs. Prince, he could not accept. Although disagreeing with their politics, he still enjoyed their society. Catron, for example, at a dinner on August 26, charmed Cutting and his family by recounting his experiences on the Santa Fe Trail in 1866. The official housewarming on September 16 was a "great success," according to Cutting's mother. Mrs. N. B. Laughlin, the mother of five daughters, sweetly remarked, "You have everything Mr. Cutting, for your home except a hostess."[9]

With the opening of his home out of the way, Bronson, like most of his friends and acquaintances in Santa Fe, turned his attention to the political scene. He considered running for councilman from his ward. He threw his support behind the Little Governor. Actively seeking the gubernatorial nomination, Otero was campaigning for delegates to the Republican convention to be held in Las Vegas at the end of September. All of the Cuttings endorsed his candidacy. From Roswell, Mike Otero told Cutting that his father had a "fighting chance," but if the ring candidate, Holm O. Bursum, was nominated, "hearsay had it" that the Republican ticket "would be 'scratched' right and left."[10]

Bronson was also associating with progressive Republicans, many of whom had organized into the National Progressive Republican League. In September 1911, Cutting sought to become a delegate to the state convention. Thomas B. Catron, the nominal head of the Santa Fe Ring, made his objections clear to the young easterner. Catron's opposition to Cutting made little sense. There was no way, thanks to the ring and its supporters, that progressive Republicans could have controlled or influenced the convention. On Monday, September 25, the Republicans of Santa Fe County gathered at the court house to name seventeen delegates to the state convention. Although Catron chaired the committee on resolutions and generally dominated the proceedings, he could not block Cutting's selection to the Las Vegas convention.[11]

On September 27, Bronson and his father departed on the 4:00 P.M. train for Las Vegas. The following day at the convention, according to Miguel Antonio Otero's analysis, the strenuous efforts of another Republican leader, Solomon Luna, secured Holm Bursum the gubernatorial nomination. Bronson was disgusted. He turned in his proxy and refused to endorse Bursum's nomination, thereby angering his fellow delegates. On October 1, the day after he returned, tired and discouraged, from Las Vegas, he had an evening conference with William C. McDonald, the Democratic candidate for governor.[12]

While crossing party lines to endorse candidates was not unknown in New Mexico, neither was it an extraordinary practice in the Cutting family, given its experience with fusion politics in New York City. Like his father and uncle, Bronson never felt strongly about party loyalty. Although he acknowledged that parties had to exist for the convenience of the electorate, he never believed that the role of voters was to serve the convenience of the party. He saw that Bursum's nomination had been "steam rollered" through the convention and that the proceedings were contrary to the wishes of a large proportion of the party. In the interest of good government, he felt an obligation to help defeat Bursum. In early September, Herbert J. Hagerman, a former territorial governor and a progressive Republican, had informed him "that the machine organization felt that they held the whip hand . . . and intended to go to the utmost limit in carrying through the slate they had agreed upon and in absolutely ignoring any independent or progressive element in the Republican party." Along with other progressive Republicans, Cutting worked for the defeat of the Republican candidate for governor in New Mexico's first statehood election.[13]

They threw in their lot with the Democrats. Without newspaper support, a progressive movement looking toward the formation of a new party would stand no chance of success. The machine, however, had one asset that progressive Republicans had to consider. Octaviano A. Larrazolo, a prominent Hispanic leader and a powerful orator, had recently left the Democratic party and endorsed the Republican ticket. Injecting race into the campaign, Larrazolo claimed he could aid "his people" better in the Republican than in the Democratic ranks.

Herbert J. Hagerman spearheaded the organization of progressive Republicans and the dissemination of their views. He and others understood that Bursum's candidacy "would start a more bitter fight than any that has ever been waged before in the Territory." Charges of graft and corruption had been leveled at his previous political and public activities.[14]

By mid-October, as the campaign moved toward its climax, the departure of Cutting's parents deprived him of their counsel and support. Before his mother left for home, Dr. Bishop returned from his stay in England. His presence assured that her son would be well looked after. His health in good order, Bronson focused on the political scene, which he continued to find most depressing. But he lent his support to the Democrats, who had accepted fusion by placing some progressive Republicans on their ticket.

With the Republican party, as a leading Democrat put it, "all split up," the leaven of reform attracted numerous Republicans into the Democratic fold. Many progressive Republicans, offered little choice but "the same old gang," followed Cutting's example and voted against Bursum. His candidacy represented to them "ring" rule—graft, corruption, subterfuge, evasion and concealment.[15]

When the archbishop of Santa Fe, Jean Baptiste Salpointe, the leading Catholic prelate in the state, opposed the blue ballot in a pastoral letter, Cutting feared that "the gang will certainly make the most of it." He wondered "how they induced him to write it." He was also amused when Catron warned R. Fulton Cutting that his investments in Santa Fe courthouse bonds might not be reimbursed by the state if the Republican ticket went down to defeat. Catron specifically noted the opposition of Bronson Cutting and his father and suggested that R. Fulton Cutting might wish to curb their activities. In a letter to his father five days before the election, Cutting wrote that the Republicans were "claiming for Bursum a majority of 250." Their prediction was a clear indication that they would try "to steal the election." So conflicting were reports, however, that he would not venture to guess the outcome, especially in light of the archbishop's opposition to the Blue Ballot Amendment.[16]

The election of November 7, 1911 gratified all those opposed to Bursum's candidacy. William C. McDonald was elected governor; Harvey B. Fergusson won a seat in Congress; and nearly half the state offices went to the Democrats. However, a gerrymandering operation that overrepresented sparsely populated counties, gave the Republicans a majority in both houses of the state legislature. The conservatives would be able to select the state's first senators. Also modified was the constitutional provision that would have favored the highest tax payers (railroad, ranching and mining interests) and that would have placed a twenty-five–year moratorium on the amendment process. Passed by a twelve-thousand–vote margin, the Blue Ballot Amendment simplified and eased the amendment of the state constitution. When the election was over and victory was assured, Cutting thanked his parents for their contributions, most of which went toward Otero's unsuccessful efforts to secure the Republican gubernatorial nomination and then to win a state senate election as a fusion candidate.[17]

Santa Fe County remained under ring control. Cutting blamed "gross intimidation and corruption at the polls" and the "misuse of the Archbishop's letter in the native precincts." He noted that even the elected candidates were in "the depths of gloom." A Democratic celebration, complete with a funeral march in front of a Republican leader's home and a burying of Bursum in effigy, aroused no fervid antagonism among the opposition. Indeed, since the election, according to a perplexed Cutting, the regular Republicans had become most "affable and genial"—charitable behavior he had not witnessed during the campaign.[18]

Throughout the campaign, Cutting's family and doctor worried that his participation, limited though it was, would jeopardize his health. Fortunately, he came through, unimpaired. His doctor observed, "Six months ago he could not have gone through the last week's exertion without grave risk." A year earlier, he could not have become involved at all. In short, living in New Mexico had strengthened his health. Despite the election results in Santa Fe County, his and his state's future appeared full of hope. Although he probably nourished political ambitions as 1911 came to a close, he had neither a job, political position nor viable political base in New Mexico. What he did possess, namely money, would be a significant asset in helping to secure a promising career in his new home.[19]

A triumph for the progressive cause, the election of the entire fusion state ticket also meant that Cutting, who assisted this victory, would be able to seek some recognition from the new governor, William McDonald. Worry about his health deterred his seeking a political appointment, but his interest in public affairs was a sign that he would advance the cause of good government in New Mexico, just as his father and uncle continued to do in New York City. Cutting, Sr. believed that Miguel Antonio Otero had contributed heavily to the progressive victory, despite the failure of his own candidacy. If he did not obtain a political appointment, "he should be taken care of adequately." Unclear is how Otero was compensated or taken care of at this time. For the rest of Bronson's life, however, he would regularly provide Otero with funds, sometimes on a monthly basis, to meet his various obligations.[20]

Progressives in both parties had much to cheer and worry about. Republican leaders, sensing Bursum's eventual defeat, had dumped money into close counties and helped to elect nearly two-thirds of the members of the legislature. In turn, these men would insure that the two United States senators and the state supreme court justices would be old-line Republicans. After the election, various candidates, their friends in the legislature, the press and others began vying for support with "Bull" Andrews, the former territorial delegate to Congress, gaining a long head start on everybody else. To Cutting at the end of November, Andrews appeared a sure bet for a Senate seat.[21]

Cutting expected to see Bursum, "the gang candidate for governor," defeated, but neither he nor anyone else had anticipated that he would lose by over three thousand votes. Under ordinary circumstances, New Mexico was Republican by at least ten thousand votes. If his loss had been foreseen, Cutting would have focused on the legislative races, "in spite of the outrageous gerrymandering by which the Republicans expected to keep themselves in power." Now the legislature would select from a large group of at least thirty "stand pat" candidates. As he viewed the pack, there were seven leading contenders: Thomas Catron; "Bull" Andrews; Solomon Luna; Holm Bursum; William J. Mills; Charles Springer; and Albert B. Fall. Cutting regarded Fall as "the most dangerous man of the bunch." If he had to choose a candidate, he would find Andrews or Springer the least objectionable, but the Albuquerque *Morning Journal,* "the most prominent paper in the Territory [sic]," had launched a personal attack on Andrews, thereby weakening his candidacy. In all, Cutting harbored little sympathy with the leadership of his party at this time. His disdain applied to the national scene as well. In

December, Cutting announced that he would not vote for Taft in 1912, although he hoped to attend the national convention. He confessed to a Groton classmate that he would not mind "seeing a change for a few years."[22]

A bitter reality quickly displaced the sweetness of victory for Cutting and other progressive-minded citizens at the end of 1911. Abundantly evident was that New Mexico would have two standpat, old gang senators. The leading candidates had plenty of enemies, but all were using "every trick they knew to get a toga." Moreover, unless progressive Republicans maintained their ranks and secured more effective press support, there was a strong chance that the old gang would control the delegation sent to the Republican presidential nominating convention scheduled for June 1912. Bronson Cutting and the small band of unorganized progressive Republicans would have difficulty making their way through the tangled thickets of the New Mexico political environment.[23]

Although New Mexico progressives were poorly organized, Cutting at least knew the direction he wished to pursue. His plans pivoted on a close family friend, the father of two Groton classmates, Theodore Roosevelt. In January 1912, before Roosevelt had announced his candidacy, Cutting proclaimed that "the Progressive Republicans of New Mexico are practically solid for you" and that Roosevelt Clubs were organizing. The progressives had "beaten the gang once" and could succeed again if Roosevelt were to be nominated, but Cutting said, "We will join anybody and everybody (for the time being) in order to put New Mexico in the Republican column next fall." He wanted to declare early for Roosevelt's candidacy. He informed the former president, "I am expecting to start a Progressive newspaper here in a few weeks, and if there is anything I could possibly do to help out, I wish you would let me know."[24]

Cutting was interested in the Santa Fe *New Mexican,* the oldest newspaper in the state. Owning the *New Mexican* would offer Cutting an entree into the public life of New Mexico at a high level. His father arrived in early February, looking well but finding "the climate very hot after New York." Cutting thought his father's appearance, as the senatorial contest heated up, would "set many tongues a wagging and alarm many a candidate." Before William Cutting could initiate negotiations to purchase the *New Mexican,* he suffered a heart attack. His wish was to return home. He boarded his private railroad car for the journey, accompanied by Dr. Bishop. Meanwhile, his wife headed west to spend the last hours of his life with him in Chicago where he died in the private car on March 1.[25]

Bronson was devastated. He knew that his father was ill, but neither

Doctors Bishop nor Massie had informed him about the gravity of his father's condition. Moreover, his mother insisted, and the doctors agreed, that the precariousness of his health forbade his traveling to New York for his father's funeral. At this time, Albert Fall and his family, renting a nearby house for the duration of the upcoming legislative session, took Cutting under their wing and offered him solace and comfort. Cutting and his father had been to tea at the Fall residence before his illness. Fall's daughter, Jouett, recalled years later that when Bronson received word of his father's death, he wrote Mrs. Fall a note "saying he was lonely" and inquiring whether he might come to visit. He called almost every afternoon. Later, though still in mourning, he took Jouett to dances. He sat patiently while she whirled about the dance floor and had a grand time. Jouett also remembered that he took little part in Santa Fe's social life, "much to the chagrin of its inhabitants," but when he did make an appearance, despite his shyness and reserve, "he was always so gracious and charming."[26]

Cutting wrote his mother, "The Falls . . . have been especially kind all through these last weeks." He added, "It is really a great deal of comfort to know how many friends one has at a time like this." Although Cutting never could abide Fall's politics, his friendship with Jouett lasted for the rest of his life. Cutting would reciprocate their kindness following Albert Fall's political disgrace and financial ruin in the 1920s.[27]

The Little Governor and Brian Boru Dunne were equally sympathetic. Numerous townspeople called on him to express their condolences. "People," he wrote, "have been awfully kind all through this terrible time." Exceedingly difficult for Bronson was remaining in Santa Fe while his mother and sisters arranged his father's funeral in New York City. Within a week, William Bayard Cutting's estate was appraised at $10,906,480, of which $9,060,242 went to his widow. His son, Bronson, received a legacy of $500,000.[28]

By March 11, the day the legislature convened, Cutting reserved his mourning for private moments and threw himself into politics. At a meeting between progressives and standpatters the previous week, efforts at reconciliation fell through. Consequently, the legislative maneuvering in behalf of the various senatorial candidates would be even more bitter and factionalized than anticipated. Cutting hoped to bring "wobbling" legislators into the progressive fold before the voting for United States senators got underway on March 19. He also expected to complete arrangements for the purchase of a paper, "just to have some means of expression." Although no acquisition was made at this time, Cutting's correspondence discussed the legislative legerdemain: the daily shifting vote for different candidates in each house; and the arrest and jailing of four legislators for bribery. Albert Fall, Cutting explained, was behind the plot to remove four Andrews supporters who willingly accepted bribes of five thousand dollars each. This incident only heightened the bitterness among the rival candidates.[29]

Finally, on March 27, the senatorial races were resolved. Fall and Catron were elected to the United States Senate. Andrews, to everyone's surprise, withdrew from the contest. Cutting surmised that "he must have been bought off, as he could have held up everything as long as he chose." The result, Cutting observed, left William J. Mills, the last territorial governor, "in tears as he had more strength than Catron all through the fight and could not see why they should have turned him down." Catron drew the longer term, leaving Fall to seek reelection by the legislature in the near future. Fall, Catron, and the president wanted the legislature to act promptly. They hoped to dominate all New Mexico patronage positions before the presidential campaign got underway in earnest.

To Fall's detriment, confusion and bad feeling prevailed among the legislators. Moreover, Andrews and Mills announced that they would challenge Fall. During the last week of the legislative session, in June 1912, he won reelection through proceedings in which, Cutting said, "money was showered right and left," while confusion and chaos reigned. Inkwells were hurled through the chamber; "the speaker was held in his chair, while members of the State Senate rushed in and knocked down Representatives." Mrs. Fall, viewing these events with Cutting from the sidelines, went into hysterics at the time of the voting and had to be assisted out of the chamber by Cutting and Dr. Bishop. Still sobbing, she was deposited in Cutting's car and driven rapidly home. Cutting considered the proceedings illegal. However, Vice-President James S. Sherman promptly telegraphed congratulations to Fall upon his election to a full term that would begin in March 1913, indicating its official recognition by Washington.[30]

After returning to Santa Fe in June from a convalescence at Westbrook, Bronson mentioned the newspaper proposition "still hangs fire." If he were to find a place for himself in New Mexico and battle for Roosevelt and the progressive cause, he had to secure control of a newspaper along the lines he and his father had discussed. While the sale of the *New Mexican* sat in limbo, Cutting presented a set of Greek books to Groton and responded to a plea from the Department of History at Harvard, which was raising funds to retain William Scott Ferguson, one of his former professors. Thus shortly after his father's death, Cutting began to follow his footsteps by endorsing, supporting or contributing to what he considered worthy causes and individuals associated with them. Wealth not only entailed responsibility, but it also became a means of achieving worthy goals.[31]

In May or early June, Cutting received from a Denver firm an analysis of the assets and liabilities of the New Mexican Printing Company. The document indicated that in 1911 the newspaper operated at a loss of just under $2,000 and that monthly operating expenses came to about $3,850. He could purchase a controlling interest—229 out of 300 shares—for $57,000 or $48,785, if the owners were willing to sell him 151 shares and majority control. These figures represented a considerable reduction in the sale price, $100,000, quoted the previous fall. But in June Cutting still thought the price too high. He asked his mother whether $30,000 was a reasonable offer. Nevertheless, he thought the time was ripe, from "the financial point of view," to make an offer. The printing company was unable to get "the administration printing . . . on account of its weak-kneed attitude and rotten politics."

The prospect of the *New Mexican* losing its printing patronage and "the terror of competition" made its major owners, Paul A. F. Walter and J. K. Stauffer, anxious to sell. Walter in particular was "badly scared by the idea of competition" and was unable to get any "substantial promises of support from the gang." Cutting had already lined up a possible editor, J. Wright Giddings, a former lieutenant governor of Michigan, while the current business manager, Charles Stauffer, was willing to remain at his post. Although Cutting's investment, no matter what the cost of the controlling shares, would be large, it was "certainly cheaper than any other newspaper scheme that has been talked of."[32]

The deal was consummated by July. Cutting purchased 229 shares of stock at $210 per share for a sum of $48,090. Miguel Antonio Otero, Sr. was made a director and the treasurer of the company. His new wife secured eight shares. Former shareholders each controlled one. On July 1, a simple statement appeared in the *New Mexican:* "Controlling interest in the New Mexican Printing Company was today acquired by Bronson M. Cutting." Details about the future editorial policy would be announced later. Cutting had finally found a prominent place for himself in New Mexico. The upcoming presidential campaign would provide an opportunity to promote the progressive cause and possibly launch his political career.[33]

The first issue under Cutting's aegis appeared on July 8, 1912. In addition to his editors, he asked Francis Wilson and H. H. Dorman to serve as directors and hoped to get Brian Boru Dunne, currently in California, back on the paper. Although the business expenses were great, more than he had anticipated, the work agreed with Cutting. The nagging cough that had plagued his health for several months seemed to disappear. Equally important was that most everybody in Santa Fe seemed "to be delighted over the new deal," and there were "lots of new subscribers."[34]

On occasion, Cutting wrote editorials for the paper, but he did not take an active role in its daily production. His company ran a weekly edition in Spanish. He devoted much of his attention to the bitter feuding within the Republican party. Old guard leaders in New Mexico, almost to a man, believed that Taft's renomination was inevitable and that his defeat was equally foretold. According to Thomas B. Catron, the two factions were so embittered that the election of either Taft or Roosevelt would be impossible. Nevertheless, Catron thought that standing by Taft was imperative. The old guard's gloom was Cutting's opportunity. "If we can get an organization in working shape," he wrote, "we shall come pretty near carrying this state for T.R."[35]

As a long-standing, intimate friend of the Cutting family, Theodore Roosevelt gained their unqualified support. Olivia Murray Cutting early contributed money. Visiting Oyster Bay, Justine convinced Roosevelt to send her brother a telegram that wished him well in his new job. Copies were widely distributed with a circular letter. The telegram helped to boost both the candidacy of Roosevelt and the circulation of the *New Mexican*. Cutting's newspaper immediately became the leading New Mexico supporter of the progressive cause. When Roosevelt walked out of the Republican party during the Chicago convention at the end of June 1912, Cutting assumed an active role in promoting the Progressive party in New Mexico. He served as treasurer of the state organization, with the Little Governor sitting as state chairman.[36]

While the enthusiasm of the Progressives mounted, the gloom of Republican leaders moved toward complete despair. In July, Albert Fall was convinced that Woodrow Wilson would be elected, that the "moneyed interests" would meagerly contribute to the Taft campaign, and that "business interests generally" would be "willing if not desirous, of seeing Wilson elected." Moreover, Fall feared that a vigorous fight for Roosevelt in New Mexico would badly split the Republican Hispanic vote and thereby impair the old gang's political base, a point that Cutting did not fully comprehend at this time but on which he would capitalize later. Fall anticipated that the courting of several prominent Spanish-speaking politicians by the Progressives would cause the loss of the heavily Hispanic and formerly solid Republican counties.[37] Cutting recognized that the "only hope of the Old Guard," nearly all of whom were financially strapped from heavy expenditures in recent campaigns, would be the coffers of the Santa Fe railroad. Symbolizing the gloom of the old gang was the death of one of its leaders, Solomon Luna. Cutting did not attend his funeral, which brought most of the state's political leaders to Albuquerque.[38]

In his capacity as treasurer of the Progressive party, Cutting sought funds with which to send native speakers and campaign workers into every "Spanish county," to maintain a headquarters, to subsidize friendly newspapers and to mail campaign literature. Cutting was not optimistic that the Progressive National Committee would commit itself to a state with only three electoral votes, but he pursued his job with enthusiasm. He attended a Progressive convention in Albuquerque on September 10 and met Theodore Roosevelt's train in Gallup several days later, talking to him "practically alone" all the way into Albuquerque. Cutting felt the former president's visit did much to smooth differences in the Progressive camp. Important to Cutting as well was that his own exertions, if anything, benefitted his health.[39]

Years later, a perceptive journalist, who would soon work for Cutting on the *New Mexican,* recalled seeing him in the Albuquerque railroad station with the Santa Fe delegation to the "Bull Moose" convention. He was the last man to step down from the train. After falling in with the delegation, he walked well toward the rear of the wildly cheering procession of delegates on their way to the convention hall. His reticence seemed strangely out of place in the "boisterous rough and tumble" politics of New Mexico. What appeared to some people as aloofness was modesty bordering on shyness. Capitalizing on his reserve, Cutting was learning how to encourage and assist others instead of projecting himself into the leadership role.[40]

As the campaign moved into its final weeks, Cutting bemoaned his lack of funds. Although there was "a tremendous progressive sentiment all over the state," he doubted whether it could be "crystallized into an effective working force" without money. The pressure of the campaign raised some concern about his health. After a trip to Roswell, he spent several weeks in bed to avoid overexertion. Although he felt Roosevelt would make "a better showing than people think," he realized by late October that "we can hardly hope now to carry the state."[41]

To meet operating expenses at party headquarters, Cutting asked his mother to make a monetary contribution that "would be most gratefully received." Mrs. Cutting, of course, was worried more about his health than the request for funds. Indeed, his health took a turn for the worse. His temperature and coughing increased. Although it was unclear whether he was hemorrhaging, he was still bedridden at the end of October. With everybody busy campaigning, he felt he was shirking his duties, but he also considered the Progressive cause doomed. He came to this conclusion because "the New Mexico corporations have deserted Taft" and were leaning toward Wilson. By throwing their strength to the Democrats, they made Roosevelt's chances hopeless. The election results showed that Roosevelt had carried only two counties in New Mexico.[42]

Once the campaign ended, Cutting's health improved. The election results did not particularly distress him. He informed his mother, "We made as good a showing on the whole as we had a right to expect under the circumstances." Taft "never had any show at all," and the "old Republican party," like the old gang in New Mexico, appeared to be finished. Its ranks had bitterly divided during the recent senatorial elections and schismed further during the campaign. Although Fall and Catron had officially endorsed Taft, they had seen the hopelessness of his cause. Cutting thought "it just as well to have the Democrats in for a while." They would give the Progressive party an opportunity to consolidate and develop its strength.[43]

After the election, Cutting attended to the details of the newspaper. While interested in local affairs and gossip, he tried to avoid the social salons of Santa Fe. At Christmas time, he personally presented each employee a present. At home with his friends, he was cheerful and entertaining. Although still coughing and sometimes bedridden, he nevertheless seemed well along the road to recovery. Whenever he overexerted himself, he regained his strength with bed rest before resuming his regular routine. When Justine arrived in Santa Fe at year's end, she noticed that her brother's coughing was negligible and that he engaged in "a good deal of exercise for him." His "constant interest" in literally every detail of publishing the *New Mexican* had "done wonders." His advice and support were in demand by many individuals. She observed his routine: a walk to the office in mid-morning; a walk home for lunch, occasionally with one or two friends; entertaining visitors at tea or discussing business with them; and possibly having one or two guests for dinner. She believed he was living "a most normal and sensible life."[44]

When the legislature convened in mid-January, Cutting became intensely interested in its proceedings. There was a slight possibility that New Mexico lawmakers would vote out Albert Fall. Or so thought Miguel Antonio Otero, Sr., who was lobbying for his own candidacy. Cutting was distressed by a rumor that Roosevelt had endorsed Fall and had urged his Progressive friends in the legislature to vote for him, if the matter was to be reconsidered. Cutting telegraphed Roosevelt to express his concern and received an emphatic denial in return.

As an honorary colonel on the governor's staff, the young newspaper publisher attended the governor's reception for the members of the legislature. He was "gorgeous in his uniform and gold braid, sword, etc., looking very tall and handsome." To his sister, Cutting appeared more mature than his twenty-four years when he dealt with various politicians. He acted quickly and decisively, "without any interior nervousness." All the while, he appeared amiable and attentive. After Fall was again elected by the legislature, he and Justine drafted editorials that attracted widespread attention. One denounced W. H. H. Llewellyn and John Barton Burg, Progressive supporters of Theodore Roosevelt, who had voted for Albert Fall. After reading the editorials, the former president commended Cutting "for the brave and manly position he was taking."[45]

With the publication of these controversial editorials, any immediate reconciliation or fence-mending between Cutting and members of the Republican leadership was out of the question. The *New Mexican* was clearly in the Progressive fold. From this base, Cutting would make his contribution to public life in New Mexico. At the outset the paper prospered, Justine reported, with "never a single back copy to be had." As the 1912 election made clear, however, it had a most precarious foundation. By themselves, Progressives could not muster enough support to win elections, although they might hold the balance of power through political fusion. As a prominent publisher, Cutting would project a powerful voice that could not be ignored, and if his health was stable, he could seek public office.

After less than three years, Cutting had found a meaningful place for himself in New Mexico, but his role and his views would be contested. Controversy, some of which he initiated, would dog him for the rest of his days in New Mexico.[46]

CHAPTER 5

CONTROVERSY
1913–1915

As the publisher of a leading newspaper, Cutting immediately
became an influential figure in Santa Fe and a person of some
repute in the state. His family friendship with Theodore Roosevelt cast him into a prominent position in the Progressive party.
As yet Cutting had not sparked any public controversy. The uproar orches-
trated against Edgar L. Hewett by Cutting and his friends appeared to many
Santa Feans as a tempest in a local teapot, but it had broad implications for the
disciplines of anthropology and archaeology. No longer were they the exclu-
sive domain of enthusiastic amateurs romanticizing ancient cultures and glo-
rifying the past. In Santa Fe, prior to the emergence of an art community,
local residents enriched their social milieu with the unique cultural heritage of
New Mexico. Most of these people were "Anglos" with pretensions to
Victorian gentility and were uninterested in the lives of native New Mexicans, but as amateurs, they were beginning to explore the Spanish past of the
community and state.

Hewett early found an appreciable audience for his popularizing of the
Southwest. Prior to the First World War, the region lacked a major university
and was yet unexposed to industrialization and urbanization. Science revolved around the anthropologist and the archaeologist, not the chemist and
the physicist. Hewett's work appealed more easily to poets and painters than
to laboratory scientists. Gentlemen and ladies with their anthropological and
archaeological interests still held fast against the university-based professionals. The research by Hewett and his associates, some of whom were
creditable scientists, was largely literary. The small but growing school of
professionals in the field became increasingly critical of them, but until
Cutting helped raise the issue, criticism of Hewett was muted in Santa Fe. He
was a highly regarded citizen who promoted the community's cultural life by
helping to restore and publicize nearby antiquities.

Cutting met Hewett, the head of the School of American Archaeology,
shortly after he arrived in Santa Fe and soon concluded that he was a pretentious fool. He was bored by Hewett's story-telling tour of the lovely canyon
in the Pajarito Plateau of the Jemez Mountains, modern knowledge of which
was first presented by Adolph Bandalier. In addition, he was outraged when
Hewett informed him that the artist, Carl Lotave, a friend, was romantically

interested in his sister, Justine, a married woman whose portrait he was painting.

From the outset of his residence in Santa Fe, Cutting had been corresponding with a Harvard classmate, associated with the Anthropology Department, who confirmed his views of Hewett. As early as September 1910, less than two months after Cutting's arrival, George Chase wrote, "I agree with you in thinking it a disgrace that such a man should hold the position he does" as head of the School of American Archaeology. Later that year, he wrote, "What you say about Hewett's methods of execution and state of the funds in the museum is certainly very damaging." Since Hewett received some support from the Archaeological Institute of America, efforts were made to cut these funds. However, Cutting and his anthropological and archaeological allies had to show that they were moved by professional considerations, a desire to see the Santa Fe operations reflect credit upon their discipline. Hewett remained convinced that Cutting's vendetta against him was retribution for his remarks about Carl Lotave and Justine.[1]

Before Cutting settled in New Mexico, Hewett had attracted the unflattering attention of university-based archaeologists. In December 1909, Franz Boas resigned as a member of the Managing Committee of the American School and of the Archaeological Institute of America, which helped to support the institution. He was unable to endorse the administrative and scientific policies of Hewett's operation. Boas criticized the policy of the American School "to encourage superficial work, to carry on a few detailed investigations that may have been technically satisfactory if it so happened that good men were in charge of it, but without any attention to the general development of the broad aspects of American archaeology." Boas also noted that Hewett had a high-handed managerial style: selecting committee members who shared his views; voting by mail without the opportunity for discussion; deleting controversial topics from the committee agenda; and withholding minority reports from presentation before the Archaeological Institute. However, Boas's chief complaint against Hewett, echoed by his university colleagues, was "based on his lack of appreciation of what constitutes scientific work."[2]

By the time Cutting entered the fray in 1913, Hewett was already a controversial figure among archaeologists but almost a venerated figure among his friends and associates in Santa Fe. Cutting challenged Hewett's credibility on his home ground and lost the battle. Hewett was too valuable an asset to Santa Fe as a cultural center in the remote Southwest. The community was grateful to him for developing a museum, restoring the Governor's Palace, promoting nearby canyon ruins as tourist attractions, and other cultural endeavors. For example, Hewett went abroad to give lectures at Oxford, Rome and elsewhere in Europe in 1912. To his dismay, Cutting wrote that "everyone feels the highest respect for him." He thought all the lectures were to be "before ladies clubs at the different places."[3]

In October 1913, H. H. Dorman, a Cutting friend and associate on the *New Mexican,* prompted the Santa Fe controversy. As president of the Chamber of Commerce, he debated the merits of the School of American Archaeology and its director, Edgar L. Hewett. Hewett disputed the accuracy of a statement, printed by Dorman on thousands of envelopes, that Santa Fe was the oldest city in the United States. Either outraged or embarrassed by the embossed claim, he secured the eviction of the Chamber of Commerce from the section of the Governor's Palace that he managed. In an interview with the *New Mexican,* Dorman declared that the school needed a new director.

Dorman's attack on Hewett and the school stirred up a hornet's nest in local cultural and scientific circles. Judge John R. McFie and Paul A. F. Walter attempted "to get up a mass meeting of citizens to denounce Dorman." Subsequent issues of the *New Mexican* followed the Dorman interview with articles that assailed Hewett and that were buttressed by letters to Cutting from university professors. Hewett was in San Diego at the time the interview was published and did not respond to an offer by the *New Mexican* to controvert Dorman's charges.

Prompted by the articles, numerous groups met to debate the issue. They indicated to Dorman and his allies that the residents of Santa Fe did not sanction the attacks on Hewett and his management of the school and that they wanted the school to remain in the community. Resolutions in support of Hewett were quickly passed by the Woman's Board of Trade, the Woman's Club, the New Mexico Archaeological Society, and several other organizations. In addition, many residents signed petitions endorsing Hewett. During a special meeting, the Chamber of Commerce endorsed Hewett, fearing that without strong community support, the managing committee of the School of American Archaeology would remove the facility to some other host city. The remarks were in response to a rumor that the city of Los Angeles was interested in having the school moved somewhere within its environs.

Cutting, a member of the chamber, enlivened the debate by stating that he considered Hewett incompetent. Adding insult to injury, he said, with Boas's earlier comments in mind, that the managing committee of the School of American Archaeology was incapable of selecting a director for any school. Hewett received support from Charles Fletcher Lummis in Los Angeles. A

Lummis letter, published in the *New Mexican,* lauded Hewett and attacked those members of the Chamber of Commerce who supported the slogan, "Santa Fe the Oldest City in the United States." Hewett, he said, was "the man who put Santa Fe on the map" and who had the distinction of being in *Who's Who in America.*

In subsequent issues of his newspaper, Cutting printed letters from Professors Roland B. Dixon and Alfred M. Tozzer of Harvard, Franz Boas of Columbia, George A. Dorsey of Chicago, and Pliny E. Goddard of the American Museum of National History in New York. One letter was more critical than the other of Hewett. In each instance, the *New Mexican* offered space to Hewett, if he wished to respond to the charges leveled against his scientific reputation. Herbert Joseph Spinden of Harvard perhaps best characterized Hewett as one who had done "little real scientific work" and was at best "a publicist and promoter."[4]

Hewett was in San Diego during most of October, helping to plan the Panama-California Exposition. His most articulate supporter was Charles F. Lummis who proposed to "skin Dorman and Cutting and the other illegitimates." In response to a wire from Hewett who thanked him for his letter to the *New Mexican,* Lummis agreed to help put "the SOB's where they belong." In a letter to Cutting, he suggested that his paper could be subject to libel litigation. Cutting immediately responded, "As you are apparently the only man between the Atlantic and the Pacific oceans who is willing to put himself on record in defense of Mr. Hewett we are especially anxious to print everything you have to say."[5]

As the controversy ran its course, its focus shifted from the age of Santa Fe to the integrity of Hewett. The fear that the institute would move the school to another location prompted a flurry of indignant telegrams and a host of resolutions endorsing Hewett. In the lead was the Woman's Club. Cutting participated in none of these activities. Although he appeared flustered upon learning that the institute might leave Santa Fe, he refused to temporize his attitude toward Hewett. He engaged in a lengthy conversation with Mrs. I. H. Rapp, the wife of a prominent Santa Fe architect, but neither changed the other's opinions of Hewett. Cutting also took the position that if Hewett's institute was removed, another would quickly replace it.[6]

Finally in mid-November the controversy came to an end when the Chamber of Commerce repudiated the controversial interview of its president, H. H. Dorman. After a bitter debate and a vote of 73 to 6, the chamber adopted a resolution disclaiming any connection with or responsibility for criticism leveled at the director of the archaeological school. Cutting, of course, voted in opposition. Although defeated in Santa Fe, Cutting continued his efforts to discredit Hewett among scientists, while Hewett, through his friend Lummis, worked to challenge Cutting and to discredit him in Santa Fe.[7]

In New York during the month of December, Cutting learned from Franz Boas what he already suspected. There was no possibility of Hewett's school moving from Santa Fe. A large portion of its support came from the state, including the use of the Governor's Palace for its headquarters. With impunity Cutting could insist, Boas believed, that the school conduct itself on a more satisfactory basis. A director should be present all the time, and he should have the confidence of the universities. What Cutting sought was a reorganization of Hewett's operation by the Archaeology Institute of America. If he failed, he then would inquire of major universities whether one or another would offer anthropological-archaeological instruction in Santa Fe, particularly during the summer months.[8]

To advance this effort, Cutting sent H. H. Dorman to a professional meeting of anthropologists in Montreal. Dorman presented a plan to reorganize the American School on a scientific basis. Cutting urged Boas to attend at his expense and to champion the cause, but in a telegram, also signed by Roland B. Dixon and Pliny E. Goddard, to several professors at the conference, Boas urged the support of the reorganization. Although Dorman's proposal made no headway in Montreal, Cutting persisted. He was convinced that the Executive Committee of the School of American Archaeology should establish a scientific school. He noted that attendance at the school's summer session was declining and that lectures were repeatedly cancelled or "had to be delivered before various local clubs in order to insure an audience." In addition, "little or no serious work" was being done by "the few men regularly employed in the museum." Finally unable to secure professional reorganization, Cutting considered undertaking an independent reorganization, an idea that attracted even less professional support. If a professionally oriented school was started in Santa Fe, Cutting was convinced, Hewett would lose his legislative appropriation. If a new school would even threaten to arise, he thought, "We should have Hewett out in a minute." By mid-1915, he gave up his crusade, but he and the professional anthropologists with whom he corresponded, steadfastly believed that Hewett at the very most was a mere promoter and propagandist.[9]

Hewett won the fight both in Santa Fe and in professional circles. The views of the academic anthropologists made little headway at the Montreal meeting. Their aggressive attacks on Hewett appeared as persecution, and his presence at Montreal only reinforced that perception. Lummis, who was preparing a pamphlet defending Hewett, was advised to let the project lie dormant, but he wanted to proceed, his object being "to get after . . . Boas and Tozzer and the bloody gang." "Cutting and Dorman and those grasshoppers," he added, "cut very little ice." The pamphlet came to naught, and Lummis had to content himself with an exchange of sarcastic letters with Cutting. Upon his return from Montreal, Hewett took the lead in seeking a successor to Dorman as president of the Chamber of Commerce.[10]

Although Cutting lost some prestige with many residents in wake of the controversy, he hardly became a pariah in Santa Fe society. He was still a publisher of a major New Mexico newspaper and the treasurer of the Progressive Party of New Mexico. Both jobs competed for his attention while he challenged Edgar L. Hewett. In early 1913, for example, Cutting and the *New Mexican* helped to expose a forgery by a prominent legislator, William H. H. Llewellyn, a former Rough Rider. He had fabricated a telegram, purportedly from his constituents, that advised him how to vote on a crucial issue. Cutting secured a copy of the forged telegram from Western Union and turned it over to the Speaker of the House. The story received national attention over the Associated Press wires. Cutting's sister, Justine, observed that the only way of gaining influence with politicians was by threatening to expose them in the press. From January 1913 through November 1914, Cutting hired private detectives to investigate members of the legislature for evidence of corruption, particularly with regard to the selection of Albert B. Fall as United States senator. Although he spent several thousand dollars in this endeavor, the detectives were unable to provide conclusive, meaningful evidence. Through the glaring light of publicity, Cutting was becoming both influential and controversial.[11]

All was not work. Many an evening, Cutting played bridge with friends, such as the Little Governor, Francis Wilson, and Dr. Massie. The ever interesting Brian Boru Dunne, the city editor of the *New Mexican*, shared Cutting's home and continually amused everyone with his wit and gossip. In addition, Cutting assumed the tuition payments of Tony Luna and Miguel Antonio Otero, Jr., who were in law school in Washington and Lee University in Lexington, Virginia. Then, too, there was the elusive Callie Hull, whom Cutting never mentioned in his extant correspondence but whom he saw when she visited Santa Fe.[12]

Progressive politics also kept him active. In the summer of 1913, when Theodore Roosevelt went to Silver City in the southwestern part of the state, Cutting tried in vain to bring the former president to Santa Fe for a day.

However, he did visit briefly with Roosevelt, who was "very tired and seedy but enthusiastic as to prospects." Moreover, the affairs of the Episcopal church always commanded his attention. In 1913, internal feuding had thus far prevented the bishops from selecting a successor to Bishop John M. Kendrick and the Episcopal district of New Mexico from holding an annual convention for the first time in its history. As a vestryman, Cutting, along with most other church members, was appalled by but unable to restrain L. Bradford Prince who used high-handed tactics to maintain prominence in church affairs.[13]

Meanwhile, the *New Mexican* was losing money. The generosity of Olivia Murray Cutting kept the enterprise solvent without serious curtailment in early 1914. The annual report showed a loss of fifteen thousand dollars. At the annual meeting of directors, the board was increased from five to seven members. Added were the Little Governor and Dr. Frederic Bishop. The new directors formed a subcommittee to detect, if possible, where the newspaper was incurring losses. An immediate result was that the size of the paper was reduced to four pages.[14] In addition, the directors hired E. Dana Johnson, editor of the Albuquerque *Evening Herald,* as the managing editor of the *New Mexican*. He replaced J. Wright Giddings, an unimaginative and limited newspaperman. Johnson soon became the best managing editor in the state, and Cutting never again had reason to question the competency or professionalism of his editors. By mid-March he was able to report, "The paper is going well and in spite of some complaint as to the loss of the illustrations, people seem to be taking to it very nicely."[15]

He was now able to devote his attention more fully to local matters such as the municipal election, which proved once again that the Republican party was invincible in Santa Fe. Cutting explained, "The Democrats seem to have gone back on us and voted Republican to keep the Progressives and the newspaper from controlling the situation." He took some satisfaction that the victors spent twenty to twenty-five dollars per vote, money "mostly put up by the saloons." To add to his woe, Dorman was turned down for reelection as head of the Chamber of Commerce. Chamber members did not even extend him a vote of thanks.

To make matters worse the April financial statement of the *New Mexican* indicated that, despite its new editor and reduced size, the paper was still losing money. Cutting now focused attention on the business manager, Charles Stauffer, a brother-in-law of the former owner and managing editor. Stauffer, who was demanding a raise in salary, was both the job printer and the business manager. Several months would pass before Cutting could replace Stauffer, and several more thereafter, before he could locate a manager amply qualified for the job.[16]

Although a minority voice in the Hewett controversy, Cutting stood with the majority at the Church of the Holy Faith. A fellow vestryman, Rufus J. Paulen, president of the First National Bank, invited Cutting "to consider taking some stock in the bank and becoming identified with it as a shareholder and a director when a good opportunity occurred." The invitation was extended in March 1914; the new board would be elected the following January. To qualify Cutting as a director, Paulen was willing to let him have ten shares of his stock. At the time, the capital of the bank, a United States Depository, was one hundred and fifty thousand dollars. Cutting thus gained an opportunity to shore up the credit of his publishing company and to learn about practical banking. Paulen assured him, "Your name would add strength to the board."[17]

Later in the spring, Cutting visited Groton and then Boston, where he caught up with friends and former classmates. By June, he was back in Santa Fe, "none the worse for wear." He noted that politics was coming to the fore as the parties prepared for the 1914 elections. The old gang insisted that Theodore Roosevelt had returned to the Republican party and that the Progressives in New Mexico should follow suit by endorsing the Republican leadership. Meanwhile, news of the war in Europe and, more importantly, stories of Pancho Villa's activities in Chihuahua competed with political news and local gossip. Most pleasing to Cutting was that the financial crisis at the *New Mexican* seemed to have subsided with Stauffer's departure.[18]

The meeting of various party conventions fueled political excitement in late August. Cutting, treasurer of the state Progressive committee, quickly became involved. As temporary chairman of the Progressive convention, Cutting was scheduled to deliver the opening address. Tensions within the party between "Rough Rider" friends of Theodore Roosevelt and the party leadership quickly surfaced. George Curry, chairman of the executive committee, was the leading spokesman of the Rough Riders, expressing the view that Miguel Antonio Otero should step down as chairman of the state Progressive committee. Both men were former territorial governors. One had resigned at Roosevelt's request; the other was appointed by Roosevelt. Curry argued that Roosevelt had no confidence in Otero and the other party leaders. Along with other Rough Riders, he claimed that he had correspondence with Roosevelt. The former president, they declared, urged the Progressives to aid the Republican organization. According to Curry, Roosevelt wanted him to take charge of the Progressive party. Partially to resolve these tensions,

Cutting was selected as the state chairman of the Progressive party at its convention in Belen. Although Cutting had no intention of leading the Progressives back to the Republican camp, his credentials as a family friend and supporter of Theodore Roosevelt were impeccable. Curry assured Cutting that Roosevelt, to whom he had written, would be pleased at his selection.[19]

Fatigued by the trip to the convention at Belen, Cutting would not jeopardize his health while serving as state chairman. Unless something very unexpected turned up, he intended to remain in Santa Fe throughout the campaign. He was delighted with the nomination of Francis Wilson, his friend, an attorney for and board member of the *New Mexican,* as the Progressive party's congressional candidate. Despite the fact that Wilson was contesting for the only major office involving the entire electorate, Cutting was also worried about finances. "The expense is terrific," he informed his mother, adding that "any contribution will be most gratefully received."[20]

Among other things, funds were needed to keep in tow the few newspapers supporting the Progressive cause. *The Republican,* published in Gallup, was threatened by Republican businessmen and officeholders with the loss of advertising and other pressures. In 1912, Cutting had purchased stock in the paper so that the Progressive editor would not lose control. In turn, the editor supplied the *New Mexican* with stories from the Gallup area. Feeling the financial pinch of the campaign, Cutting became distressed with Francis Wilson who lacked restraint "in the matter of expense." Although he believed that Wilson would make "a most excellent Congressman," Cutting soon realized that he had "very little chance of being elected." The best hope of the Progressives was "to bust the old stand pat bunch and elect a decent legislature," and that, he added, "could be a big achievement."

So high had "the absolutely necessary expenses of the campaign" risen that at the end of September, Cutting was unsure about whether he could "stand the strain unaided." Recognizing that it was "useless to try to raise any money in the State," he asked his mother, already "doing entirely too much," for an additional contribution. A Republican-controlled legislature, he said, would mean "the passage of every kind of corrupt bill" and possibly the removal of Governor William C. McDonald and Supreme Court Justice Richard H. Hanna. Both were Democrats previously endorsed by the Progressives.[21]

Managing the campaign did not overtax Cutting's health. He divided his workday between the *New Mexican* and the Progressive party headquarters. The secretary of the state Progressive committee did most of the detailed work. Cutting wrote letters to other newspapers that were endorsing Wilson and tried to shift the burden of campaign mailings to the more active county chairmen. Although he suffered a brief attack of hay fever in late September, he otherwise pursued his normal routine, which included entertaining dinner guests and playing bridge in the evening.[22]

As the campaign moved into its last weeks, Cutting's workload increased. The party dispatched the Little Governor to the northern counties "to fix things up." Cutting believed that the Progressives's only chance was to make a good showing that would break the Republican domination of the state legislature. He was concerned about the apathy among some county chairmen. Another worry was that the Republicans, "hard up throughout the campaign," seemed "suddenly to have accumulated a good deal of cash." To determine more precisely how the Republicans were managing the final weeks of their campaign, Cutting had the Burns Detective Agency in Denver hire an agent to report on activities in Republican headquarters. From these reports, he learned what he already knew. The Republicans were buying drinks and spending money freely among Spanish-speaking voters. Cutting's hard work in the last weeks of the campaign improved his health. He informed his mother that he had gained five pounds in three weeks.[23]

On the other hand, the election results were "sickening." The Progressives, Cutting exclaimed, "seem to have entirely disappeared." He found no consolation in the campaign results of other states. He wrote, "Out here it just means the total waste of two months of hard work and a great deal of money." Moreover, with the old gang firmly ensconced, future prospects, "at least for a long time to come," seemed equally bleak. The question Cutting and other Progressive leaders would have to face was whether to let the party expire.[24]

Shortly after the election, Cutting traveled eastward to stay with his family during the holiday season. He was joined by Mike Otero and Tony Luna who were breaking from their law studies at Washington and Lee University. On Christmas Eve, Cutting had distributed to all employees of the New Mexican Printing Company a five dollar gold piece with his best holiday wishes. They reciprocated with a Christmas Day telegram "from the main cheese down to the devil," thirty signatures in all.[25]

Back in Santa Fe after the holidays, Cutting noted that the Republican majority in the legislature was now trying to implicate the governor in the failure of a Las Cruces bank. The legislature, he said, "is getting worse and worse all the time." On the other hand, he noted that the *New Mexican* had come "to a crest of popularity in Santa Fe." "Even the stand patters seem to like it, as well as the Hewett set," he added. At a legislative tea hosted by Mary Prince, one of the prominent matrons in Santa Fe society told him that "it was the best paper west of the Mississippi." Such support, while encouraging, did not mitigate the fact that the paper was still operating at a loss, albeit "a good deal smaller loss than last year." Yet, Santa Fe remained attractive, despite the paper's difficulties and the depressing political scene. As Brian Boru Dunne cogently remarked, "the freedom out here, the funny people, their remarks and running the paper" lifted the cloud of financial and political distress. Among the remarks circulating during the Christmas season was that Cutting would be married at Easter.[26]

While on jury duty in March, another matter, boiling for over a year, came to a head. A. B. Renehan filed a libel suit against Cutting and the *New Mexican*. He was a prominent attorney with whom Cutting and his sister had tangled in litigation over a piano purchased shortly after their arrival in Santa Fe. To resolve the matter once and for all, Cutting took "the bull by the horns" and employed the law firm of Catron and Catron. He recognized that his bold stroke was a gamble on their integrity, but he also understood that "they are the only people in the world who can keep Renehan from bribing a jury in this county, and it would be worth their while to win this case." Cutting knew that the Catrons had both "reams of evidence on Renehan's career" and a deep personal animus against him. Cutting's gamble, which cost him twenty-five hundred dollars in legal fees, paid off. After several months of legal maneuvering, Renehan finally dropped the libel suit.[27]

While visiting the family home at Westbrook in the spring, Cutting with his sister was invited to lunch at Oyster Bay. He was unable to attend, but Justine reported the conversation with Theodore Roosevelt. In correspondence with the former president, George Curry had suggested that the Republican and Progressive parties combine in 1916 to elect David Leahy, a former Rough Rider, to the governor's office. Curry's suggestion delighted Roosevelt. Cutting considered Leahy not "the worst possible candidate," but he was still a tool of the leading corporate lobbyists, Charles Spiess and Charles Springer. Cutting thought that Leahy would be "sacrificed to Bursum in exchange for a Spiess-Springer Attorney General." Cutting had no intention of going to San Diego, where Roosevelt would be attending a "Rough Rider affair," merely to discuss New Mexico politics. Cutting was convinced that Roosevelt would return to the Republican fold, despite remarks of George Perkins, the chairman of the Progressive party.[28]

In the summer, Cutting hoped to enjoy the company of his two young friends, Mike Otero and Tony Luna, but they were so busy preparing for their bar exams in August that he did not see much of them. Instead, he had to consider buying a new printing press. The circulation of his newspaper was beginning to surge ahead of the capacity of the present machines. A more positive note, indicating his increasing acceptance in the business community, was his selection to the executive committee of the New Mexico Taxpayers Association. Although he believed himself unqualified to serve, he accepted the invitation. He quickly discovered that other committee members knew little more about taxation than he did.[29]

By fall, despite all his efforts, the *New Mexican* was "still losing money at a fearful rate." As best he could determine, another change in the business department was necessary. However, in mid-October, he had no idea about where he could find a competent person. A month later, he had a lead, a "fellow Henderson on the El Paso Herald." Although Henderson knew little or nothing about job printing, he was reported to be "a hustler," which was "the main thing" for Cutting. Imperative for the newspaper was a more aggressive policy to attract subscribers and advertisers. A competing Santa Fe weekly was planning to become a daily, indicating that it was "making money which we ought to have." The New Mexican Printing Company needed more business to stop the drain on his personal finances and his continual worrying about the plight of the paper.[30]

At the end of the year, while Cutting was in New York with his family, Ralph Henderson agreed to come aboard as business manager, a post he held most satisfactorily for several years. Henderson was appointed at a salary of twenty-four hundred dollars per year. By the year's end, both Mike Otero and Tony Luna had passed their bar exams. Mike was an attorney in the office of the attorney general, and Tony had applied for a commission in the Philippine Constabulary.[31]

In short, by the end of 1915, the plight of the paper stood the fair chance of a reversal. While Cutting's status in Santa Fe had improved considerably, the political situation in New Mexico was deplorable. Just ahead was a momentous controversy that would attract national attention, drag on for several years and drain Cutting's time and finances. The issue would be entangled with the election of 1916, which involved key New Mexico campaigns for president, governor, and United States senator and representative. Rumors that reached Senator Fall were that if invited, Cutting and Otero would return to the Republican party. Senator Catron and others were opposed to soliciting their return. The hostility among Republican leaders at the end of 1915 indicated that Cutting's vague political ambitions would be difficult to realize. It also indicated that political animosities would become involved in the controversy that soon engulfed him and the *New Mexican*.[32] The election of 1916 would be a critical one both for Cutting and the Republican party in New Mexico.

A CRITICAL ELECTION YEAR
1916

In both a public and personal way, Bronson Cutting was deeply involved in the election of 1916, which would give the Progressives an opportunity to advance the cause of Theodore Roosevelt as a presidential candidate either on the Progressive or the Republican party ticket. He and other Progressives hoped to thwart the old gang, despite their poor showing in 1914, by fusing or allying with the Democrats. For the Republicans, there was the opportunity, if the various factions could coalesce, of once again controlling and managing public affairs.

Foreign policy was injected into the campaign when on March 9, the army of Francisco Villa raided the border town of Columbus and took seventeen lives. The raid prompted the federalization of several National Guard units that included New Mexico's and led to the Pershing Expedition that invaded Mexico in a futile effort to track down Villa.

Cutting and other Republicans were enthusiastic about the possibility of Theodore Roosevelt's nomination for the presidency. Indeed Senator Albert Fall, who endorsed Taft in 1912, saw Roosevelt as the one person who, whether nominated or not, could unify the Republican party. No one, Fall believed, could be nominated without "the assurance of Roosevelt's support."[1] Before February passed, Cutting made room reservations in Chicago for the Progressive and Republican nominating conventions in June.

If presidential politics did not command all of Cutting's attention early in the year, the cause of military preparedness was partially responsible. He was on a committee seeking to raise money for a military camp patterned after the model of Plattsburg. The head of the New Mexico Military Institute offered his faculty, and the War Department agreed to send two infantry companies and enough officers to supplement the institute cadre, provided that Cutting and his associates raised five thousand dollars. This effort quickly succeeded, but events along the border soon preempted the attention of the military once units of the New Mexico National Guard were called into service.[2]

New Mexico National Guard companies were sent to the border in March following the Villa raid. Tony Luna and Mike Otero were lieutenants in those units stationed in Columbus. Cutting believed that authorities were "not keen to send the native companies, which are by far the best." Cutting expected that the troops would have an exceedingly difficult time catching Villa.[3]

In May, he sought the assistance of officials of the Aero Club of America in securing a plane for the New Mexico National Guard. If Cutting raised $2,500, the Aero Club agreed to raise $5,000. Airplanes would ease supply and other problems between Fort Bliss near El Paso and the bases at Columbus and Hachita.[4]

The attention to preparedness only enhanced the rising tide of sentiment for Theodore Roosevelt among Republican voters. Since New Mexico had provided many Rough Riders for Roosevelt's command in the Spanish-American War, he was being pressured to endorse one or another faction by former comrades in arms. Above all, clear to Cutting was that sentiment for Theodore Roosevelt was crescendoing as winter turned to spring. The question for the Progressives was whether they should hold their state convention, during which they would select delegates for the national convention, before or after the Republicans met.[5]

Cutting was distressed that with one or two notable exceptions, "the weakest and flabbiest of all the Congressional utterances" seemed to issue from the Republicans. He labeled Justice Charles Evans Hughes, a leading contender for the Republican nomination, "the German-American's candidate." Although ostensibly not an active candidate, Roosevelt told Cutting, "They ought not to nominate me unless they need me and feel they have got to make the fight along my lines." Nevertheless, the former president kept a close watch on developments in New Mexico. Cutting believed that Theodore Roosevelt remained the only person "up to the job."[6]

On April 18, the state Progressive convention met in Santa Fe to select a fifteen man delegation, including Cutting, to represent New Mexico at the National Progressive Convention scheduled to convene in Chicago on June 7. At their convention, the Republicans chose delegates for their nominating convention in Chicago, which would meet at the same time.[7] At both conventions in Chicago, caucusing among delegates was intense. The rainy, gloomy weather did not dampen the enthusiasm of Cutting and the New Mexico delegation for Theodore Roosevelt. A casual mention of Roosevelt by Raymond Robins in his address prompted the New Mexico delegation, chaired by Cutting, to start a parade complete with banners declaring, "Columbus, New Mexico, is for T.R." and "If Teddy had been President, where would Villa be?" The demonstration lasted almost two hours and set the whole place wild, much to the annoyance of George W. Perkins and other leaders. Always a realist, Cutting was quite sure that noise alone would not nominate Roosevelt.

Cutting believed that the solution was a compromise candidate acceptable to the delegates at both conventions. The most acceptable compromise candidate, Charles Evans Hughes, did not fill Cutting with enthusiasm.[8] Although the results were disappointing, Cutting stood almost alone in thinking "T.R." did the only possible thing "when he gave up the fight." Like most Progressives, he was distressed with the selection of Hughes and believed that "the Germans," the German-American Alliance, engineered his selection. Cutting foresaw that to succeed, Hughes should repudiate "as quickly as possible" the element to whom he owed his nomination. Otherwise Democratic orators would designate him "the Berlin candidate" against Wilson, "the apostle of Americanism." In a letter to Cutting shortly after the convention, Roosevelt wrote, "I am doing all I can to get Mr. Hughes to come out in such shape as to make my support of value to him."[9]

On the train returning from Chicago, Cutting had an extended visit with Senator Fall, whose conversation on Mexico he found most interesting. Fall thought that the president was deliberately trying to provoke Carranza into declaring war to secure "the *kudos*" of a war president at election time. Despite Roosevelt's assurances, Cutting reported from New Mexico that "no one out here seems to think there is much chance of beating Wilson." Unless Hughes disassociated himself from his German-American constituency, Cutting feared he might have to do the unthinkable and vote for Wilson whom he claimed to "loathe." Meanwhile, at the end of June, he became absorbed in his chairmanship of the Progressive State Central Committee. He reviewed propositions "from one or another bunch of stand patters trying to make deals for the coming campaign" and to restore harmony within Republican ranks.[10]

After a tour of military preparations on the border, Cutting clarified the dilemma facing Progressive party leaders. Should they ask their rank and file to enter the Republican primaries and select delegates for the state convention, which would certainly nominate Holm Bursum for governor and Frank Hubbell for senator? They would then be faced with the choice of swallowing these old guard candidates or with bolting the party again. Another option was "to stay out and try to rally our dwindling organization for another fight on the gang from the outside." Although Cutting hated to contemplate fusion with the Democrats, he considered Hubbell and Bursum as "too bad to be possible" and had to consider the unthinkable.

But Cutting, ever the realist, was concluding that the Progressives possibly would have to support Hughes and the state Democratic ticket. Given this dilemma, Cutting did not wish to get too heavily involved, aside from publishing the *New Mexican,* in the campaign. He noted that "there are plenty

of Bursumites to work for Hughes" and that "the state independent movement can be much better handled by somebody more in sympathy with
Wilson."[11]

Senator Albert Fall and some Republican leaders understood that party
success in November was dependent on efforts at reconciliation with the
Progressives. He intended to seek support for the Republican ticket from
Cutting and various individuals who had the success of the party at heart. In
early August, Fall urged Theodore Roosevelt to write Cutting and simply
state "that you hope that Cutting and myself will be able to cooperate in
opposition to the Democrats in New Mexico . . . ." Fall explained that
during the trip from Chicago, Cutting had "expressed his desire to cooperate
with me in political matters in New Mexico." Emerging as a prominent
figure on the national scene, Fall was making every effort to restore harmony
in the Republican party. Roosevelt, respecting his efforts, wrote Cutting a
cautious letter along the lines Fall suggested.[12]

Cutting also relaxed and socialized. Although he tried to avoid the inane
Mrs. Prince at tea parties, he enjoyed evenings of bridge with male and female
friends at his home. Whenever a Charlie Chaplin film played at a theatre,
Cutting and one or another of his friends would attend. Most enjoyable in
August was "the pond or lake on the place." Cutting allowed visitors to enjoy
the facility on the southwest corner of his homestead. The extended rainfall
during the summer had settled the dust and allowed his orchard to thrive,
adding to his feeling of relaxation and satisfaction before political campaigning got underway in earnest.[13]

Cutting, of course, understood Fall's concern that the Republicans needed
the Progressives in the days before their respective state conventions. Conferences and consultations were prevalent in offices, on the streets, and in
private residences of Santa Fe. While Cutting was not enthused about the
Democratic ticket, he nevertheless found it "very superior to the Republican"
slate and now concluded that it "must be supported with vigor." He feared
Bursum would run much better than he did in 1912 when he lost to William C. McDonald. The problem for the Progressives was how to support
effectively both the Republican national ticket and the Democratic state
ticket. To his surprise, Cutting received "an exceedingly nice note" from
Roosevelt who took "back his previous requests" and approved his stand on
Bursum and Hubbell. Cutting thought that Hughes's speeches were "pitiful"
and that if Roosevelt did not "get out and arouse the nation," nothing good at
all would come out of the campaign. Nevertheless, he felt he had no choice
but to endorse Hughes. Republican strategy, on the other hand, was "to trade

off votes for Wilson for Democratic votes for Bursum." Republican leaders openly attested, Cutting said, that they cared nothing about the election of Hughes, except for the patronage his election might secure. Only the Democrats stood to benefit from the curious and intense conflict, a point Cutting recognized at the outset of the campaign. Meanwhile, following the state nominating conventions, political fusion transpired among Democrats, Progressives and occasional Republicans. Cutting declined a nomination for the state Senate. He could not "run on a ticket headed by Wilson electors, which by a technicality of our state law, I should have to do."[14]

After attending the annual meeting of the New Mexico Taxpayers Association at Albuquerque in late September, he ran "down to El Paso" where Tony Luna was "very ill with some kind of heart trouble" and had been running a high fever that fluctuated during the day. By the time Cutting got to Fort Bliss, the doctors had given up hope for Luna's recovery. For two weeks prior to Cutting's arrival, Luna's heart had been getting steadily worse. Much of the time, his temperature was 106 and 107 degrees. With Cutting's arrival, it moderated, and on October 3, the army doctors expressed hope for his recovery for the first time. But six days later, Tony Luna died from endocarditis that had started with a mild case of tonsillitis and had infected every organ in his body. For Cutting, watching his friend die was "the most terrible experience I have ever been through."[15]

Cutting had little time for mourning. Theodore Roosevelt had invited Cutting to meet his train and accompany him to Albuquerque. The young man was pleased with the opportunity that Roosevelt's visit provided to escape the loss of Tony Luna for a few days. The hectic days following Luna's death in El Paso and funeral in Santa Fe had so deeply upset Cutting that he was overwhelmed. Enthused after his train visit with Theodore Roosevelt, Cutting believed the former president's hard-hitting speeches would help revive the lack-luster, sagging Hughes campaign. He now concluded that Theodore Roosevelt had tilted the balance and that Wilson would be defeated. At Cutting's suggestion, Roosevelt had omitted all references to state candidates in his Albuquerque and other New Mexico speeches. Cutting wrote, "T.R. was great fun all through the trip."[16]

Devoting his energies to the climax of the campaign, Cutting served as treasurer of the Independent Republican-Democratic Committee in Santa Fe County and contributed five hundred dollars to the effort of electing Hughes and the Democratic candidates for governor and senator. However, at the end of the month, Cutting was astounded to learn that Roosevelt had endorsed the entire Republican ticket in a telegram to William Gillenwater, state Republican party chairman. In a night letter to Roosevelt, he stated that his remarks were "directly at variance with everything you have said or written to me." He hoped Roosevelt would clarify his position in justice to Progressives "who wish to uphold the dignity of the nation and yet feel reluctant to turn over the affairs of New Mexico to men with corrupt and criminal records." Three days before the election, Roosevelt lectured Cutting in a lengthy telegram on the necessity of placing national goals at a critical time above state and local concerns. He scolded Cutting for supporting men "who are standing for Wilson and the dishonor and shame of this country."[17]

Cutting was convinced that Roosevelt's telegram was responsible for Wilson's carrying New Mexico in the election. Indeed, the Democrats swept all the key posts in 1916: governor; senator; and representative. Cutting's disappointment extended only to Wilson's victory in the state. He was certain that Roosevelt's speeches prior to his telegram to Gillenwater had encouraged Progressives to support both Hughes and the Democratic slate in New Mexico. Roosevelt's telegram was responsible for Wilson's capturing New Mexico for the second time, Cutting believed. Other Progressives directly attributed Hughes's loss of the state to the methods of the "old gang," which was willing to lose the election but reclaim control of the Republican organization. Disillusioned New Mexico Progressives like Miguel Otero crossed party lines and embraced the Democratic cause.[18]

Convinced of the disastrous effect of Roosevelt's telegram, Cutting in turn lectured Roosevelt about the New Mexico political scene shortly after the election. Cutting's incisive analysis remains one of the better examinations of New Mexico politics. Cutting disagreed with Roosevelt's premise that conditions were comparable to those prevailing in Pennsylvania in the nineteenth century under Simon Cameron. "The fundamental fact about New Mexico," Cutting explained, "is that it is not an American community at all." A better analogy than "Pennsylvania in the 60's," Cutting thought, would be "medieval Portugal or Modern Nicaragua." More than half the voters in New Mexico Cutting considered to be Americans only in name. "The chief duty of a citizen of New Mexico," he firmly believed, "is to make Americans out of them." Cutting said that the great mass of the natives, the pobres, had been "systematically robbed, degraded and corrupted by the Republican ring." The only way to make New Mexico an American state was to eliminate the likes of Bursum and Hubbell.

The consequences of these conditions, a feudal society with an exploited native population, were twofold. First, Cutting explained, Bursum and Hubbell represented only one of several factions of "the Republican party." Pandering "to every sectional, racial, and religious prejudice," all factions were successful "in spreading among the native people a real antipathy towards the United States." The second fact Cutting emphasized was that "few of the voters knew anything at all about national issues." Those who recognized the names of Hughes and Wilson judged them by the records of their followers in New Mexico. During the campaign, Cutting tried to convince native Progressive leaders that Hughes was neither a Bursum nor a Hubbell. Roosevelt's telegram, however, placed "Hughes and Hubbell in the same class," destroyed his efforts and "turned the state to Wilson." Cutting regretted that he found himself "in any semblance of controversy" with Roosevelt, but his course was "the only one which a patriotic citizen of this state could honorably follow."[19]

Cutting continued to ponder whether Progressives in New Mexico should follow Otero into the Democratic party or continue to battle the old gang in the Republican party. Feeling as he did about President Wilson, Cutting had to stay in the Republican party. Meanwhile the fragile health of Governorelect Ezequial C. de Baca quickly focused attention on the lieutenant governor, Washington E. Lindsey, who was considered by many to be an independent Republican. Cutting and others believed that Lindsey might lead the cleansing of the party and shut out "the gang" with the support of the *New Mexican* and with the assistance of progressive Republicans, should de Baca die. If Lindsey was truly an independent Republican, there was yet hope for the party in New Mexico.[20]

Cutting visited his family in New York during the holiday season and recuperated from the trying campaign. Possibly the greatest satisfaction came on December 30 when Cutting appeared with Theodore Roosevelt at the dining room of the Langdon Hotel on Fifth Avenue in midtown for a luncheon during which the two men reconciled their differences. It was a pleasant ending to a critical election year. Cutting then traveled to Washington. While staying with Henry White, veteran diplomat and family friend, he visited New Mexico's senior and lame-duck senator, Thomas B. Catron, "who was in good form but distinctly hostile to Mr. Fall." Cutting said he would not "be surprised to see quite a fight between them in 1918."[21]

CHAPTER 7

MORE THAN A MATTER OF LIBEL

As the campaign crescendoed during fall 1916, Bronson Cutting became deeply involved in a libel case that reflected the historical forces at work in the public life of New Mexico. An abundance of lawyers and a highly factionalized political structure made libel suits the *bête noir* of the newspaper man. Libel law was neither a clarified, coherent nor concise corpus either in New Mexico or the United States. In New Mexico's "Dreyfus affair," Cutting was slapped with the suit because of his stance against the candidacy of Holm O. Bursum in the 1916 gubernatorial campaign.[1]

At noon on October 11, Sheriff Emil James of Socorro County arrived in Santa Fe and served Cutting a warrant sworn out on the complaint of Henry Dreyfus. Dreyfus charged Cutting with libeling him in the *New Mexican* several days earlier. The story stated that "a Bursum henchman named Dreyfus in the days of Governor Hagerman, tore down the American flag in Socorro and stamped on it." Occurring in 1911, the incident was widely noted to discredit Bursum in his previous campaign for governor and was dredged up again with a similar purpose in mind. Dreyfus also brought a civil suit against the New Mexican Printing Company for libel damages in the amount of fifty thousand dollars.[2]

Cutting recognized the suit was designed to distract both him and the paper as the campaign moved toward its climax. Dreyfus was mentioned in only one sentence in the story on Bursum's career. The Dreyfus incident "was a matter of universal public knowledge." The justice of the peace, Cutting knew, could do nothing but bind him over for action by the grand jury. The fact that he was in El Paso when the story appeared in the *New Mexican* would relieve him of all criminal responsibility. To Cutting's mind, the whole thing was "a striking example of Bursum's calibre," "petty" and "low down." After some thought, Cutting decided not to go to Socorro for the preliminary examination and to let "the whole thing" go over for action of the grand jury. He recognized that he would be indicted, but he considered the case so trivial that he doubted whether it would even get to a jury. If he went to Socorro, he thought the justice of the peace would decide against him and then jail him. While Bursum no doubt intended the suit to tie down Cutting during the remainder of the campaign, Cutting successfully postponed the matter until after the election.[3]

When Roosevelt failed to endorse his candidacy, Holm Bursum was so indignant that he had the Socorro district attorney cancel Cutting's bond in the criminal suit and thereby force him to attend a hearing. Cutting decided that he would plead not guilty and show that he was in El Paso when the Dreyfus incident was mentioned in the *New Mexican*. Then, if an attempt to indict or jail him on the grounds of criminal libel was made, Cutting believed "the motive will be entirely apparent." Governor William McDonald was scheduled to speak in Socorro on October 30, the day Cutting was commanded to appear. He knew that McDonald would pardon him if the need arose. To assist his case, Cutting asked Francis Wilson, his attorney, to accompany him. The trip resulted in dropping the charge of criminal libel against Cutting but not his newspaper associates. The other civil suit against the *New Mexican* would be heard after the election.[4]

Dreyfus's civil complaint alleged that the paragraph in the *New Mexican* was in effect a criminal charge against him and that Cutting, as the president of the New Mexican Printing Company, directed and instructed the publication of the alleged libelous story. For the damage to his reputation and for his "grievous mental suffering," Dreyfus asked for fifty thousand dollars. In January 1917, Cutting engaged the Ben William's Detective Agency in El Paso to ferret out information in Socorro about the pending case. Cutting wanted Bursum's activities closely watched. After three months, Cutting had mounds of reports yielding no useful information and ended his relations with the agency.

Also in January, upon a showing duly made before the court, a change of venue was granted to Valencia County, which was dominated by Ed Otero, a close ally of Bursum and a son-in-law of the late Solomon Luna. The case was scheduled to come to trial in early March after the grand jury completed its investigation. Although the detective agency uncovered an eyewitness to the flag-trampling episode, he had been given a county job by Bursum, making unlikely that the defense could get "anything out of him." On January 19 Cutting, Miguel Antonio Otero, Ralph Henderson, E. Dana Johnson, and Austin Brady were indicted by the Socorro Grand Jury for criminal libel. Thereafter all momentarily expected to be arrested, something that did not occur in January. Since the change of venue pertained only to the civil suit against the *New Mexican,* it could involve at worst a heavy fine. The criminal case was not affected by the court order. None of Cutting's associates under criminal indictment thought they would serve if convicted in Socorro by a jury under Bursum's thumb.[5]

Whether the sheriff came to Santa Fe to arrest Cutting and his associates is unclear, but in early February they appeared in Socorro and pleaded not guilty. Judge Merritt C. Mechem met the group in the hotel lobby, shook hands and talked most amiably before the hearing. On the bench, he listened attentively while Francis Wilson presented the demurrer to the indictments. Mechem did not determine at this time whether he would continue with the criminal indictments, and the group returned to Santa Fe. Joined by his sister, Justine, and consumed by the pending libel trial, Cutting moved to Albuquerque and would commute fifty miles by automobile each day to and from the court room in Los Lunas.[6]

The trial got underway in March. Where the money came from to support the suits against Cutting and the *New Mexican* was a question that intrigued Cutting and Justine. They doubted that Bursum had enough money to initiate them and surmised that the "source" was "near the Phelps Dodge people," who were "back of most of the crooked business out here and do not want an independent paper."[7]

Two days after the trial got under way, Judge Mechem threw out both the criminal and libel charges against Cutting. The civil case now proceeded against the *New Mexican* as a corporation. Noting "the general attitude toward Bronson" in the court, Justine was convinced, as were others, that "his fight against Bursum has made him far more friends than enemies . . . ." Judge Mechem let the defendants, including Justine, sit inside the railing of his courtroom, thereby affording them the opportunity to observe more closely the proceedings as well as to take advantage of the fresh air from nearby windows.[8]

Once the charges against Cutting were dropped, Francis Wilson launched the defendants's effort to show that the alleged Dreyfus incident had taken place. "We had several old men," Justine wrote, "one who had seen the actual event himself, others who had seen the flag thrown over the fence and had joined the angry mob." Herbert J. Hagerman, the former governor whose visit to Socorro prompted the incident, testified to seeing the desecrated flag and being told of Dreyfus's actions by witnesses. Thereafter Henry Dreyfus was called to the stand. He denied desecrating an American flag and presented another "improbable" account that was confirmed by two witnesses. Justine was the first to notice that during the cross-examination by Wilson, M. C. Spicer, one of Dreyfus's lawyers and a close political ally of Bursum, was signalling the witness. Cutting himself observed that Dreyfus looked about before he responded and later remarked that he was surprised at the way Dreyfus "apparently steered out of pitfalls" with his responses. Cutting reported the irregularities to Judge Mechem who requested that nothing be said about the matter until after the case was over. Cutting obliged, and thereafter the signalling stopped.

Cutting and his associates were never in doubt that the jury, consisting entirely of Spanish-Americans, would decide against them. The case went to the jury about 10 o'clock P.M. on March 8. Before leaving Albuquerque the following morning for Los Lunas, Cutting learned that the verdict was against the New Mexican Printing Company, with thirty-five thousand dollars in damages awarded to the plaintiff on account of libel. Recourse for Cutting was to take the signalling matter to the New Mexico Bar Association and then to appeal to the state supreme court.[9]

"I don't care what anybody says, that verdict is simply an outrage—a complete miscarriage of justice," said Bernard S. Rodey, a leading Albuquerque lawyer, former territorial delegate, and former federal judge in Puerto Rico, in a memo to Cutting and his associates. He was so angry that he offered his services to Wilson "without compensation (save mere expenses) anytime." Senator Fall remarked that Mechem ought never to have heard the case. Rodey's memo and other similar responses led Cutting to think that he and his associates had demonstrated their "case convincingly to the general public." To ward off further suits that might be litigated in either Socorro or Los Lunas with Bursum-controlled jurors, Cutting had his associates, holding the first mortgage on the New Mexican Printing Company, foreclose and reorganize as a Delaware corporation. The shift of incorporation insured that any future suits would have to be brought in a federal court.[10]

Next to be considered was the hearing before the bar association involving M. C. Spicer, the lawyer who had signalled the witness. Cutting and his associates recognized that Dreyfus, Spicer, and others were "small fry," while the men higher up covered their tracks and let "these poor tools" bear the brunt of public indignation. By the end of March, the bar examiners turned down Cutting's request to consider charges against Spicer, the lawyer who signalled messages to Dreyfus. According to Cutting and his associates, Judge Mechem signed a perjured affidavit stating that Spicer was reading a newspaper during the entire cross-examination. Mechem's affidavit was contrary to what he stated on the bench. At the trial, when Cutting brought the matter to his attention, Mechem had said he was looking at the people on the witness stand and had not noticed Spicer's actions. An informant told Cutting that had Justine's testimony been offered by a man, the board "would have handed up charges to the Supreme Court." Because there were several witnesses to Spicer's signalling, the question for Cutting and his associates was how to pursue the case further. The strategy quickly decided upon was to secure affidavits from others who had witnessed Spicer's actions and "fire the charges" back to the bar examiners. Cutting, of course, understood that Mechem was a Bursum lieutenant and business associate and that the judge was virtually impregnable within the Seventh Judicial District. Nevertheless, since Mechem's affidavit challenged the integrity of Cutting, his sister and others who asked for Spicer's disbarment, Cutting felt Mechem's lie should not go unanswered.[11]

On March 30, 1917, the *New Mexican* published a long story that cited all details of the matter, denounced the affidavit as fake and declared it to be in contradiction to Mechem's statements from the bench. The article noted Mechem's close ties to Holm O. Bursum and reviewed the proceedings that had led to Attorney Spicer's "wig-wagging" secret signals to Henry Dreyfus during the cross-examination by Francis Wilson. The article neither attacked the verdict of the jury nor criticized any action or ruling by the presiding judge.

The tempo of Cutting's life increased with the declaration of war against Germany on April 6, 1917. While he assisted Francis Wilson in readying a motion for a new trial to contest the award for damages in the libel suit, Cutting dealt with the civilian side of local and state defense work in his capacity as a member of the Council of State Defense. Resigning his colonelcy on the governor's staff, he then accepted an appointment as a major in charge of the Inspector General's Department of the state militia.

In an effort to promote harmony in the state, a group of "mine managers, Phelps Dodge agents, etc." visited with the governor and sought "to patch things up between us and Bursum." Cutting called their terms, including a public apology to Mechem, "grotesque." In turn, Cutting offered what he considered "a fair proposition," one that called for a "cessation of hostilities for the duration of the war." He correctly doubted whether Bursum and Mechem would be receptive to his proposal.[12]

Mechem meanwhile had referred the story in the *New Mexican* to three personally selected *Amici Curiae,* or friends of the court. They reported that the article constituted contempt of court, whereupon a charge was lodged by the district attorney of the Seventh Judicial District against the New Mexican Printing Company, Cutting and E. Dana Johnson, the editor of the *New Mexican.* From New York Justine inquired whether Cutting needed additional legal advice since Francis Wilson was involved in the charge leveled by the district attorney. She contemplated a trip to Washington to interest *Collier's Weekly*. By mid-May, Cutting and his associates had made their first move in the contempt proceedings by raising jurisdictional questions. Following the strategy utilized in the civil suit, Francis Wilson filed a denial in his own behalf and asked for an immediate trial. However, his motion was denied because Mechem was holding court on the circuit and had to obtain the services of a lawyer to represent him.[13]

The delay gave Cutting the opportunity to attend his sister Olivia's marriage in New York to Henry James, son of the philosopher. Cutting also discussed the contempt charges with Justine and various advisers, and his interest in entering military service with family friends and acquaintances. Cutting followed up Justine's initial efforts to interest Mark Sullivan, the editor of *Collier's,* in covering the libel suit and the contempt charge. Although he reported to his associates in Santa Fe that "*Collier's* is awake," he was unable to state just when a story would appear in the national weekly. Cutting admitted that he was "prepared to go the limit" with Mechem on this issue. The contempt action might be "as quick a way as any to get rid of judicial corruption in New Mexico" and could provide Mechem an opportunity to "make as thorough an ass of himself as possible" and thereby "dig his own grave."[14]

Back in New Mexico in time to celebrate his twenty-ninth birthday on June 23, Cutting wrote his mother that "legal matters are in a bad way," but some gloom dissipated when the long-awaited *Collier's* editorial appeared in the July 7 issue. *Collier's* called the case "another example of an attempted terrorization of the press on the part of the judiciary which, in our judgment, ought to be stopped." If the court followed the usual proceedings in contempt cases, Mechem would hear the evidence. If he allowed any to be presented, he would sit in judgment of his own case and then render a verdict, possibly a fine or jail sentence or both. By giving the case national publicity, *Collier's* no doubt assisted Cutting's cause. But the Seventh Judicial District remained a tight little kingdom with Holm O. Bursum, almost phobic in his dislike of Cutting, as its ruler and Merritt Mechem as his chief minion. Cutting's family was exuberant about the editorial, but he only remarked that it "had a most profound effect on the gang."

He was "awfully busy" trying to "straighten up odds and ends" in case his anticipated commission in military intelligence was awarded. Cutting now started brushing up his rusty German with a German priest. In legal matters, he informed Francis Wilson that he had recruited Herbert Mason, a distinguished lawyer from Oklahoma City, to assist him in the suit. Wilson was a litigant cited in the proceedings, and it made sense to secure the services of a prominent out-of-state lawyer with no connection to the New Mexico scene. Wilson was surprised and possibly affronted, but Cutting reported that he had settled "the whole matter very satisfactorily with Wilson."[15]

In July, Cutting corresponded with an Albuquerque lawyer, Neill B. Field, who was party to an effort to mediate the differences between Cutting and Mechem. Cutting declared that the sanctity of a free press seemed higher than that of any court, "especially a corrupt one." He thought "the implied contract of a decent newspaper to tell the truth" of greater importance than "any possible duty to whiten judicial sepulchers." Field disagreed. Freedom of the press was not at stake in this controversy as he saw it. "The very right of the courts to exist and retain the respect of the public" and "the continuity of our institutions" were in jeopardy. Field asserted that the Constitution charged the courts, not the press, with the duty of determining "the limits of the liberty of the press."[16]

Cutting promptly responded that he was trying to impress upon the public that the proceedings were a single phase in a long controversy. He insisted, and this was central to his argument, that Mechem had no right in his judicial capacity "to pass on his own character" by initiating action to exonerate his private reputation. In addition, Cutting made clear that he could not accept Field's conclusion about the right of the press to pass judgment on the court. "Any man, good or bad, from any motive," he said, "should have the right to publish the truth about a judge as well as about any other human being." The fact that Mechem happened to hold a judicial office was inconsequential.

The fundamental question involving freedom of the press was "who is to determine the truth or falsity of statements made by a given newspaper about a given judge?" Cutting stated that "the decision should clearly be made by neither the newspaper nor the judge." Herbert Mason, after perusing the correspondence, said it was a shame Cutting was not a lawyer.[17]

While awaiting developments on the contempt situation, Cutting had decisions to make. Should he resign as inspector-general of the New Mexico National Guard or should he prepare for the necessary five-day examination if he wished to be continued in the post? He would have resigned as inspector-general if he "were sure of getting the intelligence job." Cutting passed the examination. If no other commission was forthcoming, he would leave with units of the New Mexico National Guard for a California training camp sometime in the fall. However, Cutting was commissioned a captain of infantry in the United States Army and assigned to temporary duty, starting on August 18, in the Intelligence Section of the War College Division, which was part of the General Staff in Washington, D.C. His linguistic abilities won him the commission and overrode any concerns about physical defects.[18]

One matter, however, was easily resolved. His sister, Justine, agreed to serve as president of the printing company and as publisher of the paper while he performed his military service. Meanwhile, Herbert Mason, recruited by Justine, was scheduled to arrive in Santa Fe at the end of July. She was concerned about whether Cutting would agree with her about his ability. In turn, he hoped that Mason would approve the *New Mexican*'s adopting a more aggressive, critical tone against Mechem. Many newspapers in the state reprinted the *Collier's* editorial while the *New Mexican* omitted it. Mason gave Cutting no difficulty in the matter. More important to Cutting was that he made arrangements to convey to Justine all of his real estate in Santa Fe and that he assigned to her all his mortgages and notes on the *New Mexican*. In short, when Cutting departed for Washington on the evening of August 15, he severed his connections with New Mexico for the duration of the war.[19]

As Cutting prepared to enter military service, the Supreme Court of New Mexico considered the contempt charge filed on August 9 in the office of the clerk of the district court for Socorro County. Wilson and Mason succeeded in quashing as defective Mechem's first two charges, which showed no regard for the requirements of preliminary proof necessary before alleged criminals could be brought to trial. On Mechem's third charge, contempt against the company officers, the supreme court failed to quash the motion, and the case went to trial in Mechem's court, where judgment was rendered against the New Mexican Printing Company. E. Dana Johnson, as editor of the *New Mexican,* was sentenced to serve a term of thirty days in the county jail. While finding the company guilty, Mechem refused to pass sentence upon it. He also refused to try Cutting, although Wilson and Mason demanded an immediate trial. Mechem probably wished to keep the contempt matters pending as long as possible to prevent further critical stories in the *New Mexican*. The judgment was appealed to the New Mexico Supreme Court.[20]

While still in Washington at the end of August 1917, Wilson wrote Cutting of an attempt to resolve the controversy. Mechem would drop all charges if he and E. Dana Johnson "would agree to publish a retraction and an apology." Mechem's judicial seat was being contested by M. C. Spicer. The *New Mexican*'s challenge to Mechem was strengthening Spicer's candidacy. Wilson and others agreed that if a choice was necessary, Mechem was infinitely superior to Spicer. Cutting, of course, refused to consider the proposal and was annoyed with Wilson for conveying it. What he would agree to sign and publish, he asked Wilson to convey, was that, as far as he was aware, no one on the *New Mexican* intended to reflect on the district court, to hold it in contempt or in any way to influence the presiding judge. He was willing to consider a statement expressing regret for any misunderstanding that arose with regard to these matters. However, he insisted upon a reiteration of the main facts of the Dreyfus affair as published in the *New Mexican*. As for Spicer seeking to succeed Mechem, he sarcastically concluded that his "election as successor to Judge Merritt C. Mechem would be a fitting climax to Mr. Spicer's honorable and distinguished career." Cutting's response left Mechem no choice but to follow through with the criminal contempt charges.[21]

Before he was ordered overseas on September 4, 1917, Justine kept Cutting aware of Mason's continued efforts to interest prominent eastern editors in the case. She arranged with the International Press Clipping Bureau to forward any stories that appeared. In October 1917, the New Mexico Printing Company was reorganized. The company had defaulted on the semiannual interest due on June 5, 1917. Predicated on this default, Francis Wilson, the attorney for the company, filed foreclosure proceedings in Santa Fe County. Wilson's strategy was to force Dreyfus "to adjudicate his lien in the foreclosure proceedings" should he try to collect the thirty-five thousand dollars in damages awarded in the libel suit. In addition, in the event that Dreyfus secured the judgment for damages, Wilson wanted to keep insolvency proceedings out of Socorro or Valencia counties where Bursum in effect could select a receiver for the company. "Upon the motion of Mr. Cutting, as Plaintiff," the Santa Fe County Court appointed the paper's business manager, Ralph M. Henderson, as receiver of the New Mexican Printing Company. Wilson believed that the district judge in Santa Fe County "appreciated the purposes of Dreyfus and his backers." After taking these actions, Wilson then pursued a reorganization scheme. By incorporating as the New Mexican Printing Company of Delaware and by turning over to this company all of the mortgages Justine held as well as Cutting's almost valueless stock, the new company could continue its operations "as though nothing had transpired." Future litigation, involving libel or contempt charges, could be tried in a federal rather than a county court.[22]

In London, Cutting learned of these developments from his sister and associates in New Mexico. The paper was still losing money, but less than in previous years. In October 1917 it almost broke even. Justine assured him that Mason was continuing his efforts to attract editorial attention and had interested Peter Finley Dunne, the editor of *Collier's*.

In January 1918, Justine reported discussion among the directors to sell the paper either "to the opposition" or another party and then to start a morning paper to compete with the *New Mexican*. In lengthy letters, she related her difficulties with Wilson, his lack of cooperation with her and his inability to work in harness with Mason. In the end, she said, "he came around, promptly but ungraciously, saying he would do anything I wanted done." Fortunately, Mason expressed his willingness to work with Wilson "even under these extremely trying conditions." Soon thereafter, both the foreclosure sale and proceedings to organize as a Delaware corporation occurred. When Justine left Santa Fe at the end of February, the paper was again safely in their hands, but there was still no indication of when the contempt trial would be held.[23]

Meanwhile Mason's efforts to publicize the court case began to bear fruit. Following an eight-and-a-half-hour discussion, he convinced a publicity agent in Chicago that the plight of the *New Mexican* "was a case of great importance to all the newspapers in the country." The agent agreed "to publish a special edition of his news release" that examined the issue of freedom of press with particular emphasis on the *New Mexican* and the individuals involved in the case. There was a chance that the Chicago *Tribune*, whose counsel had asked for pictures of the judges and others associated with the case, would run a Sunday feature story. Melville Stone, general manager of the Associated Press, told Henry Barrett Chamberlin that the case was "historic," and in conversation with Mason, he found that a ten-thousand-word piece had been sent "with the request that it be used liberally."[24]

Under the heading, "Shall the Press Remain Free in New Mexico?" *Chamberlin's* magazine related the story of the attempt to substitute contempt proceedings for libel action in its April issue and in the three succeeding issues. Precedents were cited and pictures of supreme court justices accompanied the account. The June and July issues presented press accounts of the proceedings, including Johnson's conviction for contempt of court. In June, the International News Service sent out a story about E. Dana Johnson's appeal of his contempt conviction before the Supreme Court of New Mexico.[25]

Cutting let Justine determine what position the paper should take and whom among the candidates seeking office the *New Mexican* should endorse in the 1918 elections. That year, Will H. Hays, chairman of the Republican National Committee, engaged in a strenuous effort to unite his badly split party organization. When Hays scheduled a one-day stop in Albuquerque to meet the leaders of the Republican party, Francis Wilson was asked by the chairman of the State Central Committee, the national committeeman and the governor respectively to attend. At the meeting, Hays proclaimed the

Republican party as "the supreme party for one hundred percent American-ism and patriotism" calling for "peace without compromise and with victory only." Hays encouraged representatives "of all shades and complexions of Republicanism and Progressiveism" to work together for victory in the fall election. After Hays finished speaking, Holm Bursum, who chaired the meeting, introduced a resolution calling for each person present to pledge himself publicly "to vote and work for every man nominated on the Republi-can ticket at the state convention of the Republican party." Wilson, when called upon, expressed reservations, whereupon "things warmed up imme-diately." After numerous speeches and much discussion, Wilson reported, one innocuous resolution that did not "bind anybody to anything except to support the principles of the party" passed unanimously.[26]

Meanwhile, behind the scenes, Hays tried to contact Justine through a mutual friend. His object was to bring the *New Mexican* "in sympathy with the party." He hoped to lure Justine and her lawyer-advisor, Herbert Mason, to Washington where he would join them for a conference with Albert Fall. Arrangements then could be devised for the paper to support the senator as well as the entire Republican ticket. In July, they met with him in New York. Although they were sympathetic to Fall's candidacy, they had difficulty with the Republican organization and were distressed at the prospect of Bursum becoming the state party chairman. If Bursum succeeded, Mason thought, there would be little chance of Progressives becoming reconciled with the Republican party. Fall was not anxious to secure the endorsement of the *New Mexican*. He demanded that the newspaper support the entire ticket and locate itself "in a position where it would be in accordance with the majority of the Republicans" in New Mexico.[27]

Fall was trying to isolate the *New Mexican* and to promote party unity in the state. With the Progressive cause all but dead as a factor in Republican party politics, Hays's strategy was to stress national issues more so than state and local concerns. The dilemma in which Justine found herself likewise became more intense when Francis Wilson resigned as vice-president and director of the Santa Fe New Mexican Publishing Corporation in August. His resigna-tion was regarded as no great loss by Justine who had continually clashed with Wilson, but his resignation was a blow to the Progressive movement and indicative of disagreement on matters pertaining to the *New Mexican*. Indeed, Justine, Mason and the *New Mexican* were becoming increasingly isolated as the campaign entered its final stretch in the fall of 1918.[28]

Will Hays, more than anyone in New Mexico, desired the support of the newspaper for the ticket. According to Fall in a letter to Bursum, Hays agreed

CHAPTER 7

that Mason and Justine had no reason not to support the Republican ticket since Bursum would not be a candidate. Fall made clear that he would publicly repudiate a *New Mexican* endorsement if it did not support the entire Republican ticket. In addition, he explained to Bursum that the *New Mexican,* although it "possessed the power to injure," had "no power to assist." Its "sworn subscription list" was approximately 600; its total claimed circulation was approximately 2,000. Fall contested Mason's claim that the *New Mexican* could control or influence "any appreciable vote" and therefore insisted that no concessions be made to it. The only way the paper could be of service would be to endorse the ticket. At that point, Fall believed, the paper might be entitled to participate in party councils.[29]

Republican politicians concluded that their best chance to win the governorship for the first time would be with a candidate of Spanish-American descent whose *compadres* probably constituted a majority of New Mexico's voters. The convention selected Octaviano A. Larrazolo, a former Democrat, as the Republican candidate for governor. Before the convention met, the retiring Chairman of the Republican State Committee informed Fall that after several conferences with Mason, an understanding was reached wherein the *New Mexican* would support the entire ticket. At the same time, Justine conferred with Reed Holloman, a supreme court justice, and with Bursum. After several meetings, Bursum phoned Justine to relate "his final definite and positive answer" that he would not seek public office in 1918. She conferred with other political leaders in an effort to seek responsible Republican candidates. With the encouragement of Will Hays and the Republican National Committee, Justine and Mason were seeking "to force the bosses to name a better ticket than they themselves wanted."[30]

The Republican candidate for governor was Octaviano A. Larrazolo. Upon learning of his nomination, Cutting informed his sister that Larrazolo "is to my personal knowledge one of the greatest scoundrels unhung" in New Mexico. His nomination prompted a fight within the newspaper. Johnson had trouble with the entire ticket and wished to endorse the more reputable Democrat candidates. Justine and Mason argued that, while Larrazolo was nominated by "the old gang," it was afraid of him and did not know what to expect, for he was "clearly the choice of the Spanish people." After conferring with Larrazolo, all members of the editorial staff, except Johnson but including Mason and Justine, came away convinced of his intention to improve the lot of the Hispanic people and that opposition to him originated "in a stupid Anglo-Saxon bigotry."[31]

The election results could not help but please Republicans throughout the nation and New Mexico. Fall's victory gave the Republicans a slight majority in the United States Senate while the Republican party in New Mexico succeeded better than ever before, even in the usually Democratic "Texas counties." A friend and associate in Santa Fe wrote to Justine, "without boasting at all," that the *New Mexican* in the general news, features and editorials supported a Republican ticket selected by the corrupt gang that the newspaper had been battling since Cutting assumed control in 1911. Her ordeal was eased somewhat when Johnson conceded that the Democrats had selected poor candidates. His bias against Hispanic nominees on the Democratic ticket made easier for him the acceptance of Justine's mandate.[32]

By the end of the year, nothing broke or disturbed the uneasy peace between the *New Mexican* and Republican party chieftains. Larrazolo, who would be inaugurated in January, had announced no appointments that angered the editorial staff. One or two, such as the retention of Clara Olsen as his personal secretary, even pleased them. Despite his dislike of Larrazolo, Cutting was aware that the Republican bosses feared Larrazolo's independence and that he might follow a path that would win the newspaper's support. Moreover, Bursum was apparently prepared to carry out the agreement made with Mason—that he would not seek to influence appointments as long as the *New Mexican* was friendly toward the Republican administration. In this atmosphere, the three New Mexico supreme court justices agreed to reverse the contempt of court decision from the Seventh Judicial District. Two justices favored reversing, without remanding, the case, in effect dismissing it, while the third wished to send it back to Judge Mechem for reconsideration. Justine learned about the outcome several weeks before the decision was publicly pronounced at the year's end. Her source was the acting managing editor who had been in consultation with Judge Holloman "about some other matters."[33]

Johnson's appeal, which had gotten underway in June, was not fully resolved, as already noted, until the closing of the year. On New Year's Day 1919 in New York City, Justine received the following telegram from Mason in Santa Fe: "Contempt case unanimously reversed and Johnson discharged. Strong opinion. Court holds no contempt charged or proved. World, Times, Tribune, Sun and many others taking specials. Have cabled London." In lead stories or editorials, papers in New Mexico and elsewhere noted, as one headline said, that "Free Speech and Press Essential to Public Good."[34]

Still to be resolved was the verdict that awarded Dreyfus thirty-five thousand dollars for suffering libel by the *New Mexican*. Cutting and his associates had moved for a new trial. One of the grounds was that the inflated size of the damages indicated that prejudice and passion ruled the verdict. Judge Mechem acceded to a new trial unless Dreyfus agreed to reduce the judgment to ten thousand dollars. Although he consented to the smaller award, the *New Mexican* appealed to the New Mexico Supreme Court. Wilson claimed that the judge had found the verdict excessive, three-and-a-half times what he deemed proper, a clear indication that the jury must have been influenced by prejudice and passion. The appeal was quickly subsumed in the contempt proceedings. In addition, Mason had asked that the libel case be allowed to drift. He needed to attend more fully the contempt proceedings and to "engage in an effort to straighten out the whole matter so that peace might reign in the future." The supreme court readily agreed. Nothing further was done until May 1919 when Justice Clarence Roberts upheld the initial award. He argued that the amount did not necessarily signify a judgment based on prejudice and passion. Mason and Wilson took exception to this conclusion and prepared a motion for reargument, but Dreyfus entered a release and a satisfaction of judgment. Following his action, the supreme court dismissed the case and withdrew Justice Roberts opinion, ending almost three years of litigation.[35]

Dreyfus's reasoning behind the dismissal was that his receiving a "trivial" sum of ten thousand dollars had compromised the case. At the request of counsel on both sides, the opinion of Justice Roberts had been withdrawn. The court "vacated and set aside the order, withdrawing the opinion from the files." While Cutting and his associates lauded the termination of the suit as a victory for freedom of the press, members of the supreme court, the governor, Holm Bursum—the boss behind Dreyfus's initial actions in launching the case—and most politicians in New Mexico understood that they had compromised to bring an end to the Dreyfus affair.[36]

With the signing of the armistice on November 11, 1918, Cutting looked forward to returning to New Mexico either before or after the legislature met. While the stance of the *New Mexican* did not please many independents, Progressives and Democrats in New Mexico, Cutting believed the Republican National Committee, especially the chairman, Will H. Hays, appreciated it and would help the cause of reform if called upon in the future.[37] Whether Cutting fully accepted his sister's decision to support the entire Republican ticket is not clear. What is known is that he would have to start over to stake out a progressive-Republican posture for himself and the *New Mexican* when he returned to Santa Fe. Before the campaign, prominent Republicans had shared doubts about how influential or important the endorsement of the newspaper really was. Now, its friends and associates doubted its integrity;

indeed the *New Mexican* had lost some standing and prestige. Cutting would have to struggle to restore its influential position in the state.

Another point is also clear. The *New Mexican*'s pro-Republican stance in 1918 cleared the way for the supreme court to dismiss the contempt suit and to accept the termination of the libel suit. If the newspaper had followed E. Dana Johnson's advice to oppose Larrazolo and others on the Republican ticket, no harmony would have prevailed in December and Johnson conceivably might have served a jail term for contempt, for two of the three judges hearing the case had partisan-Republican backgrounds. The libel case, instead of being terminated, could have prompted further litigation and controversy. What cannot be shown is a causal connection between the newspaper's posture in the 1918 elections and the favorable outcome of the litigation affecting it. No evidence is extant.[38] The favorable outcome meant that when he returned to Santa Fe, Cutting could literally start anew without any court cases hindering his activities. His military service, which will now be reviewed, was of inestimable value to the advance of his career.

CHAPTER 8

THE LONDON INTERLUDE

At twenty-nine, Cutting was determined to enter military service in 1917 despite concern that he might jeopardize his health. By late June, it was clear that he most likely could secure a commission in military intelligence and spend some time at the Army War College in Washington, D.C. Theodore Roosevelt, Senator Andrieus A. Jones, Governor Washington E. Lindsey, Supreme Court Chief Justice Richard H. Hanna and Adjutant General James Baca wrote recommendations to officials of the War Department in his behalf. Military service would enhance his credibility as a public figure in New Mexico.[1]

His proficiency in Spanish and German was an asset. Although he enlisted as a volunteer for the infantry on August 5, 1917, he was commissioned a captain of infantry in the United States Army on the very same day and was ordered to report to the Intelligence Section of the War College Division in Washington, D.C. for temporary duty in the office of the chief of staff. During late summer, he took a short course in the duties of intelligence officers and attachés. In September he embarked for London and would serve for the remainder of the war as assistant military attaché at the American embassy.[2]

After some initial confusion, Cutting reported to the staff of Colonel Stephen L. Slocum, the military attaché at the American embassy in London. The only assistant in the office at the outset, Cutting had a wide range of duties. These included processing the transfer of American troops serving with the British, questioning escaped prisoners about the treatment of Americans in German prison camps, and attending liaison work with the British War Office. In addition, he prepared reports on the economic, political and military situation in Great Britain. But as the work of the office became more organized with the arrival of additional assistants, Cutting's assignment was confined to a liaison role with various departments of British Military Intelligence.[3]

Cutting worked with the British on censorship, counterespionage, information collation and other special duties. In connection with the first of these matters, he daily visited the offices of British Military Intelligence, reviewing the British press, cable dispatches from American correspondents and occasionally motion-picture films. His object was to note segments that violated the guidelines of the Committee on Public Information in Washington and the rules of the chief censor of the American Expeditionary Force. Lacking the authority to censor anything, Cutting merely advised the British about "a fair interpretation of our rules." He was not impressed with the censorship operations of British Military Intelligence. In his opinion, censorship was their least effective department because "at the best, press censorship is a delicate job to handle" and because the "officers invalided home from the front" who staffed the operation "knew little about journalism."

One of the most interesting branches of British intelligence he had dealings with was headed by Lieutenant Colonel George Phillips. A well-known criminal lawyer in civilian life, Phillips was charged with censoring commercial cable transactions. Cutting paid weekly visits to his offices in a remote part of London and reviewed records of these transactions. The cables referred to trade matters and military shipments, concerns that Cutting generally referred to the War Trade Intelligence branch of the American Intelligence Service, "except in cases where the transaction shed light on the German espionage service or on the commercial activities of firms or individuals who were suspects from a military point of view." These cables he forwarded directly to his superiors in the Military Intelligence Division. Cutting also had to deal with the complaints of irate Americans, usually forwarded through the State Department, charging that private messages were delayed in transmission for review by British authorities and that the information thus obtained was given to British firms that might benefit by it. The British denied this charge. Cutting reported that the investigation of these and other complaints gave his office and British Cable Censorship "a great deal of toilsome and unnecessary work," given that approximately forty thousand cables passed through the censorship office everyday.

Cutting's most interesting and important work in London was probably counterespionage. He spent a good portion of each day with British officials supervising this work, and for "all intents and purposes," he was treated as part of the staff. He had full access to all files and other available information. Practically all cases were reported to the Military Intelligence Division, although the State Department occasionally requested secret information from the British.

Cutting was greatly impressed with the efficiency of the British counterespionage service, MI5, which knew the name of all German agents in England and was able to trace their daily movements. Cutting, of course, did not engage directly in such activities, but he devoted much time to "advising the British as to the best means of dealing with Americans passing through England who were suspect from any point of view." He also attended Scotland Yard inquests of suspects who offered information on American affairs or who claimed to have resided in the United States.

Cutting also worked with American intelligence, which contrasted markedly with the well-organized and efficient British service. Located in Base Section No. 3, the main American intelligence section conducted counterespionage work in England. From it were dispatched port control officers who worked with the British at major ports of entry and a police corps that undertook investigations of training and rest camps for American troops.

But the American intelligence section underwent a series of command changes that created confusion with the intelligence work of the Military Attaché's Office at the London embassy. An arrangement was concluded whereby all matters pertaining to American troops in England, as well as port control, were handled by intelligence officers at Base Section No. 3 and other matters by the Military Intelligence Division at the London embassy. The two sections mutually exchanged information and reports and jointly employed secret agents. Cutting concluded that the system of dual control was unsatisfactory. The British could never understand that two offices in London were engaged in virtually the same work and saw no reason for dealing with two sets of officers. At times they became distrustful of investigations conducted at Base Section No. 3. This joint arrangement proved a "grave handicap" to American intelligence operations in England.

A more serious deficiency of the dual organization was the failure to organize an effective system of passport control. In March 1918, upon orders from the State Department, either military or naval attachés had to approve all visas, and no citizen from a neutral nation could secure a visa without the permission of the State Department in Washington. The process involved extensive inquiries by both British and American authorities and took from four to six weeks. Once this investigation was completed, the consul general cabled the application of citizens from neutral nations to Washington for final approval. The process generally left the applicants "in a state of unsuppressed rancor towards the United States." German agents, crooks and others desiring more immediate entry to the United States could take passage to Canada and slip across the border. Cutting frequently discussed "uncontrollable travel" with Canadian authorities, who refused to act until the American system was clarified. What was important to Cutting was that authorities concentrate passport and visa matters in one office. Although such was the case in Paris, the problem was never resolved in London, where tensions between the British and the Americans were on the rise. When Cutting left London in January 1919, the situation was one of hopeless confusion.

CHAPTER 8

In addition to his involvement in what can be characterized as negative intelligence, including censorship, counterespionage, passport control and related activities, Cutting also participated in positive intelligence, or the arrangement and collation of information about foreign countries. When the Military Intelligence Division or the State Department requested statistics or other information, Cutting would take up the matter with either MI2 or MI3 of British Intelligence. He was particularly impressed with the German section in MI3. Although he was frequently in touch with the chiefs of the various branches, these contacts did not form part of his daily routine.

More fascinating and more complex were his contacts with MI1-c, the most secret of the British departments, "headed by the great genius of the British intelligence service," known only as "C." Cutting believed that "C" had developed "an organization of unusual ability and success." No reference was ever made to the existence of the department, and no name was ever officially signed to documents "except that of the legendary Capt. Spencer." Cutting "for obvious reasons" said very little about his connections with this department. He did state, however, that "we did all we could in the way of helping the British agents in various parts of the world wherever it was clear that American interests would not suffer in consequence." American cooperation included the transport of British agents through the United States to the Far East. Through an arrangement with the United States embassy, Cutting expedited the process by which British agents could secure diplomatic visas. The majority of agents "expedited in this way were Russians proceeding to Siberia to join either the Siberian Expeditionary Force or the provisional government at Omsk." Some of these agents, Cutting said, "were fairly doubtful characters." Some had shady records under the Tsar; others were supposedly interested in "planning a counter-revolution to restore the autocracy in Russia." However, in November 1917, the State Department cabled the embassy "that no more visas, diplomatic or otherwise, were to be given to Russians without previous reference to Washington." This put an end to Cutting's activities in this system. Thereafter British agents destined for Russia went through Canada, and the Military Intelligence Division lost all knowledge of the agents sent to Siberia by the British.

Cutting also participated in an effort to coordinate the activities of the Allied espionage services through a committee organized in Holland. Cutting reported that "each member of this committee was naturally prejudiced in favor of his own agents." Thus the Allies set up a second committee in London to decide general questions of policy and to review matters passed on appeal from the committee in Holland. Each committee had a member selected by the heads of the American, Belgian, British and French secret services. The American representative, Cutting served on the London committee, which functioned from October 1918 to the close of hostilities a month later. Although the London committee accomplished little, Cutting valued his experience on it because of the close and harmonious relationship he established with the British secret service.

In the lengthy report delineating his wartime service in London, Cutting gave only brief mention to what must have been the most exciting and dangerous experience he had during the war. In November 1917, during the first battle of Cambrai, he spent ten days along the British front from Passchendale south. And in October 1918, he visited the Grand Fleet in the Firth of Forth under the auspices of the Ministry of Information. Both trips, he said, "were highly enjoyable." The only account of them he ever prepared comprises a six-line paragraph in his report to the acting director of military intelligence.[4]

Social obligations were one of the pleasant aspects of the work of the Military Attaché's Office. Through the courtesy of a number of people, Cutting was made an honorary member of several London clubs that were not ordinarily open to visiting foreigners. The hospitality and courtesies extended to Cutting and his associates helped make them feel at home. Cutting took quarters in a house in Mayfair with some of his fellow attachés and returned some of this hospitality. He also attended monthly luncheons of military attachés of all the Allied nations stationed in London.[5]

Cutting saw his former physician and old friend, Frederic Bishop, who was serving with the British Expeditionary Force. In November 1917, they visited in Paris for three days "to consume the good food and enjoy both the farces and the more indigestible food of the Theatre Française." George Ward, Cutting's brother-in-law and an intelligence officer on General Pershing's staff, was also on hand "in a condition of nervous exhaustion whipped into energy and excitement at the sight of Madame with the glasses."[6] Cutting's friend, Miguel Antonio Otero, Jr., arrived in England during December with a unit of the Army Air Force and was stationed at Winchester before departing for France at the end of January. Whether Cutting visited with him is unclear from the available correspondence. Cutting maintained contact with his brother's widow, Sybil, who was residing in a villa near Florence. In January 1918, she informed him about her pending marriage to Geoffrey Scott, an English architect serving in the British embassy at Rome. When Quentin Roosevelt's plane was shot down over enemy lines with the loss of his life in July 1918, Cutting sent a letter of condolence to the family. He must have mentioned that he had seen Henry James in London because the former president commented on both matters.[7]

Shortly after the end of the war in November 1918, Cutting requested a full discharge at the earliest possible moment. On December 27, 1918, he was relieved from duty as assistant military attaché at the American embassy and ordered to report for duty to the chief of staff at the War Department in Washington. In the first week of January, Cutting received an official send-off at a London club. British friends, embassy associates and others expressed their friendship and praised his valuable cooperation.[8] In Washington, before his discharge in February 1919, Cutting prepared a lengthy report delineating his activities in London. According to the acting director of military intelligence, Cutting's "efforts and labors" had helped place the division on a "high plane of esteem in the thoughts and minds of those who are your military superiors." The British more formally expressed their high opinion by awarding him the Military Cross for distinguished service.[9]

On the whole, duty in London was a pleasant interlude in Cutting's career. He never publicly mentioned any aspects of the work in which he engaged. Yet his wartime service helped to launch his career in New Mexico in a way never before possible. It provided a route to a career of public service that, prior to his entering the military, was mired in litigation and political intrigue. In 1919, Cutting could literally start anew in New Mexico.

STARTING ANEW, AGAIN

Promises of a "New Era" or a "New Day" in New Mexico were heard with some frequency following the end of hostilities in Europe. In his 1919 commencement address at the College of Agriculture and Mechanical Arts, President W. C. Reid exclaimed, "We are about to experience in the next few years greater changes socially, politically, economically and industrially than we could, a few years ago, have dreamed would have occurred within the next hundred years." Reid based his optimism upon the prospects for growth and development, the details of which he outlined in his address. He noted that "New Mexico will have about 17,000 young men returned to us from military duty, 50 percent of whom perhaps have been overseas" and asserted that they would not be content "with less than up-to-date progress on the part of the State." Of New Mexico, an article in *Sunset Magazine* observed, "Race Prejudice and Boss Rule are Yielding to Progress in this Ancient Commonwealth." But to Bronson Cutting, visiting with his family in New York City after his discharge from military service, the "New Era" or the "New Day" meant resuming his career as the publisher of the *New Mexican* and as a promoter of civic virtue in a grudging state. New Mexico's political and social leaders yielded little indication of taking seriously the promises proclaimed by college presidents, journalists and other publicists.[1]

Before returning to New Mexico in March 1919, Cutting responded to a letter in the *New York Times* from "A New Mexican." The writer expressed the fear that New Mexico could very well become a Spanish-speaking state unless immediate steps were taken in regard "to the Americanization of the foreign elements." Since the governor's educational reform program called for instruction in Spanish and with the state bordering on Mexico, the writer thought the country was "threatened by a menace similar, if smaller and less conspicuous to that of the German language schools and newspapers within the borders of the United States."[2]

Cutting responded "as a citizen of New Mexico" and as "an editor" to correct some of the correspondent's misleading statements. He argued that the only way to teach English in New Mexico public schools was through teachers who knew both Spanish and English. He insisted that the patriotism of the Spanish-speaking citizens of the state was beyond reproach. In 1916, "when the President called for volunteers to protect the border from Mexican invasion," Hispanic New Mexicans enlisted more readily and with greater enthusiasm than their English-speaking neighbors. The same was true "throughout the present war." Cutting agreed that the teaching of English should be "compulsory and universal." It could, however, never be obtained through the employment of teachers unable to speak Spanish. He applauded the efforts of Governor Octaviano Larrazolo, a man he previously considered something of a demagogue, to raise the compulsory age limit in the public schools from 14 to 15 years and to send Spanish-speaking teachers to schools in districts where the residents spoke no English.[3]

Cutting's letter voiced a theme that would become his major concern for the remainder of his life: the melioration of the lot of Spanish-speaking citizens of New Mexico through the expansion of their educational opportunities and through their participation in the political process. He believed that they should be active citizens capable of expressing their own views, of asserting themselves more independently than in the past and if qualified, of seeking public office. Cutting now saw Larrazolo, not as a politician seeking his own aggrandizement, but as a responsible and compassionate public figure desirous of promoting the general welfare, particularly of the Spanish-speaking people of New Mexico. He also recognized that Larrazolo stood no chance of renomination by the Republican party. He would endeavor to take up where Larrazolo left off. Cleaning up New Mexico politics was his ultimate goal.[4]

However, upon his return to Santa Fe, Cutting had to reestablish himself in familiar surroundings at his bachelor quarters, now officially dubbed "Los Siete Burros," at the newspaper and in the community. He renewed acquaintances with old friends. Although he was not on hand for the dedication of the Antonio Jose Luna Memorial Building at the New Mexico Military Institute in Roswell on May 27, he was represented by Miguel Antonio Otero, Jr. Cutting had provided funds for the building, which contained a swimming pool to honor the memory of his friend who tragically died while in service on the border in 1916.[5]

In Santa Fe, he received an interesting packet from former governor Washington E. Lindsey. It contained two poorly drafted "episodes," each one-page long. They related to incidents that occurred while Lindsey was governor. Cutting expressed the hope that he would delay "a little" their publication. People might conclude that he was seeking revenge on his political enemies, "the Spieses and Springers" and others. Deferring publication for several years, Cutting explained, would make Lindsey's account more plausible. To Lindsey, Cutting indicated that the *New Mexican* would "continue the attempt to combine decency with Republicanism." In view of the national emergency, the paper would remain "regular" as long as its editors could "conscientiously do so." Despite some reservations, Cutting was encouraged by the "real courage and strength of purpose" of Governor Larrazolo whose stand against the pressure of "occult and corrupting influences" might effect meaningful changes in the leadership of the Republican party. Under these circumstances, Cutting said that he would "give him every support" in his power "and refrain from embarrassing him by criticism of immaterial issues."[6]

By August, Cutting was again involved in politics. He played host at Los Siete Burros to General Leonard Wood who was gathering support for his bid to be the Republican nominee for president and was in Santa Fe to speak. Cutting "had a large luncheon for him with all the crooks at it, and a small dinner with a few more personal friends." Cutting said that Wood "converted every human being subject to conversion." He was confident that Wood would get the New Mexico delegation to the Republican nominating convention in 1920. Although Wood was "superb" in military affairs, he had, Cutting thought, "a lot to learn about present international conditions." Nonetheless, he believed the general was capable of learning.[7]

During Wood's reception in Santa Fe, Cutting familiarized himself again with Republican leaders from throughout New Mexico. He was delighted with their enthusiasm for the prospective candidacy of Wood, a progressive Republican, and with the harmony that it created among Republican politicians. Cutting was so pleased that he made a modest contribution to the Republican State Committee, an indication that he was willing to fully enter the party's ranks.[8]

His optimism was not misplaced. M. L. Fox, the editor of the Albuquerque *Morning Journal,* agreed with Cutting and thought that "this state will go Republican beyond doubt, by the largest plurality it has ever given." Governor Larrazolo had the Spanish-speaking people with him, including many prominent Democrats. These voters plus the returned soldiers and recently enfranchised women, allowed Fox, like Cutting, to be optimistic about Republican prospects in 1920.[9]

John T. King, Wood's campaign manager, contacted Cutting to inquire about the procedure "followed in the selection of delegates from New Mexico to the Republican National Convention." Cutting promptly responded that county conventions selected delegates to the state party convention, which in turn would select the delegation attending the national convention. Because New Mexico had no direct-primary law, a popular expression in favor of any candidate was not possible. One had to deal directly with the party leaders in control of the state convention. Fortunately, Cutting wrote, "These leaders are at present unanimous [sic] in favor of General Wood." If factional differences did not erupt, Cutting thought, a delegation instructed for Wood was entirely possible.[10]

Fully apprising King of the New Mexico political scene, Cutting launched into an insightful analysis that revealed his difficulty in reconciling himself to the Republican party. In Cutting's estimation, the party in New Mexico had long been divided into two "bitterly antagonistic factions." One controlled the northern counties while the other ran the southern counties. Each group "to a large extent" was dominated by "rival corporate interests." The northern group represented the Maxwell Land Grant Company, the northern coal mines, the St. Louis and Rocky Mountain Railroad and the "powerful but unobtrusive" Atchison, Topeka and Santa Fe Railroad. Chief figures in this group were Charles Springer, manager of the Maxwell Land Grant Company and president of the State Council of Defense, Secundino Romero, sheriff and boss of San Miguel County, and Clarence J. Roberts, supreme court justice. Although associated with the group, Governor Octaviano Larrazolo had "kept free of factional alliances" since he took office.

The southern faction was controlled by the Phelps Dodge Company through the El Paso and Southwestern Railroad and allied corporations such as the Chino Copper Company. Its principal figures were Holm O. Bursum, national committeeman, Albert B. Fall, senator, W. A. Hawkins, counsel for the railroad, and Eduardo Otero, sheepman and boss of Valencia County. The issue of race permeated both sides and complicated the factionalism. Cutting reassured King that all the Spanish-American leaders were enthusiastic for Wood because he delivered a speech in Spanish during his recent visit to Santa Fe.

Cutting further observed that the northern group probably controlled a majority of the Republican voters but that the southerners, thanks to their superior political skills, had "dominated the last few state conventions and may be expected to dominate the next one." Any disaffection in Republican ranks would give the election to the Democrats. Therefore, King would have to deal with the leaders of both factions. Fortunately, Cutting believed, all but Fall were for Wood. This unanimity for Wood and Wood's progressive politics explained Cutting's willingness to align himself with the state organization. In addition, Cutting said that King could rely on the assistance of former Rough Riders, most prominently Sheriff George W. Armijo of Santa Fe, "probably the strongest leader in this county especially with the Spanish-

American voters." Cutting also evaluated other party leaders and expressed his willingness to be of assistance. By the same token Republican leaders thought that the *New Mexican* would continue to support the party and that Cutting, now back in the Republican fold, would have delegates endorsing his views on the floor of the next convention.[11]

Adding to Cutting's satisfaction with the political scene in the fall of 1919 was the fact that the *New Mexican* was beginning to show a profit. However, he was annoyed at "the most scandalous bill" he received from Francis Wilson for legal services rendered during the lengthy libel litigation. Wilson had not performed as satisfactorily as Cutting and his sister would have liked. While their friendship had cooled considerably during the trial, it now reached the breaking point. But Wilson had the last word. He wrote Cutting that "if you do not think you should pay the balance which I have stated is due me, you are at liberty to charge it off. . . ."[12]

Cutting was too involved with his own affairs to ruminate. He greeted and extended hospitality to visiting dignitaries. He hosted a reception for Admiral William S. Benson and his party in Santa Fe, and he later helped to welcome Albert, king of the Belgians, and his party in Albuquerque. By November, Cutting was fully reestablished in Santa Fe, enjoying freedom from law suits and placid relations with Republican leaders.

He left Santa Fe for an extended holiday season with his family in New York but was followed by an unexpected problem. Brian Boru Dunne informed Cutting that he had acquired business interests in Tahiti and would be departing in January. Exhausted as a journalist, he had "worn out fourteen horses in 10 years chasing around the 55 places to be visited daily . . . and written as high as 5,000 words in about two to two and a half hours. . . ." Cutting understood his situation and wished him well. He added, "You and I have had our good times and damn few bad times; we have had our ups and perhaps occasional downs. . . ."[13]

Dunne's impending departure did not impede Cutting's holiday season. After the holiday, he sailed for London to visit friends and acquaintances from his wartime service. Cutting did not return to Santa Fe until February. During his absence, New Mexico coal miners had joined a nationwide strike that the federal government rendered largely ineffective by taking possession of all coal properties. In New Mexico, the coal strike was hardly evident because there were "troops on the ground at the opportune time." Nevertheless, fear of further labor disturbances prompted Governor Larrazolo, most likely at the insistence of the mine owners, to call a special session of the legislature to provide him with the means to maintain law and order.[14]

All of this and more was brought to Cutting's attention in a letter from Herbert Hagerman, a former territorial governor, a progressive Republican and a fiscal conservative. Hagerman wanted Cutting to speak out against the groups pressuring Governor Larrazolo. However, he realized that Cutting was in favor of General Wood's candidacy and might not wish to disrupt party harmony. To disabuse Cutting of the existence of such tranquility, Hagerman explained that "the advocacy of the Republican ring here for the General" was insincere. The old gang would "trade him in" for Frank O. Lowden or Warren G. Harding. Hagerman cautioned Cutting about the seeming "sincerity and good faith of Larrazolo." While Hagerman conceded that he might be doing the governor an injustice, he alerted Cutting to the fact that the political harmony among Republicans in New Mexico was disintegrating.[15]

Cutting, if he paid attention to Hagerman's letter, did little about it and spent most of the winter and early spring in New York. By March, he had heard from others that Wood might have trouble securing delegates. While some of the southern counties were for Wood, Doña Ana County would send a delegation to the state convention pledged to Senator Fall who, it was now clear, endorsed Harding's candidacy. Cutting, however, responded to none of the letters detailing developments in New Mexico. Instead, he enjoyed the social whirl and the company of an attractive magazine illustrator, "Bibs" or Beverly Chanler. In one letter she exclaimed, "I have just been to an exhibition of about 500 photographs of all parts of Greece—and not one of them remotely resembles New Jersey. No doubt you have forgotten that you told me that Attica was like New Jersey."[16] Bibs, who was seeking a job at *Harper's,* was surprised at Cutting's disgust with Harding's nomination. She wrote, "Senator [James W.] Wadsworth dined with us the day he got back from Chicago and seemed enormously pleased." She admitted that she was "very ignorant" and asked that Cutting enlighten her. Although Cutting might have seen her again, their correspondence apparently ceased upon his return to Santa Fe.[17]

Harding's nomination indicated that Cutting's hopes for party harmony would be disappointed, although the New Mexican delegation to the Chicago convention favored Leonard Wood. He feared that he would resume his traditional role of opposing Republican candidates in New Mexico. The Republican gubernatorial nomination of Judge Merritt C. Mechem, Cutting's recent nemesis in court, drove him away from the party. Also appalled with Harding's nomination, Cutting exclaimed, "Surely no man so mediocre has ever been put up for the Presidency." He suspected that Harding was "a

good deal worse than mediocre" and was running on a platform that strad-
dled every issue. Unless the Democrats nominated a better candidate, Cutting thought that he might find himself voting for Eugene Victor Debs, the
Socialist party candidate.[18]

Although Harding's nomination cast in doubt Cutting's role in the forth-
coming elections, he was delighted with the return of Brian Boru Dunne.
Disillusioned with Tahiti, he was eager to resume bachelor quarters at Los
Siete Burros and his former job on the *New Mexican*. Shortly thereafter
Cutting left for a European vacation and did not return until late August.[19]

Republican leaders, however, were deeply concerned about the coming
election and the candidates yet to be selected. They had to consider the
women's vote for the first time. An estimated seventy percent of the Republican voters in the state were native or Spanish American. The problem was
Governor Larrazolo whose appeal to Spanish-speaking voters was enormous,
but his progressive policies and his appointments had displeased many Republican leaders, including the most powerful Spanish Americans: Eduardo
and Manuel Otero of Valencia County; Secundino Romero of San Miguel
County; and possibly Benigno Hernandez, New Mexico's lone congressman.

Opposition to Larrazolo was also evident in other counties as Republicans
selected delegates for the state nominating convention in September.[20] The
Republican convention turned down Governor Larrazolo and selected a former judge, Merritt Mechem. His nomination made certain that Cutting and
the *New Mexican* would not endorse his candidacy. Larrazolo, according to
Senator Fall, "was defeated by the heavy Mexican Republican counties with
practically solid Mexican delegations." National Committeeman Holm Bursum, with whom Mechem was allied, had little to do with Larrazolo's
demise.

Factionalism again came to the fore. As before, disgruntled party leaders
aligned themselves with the Democrats. The "condition of affairs," wrote
Fall, "is exceedingly bad." Large expenditures, bilingual speakers and Spanish
campaign literature would be necessary to keep New Mexico in the Republican fold. The women's vote, Fall believed, would help materially, for there
were "many more Republican Mexican women than Democratic women."
With local and county factional fights, however, much effort would be necessary "to get this vote out and cast for the National and State ticket." Fall, who
was devoting most of his efforts to Harding's campaign, recognized that Cutting and Carl Magee, the editors respectively of the Santa Fe *New Mexican* and
the Albuquerque *Morning Journal,* would oppose the ticket on the grounds of
boss rule.[21]

CHAPTER 9

At their convention, the Democrats nominated New Mexico Supreme Court Justice Richard Hanna, a man of integrity and ability. Their presidential and vice-presidential candidates, James M. Cox and Franklin D. Roosevelt, spoke in the state. Senator Andrieus Jones stumped every county and "practically every village." Democratic candidates bitterly attacked "all corporations and vested rights" as well as boss rule. In addition, Larrazolo, while endorsing Harding, spoke in favor of fusion with Democrats on the state level. The anti-Republican onslaught necessitated tremendous effort on the part of Republican leaders. Senator Fall started campaigning in New Mexico in late October. He thought there was a chance, given the crowds he was attracting in the southern counties, to prevent a Democratic victory if funds and other assistance were poured into the state.[22]

Cutting expected the worst in the election and he was not disappointed. "The campaign," one correspondent wrote from Roswell, "has been a series of double crosses, and it is disgusting, even locally." Richard Hanna, the defeated Democratic gubernatorial candidate, thanked Cutting for "the splendid work done by the *New Mexican*" during the campaign. Both recognized that some progress against bossism had been made "and that the work of the present campaign will bear fruit in the future." "The National ticket," explained George Curry, "was the main factor in saving the state for the Republican party." For the next two years, Merritt C. Mechem would serve as the governor of New Mexico. His party would control the legislature as well.[23]

While Cutting and the *New Mexican* endorsed Hanna and fusion candidates, he did not play an active role in the campaign. Instead, he found himself embroiled in a dispute with the arts community in Santa Fe. An editorial, "Real Bolsheviks," that appeared on September 29, 1920, charged that "three fourths of the official publicity put out from the Museum art section had been labored propaganda for art extremism of the most absurd kind." Since both E. Dana Johnson and Cutting, editor and publisher respectively, were sympathetic and supportive of the fine arts, the editorial came as a shock to the arts community in Santa Fe and generated a spate of letters and interminable hours of conversation at cocktail and studio parties throughout Santa Fe and Taos. Alice Corbin Henderson responded to the editorial in a lengthy letter that was not published. Natalie Curtis Burlin, an acquaintance of Cutting's family and a resident of Santa Fe, discussed the matter with him at a social gathering and then complained that the editorial, "with its suggestion of politically controlled art," seemed "to many of us a dangerously un-American idea."[24] Cutting responded, "Will you forgive me for saying frankly that at a time when it seems to me that the destinies of the nation and especially of this state are hanging in the balance, I am unable to take more than a perfunctory interest in the policies of the museum towards the local painters." He said that he neither dictated the policy of the art editorials nor had read this particular one before it appeared in print. When reading the controversial piece, he saw nothing in it to justify "the intense and almost hysterical excitement" that followed its publication.

Cutting wrote Burlin several days before the election, trying to make the best out of a bad situation. Arousing unnecessary antagonism, the ill-timed editorial reflected neither Cutting's views about art nor his pressing political concerns. He managed to vent his disdain on the emerging art colony in Taos and Santa Fe. He wrote, "Instead of getting down into the arena and fighting with the forces of darkness in the only way in which those forces can be conquered, they sit on Olympus, take an 'intelligent interest' in what is going on in Russia, direct a few social 'experiments,' and advise us, as both old parties are imperfect, to vote the Farmer Labor ticket." Along with his criticism of the art colony's irresponsible politics, he also revealed his despair about the forthcoming election. "We are cursed here," Cutting explained, "with the most brazen political machine which has ever disgraced this country." He admitted that while fighting this machine, the *New Mexican* had used methods that on occasion aroused public disapproval and offended high-minded citizens, but he knew "no way of defeating these men except by publishing the facts," unpleasant and unrefined though they might be. Until the disgruntled artists recognized the realities of the New Mexico political scene and sought to do something about them, he confessed that he could not take very seriously the sorrows of those who complained about the editorial entitled "Real Bolsheviks."[25]

Shortly after the election, Cutting left to spend the holiday season with his family. From the vantage point of Westbrook, he reflected on the bleak situation in New Mexico. The success of the Republicans in New Mexico "was simply the effect of the nationwide revulsion against Wilsonianism." At least ten thousand Democrats, he claimed, stayed away from the polls, and a good many more voted the Republican ticket. To effect a permanent organization, someone would have to bring together the factions within the Republican party, a process that would fail "under the present party management." The Republican leadership took the result of the election as an endorsement of its efforts. As Cutting saw things, a large majority of the party favored Governor Larrazolo's "progressive policies" and bitterly resented "the way in which he was deprived of the re-nomination." Clara Olsen, who had recently accepted Mechem's offer to serve as his secretary, agreed with Cutting. She said that "locally many Republicans who early in the campaign seemed to have their minds made up to vote for Hanna, suddenly became panicky, thinking he made too vigorous an onslaught on the big interests, without which poor New Mexico could not paddle very far." At the outset, she believed, the Republican ticket had been doomed, but about two weeks before the election, the tide seemed to turn. Like Cutting, she explained the shift as "a grim determination to get rid of the present national administration."[26]

Further reflecting on the New Mexico scene from New York, Cutting took stock of both its assets and liabilities. First, New Mexico needed an educational system that "will lead the native people to discard the dishonest leaders who have controlled them in the past." This goal, he recognized, could not be achieved within two generations. In the meantime, he feared that if the Democrats ever became an outright majority, they would be in a position "to checkmate all Spanish-American aspirations." With Larrazolo no longer a factor in the political picture, Cutting believed that there was no New Mexico leader able "to hold the Spanish-Americans together, or to look out for their interests." They could be exploited "by the most unscrupulous parts of the community." On the other hand, the Democrats had no organization. While some of their leaders had "public spirit and ability," they were unable to "inspire the rather soggy minds of their followers."

Cutting turned next to a self-evaluation. At the end of 1920, his strengths were the support of a handful of individuals and "a certain mild friendliness on the part of the native people, not including the bosses." He admitted to having "a few strong personal friends, either out of politics or with slight *political sense*." In this connection he mentioned the American Legion.

While his assets were considered under three headings, his liabilities comprised eight points:

(1) An accumulation of enmities raised up during 8 years.
(2) A hostile administration containing at least two bitter personal enemies; and completely adverse courts in district and higher jurisdictions.
(3) A local situation apparently precluding all possible advancement.
(4) Opposition of big interests.
(5) Skillfully fostered propaganda of personal animosity towards opponents, and of desire to appropriate power in any organization in which I am interested. Consequent loss of what credit I might have had with majority of posts of A[merican] L[egion].
(6) Political irregularity—unavoidable—over long period of time.

(7) Inability to swallow political crookedness of Republican organization.

(8) Inability to swallow anti-Mexicanism of Democratic voters.[27]

During this gloomy but realistic assessment of his prospects in New Mexico, Cutting received a telegram from Herbert Hoover, who provided an opportunity to be of immediate service in a new capacity. Hoover offered him the New Mexico chairmanship of the joint committee raising funds to prevent over three million children in central and eastern Europe "from being turned into the street this winter." The state was assigned a quota of twenty-five thousand dollars, and Cutting was asked to bring the campaign to a conclusion by February 15. Cutting gave the matter some thought before accepting. He recognized that many people would not contribute funds on account of his association with the movement but accepted because he knew of no one who would fill the position. Traveling about the state to the larger towns, Cutting was initially delighted at the enthusiasm he found and the ease with which prominent people accepted responsibility in their communities.

Albuquerque was the location of the state's headquarters. Cutting made additional trips there to keep abreast of conditions affecting the drive. As the February 15 deadline neared, however, his initial optimism gave way to despair. "Raising money under present local conditions," he said, "is a job I will never undertake again." Indeed, Cutting thought that "it would have been so much easier to give it in the first place than to have it come in in driblets at the most enormous cost in labor and time." The legislature and the district and federal courts were in session, and his newspaper was short-handed and under audit. Cutting now resented devoting time to Hoover's relief campaign, which was not concluded until early April.[28]

In retrospect, Cutting appreciated his involvement and observed "the types of people who take up such work, principally Jews and very poor Catholics." Nobody of any wealth, again excepting Jews, had contributed. He was unable to secure reduced rates from the railroads on food stuffs destined for the European relief. The mining corporations "cheerfully responded by cutting the wages of the miners and passing it on." In all, he concluded, "One meets and consorts with queer people."[29]

Although he was tied down with the relief campaign, he was heartened by the new administration in Santa Fe. Governor Mechem presented "an excellent message" and made "good" appointments, but he was "extremely vindictive." Cutting said that any praise he received in the columns of the *New Mexican* "evidently galls him to the limit." The crucial matter he had to consider was selecting a replacement in the United States Senate for Albert Fall, who would enter the Harding administration. In early February, Harding tendered him an appointment as secretary of the interior, a post the president-elect considered second only to the secretary of state in importance. "Since there is more opportunity for graft and scandal connected with the disposition of public lands, etc., than there could be in any other Department," Fall explained, "he wants a man who is thoroughly familiar with the business and one he can rely upon as thoroughly honest, etc., etc."

While Fall was pleased to accept the appointment, he told Governor Mechem not to appoint Bursum unless he was the freely expressed choice of a majority of Republican leaders and unless the people of New Mexico passed upon his selection to the Senate. At the Republican convention, Bursum had kept the New Mexico delegation in line for Leonard Wood after Harding's nomination was assured and would be unacceptable to the new administration. Fall explained that after some hesitation, Mechem "agreed that he would yield to my insistence in this matter and try to find someone else, at least temporarily." Moreover, Fall was upset with a *New Mexican* editorial charging that Mechem and the "Bosses" had arranged to appoint Bursum to the Senate in the event that Fall entered the cabinet. Fall was distressed when Mechem backed away from their previous agreement.[30] A loyal party man, however, Fall pledged to cooperate with Bursum.

Cutting knew nothing of Fall's unhappiness with the Bursum appointment. He too was deeply disturbed about the possibility of Mechem appointing his ally and mentor to fill out Fall's term in the United States Senate. He noted that Bursum had twice failed to win an election "under the most favorable of circumstances." Congratulating Fall upon his cabinet appointment, Cutting asked whether he would consider delaying his acceptance until after the adjournment of the legislature. He could then exert a meaningful influence on political leaders no longer constrained by legislative and patronage pressures. Although he had disagreed with Fall on state politics, he always felt that Fall's "senatorial career has been a source of great pride to the people of New Mexico." He thought that Fall should now try "to give them a dignified and worthy successor."[31]

That Fall did just that and failed Cutting never knew. Mechem and Bursum "refused to recede an inch." Bursum would not agree to "the suggestion of an election, or to any other method of obtaining the office, except by appointment of his friend Mechem." Thus, Cutting and others foresaw that Bursum would be appointed as Fall's successor. What they hoped was that Mechem might yet call for a special election to confirm Bursum's selection.[32]

Although Cutting wanted to spend several months in Europe, he changed his plans because of the possibility of a special election. Although he was convinced Bursum would be elected, he wanted to direct the editorial policy of the *New Mexican* during this campaign. The paper would favor the re-pudiation of Bursum for a third time. Meanwhile, he tried to get affairs at the paper on a sounder basis. He searched for a new business manager, and in April, he faced the possibility of a strike. He preferred to continue publication and offered the men what he considered a fair compromise, noting that "if the national managers don't interfere, they may accept it." No strike occurred. In addition, he extended a loan to former governor Larrazolo who relocated his family in El Paso. He engaged in the practice of law and devoted special attention to business affairs in Mexico, while he maintained his official resi-dence in New Mexico. Once affairs at the paper had settled down in May, Cutting departed for New York to visit his mother and sisters and enjoy the social whirl.[33]

While the Republican convention met in Santa Fe during August and nominated Holm Bursum, Cutting prepared a special anti-Bursum edition of the *New Mexican* for statewide circulation. He was shocked to learn that Larrazolo, guided by his desire to help Hispanics, would not oppose Bursum. Despite the former governor's support, Bursum's nomination widened the rift in the Republican party. His incapacity for truthfulness and reliability, according to some of his opponents within the party, was an unending source of discord and trouble. So too was the support he received from the contro-versial editor of the *Albuquerque Journal,* Carl Magee, a man whose sole purpose, Senator Fall thought, "was to array one Republican against another" or who "was simply dictated by the vagaries of a disordered intellect." Given the internal opposition to Bursum, there was the question of raising the funds necessary to turn out the vote in the heavily Republican counties. But Bur-sum had a strong ally in the "practical disintegration of the Democratic party." Unless the Democrats could unite themselves, Bursum would over-come the intense hostility to his nomination and would win the special election.[34]

During this campaign, Cutting learned about Fall's opposition to Bursum's candidacy. One of Fall's daughters responded to an editorial in the *New Mexican* titled "Has Fall Reformed?" Explaining in some detail why her father took his present position, she invoked "the pleasant friendship which existed between you and my whole family, during our short residence in Santa Fe, ten years ago" and expressed her "intense desire" to have her father's position made clear. Now that Cutting was apprised of her father's rationale, she trusted to his "personal honor and discretion" that he would refrain "from allowing your paper to couple Dad's name with the 'gangs.'"[35]

After Bursum's election, Cutting departed for an extended European vacation. He went first to London and visited wartime friends. He spent a couple of days on the Isle of Wight with Justine. Fleeing the intense fog, he departed for Paris and then Florence, where he met his old friend, the Dottore, Frederic Bishop. In Rome he and the Dottore took quarters at the Grand Hotel. In early January, they departed for Sicily. Cutting found the Sicilians "ugly and dirty and malarial and rude." On the other hand, he was enchanted with Palermo, "the most beautiful site in Europe," and with nearby Monreale, whose notable Norman cathedral and Benedictine monastery made the town "one of the few great things in the world." He returned to London in February and took quarters at Claridge's Hotel. He was "amazed" at the number of people who remembered him. In London, he began commenting on world affairs. He admitted that he was changing his opinion on the significance of the Washington Conference, hoping that it might serve "as a first lesson in international politics to some of our people." He was also pleased that the Harding administration had agreed to have a representative in Geneva where the League of Nations was headquartered.[36]

Cutting returned to Santa Fe in late April and found politicians vying to secure nominations for the fall campaign, during which all major offices would be contested. Shortly after his return, Cutting spent a few days in Albuquerque "at the meeting of the Independents" and talked with several Republican leaders. He foresaw that Governor Mechem could not get his party's nomination for a second term. Cutting wanted to determine what progressive-independent Republican sentiment remained in New Mexico. Through Felix Baca, an Albuquerque lawyer, he arranged for one or more individuals to travel throughout the state and to discern whether independents should battle party leaders to nominate progressive Republican candidates.[37]

In Albuquerque, Cutting learned of the sale of the city's leading newspaper, the *Journal*. The editor, Carl Magee, like Cutting, had opposed Mechem in the 1920 campaign. But unlike him, Magee was a maverick. His editorials were inconsistent, vituperative and inflammatory. At the time of the sale, they knew neither who had bought the paper nor what the policy of the new management would be. Magee soon reappeared as the editor of a smaller weekly paper, the *New Mexico Tribune*, and targeted Cutting in some of his editorials. As the *Journal*'s reactionary editorial policy unfolded, it was clearly friendly to Albert Fall who, as secretary of the interior, was central to the unfolding Teapot Dome controversy. Many citizens followed, as best they could, the role of Albert Fall, the first representative of the Southwest to serve in the cabinet, in the leasing and development of California and Wyoming naval oil reserves.[38]

At the time, Cutting was monitoring the conference on the distribution of Colorado River water rights at Bishop's Lodge near Santa Fe. Representing the Harding administration, Secretary of Commerce Herbert Hoover was in attendance. The question of the right to appropriate and use the waters of the Colorado River had been a "burning question" between the southwestern states for over a decade. The interested parties agreed upon a compact that paved the way for the approval, several years later, of the Boulder Canyon project and the more orderly dividing of the waters. In addition, to generate some political interest, the *New Mexican* proposed Clara Olsen for the governor's office. Cutting said the idea "made a great stir, most favorable," adding that "of course, she will not get the nomination."[39]

Cutting was not the only prominent figure in New Mexico concerned about the plight of the Republican party during Governor Mechem's tenure. Albert Fall believed that unless "great care in the selection of thoroughly competent, honest, patriotic candidates" was exercised, the party "will be defeated, as it should be, at the coming election." Such a result, he added, "might not be so disastrous . . . to the Party, and consequently to the future of the State, were it not for the firm conviction which I have that if the Republicans lose this election, New Mexico will continue for an indefinite period of time to be a non-Republican State." Although less a party man than Fall, Cutting did not hold very different views, but he did not fear fusion with progressive Democrats and other like-minded groups, diverging from Fall only in this respect.[40]

At the Republican convention, O. L. Phillips, chairman of the state committee, charged that officers of the Democratic State Committee offered Cutting a fusion proposal that would allow the Independents to select the candidates for lieutenant governor, secretary of state, state auditor and corporation commissioner. Phillips further stipulated that Cutting and his associates delay their response in order to give regular Republican leaders an opportunity to present counterproposals.

The allegations created a sensation. George Hunker, Democratic party chairman, "absolutely" denied Phillips' charges, stating, "I never had and do not now have any such authority." The Independent Republican State Committee met with Phillips at his invitation in Albuquerque to hear any proposition to harmonize the factions, but none were forthcoming. In a lengthy story in the *New Mexican,* Cutting did not deny that the Independent Republicans had consulted with the Democrats at their request. They were seeking assistance "in putting a stop to present conditions in state government." No places on the Democratic ticket were offered, although Cutting, claiming "the exact nature of the Democratic proposition was confidential," would not disclose what was discussed. In the meeting with Phillips, Cutting said the committee had sought a pledge of support "to some definite program that would assure fair play to the Independents." The Independents desired primarily two things: first, "a program of fair play for all elements of our population"; and second, that candidates for public office be individuals "whom we can trust to carry out that program." Cutting singled out only the Republican leader, Secundino Romero, "for his reasonable and moderating influence on the discussions" in Albuquerque.[41]

Cutting was disappointed with the Republican slate, which proposed Nina Otero Warren as the congressional candidate and consisted of relatively unknown political figures. The ticket indicated that the older political leaders, no longer as influential as in the past, sought new candidates to appeal to younger voters. Cutting's dissatisfaction rested in part on the fact that Larrazolo was thwarted in his effort to secure renomination.[42]

To aid Hispanics in education and public life, Cutting assumed the presidency of the New Mexico Educational Foundation and assisted the launching of *La Aurora del Nuevo Día.* The paper promoted educational advancement independent of any political or religious organization. Through the paper, the foundation urged teachers to encourage students to get through the twelfth grade and then to recommend them to the foundation. Through the foundation, Cutting would aid these "native boys and girls," selected by an impartial competitive examination, to secure a college education. The purpose of the paper and of the numerous letters written by its editor, Julian Amador, was to alert teachers of the opportunity provided by the foundation.[43]

The creation of this foundation and the appearance of its publication was not ill-timed. Announcement of its purpose came prior to the nominating conventions. Cutting was more determined than ever to help Hispanics participate, on something approaching an equal footing, in the mainstream of American life. He was seriously groping for a more active way of furthering this goal. The *New Mexican* provided a voice, but he already knew that championing causes and candidates through the press meant little unless backed with political clout. The American Legion, which had avoided endorsing candidates, provided a dubious possibility if its members could become politically active. Much would depend on the nominating conventions and the caliber of the candidates selected.

CHAPTER 10

THE AMERICAN LEGION

The American Legion made Cutting an active participant in postwar New Mexico politics. Colonel Theodore Roosevelt, Jr. initially involved him with the organization. He asked Cutting to identify possible New Mexico delegates for a caucus to be held in St. Louis. Cutting wired Roosevelt the names of forty men representing all branches of the armed forces. From this list two names, Lieutenant Colonel Charles M. de Bremond of Roswell and Private Canuto Trujillo of Chimayo, were selected by the temporary national committee chaired by the ex-president's son and namesake. In late April at Albuquerque, twelve veterans were selected to represent the state. Only ten attended the St. Louis caucus. On the morning of May 8, 1919, when Theodore Roosevelt, Jr. called the caucus of the American Legion to order in the packed Shubert-Jefferson Theater, Bronson Cutting was a participant in the general pandemonium.

The New Mexico delegation, although small, was neither inactive nor inconspicuous. Cutting, recently discharged, held the second highest rank among the ten delegates. One of their number, a former seaman first class, was elected to serve as second vice-chairman until the first national convention, scheduled for Minneapolis, met in November 1919.[1]

Approximately sixty percent of the New Mexicans volunteering for military service during the First World War were of Hispanic descent. Many could not speak the English language. Despite this handicap, so many had volunteered that the state had been unable to fill its draft quotas. Service in the armed forces had thrust Hispanic men from their restricted world into contact with the modern world. The American Legion would keep them in touch with national and world affairs and would make them aware of aspects of the New Mexico scene that had never previously concerned them. A traditional, prescribed view of the world and their place in it, already fracturing, now gave way to broader concerns.[2]

A prominent figure in the New Mexico American Legion, Cutting was a catalyst in this process. In 1919, he was thirty-one years old, older than most who joined the organization. He enjoyed the comraderie and fellowship and found that the American Legion bridged class and ethnic divisions, something he had not been fully exposed to, given his privileged and somewhat insulated experience. Given Cutting's extreme reserve and his inability to mingle easily with the rank and file, he found in the legion a wide range of friends and acquaintances with whom he could be at ease. When his participation in public life came to involve seeking public office, these contacts would serve him well.

At the outset, he focused on organizing local posts and shouldered some of the expenses. At the first national meeting in St. Louis, he served as the chairman of the New Mexico delegation. He was also elected to the permanent Executive Committee for New Mexico. In addition, he filled out the unexpired term of the first state chairman. Cutting served the national American Legion as the organizer for Zone Ten, comprised of New Mexico, Arizona, Texas and Oklahoma. His assignment was to provide speakers for posts throughout these four states when called upon. As acting state chairman, Cutting was determined that New Mexico "get busy at once with the foundation of Posts in all possible parts of the state."[3]

Organization was no easy task, given the great distances involved, the lack of adequate finances, the scattered population, the absence of accurate lists of records and the inability to reach many veterans by mail or telegraph. The efforts of Cutting and one or two others secured financial support. In addition, Lansing B. Bloom, secretary of the Historical Service of the State Council of Defense, rendered great assistance in furnishing names of ex-servicemen. The funds and the names helped the organizing secretary to found thirty-nine of the fifty-one American Legion Posts in New Mexico noted in the first annual report of the department. As of August 1920, there were 2,557 American Legion members in the state. New Mexico ranked sixth in the nation among those states subscribing their quota of new members within the time frame set by the National Executive Committee.[4]

In 1919, as the organization was getting underway, issues and an agenda also began to emerge. Its first commander, Herman Baca, a personable and aggressive former sailor, relied heavily on Cutting, a fellow member of the New Mexico Executive Committee. Writing him in November, 1919, Baca said, "Don't fail to tell me what's right and what's wrong, remember you're the Doctor as far as I am concerned and I always take your good word." Cutting endorsed, for example, resolutions adopted by the 1919 state convention favoring land settlement for New Mexico veterans. The legislature responded with a land-settlement bill but failed to provide adequate funding. New Mexico lawmakers tied their endorsement to a measure that was pending in the United States Congress and that was never approved. At the outset, the chief political concern of the American Legion in New Mexico focused on a meaningful settlement measure for soldiers. At a meeting of the National Executive Committee in Washington during May 1920, Cutting insisted that New Mexico was more interested in effective land-settlement and home-aid measures than in the payment of cash to veterans in the form of a bonus.[5] Bonus legislation was not an immediate concern of the national organization. The Minneapolis Convention in November 1919 refused to make any demands on the Congress. The New Mexico Executive Committee went on record against a bonus. Securing a land-settlement measure was its primary legislative drive, although Cutting personally believed that a vocational training provision would be a valuable addition.

While the legion would lobby for legislation in Santa Fe and members of local posts could endorse candidates, its national charter prohibited the organization from directly entering the political arena. What troubled Cutting was that an officer of the legion could not be a candidate for "a salaried elective office" but might seek nonsalaried posts such as chairman or secretary of a political committee. He would have preferred a provision that legion officers "should not be conspicuous in partisan politics" and that left to the conscience of the veteran how he should live up to the obligation.[6]

At the outset the legion was drawn into New Mexico political affairs when Carl C. Magee, the controversial editor of the *New Mexico State Tribune,* severely censured the proceedings of the annual meeting. He charged that Cutting controlled the election of officers "by reason of spending his money to round up and bring in from over the state enough of the men he OWNS to have a majority." In maligning Cutting, however, Magee had overreached himself. Several legion posts condemned him, and Cutting, after a meeting of the state committee early in 1921, was "greatly pleased and rather surprised to find that the intense political propaganda against me carried no weight in that quarter. . . ."[7]

At the national level, Cutting served as chairman of the Americanism Committee. He took a strong stand against a uniform measure, proposed by the American Legion, that called for the public-school instruction of every state to be in the English language. Cutting noted its inapplicability to New Mexico where a majority of the people spoke Spanish and where a teacher "equipped with only English was unable to teach English—or anything else." Progress resulted when instruction was offered in Spanish and when English was taught "by people who understood the native language of their pupils." An additional consequence of that enlightened educational strategy was that the legion's Americanization program, advocating the "spread of American ideas and patriotism," was advanced in New Mexico. For the present, Cutting insisted that "Spanish is still the only possible vehicle by which English can be brought to the people."[8]

Cutting argued that the reasons impelling the American Legion to call for an Americanization program were not germane to New Mexico. "We have no anti-American propaganda, no Bolshevism, no I.W.W., no disloyalty, and no organized group of foreign born inhabitants." As for Spanish-speaking natives, citizens "for more than seventy years," there was no more loyal or patriotic group in any state, in spite of their difficulties with the English language. At least half of the most active legion members in New Mexico were Hispanic. Cutting added, "The best war records made by men from this state were made by the same element." The American Legion in New Mexico constituted, Cutting explained to a friendly critic, "the one best bet for the redemption of this state."[9]

Inevitably, the legion was drawn into state politics. By the end of 1921, the New Mexico legion had given up its call for a land-settlement bill and had followed the national organization to support proposals for adjusted compensation or a bonus for veterans. New Mexico's senior United States senator, Andrieus A. Jones, was the author of such a bill. Concluding his first term, Jones, of course, was eager for veteran support of his reelection campaign. In August of 1921, he wrote Cutting to express appreciation for the attention the *New Mexican* gave a speech he delivered on the Adjusted Compensation Bill.[10]

All was placid until the fall of 1922. Serving a term as commander of the Montoya Post in Santa Fe as well as continuing his membership in the state Executive Committee, Cutting made the decision to endorse Jones and thrust the *New Mexican* and the American Legion into the forefront of his reelection bid. A form letter, either in Spanish or English, went to every ex-serviceman in New Mexico and endorsed Senator Jones as one who "has fought for us and can be counted upon to do it again." The bulk of the letter was devoted to puffing Jones, a Democrat, but two other candidates, both former servicemen—one a Republican, the other a Democrat and one a Hispanic, the other an Anglo—also received mention. The letter declared, "Forget the party labels, comrades! Vote for the Man!" Although one letter was signed by E. B. Healy and the other by Jose G. Rivera, the letter expressed the nonpartisan, fusion view that characterized Cutting's approach to politics. He may have helped draft these form letters, which were mailed to "more than 14,300 ex-service men." Moreover, Cutting assumed responsibility for furthering the cause of Senator Jones among veterans.[11]

To win an election in New Mexico, four things were necessary: political organization; the dissemination of arguments in both Spanish and English; the protection of voters at the polls; and the prevention of election fraud. Cutting was able to provide the funding to accomplish these goals. In effect, he managed Jones's reelection campaign. He wired Washington for the senator's complete voting record and provided information to veterans speaking on Jones's behalf. He requested that ex-servicemen act as poll watchers on election day and insisted that each veteran, after visiting a precinct, file a report that gave local organization plans and the names of promised workers. Cutting supervised the mailing of the form letters and kept abreast of the editorial opinion that commented on their impact and on the controversy they engendered. He carefully read letters from veterans relating their efforts on behalf of the senator. In addition, Cutting provided funds to campaign workers. At least one of them intended to use some of the money to pay "the right man to do some pre-election work for Jones" in Republican precincts in his community. By the end of the campaign, Cutting had in place a political machine that conceivably could hold the balance of power in the state. His was a personal campaign, rather than one conducted through a political organization. The effort was expensive but effective, and it was made even more powerful by his ally, the *New Mexican*.[12]

When the election results were tallied, Jones had a majority of 12,248 votes, the largest ever accorded any New Mexico candidate to that time. Moreover, Jones's astounding margin helped to elect the entire Democratic ticket. Cutting surmised that at least five thousand Republican veterans voted the straight Democratic ticket to make sure that their votes for Jones would not be discounted. Both Jones and the governor-elect, James F. Hinkle, appreciated Cutting's assistance. So grateful were they that several days after the election, Cutting was offered the Democratic state chairmanship. Cutting believed that he could easily capture the "thoroughly disorganized" Democratic party and control it for a good many years, while no outsider had "any chance of breaking into the Republican ring with any decent element." Although tempted, he declined the offer. Rather than play a direct role in the Democratic party, Cutting preferred to see that the new governor appointed worthy individuals, including veterans, to public office.[13]

As he promoted the welfare of the state's Hispanic citizenry, Cutting inevitably fell into the role of a don or patrón. His constituency was based not on ties of kinship, county rings, or courthouse machines, but on the basis of American Legion posts. Weak party attachments in New Mexico allowed veterans and other voters to cast their ballots on the basis of some other identification. An unstable party structure enabled a short term factor, the American Legion, to play a prominent role in determining voters' choices in 1922.

Shortly after the election Cutting received a letter from a former territorial delegate, Bernard S. Rodey, a Republican. Like Cutting's, his dissatisfaction with the party's candidates often drove him to vote for nominees on the Democratic ticket. Rodey explained, "It is tough on us Republicans to have to vote for and elect democrats [sic], but things got so rotten here there was nothing else left for us to do." Cutting, of course, agreed with Rodey's statement, which succinctly summarized his position as well as that of numerous similarly minded independent or progressive Republicans.

Cutting now went one step farther and became an independent or progressive Democrat. He quickly became a thorn in the party's side and antagonized successive Democratic governors as he had previous Republican party leaders. At the outset, Cutting desired only to bring qualified veterans, primarily Hispanics, to the attention of Governor Hinkle and the new Democratic administration. "Deeply grateful" for the support ex-servicemen rendered his campaign, Senator Jones was helpful in suggesting posts for which qualified veterans might apply. "If the Democratic administration should make good on its pledges to the people," Cutting explained, "it is even possible that we might think the best hopes for good government in the state would lie in that direction." Veterans and independents agreed with Cutting that the Democrats should be given a chance to provide a constructive administration in state affairs.[14]

Some Republicans, on the other hand, were anxious to have him reenter the party fold and were willing to offer "almost anything" to have him do so. Cutting did not want to discourage moves to eliminate "some of the old and undesirable elements in the party." He so distrusted "all of them" that he preferred for the time being to avoid "entangling alliances." In short, if Governor Hinkle was able to secure constructive legislation, Cutting believed, the Democrats could control the state for a good many years. More interested in good government than in party labels, he would employ a policy of watchful waiting.[15]

The 1922 campaign helped make Cutting more fully aware of the political potential of a small but influential group of largely Anglo veterans. Soldiers, some discharged and some still in uniform, came or were sent to New Mexico's dry climate to improve their health. A former military hospital at Fort Bayard near Silver City in the southwestern part of the state was home to many tubercular veterans. Immediately relating to them, Cutting could empathize with their situations. In turn, they had little difficulty in supporting his campaign efforts.

By 1923, Cutting's work through the American Legion in Senator Jones's reelection campaign had made him a political power in New Mexico politics. His goal continued to be encouraging and promoting social change. He was not seeking power to advance his own career but was following the lessons that his father and uncle had learned previously in New York City. Political reform had to precede social change: the state had to elect governors and other officials who in turn would appoint qualified individuals to the various boards, commissions and administrative agencies. Individuals, more so than partisan political organizations, were the basis of the reform impulse in Cutting's view.[16]

Now, thanks to Cutting, the American Legion in New Mexico had become an agency that allowed Hispanic veterans to participate in the political process on an equal footing with other veterans and with few, if any, ties to a patrón or boss. The legion had given them a meaningful entrance into public life and mainstream society and allowed them to keep their traditional familial base in the community. The American Legion helped to strengthen their sense of group identity and personal worth. Whereas their religion, language and ethnicity were responsible for their group identity and self-esteem in their homes and communities, the American Legion helped them to strengthen those attributes in the public sphere and to gain significant recognition in the state in a way never before achieved.[17]

CHAPTER 11

INDEPENDENT

ronson Cutting was quickly disillusioned with the new governor,
James F. Hinkle. His administration ignored the veterans once the
election was over and their help was no longer needed. Cutting
was not primarily interested in patronage positions for veterans
but in good government and an efficient and economical administration.
Unhappy with the Republican party in New Mexico, he now lost faith in
Hinkle, a former cattleman and mayor of Roswell. His administration, Cutting said, would not do much to ingratiate itself with any element of the
population "except the Texans," residents of the eastern part of the state.[1]

Cutting faced a dilemma. Although a formidable political figure, he was
powerless to promote social change through the political process until 1924
when he could work to prevent Hinkle's nomination for a second term.
Meanwhile, he would seek to develop further the confidence of the Spanish-
speaking people through the American Legion and work diligently to assist
veterans in resolving claims and securing adequate medical attention. His
independent politics and his progressive outlook made him an increasingly
attractive political figure to all but the most vitriolic partisans. Political
leaders clearly understood that he was a person to be reckoned with. Early in
the Hinkle administration, Cutting declined an appointment as colonel in the
National Guard and aide-de-camp to the governor, a position he formerly
held in the administration of William C. McDonald. He had no choice after
Hinkle acted on none of his recommendations.

At the same time, however, Cutting surprisingly found himself in accord
with the erratic, volatile and wrathful Carl Magee, the editor of the *New
Mexico Tribune* in Albuquerque. Magee published a series of articles dissect-
ing the inequities of what he called "the 'Don' System." He described how
Hispanics were "hoodwinked" and used by the dons, "who do absolutely
nothing for them, but who, on the contrary, do everything they can to keep in
practice the slogan, adopted by them many years ago, that 'an educated native
makes a damned poor sheepherder.' " Echoing Cutting, Magee noted that the
war entered a wedge between the dons and most other Hispanics. Spanish-
speaking veterans were fully aware of "the drawbacks of the old governmental conditions at home" and ought to be helped and encouraged in every way
possible. Moreover, Cutting applauded Magee's attack on the state land

CHAPTER 11

office, "a regular private enterprise for the benefit of certain people." The criminal abuse of state offices had been common in New Mexico for many years, but thanks to Magee, it was now attracting critical attention. Although Magee had attacked Cutting for his role in the American Legion in 1922, the two men, now in accord, attacked the don system and criticized the patronage policies of the Hinkle administration.[2]

Cutting did more than attack and criticize, however. He assisted needy veterans in settling their claims. Difficult cases were forwarded to Senator Jones in Washington with the request that he bring them to the attention of high officials in the Veterans Bureau. Working for the bureau in Albuquerque, Miguel Antonio Otero, Jr. facilitated the resolution of many claims. Cutting had to clear up Jones's illusions that the claims of many veterans were "gold brick" cases, that most claims were illegitimate, and that the Democratic party had given the ex-soldiers due recognition. He also brought to the senator's attention his conviction that ex-servicemen in New Mexico overwhelmingly favored a bonus, a cash option, as part of any measure pertaining to veterans affairs.[3]

The early months of 1923 were hard times for New Mexico and its leaders. Senator Jones was exhausted from a bout with the flu and unable to devote much attention to his duties. The state's other senator, Holm Bursum, reviewing the election results, did not think "that the worst is about to come, but that it *has* come!" New Mexico's most distinguished public figure, Albert Fall, would resign his post as secretary of the interior in early February and soon become a key figure in the Teapot Dome Affair.[4]

Cutting spent little time with his family during the post-holiday season and decided upon a more extended vacation in Europe. Motoring across part of France to Tours, he caught the night train south and was in Madrid at the end of April. Dr. Frederic Bishop joined Cutting in Madrid on May 1 in time for Spain's national holiday. The travelers spent four days in Seville and then went to Toledo, "the most interesting town in Europe." After attending half a dozen bullfights, Cutting felt qualified to pronounce those in Madrid the best. Cutting and Bishop enjoyed Spain but were anxious to spend time in London. Joined by Justine in Paris, they returned to the English capital. Cutting found comfortable quarters at the National Club in southwest London and spent several evenings at the theater. On June 16, Cutting, feeling "extremely well" and having had "a glorious time," joined his sister to board the *Berengaria* homeward bound.[5]

Back in Santa Fe by July 11, he was "deeply touched" at the "obvious pleasure" his return gave to "nearly everybody." Cutting thoroughly enjoyed the "unique experience" of being "without an enemy of the slightest consequence," with the possible exception of Governor Hinkle. Clara Olsen, the governor's private secretary, resigned while he was abroad. She resented "the savage animosity" Hinkle had shown toward Cutting and his friends, the people who had helped to elect him. Cutting felt confident and doubted that the governor had enough strength to do any permanent harm.[6]

Cutting returned to a number of complications. Shortly afterward, he rushed to Las Vegas and bailed out Carl Magee, who had taken on the "old combine." The district judge in San Miguel County, David Leahy, had sentenced Magee to the state penitentiary for a year to a year and a half following his conviction on the charge of criminally libelling Chief Justice Frank W. Parker of the Supreme Court. In addition, Leahy imposed a further sentence of 360 days in the county jail for contempt of court. Leahy fixed the bail so high that no one in Las Vegas, the county seat, "would dare go on the bond." Cutting's arrival prevented Magee from going to jail. Shortly thereafter, the governor pardoned Magee on both counts, libel and contempt.[7]

Cutting also came home to the failure of the Capital City Bank in Santa Fe. He feared depositors would secure at best no more than fifty cents on the dollar. Though Cutting was a director of the First National Bank, he had seven hundred dollars deposited in the failed bank, and his newspaper, "a couple of thousand." His church and the American Legion lost their money as well.[8] Another complication involved the new Republican postmistress. Cutting was convinced that she would renew the censoring of his mail. In return for his support in county affairs, Republican leaders agreed to appoint a Hispanic veteran as postmaster. Then, Senator Bursum sent word through Secundino Romero that Cutting could name the entire Republican state ticket if he and the *New Mexican* would support his reelection campaign in 1924. Nothing came of these discussions.

Cutting would have been pleased to return to the Republican party if Bursum could have been eliminated as a candidate. However, the party was too weak to dump Bursum, and the Magee case would throw the Republicans "into the arms of people and principles" he could not possibly endorse. For the time being, Cutting would stick with the Democrats, despite "the unfortunate failure of the Governor to retain the sympathy and support of those who helped to elect him." Cutting quickly recognized that Hinkle's pardon of Magee strengthened the governor with the party's rank and file and other voters as well. Although Cutting rarely saw eye to eye with Magee, he saw that the editor was arousing public opinion against "the old gang," whose leaders, Cutting believed, had committed a serious blunder. The Democrats would reap the benefits and "may stay in power a long time." Bursum's approval of the Santa Fe postmistress over a Hispanic veteran further reconciled servicemen to the Democratic party. Republican blunders had strengthened the Democratic base in New Mexico politics.[9]

The complexion of Cutting's political life changed markedly in August when fellow legionnaires elected him commander of the Department of New Mexico. He would have to remain aloof from politics until the expiration of his term shortly before the 1924 nominating conventions. Now, instead of fretting over the depressed state of politics, he plunged into legion affairs and devoted time and energy to building membership and to improving the reputation and influence of the organization. New Mexico was undoubtedly the hardest state to organize. Recruiting and retaining members in remote mountainous areas remained the key problem. New Mexico was the fourth largest state, had the fourth smallest population and had the least railroad mileage in proportion to size. The population was found in settlements remote from each other and from either railroads or good roads. In addition, the legion needed to recruit veterans entering the state to improve their health in the dry climate.

Cutting started a year-long tour of New Mexico. At the end of August, he had already visited Las Crucas and El Paso. After the fiesta at Santa Fe in early September, he visited remote communities in Guadalupe, Mora and Union counties, where he had to walk miles to attend meetings and where Spanish was the spoken language.[10]

He made a special effort to appeal to disabled veterans. Made up of hospitalized patients, the post at Fort Bayard was the largest of its kind in the country. By increasing membership, Cutting hoped to lobby more effectively for measures affecting veterans and to achieve better cooperation inside the organization. Above all, he wished to wage "a battle against apathy and indifference," stating, "We do not demand from the rest of the community any special privileges or undue advantages." But he did insist that the community acknowledge and act on veterans's concerns. Cutting would try to increase the visibility of local legion issues and to secure and enact programs that addressed them.[11]

In October Cutting attended the fifth annual American Legion convention in San Francisco, where a majority of delegates refused to repudiate the Ku Klux Klan and deadlocked on the bonus question. Although the New Mexico delegates criticized the Klan and favored a bonus, Cutting played no active role in the debates and shortly thereafter headed for New York to visit his seriously ill mother. However, he kept abreast of legion affairs through Mike

Otero, the department adjutant. Both men sought, largely in vain, to make the national organization aware of New Mexico conditions, which had "no duplicate in any other state of the Union."[12]

Cutting had sent a lengthy letter to the retiring national commander, Alvin Owsley, who made no response. In November, Otero submitted a copy of it to Owsley's successor, John R. Quinn, who also remained silent. The annual budget of the New Mexico legion was less than three thousand dollars when Cutting became commander. Most of the fifteen thousand veterans in the state resided in remote rural communities, commonly spoke Spanish and read English with difficulty. The only feasible way to increase membership was by employing a Spanish-speaking organizer who would personally explain the work of the legion. At the outset in 1919, Cutting had funded the organizer, but now as its commander, he made the trips himself. Concerned about New Mexico's declining membership, the national organization had criticized its leaders. Otero and Cutting tried to explain that the nature and location of the state's membership and the responsibility for the welfare of the nation's largest post of hospitalized veterans made the situation most difficult and unique. The existence of "the great T.B. hospital" at Fort Bayard with patients from every state should be, Cutting thought, "a national problem." Yet the problem was largely left to the New Mexico Department, which, with its sparse resources, could not give it "the attention it deserves."

Both men were critical of the policy of the Americanism Committee. As early as 1919, Cutting had noted that insistence upon the use of the English language in the classroom simply would not suffice in New Mexico. In his letter to Owsley, the architect of the Americanism program, Cutting made much of his view "that the American Legion is the one great force for good in this state, that our best pioneers in promoting true Americanism are the Spanish-American servicemen, who are most enthusiastically and intelligently working out this problem along the lines best suited to conditions in this state, and that any effort by others to interfere with the work these men are doing will disrupt the American Legion here and render impossible the spread of the very ideas you are most anxious to advance." Cutting's concluding phrase was a direct reference to remarks purportedly made by Owsley during a visit to New Mexico earlier in the year. In his estimation, no person unable to read and write the English language should be granted the franchise. A national commander coming into a state and deliberately undermining the policies pursued by his department officers, Cutting acidly observed, should be "about the last man who has any right to complain if the department makes a poor showing at the end of the year." What the New Mexico Department needed from the national organization was some sympathy for its situation and not criticism "by people in Indianapolis who understand none of our problems." If, Cutting concluded, the officers in New Mexico could not resolve their problems, "it is a cinch that no outsider can. If National Headquarters continues to buck the game, nothing will be accomplished at all."[13]

Cutting learned about another problem while in New York. Thanks to Owsley's remarks and to the national organization's emphasis on its Americanization program, plans were underway, Mike Otero wrote, "to get all the native boys to withdraw from the Legion. . . ." The new organization would be "the Spanish-American Veterans of the World War," one that would not "give a damn about the Anglos" and would make "a straight out and out race issue appeal." Otero did not believe the organization would amount "to a tinkers' damn" because few Spanish-speaking veterans would "fall for that sort of propaganda," but he resented the fact that "as usual, the Spanish American is to be made the goat." Behind this proposed organization, Otero saw an effort to get Hispanic veterans to support Bursum's reelection. He urged Cutting to "come on out here and direct things." Numerous friends had "hitched their wagons to your star" and were looking to him for guidance and support. Upon learning from Cutting that the serious illness of both his mother and younger sister made his immediate return impossible, Otero moderated his tone and said that he and others of his friends would manage the situation. He also affirmed the devotion of his friends, "your absolute and devoted followers, who swear by you through thick and thin, and who look to you as the leader in our whole movement, and it's *you* they like and look up to, and not what you might be able to do for them."[14] All talk of a rival organization ended with Cutting's return to New Mexico at the year's end and with the resumption of his travels to develop as many small posts as possible. "Had a most interesting though strenuous trip to Truchas on Sunday," he wrote his mother, explaining that he had to help push "our Ford" up the last two miles of hill. He relished the scenery, called Truchas "quite the most medieval thing in America" and was pleased with the attendance—about 120 people—at the meeting.

On January 8, 1924, Cutting concluded his term as Santa Fe post commander. "A bunch of fifty or sixty" gave him a surprise party afterward and presented him with a "large and costly" Chimayo blanket, the cost of which "must have cleaned them all out." Upcoming was a projected two-week trip through Rio Arriba and San Juan counties. In February, a trip to Mora County followed. During the meeting in Mora, Judge David Leahy, who had sentenced Carl Magee, took advantage of the occasion "to make a number of veiled but disparaging illusions [sic]" to Cutting. Responding in Spanish, Cutting denounced Leahy by name and cited him as an exemplar "of every-thing deceitful and hypocritical in political life." He later regretted the inci-dent but relished the chance of letting Leahy know what he thought of him. Although Mora was his favorite New Mexico town, Cutting thought that he would not visit it again "on Legion work." Every time he went there, he never failed "to get into a row of some sort."[15]

Cutting scrupulously avoided politics during his tenure as department commander. However, he and all political observers were fully aware that his term would end before the fall campaigns got underway. In April, one observer stated to Cutting, "The Republican party wants you back in its fold, yea more: it will welcome your return and extend you its congratulations." Cutting was "the man to represent New Mexico in the Lower House of Congress." His presence on the ticket would assure a complete Republican victory in the fall.[16] Or so he was told.

Cutting never responded. Instead, he went to New York to visit his mother, who had recently recovered from her illness. He returned to New Mexico in time to attend the funeral of José A. Baca, the Democratic lieuten-ant governor, in Las Vegas. He wrote that "nearly everyone in the state of political importance was there." Cutting believed Baca "would certainly have been the candidate for governor." Now Hinkle seemed assured of renomina-tion unless the party could organize a new slate. No Democrat would want "to make a Senatorial run with Hinkle to carry on the ticket."[17]

Shortly after the funeral, Cutting left for Las Cruces in behalf of the American Legion. He returned to Santa Fe for a meeting of the state commit-tee and, at the end of May, planned to tour the Pecos Valley and the north-west. This was followed by a trip "in the wilds to the North"—Taos and Rio Arriba counties—at the end of June. On this trip, his friend, Jesus Baca, accompanied him. Although he sought to avoid politics, some veterans saw Cutting as an ideal Democratic candidate who could easily defeat Bursum. Otero wished to nominate him for governor. Cutting's only formal contact with the Republican party during these months was an invitation to accept an honorary nonpartisan appointment as a New Mexico member of the The-odore Roosevelt Memorial Committee.[18]

Cutting was traveling in the northern counties when the Democrats con-vened in New York City to select their presidential candidate. Since mail was "almost non-existent" in the remote regions of the northern counties, he had no notion of what the Democrats were doing in New York. His hope was that "they didn't light on Carter Glass." He enjoyed his successful recruiting trip "through some of the most beautiful country in the world." Road conditions were primitive, but only twice did his car have to be hauled out of rivers or mud holes. Jesus Baca proved to be an ideal companion, "the best driver and the best fisherman in the state." He was pleased that the meetings were well attended.[19]

One issue that attracted widespread attention in New Mexico and elsewhere pertained to Pueblo Indian lands. Senator Bursum sponsored legislation that would open these lands to development. His measure prompted an outpouring of protest. Opposed to Bursum's proposal, Cutting was proud that "the *New Mexican* was the first to make a protest against the injustice of the original bill." Neither at this nor at any other time, however, did he seriously involve himself in the Indian rights movement, although he favored efforts at meliorating their lot.[20]

Politics in New Mexico and the plight of Hispanics was central to Cutting's concerns. During the last months of his tenure as division commander of the American Legion in the summer of 1924, he found avoiding the political fray increasingly difficult. Correspondents from both parties envisioned him as a candidate. Cutting recognized that the Republican party and Senator Bursum were in deep political trouble. Dissatisfied with the Hinkle administration as with the Republican party, Cutting began to consider requests that he become a candidate for public office once he relinquished his legion post.[21]

Reviewing the results of the Democratic National Convention, Cutting was pleased with John W. Davis's presidential nomination and hoped he would be elected, but he did not know how Davis's candidacy would be received in New Mexico, where William Gibbs McAdoo had been favored. If the Democrats wanted to win in New Mexico, they had to secure the support of labor. Running on a third-party ticket, Robert M. La Follette might jeopardize their chances of success. If labor leaders bolted for La Follette, they would insure Bursum's reelection in the fall. To thwart that disaster, Cutting agreed to address a meeting of the Four Railroad Brotherhoods in Santa Fe, where members would choose their presidential candidate. However, he knew very little about Davis that would endear him to his labor audience, except that the presidential hopeful had "defended [Eugene Victor] Debs and the Colorado miners." His hope was that Davis would soon make some definite policy statements on labor issues.[22]

At the state convention of the American Legion, Cutting reviewed his tenure as district commander. First giving credit to his associates, he noted an increase of 716 members. Eight new posts were chartered and two were cancelled for a total of seventy-seven posts. He noted too that the eight most active posts were "all in small and remote places, six of them off a railroad." In all of these posts "the predominant membership is of Spanish descent and speech."[23]

Along with membership, the other main issue was finance. Cutting called for a full-time "state organizer" who would visit established posts and form new ones. Improved membership and stronger finances would eventually permit a state paper that would enable posts and members to keep in close touch with legion affairs and with one another. Although not yet out of debt, the state organization would soon reach that goal, "with any luck." In his opinion, the finances came first, then the membership and finally the program.

Turning to national affairs, Cutting was pleased with the national organization's promotion of the Reed-Johnson Bill, which extended to January 1, 1925, the time limit for tracing tubercular and neuropsychiatric disabilities to service conditions. The approval of this measure would enable thousands of former soldiers in New Mexico to reopen their cases and to pursue a successful settlement. A more pressing need, however, was a Veterans Bureau sympathetic to the disabled veteran. He cited one notable exception, the Albuquerque office headed by Miguel Antonio Otero, Jr. Finally, he urged the seventy-seven posts in New Mexico to keep disagreement and dissension to a minimum and to unite around an active public role in both their communities and in the state.[24]

His legion tenure completed, Cutting could become active in public affairs. His travels throughout New Mexico as department commander and the innumerable meetings he addressed both in English and Spanish gave him a wide range of personal contacts in every part of the state and the base for a powerful personal political organization. His work with the American Legion made him an influential figure and molded him a statewide constituency. The 1924 national campaign was already under way and the state conventions were gearing up to select candidates in September when Cutting plunged back into the political arena. He attended Democratic committee meetings and was briefly in charge of the Democratic Party headquarters. Interested citizens urged him to seek the Democratic nomination for governor. Hinkle had alienated the native vote and was in deep trouble. One correspondent wrote, "The natives want you if four or five counties in this part of the state are a good index."[25]

Before the state campaign got underway, Cutting was approached by Hanford MacNider, a former national commander and now the head of the Republican Service League. MacNider wanted him to serve on its national

CHAPTER 11

committee and to back the party ticket "from top to bottom." Responding promptly, Cutting reiterated for MacNider's benefit that for four years, the Republican party had either "blocked or delayed" every congressional measure passed in behalf of the American Legion and was responsible "for the most colossal graft in American history" at the expense of disabled veterans. Those who were servicemen first and partisans second, Cutting concluded, would do everything possible to defeat "the ticket which it is humiliating to see supported by men of your type."[26]

At the same time, Cutting allowed his supporters to enter his name as a Democratic candidate for governor at some county conventions. Speaking at meetings prior to the state convention, Cutting encouraged friends "to come out in force" to the primaries in the Santa Fe districts where party members would select delegates for the county convention, which ended up "entirely in his hands." His sister, who was visiting at the time, reported that several counties apparently went for Cutting. Nevertheless, she anticipated "a tug of war at the convention" scheduled to convene in Santa Fe on September 15.[27]

When Cutting came to the state convention, he believed that beating Hinkle for the nomination would be hard. Surprisingly, Cutting's candidacy led Hinkle to withdraw from the race. To the dismay and disappointment of his friends, Cutting likewise withdrew. According to his sister, he had "all but six votes" necessary for the nomination and "a considerable number of fairly safe votes." In her estimation, he could have won, but Cutting believed that he would have greater political influence in the future if he did not hold the office of governor.[28]

Cutting, who had no desire to be governor, thought that the elimination of Hinkle was a substantial victory. He was disturbed, however, that some of the new candidates were "attempting to throw control back to the Hinkle crowd" and that Hinkle people and Carl Magee seemed allied to gain control of patronage and to build a political base for the embattled editor. Cutting's disappointed friends and political supporters felt that a Democratic ticket headed by Cutting would have swept the state by a larger majority than in 1922. To soothe bitter feelings, Cutting threw a party and plied them with Scotch whiskey, the smoothest available at any of the convention parties.[29]

When the campaign got underway in earnest at the end of September, Cutting supported the entire Democratic ticket. Neither Calvin Coolidge nor Senator Robert M. La Follette appealed to him. La Follette's candidacy made some progressives waffle in their support of the Democratic slate, which, Cutting hoped, would be the base for a reform program. The New Mexico Republican Service League, directed by J. H. Toulouse, sought funds from

MacNider, the national chairman. Toulouse claimed that Cutting was squandering thousands of dollars in "Little Mexican communities" and among servicemen in behalf of Democratic candidates. Whether Cutting dispensed money during the campaign is unknown, but he was undoubtedly asked to make contributions when he spoke at Democratic campaign meetings. In the eyes of the younger progressive Republicans and Democrats, he was still the leader to bring good government to New Mexico.[30]

Thanks to the Progressive party vote, the election was very close. Coolidge carried the state, but Holm Bursum lost, much to the pleasure of Cutting and all progressives. The Democrats won the governor's chair and most major state offices. Bursum lost his senate seat to Sam Bratton by twenty-eight hundred votes. He claimed that the Democrats stole the election. Dissatisfaction with the state Republican organization led to its second successive and stunning defeat. The La Follette vote prevented John W. Davis from carrying the state. At the state level, as Cutting had hoped and an interested observer noted, "the La Follette vote went Democratic—or practically so."[31] During the campaign, despite the charges that he was actively buying votes, Cutting played a minimal role, although the editor of the *New Mexican* worked with the publicity bureau of the state Democratic organization.

The night before the election, Mike Otero informed Cutting that he would no longer keep bachelor quarters at Los Siete Burros. Although he "hated like thunder to leave," he noted that "there didn't seem to be anything else to do." Having moved, he wanted to thank Cutting, who had paid his way through law school, for his "many kindnesses" and for the way Cutting came to his assistance when he "needed help the most." While he could never totally repay Cutting, he made his life insurance policy payable to Cutting, "so as to cover some of the money debt to you anyway." Otero wrote, "It was the best I could do."[32]

Mike's departure marked the beginning of a break in the close friendship between the two men. Whatever the reasons behind his departure, their relations would cool and their paths would diverge. Although they remained on cordial terms and never publicly opposed one another, Cutting would become increasingly dissatisfied with Mike Otero's role in public affairs. He would also break with and become openly hostile to the administration of the new Democratic governor, Arthur T. Hannett.

CHAPTER 12

DISGRUNTLED DEMOCRAT

I t should be noted" wrote Harvey Fergusson in 1925, already a distinguished novelist and a member of a prominent Albuquerque family, "that the State government of New Mexico is perhaps the most impotent and ridiculous product of the democratic theory now visible." He discussed the "political machine, probably the oldest in America," that was functioning before New Mexico entered the Union and that was founded upon "complete control of the peon class of Mexicans by the landowning aristocracy and the church." The peons or *pobres,* Fergusson explained, "were in effect owned by the landowners, primarily because they were always deeply in debt," while the landowners were dominated by the church. Over the years, especially since statehood, changes had transpired. The power of the church had declined, and "a good deal of the land passed into the hands of the Yankees." However, "most of the native people remained serfs in effect" and formed the backbone of the Republican machine, which Cutting had challenged as soon as he became involved in public life.[1]

Cutting had exploited the weak two-party system and had effectively used the American Legion to bring about the demise of the Republican party. The election of James Hinkle in 1922 and Arthur Hannett in 1924 possibly signalled a new era of Democratic control in the state. But by 1925 Cutting doubted whether the Democrats had any higher aspirations for the people of New Mexico than did the old Republican machine. Having helped to prevent Hinkle's renomination, Cutting had no choice but to support the new governor. He hoped that Hannett would bring qualified Hispanics and veterans into state government and demonstrate that he was capable of improving the administration of the state.

The new governor recognized Cutting's help in securing both his nomination and election by appointing him to the New Mexico State Penitentiary Board, whose members then selected him as their chairman. Cutting immediately proceeded to inform himself on penal reform. He contacted the noted penologist, Thomas Mott Osborne, the father of one of his Groton and Harvard classmates. A former warden at Sing Sing, Auburn and the Naval Penitentiary at Portsmouth, New Hampshire, Osborne sought to restore and maintain the self-respect of prisoners through a program of voluntary and fully remunerated prison labor. He tried to involve the inmates in decision making within the institution to the greatest possible extent. Prison authorities should not grant privileges. Inmates should request them and receive them only in return for responsibility. Cutting absorbed Osborne's views through correspondence and reading.[2]

At the outset, Cutting desired a survey of the Santa Fe prison by an outside authority. Osborne thought that most western wardens were hostile to his reform ideas but nevertheless expressed interest in coming to New Mexico. After a three-day session with the New Mexico "pen" board, Cutting had "a fairly friendly talk with the Governor," who accepted the premise that a thorough, outside inspection would be beneficial. However, the warden, John B. McManus, was firmly opposed to any changes, let alone an outside review. Cutting believed that if pressed on the matter, the governor would side with the warden.[3]

Governor Hannett's dispensation of patronage angered Cutting. The governor ignored or passed over qualified Hispanics, continuing the policy of his predecessor. With all the "bad blood" in the Democratic party, Cutting anticipated a bitter row. Prior to a meeting of the Democratic State Committee in May, he decided that he would take no office in the party, "unless under very unlikely conditions." He made a ten-day trip through the southern counties and found that "the whole Pecos Valley is ablaze with Fury" over Hannett's appointment of a close political associate to the Office of Land Commissioner, a post vacated when Justiano Baca died. Baca's deputy and close associate, an ex-serviceman, was not considered by the governor. The new commissioner proceeded to fill positions in the agency with political cronies. The *New Mexican* echoed outrage at Hannett's appointment.[4]

Cutting's criticisms of Hannett prompted Carl Magee to launch what Cutting called "the most scurrilous and personal series of articles about me" in the *New Mexico State Tribune*. In his column, "Turning on the Light," Magee accused Cutting of liberally dispensing his wealth to further his political ambitions. Cutting denied the charges but would not dignify "a creature like Magee" with "any personal discussion." Magee's columns sparked a journalistic war between the *New Mexican* and the *New Mexico State Tribune*. The *New Mexican* especially attacked Magee for consorting with the Ku Klux Klan. Magee persistently leveled his sights on Cutting's wealth. The conflict opened a chasm within the Democratic party. Magee and Hannett, the most prominent individuals, stood to one side; Cutting and the Democratic national committeeman, Arthur Seligman, opposed them. As the delineation of these factions came into sharper focus, the "honeymoon" of the Hannett administration came to an end.[5]

Cutting had not yet broken with Governor Hannett. He remained on the penitentiary board although the administration put "every possible obstacle" in the way of reforms. Although he believed that the board members were sympathetic, the warden, John M. McManus, appeared to be inflexible. McManus served two terms, the second beginning in 1923 and lasting into the Hannett administration. Cutting found him "an extremely businesslike and capable official" who ran the prison "economically and carefully." He put an end to the "unlimited graft, favoritism, riots, shooting's, etc." that prevailed in the prison during the previous Republican administration (1921–1923), but he showed little if any interest in the prisoners themselves. Cutting was certain that McManus believed quite sincerely "that no one in the world could teach him anything about the New Mexico Penitentiary." He recognized "the evils of idleness for about 60 per cent of the inmates" but believed the condition was inevitable given limited appropriations by the state. Above all, like other western wardens, he was opposed to coddling prisoners with the sentimental actions suggested by eastern penal reformers.

After talking to McManus and suggesting a survey, Cutting had another talk with the governor. Cutting found Hannett still in favor of an investigation, but he was convinced that Hannett would side with McManus in any dispute. Cutting decided to let well enough alone. His relations with the governor were already strained because of his opposition to Hannett's patronage policies. Distressed by his situation, he explained to Thomas Mott Osborne, "I have no interest whatever in the penitentiary except from the point of view of the prisoners," most of whom were Spanish-Americans.[6]

Hannett brought to a head the mounting tensions between himself and Cutting. He suggested that Cutting resign his position on the penitentiary board. The governor was responding to a July 6 *New Mexican* editorial containing phrases such as "with his dictatorship tacitly admitted by the administration" and "the continued domination of the Democratic administration by Boss Magee." Hannett thought Cutting might tender his resignation to avoid being "hampered or embarrassed" by his association with such a deplorable administration. He assured Cutting "that both the resignation and the consequences" would be cheerfully accepted.[7]

Hannett made a serious blunder and left the initiative in Cutting's hands by failing to fire Cutting or at least to call directly for his resignation. He had accepted the appointment as a member of the board "on the express understanding that the *New Mexican*'s liberty of action should be unaffected thereby." He further recalled for the governor that he had already "strongly disagreed" and "publicly condemned" some of his official acts at the time of his appointment.

CHAPTER 12

Under these circumstances, continued service on the penitentiary board in no way embarrassed Cutting. However, if his continued service on the board compromised the governor, he would be delighted to resign. Hannett had to "be fair both to me and to the people of New Mexico" and state his "real reasons" for wanting him to vacate his seat. Undergoing a change of heart, the governor asked Cutting to remain on the board and to consider the letters withdrawn. Cutting refused and published the letters, but Hannett still would not "screw up his courage and fire Cutting."[8]

In the editorial warfare with Magee, Cutting still believed he could not deal with his opponent on any rational basis. He drafted but never sent a letter that responded to some of Magee's recent accusations. He believed public sentiment was turning against the fiery editor. No newspaper in the state was with him, and Cutting was not writing the *New Mexican* editorials. In the midst of his battle with the governor and Magee, he was traveling through San Miguel, Mora and Taos counties in his new post as adjutant of the New Mexico American Legion.[9]

Cutting knew he would not be able to accomplish constructive reforms as a member of the penitentiary board. Willing neither to fire Cutting nor to let the matter stand, Hannett stated that it was not his purpose "to permit anyone connected with my administration to be disloyal to it and to remain a part of it." The best Hannett could do was to renew his suggestion that Cutting resign, something he refused to do. Taunting the governor, Cutting reminded him that "the state constitution authorizes you at any time to remove an appointee for incompetency, neglect of duty, or malfeasance in office." Since Hannett could not provide adequate reasons for removing Cutting, he tried to force his resignation and failed abjectly in his endeavor.[10]

Cutting was determined not to resign because Hannett's pretexts, "trivial and insincere," did not touch on his real motives: Cutting's insistence on a survey of the prison by an "outside expert"; and Hannett's failed attempts to force from the board "some purely political pardons" for Democratic politicians. Although Cutting wanted to effect some reform in the prison, he wanted to get off the penitentiary board. He hoped that Hannett would fire him but could not resign without impairing his own integrity.[11]

At the height of the battle, Cutting was visited by the entire Republican State Committee, whose members invited him to follow Miguel Antonio Otero back to the fold. Cutting politely declined. The press had greeted Otero's decision with "hoots and howls of derision." The comments of the native papers, Cutting said, were "untranslatable." The response deeply hurt Otero, whom Cutting expected to return to the Democrats but who had

126

"killed himself politically." Cutting would make no such mistake. But he hoped the tensions would abate.[12]

Cutting further goaded Hannett. He called to his attention illegal activities of the parole board, which released prisoners without prior recommendation by the full board of penitentiary commissioners. In one particular case, the governor pardoned a convicted felon before he arrived at the state prison and after the penitentiary commissioners disapproved the application. The general policy of the commissioners was that a convict serve at least six months on good behavior before becoming eligible for clemency. When Hannett took this action, five defendants convicted of the same crime went to the penitentiary. The pardoned prisoner later boasted that the governor's pardon had cost him six hundred dollars and that he was the most guilty party in the crime. To Cutting, that case illustrated the advisability of abiding by the provisions of the New Mexico statute. He regarded this letter as confidential and was angered when Hannett charged, without releasing its contents, that Cutting accused him of accepting a bribe.[13]

During a strenuous, soggy trip through northern New Mexico on legion business, Cutting learned that Hannett would remove him upon his return to Santa Fe.[14] Nothing happened. Back in the state capital in August, Cutting reported that "the governor had lost what little nerve he had." Hannett had been drunk, an acquaintance told Cutting, when he was interviewed in El Paso "and hence felt no responsibility" for abiding by his remarks. Cutting's position was "rather awkward." He wanted off the penitentiary board but not "under these conditions."

Through Judge Luis Armijo, Cutting received word that Magee "would stop attacking us if we would reciprocate." Recognizing that Magee's scurrilous attacks were backfiring, Cutting turned down the "rather one sided arrangement." Although Magee made his offer for the "party good," he was "about dead politically" in Cutting's estimation. In an editorial column, an indignant Magee claimed that Cutting encouraged a prominent citizen to talk to him about a truce. But his career in New Mexico was nearing the end. On August 22 in Las Vegas, Magee accidentally shot and killed a bystander during a scuffle with Judge David J. Leahy, who had sentenced him for both libel and contempt in 1924. He continued to edit the *State Tribune* until February 1927. Murder charges against him were dismissed on the grounds of self-defense, but his political career was dead.[15]

Throughout these months of controversy, Cutting continued working with the American Legion. In August at the state convention, Albuquerque posts introduced an amendment that would relocate the state headquarters from Santa Fe to the state commander's community wherever it might be. Cutting was convinced that the interests of the legion could be properly maintained only in the state capital from which the organization could reach the great number of posts in the northern counties. The anti-Hispanic amendment could prevent the election of a Hispanic commander from a remote part of New Mexico. Cutting made efforts to insure a large turnout at the September convention to defeat the proposed amendment. In addition, Cutting began to assist financially troubled editors of Hispanic newspapers that opposed the Hannett administration. By loaning money to these editors, Cutting gained some editorial support for good government and popularity, respect and affection among Spanish-speaking New Mexicans.[16]

While Cutting could strengthen his support in New Mexico, he could not force Governor Hannett either to fire or remove him from the penitentiary board. By the end of September, he was anxious to join his mother for a brief European vacation. Swallowing his pride, Cutting offered his resignation. He stated politely, "As I shall be unavoidably absent from New Mexico for a few months I am writing to tell you that I can no longer serve as a member of the State Penitentiary Board." Hannett, no doubt, was delighted. He had avoided both firing Cutting and providing an explanation. With his resignation, Cutting submitted an extensive critique of the penal system and again called futilely for a thorough survey, preferably by the National Society of Penal Information.[17]

Cutting traveled with his mother in Europe and was back in New York by mid-November and at Los Siete Burros in December. Little had changed while he was away. Senator Bratton told Arthur Seligman that the governor and his allies "were going to do everything possible to separate us politically and in every other way, and drive both of us out of the Party, if not by fair means, by foul, . . ." Maintaining a low profile, Cutting spent the Christmas season in Santa Fe. Thereafter, he left "for the north" on legion business and planned to return by way of Albuquerque, where he wanted "to take up some matters with the Veterans' Bureau." On New Year's Eve he hosted a dinner party.[18]

For much of January and February, Cutting traveled through the state with Jesus Baca, the district commander. When he was at home, he devoted a good portion of his correspondence to boosting legion membership and minimizing controversy within the organization. With "too few ex-soldiers" in New Mexico, the legion could not "indulge in the luxury of personal animosities and recriminations." To further these efforts, he tried to lower the assessment on all posts. At the end of February, the flu slowed his activities.[19]

Still avoiding political commitments, Cutting turned down the Demo-cratic nomination for mayor of Santa Fe and declined the follow-up request to name the candidate. As soon as he felt well enough, he departed for the northern counties. He found road trips both "amusing and mentally restful." However, this trip was a bit more strenuous than most, with endless hours spent digging the car out of "bottomless mud." At least seven times the car had to be hauled out by teams. Thus he was pleased that on his next trip to Raton and Clayton in northern New Mexico, all but about two hundred miles could be made by rail.[20]

As he traveled in behalf of the American Legion, Cutting was aware that he was securing a powerful base among the Hispanic people. As a major oppo-nent of the Hannett administration and as a leader of an opposing faction within the Democratic party, he could play a significant role in this election year. He also knew that thirty percent or less of the Spanish-American vote was found in the Democratic column. The patrón system made the Hispanic vote less steady than the Anglo vote in its adherence to party lines. Hispanic veterans had supported Cutting in the campaign to reelect Senator Jones in 1922, and Hispanic delegates in 1924 had endorsed Cutting's successful effort to prevent the renomination of Governor Hinkle at the Democratic conven-tion. They would look to him again in 1926, but he did not wish to be a candidate. Moreover, he understood that Hispanic voters recognized the almost complete indifference of the Hinkle and Hannett administrations to their needs and concerns. Either the Democratic party had to find a candidate strongly committed to reversing this indifference, or it would be in deep political trouble during the fall campaign.

To some Hispanic leaders, Cutting was "a man of higher education, of larger affairs, and of extended knowledge of men and political conditions." He was the public figure who could reverse the gloomy prospects of the Democratic party. He was already regarded, wrote a Hispanic Democrat in 1925, as "the best loved Anglo-American in New Mexico among the Spanish-American voters." Hispanics appreciated his "unpublished liberal-ity," his genuine comraderie and his "exceeding consideration" for the former servicemen. New Mexico was home to fifteen thousand ex-soldiers, includ-ing Hispanic veterans. Hispanic Democrats thought him the ideal gubernato-rial candidate. By replacing Hannett, he could provide new and inspired leadership and make the party attractive to a much broader electorate.[21]

Governor Hannett proposed an election code that both hindered the pro-cess of making the party attractive to more voters and that assisted in making Cutting a more attractive public figure. Hannett's stated purpose was to make the electoral process more efficient and less partisan. First, by removing the circle at the head of the ticket, the code eliminated the option of voting a straight party ticket, thereby requiring voters to consider candidates for every office. Second, and more importantly, it did away with "the assistance to voters" provision—the reading of names and propositions—of the election code.

Hannett's proposal aroused storms of protest. Section 3, Article VII of the state's constitution provided that the rights of citizens should never be restricted on the grounds of race, religion, color or the inability to speak, read or write the English or Spanish languages. By design, the amendment of this provision was almost impossible. What Hannett could not achieve directly, he could achieve indirectly, at least in the minds of Republican leaders, and of Cutting and his allies. The proposal, they insisted, was clearly designed to make difficult, if not impossible, the participation of many "*pobres*," poorly educated and largely rural Hispanics, in the electoral process. Since Anglos comprised the bulk of the Democratic voters, Republican candidates stood to lose by the approval of Hannett's proposal. In short, Hannett's election code was a political issue to most pundits. If approved, it could severely limit the number of Spanish-speaking participants in the electoral process and insure racial supremacy in the Democratic party.

Hannett presented his code in late 1925, but Cutting did not publicly denounce or attack it throughout the spring and summer of 1926. He was far too busy with developing American Legion posts across the state. In April, for example, he devoted two weeks to Hispanic veterans in the southern counties. One of his Anglo friends explained, "Without someone to lead and show them their rights they would be overridden as they have been in Arizona." He further remarked that only Cutting had "the nerve and disregard of ambition" to champion the cause of the native Spanish-speaking citizen.[22] During late spring and early summer, he toured the Pecos Valley, the southeastern counties and the northern counties. He found these trips restful in many ways, but the local obsession with politics made his effectiveness for the American Legion increasingly difficult.

In late August, he was off to Carlsbad for the annual legion convention. Since their election in 1925, Jesus Baca, the district commander, and Cutting had increased the total membership by over forty percent. They erased a long-standing debt of $2,300 and left a surplus of $1,000 to launch the new fiscal year. At the convention, Cutting resigned his post as state adjutant to participate fully and freely in political activities.[23]

Cutting had no interest in seeking the gubernatorial nomination. He had no confidence in the Republican leadership and preferred to let the Democratic leaders "have all the rope they want." The Republicans were "so completely demoralized" that they could not win in November "with—or against—anybody." Voters who saw prospects for improvement in his candidacy on the ticket of either party were discouraged. However, he remained loyal to the Democratic party, which, he believed, offered greater opportunities to the average citizen than the Republican party. Hannett, he thought, was not seeking a second term.[24]

But the September nominating conventions of both parties depressed Cutting even more. The only Democratic candidate that both he and the *New Mexican* endorsed was John Morrow, who was seeking his third term as the state's only member to the House of Representatives. With Hannett nominated for a second term, the main issue in the campaign, as Cutting viewed it, was "the proposed election code invented by Hannett, and endorsed by the Democratic convention." Now he openly discussed the proposal. He acknowledged but did not elaborate on some good features of the code. He labeled "extremely dangerous" the provision making necessary that a voter register in July, "when at least seven thousand citizens of the northern counties" would be working outside of New Mexico. Voters unable to read English would have to vote a straight ticket without assistance or be deprived of a vote altogether. Thus a large proportion of the native people would be prevented from voting the way they wanted.[25]

At the Democratic State Convention a distinguished Hispanic delegate, Judge Luis Armijo, called for an amendment designed to assist voters who could not read. Governor Hannett spoke in opposition from the platform. He said that he would not be a candidate if the amendment carried. According to Cutting, he asserted "that he would not 'pan-handle' for votes," and suggested that he literally did not care whether Hispanic voters endorsed his candidacy. A vote for Hannett, in Cutting's eyes, was "a vote to disenfranchise a large number of the citizens of New Mexico." Given this situation, he could not vote for Hannett or for a Democratic legislature. By mid-September, Cutting expected to vote the Republican state ticket, with the exception of John Morrow and perhaps two other Democratic candidates.[26]

Following the Democratic convention, Cutting went east for a brief vacation at Westbrook. Arthur Seligman reported that interested parties wanted to know when he would return. He explained that there was much talk of Democratic voters endorsing Richard Dillon, the Republican candidate for governor. Governor Hannett had visited Seligman and asked him to "get in the game." Cutting, he said, would receive "the same treatment" upon his return.[27]

Back in Santa Fe, Cutting organized a movement of independent Democrats to oppose Governor Hannett. More than one hundred people formally launched the movement in Albuquerque on October 9. The purpose of the gathering was to fuse with the Republicans and turn out the Hannett administration. The convention selected two candidates for places on the Republican ticket. They were approved at the Republican convention held that very evening. At the afternoon meeting, Cutting delivered the main address, a critical review of the policies of the Hannett administration.[28]

Thereafter, he took an active role in the campaign, spending no more than one night in four in Santa Fe. In mid-October he thought, "while things are by no means hopeless," much work needed to be done "in order to defeat the organized machine now in control." So extensive were his efforts, particularly among Hispanic voters, one of his friends observed "that if we succeed in defeating Hannett it will make you the outstanding figure in New Mexico politics."[29]

Democrats opposed to Hannett received little financial assistance from the Republicans and only scorn from the Democratic organization. The Spanish weeklies that Cutting financially assisted helped in getting his message to their readers. Hannett, however, had brought many Spanish-speaking county leaders into his machine, thereby balancing in some instances Cutting's efforts among the *pobres*.[30] Holm Bursum expressed his "gratification and satisfaction" in knowing that "you, myself and Mr. [Charles] Springer and others are actively cooperating and working in behalf of a common cause" for the Republicans on election day. Bursum appreciated Cutting's "widespread influence without which the results we hope for could not be accomplished." Bursum's encomium was a clear indication that Bronson Cutting was undoubtedly one of the most influential political figures in New Mexico.[31]

On the day before the election, Cutting endorsed Richard Dillon in Albuquerque. He denounced Hannett and Carl Magee in the harshest terms. A sheep rancher and country merchant from Encino in Torrance County, Dillon represented a new generation of Republican leaders. He had few contacts with the old guard politicians. His victory was due "more than any other factor" to Cutting and independent Democrats rallying to his candidacy. As the campaign drew to a close, Cutting sent copies of the *New Mexican* throughout the state. Its columns delineated Hannett's poor record and the reasons for opposing his candidacy. Many of the letters to Cutting made evident that the anti-Hannett voters, disgruntled Democrats like Cutting, swung the electoral tide to Dillon. He defeated Hannett by 3,771 votes.[32]

Cutting was pleased with the results, including the fact that Democrats elected the secretary of state, the treasurer, "both worthy candidates," and the attorney general, the last by a scant thirteen votes. John Morrow won by over three thousand votes. His triumph, Cutting wrote, "puts quite an additional feather in our caps." After a victory dinner in Albuquerque, prominent Republicans were putting forth Cutting's name as a senatorial candidate in 1928, but Cutting was "doing his best to throw cold water on this idea as politely as possible."[33]

Cutting considered Dillon "an excellent and conscientious man" but terribly inexperienced in "practical politics." He feared that Dillon might fall prey "to the more sinister elements in his party" and thought Clara Olsen, secretary to several previous governors, "would be the best antidote for his deficiencies." Cutting declined invitations to attend sessions of the Republican State Committee in Santa Fe. His effectiveness would be uncompromised, Cutting believed, only if he maintained complete independence. The sole recompense he accepted after the election was a letter of introduction from Holm Bursum to presidential aspirant Frank Lowden, a former Republican governor of Illinois, whom he intended to visit when returning from his holiday with family in New York. Cutting returned to Santa Fe at the end of January with the intention of remaining aloof from politics. The State Committee of the American Legion gave him the means by insisting that he keep the office of adjutant. Indeed, the opportunity allowed him to decline political appointments in the new administration.[34]

Some Hispanic leaders were upset with the Dillon administration. They wanted to make sure that "the native people" were rewarded for their support of his election. Hispanic leaders in counties like Rio Arriba, Socorro and Valencia, with populations approximately ninety percent Spanish, "threw their solid weight for the Republican party." Disappointed with their lack of recognition, they argued that both parties were controlled "by crooks," who would never give Spanish-Americans "a square deal." Although Hispanic spokesmen neither questioned nor doubted Cutting's sincerity and concern, they brought the matter to his attention and hoped that he might be able to influence the governor.[35]

Not everyone was dissatisfied. Pleasing some lobbyists, Cutting threw his support behind the abolition of a three dollar road tax, behind free textbooks for children in the first and second grades and behind the full protection for the ballots of absentee voters, all of which passed the legislature. During the push for those measures, Cutting aided the legislative representative of a railroad brotherhood, the Railway Conductors. The secretary of the Eastern

Association on Indian Affairs thanked Cutting for the *New Mexican*'s support in seeking alternative sites that would not threaten the existence of the Santo Domingo Pueblo for the Middle Rio Grande Conservancy Project. Meanwhile, deposed governor Arthur Hannett was subjecting him to editorial attacks in a column, "New Mexico Day by Day." Replacing Carl Magee as chief antagonist, he denounced Cutting as an opportunist who squandered his money to benefit his cronies, to secure favors and to realize his political ambitions.[36]

Cutting planned an extended vacation that would include attending the national convention of the American Legion in Paris. During his tenure as adjutant, legion membership had vastly increased. Writing in August, Herman Baca explained, "We were only able to get 2,562 members as compared with 2,458 shown by the records of National Headquarters for the whole of last year." Cutting assisted a delegation from New Mexico to join him in Paris.[37]

As he awaited the arrival of the New Mexico delegation in Paris during early September, Cutting spent "a very pleasant week" by going to the theater, dining at favorite restaurants, discovering new ones and wandering about the city. In all, approximately twenty thousand legionnaires, many accompanied by wives and families, poured into Paris for the convention. Cutting enjoyed all the pomp and circumstance of the convention, which was hosted by the French government. Over sixty thousand people marched in the parade as one-and-a-half-million bystanders looked on "with nothing but good feeling in evidence." About fifty people from New Mexico attended the convention. Cutting was present at a garden party hosted by Marshal Ferdinand Foch, who along with General John J. Pershing, was very much in evidence throughout the festivities and proceedings of the American Legion Convention. After the meeting Cutting, Jesus Baca and his wife motored "through Burgundy, Switzerland to Milan" and then to Venice before driving "across country" to Genoa, where they boarded the *Conti Rossi* on October 14.[38]

Cutting returned to Santa Fe in mid-November with "a touch of ptomaine." For several weeks thereafter, he was "too busy even to think" as he coped with material accumulated during his absence. In early December, he went to southern New Mexico to avoid the meeting of the Republican State Committee in Santa Fe. He explained, "I don't want any responsibility for what they may decide to do." Cutting wanted no part of any discussion of his candidacy for either senator or governor in 1928. In El Paso, he spent "a very moving couple of hours" with Albert Fall, who had requested the visit.

Cutting had last seen Fall in 1920 when they had "a particularly violent row" at a party convention. "The old man," Cutting wrote, "is completely broken in body and spirit, but his mind is as active as ever." Fall's wife and daughters deeply impressed him with their courage and fortitude during this period of adversity.[39]

Back in Santa Fe, Cutting was stunned to learn of the unexpected death of Senator Andrieus A. Jones in Washington on December 20. Jones's death changed the course of Cutting's life. Cutting had no indication of whom the governor would select to fill out the last year of Jones's term and took no part "in any of the wire pulling for the position." He was aware that his name figured prominently in rumors bandied about Santa Fe. He told no one that he would accept an offer of the seat and was quite surprised to receive the unsolicited endorsement "of practically everyone of importance in the [Republican] party—the same old crowd I have been fighting for seventeen years." On the other hand, Senator Charles Curtis of Kansas came to Santa Fe to convince Governor Dillon that Cutting was "not considered sufficiently regular by those in high places in Washington." Cutting asked his family and close friends not to aid the discussions.[40] Ignoring his wishes, J. D. Atwood endorsed Cutting as a friend of the veterans in a strong letter to Dillon.

On December 29, following the funeral of Senator Jones in Las Vegas the previous day, Governor Dillon called Cutting to his office in the Capitol and offered him the commission as United States senator. In a formal statement, Dillon said that Cutting would be able "to give New Mexico high class and effective service in the national Congress." He had the support of citizens, including a great majority of the veterans, in all walks of life. He added that at no time had Cutting solicited the post. The only promise Cutting made was to serve the people of New Mexico. Governor Dillon never inquired whether he was a Republican or a Democrat, nor did he request any legislative pledge. Cutting intended, he told his friends, to support the Coolidge administration when he believed its positions to be right. But true to his and his family's views, he made clear that he considered "loyalty to the state and nation" superior to loyalty to any party. In short, Cutting would be an independent progressive Republican joining a handful of similarly minded colleagues. In early January 1928, Cutting left Santa Fe to launch a new career as the junior United States senator from New Mexico.[41]

CHAPTER 13

SENATOR

The new senator from New Mexico was sworn in on January 4. Thirteen days later, he was assigned to four committees: Commerce; District of Columbia; Territories and Insular Possessions; and Public Lands and Surveys. In April, he was excused from further service on the Committee on the District of Columbia and joined the Committee on Agriculture and Forestry, which along with service on Public Lands and Surveys, would enable him to oversee matters of great concern to New Mexico. While letters of congratulations poured in, Cutting had to assemble a staff, get into the routine of the Senate, and locate living quarters. He was determined to establish himself as a force in legislative deliberations. In the 1928 presidential election he would have to seek election in his own right.[1]

Cutting's seat nominally gave the Republicans a one-vote majority in the Senate, which was strongly and closely divided along party lines. Progressive Republicans held the balance of power. Suspicious of Cutting, Republican leaders considered him at best an independent Republican. Editorial writers in major newspapers shared their doubts. Only time would tell whether Cutting would continue his independent ways. Upon his arrival, he was branded an independent Republican. The progressive Republicans, who professed to be "pure," purportedly neither voted for nor supported Democratic proposals.[2]

Cutting arrived in the midst of the Senate debate on the seating of Frank L. Smith of Illinois. His campaign expenditures had exceeded the thirty-thousand-dollar limit proposed in a Senate resolution. In a letter signed "W.B.," every senator was told that Cutting had spent more in previous New Mexico campaigns than either Frank L. Smith or William S. Vare, the Pennsylvania senator, similarly charged, had in theirs. The letter heightened Republican concern about the new senator's loyalty.[3]

Cutting quickly laid Republican fears to rest. A friend wrote Governor Dillon on January 17 that "the first test came yesterday and he voted on two occasions with the straight Republican side." By the end of January, most of the adverse comment had faded, and Cutting was recognized as an active, able freshman senator who neither kept quiet nor strictly followed the lead of party elders.[4]

CHAPTER 13

Delivering his maiden speech on January 19, Cutting disagreed with George W. Norris and other progressive Republicans on the case of Frank L. Smith and allied himself with Republican leaders. Elected as United States senator from Illinois in 1926, Smith had spent enormous sums on his campaign and had maintained a close association with the utilities magnate, Samuel Insull. As chairman of the Illinois Public Service Commission, empowered to regulate public utilities, Smith had accepted from Insull and other utility executives large campaign contributions. Cutting stepped into the middle of a lengthy and at times bitter debate. Appalled by the facts, he considered Smith unfit to sit in the Senate of the United States, but Cutting pointed out that no federal statute had been violated and that, despite his seamy credentials, Smith had been duly elected. Until Congress enacted legislation limiting and defining proper campaign expenditures, Cutting did not envision an end to such extravagance.[5] Cutting's remarks were favorably received by his colleagues. The vice-president and other administration supporters approved of them. Progressive Republicans were not necessarily offended by what he said. Like them, he was outraged by Smith's election, but he did not want to make a martyr of Smith by refusing to seat him. He preferred to enact legislation that would make similar senatorial campaigns all but impossible.[6]

The vice-president, Charles Dawes, and senators, such as Frederick Gillett of Massachusetts and Charles Curtis of Kansas, were fulsome in their praise. Herman Baca, who accompanied Cutting to Washington, observed from the gallery that before Cutting was recognized, "most of the Senators were out but nearly all were there soon after." His speech, incidentally, preserved harmony among New Mexico Republicans and abated criticism of Governor Dillon for appointing him.[7]

From El Paso, Albert Fall's wife forwarded a favorable editorial and said that he had demonstrated "true Western courage." She suggested that he call on their "good friends," Secretary of the Treasury Andrew Mellon, Secretary of the Interior Hubert Work, and Secretary of Labor James J. Davis, who would enjoy knowing him. From Government House in Ottawa, Alice Massey, the wife of the Canadian minister to the United States, wrote his mother about the compliments that his speech had received from the vice-president and from Democratic and Republican senators. All were "exceptionally keen about his independent stand." Cutting responded pompously to a constituent, "No doubt I will be criticized severely for my action, but that is to be expected by a representative of the people." His ego no doubt was inflated by the praise "from nearly all the people whose opinion I value in the Senate."[8]

Cutting had little time to bask in the glory. He was quickly involved in "daily and nightly hearings on flood control" and was deluged with patronage requests. He suggested that job applicants not expect "too much too quickly." He also received inquiries about his seeking election in the fall campaign. He told correspondents that he had made no plans. Only the backing of friends, who had been kind to him in the past and who were currently counting on him, would move him to run for the office.[9]

In early February, he attended a dinner in his honor at the Harvard Club in New York. Old friends from Groton and Harvard, including Grenville Clark, Harry James, George W. Wickersham and Vanderbilt Webb, came to honor him at a sumptuous dinner. Invitations went only to those considered "good company and not afflicted with giving advice or a message to the world."[10]

Shortly before he attended this dinner, the Committee on Public Lands and Surveys began hearings for the second time in six years on the Teapot Dome Affair, which had ended the political career of Albert B. Fall. Once again the prosecutor, Thomas J. Walsh, probed the activities of the Continental Trading Company, a Canadian firm that purchased and sold barrels of crude oil. Walsh unearthed the fact that Harry F. Sinclair had paid off the outstanding debts of the Republican party with profits from one of Continental's transactions. Walsh also examined Robert W. Stewart, one of the organizers of the Continental Trading Company and the president of Standard Oil of Indiana in which the Rockefellers had heavily invested. Stewart declared that he had received none of the company's challenged profits, had no hand in the transaction, and could not recall whether Fall had received a portion of the profits.[11]

Cutting played only a minor role in questioning Stewart. Although he found it "inconceivable" that Stewart could not recall the disputed transaction, Cutting did not believe, as some newspaper reporters suggested, that Stewart committed perjury. More importantly, Cutting arranged for John D. Rockefeller, Jr. to testify before the committee and to confer with Senator Walsh prior to his appearance. This conversation, Rockefeller explained, "cleared up in my mind, as I hope it did in Senator Walsh's, any little misunderstandings that might have existed prior to our meeting." During his testimony, Rockefeller, a friendly witness, expressed his indignation at the practices of the Continental Trading Company and of Stewart in particular.[12]

Appalled at Sinclair's bailing out of the Republican party, Senator William E. Borah launched a drive "to clean up the Republican campaign debt to Sinclair," a venture that received Cutting's complete support. The young senator endeavored to interest his uncle, R. Fulton Cutting. Cutting believed Borah's drive would allow the Republican party to clean "its skirts in some rather dramatic and sensational way" and to prevent the Democrats from making the financial scandal an issue in the upcoming national election. He said, "I don't believe that any $160,000 could ever do the Party so much good as this particular $160,000 if raised properly." To assist in raising this sum, Cutting, along with Senator Guy D. Goff of West Virginia, pledged five thousand dollars. Borah's drive, while securing numerous small contributions, attracted few large donors and soon disappeared from view. Cutting concluded that those in charge of party affairs were not sufficiently interested.[13]

Cutting's attention was also diverted by a bitter fight over the Middle Rio Grande Conservancy District. As early as 1913, citizens of New Mexico had petitioned for the establishment of a drainage, irrigation, and flood-control district from the Elephant Butte Reservoir in the south to the northern border of Sandoval County. Included in the district were the city of Albuquerque and numerous Indian pueblos. In the measure under consideration, the northern boundary of the district was extended to include Santa Fe County and several additional Indian pueblos, the structure of the conservancy board was slightly modified, and concessions were made to farmers to encourage irrigation. The main focus of the bill was to benefit the Pueblo Indians, a concern that brought the matter to the attention of Congress. The establishment, operation and development of the district had been exclusively a state matter.[14]

Friends of the Indians feared that the Pueblos could not possibly reimburse the Department of the Interior for irrigating and improving their lands. Cutting was amazed. Although authorities had "guaranteed to make no attempt to enforce their reimbursement clause," he noted, John Collier and others "prefer to have no Conservancy legislation at all (which would mean that the Indians would lose a million and a half dollars from the Government) rather than accept the present bill," which he believed to be the only measure able to gain Congressional approval.[15]

On March 1, Cutting gained the floor and asked the privilege of reading two telegrams. In one, Governor Dillon said that citizens in New Mexico wanted the conservancy bill and were unconcerned with its reimbursable features. In the other, the chair of the Committee of Indian Welfare of the New Mexico Federation of Women's Clubs also endorsed the passage of the bill, "with or without reimbursement." Cutting stated that opponents of the measure were not fully cognizant of the conditions along the Rio Grande Valley in New Mexico. They were misinformed in believing that the pueblo tribes were "treated in anything like the same manner as the Indians in the rest of the country."

He explained that the 150-mile-long conservancy district was in most places about one-mile wide. There were a few broader tracts settled in prehistoric times by various tribes of Pueblo Indians, six of them within the conservancy district. They inhabited "exactly the same area, with the same lands, with the same architecture and buildings that they were living in when Europeans first came out there" in the sixteenth century. Well in advance of modern scholars, Cutting explained that the Spaniards, even after the Pueblo Revolt of 1680, neither dispossessed, nor drove the Indians off their lands, nor revoked any of their privileges. These guarantees were later assumed by the United States and then preserved in the enabling act and in the constitution of New Mexico. In these remarks, Cutting indicated a deep knowledge of the history and current state of Indian affairs in New Mexico. He observed that the proposed bill "will benefit the Indians in proportion far more than the white settlers." For example, while whites paid taxes and interest, the Indians paid none. Whites would pay the principal in forty years; Indians could have the time extended. In every category, Indians benefited more than white land-owners within the conservancy district.

During the debate, Cutting exchanged polite barbs with the junior senator from Wisconsin, Robert M. La Follette, Jr., who would become one of his closest friends. Cutting and his colleague, Sam Bratton, felt that following the previous policy in New Mexico, reclamation work should be reimburs-able. La Follette and other critics said the measure should contain a gratuity feature. Cutting and Bratton argued that a measure with a gratuity feature would never gain full Congressional approval. They were correct. Congress approved the amended bill with the reimbursement stipulation. Even without the gratuity provision, Cutting agreed with the assistant commissioner of Indian Affairs that the measure was "the most generous piece of Indian legislation" that had passed Congress in the last fifteen years.[16]

Since 1928 was an election year, Cutting had to keep abreast of political affairs in New Mexico. Clara Olsen and Herman Baca assisted him. Secretary to Governor Richard Dillon, Olsen was prudent, judicious, circumspect and well informed. Associated with Cutting from their work in the American Legion, Herman Baca was the United States property and disbursing officer in Santa Fe. He kept Cutting informed about developments in the American

Legion and in the Hispanic communities throughout the state. Cutting confided the management of the weekly Spanish edition of the *New Mexican, El Nuevo Mejicano,* to Baca. On measures pertaining to New Mexico, Cutting always sought Governor Dillon's advice.[17]

Aside from political developments, Cutting took great interest in a Santa Fe tempest that had broad cultural ramifications. John D. Rockefeller, Jr., through the Rockefeller Foundation, wished to establish an anthropological laboratory and museum in Santa Fe that would be distinct and separate from the Museum of New Mexico and the School of American Research directed by Cutting's old adversary, Edgar Lee Hewett. In a meeting with John D. Rockefeller, Jr., Cutting expressed his support for the project. He learned, however, that the president of the University of New Mexico, James F. Zimmerman, where Hewett was a faculty member, opposed the creation of another museum. His resistance accounted for Rockefeller's reluctance to proceed with the project. Hoping to keep the laboratory and museum in the state, Cutting sought ways of mollifying Zimmerman and removing his opposition.[18] Clara Olsen and Francis C. Wilson, Cutting's former lawyer and close associate, helped to convince Zimmerman that the university would attract outstanding scholars by becoming a trustee of the Museum and Laboratory of Anthropology. Wilson's support of this proposal brought about a reconciliation between the two men, although they never resumed their friendship.

In January of 1929, Cutting was relieved to learn that Santa Fe officials had accepted the Rockefeller gift, a sum "approaching nearly a million dollars," for the new museum. He was also delighted to serve on the board of the new institution. The directors of the new museum wanted to avoid a conflict with Hewett. Cutting wrote that he visited with "some of the people directly interested" and said that "as a sop to Hewett," there would be "a donation of some $25,000 or $30,000 to one of his pet schemes, to show that the Rockefellers are not trying to slam him or his institution in any way." The solution, he said, was "entirely satisfactory to all of us."[19]

Cutting emerged as a strong senate friend of the veterans when he endorsed a pension measure for disabled officers who were not part of the regular army. They were men who, like Cutting, entered the service during the war. Having incurred physical disability in the conflict, many were still in service and being cared for in veterans hospitals. The measure provided a pension that would make them eligible for retirement. "For nine years," Cutting explained, "I have been working for this bill and for other legislation fostered by the ex-service men's organizations." The measure would affect no more than three thousand emergency officers. The United States owed a debt to these emergency officers who served in time of war and had recognized such an obligation after all previous conflicts. Cutting claimed that among the eighteen thousand ex-servicemen in New Mexico, no more than twenty-five or thirty would benefit from this measure. Nevertheless, he found "that all the rest are thoroughly in favor of it, and that they want it brought to a vote." He called for its approval "because as far as it goes it is right in principle, even though it may not go as far as some of us would like."[20]

Because all major offices in New Mexico would be contested in 1928, Cutting could ignore local developments only to his detriment. Asked about whether he would become a New Mexico delegate to the Kansas City presidential nominating convention, Cutting gave an indefinite answer. He was disturbed by Clara Olsen's report that Governor Dillon "for some time expressed himself as desiring to get out of the game." He could no longer afford to neglect his business, nor did he appear to have enough funds to wage a reelection campaign. Olsen urged Dillon to stay on. She explained that his harmonious administration was at a turning point in New Mexico's political history and that prosperity and decent government had a chance to entrench themselves along with the Republican party. Olsen's information caused Cutting "a great deal of anxiety." Dillon's integrity and progressive stance had incurred the opposition of "some of the old gang leaders." He had helped Cutting find a solid political base and had given him an opportunity to champion progressive causes in an effective arena. Dillon's dropping out of "the game" would cast Cutting loose from any stable political mooring. Therefore, he informed Clara Olsen that Dillon's financial embarrassment could "be taken care of without any great difficulty." Under no circumstances would Cutting run on a ticket without Dillon.[21]

Meanwhile, Herman Baca kept Cutting informed of his support among Hispanics. Baca loaned small sums to many in distress and occasionally to individuals who would devote time to strengthening Cutting's support among Hispanic voters. In lengthy letters, he made clear that Democrats were following the same practice. "The democratic state organization gave them a big wad of money here for the election," he explained. He also urged Cutting to dispatch "more and more publicity" of his activities in Congress, as "people are eating it up." They claimed Cutting had done more in three months than previous incumbents had done during their entire tenure.[22]

Cutting was busy with "three or four months discussion and debate in Committee" on "the enormously complicated Flood Control bill." The measure appropriated $325 million and received unanimous Senate approval

"after an hour's debate." The rapidity of its passage and the upcoming nominating conventions led senators, Cutting not among them, to predict an
adjournment in mid-May. He thought "farm relief, the Boulder Dam, and
other controversial subjects" would delay adjournment. Largely for this
reason he avoided the Republican state convention in Santa Fe on April 14,
where delegates to the presidential nominating convention were selected.[23]
Cutting continued his interest in penal reform, expanded his interest in Indian
affairs, developed an interest in services for the blind, and involved himself
unenthusiastically in patronage matters.[24]

In the last weeks of the session, Cutting became an outspoken critic of
corruption in the electoral process. His call for clean elections, coming before
the nominating conventions, received little attention and resulted in no re-
medial legislation, but he pleased the handful of progressive Republican
members, who now saw him as an ally. Cutting called for changes in the
Federal Corrupt Practices Act, which purported to limit campaign expenditures but whose many loopholes erased "any real equality between a rich man
and a poor one." Moreover, the law contained no effective enforcement
provisions.

To resolve the law's inadequacies, Cutting introduced five measures and
discussed them on the senate floor. He admitted that they were unsatisfactory and that they would be unacceptable to the Judiciary Committee without amendment, but he nevertheless believed they represented a substantial
advance over the prevailing situation. First, he called for a constitutional
amendment that would grant "Congress authority to legislate concerning the
nomination as well as the election of candidates for Congress." Second, he
wished to amend a section of the first article of the Constitution. He argued
that candidates who violated the laws regulating the nomination and election
process should be ineligible for membership in either branch of Congress.
Next, he proposed the creation of an electoral commission—a continuing
auditing body that would function as an agency of Congress. It would have
no authority but would provide Congress with information on expenditures,
credentials of candidates, and the facts in contested elections. Fourth, he
proposed a more effective Corrupt Practices Act dealing with the nomination
and election of members of Congress. It specified more precisely than in the
past what constituted legitimate expenditures. These were confined to presenting "information, arguments and advice to electors as to the issues of the
campaign, and the qualifications of candidates." And the act also called for a
precise and prompt method of reporting campaign contributions, placing
responsibility for doing so entirely on the candidate. Finally, his last bill called

for a similar measure pertaining to campaign expenditures by candidates for president and vice-president.[25]

Cutting claimed that his proposals represented an advance over the prevailing legislation. However, he would be "glad to have the Judiciary Committee take them and tear them to pieces and substitute something else which might be more adequate to meet the purposes in view." The chairman of the Judiciary Committee, George W. Norris, told Cutting that the committee would be unable to consider his proposal, despite the sense of urgency Cutting expressed. Nevertheless, Norris said that he was interested in the measures and, regardless of the difficulties involved in amending the Constitution, he assured Cutting that he would be glad to cooperate in securing "proper legislation."[26]

The improper and extravagant use of money in politics presented a vital problem to representative democracy in 1928. Cutting's proposals, while incomplete in some respects, were a commendable attempt to bring a serious matter to public attention. That one of the newest and youngest members of the Senate would take the lead in election reform indicated to his progressive colleagues that Cutting was a man of independence and courage. Maintaining a temperate and modest stance, he inspired confidence in Norris and other like-minded reformers.[27]

Cutting, however, had little time to rest on his laurels. In the Senate's rush to conclude its business by the end of May, he was overwhelmed by "sessions practically every night." He so exhausted himself that when the session ended, he rested and regained his stamina at Westbrook, the family estate on Long Island. Before leaving Westbrook, Herman Baca informed him of the disarray among the Democrats at their convention. "About 15 natives [were] in attendance," indicating that once again the Democratic Party would not exert widespread appeal to Hispanic voters. Moreover, he indicated that Cutting's support among veterans and Hispanics was in good order and that the small-town editors, many of whom Cutting had assisted, were favorably disposed toward his candidacy.[28]

Rather than attend the Kansas City convention, Cutting decided to remain "quietly" at Westbrook, "basking in the sun and salt breezes." He listened to some of the speeches over the radio, and he kept his eye on political developments in New Mexico. Before returning to Santa Fe, he journeyed to Cambridge. Cutting and his mother dined with Harvard president A. Lawrence Lowell. During the Harvard commencement exercises on June 21, he was awarded an honorary degree, an M.A., to compensate for the bachelor's degree he never received. Lowell honored Cutting as one "who has made his home in New Mexico and carried on in the press there a courageous political warfare."[29]

Unknown to Cutting at this time, the director of the People's Legislative Service in Washington recruited him additional support. Richard Hogue recommended Cutting for editorial backing in *Labor,* the weekly newspaper of the Railroad Brotherhoods, edited by Edward Keating, a former Congressman from Colorado. Hogue, who had previously interviewed Cutting, was "impressed by his informed attitude and outspoken friendliness toward organized labor" and by the fact that his secretary, Edgar Puryear, had formerly served as the Democratic leader in the Senate of New Mexico. Cutting's appeal to labor, his nonpartisan approach, and his bills "in behalf of clean government and uncorrupted popular franchise," Hogue insisted, would appeal to members of "the Big Four Brotherhoods in New Mexico."[30]

Back in New Mexico in early July, Cutting began touring the state. He attended banquets and fiestas and spoke frequently, despite his trouble with "pre-mature hay fever." On occasion, he accompanied Governor Dillon. At Raton on July 4, before an audience of about three thousand people, Cutting competed with "a million firecrackers and automobile horns." That night at the Cowboys' Ball in Las Vegas, former governor Arthur Hannett, drunk at the time, insulted Herman Baca's wife and was badly pummelled by her husband. Knocked out, Hannett was carried away by some friends. About a half hour later, he returned with a gun and tried without success "to resume operations."[31]

Once the presidential candidates were selected, Cutting quickly concluded that Herbert Hoover was "the abler and better man of the two" and was "bound to appeal to the average sensible voter." Responding to a congratulatory telegram, Hoover thanked Cutting "for the fine vote of friendship" and for the support given him in the past months. Alfred E. Smith's candidacy, however, posed a delicate problem in New Mexico. The first Catholic to receive a presidential nomination, he would appeal to Hispanic voters. Cutting would have to hand out endorsements with caution as he campaigned throughout the state.[32]

In late July, while Cutting was traveling through the northern counties, the chairman of the Republican Executive Committee moved that a committee be appointed to ascertain the purity of his Republicanism before the party considered him eligible for the senatorial nomination. The motion, which received wide attention, received no second and was withdrawn. When he learned of the motion, Cutting was reported to have "merely chuckled." He recognized that the "old guard," now comprising a minor faction in the party, was antagonistic to his receiving the nomination at the state convention.[33]

In a letter, a well-respected ex-serviceman from Bernalillo County indicated the extent of Cutting's support in New Mexico. Between his "maternal side" and his "paternal side," Cutting could count on seven hundred votes. If these veterans and their families supported Cutting, he would have "a good substantial majority."

Meanwhile, his Washington staff, Edgar Puryear and the efficient clerk-stenographer, Florence Dromey, returned to New Mexico and prepared, among other things, a wide distribution of Cutting's speeches on Conservancy and Corrupt Practices.[34] With the Republican nominating convention scheduled for September 12 in Albuquerque, "Things," Cutting wrote, "are getting busier all the time." On August 16, Cutting and some of his friends went to Taos to visit Vice-President Charles G. Dawes. On Saturday, August 18, Cutting met Herbert Hoover in Gallup and traveled with him to Albuquerque, where he introduced the presidential candidate at a political rally. Cutting explained that Hoover "has blossomed out since his nomination into a very pleasing and human personality" and was convinced that Hoover won votes during his various stops and back-platform talks. At El Paso, he and Hoover met Governor Dillon and reviewed the National Guard. Hoover proceeded into Texas. Cutting covered "the East side" of New Mexico for about a week and then intended to cross the state for the Indian Ceremonial at Gallup. He was due in Santa Fe on the first of September, a Saturday, for a brief rest before proceeding to Silver City for Labor Day and then to Las Cruces, all prior to the state nominating convention.[35]

In Santa Fe in early September, Cutting responded to urgent requests from Hanford MacNider, the head of the Republican Service League, who was seeking the votes of veterans. In 1924 Cutting, then supporting the Democratic candidate for governor, had denounced MacNider's vote seeking. Although he now appeared willing to accept MacNider's efforts, albeit hesitatingly, he feared that a branch of the league in New Mexico might offend Hispanic veterans. But he was a veteran, a Republican candidate and a Hoover admirer and did not openly oppose efforts of the Republican Service League in the campaign.[36]

The Republican campaign was launched officially when the party selected its candidates in Albuquerque on September 12. By New Mexico law, Cutting had to resign his seat prior to the convention since he would be nominated for a full senate term. He allowed the delegates to nominate Octaviano A. Larrazolo to the short term of Congress, the remaining months of the term to which Andrieus A. Jones was elected in 1922. In nominating Larrazolo, the Republican convention selected a prominent Hispanic leader to head the ticket along with Governor Richard C. Dillon and Cutting. The party and the candidates, judging from the convention oratory, solidly backed the national ticket, but all candidates knew that a large portion of Hispanic voters would lean toward Alfred E. Smith, the Democratic presidential candidate, on the basis of his Catholicism. Cutting in no way wished to offend Hispanic voters by strongly endorsing Hoover. Only very guardedly would he endorse the national ticket. Thus, Republicans focused their efforts on electing the state ticket and merely hoped that Hoover would garner New Mexico's three electoral votes.[37]

Cutting's campaign got off to a good start. A strong editorial ally, T. M. Pepperday printed his acceptance speech in full in the *Albuquerque Journal* and commented favorably on it in a Sunday edition. Pepperday provided a powerful editorial voice in the state's most populous area, an outlet Cutting never previously enjoyed. His opponent was characterized "as a foe to labor and to the native people as well." An Alabamian, he was " 'agin' the colored race, that includes Mexicans and they know it." Cutting knew that he could relax a bit before launching a vigorous campaign in the final weeks.[38]

Nevertheless, his campaign was in full swing. Edgar Puryear, Herman Baca and others continued at their appointed tasks. Puryear predicted in mid-September that Cutting would be elected by ten thousand votes. Cutting could afford to remain in Santa Fe because his strategy did not involve him directly with other candidates or with the overall management of the Republican campaign.[39] While he was resting in Santa Fe, the Railway Labor Executives' Association in Washington agreed to inform the members of the Railroad Brotherhoods in New Mexico that the best interests of labor would be served by electing Bronson Cutting. This endorsement meant that at the height of the campaign, the weekly newspaper of the Brotherhoods, *Labor*, would blanket New Mexico with an editorial endorsement of his candidacy. Edward Keating, the editor, had to be assured, however, that Cutting was not responsible for a series of *New Mexican* editorials critical of labor.[40]

Although Cutting was not overconfident about his prospects, the chances for a Republican sweep were good. He was recognized throughout the state; the popularity of Governor Dillon was strong. While there was Smith sentiment in "the native counties," it was "very much sub-rosa" and therefore hard for Cutting to evaluate. However, he had prepared his candidacy well in advance of this campaign through his American Legion work and through numerous trips, particularly in the northern counties. One acute observer remarked, "For years he has used his great wealth to carry on a sort of welfare work among the natives of the state. . . . He has buried the dead, paid for the doctor for the arrival of the children, built homes for the poor, (and American Legion club houses) in fact carried on a philanthropic work that has made him countless friends among the natives of this state." Many natives might vote for Smith, but almost all would support Cutting. While critics insisted that Cutting engaged in these endeavors for crass political gain, some observers and most of his friends and associates considered them altruistic. Claiming indifference, Cutting explained, "I have no idea what the results will be and don't particularly care."[41]

He was not indifferent, however, to the plane trip, the first by any candidates in New Mexico, that he and Governor Dillon took to San Juan County. Normally it was a three-day trip by train and two by road. Cutting and Dillon "went over in two hours, and back in one hour and a half." Cutting was ecstatic. Never had he seen "anything so beautiful as this country from the air." At this point, Cutting spoke as often as possible, while Puryear and Herman Baca managed the campaign. They were delighted to learn that a special edition of *Labor* endorsed Cutting at the end of October. They planned to distribute ten thousand extra copies. Toward the end of the campaign, Jefferson D. Atwood, a Roswell lawyer and a former commander of the New Mexico American Legion, cultivated the votes of veterans and businessmen in the eastern counties for Cutting. To counter the impact of Senator Joseph T. Robinson, the Democratic vice-presidential candidate who spoke to about nine hundred people in Roswell, Cutting asked Senator William E. Borah to speak in New Mexico as a favor to him and as "a great service to Hoover's cause."[42]

Cutting devoted his speeches equally to previous Democratic misrule and to his service in Washington. He also insisted that Herbert Hoover could do more for New Mexico, given the fact that western members controlled the Senate, than Alfred E. Smith. When he spoke before the state convention of the American Legion, he confined his remarks to the status of measures pertaining to veterans and to his efforts for moving them along. Nowhere in his speeches did he mention his campaign. Nor did he mention his opponent. His oratory, temperate and judicious, appealed to the heads and not the hearts of his audience.[43]

Cutting appeared the likely winner as the campaign reached its climax. However, at the end of October, a most unlikely source seemingly offered his opponents ample ammunition to use against him. Cutting's maternal uncle, in behalf of several family members, contributed twenty thousand dollars to the Republican campaign in New Mexico. Thereafter, the Democrats pounded away at the issue of Cutting's wealth. Campaigning throughout the state, Cutting possibly was unaware of the family contribution until the very end of the campaign.[44]

After hearing him speak in Las Cruces, Jouett Fall wrote to tell him of the "splendid impression" he made on every side. She heard "the finest things" said about him and had never seen "more intense interest and enthusiasm." At a rally in "Old Mesilla," Cutting made a point to seek out and sit by Jouett Fall while Dillon and other Republican candidates spoke. Beside pleasing the Fall family, Cutting's gesture indicated to all of Albert Fall's friends and former neighbors in his home area of southern New Mexico that he, unlike others, was not ignoring Fall now that he had been discredited and would soon be jailed.[45]

While Cutting was campaigning in the southern counties, "a young and enthusiastic woman supporter" prepared a circular that endorsed Hoover and Cutting and that was mailed to thousands of women throughout the state. Soon thereafter came a letter from Herbert Hoover, who declared "the extraordinary importance" of Cutting's returning to the United States Senate. Hoover commended his "fine constructive service" and expressed the hope that the voters would recognize "the distinction that comes to them because of so able a representative."[46]

No doubt pleased with Hoover's endorsement, Cutting returned to Santa Fe "from a pretty strenuous trip in the south," prepared to go to the "East Side," and then traveled back north with big rallies at Albuquerque and Las Vegas on the last nights. Although he met with "good meetings every where," he also noted that "the Democrats are indulging in falsehood and personal abuse" and that they were "well backed in a financial way." He refused to comment on his chances primarily because of the "R.C. danger," stating that "one can tell nothing about it till the votes are counted." Back in Santa Fe on election day, Cutting admitted to being "thoroughly exhausted" and anxious "to get away somewhere as soon as possible." Despite Cutting's reticence, some of his friends continued to predict that he would carry the state by at least ten thousand votes.[47]

He won by a majority of 18,157. His decisive victory was the largest received by any New Mexico state official to that time. For several days, an overwhelmed Cutting was unable to get a handle on the dimensions of his victory. He carried 24 of the state's 31 counties, surpassed only by Hoover who carried 30 and won the state by a majority of 21,434 votes. In Santa Fe, his home county, Cutting's majority (2,904 votes in the final tabulation, and 2,895 when he wrote) was "the largest one ever given anyone in any county of New Mexico." He had even captured the nominally Democratic "Anglo" counties in the East End. Moreover, Cutting believed that he was the first Republican ever to carry the cities of Albuquerque, Roswell and East Las Vegas.

Cutting saw possible problems arising from the election results. The Republicans gained control of the state legislature, "two-thirds in the House and three-fourths in the Senate," majorities that "were too big for good government," Cutting believed. Fortunately, Governor Dillon, New Mexico's first reelected governor, was aware of the danger. Cutting believed that Dillon's large majority, over thirteen thousand votes, would make him "quite independent of the bosses." To guide progressive measures through the legislature, a task Cutting hoped to be involved with before the new Congress convened after Hoover's inauguration, would "mean work." But before he started lobbying the New Mexico legislature, Cutting wanted to get away for a rest.[48]

After the election, Cutting tended to his correspondence, chiefly answering letters of congratulations. Anxious about his status at the convening of the Seventy-first Congress, he inquired of James E. Watson, chairman of the Senate Committee on Committees, whether Larrazolo could take over his assignments so that he could assume them when he returned to Washington. Of the three committees on which he served—Commerce, Agriculture and Forestry, and Territories and Public Lands—if one had to be yielded, both he and Larrazolo agreed that Commerce interested them least. He was delighted when Watson assured him that Larrazolo would assume his assignments for the short term and that he would "then be reinstated in all of them without loss of prestige or position" when he again entered the Senate.[49]

Rather than return to New York for the holiday season, Cutting briefly vacationed in Mexico City. Upon his arrival in early December, Cutting dined with Ambassador and Mrs. Dwight W. Morrow at the embassy one night and met the diplomatic corps. Through the ambassador he met most of the prominent Mexican officials. He attended the inauguration of President Emilio Portes Gil and addressed the Cortes in Spanish. After his address, the Senate hosted a reception in his honor, "the first time anything of the sort had been done." One of the Mexican officials, Manuel Gamio, a former secretary of education and a leading Mexican archaeologist, took Cutting and his friends over the pyramid of Teotihuacan. Although Cutting found Mexico City interesting but "somewhat noisy," he was charmed by the countryside and the smaller towns. He attended a bull fight that had "the finest matadors in Spain as the principals." Then he briefly visited Vera Cruz and Cuernavaca before returning to Santa Fe just before Christmas.[50]

In Santa Fe at the end of the year he was able to fend off job hunters, well-wishers, and people desiring interviews. A cold and the prevalence of numerous cases of the flu provided excuses for remaining at home. At the year's end, Cutting was much better. He enjoyed walking on the mesa but avoided going to town. He was not certain about whether he would attend the inauguration ceremonies for Governor Dillon's second term. However, he wanted to be on hand when the legislature convened. He intended to lobby for the approval of planks in his party's platform before departing for Washington to attend Hoover's inauguration and to be sworn in as a duly elected United States senator.[51]

Nineteen twenty-eight was the "golden year" for Cutting in New Mexico. The election showed that by curbing factional and other differences, political harmony could produce a Republican victory that was unmatched in the history of the state. As for Cutting, he had found a meaningful, constructive and influential place for himself by serving New Mexico in the United States Senate. He had broad support among Hispanics, labor, and veterans. In Richard Dillon, Cutting found a governor with whom he could cooperate and whose administration he could endorse. Although a new and satisfying situation, it was unfortunately a short-lived one. In the early months of 1929, Cutting again found himself adrift in the quagmire of New Mexico politics and his place in the Senate pecking order in jeopardy.

Bronson M. Cutting at Groton, ca. 1901. (Courtesy, Library of Congress.)

The Bronson and Murray clans dining at Westbrook. Bronson is the boy wearing the wide white collar and glasses and seated between two girls on the near side of the table. (Courtesy, George Roussos).

(*left*) Bronson M. Cutting while a student at Harvard, ca. 1908. (Courtesy, Library of Congress.)

Bronson M. Cutting, ca. 1913. (Courtesy, Library of Congress.)

Bronson Cutting's home on Thirtieth Street, Northwest in Washington, D.C. (Courtesy, Library of Congress.)

(*top opposite page*) Cutting visits troops of the New Mexico National guard at Columbus New Mexico during the Pershing Expedition in summer 1916. Cutting is second from the right. (Courtesy, Library of Congress.)

(*bottom opposite page*) Captain Bronson M. Cutting during World War I. (Courtesy, Library of Congress.)

Westbrook, the Cutting home on Long Island, New York. (Courtesy, George Roussos.)

The Cutting family in New York, ca. 1909. *Left to right:* Justine Cabot Ward
(sister); Bronson Cutting; Olivia Cutting (sister); Olivia Murray Cutting
(mother); William Bayard Cutting, Sr., (father). (Courtesy, Museum of New
Mexico, Santa Fe, Neg. No. 7118.)

Cutting's residence, Los Siete Burros, in Santa Fe, New Mexico. (Photograph by T. Harmon Parkhurst, Courtesy, Museum of New Mexico, Santa Fe, Neg. No. 54293.)

(*top opposite page*) Interior view of Cutting's Santa Fe residence, Los Siete Burros. (Courtesy, Museum of New Mexico, Santa Fe, Neg. No. 47773.)

(*bottom opposite page*) A view of the study at Cutting's Santa Fe residence, Los Siete Burros. (Courtesy, Museum of New Mexico, Neg. No. 47781.)

Safford H Hoover   B M C.   Gov Dillon

Hubbell

Cutting with President-elect Franklin D. Roosevelt in Warm Springs, Georgia, December 1932. (Courtesy, Library of Congress.)

(*top opposite page*) A Hoover campaign rally at El Paso, Texas in August 1928. *Left to right:* Ed Safford; Herbert Hoover; Bronson M. Cutting; Frank Hubbell; and Governor Richard C. Dillon. (Courtesy, Library of Congress.)

(*bottom opposite page*) At the Capitol, Senator Bronson Cutting poses with three senate colleagues who are also newspaper publishers, ca. 1928. *Left to right:* Arthur Vandenberg; Carter Glass; Bronson Cutting; and Arthur Capper. (Courtesy, Library of Congress.)

Senator Bronson M. Cutting, 1934. (Courtesy, Library of Congress.)

Left to right: Senator Robert M. La Follette, Jr.; Senator William E. Borah; and Senator Bronson M. Cutting. The photograph was probably taken in Borah's senate office, ca. 1929. (Courtesy, Library of Congress.)

Senator Bronson M. Cutting, Santa Fe, New Mexico, ca. 1934. (Photograph
by T. Harmon Parkhurst, Courtesy, Museum of New Mexico, Santa Fe,
Neg. No. 51498.)

Bronson Cutting and Clifford McCarthy, ca. 1934. (Photograph E. Boyd or persons unknown, Courtesy, State Records Center and Archives, Santa Fe, New Mexico.)

Memorial bust of Bronson Cutting on the grounds of the Department of Education in Santa Fe, New Mexico. (Photograph by T. Harmon Parkhurst, Courtesy, Museum of New Mexico, Neg. No. 47408.)

CHAPTER 14

DISGRUNTLED REPUBLICAN

After the Republican victory in 1928, the party, led by Dillon and Cutting, dominated the political scene in a way previously unknown in New Mexico. Despite the contending party factions, Dillon and Cutting had a chance to consolidate the position of both themselves and the Republican Party in the coming years. Before Cutting was officially sworn in as a United States senator in his own right, however, the harmony between the governor and senator was in shambles, and factionalism wracked the Republican and Democratic parties. From this disarray, Cutting emerged as the most powerful public figure in New Mexico politics. He was a patrón and a leader, whose power and influence played a prominent role in the decisions of both major parties in New Mexico.

As the New Year got underway, Cutting technically was no longer a United States senator. Already seriously ill, Octaviano Larrazolo would fill out the unexpired term of Andrieus A. Jones during the lame duck session of the Seventieth Congress concluding on March 3, 1929. As senator-elect, Cutting anticipated the inauguration of Richard C. Dillon on New Year's day. Dillon was the first governor of New Mexico to succeed himself and generated a great deal of enthusiasm. Receiving a great ovation, "he became rattled and had a hard time getting through his speech." Fearing that exposure to the crowds would impair his recovery from the flu, Cutting stayed at home and avoided contacts with swarms of office seekers and politicians. The new legislature with its overwhelming Republican majorities in both houses, would be "a hot bed of intrigue." Nevertheless, if the legislature translated campaign promises into reality, Republican hegemony would be assured.[1]

On January 8, the legislature convened. Following the usual "log rolling and intrigue," the two chambers organized "very satisfactorily and without too much old guard control." Besides following developments in Santa Fe and keeping up with constituent mail, Cutting tried to rest and observe regular hours as a preliminary to strenuous times ahead in Washington. In mid-January, he decided to attend Hoover's inauguration and purchased tickets for a preinaugural dinner hosted by members of "various former Hoover organizations."[2]

Cutting's desire for rest and regular hours abruptly ended in early February when he involved himself in a New Mexico legislative controversy. During the campaign, both Cutting and Dillon endorsed a plank, unanimously adopted at the Republican State Convention, that pledged the creation of the Office of State Labor Commissioner. The measure was one of the chief reasons the Railroad Brotherhoods and other labor groups had endorsed the Republican ticket.

Initially, the House of Representatives turned down the Labor Commissioner Bill by a 29 to 13 vote. Cutting insisted that Republican legislators had an obligation to enact a major campaign promise, requested permission to appear on the floor and addressed the House members. His defense moved them to pass the bill by a 31 to 15 vote. Cutting recognized that lobbyists exerted greater pressure on the Senate than on the House of Representatives. He explained, "I am quite prepared to resign my own position, if it should be necessary in order to wage an effective fight," but he thought the threat would be sufficient. Once the Senate killed the measure, an editorial in the *New Mexican* listed the senators who had helped to draft and campaign for the pledge but who now opposed the Labor Commissioner Bill. The writer called their actions "the most hard-boiled double cross we have seen in New Mexico politics."[3]

During the tense debate before packed galleries, opponents of the measure took turns denouncing Cutting. Only a handful spoke in defense of Cutting's insistence upon the fulfillment of a party pledge. At one point in this extensive controversy, Senator Oliver Lee asked Cutting, who was again granted floor privileges, "Is it not true that you recently wrote out your resignation as United States Senator and handed it to Governor Dillon?" Refusing to answer, Cutting stated, "Governor Dillon is here and if you care to ask him that question he may answer." Resuming his remarks, Cutting stressed the sacredness of party pledges. He was followed by a host of senators, most of whom made a point of denouncing his interference in their affairs and of noting his previous desertions from party platforms. Anticipating these barbs, Cutting said, "I have always made my position clear before the people went to the polls to vote." A political platform pledge, he explained, was as binding as a legal contract. If elected officials did not abide by their pledges to the people, Cutting said, they should be turned out at the next election. While he had some support in the Senate, he lost the fight for the Labor Commissioner Bill.[4]

Cutting did not give up. With a strong group of supporters, he would try to win over enough legislators to pass some kind of bill before the sixty-day session came to an end on March 9. To Cutting, this fight was not so much a question of the labor bill itself "as of the future of the party, and whether I or the old gang remain in control." The stakes were high because "it is really a life and death struggle for them [the old gang], and they will stop at nothing to win." Would the Republican Party in New Mexico continue as a progressively oriented party, the image projected during Governor Dillon's first term, or would the old gang reassert control?[5]

In mid-February Cutting doubted that a renewed push could change the senate vote, but he made the effort. Before the battle was over, the Labor Commissioner Bill was defeated four times by the Senate. According to Cutting, the press of the state was practically unanimous in denouncing that body. So intense was the fight that Cutting cancelled all of his plans to attend the inauguration of Herbert Hoover. He feared that his fight would bring him undesirable committee assignments in the United States Senate, a point he labeled "a very minor consideration right now." In addition to lobbying the legislature, Cutting drafted an article, "Party Allegiance," for the *New Mexican*. The story, he said, caused "a good deal of resentment." But Cutting added, "The time has come to call things by their real name."[6]

Throughout the debate on the Labor Commissioner Bill, Governor Dillon faced a difficult predicament. The fight over the measure consumed so much of the legislature's time that the session ended on March 9 without consideration of appropriations and other items on the legislative agenda. The Governor called a special session for March 14. Cutting understood Dillon's desire to conclude a legislative agenda, but until late February, he labored under the impression that Dillon endorsed his fight for the Labor Commissioner Bill. After Dillon called for harmony and an end to the controversy, he concluded, "The governor had acted in bad faith in requesting me to continue the labor commissioner fight." With a bitter taste in his mouth, Cutting tendered his resignation. As the news spread, Dillon discussed the matter with legislative leaders and contemplated accepting the resignation and succeeding Cutting in the United States Senate. According to an account prepared after Cutting's death by his administrative assistant, Cutting and Dillon had earlier agreed that they would jointly resign if the legislature failed to pass the Labor Commissioner Bill. In handing over Cutting's resignation, Edgar Puryear asked the governor to fulfill his part of the agreement. Dillon took the letter of resignation but gave no response to Puryear's query.

Dillon, however, refused to accept his resignation, and Cutting finally withdrew the offer. During "some pretty frightful sessions," Clara Olsen, the governor's secretary, mediated an accord between the two men. She tearfully asked both men to quit acting like children. Responding to her pleas, Dillon returned Cutting's letter of resignation, all the while insisting that he had never agreed to resign if the Senate failed to approve the controversial measure. Cutting responded that since Dillon had initially appointed him to his post as United States senator, he "could hardly fight his politics without first offering to resign." Despite the restoration of peace between Dillon and Cutting, the battle over the Labor Commissioner Bill destroyed harmony within the Republican Party in New Mexico.

In Cutting's eyes, the moment Dillon dropped his support of the Labor Commissioner Bill, "the fight was quite hopeless." The governor's move facilitated the passage of numerous "petty graft measures." Cutting and other pundits observed that Dillon had now cast his lot with the old gang. Cutting was "a little disgusted with Dillon" but was pleased with the "significant support" his stance received. Cutting demonstrated to New Mexicans that he was a party leader who would battle against old guard Republicans and stand up for the welfare of the people as expressed in party pledges. "We had a great meeting at Albuquerque," he wrote shortly after his confrontation with Dillon. Fully aware of his support, Cutting, not wishing "to over do the thing," headed East to an engagement at Harvard and a brief visit to Groton before assuming his seat in the United States Senate.[7]

He kept in touch with developments in New Mexico. Herman Baca informed him that in the legislature, "our friends stayed with us better than ever." To a friend in Albuquerque, Cutting explained, "I think it is only a question of time before our fight will be successful." He made clear to Dana Johnson, the editor of the *New Mexican,* that "there is no use in keeping a chip on one's shoulder, and certainly as far as personal relations go, there is every advantage in being on good terms." However, the paper should not go out of its way to support administration policies "unless [they were] in complete line with our own views."

Meanwhile, in Washington, Senator Bratton filed Cutting's credentials as the junior senator from New Mexico for the term commencing March 4, 1929. A friend wrote to key senators recommending Cutting for a place on the Foreign Relations Committee in the Seventy-first Congress, an assignment he failed to receive when Congress officially convened on April 15. He was delighted with the bouquet sent by Mike Otero "and the rest of the bunch" at the opening of the session. "Everything," he said, "went off in good shape" except for the fact that he was "in the kindergarten class again." Nevertheless, he looked forward to working with colleagues in the Senate where his party enjoyed a 56 to 39 majority and where three of his fellow senators, Arthur Vandenburg, Carter Glass and Arthur Capper, were also newspaper publishers. With a devoted staff of four members, three of whom had maintained continuity by staying on with Octaviano Larrazolo, and with a commodious residence rented and another soon to be purchased, Cutting was ready for what turned out to be a long, arduous and disheartening session of Congress.[8]

At the outset, Cutting endorsed Senator Larrazolo's bill, introduced in the previous Congress, that sought an additional allotment of federal land for the Spanish-American Normal School at El Rito, New Mexico, in remote Rio Arriba County, long "the black spot on the educational map of the state." The sale of this additional land would provide additional funds to maintain the program of the woefully underfinanced institution. As he contended with unending, fierce patronage pressures, he introduced a bill that would assist New Mexico's depressed economy by developing the roads in the state's forest reserves. His legislation was widely noticed in the press and led many to conclude that he was indeed doing "something for New Mexico."[9]

On the other hand, Attorney General "Mike" Otero, Clara Olsen and Herman Baca kept Cutting up-to-date on state affairs and Santa Fe gossip. They informed him that Governor Dillon was growing dependent on Charles Springer, the state road commissioner and chief dispenser of local patronage through the Highway Department. Through their vigilant eyes, he learned about the selection of a land commissioner, about legion affairs, and about the political activities of various New Mexicans. Clara Olsen, in particular, reported on the politics of the developing oil industry in the southeastern part of the state. Another acquaintance, Mary Austin, continually sought his advice and support for her numerous efforts to revive and promote the cultural heritage of the Hispanic and Native American peoples of New Mexico. Cutting was able to examine New Mexico affairs more carefully than he had expected during the spring months. The legislative process was moving slowly, owing to "a complete lack of leadership on both sides of the [United States] Senate." He was bored with the slow pace of the tariff debate and looked forward in early June to the recess, which would allow him to return to Santa Fe.[10]

Cutting discussed with President Hoover oil drilling on public lands. The Hoover administration was trying to curb the overproduction of crude oil. Although Cutting was pleased that Hoover was seeking a practical method of regulating the remaining oil production, drilling on the public domain produced only three percent of the total oil supply. "Exceedingly sympathetic," Hoover told Cutting that he would review the action of the Department of the Interior, which was rejecting, without consideration of the expenses incurred, all applications for permission to drill on public lands. This order reversed a previous one that encouraged the development of these resources and left many oil drillers in New Mexico in a most precarious situation that was "indefensible from the point of view of ethics or sound policy." The courts were cluttered with New Mexico oilmen who, in good faith, endeavored to tap the public domain in accord with the policies of the Department of the Interior. Cutting now believed that Hoover would put a stop to further injustices against applicants.[11]

While Hoover sympathized with the plight of these oilmen, he intended to bar further prospecting on public lands. The president called the governors of the oil-producing states to a conference held in June. Mark L. Requa, Hoover's representative and the conference chairman, ruled out of order a resolution calling for the rescission of the Department of Interior order. On the senate floor, Cutting objected to Requa's action. Appealing to senators of the oil-producing states, he hoped that this "policy of coercion will be bitterly resented and repudiated." Cutting omitted the president from his remarks. He was distressed with the "wishy-washy attitude" of the New Mexico delegation, which initially endorsed Hoover's order. "Not understanding the situation," Governor Dillon acted quickly and then had to reconsider.[12]

Cutting found himself with time on his hands. The tedious discussion of the tariff did not directly involve New Mexico's interests. Cutting and his mother rented the residence of Hugh Wilson, the United States ambassador to Switzerland. They dined at the White House, took short trips to historic sites and enjoyed the Virginia countryside. When the Senate recessed on June 19, Cutting promptly departed for Santa Fe. While he was absent, his mother purchased a spacious residence on Thirtieth Street, which would be his home for the remainder of his career.[13]

During the session, Cutting and Robert M. La Follette, Jr. struck up a friendship that improved with each succeeding session. The youngest members of the body, they were regarded as two of the more perceptive senators in the small but influential progressive-Republican camp. Both had experienced serious illness and were constantly concerned about their health. La Follette's ailment was "an infection which might break out anywhere or everywhere." As a sign of their growing friendship, Cutting invited him to visit Santa Fe as his guest. At the very end of this letter, Cutting added, "With regard to the tariff fight I suppose you will let me know what you want me to do."[14]

In Santa Fe, Cutting could not avoid public affairs. He was concerned about an address in Albuquerque to Rio Grande farmers on conservancy, "a subject full of dynamite." Cutting hoped he could confine his remarks to his congressional bill calling for the approval of the compact signed on February 12 in Santa Fe. The accord authorized funding for the construction of a drainage channel and for locating a reservoir site both in the San Luis Valley. The Reclamation Service angered proponents of the plan. Although the service endorsed the drainage channel, it opposed locating a reservoir in the valley. In addition, Cutting was worried that Francis Wilson's recent endorsement of the administration's oil policy would necessitate his responding against it during the summer recess.[15]

Cutting relaxed in the New Mexico mountains and attended "the big Santiago fiesta at Tierra Amarilla." He visited with the Spanish ambassador, Don Alejandro Padilla, who at the end of July stopped in Santa Fe enroute to Washington from San Diego. During the entire recess, he underwent "the torments of the damned from hay fever," which brought in its wake the "intense inflammation of the eyelids."[16]

Spending the summer in Santa Fe brought him into close contact with Mary Austin. As she had done before, she sought his support for Hispanic and Indian causes in New Mexico. She hoped that he could examine "the Mexican problem north of the border" in an article for a special issue of *Survey-Graphic*. Although Cutting did not accept her invitation, he did agree to talk with her about it and other matters when he returned from his trip to the northern part of the state. During his travels, Cutting was greatly distressed to learn of the murder of "one of my best friends, in fact my chief lieutenant in northern Santa Fe county." Although he tried to initiate an investigation, "the alibis were so cleverly laid" that he was sure the whole affair would be dropped.[17]

In August, he served as a pall bearer at the funeral of "the last of the old-time native leaders," Secundino Romero in Las Vegas and Frank Hubbell in Albuquerque, who died within a week of each other. They were devoted supporters of Cutting, his "only friends among the 'old guard.'" Their passing, he believed, strengthened the opposition. Their deaths served to remind him that the political situation in New Mexico was his most pressing concern.[18]

An exposé in the *Albuquerque Journal* reinforced this perception. The *Journal* began "an exposure of appalling graft and corruption in the Highway Department." Cutting could not believe the lack of decisive action from Governor Dillon. By failing to remove Frank Springer and other key officials, the governor displayed "the same lack of resolution that he manifested during the Legislature." When the governor chose to focus on Springer's subordinates, Cutting exclaimed, "It is a pity there is so little backbone in public life." Cutting shifted his attention from the fortunes of the Republican party to those of families along the Rio Grande. In August, the river flooded and wiped out several villages, inundating and threatening others, leaving hundreds homeless and destitute. Cutting immediately called for assistance. Before he left for Washington, he attended the annual convention of the New Mexico American Legion in Las Cruces, all the time complaining about the intense heat and hoping that "Washington will have cooled off."[19]

Cutting returned to the seemingly interminable tariff debate. While he carefully followed the tariff issues, he seemed "somewhat uncertain as to what action should be taken in protecting our own sugar beet industry in this country against the Philippines," according to a visitor. At the time, Cutting was in the process of preparing a measure that called for Philippine independence.[20]

On one dimension of the tariff debate, Cutting came to the national forefront. During the summer, while in Santa Fe, Cutting denounced the Customs Bureau for barring the entry of Erich Maria Remarque's novel, *All Quiet on the Western Front*. The bureau deemed the contents obscene. The ruling served to draw attention, Cutting said, "to the danger and folly of giving customs officers the right to dictate what the American people may or may not read." The source of their authority was an obscure provision, Section 305, of the prevailing tariff. The House version of the tariff measure under consideration in the Senate extended the provision to include seditious and insurrectionary, as well as obscene, literature. In the past, Cutting said, Section 305 had been enforced "with comparative common sense," but over the years the Customs Bureau had blacklisted "many of the most famous works of ancient and modern literature" because "in some mysterious way" they might be "detrimental to American morals." Unfortunately, Cutting noted, "The federal courts invariably have backed up the bureau in its preposterous ruling."

On the senate floor, Cutting opposed the extension of Section 305 by the Customs Bureau and the House of Representatives. He argued that "the way to deal with subversive literature is not by suppression, but by complete exposure, and, if necessary, by refutation." He doubted whether censorship had ever proven itself beneficial to public morals. "To decide what an intelligent adult may read," Cutting concluded, "is a task for a superman, and supermen are not apt to be found in the poorly paid Bureau of Customs."[21] Resuming the senate fight in October, Cutting expressed his fear that an enlarged Section 305 would cut off the American people from European literary culture. Cutting inserted in the *Congressional Record* a statement by Zechariah Chafee, a distinguished Harvard Law School professor. Regarding the effect of Section 305 on students and others seeking an understanding of the Russian Revolution, Chafee wrote, "This law is a kindergarten measure which assumes that the American people are so stupid and so untrustworthy that it is unsafe to let them read anything about revolution because they would immediately become converted." Cutting noted that the term *obscene* was impossible to define and to agree on. He cited the incongruities in the recently compiled customs list of 739 books. More than half were in editions other than English and were considered unfit for Americans to read. He redirected the debate from the question of immorality and obscenity to whether Congress should continue to delegate to customs clerks guardianship over the minds of the American people.

Cutting held the floor for the better part of two days. On October 11, the Senate accepted Cutting's amendment opposing the inclusion of Section 305 in the tariff bill by two votes. His opponents cast him and his supporters in the role of pandering obscene literature and of sympathizing with seditious ideas. Cutting's supporters, on the other hand, contended that censorship at customs houses was unsound in principle and oppressive in practice. The final vote of 38 yeas, 36 nays and 21 abstentions crossed party lines. Senators voted their convictions more so than their constituencies.[22]

While Cutting's fight brought him national attention, it received only limited response from New Mexico. He was greatly pleased, however, that the State Federation of Labor unanimously endorsed his strong support for organized labor. The strength of the endorsement reassured Cutting that his fight for a state labor commission had considerably broadened his political base and that the recent scandals in the state Highway Department would only enlarge it. He believed that "the native people" now were "pretty well" aware that Frank Springer, the highway commissioner and the power behind the governor, was unsympathetic to their needs and interests.[23]

Nevertheless, the exasperatingly slow tariff debate consumed Cutting's time and attention. Although he again took little part in the discussions, he was now constantly alert to schedules that affected his constituency. Along with other western senators, Cutting was opposed to any "reduction in our wool protection" and hoped a strong schedule would be in place before the end of the year. At the end of November, he was able to wire Governor Dillon, a former sheep rancher, that the Senate voted for a thirty-four cent duty on wool, three cents more than the Senate Finance Committee proposed. The 44-to-26 vote guaranteed that there would be no contention of this schedule in conference since the house measure contained the same duty on wool.[24]

During the tariff debate, Cutting reinforced his long-standing friendship with the Fall family. At the request of Albert Fall's wife, he responded to Senator Thomas Heflin's charges against Fall. On the senate floor, Heflin stated that during a visit to an ill President Woodrow Wilson in 1919, Fall pulled the covers from Wilson's bed to see the president's condition for himself despite the protests of an attending doctor. To discredit Heflin, Cutting cited the statements of Admiral Cary Grayson, the personal physician of President Wilson, and that of Senator Gilbert M. Hitchcock, both present with Fall in the room. According to both men, Fall did nothing more than shake hands with the president. Grayson stated that Heflin was not one of the senators who visited the president that day. Cutting laid to rest an ugly rumor.[25]

Cutting also kept an eye on the negotiations for the Rio Grande Compact. According to newspaper sources, the state delegation agreed that the entire appropriation for the drainage channel and reservoir should be spent in Colorado as compensation for the development of the San Luis Valley, which was located largely in New Mexico. Cutting wired Francis Wilson, a commissioner who helped to draft the compact, for clarification.[26]

Wilson implied that there was a misunderstanding. If Congress approved the compact, it would not necessarily legislate an appropriation for the drainage channel and reservoir. Cutting had read press accounts by Colorado developers who wanted to secure as much Rio Grande water as possible to the detriment of users in both New Mexico and Texas. They wanted federal funds spent in their state to compensate for the federal appropriations that built Elephant Butte Dam in New Mexico. The Rio Grande Compact would in effect postpone the financial matters until the drainage channel was constructed and a dam site could be agreed upon. Wilson further explained that the delay afforded by the compact would provide time for the development of the Middle Rio Grande Conservancy District, which could remedy some of the state's water problems and also put New Mexico in better shape "to litigate our rights as against the rights in Colorado than we are now." New Mexico wanted to insure that Colorado did not deplete the flow of the Rio Grande during the five-year life of the compact. The drainage channel was a mere sop to Colorado. Once the compact was ratified and confirmed by Congress, the appropriation for the drainage channel could receive attention.[27]

Mary Austin also pressed Cutting to support her projects in New Mexico. She remarked to a close friend, soon after Cutting was appointed United States senator, that she had "made a coalition with him." They would work together "on our various schemes for the good of the community." In early

December 1929, as she arranged for her annual lecture trip, she related some of her plans to Cutting "so that we may continue to work together harmoniously." She was interested in gathering information about Indian dances and "the pattern of the Spanish Arts in New Mexico." She also was seeking funds to purchase "the beautiful—and the oldest—triptych of the creation, from the old convento at Tesuque" so that it would not leave the state. In addition, she was continually on the lookout for "authentic versions" of old Spanish plays. She hoped that Santa Fe would construct a public hall "for the use of the Spanish people for a reasonable sum."[28]

Cutting had already provided her with funds for her various cultural affairs. He was always pleased with her endeavors and ready to be of assistance. He was equally pleased when Austin selected him as a trustee for the association she organized to preserve and restore Hispanic culture in New Mexico. Cutting invariably was sympathetic to her efforts to assist Indians and Hispanic peoples in exploring their cultural heritage and their history.[29]

Shortly before the Senate recessed for the holidays, it considered a resolution offered by George W. Norris to deny William S. Vare of Pennsylvania a seat in the chamber. Cutting's maiden speech in the Senate two years earlier had been devoted to endorsing Frank L. Smith of Illinois, whose election was challenged on the grounds of excessive expenditures. In this instance, however, Cutting said that he would support the resolution offered by the senator from Nebraska on the grounds of fraud and corruption. He insisted that he was not voting for the resolution "on the ground that the amount of money spent by Mr. Vare was ipso facto a ground for reversing the decision made at the polls by the people of Pennsylvania." As he had argued earlier, a duty of Congress was to generate clear standards for proper campaign expenditures. While he preferred the public financing of elections, Cutting recognized that such a proposal was ahead of its time. In the meantime, he would merely call for congressional limits on election expenditures. Cutting agreed that Vare's election was fraudulent and thus invalid. He noted chain voting, registration by mark without affidavits, the use of unregistered voters, repeaters, and dead men, the excess of ballots cast over listed voters, and numerous other violations in Vare's election victory. He could not vote to seat William S. Vare as the victor in the 1926 Pennsylvania election.[30]

Among the final items in the session, Cutting endorsed and the Senate promptly accepted a joint resolution calling for the relief of flood victims in areas overflowed by the Rio Grande in New Mexico during the late summer. The Department of Agriculture would conduct the work and would secure a first lien on crops for the assistance, which could not exceed one thousand dollars per person. During these hectic days, Cutting had "requests from a number of people, all good and loyal personal friends, amounting altogether to nearly $70,000."[31]

Requests for financial aid from friends and supporters were a fact of life throughout Cutting's senatorial career. In many instances he opened his purse to them. But the pressure of business during the session turned Cutting away from individual requests. That he was exhausted and yearned for the rarefied atmosphere of Santa Fe helped account for his turning down the plea of former territorial governor Miguel Antonio Otero, although Cutting usually was receptive. In later years, he would comply with almost all of the former governor's pleas for assistance. Otero was perhaps Cutting's oldest friend in New Mexico. He was a progressive and consistent supporter. He had guided Cutting and his family through the intricacies of the social and political scene in New Mexico. Gradually, his advice and suggestions proved irrelevant to Cutting, and Otero, continually down on his luck, became a supplicant, who, while he might have bored Cutting, usually received a sympathetic response.

As soon as the Senate recessed, Cutting fled to Santa Fe, where his spirits and health rebounded. "This air," he wrote at year's end, "is doing me so much good that I should like to store up as much as possible to last through the dreary months of February and March." He enjoyed Christmas with Brian Boru Dunne and his children at Los Siete Burros. Dunne's wife, who was seeking a divorce, was not present. Dunne undoubtedly briefed Cutting on developments, both personal and political, occurring during his absence.[32]

By any standard, 1929 was momentous for Cutting. His harmonious relationship with Governor Richard Dillon underwent a serious disruption that put them at odds. Cutting became a disgruntled Republican, the leader of a powerful and growing faction within the party. His following included labor, Hispanics, veterans, and progressive-minded citizens and independent voters. Cutting's place in New Mexico at this time was carefully noted by Clyde Tingley, the Democratic mayor of Albuquerque. In a letter to Franklin D. Roosevelt, the governor of New York, he wrote, "There is a fight in the Republican ranks for control of the party between Senator Bronson M. Cutting and the so-called old guard." Cutting's political following, Tingley continued, was largely "among the native people" and among those Democrats who left the party "during the Al Smith campaign." Another of the New York governor's correspondents from New Mexico informed him that "our state administration is the weakest and most vicious the state has known in 20 years or more. . . ."[33]

Disgruntled Republican

Though he was at odds with Republican party leaders in New Mexico, he was in good standing with his party in Washington, voting on occasion with the progressive group. In the Senate, Cutting was an independent-minded member of ability and integrity. He stated or defended his positions with clarity, logic and intelligence. Nevertheless, owing to the tedium of the session and the state of affairs in New Mexico, Cutting remained a disgruntled Republican, who faced a showdown with the party at the 1930 state nominating conventions. Cutting did not relish the prospect of a gubernatorial campaign that could pit him directly against Dillon, Springer, and the old guard in the party.

CHAPTER 15

STILL DISGRUNTLED

While Cutting was resting in Santa Fe, his secretary, Edgar Puryear, was planning the fall campaign from Washington and thinking of a way "to eliminate Dillon" through a federal appointment. Mrs. E. A. Perrault, the secretary of state and a Cutting supporter, would succeed him. Then Puryear exclaimed, "We could 'clean house.'" Of course, Dillon would have to accept the proposal and Cutting would have to involve himself in the election of a ticket with some of "the Republican mistakes." Puryear had doubts about his scenario, but thought Cutting, if he was not too busy, might investigate the proposition.[1]

Puryear's scheme was more than a political fantasy. He was asked to confer with Senator George H. Moses, senate majority leader, about the New Mexico situation. Moses claimed that he was Cutting's best friend in the Senate. According to Puryear, the senator was "scared to death about the situation" in New Mexico and recognized that Cutting was "the one man" who controlled it. Without Cutting's support, Moses believed, the Republican cause in the state would be hopeless. So impressed with Cutting's political power was Moses that he related his understanding of it to the president and the post master general. Puryear related that Moses intended to visit New Mexico and offer Governor Dillon an appointment, thereby eliminating him from the political scene. Moses wanted to see Cutting "in complete control."

Puryear's scenario was now beginning to appear less fantastic, but he foresaw a dangerous price if Moses succeeded with his plan. Cutting "would be placed in a position of electing the ticket and carrying the burden of dozens of Republican mistakes," something Puryear did not believe possible. George Moses, as majority leader in the Senate, insisted that Cutting's control of the state's party would guarantee a Republican replacement for Sam Bratton, Cutting's Democratic colleague, and would compensate for "several losses elsewhere." Moses was concerned that the Republican party would pay for the bleak economic aftermath of the stock market crash by losing control of the United States Senate. To Puryear, however, the assessment of the New Hampshire senator still bordered on the fringe of fantasy.[2]

Meanwhile, Cutting postponed his return to Washington. The Senate had taken up the sugar schedule, the rates of which affected his constituency in no direct way. In early January 1930, Hoover sent to the Senate the name of

A. M. Bergere for reappointment as registrar of lands in New Mexico, without consulting Cutting. He had angered the administration by voting against the appointment of Joseph Grundy to replace William S. Vare as the senator from Pennsylvania. Although Cutting had no intention of opposing Bergere's appointment, he would realign himself closer to the progressive Republican members of the Senate.[3]

Back in Washington by mid-February, Cutting rejoined the tariff debate. Endorsing a tariff on oil, he won the plaudits of oilmen and others worried about the effects of overproduction. In eastern New Mexico, the development of new wells had practically ceased, and some producing wells were shut down. The demand for petroleum did not warrant the construction of a pipeline to carry the product to national markets. As long as overproduction prevailed, the oil industry in New Mexico would suffer. Moreover, the United States imported one hundred million barrels of crude and ten million barrels of refined oil from Mexico, Venezuela and Columbia in 1929 and thus hurt American producers, especially independent operators and small companies that flourished in New Mexico. Some producing wells went to water and were no longer able to produce oil when they were shut down.

Cutting believed that shutting off the flow of foreign oil would not resolve the difficulties of producers in New Mexico and elsewhere but was a first step in developing a more rational system of production. Interested parties could then negotiate production quotas based on national need. Such interstate agreements would allow for orderly development of the industry in New Mexico. Unfortunately, as Cutting explained, "we lost out on the oil tariff," largely because unsavory revelations about "the oil lobby and the general trade" had come out just before the vote. The best that could happen, Cutting thought, would be a reconsideration of the schedule before a final vote occurred later in the session.[4]

In early March, Senator Harry Hawes and Cutting jointly authored a bill on Philippine Independence. Introducing the bill in the Senate, Hawes requested that it be referred to the Committee on Territories and Insular Affairs, on which both senators served. Hawes and Cutting, a Democrat and a Republican respectively, hoped to avoid partisanship and to discuss Philippine independence upon its merits. In his introductory remarks, Hawes said that the measure would satisfy neither those desirous of "immediate and unqualified" independence nor those who desired a tariff upon the imports and exports of the islands prior to a transition period under American sovereignty.

The measure provided for the submission of a constitution to the Philippine people and for its subsequent submission to the Congress of the United

States for approval or disapproval. It provided for the assumption of financial obligations by the Philippine government and called upon that government to protect religious liberty and to maintain a school system conducted in the English language. A transition period of five years, accompanied by the gradual cessation of the prevailing free-trade relations, would provide the people of the Philippine Islands "an actual practical demonstration" of the cost and other responsibilities of freedom and would give them an opportunity to change their minds.[5]

The bill went to the Committee on Territories and Insular Affairs where Hawes and Cutting listened to a long list of witnesses: representatives of the federal government and the Philippine people; economists; businessmen with interests in the Philippines; and others. After listening to testimony that filled nearly seven hundred pages, the committee favorably reported on the Hawes-Cutting bill to the Senate in early June. Both senators submitted extensive reports endorsing the measure. Hiram Bingham submitted an equally extensive minority report. But no vote was taken during the remainder of the Seventy-first Congress.[6]

Although Cutting endorsed the measure, Hawes was the chief spokesman for the bill. He plugged, explained, and defended it to his colleagues and the public. The debate over Philippine independence, like the tariff debate, became a protracted, tedious affair that tested Cutting's patience.

Meanwhile Cutting's opposition to Section 305 of the tariff bill, empowering customs officers to seize obscene or seditious printed imports, attracted additional attention. On February 15, Poets, Essayists, and Novelists (PEN), an international organization of poets, playwrights, essayists and novelists, honored Cutting at the National Arts Club in New York. At about the same time, one of Cutting's friends in Taos, Willard H. (Spud) Johnson, devoted the February issue of his magazine, *The Laughing Horse,* to "A Symposium of Criticism, Comment and Opinion on the Subject of Censorship," a copy of which went to every member of the Senate. All twenty-nine contributors endorsed Cutting's opposition and congratulated the Senate for its approval of his amendment to the controversial section. In *Poetry* magazine, Ezra Pound expressed "by all means *et de tout mon coeur*" his thanks, noting that "Cutting has put New Mexico on the map."[7]

Buoyed by this support, Cutting fought the issue of customs censorship once again when the tariff bill came before the Senate for final action. He presented a petition, signed by more than five hundred ministers, librarians, authors, educators, editors and other intellectual leaders, that protested the system of censorship by customs inspectors. Although the Senate, sitting as the Committee of the Whole, had already approved a Cutting amendment that drastically modified Section 305, it had not yet formally adopted it. In vigorous opposition to Cutting, Senator Reed Smoot denounced *Lady Chatterly's Lover* by D. H. Lawrence as a novel that customs officials should deny admission. The secretary of the treasury should have the authority, he proposed, to admit the "so called classics" for noncommercial purposes only. The Senate voted down Smoot's proposal. Regaining the floor to defend his amendment, Cutting noted that "the attempt to suppress individual books simply promotes their circulation and reputation." Throughout this discussion, Cutting revealed his erudition in classical and modern literature. In addition, he mercilessly took to task Smoot's vilifying remarks that made D. H. Lawrence's novel a classic along with similar "grossly indecent" plays by Shakespeare, such as *King Lear, Hamlet,* and *Romeo and Juliet.* According to Smoot, reading one page of Lawrence's novel sufficiently indicated that it was disgusting, dirty and vile and ought to be denied entrance to the country. Cutting observed, "The courts of the United States say that the reading of one page is not sufficient, and that the book must be read as a whole." "The passage of a law," Cutting added, "does not necessarily abolish the evil which the law is meant to correct." Indeed, in many instances, it had exactly the opposite effect.

Since the Senate already had debated and voted on his amendment after "a complete and sane deliberation which lasted the better part of two days," Cutting had no desire "to reiterate or rehearse" previous arguments. Nevertheless, Cutting continued to discuss the matter. He read excerpts from his extensive mail and from newspaper articles and exhibited volumes, secured from the Library of Congress, that were banned by customs officials. After he concluded his arguments, his colleagues went on with the discussion. Finally, Cutting's views won the day. Section 305 was again modified, this time in the final version of the bill, to limit censorship of imported literature by customs officials, who henceforth would have to submit suspect books to the federal courts.[8]

Although he prevailed on the issue of censorship, Cutting was distressed that the Senate had had to reconsider the matter and worried that it might reverse itself as it did on the sugar and cement sections of the tariff bill. The tariff sessions were so demanding that Cutting found little time for anything else. He did meet Arturo Toscanini, the famed conductor, at the Italian Embassy "and came within an ace of missing the vote on sugar!" He concluded that he could not stay away from the senate chamber for any length of time because "every rate set with so much care and trouble in the Committee of the Whole is now being torn to pieces in the Senate." Extreme protection-ism, he felt, was "completely in the saddle—thanks to the treachery of some of our Democratic friends." It seemed "a pity to have spent so much effort over nothing at all." Cutting now admitted that he was returning to the low opinion of the Senate "which I always held in private life."[9]

Cutting's stature rose enormously in some quarters. Henry Seidel Canby, a leading literary critic, praised Cutting for having kept the subject of censor-ship on such intelligent grounds. Others were delighted to find a senator who could discuss books "as literary people discuss them." Some who attended the PEN dinner applauded his speech and remarked on his handsome appearance. Mary Austin added that in her lifetime, "there have not only been no Sena-tors, but only two Presidents who could" discuss literature intelligently.[10]

The Easter recess allowed Cutting a chance to buoy his spirits in Santa Fe. Fighting "an attack of hay fever," he briefed himself on the political situation and had a long talk with Clara Olsen. In general, he found that "nearly everybody's sore and bitter beyond the ordinary limits of even New Mexico politics." He could not see his old friend, Arthur Seligman, Democratic state chairman and possible candidate for governor, who was ill with the flu, but he did call on other politicians during the brief recess. In all, he kept "fairly well out of the political maelstrom" and despite "the troubles of many friends," had a good rest "from the Washington sort of things."[11]

While Cutting took a vacation from the political scene in New Mexico, other politicians were plotting to garner his support in the upcoming state election. New Mexico congressman Albert Simms held discussions with Governor Dillon, who would most likely oppose Sam Bratton, the Demo-cratic incumbent, for the Senate. Dillon thought "it would be a mistake to remove Senator Bratton by presidential appointment" from the forthcoming campaign. The governor feared that Arthur Seligman would then become the Democratic candidate. Cutting's "long standing friendly relations" with Se-ligman would guarantee his support for the Democratic nominee. Simms concluded that Dillon could probably defeat Bratton with Cutting's help.[12]

Back in Washington, Cutting involved himself in the debate to tighten immigration restrictions, an issue that was important to every southwestern state, he believed. Under consideration was a bill that would extend the quota system to the countries of the Western Hemisphere. Under the prevailing system, the State Department negotiated immigration quotas with the Mexi-can government. Although Cutting supported the principle of immigration restriction, he opposed an amendment that would admit immigrants seeking farm work after an employer informed the secretary of labor of his need for field hands. If the federal government could enforce the provisions, it would place the immigrant "under a state of peonage." Cutting believed that the measure was unenforceable and would open the gates wider for Mexican immigrants to enter the country. Once a laborer entered the country under the proposed amendment, Cutting said, "we no longer have any hold on him at all."

Cutting was not unsympathetic toward Mexico. He praised the virtues of its people, but at the same time, he insisted that unrestricted immigration was in the permanent interest of neither the Mexican nor the American people. Border-state citizens suffered from the influx of Mexican immigration, the crux of Cutting's opposition to the proposed amendment. Mexican immigrant and New Mexican Hispanic labor competed for jobs "in the beet fields, in the cotton fields, and in other industries in the Southwest and the Western States." Hispanic citizens wished to labor under "an American wage scale," that Mexican immigrant competition undermined. Cutting was convinced the proposed amendment would only exacerbate the situation, and if the measure could be enforced, it would legalize a system of peonage. Cutting envisioned that Mexico would have a tremendous need for manual labor in its developing industries once its political conditions stabilized. By a two-vote margin, 32 to 34, the amendment was defeated and Cutting prevailed. [13]

Cutting was immensely satisfied when the Senate turned down the nomination of Federal District Court justice John J. Parker for a seat on the Supreme Court by a vote of 39 to 41. Although he did not participate in the debate, he considered the defeat of Parker "our one big victory," indicating that he now was part of the small group of progressives who opposed much of what the Hoover administration proposed. After finishing Senate business, he relaxed with music and attended the concert of the distinguished black vocalist, Roland Hayes. Even more enjoyable was the play, *Abie's Irish Rose,* which was "rather graceful in a naive folk-lorish sort of way." [14]

On May 24, he attended the services honoring John Campbell Greenway in Statuary Hall at the Capitol. A likeness prepared by Gutzon Borglum, the notable American sculptor, was placed in the rotunda representing Arizona. Greenway's widow, Isabella, was a childhood friend upon whom Cutting's father had bestowed a bequest of one hundred dollars per month. She recalled that the gift helped enormously "when our margin was small and our burdens many." [15]

In late June during the last weeks of the session, the Senate took up a veterans bill of utmost concern to Cutting. The legislation provided veterans an allowance for any permanent disability acquired outside military service. It was, as Katherine Mayo remarked, "a free sickness-insurance policy." Both the House of Representatives and the Senate approved the bill by a lopsided vote. In a lengthy message on June 26, Hoover vetoed the legislation. The House of Representatives sustained him. Following the veto message and a White House conference, congressional leaders introduced and approved a new disability-allowance measure. Under this bill, a claimant must have been exempt from federal income tax in the year prior to filing for a pension and could not have contracted the ailment by willful misconduct.[16]

On June 21, Hoover wrote Senator James E. Watson that the expenditures in the bill would create "grave inequalities, injustices, and discriminations among veterans. . . ." To Cutting the bill was a means of providing assistance to veterans suffering illness and debilitation in a depression-ridden economy. The president's "smug" remarks filled Cutting with indignation, those of General Frank T. Hines, administrator of the Veterans Bureau and Hoover's source of information, were "even worse, because Hines knows better and is deliberately trying to deceive the public. . . ." In Cutting's eyes, Hoover was just plain "ignorant" like "the general public" about the "disabled today." The indignant senator was bewildered by such apathy "in a professional humanitarian."[17]

Cutting was silent during the debate prior to Hoover's expressed opposition to the disability measure. On June 23, his forty-second birthday, he spoke out against the Veterans Bureau's arbitrary classifications that had excluded many New Mexico veterans from pension eligibility. Expressing his disillusionment with Herbert Hoover, Cutting lamented, "I think he has been misled, but his great personal reputation, as well as his high office, would seem to require that, even though misled, he do [sic] not mislead the people of the United States." Although Cutting heard "no conscious misstatements" in Hoover's press conference on June 24, the senator said the president's statements were "full of error," misleading and inaccurate to anyone "who has been engaged in work for the disabled."

Although Cutting believed in economy, he did not think "that the tax payers of the country believe in economy at the expense of the disabled veterans." If anything, the federal government could save dollars reorganizing the bureaucracy of the Veterans Bureau. Tubercular veterans were frequently summoned to local offices of the Veterans Bureau for medical reexamination and pension review. Now, Cutting was afraid that the president had lulled the press and the public into believing the government generously provided for the disabled veterans and Congress had enacted "just bad legislation." Cutting expressed extreme disillusionment in his concluding remarks on June 26: "I can only say that upon the President and any Members of the House who vote to sustain his veto will rest the responsibility for the lives of those innocent men who gave all that they had in order that the Nation might be preserved."[18]

To sustain his veto, the president persuaded a substantial number of House Republicans to accept a weaker and less expensive disability allowance bill. When the watered-down measure came before the Senate on July 1, Cutting reviewed what he called "the close of a chapter in veterans' legislation." "Owing to the stubbornness, the lack of generosity, and the pettifoggery" evident in administering the laws, Congress had had to amend and modify them continually. Now Cutting said, "Within the past week we have changed all that."

He argued that the president had vetoed "the soundest, the most just, the most carefully considered measure of veterans' relief which has ever been passed by Congress." Adding to his disillusionment were his congressional colleagues who had overwhelmingly approved the original measure but were now accepting a weak administration bill without any serious debate. Cutting reviewed the thirteen-year-old system of handling disabilities. One theory predicated compensation on the principle of service disability. The other, "the so-called pension or gratuity theory," called for assisting disabled ex-servicemen "on an exact equality with those who were similarly injured in action." Both theories had been approved by Congress, upheld by various attorneys general and the comptroller general, and sanctioned in Treasury Department rulings. However, the Veterans Bureau either disregarded, mal-administered, or narrowly interpreted legislation and thereby necessitated further congressional action—all at the expense of disabled veterans. Cutting sprinkled his remarks with asides to the problems of veterans in New Mexico and to his own exposure to the plight of disabled veterans. In what must have been a painful moment, he criticized the American Legion's changing attitudes toward pensions and its failure to lobby for the original disability measure.

According to Cutting, the president, the Veterans Bureau and the American Legion would be evading their responsibility to disabled veterans if Congress approved the president's measure. Hoover's bill would alter the system established in 1917 by applying a means test, narrowly defining services, and markedly reducing compensation rates offered to disabled veterans. Cutting queried, "How can we expect to go before the people of the United States and justify any such action?"[19]

Cutting held the floor longer and spoke more extensively during this debate than on any previous occasion. A disgruntled Republican, he was at odds with the Hoover administration in Washington and the Dillon administration in New Mexico. Yet in both New Mexico and in the Congress, Cutting believed he was espousing the views of his constituency.

Shortly after approving the veterans measure, Congress adjourned the session on July 3. Cutting immediately headed for the family estate on Long Island and then departed for a European vacation. While he recovered from the long, arduous session, he would sequester himself from candidates seeking nomination in New Mexico. Although he would endorse no statewide candidates for reasons of propriety, friends and supporters could line up behind political hopefuls. He reiterated his view that "state conventions should not be dominated by national office holders." He explained, "A rest means for me a complete cessation of political activity."[20]

During and after the Congressional session, Cutting made several substantial contributions. He gave ten thousand dollars to the University of New Mexico for the establishment of a demonstration-project school devoted to the education of Hispanic children. A member of its advisory committee, he recommended Mary Austin for membership "in addition to the Spanish-American names" he had previously submitted.[21] Prior to boarding the *Ile de France* with his mother on July 11, Cutting contributed to Philip La Follette's campaign for governor in Wisconsin and to George Norris's reelection campaign in Nebraska.

After Cutting and his mother traveled to Paris, he went to Munich, Germany, and she to Italy. According to Cutting, the Germans were hardly "cocky and arrogant and preparing to reconquer the earth." Instead they were "crushed and underfed and depressed (and also depressing)." The food was vile "and good Rhine wine prohibitive in price." Looking on the bright side of a rainy vacation, Cutting enjoyed "good pictures and music, and an occasional good piece of Romanesque or Baroque architecture." On occasion, he indulged in a good bottle of Rhine wine.[22]

From Munich, Cutting went to Berlin, where he met Senator Burton K. Wheeler. Along with another colleague, Alben Barkley, they accompanied a tour to the Soviet Union. Although neither Cutting nor Barkley publicly expressed their views about what they saw in Communist Russia, Wheeler provided a brief account in his autobiography. The group toured rural areas, observed some cooperative farms, visited with several high-ranking officials, coped with bed bugs and met with Russian workers. They saw as much as they possibly could in a guided tour lasting about three weeks. A member of the group later recalled that Cutting observed everything but said very little. He sought to "grasp this new and different culture."[23]

At some point on this tour, the three senators and others accompanied Albert Rhys Williams, a Soviet specialist, on a trip into the rolling plains of Vladimir, some hundred miles east of Moscow. The rough roads "battered, pitched and tossed" the party, and the cars broke down. Under a boiling sun, the group "hauled them out of muck holes, pushed them up long hills, and poured endless buckets of water into the radiators leaking at every seam." In some of the villages they visited, the peasants gazed in awe at the automobiles and Americans, the first they had ever seen. Some old women "violently crossing themselves fled into their houses crying out that we were Anti-Christs."

Cutting most likely was able to converse in German with some of the collective farmers. He was interested in comparing the old and new ways of farming. In one field, he saw women bent over reaping rye with a sickle, while in another, he witnessed a mower cutting the crop in clean, wide swaths. In one instance, a peasant family would beat out the grain "with flails winnowing it with the wind; on a collective farm a thresher with a stream of grain flowing from its chute, and the flying straw piling up into stacks." During their three weeks in the Soviet Union, the senators gained an insight into Soviet agriculture, the old and the new. The new methods were slowly supplanting the old ways and promised a release from isolation and insecurity for millions of peasants into a collectivized order of mutual aid and dependence.[24]

From Dresden, Germany in late August, Cutting exclaimed, "It is delightful to get out of Russia in spite of the interest of Moscow and especially of the peasant villages." He had visited more than 150 of them. While he had no intention of fully analyzing his observations at this time, his impression of the Soviet Union was "that the present system will pull through its troubles" and last "a good long time." Devastating droughts or even excessive prosperity might cause serious problems, but Cutting believed, "The organization, and more especially the spirit and enthusiasm are superb and ought to see them through." On the other hand, he noted the lack of freedom, the general discomfort and poor diet prevailing throughout the country. He was glad to be in Germany, where Berlin appeared to him "strangely neat and dignified and luxurious."[25]

In a letter to Mary Austin who had just returned from a trip to Mexico, Cutting said that Russia was "enormously important and absorbing" but that the cultural manifestations of the Mexican Revolution might eventually mean more to the world. Referring to the Marxist-Leninist revolution in Russia, he doubted "whether the worship of smokestacks and tractors can furnish, by itself, a permanently satisfactory faith for suffering humanity." However, for the next half century, Cutting said, the United States had best "look out for the Soviets and what they will do!"[26]

On August 30, he dined at the American embassy in Berlin with Ambassador and Mrs. Frederick Sackett and the head of the Russian branch of the State Department. Since Cutting believed nonrecognition of the Soviet Union was "hurting no one but ourselves," he hoped his fellow guest would not be "too set in his ways." Thereafter, he departed for Paris with a possible stopover in Antwerp to see an exhibition of Flemish art. He expected to arrive in London about September 9. He wanted to be in New York before the New Mexico Republican Convention opened on the twenty-third. Since he did not plan to attend the political gathering, he wanted to conceal his whereabouts. Meanwhile his mail accumulated in New York, at Morgan-Harjes in Paris and elsewhere. Aside from brief letters to his mother and a few friends, Cutting had written nothing since entering the Soviet Union in early August.[27]

When he sailed for New York, Cutting's strategy was to remain aloof above the battle. He found little to support in Governor Dillon's administration. His silence alone would inform his friends and supporters that he did not endorse the Republican state ticket in 1930. Yet some Republicans felt optimistic about the fall election. According to Congressman Albert Simms, the state was not experiencing drought and was enjoying "a fair degree of prosperity." Simms believed that Governor Dillon would receive the senatorial nomination and stood a good chance of defeating Sam Bratton, who would be seeking a second term. Simms also anticipated that Cutting would support the ticket. "Goodness knows," he added, "we need his regularity in our state where we would, if he were regular, never have any political problems."[28]

Edgar Puryear, Cutting's secretary, disagreed. Early in September, he wrote Cutting that "the state looks more and more Democratic" and that key Republican leaders recognized that "the fate of all candidates in New Mexico rests with you." Several county conventions, including the Democratic one in Albuquerque, had praised him and most every paper in the state appeared "very friendly." Puryear facetiously wrote about the persistent Dr. Boggs "who awaits with all tenderness, and fond anticipation, full of her generous, and abundant love your early home coming." Puryear sent the letter and a stack of clippings to a cable address, not knowing Cutting's exact whereabouts, to brief him before he returned to New Mexico.[29]

To everyone's surprise at the New Mexico Republican convention, Governor Dillon refused the senatorial nomination, although, according to an observer, he could have had it by acclamation. The Republican party selected state senator H. B. Holt to oppose Senator Sam Bratton and Judge C. M. Botts of Albuquerque to oppose Arthur Seligman, a Santa Fe banker and longtime Cutting friend, in the governor's race.[30]

By the first of October, Cutting was at Westbrook briefing himself on the New Mexico political scene. He intended to make no declaration of support for the Republican state ticket. H. B. Holt and others suggested that Cutting attend to the duties of his office in Washington. New Mexico Republicans wanted him removed from the state unless he actively supported the party ticket. Prior to his departure for Santa Fe from Washington, he found Republican leaders "as evasive as all the others who are close to the White House" about his few patronage requests. Their evasive behavior convinced Cutting that "it may be as well to be on the outside." He told Robert M. La Follette, Jr., that "between a rotten Republican state ticket and a fairly good Democratic one, I am trying to maintain a dignified silence."[31]

The political race in 1930 brought Cutting some surprises. His close friend and associate, Jesus Baca, was nominated for sheriff of Santa Fe County, and then his Democratic opponent dropped out of the race. About the same time, two Republican senators, George Moses of New Hampshire and Frederick Steiwer of Oregon, visited Cutting in Santa Fe. Steiwer, in charge of the western Republican campaign, certainly had reason to be in New Mexico. However, both Cutting and Steiwer resented the intrusion of Moses. During dinner at Los Siete Burros, Moses offered Cutting the post of secretary of the interior, suggesting that Ray Lyman Wilbur would be released from the office, if Cutting would come out for the state ticket. When Cutting was evasive, Moses promised him the sum allocated to New Mexico for the senatorial election. When Moses asked Cutting to endorse Holt on the third day, he offered Cutting the choice of an ambassadorship or the vice-presidential nomination in 1932. In Cutting's mind, Moses's incredible offers indicated his fear, and possibly that of the Hoover administration, that the forthcoming election would either weaken or lose the Republicans' precarious hold on the Senate. Cutting did not see "how Holt can beat Bratton." Although he was puzzled by the visit of George Moses, he finally concluded that Moses "was no doubt told to feel out and see what looked attractive to me."[32]

By sitting out the election, Cutting reinforced his controversial reputation. When the Democratic party won a stunning victory, Cutting was denounced as a traitor in some circles. Some observers suggested that the broken pledges, selfish policies and mercenary patronage practices of the old guard incumbents were responsible for the demise of the Republican party. The Democratic majorities were so large that Cutting's few supporters on the Republican ticket "went down in the avalanche." Arthur Seligman defeated the Republican gubernatorial candidate, Clarence M. Botts, by eight thousand votes. Senator Sam Bratton overwhelmed his Republican opponent, Herbert Holt, by an "almost incredible" twenty-one-thousand-vote majority. Surveying the election, Cutting exclaimed, "I wonder what George Moses thinks about it."[33]

Gratified with the outcome, Cutting said, "It is the first time I have tried passivity as a political weapon, and it seems to have worked like a charm." So upset were Republican leaders with his silence and inactivity that two of them, shortly after the election, departed for Washington to convince the Hoover administration that Cutting should be denied further patronage. For his part, Cutting announced, "Since I am not interested in patronage or Embassies, I don't care whether they succeed or not." The defeat of the Republican old guard left Cutting the dominant leader of the Republican party in New Mexico. That thousands of his supporters accepted his passivity as a denunciation of the Republican ticket and voted the Democratic ticket proved he was now a significant figure in that party as well. In short, Cutting had become the ring master of New Mexico politics.[34]

Republicans believed the party "was betrayed and dynamited by Senator Cutting, who without difficulty could have elected the whole ticket." Defeated in his bid for a second term in Congress, Albert Simms added, "I believe the whole ticket could have been elected without his help if he had not contributed very large amounts of cash, which were distributed in the river counties the night before election." Nevertheless, Simms acknowledged the critical condition of the Republican party in New Mexico. If the White House abandoned the New Mexico party, if patronage appointments were delayed and not forwarded for confirmation, Simms believed, "Senator Cutting will have possession of both the Republican and Democratic Parties."[35]

By the end of 1930 Cutting had established himself as a progressive Republican critical of the Hoover administration and New Mexico state politics. One Cutting friend stated, "The old timers have become rancid in office, and domineering." Cutting played a large role in bringing about their downfall. Cutting, as his friend explained, was "the patron and whatever you do is alright [sic]."[36] While he had maintained his political integrity, he had also expanded the base of his support from the American Legion to include organized labor. In addition, he attracted fair-minded citizens to his long-standing fight against corrupt political practices. When he battled censorship, he won the support of many members of the arts community in Taos and Santa Fe. He sought no privileges or favors for himself through public service. Cutting loaned money to Hispanics and veterans down on their luck and became the leading dispenser of welfare in New Mexico prior to the New Deal. In addition, at election time, Cutting financially assisted candidates, particularly those seeking local or county offices.

What made Cutting a most unusual political leader is the subject of the following chapter. He was no longer the disgruntled politician but instead a dominant political figure who could determine the course of New Mexico politics. In Washington, he helped progressive Republicans in the Senate hold the balance of power during the next session of Congress.

CHAPTER 16

BRONSON CUTTING AND HIS FRIENDS

The late 1920s were momentous years for Bronson Cutting. His political career had reached a commanding position by 1930, and his private life had also become rich and rewarding. A private individual, Cutting rarely exposed himself to public scrutiny, and most of his correspondence, including that to his family, was confined largely to current developments and gave sparse mention of his personal life. He was a complex and brilliant individual who gave the public few indications of his astounding erudition.

When Cutting entered the United States Senate, he was thirty-nine years old. A bit over six feet tall, he weighed close to two hundred pounds. He was quick of step, athletic and vigorous. His complexion was dark, his eyes were brown, and his hair was brown-gray. His nose was straight, his face round, and his forehead broad. He was considered both charming and handsome. Some of his friends considered his appearance cherubic and among themselves called him "baby," short for baby face. While his handshake was firm and his smile gracious, Cutting was a modest man, almost shy on first acquaintance, possibly because he spoke with a slight lisp. Although actively concerned about and involved in veterans affairs, for example, he rarely talked about his wartime service. He seldom mentioned his years at Groton and Harvard, but he established a Harvard Club in Santa Fe. Yet his preferred associates were the citizens of the community, both Anglo and Hispanic, his colleagues on the *New Mexican,* and politicians who were ever present in Santa Fe.

Like every politician, Cutting was a joiner, but few successful politicians would list his affiliations: the New Mexico Taxpayers Association, Archaeological Institute of America, Southwestern Anthropological Society, American Legion, Phi Beta Kappa and Harvard Club in New Mexico; the Knickerbocker Club, Century Club and the Union League in New York; the Cosmopolitan Club in Washington, D.C.; and the Travelers Club and Union Club in London. In addition, he subscribed to a wide range of periodicals and newspapers, including several English publications.

Cutting's birthright was what was popularly supposed to bring happiness: wealth; social standing; good looks; an Ivy league education; and ample opportunities for travel. The one thing he did not have, however, was good health. His concern for his health, indeed his very life, brought him to New Mexico and led to the broadening of his horizons. Cutting made the transfer with ease and grace, never yielding his aristocratic background nor imposing it on others. He was equally at ease with Hispanic friends in New Mexico, with family and former classmates in New York or Boston, and with military acquaintances and family friends on the Continent. His intelligence was sympathetic; his enthusiasms, aside from music, were tempered; and his tolerance and humanity were unmarred by any patronizing air.[1]

George Santayana, who taught Cutting at Harvard, recalled his impressions of his former student. Cutting's brother had been one of Santayana's prized pupils. He thus took special notice of Cutting when he appeared in one of his classes. Santayana told Iris Origo, Cutting's niece, that although a shy pupil, "he showed the same clear intelligence, perhaps less full and enthusiastic" than that of her father. He further recalled that Cutting's "comments on philosophical ideas were inclined to be meager" but that "he went at once to the essence of things, not always to their advantage." Decades later in Rome when Santayana again met Cutting, now a United States senator, he saw the same traits vigorous as ever. Santayana "felt as if his splendid victory over the threat of ill health had made him very exacting in his principles and very precise in his objects," characteristics "that must have been of the greatest value in political life."[2]

To Cutting and his family, wealth entailed responsibility. Through his contributions, gifts and loans to needy veterans, Hispanics and others, Cutting was possibly the chief dispenser of welfare in New Mexico prior to the New Deal. Moreover, he contributed to a host of other institutions and individuals concerned with advancing the education and the arts of the Indian and Hispanic populations. By 1934 he contributed at least twenty-five hundred dollars semiannually to the San Jose Training School in Albuquerque, an experimental school concerned with the problems of rural education in a bilingual culture. As previously noted, he worked closely with, and in many instances was guided by, Mary Austin in these endeavors.[3]

As his battle against censorship demonstrated to Mary Austin and others, Cutting was a cultured, urbane individual. When Iris Origo visited him in Santa Fe, she found his book shelves stocked with all the classics, not only English, but Greek and Latin, and French and Italian. She recalled that without speaking, he handed her a new poem by William Butler Yeats. But when in the company of his New Mexico friends, he hinted at none of these interests. She also remembered that when no one was about, he would sit at the piano and play Bach. Classical music was his passion, yet he rarely indulged it in the company of others, at least until he went to the Senate at the end of the 1920s.

In a rambling set of recollections of Cutting, Brian Boru Dunne commented on the endless array of books that Cutting read. Principally he mentioned works on art, architecture, history and especially biography. He also read murder stories and frequently perused travel and guide books. Dunne recollected Cutting reading books by H. G. Wells, Joseph Conrad, John Galsworthy, and other English and American authors. Honore Balzac was a particular favorite of Cutting's. He even read dictionaries and not merely to seek definitions. Dunne saw his collection of music books, "books of songs and classical compositions and a few non–classical selections for the piano, which he played two to three hours a day as a rule."[4]

Cutting had a natural distaste for showing off. According to his sister, Justine, he bore especial "indignation at any form of inequality between human beings, including inequality of education or opportunity." He would rarely force his worldliness upon his Hispanic friends. He firmly believed that they had a right to their opinions. In social situations, he never sought to "use his superior knowledge to put anybody on the right track." He scrupulously avoided taking unfair advantage of others with his superior education, his spacious home and his inherited wealth. His capacity for silence, Justine recalled in 1939, "was infinite."

Iris Origo mentioned another telling instance of Cutting's sensitivity to social justice. While visiting at Westbrook, he took a walk with his mother along one of the paths in the arboretum. As they passed one of the grounds crew, an employee of some forty years, his mother greeted him with a few pleasant words but Cutting looked the other way. When asked why, as Iris Origo related, Cutting responded that he was "ashamed to think that a man's whole life should have been spent in tidying paths for us to walk on." His sense of guilt about the benefits and privileges of wealth and his sensitivity to the feelings and opinions of others, help to explain his alignment with the progressive camp when he became a senator.

Among those who knew him well, Cutting also displayed a delight in the grotesque and the ridiculous. Prior to his cultivation of a handful of friends associated with the Santa Fe arts community, only his sister, Frederic Bishop, a few school and family friends, and possibly Brian Boru Dunne were fully aware of this dimension of his personality. When he indulged it, his cherubic face would expand into "a slow irresistible smile." Behind the smile, as Iris

Origo intimated, was a deeper and darker pessimism of which delight in the grotesque and ridiculous was only the surface manifestation.[5]

His long bout with tuberculosis was undoubtedly a factor in shaping this facet of Cutting's personality. Dr. Bishop often remarked to Gordon Gardner, a mutual friend and a victim of tuberculosis, that Cutting's survival and eventual recovery were "due more to his calm, unvarying fortitude than even to the wonderful New Mexican climate." At a memorial meeting a year after Cutting's death, Gardiner related that during prolonged pulmonary hemorrhaging, "when death was literally in his nostrils," "Bronson would continue to read—his book propped before him—as though nothing untoward were in progress."

While visiting Cutting in Washington, Gardiner recalled extended conversations which "never ended until long past midnight." They took numerous trips to museums, galleries and other interesting places. Indicating Cutting's eccentric sense of humor, Gardiner remembered a notable visit to the zoo. On an extremely hot afternoon, Cutting roared with laughter for "the best part of ten minutes" at the sight of "a large bird, pompous, solemn, yet remarkably sly looking and quick on his legs." The bird's antics reminded Cutting of a political acquaintance, possibly a senate colleague.[6]

Cutting was equally intrigued with the human comedy around him. Like an inveterate theater patron, he enjoyed looking at and listening to the performers on stage but had no desire to participate in the proceedings. Yet with all of his observing, Cutting rarely passed final judgment on an individual. One who knew him well recalled, "He certainly had fewer strong dislikes among people than the average citizens." His charitable nature in part stemmed from his own and his family's history of tuberculosis and helped to produce in him "the kindest, gentlest and most civilized attitude toward everyone," except possibly some of his political enemies. But once the fray was over, Cutting bore no ill will. In many instances, as was the case with Albert Fall and Richard Dillon, a reconciliation was effected.[7]

As with most public figures, Cutting's friends fell into two classes, personal friends and political associates. His personal friends stretched from the British Isles across the Atlantic to New Mexico. His brother's brief career in the State Department, his tenure as a secretary to Ambassador Joseph Choate in Great Britain, and his marriage into the Anglo-Irish nobility gave the Cutting family a wide range of friends and acquaintances in England. During his education at Groton and Harvard, Cutting developed an equally wide social circle among the eastern establishment. His family was on a first name basis with both the Oyster Bay and Hyde Park branches of the Roosevelt family.

Cutting never exploited this relationship, and once settled in New Mexico, he saw these friends only on occasion.

Cutting quickly made friends shortly after his arrival in New Mexico: Miguel Antonio Otero; Brian Boru Dunne; Harry Dorman; Francis Wilson; and others. Mike Otero and Tony Luna, two recent graduates of the New Mexico Military Institute, became very close friends. Cutting paid their way through Washington and Lee Law School. His acquisition of the Santa Fe *New Mexican* and his work with the American Legion enormously enlarged his social and political range. Although he learned Spanish shortly after his arrival in Santa Fe, he gained a much fuller exposure to and appreciation of the Spanish-speaking community in the state through the American Legion. In New Mexico, personal friends were often political friends.

Finally Cutting made friends in the arts community of Santa Fe and Taos. Upon his arrival in 1910, only a handful of artists lived in Santa Fe. Its development as a center of the arts did not directly involve him, but Mary Austin made him aware of the serious social and cultural concerns of some members of the arts community. At first, she regarded Cutting as a source of funding for her various efforts in reviving and promoting Indian and Hispanic culture. She realized, however, that Cutting was genuinely interested in the welfare of the native people of New Mexico and had an equal if not greater understanding than her own. He condoned practices of the Penitentes and attended their rites as one of the group. Although Austin's esteem for Cutting grew, their friendship never developed beyond her seeking his assistance for her several cultural activities. Nevertheless, they shared a sympathy for the "sorrows of the lonely" and a sensitivity "to those elements in their natures and cultures" most lacking in theirs.[8]

Among his closest friends were several Hispanics. At the outset Mike Otero and Tony Luna were the most evident. Luna died while in the service on the border in 1917. Otero worked closely with Cutting in the American Legion and in political affairs. As Otero's own career developed through the 1920s, they drifted apart, and their friendship, though never broken, waned.

With the two Bacas, Herman and Jesus, his friendship, if anything, deepened over the years. Although unrelated, both Bacas met Cutting in the American Legion. A rare blue-eyed, blonde Spanish-American, Herman became Cutting's closest political associate and informally served as his secretary in New Mexico. Baca kept Cutting informed about developments in the American Legion, Veterans Bureau, and other organizations throughout the state. When Cutting was in Santa Fe, individuals who wished to see him usually did so through Herman. As Cutting's eyes and ears in New Mexico,

Herman would suggest, if Cutting had not already done so, that a message of congratulations or condolence or that flowers or a gift might be sent to a friend or family on the appropriate occasion. To the extent that Cutting maintained a political organization, Herman managed its affairs on a day-to-day basis, providing funds when needed for meetings and for political expenses. Through his travels and correspondence, Herman kept Cutting informed on state political affairs. Their relationship was deeply personal. Cutting relied heavily on Baca's political judgment, which, owing to his broad social connections and canny political sense, was of inestimable value. On holidays, when Cutting was in Santa Fe, he occasionally had dinner with Herman and his family.[9]

Cutting's friendship with Jesus Baca was even more immediate and more personal. Jesus served as Cutting's driver and companion on the innumerable trips Cutting made in behalf of the American Legion and while campaigning. Accompanying Cutting to remote areas, Jesus would be away from his home and family for extended periods of time. When Cutting entertained at his spacious residence, Los Siete Burros, Jesus's wife, Julia Strong Baca, occasionally served as the hostess. Jesus was blessed with a genial personality and a perfect memory. He was able to find good qualities in almost everybody and was remarkably free of vindictiveness. Cutting found him a most congenial companion. In his will, Cutting left Jesus Baca both a generous monetary gift and the Santa Fe *New Mexican*. In 1935, Cutting's family sold him Los Siete Burros for a trifling sum.[10]

Eugene Manlove Rhodes was as devoted to New Mexico and as concerned about its native peoples as Cutting. Although no Republican, he nevertheless concluded, "I'm for him." Rhodes, author of several distinguished "western" novels, explained why:

> Senator Cutting has given his money freely to nonpartisan, or more accurately, bipartisan societies—and to American Legion Posts, etc. Not cash to divide. A hall to meet in, a billiard table, a tennis court, a baseball diamond, expenses of delegates. Also Legitimate [sic] travel and hotel expenses of candidates, committee men, etc., in actual campaigns. He has asked for nothing—and it seems, has got a good deal. A thousand details to be told by the moonlight alone—Most of all—he has never high-hatted any body—And that includes—any Mexican. —This is a conquered race—and a proud and sensitive race—when you take 'em where they were born and raised. They may forgive you for taking a shot or two at them—but *never* for high-hatting. Cutting has won more votes from this course alone than from all the money he has spent.[11]

At the end of the 1920s, Cutting made several new friendships that were predicated upon a common love of serious music, that had no connection at all to politics or public affairs, and that added an enriching dimension to Cutting's life. He met these people at a party hosted by Witter Bynner, a Harvard graduate several years ahead of Cutting. Since his arrival in Santa Fe in 1922, Bynner had become a leading member of the arts community. Bynner, or Hal as he was known to his friends, was a distinguished literary personality, who like so many other creative artists, was attracted to the ambience of northern New Mexico. He was soon known in the arts community for his numerous parties. Mary Austin explained that Bynner hosted at least two types of parties: "I never go to Hal's drinking parties, but to those irreproachable ones when he entertains Senator Cutting and the Governor." Haniel Long, another Harvard graduate residing in Santa Fe, wrote that Bynner's parties sometimes included as many as two hundred people. Describing one bash, Long recalled, "You should have seen the assortment that were there. Flapper types, thin, and hats on the back of their heads, and smoking as though life depended on it."[12]

At one of Bynner's more respectable parties, Cutting met Phelps Putnam, a published poet recently awarded a Guggenheim Fellowship; Una Fairweather, his wife and an aspiring singer; Frederick Manning, a history professor at Swarthmore College and son-in-law to former president and chief justice William Howard Taft; and Clifford McCarthy, also known as Don, a brilliant, witty, erratic young man in his twenties, who at the time was companion and secretary to Witter Bynner. McCarthy spent at least a week with Cutting at Los Siete Burros while Bynner was away. Cutting assumed the responsibility of trying to help McCarthy find a satisfactory place for himself. The young man's penetrating mind, witticisms, versatility and capacity as a mimic helped to account for Cutting's interest. McCarthy threw himself on Cutting's mercy, leaving his arrangement as Bynner's secretary and companion. Thereafter, Bynner experienced a bout of severe depression, which he did not resolve until he established a durable relationship with another secretary and companion in November 1930.[13]

While Cutting, the Putnams and Manning founded their relationship on music, all were concerned about McCarthy and hoped, as Cutting expressed it, "that somehow or other an atmosphere may be created in which the Boy can develop himself." He added that "certainly he will not fail for lack of friends." Cutting's new friendships allowed him to play duets, to express musical opinions and to comment on concerts, things he had not done previously.[14]

Cutting's friends were not unaware of his musical concerns, which even his enemies made the subject of jibes. "They tell me," quipped ex-Governor Arthur Hannett, "that when crossed he would play the piano all night." On occasion Cutting would entertain guests at Los Siete Burros with selections from Bach, Beethoven or Wagner. More rarely, long after midnight, an eavesdropper could have heard through the open windows at Los Siete Burros, "the thunderous crescendos, in magnificent succession of Franz Lizst's *Concerto in E Flat Major.*"[15]

Cutting's tastes ranged beyond classical music. Nowhere else in the United States was the study of Spanish-American music more seriously followed than at the University of New Mexico. With funds provided by Cutting and the Rockefeller Foundation, Dr. Arthur L. Campa made recordings and subsequent transcriptions of different types of folk songs found within New Mexico. Cutting was an equally generous patron to other similar cultural endeavors within the state. Only in the company of his newly found friends, however, could he relax and discuss music and other matters in a congenial and convivial setting.[16]

Cutting never compartmentalized his friendships. All of his friends, personal and political, intermingled and usually enjoyed one another's company. Both Bacas, for example, hosted dinners for Cutting's new friends and others when he was in Washington. All at one time or another were guests at Westbrook or in the New York City residence on East Seventy-second Street hosted either by Cutting or, if he was not on hand, by his mother. Visiting in 1918, E. Dana Johnson found Mrs. Cutting "a most beautiful old lady" with "pure white" hair and her city residence "the most beautiful home I ever saw." He stayed in "a gold trimmed boudoir with valets lurking around in all dark corners outside and Lord knows how many men, women and children in the servants' quarters." Johnson's room contained old-fashioned mahogany furniture including a massive wardrobe, a great white-tiled fireplace, a brass coal bucket, electric lights like candles ensconced on the walls, buttons to call the butler, the valet or the maid. The room was "all furnished in white." There were three floors "and a cute little elevator that holds two people and runs by just pressing a button."

Johnson dined in a large room lined with tapestries, each as large as the side of the room. The other guests included Theodore Roosevelt's sister, Anna Roosevelt Cowles. All wore evening dress except Johnson, who had failed to pack a pair of black shoes. Yet Mrs. Cutting "never let on that I wasn't dressed in the latest cut of evening clothes." Other guests were similarly put at their ease and made to feel at home despite the sumptuousness of the surroundings.

Not only were Cutting's friends made to feel at home, but both Mrs. Cutting and his sister, Justine, were interested in everything that the guests cared to impart about New Mexico.[17]

The formalities that prevailed among Cutting's established friendships tended to give way among his newly found friends. Because of his cherubic face, he was called "baby," and McCarthy, the youngest of the lot, used the salutation in his letters. His immediate concern in March 1930 was "to get a room some place away from Hal's house" and to find meaningful work. He was no longer interested "in the hordes that came there to parties." He wrote Cutting, "The week I spent with you there [at Los Siete Burros] was the happiest I've ever had." He also promised to prepare "a daily report" and had every intention of putting his life in meaningful order. He concluded the letter with "Love to you, baby, forever" and signed it "Don."[18]

Such a letter could quickly lead to speculations that Cutting and McCarthy had established a romantic relationship and that the latter was in love with Cutting. Although McCarthy undoubtedly loved Cutting, no conclusive evidence proves that Cutting was gay. The circumstantial evidence in McCarthy's effusive letters indicates that Cutting was a homosexual, but Cutting's letters to McCarthy, some of which have been retyped and edited, are more formal and relate his daily activities more so than his reflections or musings. Whether they contained affectionate remarks can only be suspected, but several points are clear. For one, as was the case with Tony Luna and Mike Otero, Cutting was interested in helping McCarthy secure some further training or education and ultimately a livelihood. For another, in the remaining years of Cutting's life, the two men saw little of one another. McCarthy had family in Kansas City, and Cutting soon sent him to Europe. Earlier Manning took him to Canada to vacation with his family. Manning was equally interested in his welfare, though Cutting was the only one who could be helpful. Putnam was concerned but was more interested in using his Guggenheim award to further his creative ability by writing poetry.

In 1939, several years after Cutting's death, McCarthy commented on this relationship. Of its essence, he wrote, "Senator Cutting gave me his friendship at a time in my life when only his disregard for usual opinions, as against his own beliefs of good and bad and right and wrong, could have permitted him to do so." While he recognized that he never gave Cutting "much for his faith to go on," Cutting's friendship was unfaltering and beyond doubt. Although a burden and a bother, McCarthy said Cutting saw him "through every imaginable kind of difficulty—quarrels, illness, nerves, family difficulties, financial difficulties and God knows what!—And always with understanding, patience and affection." Never once, McCarthy recalled, did Cutting pass judgment on him or any other individual. McCarthy never pinpointed the source of this inability, but "whatever it was produced in him the kindest, gentlest and most civilized attitude toward everyone."

If one accepts McCarthy's letter at face value, it casts doubt upon a homosexual relationship between the two. What then emerges is a close and caring older friend, a parent or an older brother, concerned about a wayward and distressed son or younger brother. Added to this interpretation is McCarthy's statement that the deleted passages from Cutting's letters to him contained "for the most part some mention of my own personal problems or affairs."[19]

In their correspondence, Cutting, Phelps and Manning always commented on "inspirations as to jobs for D," and remarked on cultural interests, chiefly music. In one letter Cutting inquired of "Put," "What do you play now besides Schubert's Unfinished? The first in the same volume (in C Major) is not bad—the 4 hand arrangement." In short, the correspondence between Cutting, and Putnam and Manning indicated no deeper relationship with McCarthy than a genuine concern, which they all shared, for his general welfare.[20] Since Manning, in particular, related to Cutting his own personal torments and Putnam's relationship with Una Fairweather, one might presume that if Cutting had a homosexual relationship with McCarthy, he, Manning, and Putnam might have hinted at it in their correspondence. Instead what appears is evident concern for an attractive, sensitive, brilliant but confused, erratic and at times disturbed young man.

That McCarthy was in love with Cutting is clear. In February 1930, McCarthy was taking business courses, shorthand and typing in Kansas City, his home town. He signed one letter "Love to you, partner" and another "affectionately, always." He used Don in one letter and Cliff in the other. From Denver in the same period, he wrote a letter on Brown Palace Hotel stationery. McCarthy had set Cutting's picture on the dresser and explained that he had not taken a drink all day. He wrote, "Please don't think I'm going to hang on to you because I'm not. . . ." His life, he claimed, "is an open sewer and except for one defalcation I think there is nothing in it of any particular interest to 'agents.' " In this same letter, he also promised "not to get excited again."

Cutting had told McCarthy that he "trusted" and wanted to help him, and McCarthy made an effort to justify that trust. He took business courses but hated them and soon gave them up. He tried to stop his excessive drinking. He purchased a volume of William Butler Yeat's poems and sent it to Cutting. Of a visit to New York City, he told Cutting about lunching with Max

Eastman, meeting Sinclair Lewis, visiting the Steiglitz gallery, viewing the paintings of Georgia O'Keeffe, and visiting with John and Dolly Sloan. He also discussed music he had heard and commented on the concerts he had attended. On occasion he requested further funds, explaining how he spent the previous seven hundred dollars Cutting had provided. All the letters expressed either his love or affection. Almost all noted that he either thought about or missed Cutting. The one-sided file of letters present a portrait of a young man, trying to find a meaningful role for himself, expressing in effusive terms love and affection to a patron who, like himself, had a keen appreciation of art, literature and music.[21]

Cutting was careful to sign all his letters to McCarthy with the letter *B*, but in his correspondence with Putnam, for example, he wrote, "I miss you like hell." He commented on themes found in the McCarthy letters: the theater; literature; music; and his observations on the Washington scene. Cutting called Putnam "partner," the term used by McCarthy as well, while almost always asking to be remembered to Una Fairweather. In a comment about McCarthy, Cutting wrote, "I refuse to worry about problems which I am unable to take any hand in solving. A tough one, that!" In December 1930 when Putnam planned to visit Cutting in Washington, he rented a second piano. Once again, as in Santa Fe, they could play as partners in a duo piano team. Manning, like McCarthy, occasionally addressed Cutting as "Baby." He also kept Cutting abreast of McCarthy's activities and was equally interested in encouraging and assisting him. He too wrote about music.[22]

Cutting was a lifelong bachelor, and his sexual preference was the subject of rumors generated most notably by his political enemies. On occasion, his detractors openly discussed the subject in a futile effort to discredit him among the voters. Although he had proclaimed his intention of remaining a bachelor in the horoscope he prepared shortly after arriving in Santa Fe, he also indicated that he was interested in women and that he found them attractive. And most assuredly, he had many female admirers.

During his early years in Santa Fe, Cutting became acquainted with several young women. One became a life-long friend, Jouett Fall. The youngest child of Senator Albert B. Fall, she met Cutting in 1912 at the time of his father's death. Her parents befriended and solaced Cutting whose precarious health prevented him from attending his father's funeral. Although Cutting accepted Jouett's friendship, their relationship never progressed beyond that stage. Later, unhappily married and then divorced, Jouett Fall Elliott remained interested in and in love with Cutting. She devoted herself to her father and supported him throughout his long political ordeal: the Teapot

Dome Affair; his resignation from the cabinet; a term in jail; the loss of his beloved Three Rivers Ranch; and his reduction to abject poverty. At one point during her vigil, she broke down from the strain of constantly attending her father. Throughout her trial, she received solace and support from Cutting. "I appreciate you 'standing by,'" she wrote in one of her numerous undated letters. In another, while in El Paso with her parents, she wrote, "You were a dear to come down, I haven't the words to tell you how I feel or my gratitude."

Jouett's friendship with Cutting was an extension of his relationship with her father, Albert, but she was pleased with the attention Cutting extended to her. Cutting's visits to her father in the New Mexico State Penitentiary during 1931 buoyed his spirits. Jouett remembered that Cutting called on Fall every Sunday afternoon. He often tramped "through the snow, dressed in boots and riding clothes, looking so rugged and wholesome and cheery." The three of them would sit for hours, discuss national and state affairs and talk about individuals. Jouett enjoyed Cutting's sense of humor, "one of the most delightful things about him." He left her, she said, "with the courage to go on and meet the world."

Although she could not gain his love, she could always count on his friendship and understanding. She confided her troubles to Cutting "as a friend—the only one I can trust," and she sought his "honest opinion and advice." He was "the one person owing us nothing—who has 'stood by.'" She was distressed by the plight of her father and about her parent's deteriorating health and growing poverty. Cutting clearly did not respond to or reciprocate her romantic overtures.[23]

After his PEN speech in New York City, Mary Austin began to see something more in Cutting than merely a sympathetic friend and steady patron. Although twenty years older than Cutting, she occasionally flirted with him, remarking in one letter, "I thought only of your charm." And in a postscript, she added, "I think you should know, being as you are a shy man, that I have changed my style of hair dressing. Where I used to have a thousand pins to keep up my wealth of gorgeous locks, I now have only one pin which can easily be drawn by that brave who deserves the fair."[24]

Other women also found Cutting equally charming and handsome. As a United States senator and a bachelor in his early forties, Cutting was an eagerly sought dinner guest. In letters to Clifford McCarthy, he commented on these parties and the various people in attendance. He mentioned a Dr. Boggs, a physician in Washington. When he was in Europe in 1930, she continually phoned his office and inquired after him. When she sent him a "magnificent photograph," he quipped to McCarthy, "An invitation to her tent?" And Dolly Sloan, ever seeking funds from Cutting, stated in the conclusion to one of her letters, "My affection for you is not based on your generosity in the things I am interested in, but because I am really very, very fond of you."[25]

Cutting and marriage were also the subject of public rumors. Following a "confidential tip," a reporter in Washington, Fulton Lewis, called on Cutting at home to verify news from "very reliable sources" that Cutting and Alice Roosevelt Longworth were "to be married shortly—within the next few days or weeks." Far more revealing of Cutting's interest in women is a statement by his mother in 1946. She admitted that she had destroyed "the whole long box of letters which were written to Bronson from Callie Hull." After his death, she destroyed them at Callie Hull's suggestion. Later regretting her action, Mrs. Cutting claimed that the letters "showed how much he cared for her, and how he had decided to give her up because of his illness." The letters also indicated, according to Mrs. Cutting, that Callie Hull "had begged him not to think of other people but of himself in this." They last saw one another in Washington before Cutting went overseas in 1918. Mrs. Cutting concluded, as had Cutting himself shortly after he arrived in Santa Fe, "that he knew he could not get well, and so gave up matrimony."[26]

In spite of his reticence, Cutting was engaging to children. According to Iris Origo, Cutting would sit on the lawn at Westbrook with her beloved son and carry on a serious conversation with him. Jouett Elliott recalled how after a political address in New Mexico, "a tiny bit of a girl—all dressed up in frilly white, with a large, pinky bow on her hair," following a Spanish-American custom, marched up to the platform and presented Cutting with an enormous bunch of flowers. "At first," she wrote, "he looked as though he wanted to run—then he bent over, shook hands and led her to a seat by him." For "the rest of the evening," he talked to her in a serious and interesting way.[27]

Two or possibly three themes help to understand Cutting and his relationships: his wealth; his health; and his deep, abiding interest in music. His family's friends and acquaintances at home and abroad allowed him to feel at ease in a wide range of social environments. The efforts of his father and his uncle to elect good men and to achieve honest government influenced him to ignore party labels when he sought similar political goals in faction-ridden New Mexico.

The long battle to regain his health fostered tolerance for eccentric behavior, an appreciation for humor, the grotesque and the ridiculous in life.

Self-confident possibly to a fault, he rarely tried to impose his views on others and sought to comprehend their views and to understand their motivations. He possessed an ability to mingle work with play, the deadly serious with the utterly trivial, in a continuous flow that intrigued his associates and friends. He found respite and relaxation in travel and especially in music. Putnam, Manning and McCarthy allowed him, as never before, to find solace and fellowship in his private passion.

What emerged in 1930 was an engaging, shy, handsome and brilliant public figure. Although he found little in public service to attract him, he felt a deep sense of obligation to represent as best he could the interests of his constituents. By 1931, with the depression fully unleashing its devastating impact, he had become a critic of President Hoover and a member of the small band of progressive Republican senators who would soon hold the balance of power in that chamber. At the same time in New Mexico, this reluctant politician was already recognized by leaders in both major parties as the dominant political figure in the state.

CHAPTER 17

PROGRESSIVE REPUBLICAN

Following the election of 1930, Cutting had no reason to be disgruntled. He had engineered the election of a Democratic governor sympathetic to his ideas for clean, honest government. As Cutting prepared for the concluding session of the Seventy-First Congress, he was already recognized as a prominent progressive in the United States Senate.

Before leaving for Washington, Cutting drove to Albuquerque with Mary Austin and participated in a conference on the newly established San Jose Training School. Established with assistance from the Rockefeller Fund, the school sought an effective way of educating Hispanic and Indian children. The school would operate under the auspices of the University of New Mexico. Both Cutting and Austin were members of the board of directors. The program supporters hoped that the school would be a focal point of cultural integration, would help to instill pride and hope among native children and would reinvigorate a sense of community among their parents.

At least Austin and Cutting carried those hopes for the program, but Austin also entertained reservations about some of the board members and about the president of the University of New Mexico, J. F. Zimmerman. She believed that they were largely unacquainted with the "history, culture, capabilities, racial and social background of the children." They believed, she feared, "that an educational problem is solved when it can be reduced to a tidy statistical chart." While in accord with Austin's views, Cutting was unable to act directly on the school board but lent his support to the development of its program.[1]

Cutting wanted to leave Santa Fe as late as possible, since "state politics are so entertaining and national politics so dull." He was amused by the bitter factionalism within the Democratic party. While the leaders of one faction cast him as the villain, the divisions also enhanced his political influence. According to former Democratic governor Arthur T. Hannett, Cutting was the spoiler in New Mexico politics and was the key figure in what he called a "Cutting-Seligman" administration, a coalition between these two friends of different political persuasions. Hannett argued that "approximately 55,000" registered Democrats held "very close to a majority of the voting strength" in New Mexico but that "neither a Democratic party nor a Democratic organization" existed. The Democratic organization, Hannett believed, had been "sold and delivered" to Cutting at the 1930 Democratic State Convention. Cutting was the master of the party and Governor Arthur Seligman was his minion. Those loyal Democrats who "refused to knuckle and bend" to "the arrogance of Cutting's wealth" had been driven from the councils of the party. With variations, this view of a Cutting-Seligman coalition gained credence among many New Mexicans at the time and among historians and others thereafter.[2]

Whether Governor Seligman was a pawn of Cutting is open to serious doubt. Seligman's views were in accord with Cutting's only in their mutual desire for honest, efficient government. Seligman was soft-spoken and serious-minded. But as a conservative banker-politician, he had no sympathy for progressive change, and Cutting had no desire to impose his views on the new governor. When Seligman asked Cutting to evaluate a number of applicants for office in his administration, Cutting gave him "as frankly as possible" his opinion of "the merits and demerits" of some "twenty or thirty individuals." In addition, he suggested the names of two men who held minor offices in the previous administration and who "would render efficient service in the positions which they held." Heavily involved with senate business several months later, Cutting was unaware of how the governor had acted on his recommendations.

Of course, he recognized that Seligman was "holding an office of enormous responsibility and importance" in troubled times. Cutting was "sure that neither of us would wish to interfere in any way with matters which have nothing to do with our respective offices." His chief interest in New Mexico politics, he explained to Herman Baca, was not "to control people's opinions, but to get them to think for themselves." Moreover, he had "so many friends throughout the state" that his endorsement of particular individuals "would seem like discrimination against the others."[3]

Although he was reluctant to give his views on individuals to Governor Seligman, he had no hesitation when he commented on colleagues in the Senate. Ezra Pound, impressed with Cutting's stand against censorship by customs officers, asked whether he would seek to amend article 211 of the penal code, which fined and/or imprisoned importers who attempted to bribe revenue officers. This section was related to section 212 of the tariff act that Cutting had vigorously opposed. Pound believed that Cutting could now strike another blow against custom's censorship of wares entering the United States.

Equally opposed to this section of the penal code, Cutting explained to

Pound that "owing to an anomaly of our constitution the fauna whom you mention, though retired by the voters, are still with us." Changing the code would be impossible until the new Congress, "which promises to be considerably more liberal," convened in December. Sizing up his opposition, Cutting first mentioned literate senators whom they could count on to "sin against the light": George Moses; Hiram Bingham; and David A. Reed. Literate senators opposed to censorship were William Borah, George Norris, Hiram Johnson, Millard Tydings, Robert La Follette, Jr., Burton K. Wheeler, Thomas J. Walsh and possibly Dwight Morrow "and not much else." Cutting concluded his handwritten letter to Pound, "But don't say that I said so."[4]

The correspondence with Pound helped Cutting to launch into what promised to be "a busy and rather dreary session." His mail from New Mexico indicated that his constituency was in need of federal drought relief, a point that the Hoover administration would not accept. President Hoover was coping ineffectively with the deepening depression crisis. Cutting noted Hoover's paralysis when he opposed controversial candidates for high government posts in the "Lame Duck" session.[5]

Seeking to win Cutting over to the administration, the president invited him to the White House on January 15, 1931. "H.H. was never so cordial," Cutting wrote. He continued, "[Hoover] held my hand so long (patting it) that it became quite embarrassing." The next day on the senate floor, Cutting widened his breach with the administration by criticizing the activities of Robert H. Lucas, executive director of the Republican National Committee, who had requested information about the political affairs of administration critics from employees of the Internal Revenue Bureau. Cutting and several others concluded, "Mr. Lucas, the Republican executive director, attempted to use these revenue experts as political agents, political spies, if one wishes to use that word, in their respective committees to furnish the Republican National Committee with information which they think may be of political benefit." In addition, Cutting noted that Lucas used fake letters to denounce political appointees. Lucas was employing these measures and "the money of the national committee" to promote the renomination of Hoover. Cutting concluded that the president was "to be pitied and condoled with" if he could not separate his candidacy from an individual "so completely discredited and disowned by the decent element of his own party." Not only the president but all office-holding Republicans should "take a stand as between right and wrong." In short, "through the men who are actually in power," the Republican party ought to repudiate the "disgraceful and outrageous methods" Lucas "practiced and publicly endorsed."[6]

CHAPTER 17

At the request of the Author's League, Cutting was busy with Patent Committee hearings on the general revision of the copyright law. He attended hearings and testified to endorse the principle of the automatic copyright that would provide protection "without going through a long formality of registration and notice and what not" as well. The measure under consideration was loaded with many technical features, some ambiguous and some "really objectionable," and developed "a good deal of unnecessary opposition." "Unless one has actually worked on this type of measure," he explained to Ezra Pound after the Copyright Bill lapsed without consideration at the end of the session, "it is inconceivable how many complications come up."[7]

Devoting close to seven hours a day to the copyright hearings, Cutting had little time to prepare for a scheduled address that he gave to the National Republican Club in New York on Saturday, January 31. In his speech, he advocated United States recognition of Soviet Russia. Following the suggestion of Ezra Pound, Cutting claimed that opening official relations with the Soviets would follow the precedent of Thomas Jefferson who, as the secretary of state in 1793, had recognized the republican government of France. "After fourteen years of varying fortunes," Cutting said, "the Soviet Government has established itself as one of the emphatically stable governments of the world." Recognition would allow for fair discussion and competition between differing economic, political and social systems and could prove beneficial by making "possible that some new social order may arise superior in essence and in detail to either one."[8]

The most tedious and dreary senate matter stemmed from an unfortunate misunderstanding. In January 1931, Senator Lynn Frazier, chairman of the Indian Affairs Committee, sought the removal of Herbert J. Hagerman from the federal payroll for the incompetent performance of his duties. A former territorial governor and more recently a special commissioner to the Navajos and a member of the Pueblo Land Board, Hagerman had agreed to the sale of over forty thousand acres of Pueblo lands for either inadequate or no compensation. In one instance, he gave away nineteen thousand acres. At the same time, Hagerman neglected to purchase new property as the Pueblo Lands Act stipulated.[9]

Miguel Antonio Otero, Sr. informed Cutting that Frazier had requested from him information about Hagerman's "work for Government on Indians and in oil leasing matters." According to Otero, only Hagerman's friends "seemed to profit in that oil matter on the Navajo Reservation"—the purchase of "Rattlesnake Dome" reserve lands. After receiving Otero's reports, Cutting began attending the Frazier hearings, which concerned New Mexico and some of its prominent citizens. Soon thereafter on the senate floor, he clarified a misunderstanding over Theodore Roosevelt's removal of Hagerman as territorial governor. He also argued that Hagerman auctioned the Rattlesnake oil field lease in a legal manner despite the fact that the purchaser resold the lease at an enormous profit to the Continental Oil Company.[10]

In his discussion of the sale, Cutting first traced the tortuous history of the Pueblo lands through three centuries. Their status was so convoluted that both sides, Indians and settlers, had "a real right in equity." Congress established the Pueblo Lands Board to decide conflicting claims as fairly and equitably as humanly possible and granted the right to appeal a board decision in federal court. Recognizing that "in most parts of the United States the Indians have been disgracefully treated," Cutting was inclined to "think on the whole that they have come nearer receiving fair treatment in New Mexico than anywhere else." Although he had not followed Hagerman's actions on the board, Cutting thought that the testimony of the people who were "sincerely interested in the Indians should be taken into consideration," before Congress judged Hagerman's record.[11]

Cutting acknowledged that acceding to low awards in settling land claims would "always be a certain smirch on Hagerman's reputation," no matter what Frazier's committee decided. In Cutting's estimation, John Collier was "a far more serious menace to New Mexico, and especially to the native people, than Hagerman ever could be." The Frazier investigation, as Cutting saw it, was "simply a means to let Collier get some of the venom out of his system." Otherwise all the hearings could demonstrate was that Hagerman had shown poor judgment as the Navajo commissioner and as a member of the Pueblo Lands Board.[12]

When the Hagerman matter first came up, Cutting thought it too trivial to notice, but too many "coincidences" surrounded the Rattlesnake lease. Hagerman claimed on the basis of reports he reviewed that the land was a poor prospect, while a more recent report, unknown to Hagerman, indicated the opposite. The members of the investigating committee were left with "a very suspicious attitude" that only intensified when they learned that friends of Hagerman benefitted from the transaction and that the Continental Oil Company began drilling on a site Hagerman deemed worthless. Finally the committee caught Hagerman in an outright lie that cast "grave doubt on every other statement" made by him throughout the hearing. Cutting considered Hagerman a fool who was innocent of any criminal action. "Don't take the matter too seriously," he cautioned his colleagues. At best the Rattlesnake-lease controversy was "a tempest in a teapot" that simply puffed John Collier

---

and exhibited Hagerman's ineptitude and that had little impact on Herbert Hoover's New Era in Indian policy.[13]

While Cutting was playing down the Hagerman affair, he was bitterly attacked by old guard Republican senators in Santa Fe. They accused him of aligning with the Seligman administration and for having "bought the 1930 election in New Mexico." Republican and independent members of the New Mexico House of Representatives promptly repudiated the remarks and declared their confidence in Cutting. Similar expressions of support for Cutting indicated that independent and progressive Republicans throughout New Mexico had county organizations in place or were in the process of building them and that their organizations stood ready to aid Cutting's political endeavors.[14]

Cutting did not respond to the Republican charges. In the waning days of the lame-duck Seventy-first Congress, he battled for assistance to disabled veterans. He attacked the Hoover administration's claim that federal aid to the veterans would constitute a financial burden and a serious embarrassment to the government and to the country. In spite of Hoover, Congress approved an adjusted compensation measure that provided loans to veterans against their insurance policies. Cutting endorsed the bonus as a means of providing ex-servicemen with a cash option, "something to tide them over their immediate necessities" rather than waiting until 1945 when their government-provided insurance policies would mature. He noted that relief funds were inadequate to meet the needs "of those suffering from the present economic depression" and "that the proportion of ex-service men out of employment is greater than the general proportion of ex-service men . . . in the total population." In his estimation, a bonus to veterans was a rational proposition, one calling for immediate action.[15]

Hoover vetoed the bonus measure on February 26, 1931. The following day, the Senate overrode the veto by a vote of 76 to 17. Cutting challenged the "two fundamental misconceptions" in the president's veto message: that ex-servicemen constituted "a group of special privilege"; and that "loans from the money which is theirs," would tend to open the federal treasury and help to break "the barriers of self-reliance and self-support in our people." Cutting insisted that veterans were mindful of the nation's welfare and that only veterans experiencing economic distress would apply for loans. Given the opposition mustered against the measure, Cutting considered it "a source of gratification not only to the veterans but to the country as a whole" that the measure gained enactment.[16]

Cutting was dissatisfied with the administration of the Veterans Bureau under General Frank T. Hines. At the end of the session, the Senate considered a resolution that would provide a retirement salary for the director, thus giving Cutting an opportunity to express his opinion. From the point of view of the disabled veteran, the bureau under Charles R. Forbes's "genial incapacity and graft" offended less than "the narrow honesty and lack of sympathy which has been shown by the bureau from that day to this." Its policy, Cutting argued, was "to save the taxpayers' money, not through administrative economies, but at the expense of the disabled veterans." He decried the bureau's red tape. He blasted its innumerable decisions against veterans in "benefit of the doubt" cases, although the law directed that in such instances, the ruling should be to the veteran's advantage. Cutting said that in ninety-five percent of such cases the decision went the other way. Cutting did not hold General Hines personally at fault, but in his opinion, the bureau had become a large, unwieldy organization. Rectifying its objectionable conditions had become a monumental task.[17]

Cutting maintained his position as one of the staunchest friends of the former soldiers in Congress. He did not shy away from criticizing both the president and the Veterans Bureau and voicing his dissatisfaction with the inability of the administration and the Congress to cope effectively with the depression crisis. Before he could escape from Washington and return to Santa Fe, he had one further commitment to fulfill.[18]

Shortly before Congress adjourned, five senators, Cutting among them, announced a Conference of Progressives to discuss and outline a program of legislation for presentation at the convening of the Seventy-second Congress. Senators George Norris, Robert M. La Follette, Jr., Edward Costigan, Burton K. Wheeler and Cutting believed that the nation was lacking effective political and economic leadership in the crisis. Hundreds of participants sought constructive legislative proposals during the conference at the Carlton Hotel on March 11 and 12.

They discussed five subjects: unemployment and industrial stabilization; public utilities; agriculture; the tariff; and a return to representative government. Norris chaired the conference, while Cutting headed the Committee on Representative Government. In his address, Cutting recognized that a hastily called two-day conference could not rectify long-standing difficulties of enhanced executive authority, excessive campaign expenditures and judicial curbs on civil liberties. His remarks, like those of all the participants, were critical of the programs and policies of the Hoover administration.[19]

At the round-table discussions, spokesmen analyzed the issues. On the afternoon of the final day, each chairman provided the report of his round table. Cutting presented a nine-point summary that called for legislation to place further limits on excessive campaign expenditures, for the submission of the "Lame Duck Amendment" to the states, and for an anti-injunction law that would curb the power of the courts. Underlying all of the proposals, the committee report noted, "is our fundamental demand that liberty be restored to the American people, that we vindicate by legislation our faith in the liberal traditions of our country."[20]

Journalist Edmund Wilson, covering the conference, commented perceptively on Cutting. He "is so much a New Yorker," Wilson wrote, "that one forgets he's Senator from New Mexico. He's rather like an English liberal—like some of the men in the Labor government—we've never, so far as I know, had that type in the Senate before." After listening to Cutting's remarks, Wilson concluded that "he sounds as if he were aiming at something like the English system, the President and the Cabinet responsible to Congress, a congressional majority controlling policy." If Congress were composed of "Cuttings and La Follettes," the system might work, but Wilson saw only professional politicians.[21]

Wilson was not the only observer to take note of Cutting's keen intellect and his leadership in the progressive Republican camp. Douglas Gilbert, a reporter, had two lengthy talks with Cutting in the waning days of the Seventy-first Congress and labeled him the body's "extreme liberal." Cutting believed that the subservience of politicians to big business had merged the two political parties beyond differentiation. Cutting suggested as more meaningful, a Liberal-Conservative realignment. Gilbert affirmed what Wilson only implied, namely, that Cutting favored the British parliamentary system. In his eyes, it was more national in outlook and accordingly less selfishly insular. The Constitution was outmoded, he believed. A "community document," it established a form of government unable to provide constructive leadership. During his service in the Senate, he had learned that "our government is quite without tradition" and that "shop worn," hackneyed arguments had not, indeed, could not, resolve the economic difficulties overwhelming the American people in 1931. His criticism of the Hoover administration and his participation in the Conference of Progressives brought Cutting to national attention as a most unusual legislator, a "Lochinvar libertarian riding in from the West."[22]

Attention was the last thing Cutting wanted as the Conference of Progressives adjourned in the late afternoon of May 12. He left Washington for a period of respite at Westbrook and at the family residence in New York City. Returning to Santa Fe at the end of the month, he found politics "in about the state I expected to find them." Factionalism in the Republican party now involved a new combination. Albert Simms and his wife, the former Ruth Hanna McCormick, were attempting to gain control of the party. Both were former members of Congress, he from New Mexico and she from Illinois. Cutting found their antics "rather ludicrous." He noted that Mrs. Simms, the widow of former Illinois senator Medill McCormick, was "in daily consultation with the Republican organization in Washington and has already guaranteed my overthrow."[23]

On the other hand, he found the opposition of his former friend and ally, Miguel Antonio Otero, Jr., serious, persistent, and possibly "very formidable." Mike was a former attorney general of New Mexico and now a district judge in Santa Fe. For reasons Cutting never explained, Otero was in opposition to him, although he was "not yet ready to start a fight in the open or on a state-wide scale." The most that Cutting could hope for was that Otero would "come to his senses before long." Cutting recognized that his former friend was now part of the opposition he had to contend with in the Republican party.[24]

While devoting his efforts to disentangling the political situation in New Mexico, he found time to offer his condolences to Alice Roosevelt Longworth upon the death of her husband, Nicholas Longworth, the Speaker of the United States House of Representatives. He also helped Mr. and Mrs. William Allen White celebrate their thirty-eighth wedding anniversary, attending a dinner hosted by Mary Austin in their honor at which "we talked of Russia till all was blue." In addition, he traveled with members of the Committee on Indian Affairs, who were seeking "some final settlement of the Pueblo problem, if not the general S. W. Indian question as well." At one of the hearings, Mary Austin impressed the senators with her profound knowledge of Native American culture. Awing them, she stalked off after stating that John Collier was the driving force behind bringing them to New Mexico to learn the truth about the Indian problem from her.[25]

To round out his activities, Cutting spoke at an Episcopal convention in Albuquerque, met with the national commander of the American Legion, visited with members of the House Committee on Interior Appropriations, and traveled to Taos with Mary Austin to meet Carlos Chavez, the Mexican composer and conductor who was staying with Mabel Luhan. He then went to El Paso where he accompanied Albert Fall to the hospital. "A fool trip," he called it, but he could not "turn down a guy who is as much up against it as he is." Back in Santa Fe, he looked forward to musical evenings following the arrival of Frederick Manning and Phelps Putnam in early June.[26]

Overriding all of these engagements were the judicial decisions of Mike Otero, who was conducting "a Reign of Terror in the form of a term of court." According to Cutting, Otero was rendering decisions of which "Lord Jefferys or Judge Webster Thayer might well be envious." Cutting lost faith in Otero. After several "long and pretty satisfactory" conversations, Otero seemed "ready to be reasonable" but then broke "every damn agreement." Cutting was distraught by Otero's appointment of former governor Arthur T. Hannett's "chief legal advisor and political tool," Fred Wilson, to prosecute Hannett's enemies. Rather than discuss matters with Otero, Cutting decided on "open warfare" and drafted an editorial criticizing Judge Otero's action. The appointment, he remarked, "was only a peg to hang a hat on." Otero had deprived the defendants of a right to a fair trial. His act was "reprehensible." Cutting made a clean break with Mike Otero, one of his closest friends in Santa Fe, a friend whose legal education he had subsidized and whose friendship was strengthened through work in the American Legion and in earlier political battles.[27]

Cutting paid for his numerous involvements with his health. He rested little during his trip with the senate committee and worried constantly about his deteriorating relations with Mike Otero. What he first considered neuritis or rheumatism in his right arm, the doctor informed him, was "merely a matter of nervous strain due to over-exertion and worry." At times, the pain was so severe that he had trouble writing. His editorial so angered Judge Otero that he considered jailing Cutting for contempt. Only the intercession of his father, Miguel, Sr., dissuaded him. Cutting thought that "the jail sentence would have been restful." While the pain in his arm eased after the break with Otero, he was still plagued with bouts of hay fever, mild and minimal at first but "the worst hay fever I ever had in my life" by July.[28]

So severe was his suffering that he could not fully enjoy the company of Frederick Manning and Phelps Putnam, who arrived separately in June. The three men attended a singing fiesta in Mora. Manning and Cutting visited with Carlos Chavez at Mabel Luhan's home in Taos. However, Cutting and his friends attended no more fiestas or other musical events. Seeking relief from his hay fever and the chance to rest, Cutting decided to attend an August meeting in Prague of the Federation Interalliée des Anciens Combattants (the Allied Veterans Federation). He made reservations on the *Ile de France* for Putnam and himself and secured a place for Herman Baca and himself on the American Legion delegation.[29]

His severe hay fever and a sinus infection put him in bed during the last weeks of July before departing for New York. On July 30 at 10:00 P.M., he was operated on to relieve his infected antrum and sinus cavity. On August 12, he sailed on the *Mauretania* and was ill the entire voyage. Upon his arrival in Paris, he visited Dr. Fernand Lyani, who was recommended by Justine and who cabled his mother the following day that he was well. Quickly establishing rapport with Dr. Lyani, Cutting later explained that he "was the only doctor who had ever understood him."[30]

With Lyani's approval, Putnam and Cutting departed for Vienna. Cutting expected "to put in a perfunctory appearance at Prague" and sail for home as early in September as possible. In Paris, Cutting spent most of his time visiting specialists to determine why he became so ill aboard ship. He thought the cause was "purely digestive." Others suggested heart trouble. The Parisian specialists confirmed Cutting's diagnosis, but they also noted that he was "still in a high state of nervous tension" and needed "lots of mental repose and calm and no worries." One of the ways he sought to relax was to write no letters until he returned to New Mexico.[31]

While Cutting was in Europe, the Republican party in New Mexico sought to put its house in order. The new chairman of the central committee was a former district judge, Carl Dunifon. He had kept aloof from state politics and believed that his duty was to restore party harmony. He immediately saw that Cutting had "the respect and admiration of the vast majority of the citizens of New Mexico, regardless of party." Dunifon was convinced that the party's best interests would be served by placing all federal patronage in Cutting's hands, something that neither the Hoover administration nor most state leaders were willing to accept. Albert Simms, for example, concluded that Cutting was "very much interested in seeing Franklin Roosevelt nominated on the Democratic ticket," that he had utilized his great wealth to control politics and that he had caused the bitter divisions within the state party.[32]

Back in Santa Fe after his European trip, Cutting again had hay fever and had to sleep in a pollen-free room. He visited the penitentiary and spent "half an hour with poor old Fall," whom he found "quite pitiful and in a wretched physical state." Fall was afraid the Hoover administration would try to block his parole in November. Cutting did not see how justice could be served by denying Fall's parole. In December 1931, Emma Fall pleaded with Cutting to intervene with the United States attorney general in behalf of her husband. Cutting said that Attorney General James Mitchell acted only on "orders from higher-up" and that "there was no earthly use in talking" to him. Cutting and Senator J. Hamilton Lewis secured an appointment with the president. Cutting wrote Mrs. Fall, "I cannot in a letter describe the degree of discourtesy with which the President received us." He added, "It is almost incredible that a man in his position can be vindicative in so petty a way." Cutting worried that his intercession might have further antagonized the president against her husband.[33] Fall would serve until May 9, 1932, a total of nine months and nineteen days.

As the pollen count declined in Santa Fe during fall 1931, Cutting resumed an active life. He had Albert Simms and his wife, Ruth Hanna McCormick, to lunch and on another occasion dined with Richard Dillon. "A lot of hatchets are being officially buried," he wrote of these cordial and informal luncheons with the factional leaders of the Republican party. He spoke at the American Legion post in Old Albuquerque and at Roswell on Armistice Day. He tried to rest "as much as anyone could ask." He found "little going on that is harmful," except for the activities of Mike Otero on the district court. Before departing for Washington, Cutting enjoyed Thanksgiving dinner with Ernest Thompson Seton at his "Indian Village" about eight miles south of Santa Fe. The village was furnished with Navajo hogans, brush houses and wild animals. Cutting found the arrangement "quaint" but also "a little artificial."[34]

As the Seventy-second Congress got under way, Cutting sought rest and "some calm" by keeping busy "with trivial things for the most part." At the behest of Roger Baldwin of the American Civil Liberties Union, however, he agreed to introduce a bill intended to overturn a recent 5-to-4 Supreme Court decision. The legislation would admit pacifists to citizenship regardless of their views on bearing arms in time of war. The bill was drafted in the office of John W. Davis, attorney for Douglas Clyde Macintosh, a Yale Law School professor and the defendant in the Supreme Court case.[35]

Cutting spent Christmas with his mother, Phelps Putnam and Clifford McCarthy in New York. He was on hand in early January when his niece, Iris Origo, her husband and young son arrived from Italy. These visits were distractions from the business of the Senate in which the Republican party held a precarious plurality of one, leaving the twelve progressive Republican senators holding the balance of power. With the House of Representatives under Democratic control for the first time since the Wilson years, the Hoover administration's efforts to cope with the economic crisis could be subject to modification or defeat. In this session, Cutting was regarded as a key member of the progressive group and received a coveted seat on the Foreign Relations Committee. His initial comments on the senate floor put him in opposition to one of Hoover's notable foreign policy accomplishments, the German moratorium or postponement of intergovernmental debts.

Cutting was not critical of the moratorium but of the president's securing senate approval by Western Union telegram in June when Congress was not in session. James Watson, the senate majority leader, compiled a list of sixty-eight colleagues who responded favorably to Hoover's telegram, more votes than necessary for the approval of a joint resolution. Cutting complained that the details of the proposal had not yet been resolved in June and that any positive response to the Hoover telegram was tenuous at best and should not have bound him to a specific arrangement in December. He opposed the whole scheme of war debts. He favored the British policy of the Napoleonic Wars— "subsidizing its allies for what war expenses they were unable to pay themselves." The complications emanating from reparations and war debts only added to the economic distress "which is universal and which particularly affects the people of this country." In canceling many of the war debts, "the United States had to give everything without getting anything in return." The source of the trouble, according to Cutting, was "the Versailles treaty with all its ramifications." The moratorium, necessitated "by the logic of facts," represented to Cutting "the first step in a process of world adjustment."[36]

In behalf of Cutting and himself, Senator Harry Hawes reintroduced a bill calling for the independence of the Philippine people. Cutting offered a few favorable remarks on the measure. Both men sat on the Committee on Territories and Insular Affairs, which positively endorsed the bill. Commenting late in the session, Cutting noted that "the islands have cost us more than they have repaid us," that they were neither "necessary nor advantageous to us as a 'spearhead' to our commerce in the Far East," and that they possessed dubious military usefulness to the United States.[37]

Several days later when the Senate considered the Philippine-independence measure under a unanimous-consent agreement, Cutting made his most extended explanatory remarks on its contents: the establishment of the government; trade and tariff provisions; and immigration clauses among other sections. Cutting explained that some committee members favored immediate independence instead of a fifteen-to-seventeen-year trial period after which the residents of the islands would take a final vote on their independence. Others preferred a more detailed and restrictive proposal presented by Arthur Vandenberg. Cutting asserted that the question "is for the Philippine people to decide" and that the promise made "the Filipinos to give them independence at least implies that they themselves desire independence." They should have a chance, Cutting said, to decide the matter for themselves. The trial period was designed to allow them "a chance to create a new economic system suitable for the new conditions under which they will have to exist after independence." Owing to the lateness of the session, the decision on Philippine independence was postponed until the second session of the Seventy-second Congress.[38]

Ever concerned about the plight of the veterans, Cutting took the floor to castigate the *Washington Post*. The paper reported that the American Legion agreed with the insistent calls by the administration for the curtailment of federal expenditures until the national budget was balanced. According to Cutting, American Legion officials had denied the story and intended to seek a pension bill for the widows, orphans and dependent relatives of former servicemen. The inaccuracy of the story, stated Cutting, "is due to the White House itself." He also called attention to the need for a senate Veterans Committee comparable to the one already functioning in the House of Representatives.[39]

In nearly all of his remarks, Cutting opposed the Hoover administration, whose retribution came with the loss of patronage. Cutting concluded correctly that Hoover was awarding New Mexico patronage to the state chairman. "I am really glad to be able to wash my hands of it," he wrote in January, "as it was an intolerable nuisance and I think more of a liability than an asset." The administration also excluded him from the White House reception for members of Congress.[40]

Cutting labeled the mass of congressional legislation "mostly futile." Either the administration opposed helpful measures or supported those that fell far short of resolving the crisis. The pressure of senate business was so great that he had not thought ahead to the 1932 elections. Politics, he said, "are so tangled up, that it is pretty hard to see any distance ahead."[41]

Cutting endorsed the distress relief measure sponsored by Edward Costigan and Robert M. La Follette, Jr., but he thought a public works bill "very much more fundamental." Although neither measure stood much chance of success, Cutting believed the effort would be a first step in arousing public sentiment for an adequate program of public works. The Senate's paralysis moved *The Nation* to powerful editorial criticism on March 2, 1932. In a bitter article, "Let Them Starve," the editor concluded that the august body had decided "the unemployed workers and their families must not look to the government in Washington for aid."[42]

So discouraging did Cutting find this session that on March 9 he left Washington for New Mexico to be on hand for the primaries. Despite the cold and snowy weather en route, the trip was "soothing to the nerves." In the Santa Fe primaries, he wrote, "our friends carried every ward." He noted similar results in Albuquerque and elsewhere. At the Republican State Convention later in March, Jesus and Herman Baca completely outmaneuvered "all the veteran political strategists of the past forty years." Cutting witnessed the defeat of Holm Bursum, "an unheard of occurrence in a convention" and one that "completely flattened out the old guard." When appointed to escort Cutting to the podium, the outraged Bursum "could barely speak." Although the convention was only selecting delegates to the presidential nominating convention, it was, Cutting remarked, "a pretty damn impressive demonstration of confidence and affection."

Old Guard Republicans were pressuring some county conventions that were selecting delegates for the state nominating convention in September. They were canvassing "desperately all over the state and through the railroad and coal companies as well as through Federal patronage" and were gaining support from "everyone who can't afford to lose a job." Nevertheless, when Cutting departed for Washington, he was confident that his forces would have "a comfortable majority" at this convention.[43]

He again immersed himself in his committee assignments and attended sessions of the Senate, but he did not join the debate until May. He considered attending an upcoming Bach festival and a concert in Philadelphia with Frederick Manning and spending a weekend in New York with his family. Manning suggested, "If you get too fed up with the Washington boys, pull out for a night. We could take Danny [Clifford McCarthy], op. 59, fly to Montreal and hire a piano."[44]

In May, Cutting breathed a sigh of relief. He hoped that Congress now was on the last lap "of the busiest and most futile session in history." Both Democrats and Republicans blamed "each other for the fiasco." He was concerned that in the confusion, Herbert Hoover possibly could "forge ahead with another mandate from the Great American people." For two years, Cutting argued, Hoover had successfully blocked meaningful relief measures. The president's proposals had failed to ease "distress in any substantial respect." Some of Hoover's constituents still admired him, but in Cutting's opinion, only the senate progressives were seriously shaping proposals that would cope in a meaningful way with the depression crisis. Unfortunately, they were in a hopeless minority in the Seventy-second Congress.[45]

Cutting did not give up. As the session came to an end, he again spoke out in the Senate. On May 23, barely a week after having a large cyst removed from his left eye, he introduced legislation for a five-billion-dollar expenditure to provide work for the unemployed and to assist in stabilizing business.[46] The federal government should step in when state and municipal governments exhausted their funds. Cutting said that "all measures enacted by the congress, including the Reconstruction Finance Corporation and the

National Credit Association, have failed to remedy the situation, or even to check the downward trend of business, the fall in security and commodity prices, and the rise in unemployment." The time had come to test a public works program on a scale adequate to meet the present emergency. For the past two years, Cutting said, Congress had been "approaching this problem from the wrong end, i.e., pouring the money in *at the top,* instead of re-establishing purchasing power *at the bottom.*" A federal public works program pursued "with the energy and boldness of war times would check the depression" and launch the economy on an upward course. Nothing less would do the job. His final statement upon the introduction of this bill concluded, "The time is short in which to make the effort."[47]

During his remarks, Cutting took special care to excoriate the president's handling of the depression crisis. In careful detail, he showed how earlier in his career and even at the outset of his presidency, Hoover had endorsed public works to ward off unemployment in lean years. Now the president expressed excessive concern for a balanced budget and for stabilized national credit, while others called for a massive federal program of public works.[48]

A week later, he resumed the attack. A recent address by Andrew Mellon, the American ambassador to Great Britain and the former secretary of the treasury, provided the occasion. Mellon's emphasis on a balanced budget only added to the "critical situation which has been stirred up by forces not under the control of the legislative branch of the Government." A balanced budget, Cutting argued, would impede "the relief of our starving population" and would fail to provide them with the "opportunity for profitable employment." Neither in Mellon's nor Hoover's current "philosophy" was there any place at this critical juncture for public works of any kind. Cutting anticipated that as the presidential campaign approached its climax, Hoover would endorse a public-works fund as a means of combatting unemployment. Now a leading critic of the administration, Cutting concluded, "If this country is going to continue to retain the respect of the civilized universe, it will devote a little less of its attention to the mere question of balancing the Budget . . . and will devote an infinitely greater proportion of its attention to the question of restoring the purchasing power of the consuming population of this country, of maintaining the American standard of living, and of preventing misery, unemployment, distress and starvation."[49]

By the end of May, Cutting and his senate colleagues were very tired from the twelve-hour daily sessions. On May 31 the president proposed to the Senate a program that sought to avoid "wasteful expansion of public works." Finding little to applaud, Cutting considered the program totally inadequate and the address a soporific, "about the only one we get these days." The trouble, he explained, was that everyone was "pulling in a different direction, with the President in the middle, all tangled up, and trying hard to make a face like a Mussolini."[50]

In June, Cutting favored a Veterans Bureau measure that provided assistance to "those who have incurred tubercular or neuropsychiatric complaints as the result of their service connection." These veterans, Cutting maintained, "on the whole are suffering even more pitifully than those who suffered loss of limbs in action, far more than those who were mercifully granted death at the front." He criticized the Hoover administration for having insisted in 1930 on a limited provision that made veterans with nonservice-connected disabilities eligible for compensation. Cutting urged the Senate to develop a comprehensive general disability plan that could be debated on its merits.[51]

As veterans trickled into Washington in search of their bonus, Cutting observed that he had favored a bonus since his term as commander of the American Legion for the Department of New Mexico in 1924. He and others who had witnessed their parade through the city were "profoundly moved at the idea that a whole generation of men whom the Congress of the United States took out of private life and put into the war is now at our doors pleading for the elementary right of citizens to be allowed to work or, if that is not given to them, for the payment of a debt which they feel to be just." However, he did not think the arrival of ex-servicemen would aid their cause.

Cutting claimed his proposed public works measure calling for a bond issue of five billion dollars would provide a more meaningful response than a bonus to the crisis situation. Although he doubted whether even that vast sum was adequate, he was sure that reducing federal appropriations all along the line, as the administration desired, was not the proper course of action.[52]

During his final remarks on June 15, he spoke in favor of a senate standing committee to handle veterans affairs and promised to push for a resolution that would create one before the close of the session, but he never got the opportunity. Cutting had been "pretty fatigued" during the past weeks, and on June 16, he took to his bed, feeling "very weary." Three days later, he went to Baltimore where he had an eye examination. "All is in excellent shape," he reported, although the doctor changed his glasses and repeated that his right eye, while "entirely normal," could be improved if he read with it for at least two minutes every day. The following day, June 20, he spoke to the Senate in favor of Philippine independence and then returned to his bed, where he spent his forty-fourth birthday on June 23.[53]

That day, his fever was 101 degrees, although he experienced no aches or pains. Upon the advice of Robert La Follette, Jr., Cutting called in another physician. Dr. Worth Daniels discovered a queer rash that he diagnosed as a rare blood complaint and recommended two eminent blood specialists. After a sampling of specimens and a thorough analysis, they decided the rash was a rare form of purpura, a disease marked by purple or livid spots on the skin. The platelets in the blood had broken down and had allowed the blood in the small vessels to wander at random over the tissues. The disorder was not serious unless a major organ was involved and could be cured through the ingestion of calcium.[54]

However, his condition further deteriorated, his temperature rising to 102 degrees. The doctors made additional blood tests. On June 28, they concluded he had jaundice. The purpura was no longer visible. On July 2, he received a blood transfusion, but his fever did not fully abate for several days. Concerned about his health, his mother and younger sister came to Washington, stayed several days, and returned to Westbrook once reassured. When his mother returned on July 20, she found that he was taking dinner downstairs but that he was depressed and wanted to escape the terrible heat. Managing to find some humor in his situation, he labeled himself a "medical freak" certain "to be written up in the medical journals." An attack of purpura complicated by jaundice was an unknown combination and had "stirred several sets of doctors into a frenzy." And he was no doubt pleased that some of his colleagues received almost daily bulletins about his condition from La Follette and inquired after him.[55]

On June 22, accompanied by his mother, Cutting left Washington for New York and the family estate at Westbrook. Here his temperature abated, and he was able to sleep well. By the end of July, he was lunching with Alice Roosevelt Longworth and sailing on the bay with his mother and Clifford McCarthy. His blood tests, while erratic, showed improvement, and the jaundice began to disappear. Cutting's spirits improved as well. Having luncheon guests and sailing in the afternoon indicated that his health had been restored and that he was feeling fit once again. On August 19, he departed by train for Santa Fe, ready and eager to engage in the political fight "at least locally." He did not see how he could do much for either Hoover or the national administration. His secretary, Edgar Puryear, informed him that neither the Reconstruction Finance Corporation nor the Home Owner's Loan Corporation were of much help in New Mexico. When his train departed from Grand Central Station, he had no notion that he would emerge as the leading figure on the New Mexico political scene and would play a dominant role in both political parties.[56]

CHAPTER 18

CAMPAIGNING
1932

In 1932 New Mexico politics were more tangled and confused than in previous election years. As the presidential contest and the failing economy interjected themselves into New Mexico by the time of the state conventions, Cutting played a major role in compounding the tangle. His behavior, however, paralleled that of other progressive Republicans who placed principle above party in 1932.

As usual, party factionalism was rampant in New Mexico. Governor Arthur Seligman, the Democratic incumbent, was bitterly opposed by an old guard faction in which two of his predecessors, Arthur T. Hannett and James F. Hinkle, were prominent. They resented, among other things, Seligman's appointment of progressive individuals to political offices—"Cutting Democrats," or, even worse, "Cutting Republicans." They charged that an alliance existed between Seligman and Cutting and that Seligman had been taken in by Cutting and therefore was neither a Democrat nor of any use to the party.

For his part, Seligman had considerable factional support. While Cutting was a personal friend and a member of the board of the First National Bank of Santa Fe, Seligman was a conservative banker and traditional Democrat. His political views were hostile to Cutting's progressive challenges to the Hoover administration. When Cutting reflected on Seligman's performance as governor, he was unimpressed. Herein lay the seeds of his dilemma.

To be sure, the progressive wing of the Republican party, the "Cutting Republicans," were a powerful group. Hispanics, comprising a majority of the state's population, mostly voted the Republican ticket and filled the ranks of the "Cutting Republicans." Their standing was bitterly contested by the stalwarts, who were supported by the Hoover administration. Moreover, thanks to Albert Simms and Ruth Hanna McCormick, the old guard could maintain close ties with both the Hoover administration and the national Republican organization. If Cutting found his position in the Republican party jeopardized, his option of shifting to the Democratic party, neither faction of which appealed to him, was foreclosed. His dilemma led him to follow the example of Theodore Roosevelt in 1912 and leave the Republican ranks to create his own political party.

The first skirmish came in January with a call for a meeting of the Republi-

213

can State Central Committee to be held on February 6. The committee would select the date for the convention that would elect both delegates to the national convention and would select the national committeeman. Albert Simms, who had lost his seat in the House of Representatives to Dennis Chavez, a Democrat, reported that Cutting's friends intended to forward his name as the national committeeman and that he believed Cutting would likely be elected. As long as Cutting was denied patronage, the old guard could retain control of the party apparatus and thwart the challenges of independent or progressive forces.[1]

When the state committee met, the "Cutting Republicans" won two signal victories. The first was determining the method of apportioning county delegates to a state convention at which nine delegates to the Republican National Convention in Chicago would be selected. The second came in selecting March 26 as the date for the convention rather than the latter part of May as preferred by the old guard. Cutting had suggested the date in a telegram to Carl P. Dunifon, the state chairman. The victory was impressive because the committee had been selected two years previously when the old guard controlled the party machinery. The vote, 63 to 51, indicated a change in sentiment, leading the Cutting forces to believe that for the first time they could gain control of the party.[2]

While pleased with these victories, Cutting recognized that the old guard would yield power only after a hard, desperate fight. Acknowledging its clout, Cutting wrote, "Through the Santa Fe Railroad and the coal companies, they have a hold on so many people who would like to be friendly but can't afford to lose their jobs." Members of the state committee feared an anti-Hoover delegation would be selected at Cutting's behest and would go uninstructed to the national convention. Albert Simms, a staunch Hoover supporter, was selected as a delegate to the state convention with instructions to support Cutting for the Republican National Committee, an indication of the disarray of the state organization and of the strength of the Cutting forces. A week before the state convention, all of the Bernalillo County delegates were instructed to endorse Cutting as national committeeman.[3]

When the state convention met in Santa Fe on March 26, Cutting told the delegates that he hoped the Republican National Convention would nominate a candidate who would consider "the interests of New Mexico and the nation." The convention then elected him Republican national committeeman by acclamation. He candidly stated that he did not favor the renomination of President Hoover. As long as he conscientiously could support the interests of the Republican party he would do so. Otherwise he would get out. Cutting also made clear his opposition to an instructed delegation to the Republican National Convention. By a vote of 24 to 3, the resolutions committee then turned down a proposal to instruct the state delegation for Hoover. In his remarks to the convention, Cutting stated that he had no personal stake in the matter, his chief interest being the welfare of the people of New Mexico. He explained, "Whether in private or public life, I hope you will know that, it is your interests which I am trying to promote, so long as life may endure."

Without reservation, the Santa Fe convention turned the Republican party over to Cutting. He was one of nine delegates chosen to attend the presidential nominating convention. He was especially appreciative of the support he received in the primaries when voters selected delegates to the county conventions. He wrote, "The youth has come forward to testify to what I consider a vote of confidence in the new deal that we are going to have in this state." Cutting wanted Hispanics to have an enhanced role in the political process, a prospect anything but pleasing to some of the party leaders.[4]

Cutting's victory further complicated the complex political situation in New Mexico. For example, his alternate to the national convention, Manuel Gallegos, held a post in the Seligman administration. Since Cutting now dominated the Republican party, whether his supporters would endorse Seligman for a second term was now in doubt. Following Cutting's election as national committeeman, a movement got underway to "unseat from control the Cutting faction in the Democratic party." Within Republican ranks, at least four of the nine delegates selected in Santa Fe would vote for Hoover only, indicating that the old guard was still a potent faction and could take advantage of any crack in the Cutting ranks. Complex as the situation was, when Cutting departed for Washington, his frank, clear and impressive remarks left few, if any, doubts about where he stood on critical public issues.[5]

Until his return in August, Cutting had little time to devote to political affairs in New Mexico. He was probably amused when, at the Jefferson Day rally of Democrats in Santa Fe, he was lauded for his national leadership. But more importantly, he was aware that the progressives now held a majority in the Republican organization and had to select a slate "which we can offer the voters with self respect." Cutting told an old friend that he was "not interested enough in remaining in office to be willing to compromise on matters of principle." Meanwhile he left the nuts-and-bolts political work largely in the hands of his key political aides, Herman Baca and Jesus Baca.[6]

Cutting's dilemma was that, while unhappy about Hoover's renomination, he was unenthusiastic about the Democratic performance in both Washington and Santa Fe. His supporting Democratic candidates in New Mexico would provoke uproars among factions in both parties and would further muddle the political situation. Agreeing with his assessment of the Hoover administration, many progressive citizens and Cutting supporters in New Mexico faced a similar dilemma and awaited his return for guidance in the coming campaign. On the other hand, old guard Republican leaders recognized that Cutting's support of the ticket could prevent a party split that would benefit the Democratic party.[7]

When the newspapers learned in July that Cutting was ill, some carried stories that he had suffered a nervous breakdown. After the public learned that jaundice was responsible for his illness, the rumors subsided and both friend and foe awaited his return to the state political wars. Meanwhile, on the precinct level, Cutting's friends were canvassing voters in counties with large Hispanic populations and building membership in organizations loyal to him. Throughout the summer months, national and state political tensions became hopelessly entangled with Cutting in one way or another.[8]

In mid-August Cutting returned to Santa Fe. He had recovered from jaundice but was concerned about hay fever. He immediately went to the pollen-free room at Los Siete Burros. After a day and a half in isolation, he ventured forth and gradually increased the time he spent in the open air. An injection every fourth day helped to ward off a serious pollen reaction. Following this regimen, he was able to conduct interviews. He learned firsthand that politics in the state was "almost as mixed up as [it] seemed at a distance." The condition of the First National Bank, over which Arthur Seligman presided, was so "disgraceful" that Cutting could not "conceive of the Governor being a candidate for reelection."[9]

Republican leaders visited Cutting during this period. From these interviews, he discerned that "it won't be any cinch to elect a state ticket" and that there was "a close understanding between the reactionaries in both parties," but he said, "It is doubtful which way they intend to jump." Immersed as he was in the political situation, Cutting responded to a plea from Robert M. La Follette, Jr. for an additional contribution to his brother's gubernatorial campaign, a sum Cutting previously promised to forward if needed.[10]

An indication of the eruption to come soon appeared. At the August meeting of the Republican State Central Committee, Francis Wilson was not permitted to read a statement delineating the damage inflicted on the party by Cutting and his paper, the *New Mexican*. Wilson was distressed that Cutting had "said privately that he will not support the President and yet the party leaders in New Mexico, hopeful that he will support the State ticket, are willing to accept him on that basis." Wilson opposed surrendering Republican national policies to a "Cutting party masquerading under the name of the Republican party."

Wilson was angered by a *Nation* article reprinted in the *New Mexican*. The author, Paul Y. Anderson, was critical of Hoover's deployment of troops against the bonus marchers in Washington, D.C. He charged that Hoover had deliberately schemed to persuade the people that their government was threatened by revolution. In his statement and more directly in an open letter to Cutting, Wilson suggested that Anderson and Cutting might be communist sympathizers. According to Wilson, Cutting, given his known opposition to the Hoover administration, should not serve as Republican national committeeman.[11]

Still convalescing, Cutting did not attend the meeting of the central committee at which Wilson sought to make his presentation. Instead, he sent a letter expressing the hope "that individual differences of opinion may be subordinated to the kind of vigorous and united cooperation which will insure victory for the party in New Mexico." From Los Siete Burros, he kept himself informed of plans for the state nominating convention that would be held in Albuquerque on September 22. He noted that Hoover-Curtis clubs had appeared around the state and that the Bernalillo County chapter had scheduled a banquet for August 29 in the largest dining room in Albuquerque. Holm Bursum, still an old guard leader, was the state chairman of the Hoover clubs and a firm believer that independently wealthy Cutting would try to betray the Republican party in some underhanded way.[12]

In early September, Everett Sanders, the chairman of the Republican National Committee, heard from the state chairman, Carl Dunifon, about the "difficulties within our party ranks in New Mexico." Dunifon suggested that "some absolutely disinterested person from National Headquarters" conduct an investigation before irate Republican leaders took any drastic measures, "such as the removal of Senator Bronson Cutting as National Committeeman." If the party jettisoned Cutting, Dunifon worried, it would lose the support of the *Albuquerque Journal,* which had "by far the largest circulation of any paper in the state." Cutting was reputed to be part owner, and its publisher was his ally. If Cutting was "put on the pan," Dunifon declared, enough Republican voters would stray from the party ranks to cause defeat in November. Sanders never responded to the letter.[13]

While organization leaders wrangled over the dilemma, Cutting pondered his strategy for the state convention. In Socorro County, dominated by Holm Bursum, old guard delegates won every precinct election. Maurice Miera, leader of the opposition, claimed that the delegation was fraudulently selected. The Cutting organization concluded not to initiate costly court challenges that could not be concluded prior to the nominating convention and decided to accept the delegation at the state convention. Also involved in this contest would be the disposition of campaign funds in the county and the distribution of patronage if the state ticket prevailed in November.

Cutting accepted the agenda and agreed to support it. The old guard was using all available means to gain control of as many county delegations as possible. Their success would allow them to select county candidates and then to challenge Cutting's control of the state convention. In Socorro County, Miera understood what was involved. He agreed to let the old guard control the county nominations and then battle them for recognition at the state convention. Since a similar situation prevailed in two other counties, the state convention, scheduled for September 23 in Albuquerque, promised to be a lively affair.[14]

While Cutting pondered a Republican slate, Richard Dillon informed him that he would accept the party's gubernatorial nomination if the convention offered it. Cutting was not surprised. He told an ally that if nominated, Dillon would receive his support. However, he believed Dillon would face certain defeat. He could win the votes neither of Republican workingmen who would recall his opposition to the creation of a labor commission nor of the residents of the largely Hispanic northern counties.[15]

Following a careful regimen of diet and rest since his return, Cutting conducted political affairs from his porch and at his dinner table and, as ever, got "a vast amusement out of the transparencies of his fellow men." He closely watched the county elections in which delegates and local candidates were selected. Although Cutting's health improved, the political situation went from "bad to worse." In early September, Maine, traditionally a Republican state, went for Hoover by slightly less than thirty-six thousand votes. Cutting did not see how "New Mexico could go Republican" and thought that "perhaps Dillon might as well be defeated as the next man." The prospect of losing control of the Republican organization in the likely event of a Democratic landslide did not please him after the long and arduous battle waged to gain it.[16]

Cutting came to his gloomy conclusion despite the equally sharp divisions within the Democratic party. Governor Seligman had antagonized Democrats with his appointment of some "Cutting Democrats" to his administration. Moreover, pundits speculated that if Cutting named a Republican state ticket, he would drive many old guard Republicans to support a Democratic nominee other than Seligman, whom they regarded as a Cutting ally. Many Democrats, following the same logic, sought a candidate other than Seligman. The leading challenger for the nomination was John Simms, the brother of former Republican congressman, Albert Simms. Despite Democratic feuding on a scale comparable to that within Republican ranks, the failing economy and the inability of the Hoover administration to cope with the crisis led Cutting to conclude that his party's prospects were bleak. He could not say so publicly before the state convention, however, where in some sense, damning with faint praise, he would have to support Herbert Hoover for reelection.[17]

In the days before the Albuquerque convention, he feared that his strategy might go awry. In several counties, Cutting delegates won handily, but the old guard intended to contest their seating. With delegations challenged by both the Cutting forces and the old guard, the nominating convention promised to be lively. Cutting debated whether he should "wash his hands of the whole affair" and "let the ticket take its inevitable defeat," or whether he should put up as good a ticket as possible "and let the voters take it or leave it." Either way, he envisioned a Roosevelt landslide in New Mexico.[18]

The Albuquerque convention was a pyrrhic victory for the old guard Republicans, who regained control of the Republican party. Ironically they catapulted Cutting into a more powerful and influential role in both New Mexico and national politics. The war began on the morning of September 23, before the convention got under way at the armory. Shortly after nine, Cutting appeared before hundreds of delegates gathered in the nearby courthouse. Cutting categorically stated that "he would not stand for fraud and political chicanery," that the central committee's seating of delegates from rump conventions was thwarting the wishes of qualified voters and that he would not abide by their decisions. The way was now open "to vote for any ticket put in the field after such action," but Cutting did not urge voting for the Democratic ticket. In addition, he said that he was ready to step down as national committeeman.[19]

The convention merely played out the scenario presented in the courthouse, with Cutting holding center stage in both instances. He tendered his resignation as national committeeman, and the county delegations from Rio Arriba and Santa Fe counties and Maurice Miera's Socorro group walked out of the hall. Dennis Chavez, a Democrat, later estimated that about sixty-five percent of the delegates departed with Cutting. The remaining delegates by acclamation nominated Richard C. Dillon for a third term before recessing for the day. The next day, the convention selected other candidates and adopted a platform.

The Cutting delegates bolted after the convention sustained several controversial decisions of the credentials committee by a vote of 682½ to 368½. In the Rio Arriba and Santa Fe contests the committee upheld the old guard challengers. In the Socorro County contest, it turned down the challenge by the Miera faction. After the roll call was concluded and the result announced, Cutting mounted the platform. He declared, "As one of the members of this convention, who has been unseated by the action of the convention, I hereby submit my resignation as national committeeman." In a ringing, hour-long address, Cutting warned the delegates that only just action would entitle the convention to public support. At the same time, he assailed the age-old control of New Mexico by corporations and their attorneys. He said that sitting in the convention were delegates who would dictate politics to the voters and would deprive the people of their rights. Cutting insisted, "I cannot be a party official responsible for electing a ticket I believe was founded on fraud." While he might support "some or all of the candidates" as in the past, he would also tell the people exactly what he thought.[20]

Old guard Republicans were delighted. Although they won a self-destructive victory, they regained control of the party. That very day, Ruth Hanna Simms phoned the White House to announce that Cutting had been beaten "to a frazzle" and that he had resigned as national committeeman. She wanted to interest Hoover in the selection of her husband to replace him. However, the initial response of the Republican National Committee to the news was that "it does not seem advisable to spend a great amount of effort in New Mexico."[21]

Explaining the convention's actions, Holm Bursum said, "Cutting was all wrong in what he tried to do—he simply tried to manhandle the Convention and when he failed he squealed like a spoiled child—resigned, walked out and wouldn't play. He showed himself a bum sport." Bursum was convinced that Cutting and Democratic governor Arthur Seligman "had planned the job to bust up and destroy the Republican party in the interest of Seligman and Cutting bipartisan control of the state." Although Bursum's analysis of Cutting's motives was faulty, his indirect statement about the demise of the Republican party was preeminently correct. His flawed analysis became the official Republican view and was presented in a lengthy statement released on October 29 by Republican State Chairman E. L. Safford when the party realized that it could not carry the state.[22]

Equally delighted by Cutting's action, New Mexico Democrats commended him. On September 24, a county convention complimented Cutting for his courageous resignation when "the Republican party of New Mexico became so rank that honorable Republicans could not support it." Many Democrats believed that he could rejoin their party. Even before the Albuquerque convention, the Democratic standard-bearer, Franklin D. Roosevelt, contacted Cutting about meeting him secretly on September 27 when the presidential-campaign train entered the state. Noting that secrecy "for either of us" was impossible, Cutting said, "Of course I shan't go."[23]

Cutting would not join the Democrats. Instead he announced that his organization would file a third state ticket, a task completed on September 26. He was confident that his independent stance would win him hundreds of new and loyal friends. He and his organization believed that by creating a third party, a Progressive party, he could institutionalize his hold on the balance of power in New Mexico politics. Franklin D. Roosevelt acknowledged Cutting's power and influence and hoped to win his support in the presidential campaign.[24]

On September 27, the Roosevelt Special, returning east from the successful trip to the Pacific Coast, stopped at Lamy, the junction point of the fifteen-mile spur line into Santa Fe. With his remarks, Roosevelt endeavored to win the support of Cutting and the new Progressive state organization. Turning to the "left," he asserted that there was no longer room for two major parties, both of which were conservative. At Roosevelt's invitation, Cutting joined him on the rear platform and waved to the crowd. Talking with reporters, Cutting did not declare himself for Roosevelt but said that his actions spoke for themselves. Given Roosevelt's statement that the Democratic party was the progressive party, the way was open for Cutting to endorse his candidacy. With a third party, as Albert Fall suggested, "the surest way to defeat those who have connived to defeat you, is to let your supporters go to the Democrats."[25]

While Cutting neither spoke to Roosevelt nor stayed very long on the rear platform, he did "have a talk with Eleanor in the car while the speaking was going on" and explained the local situation to her. He was not enthused about Roosevelt's farm speech but thought "the railroad and especially the power speeches were a great improvement." When the campaign special departed from Lamy, Roosevelt must have felt confident that Cutting would endorse him.[26]

Word quickly leaked that Cutting was considering Frederic Howe's invitation to join the executive committee of the progressive organization that was working on behalf of Roosevelt. Joining the organization, Robert M. La Follette, Jr. told Cutting, not only would he strengthen Roosevelt's progressivism but it might serve as a nucleus for future progressive political activity. Cutting, like La Follette, was inclined toward Roosevelt primarily because of his own adamant opposition to Hoover. Both men sensed from Roosevelt's speeches a lack of breadth and depth in his progressivism and were concerned that their support for Roosevelt might be taken as support for the Democratic tickets in their home states. They concluded that criticizing the Hoover administration was the best way to support Roosevelt.[27]

Although admitting to some disappointment in early October, Cutting was relieved that he did not have to nominate a Republican ticket that "surely would have been knifed by the Old Guard." Throughout the convention, Cutting believed that delegates had been in touch with the White House. "Even in the old days of the Gang," he said, "there was never anything quite so brazen as the seating of the Rio Arriba contestants." Freed of his post as national committeeman, Cutting was no longer constrained by questions of party loyalty or discipline. He found Hoover impossible as a candidate, but he deemed "it unwise to come out for Franklin so soon after the convention." He recognized that he would have to issue a public endorsement at some stage and get behind the state Democratic ticket as well, "a rather distasteful alternative."[28]

The campaign would be a hard one, "both on account of Dillon's popularity and Simms's contributions." Whenever possible, Cutting intended to avoid public appearances. He would campaign, only at the "end of the period." He was willing to say that he saw no future for himself in the Republican party only to "the few people" who valued his opinions. If the Progressive party did not survive the election, Cutting thought that he would leave "public life, unless the Democrats put on a much better performance than I expect of them." Existing in name alone, the new party quickly withdrew its state ticket to insure the defeat of the old guard slate, a maneuver that drove the Republicans to continue denouncing a Cutting-Seligman alliance. More to the point was the question of whether he was not "under some moral obligation" to endorse Roosevelt over Hoover as "the lesser of two evils." Certainly, he concluded, "I am no longer under any moral obligation not to say so."[29]

Campaigns left Cutting little time to contemplate moral imperatives. If the Progressive party was to survive, it had to find places for supporters who in the future could rally to the new party. Since it was rather "late in the day" to build a satisfactory party organization, Cutting reluctantly concluded "to pick the lesser of two evils" and fuse with the Democrats on the county level. To accomplish this goal, he engaged in "innumerable conferences and intrigues" and then patiently awaited the results of various county conventions. Enormously strengthening the Democrats, fusion occurred primarily in the heavily Republican northern counties, the largely Hispanic area whence Cutting derived his support. Cutting recognized that these efforts, plus "luck and a national landslide," would carry the Democrats to victory in the state, "though they certainly don't deserve it."[30]

On October 18, Robert M. La Follette, Jr. phoned Cutting that he intended to announce for Roosevelt on the following day. Cutting thought that he would wait until later in the month. He wanted to complete the fusion process and to help manage the local campaign in Santa Fe County. By October 22, Cutting concluded details with the National Progressive League and agreed to speak over a NBC hookup at 10:30 P.M., Eastern Standard Time, on Wednesday, October 26, in Albuquerque. Hiram Johnson, whom Cutting informed of his decision, promptly responded that in California, he had already endorsed Roosevelt. The remaining progressive Republican leader, George W. Norris, was on a national speaking tour in behalf of Roosevelt. Owing to illness, Norris was responsible for Cutting's speaking on the twenty-sixth.[31]

By the end of October, Cutting was convinced that Roosevelt would carry New Mexico. Unless he carried it by at least twenty thousand votes, he thought, Seligman would lose to Dillon. Seligman was "personally very unpopular, especially with the Anglos," and everyone liked Dillon, but the election of Dillon would mean "the return of the Old Gang." The fusion movement and a Roosevelt landslide could turn the tide. This was the context in which Cutting viewed his radio address. He felt some urgency about the matter because in September, he had given "a rather trivial interview," one with no political significance, that appeared in the Hearst papers as a ringing endorsement of Roosevelt. Cutting counterbalanced the two hundred thousand dollars that Mrs. Simms was reported to have given the Republicans by borrowing "a modest amount which will go a long way" in preventing the return of the old gang.[32]

Senator Norris was scheduled to speak in Denver over a national network on October 26 but had to cancel the engagement. At the last moment, with barely time to catch the train for Denver, Cutting agreed to take his place. "Suffering from stomach trouble or nervous indigestion," Cutting claimed that he was unprepared when he boarded the train. He spoke first over the radio and afterwards in an auditorium before a large crowd for an hour and a half. His endorsement of Roosevelt embodied a penetrating critique of the Hoover administration's failure to cope with the depression crisis. His national audience heard a progressive who sought an honest, efficient government that would provide equal opportunity and equal justice to all of its citizens.[33]

Cutting criticized Hoover for having "no idea of the real causes of the depression." He made suggestions for a sensible relief program: the immediate relief of starvation; the formulation of a public-works program to provide jobs; the shortening of working hours to extend employment; the extended use of taxation to produce a better distribution of wealth; the utilization of national planning in formulating industrial policies; and the provision of equal access to credit. In all, he found a president "completely subservient to anti-public interests."

After reviewing Hoover's failures as a president, he noted the real temptation of many liberals to support Norman Thomas, the Socialist presidential candidate. Cutting thought that a ballot cast for Thomas would be a vote thrown away. He saw genuine hope in the candidacy of Franklin Roosevelt, whose record of public service was praiseworthy. In addition, Cutting mentioned his personal knowledge of the candidate as a "hard working, honest and open-minded citizen." Above all, he concluded, "In this crisis there can be no thought of things so trivial as party alignments." The welfare of the country took precedence. Cutting summoned "all who believe that the common people of America have the right to share in the benefits of our civilization" to vote, as he was going to vote, for Franklin Roosevelt.[34]

Unhappy with his address, Cutting wrote, "I thought it very conventional when I read it after dictating it. . . ." The response, however, was more than satisfactory, and Cutting immediately found himself in demand as a speaker. For over two weeks, he received each day about five hundred letters referring to the Denver speech. He agreed to deliver one further radio address, although he was not enthused about the prospect. For one thing, he felt that he had said all he "had to say the first time," and for another, he confessed, "My nerves are all shot to hell." Therefore, he decided to remain in New Mexico "where the fight is getting very bitter and the results greatly in doubt."[35]

He soon departed on a trip to Socorro and Valencia counties, making three or four speeches a day, some in Spanish and some in English. He gave one address in Spanish and English over the radio at Albuquerque on the evening of November 4. The following day in Santa Fe, he hastily prepared for another national radio address that he would follow with another on a local station to discuss state affairs. He was now so exhausted that rather than depart on a Mexican vacation "after the election on November 8," he considered barring the house to visitors and resting at home.[36]

On Sunday evening November 6, Cutting spoke briefly over an Albuquerque station, again sponsored by the National Progressive League. He reiterated the chief theme of his Denver address that had criticized Hoover more so than it had praised Roosevelt. He appealed "especially to Republicans" to rise above partisanship, and he spoke only about the presidency, "of two men, one of whom thinks it is too expensive to put the unemployed to work and the other of whom makes it the main item of his program." His second address delivered to a statewide audience was not favorably received by some stand-patters in the Republican party. One party loyalist said that unlike in his earlier address, "he talked about himself and his affairs all the time" and that the title of his speech "should have been 'I—Me—Myself.'"[37]

The election resulted in a Democratic triumph in both New Mexico and the nation and left Cutting, like most of his friends, completely exhausted and eager to take things as easy as possible. He turned down three invitations to deliver Armistice Day addresses. Although the victory was pleasing, it was "a little too extreme to be really satisfactory," according to Cutting. While he wondered "what the Democrats will do with it," he recognized they could not do much worse than the Republicans. In New Mexico, Hoover carried only three counties; in 1928, he had lost only one county. Dillon carried only six counties in his race for governor, losing to Seligman by over sixteen thousand votes. The state Senate went three-fourths Democratic, as did eight of the nine judicial districts in which only district attorneys were elected. In short, Cutting noted, "The old gang is left without anything to hang onto." Mrs. Simms's money could not turn the tide. Cutting noted that she broke down in the middle of an election-eve radio talk. She started an appeal to the voters of Illinois and then claimed that she had lost her manuscript. A phonograph record filled out the remaining time.[38]

As he contemplated the changes in Congress, Cutting was almost ecstatic. "Think of the senate without [Hiram] Bingham, [Wesley L.] Jones, [George H.] Moses, [Tasker L.] Oddie, [Samuel M.] Shortridge, [Reed] Smoot or [James E.] Watson," he wrote, while noting that Simon D. Fess and David A. Reed would be "the only real old-guarders left." Nevertheless, he wished that he "felt a little more real confidence as to what the new administration will do." Although he had some hesitations, he received little but praise from many quarters for his role throughout the campaign.[39]

A friend in New Mexico observed that his stand for "honesty and regularity in party procedure" had been "conclusively and emphatically sustained at the polls, by the complete retirement of the O[ld] G[uard]." The Democratic mayor of Albuquerque, a rabid partisan, admitted that Cutting "did a great deal to carry this state." As a further indication of his increasing national significance, a telegram from the president-elect invited him to stop over at Warm Springs, Georgia, while enroute to Washington for the lame-duck session of the Seventy-second Congress.[40]

With Congress scheduled to reconvene in early December, Cutting had little time to rest and enjoy "this wonderful air." Key Pittman and Burton K. Wheeler, powerful Democratic senators, appeared in Santa Fe. John Collier joined Senator and Mrs. Wheeler at lunch with Cutting and discussed his preferences for Indian commissioner. State Progressives held a conference to perfect the organization of the new party. Over six hundred people "showed up from every corner of the state." At least two of Santa Fe's many artists inquired about painting Cutting's portrait. Cutting attended a dinner at Witter Bynner's home, the first since Clifford McCarthy departed from it in 1929, and patched together a friendship that Bynner sought to renew. Cutting escaped with Jesus Baca for a five-day automobile trip covering over fifteen hundred miles, mostly in Arizona, a journey that managed to smooth out "both sets of nerves." He enjoyed this respite, "glorious warm days, and a full moon at night," but he wondered "why this successful election should have us all so jittery except that one had to have so many dealings with cheapskates and sons of bitches."[41]

Of all the activities Cutting engaged in during this period of respite, the conference of Progressives was easily the most significant. On November 16, 1932, a platform for the Progressive Party of New Mexico was adopted at the convention assembled at Santa Fe. It proclaimed "that the government of this state should be brought closer to the people" and stressed that the new party had been organized "for the sake of principles and not for the sake of obtaining political appointments." Toward this end, the final sentence of the platform recommended that "the state organization should refrain from official endorsement of any candidates for public employment under the present or incoming state administration." Reflecting Cutting's views, the platform emphasized the independence of the new party and officially severed whatever ties might have existed with both political parties in New Mexico. Cutting believed the Republican party would need something "more than money" to revive itself and that the Democrats would prove a disappointment because their leaders showed "no understanding whatever of what is going on." In his opinion, the Progressive party possibly had a future in New Mexico.[42]

Maurice Miera, who had headed the challenging delegation from Socorro County at the Republican State Convention, became the chairman of the new party. He tended to organizational details such as opening a headquarters, distributing copies of the party platform, meeting with legislators, and in general representing the Progressive party. To engage in these activities required funds that the party did not possess. Miera was willing to devote as much time as necessary to the job. Cutting asked that he keep expenses down "in order to save what little is available these days for the really vital things" but that he let him know what his personal expenses were.[43]

On the evening of November 29, before departing for Washington, Cutting announced that he had received an invitation from the president-elect to stop off at Warm Springs. The announcement elicited a spate of rumors that he would be offered a cabinet post, a matter that was not clarified following his visit with Roosevelt. Upon his arrival at Warm Springs Cutting spoke to the press. He indicated that he was ready to support the newly elected president on progressive legislation. He said he had no reason to believe that he and the progressive Republicans who endorsed Roosevelt would receive any patronage from the new administration. He was then taken by automobile to the cottage of the president-elect.

Cutting spoke again with the press before his departure. More specifically, Cutting said that he had discussed legislation, agriculture and reforestation in detail with Governor Roosevelt during the two-hour conversation. He added that the subject of the Indian Bureau, in which he had a particular interest, was also explored. Cutting gave vague, evasive answers to all other questions: whether the Republicans would punish him for bolting President Hoover; whether there would be a new party alignment along liberal lines; and whether the Democratic party was on trial. He then boarded a train for Washington, which he reached on December 6. He had left the nation's capital on July 22, recovering from jaundice and a blood disease. When he returned, he was bronzed and in good health, ready to face the rigors of the last months of the Hoover presidency while awaiting the advent of the Roosevelt administration.[44]

Cutting underwent a thorough physical examination shortly after his return to Washington. "No abnormality of any significance," reported Dr. Worth Daniels. Cutting, he said, was somewhat overweight but less so than formerly. He believed that during Cutting's illness, "there was slight damage to his liver." The doctor advised his continued abstinence from alcohol and his following "a proper diet." He also urged Cutting to get away during the Christmas recess, "probably to the Caribbean." Freedom from responsibility and an opportunity to rest would do him good. Although Dr. Daniels did not "feel apprehensive" about Cutting's condition, he wanted to check it again at the end of several months. [45]

Commenting later on his Warm Springs interview, Cutting was pleased that Roosevelt had "kept his sense of proportion" and that the victory "had not gone to his head." He was amused that Alice Longworth was "very indignant" with him for supporting her fifth cousin. He did not inform her of his recent discovery that the new president was in fact his fourth cousin. [46]

Cutting's newly discovered relative had helped him to gain national prominence during the past campaign. The lame-duck session of the Seventy-second Congress, the opening day of which Cutting missed because of his stopover at Warm Springs, felt the incoming administration hovering over its proceedings. Cutting had not fully made up his mind about Roosevelt's and the Democratic party's capacity for leadership in time of crisis, but he looked forward to this session and the likely special session that would follow Roosevelt's inauguration.

CHAPTER 19

NO NEW DEAL

With the election over, Cutting hoped that the new president would present a program enabling the nation to overcome the depression crisis. The inadequacies of the Hoover administration served only to reinforce his view that government owed its people the obligation "to find ways and means by which they can at least keep themselves alive." He never blamed Hoover for causing the depression, but he did fault him for failing to cope with starvation in the midst of abundance.[1] However, until Roosevelt took office, Cutting's immediate concern was the lame duck session of the Seventy-second Congress, which got underway the day before he arrived in Washington from his visit with Roosevelt at Warm Springs.

Almost immediately he plunged into the final debate on the Philippine Independence Bill, which his colleague, Harry Hawes, took the lead in shepparding through the chamber. Cutting defended the provision that established a quota of one hundred Filipino immigrants to the United States per year, once American sovereignty over the islands had been withdrawn. In doing so, he encountered the opposition of senators who wanted the total exclusion of Filipino immigrants like other Asiatics. Cutting argued that while under the American flag during a commonwealth period prior to achieving complete independence, the Philippine people should suffer no discrimination on account of race. After final independence, however, he had no objection to full restriction.[2]

Throughout the extensive debate, tariff rates on sugar imports, racial prejudice and a desire for disentanglement from the Far East vied one with the other on the senate floor. The motive of Cutting and a handful of senators for granting independence was opposition to the acquisition of an American empire. Cutting was unwilling to grant independence, however, until the Philippine people had "stated in the most forceful way open to them that they desire it." Unlike Cutting, some in Congress would automatically grant independence after an interim period.

The Hawes-Cutting measure provided three opportunities for input by the Filipinos. First of all, the Philippine legislature would have to ratify the bill. Then, after a convention drew up a constitution, it would submit the plan to a plebiscite of the Philippine people. If adopted, this constitution would guide the Filipinos during the commonwealth or interim period. Finally, the people would decide whether they should sever their connections with the United States. In brief, the United States should not "step out" until the Philippine people had ample time to weigh "the pros and cons" of independence "regardless of any economic disadvantages which might come to them from so doing."

"Tariff barriers" and "free trade" with the United States had given the Filipinos a better-than-average "standard of living" in the Orient. During the interim period, they would gradually replace their free-trade status with an export tax that would pay their national debts. The trial period would provide them firsthand opportunities to learn "the disadvantages" of "independence" before they cast their final vote.[3]

The bill cleared the Senate on December 17 and the conference committee on December 22. After final approval by both houses, Cutting departed to spend Christmas in New York. During the following week, he attended the opera and visited with Don McCarthy, Phelps Putnam and Frederick Manning. He also met John Strachey, who was visiting from England. On New Year's Day, he returned to Washington, leaving behind two of his friends to enjoy his mother's hospitality for several more days.[4]

Meanwhile, President Hoover vetoed the independence bill. In a carefully constructed message, he argued that the Filipinos were unprepared for independence. Cutting mustered the Senate to override the veto. He noted that "for the first time in history," so far as he knew, thirteen million people were "acquiring liberty, not through physical violence and blood shed" but by the vote of Congress in harmony with the desires of the people. He reassured his colleagues that the Filipinos had ably demonstrated their capacity for self-government. Neither the veto message of the president nor the supporting documentation of the cabinet members provided "compelling" grounds for postponing the independence process.

Cutting delivered a stinging rebuke to the president. Philippine independence was hardly a "spiritual" issue as the president said but was a "purely material or practical" matter. According to Cutting, it was the fulfillment of a "plain pledge" made by the American Congress to the Philippine people. Cutting recognized that no single bill could please all people either in the Philippine Islands, in the United States or in the world. At no point in his message did Hoover mention that the bill carefully safeguarded American authority and sovereignty during the transition period. Finally, he noted that the bill had not been hastily drafted. That sectors of the American and Filipino people would experience hardships was a given. Cutting insisted, "The main purpose of the bill has been to do justice to the Philippine people, whom we regard as our wards and for whom we have the primary responsibility of living up to a promise which we made to them." The ultimate force behind the legislation was "the late Senator from Massachusetts, Mr. [George F.] Hoar, [who had] protested in this body against the imperialistic venture on which the United States entered in his time." Thus, Cutting protested that "we should never have gone into the Philippine Islands in the first place." Why quibble over the details when the American people through the Congress had awarded "the people of the Philippine Islands the right to determine their own future destiny"?[5]

On January 17, the Senate following the action of the House of Representatives by a vote of 66 to 26, two votes more than the necessary two-thirds, approved the Philippine Independence Bill, or Hawes-Cutting Act, over the objections of the president. Ten months later, in a resolution of October 17, 1933, the Philippine Legislature rejected the terms of the independence bill.[6]

While Cutting was calling upon his colleagues to endorse Philippine independence in January, the president-elect was selecting a cabinet. When Cutting visited Roosevelt at Warm Springs, the cabinet had come up in their discussion. Roosevelt had remarked that the State Department already was settled. Still vacant, the interior would administer Roosevelt's public-works program. Whether he offered the post to Cutting was unknown, but Roosevelt asked him to consider his proposed changes for the Interior Department and to offer any suggestions he deemed worthwhile. Given Roosevelt's outlook for the department, Cutting, as the author of a comprehensive public-works measure, was an ideal candidate. Thereafter, Washington buzzed with rumors that he had been offered the post of secretary of the interior. When asked during the Christmas recess by family and friends what he would do if offered the position, Cutting said that he did not know and that he did not want to decide.[7]

During the second week of January, Cutting visited the president-elect at his New York City residence. During the meeting, Roosevelt invited him to join the cabinet as secretary of the interior. He added, however, that Cutting should withhold his answer until he could give the request due consideration. No sooner was the offer made than Cutting had to gird for battle to override the president's veto of the Philippine Independence Bill. In deciding the matter, Cutting had to resolve two concerns. Would he be more useful in the cabinet or in the senate, where he was a free agent? And would he overcome his hesitations, even distrust, about Roosevelt's ability to cope in an effective way with the depression crisis?[8]

CHAPTER 19

In late January, Cutting again spoke briefly with Roosevelt in Washington. The president-elect invited both him and Robert M. La Follette, Jr. to Warm Springs. He wanted to discuss the cabinet post and his intended progressive policies. Cutting was reticent about the cabinet offer and his conversations with Roosevelt, but he made clear to the president-elect that his decision would be influenced by the possibility of Philip La Follette, the former governor of Wisconsin, becoming attorney general. Cutting wrote few letters during this period. However, he did note on February 10 that "the undercover man, [Raymond] M[oley][,] was down here this week and at his request I am still keeping the matter open."9

Prior to this visit, Moley had briefly met Cutting at the Conference of Progressives in March of 1931. He recalled Cutting as "a man of deep passions and great daring, but outwardly so taciturn, so inarticulate, that there was none of the conversational give and take that characterizes most practical politicians." Nevertheless, Moley warmed to Cutting once he discovered that both had gone to New Mexico to recover from tuberculosis. Cutting's unstable health weighed against his acceptance of the cabinet post. In addition, Moley detected in him "something less than complete confidence in Roosevelt as a progressive leader" and informed Roosevelt that Cutting would turn down the offer. At the Washington terminal with the president-elect on February 17, 1933, Cutting formally declined the invitation to join his cabinet as secretary of the interior.10

After turning down the post, Cutting was reluctant to volunteer recommendations to the incoming administration. He did, however, forward letters of job applicants to Roosevelt officials and suggested to job seekers that they could quote him when presenting their applications. He was aware of the opposition among both his constituents and westerners to the appointment of Senator Thomas J. Walsh of Montana as attorney general, but did not bring the matter to Roosevelt's attention.11

Throughout these discussions, Congress grappled in the last month of the Hoover presidency with its final appropriation measures. Cutting argued that "instead of balancing the Budget what we should be trying to do is to balance the consuming power on the one hand with the productive power which has so excessively outgrown its possible usefulness to the country." He announced that he would vote "in favor of cutting expenditures which go to increase producing power" and against "any cut which goes primarily to the purchasing or consuming power of the country." One bureaucracy he singled out for reductions was the Department of Commerce. He complained that it was "principally engaged in trying to create a demand in foreign nations for things which those nations did not really require, and which they have had to give up with disastrous effects to American industry as soon as the depression hit them."

Cutting opposed reducing the salaries of federal employees. A shrinking federal payroll would only intensify the depression and set "a bad example to private industry all over the country." Indeed, he argued, "the Government should expand its activities, place more people on the pay roll." The depths of a depression was no time "to cut down the wage scale and put upon such a cut the sanction of the Congress of the United States."[12]

His final comments during the session touched on the plight of transients and their need for assistance. Cutting insisted that the economic and social crisis was national in scope and that the federal government had a "responsibility . . . to see that its citizens do not starve." Here again, Cutting diverged sharply from the Hoover administration, which laid the burden of relief on the shoulders of the states and their municipalities. To Cutting, both the national government and society owed the American people the fundamental right of staying alive.[13]

His remarks reiterated his analysis of the depression crisis and his call for a public works program to combat it. His progressive ideas on public works had brought him to Roosevelt's attention as a possible cabinet member, and, as we shall see, they would lead him early on in the New Deal to break with the Roosevelt administration.

Cutting was not on hand for either the end of the Hoover presidency or the onset of the New Deal. In late February, he embarked on the French liner, *LaFayette,* for a nineteen-day Caribbean cruise to recoup his energies. While his senate colleagues assembled for the special session called by the new president, Cutting enjoyed warm, sunny days, "a boatload of dull but quite inoffensive people, and some really marvelous landscapes, especially at Martinique and in Venezuela."

He was also down to his last dollar bill by March 8. Consequently, until he resolved the problem, he had to remain aboard the boat. In doing so, he rated a wire-service story. When called by the steward to join the line up for health inspection at quarantine in Colon in the early morning of March 8, Cutting replied that he would do so when "good and ready." He appeared on deck a half hour later, after which the vessel was allowed to dock for the inspection.

While in Venezuela, he read Roosevelt's inaugural address. Since he did not sit on the banking committee that would investigate legislation dealing with the banking crisis, he determined to continue his cruise. "If I don't take the rest now, I shall probably have to take it later when it may be even less convenient," he concluded.

In Panama City, with his finances restored, Cutting was "almost constantly on the go, inspecting new constructions, seeing the locks getting overhauled, flying over the Republic [of Panama], and even attending Rotary luncheons." He also lunched with the chief of staff of the military forces before returning to the *LaFayette,* which was docked in Colon for passage through the Panama Canal. While he found the people and places "pretty interesting," he thought the food and liquor available on the Isthmus "beneath contempt."[14]

Cutting left the *LaFayette* when it docked in San Diego and motored with an old American Legion friend, Fred Humphrey, to Los Angeles where he boarded a train for Albuquerque. He was back in Santa Fe early Sunday morning, March 19. After catching up with local news and gossip, he turned his attention to the national scene and wondered whether he should return to Washington. He would prefer to "stay a couple of weeks if at all possible" in New Mexico. In one sense, he thought, "Individual senators were of very little importance at the moment," but then again, he wondered about "things going on beneath the surface which are important to be in on." He considered calling Robert M. La Follette, Jr. to "see what is what."

La Follette was "pretty disgusted" with the president's program and saw no reason for Cutting to hurry back. Cutting concluded from the phone conversation that "this is no session for individualists." From what he could determine, he thought that Roosevelt had handled the banking problem well, but the rest, he lamented, rang "a trifle hollow." He would not complain or criticize the Roosevelt administration since he had been doing nothing "except soaking up sunshine." His most immediate concern was whether the artist, Russell Cheney, should paint his portrait.[15]

Since a reporter from an Albuquerque paper saw him get off the train, Cutting had had "to talk to at least five hundred individuals." The lack of privacy impeded his rest and would drive him back to Washington by the end of the month. But he was not enthused with the prospect. The Roosevelt program, "so far as I have been able to discover what it is," did not arouse any enthusiasm. Cutting doubted that he would be able to accomplish anything significant "at this kind of a steam-roller session." Before leaving Santa Fe, Cutting wired Harold Ickes, the secretary of the interior, that John Collier "by all odds" was the person best qualified for the post of commissioner of Indian affairs. Aside from this endorsement, Cutting reiterated that he would not volunteer any recommendations to the new administration, although if consulted, he would be glad to endorse a qualified candidate.[16]

On March 31, Cutting took his senate seat for the first time in the Seventy-third Congress. After several days, he was able to report that "things keep pretty busy and from my point of view pretty unsatisfactory." The new administration, he thought, had lost a great opportunity to accomplish "something constructive" and had frittered away its first month "on non-essential or positively harmless measures," such as the "beer bill" ending prohibition. The Economy Act would achieve a measure of budget balancing that only Hoover supporters could envy. Cutting's one satisfaction was that by turning down a cabinet post, he had no connection with or obligation to support the emerging New Deal. He also participated in the Washington social whirl. Dinner guests engaged in earnest discussions on the topics of unemployment, costs of government, waste in business, and others until late in the evening.[17]

Surprisingly, he found that he could enjoy some favors from the Roosevelt administration. In late April, he visited Secretary of the Interior Harold Ickes to discuss patronage matters. Ickes recalled that Cutting was "a very reserved person" and that he "never asked me for anything." From respect and admiration for Cutting, Ickes concluded, "I do not intend to make any appointments in New Mexico that won't help him." In the United States Land Office at Santa Fe, Ickes went even further by firing a registrar antagonistic to Cutting and asked that he select a replacement. In fact, Ickes gave Cutting more patronage during the New Deal than Hoover had in the last years of his administration.[18]

While Cutting maintained a friendly relationship with Ickes, he was displeased with the Economy Act that Congress approved during his absence. He considered it "the most indefensible piece of legislation ever passed by Congress." He said that "the spirit in which its provisions are being carried out" was "far worse than even the Act itself," particularly with regard to reducing pensions for disabled veterans. The veterans cases that came to his attention deeply distressed him. In turn, he brought many of them to the attention of the Veterans Administration, and in one instance, he expressed hope that "personal consideration at the White House" might favorably resolve the matter.[19]

On May 10, more than a month after his return to Washington, Cutting took the senate floor to discuss a minor measure calling for the protection of government records. Agreeing with his colleague, Tom Connally, that "there is not very much in it," Cutting suggested that an "apparently trivial" measure "may nevertheless have serious consequences." He showed that the bill's language was "ungrammatical, unintelligible, ambiguous, and therefore dangerous." In one instance, he demonstrated how the word *whoever* governed three sets of verbs without any "grammatical connection between them." Acting as a schoolmaster, he illustrated the measure's infelicities on a wall chart in the chamber. The text, not the measure, concerned Cutting. To decode its meaning, he offered a clarifying amendment. As Cutting showed the importance of grammar in framing even an inconsequential measure, he made abundantly evident the haste in which early New Deal measures were prepared.[20]

With Senators La Follette and Edward Costigan, Cutting prepared a bill that would create an Administration of Public Works. The measure called for a six-billion-dollar program "to provide for the construction, extension and improvement of public facilities and services, to relieve unemployment and for other purposes." Cutting recognized that the National Industrial Recovery Act (NRA), a more comprehensive administration measure, would supercede his bill and would provide some immediate assistance through its public-works title. Nevertheless, along with most Republican progressives, he voted against the recovery act because its business codes would allow exemptions from antitrust legislation.[21]

One of the measures under senate consideration called for reductions in the compensation and pensions of veterans under the administration's economy program. Cutting took the opportunity to express publicly his disillusionment with some parts of the New Deal. In June, during the debate on appropriations for the Veterans Bureau, Cutting proposed an amendment that ultimately prevailed. Slightly modified by Tom Connally, it took from the president authority to reduce the pensions of veterans with service-connected disabilities of more than twenty-five percent.

As he did during the Hoover administration, Cutting reviewed the necessity of pensions and compensation for veterans. While he admitted that many undeserving veterans received pensions, he argued that the publicity of a few bad cases had built general sentiment against the entire class of veterans. The recently approved Economy Act, while seeking to "save between four and five hundred million dollars," would eliminate from the rolls more veterans than the few undeserving ones. At best, the indignant senator estimated, "perhaps a hundred and twenty-five million dollars was [sic] saved by cutting out the non-service connected cases."

Moving in his remarks to the Economy Act itself, Cutting denied that it provided a means of preserving the credit of the United States. In the last analysis, Cutting argued, the nation's credit depended "on the labor, the production, and the purchasing power of the individual . . . and on nothing else." The erosion of purchasing power through pension cuts only helped to intensify the depression in the United States. When Congress bestowed favoritism on some veterans in the belief that millions of dollars would be saved, it had in fact neither economized in a meaningful way nor meted out justice. Cutting argued, "The distinction which is habitually made between service-connected and non-service-connected cases [is] in many respects a misleading one."

While Cutting believed a twenty-five percent cut in service-connected cases was too great, he also thought that keeping on the rolls "the men who ought to be there" was more important. Striving for temperance, Cutting said that in his judgment "the Economy Act was drawn up so as to exclude from the rolls every individual veteran who could possibly be excluded." Any liberal-ization of that law would be an improvement "on the language of the Economy Act as we passed it in March."

Cutting cared deeply for the plight of the disabled or impaired veteran. In New Mexico alone, he claimed, the government would put "on the streets" approximately five thousand tubercular veterans who could not prove their affliction was service related. In every veterans hospital in New Mexico and Arizona, "there have been catastrophic epidemics of hemorrhages and there have been suicides" among those affected by the regulations that the Veterans Bureau adopted after the approval of the Economy Act and that the appropri-ation measure for the agency now reinforced.

Alarmed veterans forwarded their cases to Cutting "day after day by the score and by the hundred." Cutting insisted that he was speaking "with no partisan purpose in view." He made clear that he was not criticizing the president as an individual. He was leveling his displeasure at a machine in which "some clerk down in some bureau" issued a regulation or carried "out a precedent laid down by some other regulation made by some other clerk with no more authority than he has." The best that could be achieved, Cutting recognized, was to amend the appropriation measure and thus to mitigate its disastrous impact on disabled veterans. After extended debate, the Senate restored $150 million to the appropriation measure for the Veterans Bureau.[22]

While Cutting expressed only admiration for Franklin D. Roosevelt, he showed only antipathy for Louis Howe, the president's secretary. During a radio interview, Howe said that the Senate's reduction of the proposed cuts in veterans allowances would add up to $1.25 more in taxes each year for every citizen. Cutting seized on Howe's address to personalize his criticism of the White House. He called the secretary a "purely ministerial clerk, a man unknown to the constitution, not responsible to the voters." How could he present his views to a broad audience while members of Congress directly responsible to the people were unable to air theirs? If the president had something to make public, "he should take it on his own responsibility" and express his views "in his own name." The White House secretary certainly should not "be discussing directly with the people of the United States an action taken by the Congress of the United States."[23]

To illustrate the seriousness of the situation, Cutting cited the injustice unfolding in New Mexico. The bulk of three to five thousand tubercular veterans who would lose their federal aid on July 1, 1933, were not native New Mexicans, yet they would become a burden to a state that could barely assist its own distressed citizens. The governor of New Mexico wanted to assist these veterans, but the Veterans Administration would not provide him with a list of the men receiving federal compensation in the state.

Cutting received a disturbing letter from the adjutant of the Disabled American Veterans of the World War at Fort Bayard, New Mexico, a large tubercular hospital. He informed Cutting that of the fifty men he contacted at random, the pensions of more than half were cut one hundred percent. Distressing reports like the adjutant's added fuel to Cutting's anger over the administration's treatment of disabled veterans. He too was unable to obtain a copy of a presidential order from the Veterans Administration. After Cutting's remarks, the administration made the order public and presented it to the Senate, thereby curbing for the moment further comment until he analyzed the executive order.

Before yielding the floor, Cutting applauded the senate action that modified the president's power to cut veterans disability compensation. He hoped that the increased pressure from the White House, the National Economy League, constituents and others would not force a senate reversal that would leave the disabled veterans high and dry.[24]

On June 8, Cutting again took the floor to dissect the executive order in which the president "purported to initiate great modifications" in previous veterans regulations. To the contrary, Cutting found no great modifications. Almost everything remained intact under the so-called new regulations. After analyzing them in some detail, his conclusion was "that these regulations, which were refused me yesterday morning, and which after a change of heart were presented to the Senate yesterday afternoon, show on the face of them that they were written in bad faith and with the intention of fraud."

In short, senators could not trust executive orders that were "promulgated and written by some subordinate in the Veterans' Administration under the pressure of the Director of the Budget," Lewis Douglas, who was "trying to cut down veterans' compensation to the lowest conceivable point." Veterans officials were unsympathetic to disabled veterans and were "willing to act in bad faith with the Congress of the United States." Cutting's biting remarks alerted his colleagues to interpretations of executive orders by the Veterans Administration that would nullify the will of Congress.[25]

Cutting restated many of his previous arguments when the Senate reviewed amendments to the Independent Offices Appropriation Bill on June 12. He protested a house amendment that could be interpreted to reduce pension payments more than twenty-five percent, the amount the Senate agreed upon. And he dissected other proposed amendments he found harmful to the best interests of disabled veterans. From his study of the house compromise, Cutting said, "I think there is nothing in it . . . that if that is all we can get, we had better go home and tell the veterans in our States that we would not stultify ourselves by voting for something which was patently fraudulent and patently a sham."

Cutting despaired at obtaining justice "for these helpless veterans of war." The American people were deluded by the propaganda that men on pension rolls were grafters and were simply misled about the issues involved. "The subject," he said, "is dull and it is hard for most people to realize that the difference between one adverb and another adverb may mean the difference between life and death." He related the case of a terminally ill tubercular veteran wounded in battle and cited for gallantry in action. The Economy Act and Veterans Administration regulations had cut his pension from $100 to $20 per month effective July 1, 1933. Cutting's analysis, corroborated by two senators who were also medical doctors, was that the situation of this veteran was typical of many more terminally ill tubercular veterans at Fort Bayard whose suffering and wounds were not readily visible to the layman. He read letters from physicians citing other distressing cases and discussed others that had come to his attention. All the cases he cited involved men whose pensions were curtailed. Throughout these remarks, Cutting blasted Veterans Administration doctors, most of whom only cursorily examined tubercular patients and acted under orders "to cut expenses whenever they can."

Concluding his lengthy remarks, Cutting insisted that the compromise to be discussed in the conference committee harbored no benefits to anybody. Although he did not charge the president with deception, he said, "We have been treated in bad faith." Roosevelt was much "too busy with other matters to give this matter the detailed attention which is required if justice is to be done." The people who acted in his name, however, the men who wrote the executive order of June 6, "knew exactly what they were doing." Balancing the budget had taken priority over "human flesh and blood." After more than four hours of continuous battle, Cutting was unable to convince his colleagues to approve and send to the conference committee a more appropriate amendment pertaining to disabled veterans than the compromise measure the house members presented.[26]

Since early June, Cutting had devoted all of his efforts to battling budget balancers. As the arduous and debilitating special session ground to a halt, he had his final say on July 15 when the Senate considered and approved the conference report. At the outset he found himself involved in a highly charged emotional debate with Virginia's peppery and fiscally conservative little senator, Carter Glass. The previous day on the floor, Glass accused veterans of greed. Cutting complained that each of the three times he asked Glass to yield, he declined. Reading the transcript of Glass's remarks in the *Congressional Record,* Cutting spotted the word "laughter" following some of the Virginian's remarks. He complained that the word was "the most disgraceful word which has ever been written into the Congressional Record." He had heard no laughter and wondered "whether the Senator from Virginia revised his remarks in the Record."

Glass was outraged. Cutting's "infamous suggestion" was "nothing less than mendacious." The wrangle proceeded with the two senators exchanging barbs until the presiding officer ended the quarrel with a blow of his gavel. He advised Cutting to proceed so that the Senate could vote on the conference report.

Cutting resented house Democrats for enforcing strict party discipline to approve the committee report. The majority of senators had previously objected to most portions of it. The ambiguous verbiage of its provisions would allow the Veterans Administration to remove cases from the rolls, to make drastic reductions in compensation, and in general to deny adequate protection to tubercular, mentally disturbed, and other veterans. Again he denounced Budget Director Lewis Douglas's "handling of straight combat-connected cases." He had directed that pensions be cut anywhere from fifty to eighty percent.

Cutting noted that many senators had defied President Hoover by voting to increase compensation for all veterans claiming a disability. Now these same senators were endorsing a report that would wreak havoc on the truly disabled. Despite his lengthy address, Cutting convinced few, if any, senators to change their vote and to oppose the pressure of the Roosevelt administration. Cutting was bitter, disillusioned and angry at the deplorable treatment of disabled American veterans in the name of economy.[27]

The next day, Cutting apologized to Carter Glass, who was still upset over their contretemps. He had not "the slightest idea" that his comments reflected on his colleague's integrity. The issue that had prompted the clash was not a personal one. Glass and James F. Byrnes, as members of the conference committee, had agreed with colleagues from the House of Representatives to oppose "the attitude which the Senate had taken." In the next session, Cutting hoped, the Senate would insure that its conference representatives were "genuinely and firmly and sincerely convinced of the soundness of the positions taken by the body which they represent." Although his emotions never overcame him, these final words to the Senate again suggested his disgust with the callousness of the Roosevelt administration.[28]

Like everyone else in Congress and the White House, Cutting was utterly exhausted at the end of this hectic session during which the New Deal took shape. Cutting struggled with the intense heat—"the worst I have ever felt anywhere"—and with the daily sessions "lasting from ten till midnight." He further complained about the "impossibility of ever being off the floor for fear of something being slipped over you." He was revolted by the way Roosevelt "lashed the House into line on a meaningless veteran's compromise." About the only positive thing during the session was that his doctors gave him a "one hundred percent clear bill of health." Nevertheless, when the session came to an end in the late evening of June 18, Cutting said that he was "very tired and in a bad nervous state." The visit of Phelps Putnam and Frederick Manning during the last days of the session only created "pandemonium" at home and deprived him of time "to think."[29]

Roosevelt's initial steps to cope with the Great Depression confirmed Cutting's initial impression that the new president would be no more effective than Hoover. Cutting's sizzling harangues, according to Raymond Moley, visibly affected the "poise, self confidence, and good humor" of the president. Otherwise, throughout the hundred days, Roosevelt appeared an "ebullient, easy, calm man." Although the president and Cutting hailed from similar backgrounds, were personally acquainted and functioned on the same social level in New York, they could neither forgive, forget nor ignore the acrimony and recrimination this fight engendered.[30]

To Cutting, his fight produced at least two positive results. First, the publicity given the "barbarous treatment" of the wounded and tubercular veterans had called attention to the "criminal shortsightedness" of the Veterans Administration policy. Both the president and his bureaucracy would have to use their powers with restraint and would have to be wary of perpetrating similar outrages. And second, "an overwhelming majority of both houses of Congress" obviously favored just treatment of disabled veterans, "regardless of votes inspired by misguided partisanship." Congress would resume debate on the issue when it reconvened. Cutting expected that in the interim, "rank and file" veterans would express their displeasure to their representatives in both houses of Congress.[31]

With the session concluded, Cutting spent two days clearing his desk, which was littered with unanswered letters. He then bade farewell to his house guests and hurried to visit his mother, who was recovering from a minor operation. While en route to Santa Fe from New York, he stopped over in Chicago in ninety-five-degree heat and got a bird's-eye view of the World's Fair. He walked no further than the science building, the first one he entered. He enjoyed his hour and a half of visiting the exhibits before he left to catch his train. He was back in New Mexico by June 23.[32]

Here too he faced a hectic schedule. In Santa Fe, he found Clifford McCarthy enjoying his new job as supervisor for several New Mexico Indian tribes. He quickly caught up with the activities of other friends, and on June 27, Herman Baca drove Cutting to the village of Tyrone in southwestern New Mexico where he was an honored guest at the wedding of Baca's daughter. Thereafter he addressed a new Veterans' Council in Albuquerque. He returned to Santa Fe, enjoyed the "wonderful air," and sized up conditions in the state. On the Fourth of July, he spoke in Tierra Amarilla.[33]

Although absent from New Mexico at the end of May and early June, Cutting was saluted by the fifty-nine graduates of the Española High School, their teachers, their families and their friends. He had sent a check so that the junior and graduating classes could enjoy a luncheon at the local hotel. He also helped to fund for the community a late-summer pageant celebrating the anniversary of Juan de Oñate's arrival in the Española Valley on June 11, 1598. Cutting was "saluted" by the salutatorian. The community, engaged in constructing additional school buildings, proposed to invite him to their formal dedication. Incidents such as this one in Española were not unique, but Cutting never publicized his gifts. His critics, however, often claimed that he was squandering his wealth to buy votes and to influence elections.[34]

Although anxious to get away, Cutting was disturbed that the Roosevelt administration had not yet made various state appointments. At the time, there was no one to execute in New Mexico the legislation approved by Congress during the past session. Nor had Governor Seligman yet named a replacement for his senate colleague, Sam Bratton, who had resigned to become a federal judge. Cutting thought he ought to remain in Santa Fe until the appointments were made "so as to be able to map out some intelligent procedure for the all-important months immediately ahead." One likely appointment was Jesus Baca to the federal marshalcy.[35]

But in July, key federal appointments for New Mexico were still pending. Interested parties were submitting names to Postmaster General and Democratic National Committee Chairman James A. Farley. In several instances he received the names of Cutting supporters, but Farley was warned, for example, that Governor Seligman and some of his associates were Cutting's agents. Any chance for Cutting to formulate plans or respond to federal appointments faded when he left for his European vacation.[36]

As Cutting pulled out of Santa Fe, he literally had severed all political ties. He had broken with Roosevelt over the Economy Act and its treatment of veterans. He was highly critical of the policies of Governor Seligman, whom contrary to prevailing opinion, he had never sought to control. His tongue lashing of Hoover had made him a pariah in the Republican party. Within both major parties on the state and national levels, Cutting had powerful enemies who would endeavor to end his senatorial career by preventing either his renomination or reelection in 1934. Besieged on all sides, he entered a state of political limbo, but headed for Europe, Cutting only looked forward to an extended period of rest and relaxation.

CHAPTER 20

LIMBO

On the afternoon of July 22 in Brooklyn, Cutting boarded the liner *Europa* for an extended vacation first in London and then, as he wrote while still on the high seas, "Lord knows where." The "cloudless and waveless trip" was enlivened by the presence "of the Odgen Millses and a few minor celebrities." Although "too palatial to be much fun," the *Europa* served fair food and excellent wine. Cutting felt pangs of guilt about going to Europe when he really should remain in New Mexico, but the onset of debilitating hay fever hounded him out of the state. Having made the decision to leave, he was determined to make the most of the trip.[1]

In London, he dined most every night with his old friend and former physician, Frederic Bishop. They laid plans to travel to Paris, Salzburg, Vienna and Budapest. His niece, Iris Origo, and her husband, traveling through Scotland and Scandinavia, wanted to rendezvous with him in Germany later in the summer. According to another old friend, Gordon Gardiner, Cutting was in the best of spirits. Gardiner "found difficulty in recognizing the rather taciturn Bronson of other days." One hot Sunday afternoon in Greenwich, they met "in an extremely squalid little shop hemmed in by incredible numbers of the proletariat eating scones and swatting flies." For two solid hours, Cutting related to Gardiner his Russian adventure of 1930. As he listened, Gardiner was struck by his "detached and far seeing attitude." Cutting's sympathy and understanding were evident not only in his perceptions about Russia but also in his views on world affairs and, most particularly, on American problems.[2]

In London, Cutting replenished his wardrobe but the inequitable rate of monetary exchange prevented him from buying very much. In addition, he found that the recently concluded economic conference, from which the president recalled the American delegation, had "not endeared us to any of the European countries" and engendered much skepticism about the New Deal. On August 7, after a week together in London, Cutting and Bishop, "the Dottore," left London for Paris. They spent a few days in the French capital and departed for Budapest. Although they had hoped to escape the intense heat engulfing western Europe, they unfortunately encountered one hundred-degree heat for the first day or two in Budapest. Despite "some fine pictures," Cutting was disappointed with the Hungarian capital. Looking forward to Vienna and Salzburg, he and Bishop planned to attend the last week of the music festival.[3]

In Vienna, the heat eased considerably. Cutting complained that aside from Clifford McCarthy, none of his friends had bothered to write. Hungry for news from New Mexico, he was unable to make out "head or tail" of what he had received and hoped to hear more soon. After a week in Vienna, Cutting and the Dottore motored to Salzburg. Cutting enjoyed the music, heard from several of his friends, and caught up on public affairs in New Mexico. He visited with Antonio Origo and Percy and Sybil Lubbock. Mrs. Lubbock was first married to his deceased brother, Bayard. Cutting was now having a good time, "quiet and unexciting." He "put on a few pounds" from the splendid food and wine. The production of *Faust*, staged by Max Reinhardt, was "impressive in a gaudy and tasteless sort of way," but he confessed that the genius of Goethe did not strike him as did that of Mozart. He was now anxious to see how Reinhardt staged the tale of Everyman.[4]

Through an American friend in Salzburg, Cutting arranged an informal meeting with the German "Reich-chancellor," Adolf Hitler. In the Rhineland, Cutting learned that his meeting with Hitler, "on account of the big Nazi reunion," was shifted to Nuremburg. Reluctant to travel that distance, he canceled the appointment. Most Americans coming from Germany, Cutting reported, were enthusiastic Hitlerites. He concluded that the German people were "childish politically" and that Hitler offered "the only kind of Government they can be expected to understand."[5]

On September 2, Cutting and Bishop motored from Strasbourg, enjoying "the most exquisite beauty of landscape and architecture." After resting at Nancy for a day or two, they entrained for Paris. On the Avenue de l'Opera in Paris, Cutting met Senator Joseph Robinson, who was recovering from "a complete nervous breakdown" and looked "old and rather ghastly." He heard French lawyers "make their plea for the [German] Reichstag [fire] defendants," an appeal they were forbidden to deliver in Leipzig. One of the lawyers was kind enough to send Cutting an "otherwise unprocurable" reserved seat.[6]

Meanwhile in New Mexico, the political scene underwent a drastic change. On September 25, Governor Arthur Seligman died, and an old-line Democrat, A.W. Hockenhull, the lieutenant governor, stepped up to replace him. Clyde Tingley, the Democratic mayor of Albuquerque and a rising power in the party, now jockeyed for position, "pulling every string" within his reach. He pushed his protege, Dennis Chavez, for the post of national committeeman and for the nomination to Cutting's senate seat in 1934. He threw his endorsement behind Carl Hatch of Roswell to fill out Sam Bratton's term in the Senate, and prepared to contest that office when it came up for election. Uninterested in working with progressive Republicans, anti-Cutting and anti-Seligman Democrats controlled the party. Clyde Tingley and former governor Arthur Hannett were its dominant figures. In the Republican party a similar situation prevailed. Old guard leaders, anti-Cutting to the core, were in charge of the party machinery. Both organizations had cast Cutting into a political no-man's land.[7]

The highlight of Cutting's return voyage in late September was watching Emil Ludwig and Marlene Dietrich waltz in the Grand Salon. Upon his arrival, Cutting spent "a somewhat strenuous day" in Washington briefing himself on national developments. He concluded that the social and economic situation was "pretty bad," but he hoped that it might clear up before Congress convened to examine the results of the various New Deal programs. He thought New Mexico would have to wait "for any solution of its problems." But rather than return immediately to Santa Fe, Cutting headed for Chicago to attend the Fifteenth Annual Convention of the American Legion. On the train enroute to the Windy City, he listened to former Senator Charles S. Deneen talk about political affairs till the late evening and wondered whether the president would attend the convention.[8]

Since the convention did not get underway until October 2, Cutting went on to Madison to visit at the La Follette farm, a "very pleasant, simple, old-fashioned place" overlooking a lake. He found the La Follette brothers "totally at variance about the present situation and outlook." Philip thought that Roosevelt was losing public confidence, while Robert Jr. believed that "the public are as strongly for Roosevelt as ever." Their diverging views further convinced Cutting "of the chaotic condition of American politics just now." Public life, he mused, seemed "a damn heartbreaking game," and the news from New Mexico indicated that he was "completely out of the running." Indicative of his mood at the time, Cutting concluded, "and damn good riddance if I do say so myself."[9]

At the Chicago convention, "in an atmosphere of bombs, booze, fireworks and buglers bugling out-of-tune," his despair, if anything, intensified. He learned that a fellow delegate, an old guard Republican, had filed charges against him for "corrupting the Legion." His action virtually suspended the "Department from any voice on the floor." For this service, Cutting believed, the delegate, Roy Cook, had been rewarded with an appointment as postmaster at Albuquerque. "The whole damn Federal patronage" had been turned over to his "bitterest enemies," and with Seligman's death, all state appointees would be members of his opposition. Adding insult to injury was the ovation Roosevelt received, despite his shabby treatment of veterans, when he addressed the convention. Cutting was saddened that two of his closest friends in the American Legion, Osborne Wood, the commander, and Herman Baca were engaged at the time with the National Guard in suppressing a miners strike at Gallup. Their participation did not provide "the kind of issue on which I should care to run for office, even assuming I should have that opportunity."[10]

In Santa Fe, Cutting confessed that he would have skipped the Chicago convention had he foreseen his reception. He was never given an opportunity to take the floor in behalf of disabled veterans and "had all I could do not to get thrown out of the Legion." The National Executive Committee might expel him later in the year. When he closely examined the New Mexico political scene, he saw little to dispel his gloom. The appointment of Carl Hatch, "certainly as mediocre a choice as could have been made," gave further evidence that old guard politicians, hostile to his progressive views, had repudiated him. His friend and ally, Jefferson Atwood, had been Governor Seligman's apparent choice for the post. Moreover, Cutting believed the president was behind his difficulties with the American Legion and had made their instigator the Albuquerque postmaster. The only bright spot was the brief visit of Philip La Follette, who made a series of Columbus Day speeches in which he pointedly praised Cutting.[11]

While concerned about his political fortunes, Cutting also became distressed about New Mexico and its people. The state, for example, was unable to qualify in any large way for Public Works Administration (PWA) projects. Federal law required the state to repay the federal government seventy percent of its advances for any nonfederal project, such as the extension of the secondary road system. With "perhaps the lowest economic standard" in the nation, New Mexico desperately needed federal aid. By October 1933, 5,753 families were receiving public relief and represented only a small fraction of the families in need. Few jobs were available, and most New Mexicans were engaged in their own food production on a noncommercial basis. One half of the state's one hundred thousand families were bereft of cash and were unable to purchase minimum subsistence items—shoes, jeans, sugar, or coffee—particularly in the northern counties. The drought in the eastern counties, the failure of the fruit crop and the declining prices of agricultural produce exacerbated their inability to raise cash. The small jobs and the occasional jobs, such as fruit picking, had provided the margin between limited sufficiency and dire necessity, but now were virtually dried up. The state's crisis conditions made essential that Cutting, as the senior senator from New Mexico, cooperate with state leaders. Setting aside their political differences, they had to seek some modification of federal guidelines to secure aid from the Public Works Administration.[12]

The political developments following Governor Seligman's sudden death consumed Cutting upon his return. Severino Trujillo, a member of his office staff, reported a conversation with Dennis Chavez. The state's lone representative in the House, Chavez was the rumored choice of the Tingley-Hannett faction to run against Cutting in 1934. Chavez assured Trujillo that "Hannett-Tingley *et al.*" could not wield him to slay Senator Cutting. Affirming his admiration for Cutting, Chavez stated that "he would never fight" him and that he would like to run on the same ticket with him. The suspicious Trujillo was unconvinced, explaining, "This is the same line of conversation that he has always handed me."[13]

Like Trujillo, Cutting doubted Chavez's sincerity. He chatted with the congressman shortly thereafter in Santa Fe. Neither uttered a word about the senatorial situation. Cutting remarked that Chavez "seemed very friendly, but of course he is playing with the other crowd and doing everything that he can to injure my friends if not myself." He was convinced that Chavez intended to contest his senate seat in 1934. Indeed, Chavez had boasted to Maurice Miera, a close ally of Cutting, "that he could split the Native vote 50-50, could count on the entire Democratic Anglo vote, and also the Republican old guard." In all, Chavez claimed, he could capture close to seventy-five percent of the total state vote.[14]

Chavez was not the only person he chatted with in Santa Fe upon his return. Cutting visited with Gugliemo Marconi, the inventor of wireless telegraphy, and Prince Louis Ferdinand, the last of the Hohenzollerns. Cutting found both men "intelligent and engaging." However, the pleasure of social calls sagged under the oppressive political situation. Neither he nor his friends could mitigate the damage inflicted by his political enemies, who controlled "all the strings." Their actions included, in the words of one associate, the "uncalled and unwarranted mistreatment you received at the hands of the Legion's National Organization."[15]

While depressed about the American Legion, Cutting still held out hope for a satisfactory resolution of the charges against him. In Chicago, he had had "a very nice talk" with the new national commander, Edward Hayes. Unlike his predecessor Louis Johnson, Hayes was "one hundred percent for the disabled" and was sure "to make a fight instead of lying down." Although Cutting had neither seen a copy of the charges leveled against the Department of New Mexico nor had been permitted to appear at any of the hearings, he was briefed on the most serious charges by a member of the investigating committee. One accusation was that some New Mexico members spoke no English. Another charged that the words "for God and Country" were absent from the state constitution, thereby proving to some committee members that legionnaires in New Mexico were both atheists and disloyal Americans. Whether the national committee would heed such reactionary blather remained to be seen.

Cutting's hopes may have dimmed when Edgar Puryear, his chief of staff, reported that Hayes came out "100 per cent" for Roosevelt after visiting the White House. Puryear could only state that "no one could be worse" than Louis Johnson toward disabled veterans and toward the Department of New Mexico. If the veterans who directed the national conventions were at all representative of the rank and file, the prospects of "getting any justice" were dim indeed.[16]

Cutting's outlook remained gloomy throughout the remaining months of 1933. He spent most of his time in Santa Fe. Although he found "great friendliness from the rank and file of both parties" when he did venture forth, he anticipated little chance of his receiving a nomination unless he was willing to make "impossible concessions" to the Republicans. His options were to stay out of the race altogether or to run on an independent ticket and meet "certain defeat." An independent fight might be an asset in the long run if "the whole debt structure of the nation" collapsed in 1935 and 1936, as was happening in Central Europe. From Cutting's perspective, politics, both in New Mexico and the nation, were a convoluted mess.[17]

What kept him on an even keel in these months, during which his mother had to assist him financially, were his almost daily meetings with close friends at Los Siete Burros. Here, he could enjoy good music, playing duets, for example, with Prince Louis Ferdinand on his Steinway grand piano. His work load was so heavy that by the end of October he asked Florence Dromey, a secretary in his Washington office, to travel to New Mexico and help ease the burden. On November 4, a meeting of state Progressive leaders, "a council of war" called by Cutting, met in Santa Fe to discuss the political situation. In subsequent days, Cutting traveled throughout the state and sounded out political opinion. Upon his return, he reported few cheers for either Roosevelt or Chavez, but he added that the public humor could change markedly at any time.[18]

In November, Cutting's suspicions about the trumped-up charges against the Department of New Mexico materialized. They were designed to show that he was a scoundrel using the legion for self-aggrandizement. All thirty-seven charges were "pure piffle," but the national committee would evaluate them in Indianapolis and not in New Mexico, where hundreds of veterans could refute them. The American Legion, Cutting was certain, meant "to throw us out." While Cutting claimed that "it does'nt [sic] really make a hell of a lot of difference," he did not want "to give Frank[lin D. Roosevelt] and [James A.] Farley that degree of satisfaction." He firmly believed the proceeding was part of an administration effort "to eliminate me with regard to a renewed veterans' fight at the next session."[19]

As he expected, the National Executive Committee suspended the New Mexico Department. Its swift punishment ended his ties, as well as those of many of his friends and supporters, to the state legion organization that they had created and that had launched his political career. The "cut and dried" decision, Cutting bitterly remarked, was a "direct punishment" for his opposition to the president in the senate debate on pensions. He doubted that the national committee wanted to hear true evidence, a view confirmed by Jefferson Atwood, the department's representative at the hearing in Indianapolis. He reported that "we were voted out of the Legion upon perjured affidavits and hearsay evidence." The national committee did not bother "even reading the charges or hearing the evidence." Like Cutting, Atwood believed that the former national commander, Louis Johnson, had influenced the decision. Whether the suspension would be a meaningful punishment remained to be seen. Whether within or without the American Legion, Cutting would continue his battle in behalf of disabled veterans when Congress convened in January 1934. Until that time, he would continue to evaluate the political scene and the impact of the New Deal in New Mexico.[20]

Shortly before Thanksgiving, Cutting returned from an extended trip through southern and eastern New Mexico, territory almost entirely Democratic. He reported that its constituency exhibited "little enthusiasm" for either Roosevelt or Chavez. A candidate could effectively exploit the dissatisfaction, Cutting speculated, by moving politically toward the left. Although the Republican party could not capitalize on the feeling, he could. In Washington, Harold Ickes, both the publics works administrator and secretary of the interior, was seriously studying relief proposals that Cutting had endorsed. Sometimes, Cutting allies successfully challenged key personnel appointments favored by his opponents. Of course, he exerted all possible effort in behalf of projects beneficial to New Mexico, such as one calling for canalization of the Rio Grande.[21]

Although PWA projects would provide badly needed aid to New Mexico, drought relief was a more immediate concern, particularly in the eastern counties. The state-approved plan in New Mexico was to place needy farmers on road construction that would enable them to earn about fifty dollars a month. The distress of many dry-land farmers was so serious by the end of 1933 that federal relief workers bypassed some of the requisite paper work to distribute feed grain. Presenting a far rosier perspective from Washington, Cutting's secretary claimed, "The trouble in the agricultural districts is gradually passing away." Under Harry Hopkins, the Civil Works Administration (CWA) was putting millions of men on the payroll. The Department of Agriculture was now "sending out millions" to farmers for plowing up their acreage. Business was stabilizing. The National Recovery Administration was of great assistance. Puryear believed that if Ickes were more aggressive in the public works program, New Mexico would be further along the road to recovery.[22]

At the end of November, Cutting awaited the arrival of his senate colleague, Robert M. La Follette, Jr., who was scheduled to speak in Albuquerque. Thereafter, he and Cutting boarded a train for Chicago where they would attend a small meeting of prominent progressives. The discussion focused on whether they should formally challenge New Deal programs whose modest success made an effective opposition to Roosevelt difficult. In the coming session, members of the House and Senate would most likely not take issue with the president, except on the veterans question. Cutting would follow suit. He let others know that a "good many friends" had inquired about whether they might suggest his name as the first American ambassador to the Soviet Union. His response was that a couple of years in New Mexico would do his health more good than a stint at any foreign mission.[23]

With conditions improving across the country, the Chicago conference could not promote effective opposition to the New Deal. Indeed, one of the more prominent progressives issued a strong statement in support of the president. At the time, Cutting was a member of a committee provided with federal monies to fund a public arts program in New Mexico. Even he could discern positive results from the New Deal. By the end of 1933, the committee was employing "thirty artists at forty dollars a week, and twenty at twenty five." However, Cutting had cause for concern. As opposition to Roosevelt's policies evaporated, the stature of the Democratic party was bound to improve.[24]

Cutting had every intention of fighting for his senate seat. Unlike previous holiday seasons, he stayed in New Mexico. In the evening of December 16, he spoke at a meeting of the newly created Veterans Council in Albuquerque. "Not an unqualified success" was the way he characterized his speech, but he had to make a public address on veterans issues if the legion was to remain a viable organization in New Mexico. During the Christmas season in Santa Fe, Cutting entertained guests and tried to provide assistance to distressed citizens. For instance, Hispanic settlers on Pueblo lands had been given notice to vacate their premises in one month, after which they would be turned upon the community as charity cases. He listened to well-intentioned acquaintances, such as Cornelius Vanderbilt, Jr. and Edgar Puryear, warning him that his opposition to Roosevelt was a terrible mistake.[25]

The loyalty of his constituents gave Cutting a base of support that was unaffected by political maneuvering. As one follower wrote, "You perhaps will never know the service you have rendered the thousands of farmers in the Ninth Federal Land Bank, in your tireless fight to force the Land Bank to carry out the intent of Congress." Cutting had secured the removal of the Land Bank District president and earned the gratitude of many hard-pressed, debt-ridden, drought-stricken farmers in New Mexico. As he soaked up their praise, he was convinced that his criticism of the New Deal had impaired his standing among "the Washington Bureaus." He was determined to reject the "bunk that bureaucrats in Washington are willing to hand out" when they turned down requests from Capitol Hill offices. He appreciated the New Mexico veterans groups that, unlike the National American Legion, acknowledged his efforts in their behalf. The American Legion post in Santa Fe held a party for those who opposed the Economy Act, briefly delaying Cutting's return to Washington.[26]

Cutting was pleased that some of his donations were well utilized. At Española High School, vocational students used his gift to craft reproductions of Spanish colonial furniture. Private charity was particularly beneficial to the northern New Mexico counties, which could not apply, owing to matching grant provisions, for government-aided vocational work funds.[27]

At the year's end, Cutting still did not "know what to say about the New Mexico situation." He believed that he could be reelected if either the Republicans or the Democrats nominated him. But could he be nominated? Cutting thought that he would receive a party nod on the condition that he agree to the rest of the ticket, something he was unwilling to consider at this time. His preference was "to have nothing to do with either of them, but to run on a ticket of my own," although such a course would spell certain defeat. In short, he was still in a state of political limbo, cast on the horns of a dilemma that appeared insoluble. He could rationalize his impending doom only by remarking that "there are a lot worse things than defeat at this particular stage of the game."[28]

His strategy, indeed his only recourse, was to plunge into the business of the Senate, to keep close tabs on political developments in New Mexico, and to hope that by the end of the session the situation would have sorted itself out. He could then make a reasoned decision, one that would provide him a fighting chance for reelection. The Second Session of the Seventy-third Congress would be a crucial one for Bronson Cutting.

RELEASE

As the session got underway, Cutting heard rumors that pointed toward a possible solution to his dilemma. Whether Dennis Chavez would oppose him was unclear, but that he would run only with the assurance of Roosevelt's backing was becoming evident. On the Republican side, Cutting learned that many members of the old guard, acknowledging the impact of the New Deal, were prepared to cooperate with him on any reasonable basis and to forgo control of the party. Although the rumors did not solve Cutting's problems, they suggested that their resolution would be within the folds of the Republican party.[1]

Albert Simms, Republican national committeeman, agreed with this view. He recognized that his party stood no chance of success in New Mexico unless it reached an accord with Cutting. Simms personally abhorred Cutting's senate candidacy, but through friends, he let Cutting know that he would avoid "a money fight" to defeat him.[2]

On January 19, 1934, Senator George W. Norris, the venerable Nebraska progressive, complained to President Roosevelt that all federal appointments in New Mexico had been filled "almost invariably" by Cutting's political enemies with the view "of laying the foundation" for his defeat in the fall election. Norris explained that Cutting wanted no control of "patronage in New Mexico." "The appointees," Norris believed, "should be friends, rather than enemies, of Senator Cutting." Given Cutting's support of Roosevelt's candidacy in 1932, the president could not possibly approve of the adversarial appointments. Roosevelt responded that he did "not want to do anything to hurt" Cutting but that "a lot of Bronson's retainers in New Mexico are not considered especially fine citizens."[3]

Although Cutting was powerless in patronage affairs, he found some leeway through the New Deal programs in New Mexico. He was pleased to learn that New Mexico would be the site of a large-scale demonstration project by the Soil Erosion Service. In addition, the service would extend erosion-control operations on the New Mexico drainage of the Gila River as soon as funds were available. He asked the governor for his advice and suggestions about the desirability of the Taylor grazing bill, which had passed the House of Representatives and which would soon come before the Senate. The controversial measure would withdraw from inappropriate public use, federal lands in the West and lease them for grazing under careful supervision. Governor A.W. Hockenhull was afraid that the bill would impede New Mexico's ability to acquire all public lands within its boundaries, but he recognized that public opinion was divided on the matter and suggested that Cutting should "await developments and defend our position step by step." Like the governor, the Public Works Administration preferred to move slowly. Cutting was disappointed to learn that of the original six million–dollar PWA appropriation New Mexico was entitled to receive for non-Federal projects, less than three hundred thousand had been awarded.[4]

His main concern, however, was legislative business. Although Cutting was at odds with Roosevelt, he was contacted by the president about the extension of the Hawes-Cutting Act. The law called upon the Philippine legislature to approve the independence measure before January 17, 1934. In March, Congress, with Roosevelt's approval, extended the time frame to October 1, 1934.[5]

Following his discussion with the president, Cutting endorsed the administration proposal sponsored by Senator Millard Tydings. "A slight improvement," the measure left out "an objectionable sentence which gave the United States permission to maintain military bases after independence." Cutting said that the proposal "has been essentially endorsed by both Houses of Congress" and has been accepted "with considerable enthusiasm in the main by all responsible elements of the Philippine people." During this rare condition of relative unanimity, his colleagues should "sink their personal likes and dislikes" to secure a measure that would grant independence to the Filipinos within a definite period of years. Cutting called for the rejection of all amendments and all substitutions. With the support of the administration, the measure granting the Philippine Islands independence after ten years met no serious opposition in Congress and quickly gained Roosevelt's approval.[6]

Cutting's chief effort during the session was a proposal that would nationalize credit through a national fiscal system. A Federal Monetary Authority would control the expansion and contraction of credit with the goal of restoring a base of prosperity to the nation. It would raise demand deposits in banks to the level of $250 per capita. Such an expansion of the national currency would wipe out the money famine that was stagnating business. To achieve this goal, Cutting's proposal authorized the government to nationalize the sixty-five hundred member institutions of the twelve Federal Reserve Banks and to operate them under a central bank.[7]

At the time, Cutting was reading widely in the literature on money and banking. He had consulted a group of University of Chicago economists and lawyers to develop his ideas. He claimed that his proposal for a government monopoly on credit was a logical step in the nation's financial history. Through the Reconstruction Finance Corporation, the government was functioning as the chief credit-dispensing bank. In addition, Federal Reserve Bank gold had been taken over by the government, which now determined its value. A publicly owned and operated banking system made good financial sense. It would "furnish cheaper money, lend itself to national planning, tend to prevent disastrous depressions and centralize responsibility." A credit system in the hands of the private bankers, Cutting said, could achieve none of these essential controls.[8]

Cutting recognized that his proposal would not receive serious congressional consideration and sought a national forum in *Liberty Magazine*. He hoped to spark a national debate that would lead to congressional legislation. "Without Government employment of surplus labor and Government control of credit" Cutting argued, "the New Deal must fail." To bring the government into alignment with modern needs, Roosevelt should have nationalized the banks on his first day in office. If he then implemented a federal program that equalized consumption and production, he would resolve the economic crisis. The federal government should employ surplus labor to raise consumption levels and should install credit controls that would force industry to balance production with consumer demand. Cutting wrote, "The failure of consumption through unemployment and the wild gyrations of private banking control brought on the 1929 crash." He envisioned even greater havoc wrought on the economy unless the federal government took decisive action.

Cutting insisted that financial stability would force no great change on the national political system. He reassured the American people, "We are capable of national economic planning without the shackling of human intellect now practiced in Russia and Germany." However, the economic doctrines, "absorbed second hand from Adam Smith, John Stuart Mill, and the others," in no way applied to the United States in the twentieth century. The nation had to modernize both its government and its economy.

Cutting discussed the employment of displaced workers and the control of credit by the federal government. Through hypothetical examples, he demonstrated how private bankers exercised "an uncontrolled and capricious power of credit" that was sometimes beneficent but was "more apt to be destructive." The government control of credit was the "only tool by which we can have national planning." Commercial banks would continue to serve individuals and industrial enterprises in all areas except the loaning of credit. Cutting anticipated that private banks would not yield control of credit without "a mighty struggle" and regretted that President Roosevelt did not bring about the nationalization of banks on March 4, 1933, when "even the bankers were thinking the whole economic system had crashed to ruin." This feat "could have been accomplished without a word of protest."

Cutting then tried to outline a framework of accountability for his program. The two-party system would work, he believed, "if there was a distinct line of cleavage" between them. The American consumer should form a consumers' party that would provide the necessary balance and accountability. For this to happen, the American people had to recognize "that we are not labor or capital, a broker or a store proprietor," but consumers. By abandoning the futile fight between capital and labor to obtain a more equitable distribution of wealth, they could achieve "in the long run greater prosperity" for all. If, as Thomas Jefferson observed, "the earth belongs to the living," then Cutting concluded, "We must throw away the old shibboleths and look to the future instead of the past." And this specifically meant that "the success of any new deal depends primarily on Government control of credit and Government employment of the surplus labor on national projects."9

Cutting prepared the credit measure (Senate Bill 3744) with the assistance of Roger Baldwin of the American Civil Liberties Union and introduced it on June 6, 1934. As he expected, the bill died in the Committee on Banking and Currency. Nevertheless, his article in *Liberty Magazine* had launched a national debate and had created a yard stick by which to measure the New Deal. The credit bill was the first step in his campaign for a rational economic system predicated upon national planning.10

Although he refrained from endorsing his measure on the senate floor, he spoke in behalf of some of its components. Early in the session, he had observed that "in normal times nine-tenths of the money of the United States consists not of currency but of credit." While he admired "the golden cobwebs spun by Professor [George] Warren and Professor [James Harvey] Rogers," he was concerned that their proposed gold reserve bill would provide credit to the wrong people—bankers and not consumers.

In January, 1934, he noted that only two components of the New Deal were attacking the depression crisis in a meaningful way. One, the Civil Works Administration (CWA), was already "talking seriously" of reducing its rolls by four million people, all active consumers. The second was the Agricultural Adjustment Act (AAA). Although it operated under a preposterous theory, it brought help to "people who are going to spend their allotment checks in consumption." Otherwise he saw no teeth in the New Deal. The Public Works Administration had made a promising start but had expended fifty million dollars in seven months. By contrast, the Civil Works Administration had spent two hundred and fifty million dollars in a few weeks. As for the National Industrial Recovery Act, Cutting said that it increased prices more rapidly than wages and thus decreased purchasing power. In short, the New Deal generated little positive change. Cutting declared, "We have got to get results, and we cannot afford to postpone them until it shall be too late."[11]

He intensified his drumbeat of criticism by introducing an amendment that would increase the CWA appropriation. He concluded that the agency was Roosevelt's "most successful effort" to enhance consumer power. Cutting urged the administration to launch new economic experiments to cope with the depression crisis. Except for the Economy Act, Cutting had voted for all of "the experiments suggested by the administration." In his view, however, most of them had failed. He wanted to extend the life of the CWA beyond May 1, 1934, the agency's expiration date. He hoped that Congress would fund the agency at least until the convening of the next regular session of Congress in January 1935. The CWA programs, Cutting said, were the only ones that "ameliorated the situation in any way," and he believed the same was true for the majority of states west of the Mississippi River.

Cutting took a pessimistic view of the country's immediate future. Federal budgets would only increase "for a long period of years." The states and municipalities were "practically bankrupt." The federal government alone controlled the distributive system of the United States and would have to assume the state and local share in providing basic services. Only it could "in any measure" balance "the consuming power of the country with what is acknowledged to be the overwhelming productive power of the United States." A democracy, Cutting believed, was a commonwealth of all citizens. The government could secure their well being "by putting purchasing power" at the foundation of their society until "we find some better method of accomplishing the same results." Congress rejected his amendment.[12]

The distinguished poet, Ezra Pound, offered Cutting suggestions during the session. Pound basically agreed with Cutting's views, but he complained that they did not make clear "that a National Bank is really a National Bank— i.e., one which makes dividends for the nation, like the banks of medieval Genoa, Venice and Naples." Cutting replied, "You can't settle the universe in 18 minutes." His proposal was a prudent first step. If he argued that a properly functioning national banking system "might do away with the need for taxation altogether," he would be "branded as a lunatic" and would hurt his "chances of election in a doubtful year."[13]

Cutting took his plan for a national banking system to the People's Lobby at the Cosmos Club on May 19. His remarks were carried over the National Broadcasting System. The creation of a national bank that would eventually gain a monopoly on the control of credit, he declared, was the most vital need of the country and a necessary first step in conquering the depression. His senatorial task was to arouse interest and understanding in the citizenry. He hoped that public pressure would force Congress to consider his proposal.[14]

Throughout the session, Cutting kept in touch with developments in New Mexico. According to Jouett Elliott, his popularity, particularly in the southern counties, had grown tremendously. In Santa Fe, former governor Miguel Otero drew similar conclusions based on his observations. What was more important to Cutting, however, was expediting PWA projects in the state. The delay lay in Washington where PWA bureaucrats processed applications at a glacial pace. The New Mexico constituency, miscomprehending the situation, tended to place the onus on Cutting and the other members of the state's congressional delegation. Cutting's congressional drive to increase the CWA appropriation in part reassured voters.[15]

At the same time, Congress was challenging Roosevelt's Economy Act. Cutting closely studied the Veterans Administration reports of General Walker D. Hines. Thousands of veterans had altogether lost their benefits, while thousands more were struggling to live on their reduced pensions. Backed by the American Legion in February 1934, national lawmakers approved the Independent Office Appropriation Bill. The act increased pensions for disabled veterans and returned to the pension rolls some four hundred and eighty thousand beneficiaries whom the Economy Act had removed the previous year.[16]

Cutting took no part in the debate over the appropriation measure until the Senate sought to override the executive veto. During the debate in late February, Cutting took the floor to argue, as he had previously, in behalf of veterans with a presumptive service disability. Although never physically wounded in action, these men suffered from tuberculosis or psychological disturbances whose origins lay in their military service. A majority of these veterans had been cut from the pension rolls under the Economy Act. Cutting discussed the injustice of this policy and praised the reevaluation that "restored 40 percent of the cases which had been eliminated by the Economy Act last March."

He now focused on the other sixty percent and illustrated the discrepancies in the rules and regulations of the evaluation process. They were vague, contradictory, and incomprehensible, he argued. In other countries, a disabled veteran, "who knew at first hand something of what they were dealing with" sat on the evaluation boards, but in the United States, none were members. To make his case for disabled veterans sitting on the review boards, Cutting employed charts and tables and presented correspondence between General Hines of the Veterans Administration and Edward E. Spafford, former commander of the American Legion.[17]

Cutting was disappointed by the amendments his colleagues offered to the appropriations bill. On March 26, he expressed his dislike by voting against the conference report, which passed the Senate. The following day, Roosevelt vetoed the measure. Over the president's veto, the House voted 310 to 72 on March 27, and the Senate, 63 to 27 the next day. Cutting voted "Yea." Reversing the application of the Economy Act to disabled veterans, Congress handed Roosevelt his first serious defeat. Reversal meant that government salaries and veterans allowances would be increased by a total of three hundred and fifty-eight million dollars. The scene in the Senate, with people in the "galleries yelling and no attempt at control by the presiding officer," was the most exciting that Cutting had witnessed. Although he played a peripheral role in the override, the president never quite forgave him for the embarrassment of his administration. Over the next few months, Cutting would try to smooth the differences between them.[18]

The president, of course, held the upper hand, and Cutting understood that securing any significant legislation would be impossible unless the administration favored it. Although introducing bills was easy, passing them was difficult. For instance, the proponents of social-credit legislation sought "to get in touch with prominent members of the Administration in order to convert them to some form of social credit." In April 1934, Major Clifford Hugh Douglas, the British mechanical engineer who formulated the social-credit theory, planned to visit Washington. During his stay, Cutting hoped "to get him an interview with some of the higher-ups." His basic concern, however, was to help develop "a determined and intelligent public demand" that credit money "should be mobilized to aid the consumer to buy and use goods and not merely to build a costly tomb for production profits."[19]

Although he kept one eye on banking and pension legislation, Cutting firmly fixed the other on New Mexico affairs. Governor Hockenhull appreciated his efforts to obtain drought relief but really wanted funding for road construction that would put people to work and that would largely eliminate the need for relief allocations. Moreover, Cutting learned that federal projects alone would not alleviate the acute unemployment in New Mexico. Nonfederal projects, he was informed, "are absolutely necessary" to put people to work. Cutting cosponsored a bill that would create a new Federal Land Bank District from Wyoming, Colorado and New Mexico, whose farmers shared agricultural problems. From her vantage point as secretary to the governor, Clara Olsen fed Cutting reports of the political jockeying in New Mexico. Her letters, as she remarked, were in essence "a confidential chat."[20]

Cutting was walking a political tightrope as spring approached. In late March, he dined at the White House two successive nights. Socially, he remarked, "all goes well." Politically, however, he received the distinct impression that the administration would offer him no support unless he agreed to run on the Democratic ticket. Such a "fine type of non-partisan statesmanship," Cutting ironically quipped, made him "feel like swallowing the Old Guard at their worst." Cutting was not prepared to follow his destructive impulse, but a February issue of the New York *Herald Tribune* had carried a story predicting Cutting's reelection with unified Republican support. Several weeks later, the *New York Times* carried a story that progressive Republicans in New Mexico had been invited by the Republican State Central Committee back to the party. Cutting proposed to discuss the rapprochement during a brief Easter recess in Santa Fe.[21]

When he arrived home in the late evening of March 31, he found the political situation "pretty badly scrambled." Most of his friends were wary of accepting "the Old Guard olive branch," which would award the Progressives "approximately 70 new members" and add them to the 159 members serving on the Republican State Central Committee. By a vote of 86 to 52, with 21 members absent, the committee voted to make the offer. Following the vote, former senator Holm Bursum remarked that he was now taking Cutting's place as the bolter of political parties.[22]

The overture to Cutting frightened New Mexico Democrats. A united Republican party heretofore had always foretold defeat for the Democratic party. A divided Republican organization, on the other hand, would insure a Democratic victory, provided, as in 1932, the Progressives supported them. If three tickets invaded the field, the election would be hard to predict, although Roosevelt's popularity would aid Democratic candidates. A Democratic avalanche might permanently bury the old guard Republicans whom Albert Simms and his wealthy wife, the former Ruth Hanna McCormick, now controlled. Cutting was the linchpin in the 1934 state campaign. His decision about whether to return to the Republican fold, to run on the Progressive ticket, or to stick with the Democrats would probably determine the outcome of the election. Whatever he decided, he no longer occupied a space in the nether regions of the political landscape. Through no conscious efforts of his own, he had returned from his banishment to occupy a commanding position in New Mexico state politics.[23]

Before Cutting departed Santa Fe, city voters turned out the incumbent mayor, David Chavez, brother of Dennis Chavez, and replaced him with Jesus Baca, Cutting's close friend and confidant. Political observers attributed Chavez's defeat to Cutting's money. Miguel Antonio Otero, however, enlightened the cynics. He noted that Cutting never participated, "never put up a dollar," in the city elections. Baca's election led Otero to conclude that the Progressives and the old guard "will never mix," and that the old guard would never vote for Cutting. Only a resurrection of the Democratic-Progressive alliance of 1932 would insure the defeat of the old guard Republicans, who were solidly united. With the Democrats disorganized and divided, a Progressive ticket might draw "the best" from both parties. In short, Otero's views reflected the ambiguity of the New Mexico political scene in 1934.[24]

In Washington, Cutting reflected on these developments. He could not "count on good faith from the Old Guard in either Party," and he was afraid that the state election laws would prejudice a straight Progressive ticket. The best approach at the moment was to wait and watch. He could make an informed decision when Congress adjourned and when he returned to New Mexico.[25]

Meanwhile Cutting was exasperated with Roosevelt. He felt that "the gent in the White House" was pushing him "in sixteen directions at once." According to Cutting, no one "could explain what is going on in his mind." He doubted whether Roosevelt knew. With all the power at his command, Cutting lamented, the president still failed to "think up something sensible to do with it."

Taking the policy initiative, Cutting invited "35 or 40" senators and congressmen, plus Father Charles Coughlin and George Peek, to a supper at his home on Thirtieth Street. The honored guest was Major C. H. Douglas, who was visiting Washington to study the New Deal with his social-credit analysis. Cutting was a bit dubious about some of his guests on April 26, but he invited all whom Douglas wished to meet, including the Speaker of the House, Henry Rainey, and the senate majority leader, Joseph Robinson. Although Cutting had not committed himself to the "mechanics of the Douglas" social-credit plan, he thought his analysis "entirely sound." He had no idea how his guests would respond to Douglas's presentation. Many were committed to the president's proposal for twelve intermediate credit banks that would provide only an "improvement in the diffusion of credit." On the other hand, Major Douglas and others wanted both to alter "the fundamental method of credit creation" and to improve "its distribution." National economic stability was out of the question until the government actually controlled the credit of the country. Cutting, however, intended to support the Roosevelt banks on the grounds that some slight progress was better than none at all.[26]

Several weeks later, Cutting listed for Ezra Pound the members of Congress who might be converted to the social-credit views of Major Douglas. About halfway down his list, Cutting drew a line across the page. Those above the line were "open minded," while those below "have mostly crank notions of their own, but could perhaps be converted." Many of the congressmen had attended the supper party for Douglas. Of the fifteen senators Cutting mentioned, seven names were above the line. Of the nine representatives, five were above the line.[27]

At this time, Cutting learned about the efforts of his enemies to compound the disarray of the American Legion in New Mexico. The cancellation of charters, the investigators alleged, was not politically motivated. The lack of cooperation and "an entire lack of any activity" caused their demise. If post commanders in New Mexico would cooperate with the national officials, they would be guaranteed a "field for Legion activities." The National Executive Committee had withdrawn the charter of the Santa Fe post to which Cutting belonged, along with "practically all of the Spanish posts in New Mexico." He firmly believed that politics were at the root of the attacks on the New Mexico legion. A former national commander, Edward Hayes, agreed. He complained that "the American Legion has kicked out of its membership the man who has done more for the disabled man than any man in Congress today or who ever was in Congress."

Edward Spafford recognized that the Democratic party had used the American Legion to retaliate against Cutting for his opposition to the Economy Act and to the administration's policy toward disabled veterans. Spafford knew that the Roosevelt administration had rewarded the instigator of these activities with a political plum, the office of postmaster at Albuquerque. He grumbled, "I have never felt so humiliated at any Legion action." His New Mexico contacts informed him that fifteen years of conciliation would be necessary "to undo the harm."

Spafford concluded that Cutting was no mere "partisan political figure." Factions in both major parties claimed him. Other Democratic and Republican regulars would like to "slay him." Above all, Spafford said, "Bronson Cutting has been loyal to the veterans." He had fought their battles "in season and out of season." The shabby treatment meted out to him by the Roosevelt administration was undeserved. Pleased with Spafford's remarks, Cutting recognized that his political future would suffer minimally from the cancellations. The American Legion was the real loser among those who knew about the political manipulation of its membership.[28]

Although Cutting had not devised a campaign plan, he had received the summons of groups in both parties in New Mexico. Miguel Antonio Otero was confident that "Cutting will win out on any ticket he runs on." Republicans and Democrats waited to see whether Cutting and the Progressive party would engage in fusion or would field an independent ticket.[29]

Before Congress adjourned, Cutting and President Roosevelt attended the fiftieth anniversary of Groton. At the school, Cutting spent three days participating in the ceremonies. He admitted to being "charmed by the reactionary gents with whom we dined (on some admirable white wines)" and who looked on him "as the devil with horns." Nevertheless, he enjoyed the formal dinner and the visit with his former classmates. However, he labeled Roosevelt's address "the bummest speech on record." While in the neighborhood, he addressed both houses of the Massachusetts legislature and "reveled in the disapproval of the members."[30]

During the debate on reciprocal tariff agreements, Cutting criticized the Finance Committee, which offered an amendment that would grant the president power to determine whether an existing duty or import restriction was unduly burdensome and restrictive. The president could raise or lower tariffs by fifty percent. His power would be comparable to the authority Congress granted him under the Economy Act. Cutting said, "We are delegating away the taxing power, the power to regulate commerce, and the power to ratify treaties or agreements." Cutting cautioned his colleagues to "remember in the meantime that powers surrendered can be regained only by a two-thirds vote." He further argued that the revival of foreign trade under reciprocity agreements held out little hope for American agriculture. No one "has pointed to any single commodity as to which the United States would obtain more favorable treatment through the passage of the bill than it is able to obtain at the present time."[31]

Cutting's primary objection to the tariff legislation amending the Hawley-Smoot Tariff Act was not that the measure granted unwarranted power to the president. Instead, he based his opposition on two assumptions basic to his understanding of the depression crisis. The first was his often expressed belief that the national economic "evils were due primarily" to insufficient "purchasing power." If the American people could not buy American goods, neither could they purchase the commodities that "some foreign country is willing to exchange." The federal government must balance industrial production and consumer power. An international agreement could in no way remedy the plethora of empty billfolds in the United States.

His second assumption was that international trade involved "essentially an exchange of the goods and services of one country for the goods and services of another." Extending credit to a foreign country merely postponed "the day of reckoning." He believed that "the credit" granted the foreign country would "never be made good by any real exchange of commodities." Reciprocity, according to Secretary of State Cordell Hull, would provide expanding markets for burdensome surpluses. No surplus was "burdensome," Cutting explained, "with millions of our own people underfed and underclothed." Reciprocal trade would put American surplus goods "into the hands of somebody else somewhere else, and leave our own people to starve." Cutting queried, "If we are going to increase purchasing power, why do we have to confine ourselves to foreign purchasing power?" Filling the American purse should be the federal government's first priority.

Cutting was no protectionist. He believed that many of the duties in the Hawley-Smoot Tariff Act were "entirely too high." The only purpose for lowering the tariff rates should be to increase "our own defective purchasing power." A good "Yankee horse trade" for foreign commodities was a poor basis for an international trade policy. Congress should not shape legislation "to create foreign purchasing power." The Hawley-Smoot tariff already authorized the president to reduce rates by as much as fifty percent. Why should Congress again bestow the power on him as part of a series of foreign trade agreements?

Loaning money to foreign governments would fail unless the American consumer had the means to purchase both domestic and foreign goods. Cutting's premise was that reinvesting "surplus capital" overseas had "helped create the current crisis." Further expenditures on domestic production and foreign trade would only enlarge "the gap" between the purchasing power of the American people and the production capacity of their industry. Why should the federal government invest money abroad to create markets when American voters will "have to pay" for the default?

Seeking a favorable balance of trade meant depleting "our country of its goods and services" and receiving nothing in return. In Cutting's opinion, the United States produced "almost everything" but struggled to locate "sufficient noncompeting foreign goods to pay for its exports." The reciprocal trade agreement was a "policy of madness." Within United States borders lay large, profitable markets. Cutting asked, "Why should we not help our own consumer?" Why not "distribute our surplus among the needy and the starving right here at home?" Dumping goods on foreign consumers, "who will never in the long run be able to pay for more than an infinitesimal fraction of them," was absolute folly.

Cutting's proposal was to devise "some method" of liquidating "our industrial and agricultural surpluses" by providing relief to "our starving underclothed consumers." Upon resolving this dilemma, Cutting said, the United States could "face foreign nations with equanimity" and enter into agreements of mutual profit. Until the federal government boosted the nation's "internal purchasing power," reciprocal trade agreements were "not only injurious" but also "perilous to the interests of this country."[32]

In its haste to adjourn, the senate postponed acting upon "the so-called 'Wagner' bill" that would extend the labor provisions of the National Industrial Recovery Act. Cutting was again in the opposition. In the beginning, he had voted for the National Recovery Act. The measure was a refusal "to accept the anarchic condition" of American industry at that time. No other "definite proposition" was available for consideration. Cutting, however, always thought the NRA a "highly doubtful piece of legislation." The one chance for the NRA to have been successful, Cutting remarked, was in shoring up American purchasing power. He meant that "wages would have to rise more speedily than prices," a process that did not occur. The intent of Section 7A of the NRA was to insure that labor would be represented by its chosen agents, but labor was not granted the same rights as employers. Cutting believed that Section 7A ought to be amended. Members of Congress were walking away from a fight that "could have put over the major portion of the program" still on the senate calendar.[33]

A fight that the Senate took up in its final days was the confirmation of Rexford Guy Tugwell as the assistant secretary of agriculture. Endorsing Tugwell, Cutting defended him against the charges of his critics. He insisted that Tugwell's ability was unquestionable and that his character was unimpeachable. Cutting said that Tugwell's detractors attributed to him the policies that originated with persons higher up in the administration. Although Cutting did not approve of all so-called Tugwell policies—crop reduction, for example—he would vote for him.[34]

Although "busier than hell" during the last days of the session, Cutting was able to relax at home on Thirtieth Street with Clifford McCarthy, Jesus Baca, Frederick Manning, Russell Cheney, and F. O. Matthiessen. He also attended the congressional reception at the White House. He characterized the affair as "unspeakably dull and crowded," but these social occasions eased the intensity of his lonely opposition as a critic on the left to New Deal programs.[35]

By the end of the session, Cutting had emerged as one of the more perceptive critics and insightful analysts of New Deal policies and programs. His criticism, evident already during the Hoover years but more carefully honed during the New Deal, was almost entirely of one piece. On the triad—relief, recovery and reform—often used to describe New Deal legislation, Cutting focused on recovery, in other words, the expansion of purchasing power. The federal government had to balance mass production and mass consumption. Most New Deal programs ignored strengthening the consumer's pocketbook. Although he supported most of the New Deal, Cutting was unimpressed with Franklin Roosevelt. In fact, he doubted that the president understood much more than Hoover about the causes of the economic crisis.

Cutting advocated radical measures like banking and credit reform to attack the depression. He was disappointed with Roosevelt who had failed to exploit his electoral mandate to reverse the economic spiral. Cutting promoted reform to achieve recovery. Federal relief efforts had been too minimal to eliminate distress, let alone to enhance purchasing power. Cutting had traveled far from the good-government values of his family background. Some considered him a radical, but he was at most a perceptive, outspoken progressive seeking to resuscitate a badly flawed economic system. Despite his great wealth, he fully comprehended the human suffering that followed the economic collapse of a modern industrial society.

When the congressional session concluded on June 18, Cutting turned to the 1934 campaign. He debated whether he should run on the Republican or Democratic ticket, and he pondered the terms. Back in New Mexico by the end of June, he took stock of the political affairs and drove "constantly" with Jesus Baca. On July 1, he delivered the opening address to the National Convention of the Disabled American Veterans at the Antlers Hotel in Colorado Springs. Departing immediately, he traveled to Clovis, New Mexico for an Independence Day speech. His period of watchful waiting had ended. His political realignment would now begin in earnest.[36]

CHAPTER 22

REALIGNMENT

When Cutting returned to New Mexico at the end of June 1934, the state was experiencing a terrible drought, the worst in twenty years. For nine months, there had been little precipitation. Farmers were about to tap reserve supplies of water for the irrigated lands along the lower valley of the Rio Grande and the Pecos River. The outlook was bleak in the dry-land sections, which had about three fourths of the state's total crop acreage. Farmers and ranchers faced disastrous losses of crops and livestock. In addition, the state had made no provisions for unemployment relief. The counties expected to raise ten thousand dollars per month from an indigent levy. What assistance New Mexico received in the summer of 1934 came from the federal funds authorized by various New Deal programs. In August, with 59,956 people on the relief rolls, the state received $750,000 from federal government. Two hundred thousand dollars went for general relief; $500,000 for drought relief; and $50,000 for miscellaneous purposes. In the second quarter of 1934, the federal government provided 98.5 percent of the state's relief expenditures.[1]

Cutting recognized that the Democratic senatorial candidate, indeed the entire Democratic ticket, would benefit enormously from the New Deal largesse and the president's popularity. He still had to decide how he should align himself for state law made launching a third party exceedingly difficult. On July 7, a three-hour "seance" with "a conference committee from the G.O.P." did not clarify Cutting's future. One thing was certain, the state Democratic administration, since the death of Arthur Seligman, was "unspeakable." Cutting doubted that he could work with the Democrats even if they invited him. The alternative was equally distasteful. Running on a Republican ticket would mean swallowing the old guard. With resignation, Cutting said, "One acquires a good swallowing capacity after a few years of this sort of thing."

In early July, the Democrats had not selected a party chairman to replace Ed Swope. The search for a new chairman would involve a fight. Cutting knew that some of his supporters would want him to run on the Democratic ticket, while others would endorse him regardless of his party affiliation. From what he could discern after a week in New Mexico, the outlook was not as uncompromising as his secretary, Edgar Puryear, had suggested. In a fit of pessimism, Puryear had insisted that Cutting would lose the election unless he aligned himself with the president. The senator was pleased to learn that Mabel Dodge Luhan had started a "Cutting for Senator Club" among the intelligentsia of Taos and that another pro-Cutting club was organizing in Santa Fe.

Writing from Italy, Phelps Putnam expressed an interest in limiting the suffrage "to the select kind of voters." Cutting disagreed. While he might favor "limiting the subjects on which they were to vote," Cutting thought that "the ignorant voters are apt to be at least as sound as the cultured boys." The question, of course, was meaningless because no people would willingly deprive themselves of any political rights. As much as Cutting disliked Roosevelt, he preferred "the Franklin type of democracy" to the bloodthirsty mobocracies that Mussolini and Hitler were nursing in Europe. Cutting, however, was rankled by the foreign "hero-worshippers"—John Maynard Keynes, H.G. Wells and John Strachey among others—who applauded Roosevelt and his policies. "The grin," Cutting said, "bowls them over every time."[2]

Much to Cutting's dismay, the Democratic State Committee unanimously conferred the party chairmanship on John T. Miles, the favorite of the Arthur T. Hannett-Dennis Chavez forces. Cutting was appalled. In 1924, Miles had been charged with stuffing county ballot boxes three days after the election, and had recently been discharged from his job with the Internal Revenue Service. Under his direction, the state committee urged the removal of all "progressive employees and all non-political welfare workers" from the state payroll. Cutting now had no choice but to align with the Republicans on the best possible terms. To make matters worse, he learned that the Democrats expected at least thirty-nine million dollars in federal relief funds to pour into the state before the election. In no way could Cutting match this "formidable weapon," but he thought that public sentiment for the New Mexico Democrats was thinning, given the kind of administration they had been giving the state.[3]

Whether the visit of James A. Farley, postmaster general and chairman of the Democratic National Committee, to New Mexico altered the political climate was a matter of dispute. John Dempsey and Dennis Chavez met Farley at Lamy on the morning of July 17 and rode with him to Santa Fe. At Dempsey's home outside the city, Farley breakfasted with leading Democrats from all parts of the state. Before departing, Farley was presented with a hand-crafted blanket by the head of the county Democratic organization, David Chavez. Later that morning, he discussed politics with newspapermen but said nothing to encourage or discourage any faction in the state. Indeed, Farley reiterated throughout the day that Democrats would have to settle their differences themselves. In Albuquerque, he spoke to an audience of statewide postal employees. That evening, after an extended afternoon conference at his hotel suite, he delivered a political address before six hundred people. Democratic leaders were delighted with the encouragement and support he offered during his hectic, daylong visit, one stop in his extensive western tour.[4]

Farley's visit reenforced Cutting's pessimism about his election prospects. Alignment with the old guard Republicans would be difficult, and there was a distinct possibility that he might lose in the process. As if preparing himself for eventual defeat, Cutting wrote his friends about how relieved he would be should his tenure as United States Senator come to an end. Cutting complained that the Associated Press had given no attention to his senate speeches on its western wire. Ironically, as he voiced his disillusionment, a young Republican expressed the hope that a candidate like Cutting, who boasted an exemplary voting record, would provide "A Recipe For Republican Success In 1936." While expecting the worst, Cutting intended to wage as strong a campaign as he possibly could.[5]

Old-line Democrats controlled the state central committee, but by the time of Farley's visit, rank-and-file Democrats, some prominent party leaders, and several county committee chairmen had come out for Cutting and threatened to disrupt the party if its leaders did not dampen their hostility. Progressive Democrats wanted him returned to the Senate regardless of his political affiliation. In their view, Cutting held the balance of power in the coming election campaign. However, Farley had been silent about whether the Democratic party should support Cutting. New Mexico pundits concluded that the party would fight him. Cutting agreed, as did Dennis Chavez, the newly elected national committeeman, who wished to contest Cutting for his senate seat.[6]

Chavez and other Democrats recognized that old guard Republicans were resisting fusion with Cutting and his associates. Equally resolute, the Democratic regulars proceeded to expel "the Cutting office barnacles," Herman Baca among them, from any post in the party organization. Leaders of both parties and most prominent businessmen stood shoulder to shoulder in their opposition to Cutting. Democratic leaders talked of fusing with Republicans in every county, and in mid-July, they thought they could carry Bernalillo County (Albuquerque) by at least five thousand votes and knew that they would have ample funds at their disposal. Their confidence extended to the press, Cutting's only strength, they believed. The Democratic party argued that it had Roosevelt and the New Deal behind it. All that remained was for both parties to select their candidates at their state conventions. The outcome of factional battles in the Republican party would determine whether Cutting would rejoin the Republicans or would run as a third-party candidate.[7]

After Farley's visit, the Democrats were "very cocky." Roosevelt's popularity and the huge relief funds were behind their optimism. Cutting's hope was that the Progressives and the Republicans could unite. He anticipated "a lot of knifing." His task would be to mobilize popular sentiment against "the dictates of immediate self interest."[8]

At the Progressive meeting on July 20, 1934, Cutting told the six hundred cheering delegates that the issue of fusion was entirely in their hands. He asked only that the basis of any agreement be the Progressive principles expressed in the 1932 platform: the initiation of election reform; the improvement of the school system; the dispensation of social welfare and health services; and others. Cutting declared, "The keynote of the platform is that government must be brought closer to the people."

The next day, Cutting and the Progressive leaders were invited to meet with the Republican State Central Committee. Former Governor Richard Dillon led the welcoming party. In an earlier conference, Cutting and Dillon had agreed upon a platform largely based on the Progressive party platform of 1932 and acceptable to both groups. The Progressive chairman, P. L. Rapkoch, was elected to the chairmanship of the central committee of the united party. The Republican leadership reorganized the state central committee, doubling its membership with the addition of Progressive members. Most old guard members either absented themselves from the meeting or reluctantly agreed to these developments. No dissenting voices were heard when the crucial question of fusion was decided.[9]

Cutting's address to the members of the new state central committee denounced the sales tax imposed by the Democratic legislature, reiterated some of the points from the Progressive platform and called upon the delegates to forget past differences. The fusion of the two organizations would not necessarily translate into votes come November. Winning would require, Cutting explained, "a campaign of education" conducted by "the individuals who are sitting today in this hall." The first hurdle would be to secure at the Republican State Convention in September the progressive program adopted by the reorganized state central committee.[10]

Democratic observers concluded that Cutting had taken over the Republican party and would go "straight down the line for the whole ticket." The old guard assured the Democrats that it would actively support Democratic candidates, provided the party had nothing to do with Cutting. Democratic leaders were cheered by these developments. Members of the old guard immediately started to raise funds for the coming campaign.[11]

Cutting thought that the old guard defection had "a certain advertising value" and that many Democrats would support him despite their party leader's counsel. While public sentiment was "very fine," the "mathematics of the situation" were against him. The New Deal would pour "39 million Democratic dollars . . . into the state between now and election." Cutting said, "We shall all have a man sized fight on our hands." His chances were slim, he realized, but he added, "I shall shed no tears if destiny intends my remaining years to be in Santa Fe instead of the stinking Senate Chamber." Before he engaged in what promised to be "an interesting fight," however, Cutting took an Alaskan cruise.[12]

With a strike of stevedores tying up Pacific Coast ports and a general strike in San Francisco, Cutting would wait until early August before leaving Santa Fe. In the interim, he attended fiestas around the state. He concluded that "the Democratic organization has been used to solicit campaign contributions from Federal employees." Departing by plane, he spent a day at the Pacific Palisades home of his senate colleague, Hiram Johnson. In Seattle, he boarded a cruise ship, the SS *Yukon* for Alaska.[13]

Old Alaskans, Cutting reported, considered August "an impossible month for weather." They were not trifling with him. At the outset, Cutting experienced "days of penetrating cold, fog, rain and cloud, and precipices looking black as far as you can see." The boat, which could comfortably hold one hundred people, had almost twice that many passengers. There was neither privacy nor wine. The beer was "scarcely drinkable," and the whiskey, "old Guckenheimer would promptly disown." Among his table mates were the national secretary of the Elks and his wife, the Internal Revenue collector for Alaska and a couple from New Mexico. A crooner entertained them during their meals, between which sounds from a radio permeated every corner of the SS *Yukon*.

On deck Cutting had to pick his way through piles of supercargo: "potatoes, tin cans, Ford trucks, airplanes, and drilling machines." At every change of course, the vessel listed heavily. The pilot, laid off for sinking his last boat, was "doing his best to live up to reputation." And there were "no telephones or doorbells." The privations and inconveniences aside, the cruise was "pretty jolly," Cutting concluded. If not exactly restful and relaxing, it provided an escape from what he considered to be a most depressing political situation. The majestic Alaskan waters and stunning coastal scenery could not tear his mind from New Mexico. He plaintively wrote, "I wish I could stop thinking about it all."[14]

Cutting's outlook brightened after motoring three days to Valdez. The interior was less damp than the coastal region. He found solace in the snow-capped mountains, the rivers and the glaciers. Three weeks without "telephones and front doorbells and discussions" now became a salve to his anxious soul. His spirits revived somewhat, but his mind still harbored menacing doubts about the election. He expected a hard fight. "Bursum, Farley, Hannett, Magee and the Simms[es] make quite an unholy alliance to buck," he explained to his mother. By the end of the cruise, he was determined to battle for and to accept renomination.[15]

While in Alaska, Cutting received the endorsement of several leading national progressives. Senators Henrick Shipstead, Gerald Nye, Robert M. La Follette, Jr. and Edward P. Costigan praised his record and encouraged his candidacy. Costigan spoke to a meeting in Raton. Through the Scripps-Howard newspapers, Robert Scripps declared that Senators Cutting and La Follette had realistically assessed the grave economic plight crippling the country. Shortly after his return from Alaska, Cutting wrote Mayor Fiorello La Guardia of New York City, ". . . if you feel like making any statement in my behalf, it will be extremely valuable to me."[16]

Returning to Seattle four days later than scheduled, Cutting was met on the pier by Senator Homer Bone. They lunched with Edward Scripps, the nephew of Robert Scripps. Flying to Portland, Cutting caught the fast express for San Francisco, where he dined "with the Johnsons." Thereafter, he flew to Albuquerque. On his return, he surveyed the political scene. The Democrats were "very cocky," and his friends, "correspondingly gloomy." He thought that he had "a 40-60 chance, and the rest of the ticket at least a fighting chance." The Alaskan trip had dispelled his black cloud. Cutting had an exciting fight on his hands. Refreshed by his vacation, he rolled up his sleeves and eagerly waded into the fray.[17]

His presumed opponent, Dennis Chavez, was canvassing the state. As Chavez made the circuit of the state, he visited places that were "in need of some attention." Most Democrats knew that Cutting would make the senatorial race difficult by spending "many thousands of dollars." Some Democrats were confused by Cutting's veiled references to removing himself from the race. Most, however, waived aside those defeatist statements. They believed that Cutting was the Republicans' only hope in the coming campaign. As Cutting had sensed upon his return, the Democratic leadership was cocksure about its party's chances in the coming campaign.[18]

Many rank-and-file Democrats were loyal to the New Deal but critical of the Democratic state administration, especially its recently imposed sales tax. Some organized Cutting clubs, while others broke their party affiliation and entered the Republican ranks to support Cutting. Likewise, old guard Republicans, Holm Bursum and Albert and Ruth Simms among them, broke party ranks in desperation to defeat Cutting. These renegade Republicans wanted to make the controversial Cutting the chief issue in the coming campaign. On the other hand, Democratic leaders, particularly Dennis Chavez, hoped to generate the popular Roosevelt and the New Deal as the main themes of their campaign. The key issue for the Republican party, now firmly under progressive control, was "Shall we get a new deal in state affairs?"[19]

At the end of August, Cutting was certain that Dennis Chavez would be his senatorial opponent. Either Clyde Tingley, the mayor of Albuquerque, or John Dempsey, a New Deal administrator, would receive the Democratic nomination for governor. "Either one [Tingley or Dempsey]," Cutting explained, "would be easy to beat in a different kind of year, without the White House propaganda and backing behind them." What bothered Cutting was that the Republicans had no obvious gubernatorial candidate who could wage an effective campaign and who if elected, would promote a progressive program.[20]

Although concerned about the party tickets, Cutting did not ignore his own campaign. He spoke at a Labor Day rally in Raton. Afterwards, he planned a tour of the drought-stricken areas in Union County, part of the "Dust Bowl," in northeastern New Mexico. He also asked the Public Works Administration in Washington to survey the development potential of the enormous natural gas fields in Lea and San Juan counties. An energy program utilizing these natural resources would generate power to pump water for agricultural industries and thereby would render much of New Mexico "virtually immune from crop failure due to drought conditions." Now assisting Cutting from Santa Fe, Edgar Puryear wrote senior citizens to remind them that the senator had introduced a bill providing "proper pensions for aged people" and that he intended to secure its passage in the next Congress.[21]

Both parties scheduled their nominating conventions for September 24. The Democrats met in Albuquerque; the Republicans, in Santa Fe. Surveying the situation before the conventions, Cutting still believed that public "sentiment is with us, but all the munitions of war are the other way, as well as all the organizations." On a positive note, he reported that about eighty percent of the county newspapers favored his candidacy and that "most of the silent vote" would fall into his column. He also recognized, however, that "one quarter of the people of the state will be working for the government by election day." When his mother offered him a contribution to help overcome the heavy odds, Cutting urged her to keep her money. He wrote, "Confidentially, I no longer see the remotest chance of carrying the state." A member of Roosevelt's "inner circle" informed him about the "deep hostility" towards him boiling up "over Hyde Park."[22]

Nevertheless, Cutting continued to expedite federal funding for New Mexico projects. The head of the Public Works Administration, Harold Ickes, was friendly to him. His requests for PWA funds usually received a favorable hearing. Although the odds were arrayed against him, Cutting intended to wage a strong campaign. At this time, Clyde Tingley informed James A. Farley that Chavez could defeat Cutting "as the Old Guard Republicans will go with the Democrats in every county in this state."[23]

The weekend before the Republican state convention, Cutting wrote a letter to his closest friends in the United States Senate. To Hiram Johnson, he explained, "The fight is going to be pretty tough." He counted on "the unorganized rank and file in both parties" to counter the massive funding of the old guard Republicans who were in league with the Democratic machine to bring about his defeat. To Robert M. La Follette, Jr., Cutting added a more personal observation. His own hope was "either that both of us get elected, or that both of us get whipped." If they were relegated to private life, Cutting believed, they "could start something in this country which would go a long way." He wrote these letters during the Santa Fe County Republican Convention, which selected delegates for the state convention scheduled to meet two days later on September 24 in Santa Fe.[24]

In his acceptance speech at the Republican State Convention, Cutting praised the party platform as a first step in redeeming New Mexico from its "completely political setup." He recalled his efforts to increase purchasing power, to promote employment and to relieve human misery—the heartfelt concerns of the farmer, the laboring man, the small businessman and professional man. Making no claim to partisanship, he had always stood by specific principles. Foremost among them were "the rights of the people of the state of New Mexico." If he had failed in this undertaking, Cutting said, "I hope you will vote for somebody else."

He indicated his agreement with the last words of a seventeenth-century English martyr. Facing death on the scaffold, the condemned man spoke words "something like these: 'I have never subscribed to the doctrine that the masses of mankind were born with saddles on their backs, and a few men born with boots and spurs to ride them.'" The bosses of both parties, Cutting said, too often had imposed that doctrine on the people of New Mexico. The Republican platform incorporated the view of the martyred Englishman and encompassed Cutting's political philosophy. Cutting concluded, "All of us together shall eventually establish in this state a government which will maintain the rights of our own people."[25]

To flesh out his views and those of the Republican party, Cutting endorsed a campaign document, "An Economic Plan for New Mexico." The pamphlet argued that the state Democratic administration had failed to bolster New Deal programs that would benefit New Mexico: hydroelectric expansion; the transfer of population from unproductive to productive lands; and public-works unemployment relief. The Republican program for New Mexico was both practical and utilitarian and dovetailed with Roosevelt's New Deal. The proposal addressed three topics dear to New Mexico: water; natural resources; and state highways. If successful in the coming election, Republicans pledged themselves to implementing these policies. The pamphlet concluded, "Government rather than the individual citizen must be effective."[26]

With his nomination in place and with a platform and a ticket dominated by progressive Republicans, Cutting could now throw his energies into the upcoming campaign. Writing to his sister several days later, he said, "Even now I am not sure which day it is." So involved was he with the "grueling activities" leading to the convention that he forgot his own birthday. Six days after the convention, he felt like "a dish rag," gloom once again pervading his outlook. "There is no way," he wrote, "in which a victory can be figured on paper." The sources of his pessimism were Roosevelt's popularity, federal funds and relief recipients, twenty-five percent of all New Mexicans, who would be told how to vote. In addition, he had trod on too many "prominent toes" over the years. Practically everyone who controlled votes or who had been a party leader in the past had combined against the Republican ticket. After reviewing reports from all thirty-one counties, however, Cutting could not "figure out a majority in the state." He placed his hope in the "silent" voters, "the unimportant people whose names don't get into the head lines." On the positive side, the Republican ticket was much better than he expected. Taking several days of rest before stumping the state, Cutting believed that he would survive the remaining thirty days, "somehow." While he saw no reason for undue expectations, many of his congressional colleagues were more sanguine about his bid for reelection. Several even offered to speak for him during the campaign.[27]

Cutting's assessment was much more realistic. In an incisive letter written before the state convention, he reflected, "I don't suppose one has any right to expect gratitude in public life. People have such a false idea of the delights of holding public office that they could never stop to consider that there is any debt at all on their own side. I shall undoubtedly 'get mine,' if not at this particular election, then surely one of these days ahead." Then he added, "Public service is its own reward—and a measly bitter little reward it seems at times." Anyway, he continued, "If you don't care much about the job, you can view its loss with a great deal of philosophy." He carried that flinty attitude into the campaign. He was struck by "how nice it is to live in Santa Fe (or anywhere else in New Mexico)." Maybe he ought to "let others move about the vast corridors of Washington." In short, Cutting confessed, "I've never learned to be a politician."[28]

Nevertheless, this matter of learning "a little more by going on living" had carried Cutting, within the space of two years, from political limbo to political realignment in New Mexico, a process that he personally engineered. Read out of the Republican party in 1932 when he resigned as national committeeman, Cutting had come back as the leader of the "new" Republican party controlled by the progressives. Now he would campaign for reelection against what appeared to be insuperable odds.

CHAPTER 23

REELECTION

A ll issues are clearly drawn between the selfish interests on the one hand and the independent vote on the other," Cutting wrote shortly after his nomination at the Republican State Convention. Now his job was to appeal to independent voters. He was convinced that "party labels no longer mean anything in our state, or for that matter in the nation." To succeed, he would need help from state and national supporters. Endorsements from prominent progressives throughout the nation were forthcoming. Although their reception by New Mexicans was highly problematical, Cutting welcomed all endorsements for his candidacy.[1]

Edward Prentice Costigan, a Democratic senator from Colorado, was anxious to speak in New Mexico in Cutting's behalf early in the campaign in case the Roosevelt administration pressured silence from Cutting's Democratic friends. His secretary, Edgar Puryear, actively solicited endorsements from sixteen senators and four representatives.[2]

While Cutting was seeking endorsements, Democrats were gathering influential support for Dennis Chavez, his opponent. Chavez's son, residing in Puerto Rico, was informed that "the Republicans have nothing to offer the people and our record, State and National, is an open book and approved by the masses, all the corporations, the Santa Fe R.R., Chino Copper Co., and Cerrillos and Raton Mines." In addition, most old guard Republican leaders and many others endorsed "your daddy." Many, like this correspondent, did not "see how he can loose [sic]."[3]

At times in October, Cutting agreed with this prognostication. After "jerking about from Tucumcari to Clovis and then back to Fort Sumner and Albuquerque," Cutting was already looking forward to the campaign's end, which would bring him time to devote to his cultural interests. On the one hand, he thought that he would "be much happier if not elected." On the other, his pride and determination coaxed him to confess, "I shall be a little sore at Frank [lin D. Roosevelt] for putting it over." His resolve to thwart the designs of the Roosevelt administration was what people saw in Cutting during his campaign for his reelection.[4]

Holm O. Bursum was one of the prominent old guard leaders supporting Dennis Chavez. He was certain that Cutting would wage a desperate campaign. He reported to Herbert Hoover that Cutting would spend three hundred thousand dollars on his reelection bid. Bursum and other "substantial citizens" believed that Cutting was "as much a menace to free and orderly government as Mr. Huey Long is to Louisiana." Although Cutting's defeat would result in the election of the Democratic ticket, it would be beneficial, Bursum explained, "to the future of the Republican Party, the State of New Mexico, and to Washington." Bursum, Republican National Committeeman Albert G. Simms, and other "reliable Republicans" were mustering their resources to elect the Democratic ticket. Bursum inquired of the ex-president "if there is any way you might feel disposed to lend a helping hand, or put us in touch with a source from which we might obtain some help." Bursum made his request with complete confidence. Men such as Cutting, he explained, were not "politically conducive to healthy, virile, sound government and their retirement from positions of power and influence would improve the service of the country."[5]

As he stumped the state, Cutting compared his and Chavez's voting record in the United States Congress. He claimed that he was a better New Dealer than Chavez, who was preaching party regularity. Cutting insisted that "party labels mean nothing, but that you have got to vote progressive or reactionary according to your own beliefs." At each rally, he usually endorsed Jaffa Miller over Clyde Tingley, the mayor of Albuquerque, for governor. He declared that electing "a chief executive who will do the right thing by the people" was "more important" than sending him or anyone else to Congress. In Washington, "if we go wrong on you," there would be others trying to do "the right thing."

On October 16, in Santa Fe, Cutting was followed on the platform by his Republican senate colleague, Frederick Steiwer, who praised his championing of disabled veterans in the Senate. Cutting delivered his progressive message to all parts of New Mexico in both Spanish and English. He always insisted that progressive principles were best represented in the Republican platform and in the records of the Republican candidates.[6]

That the Roosevelt administration sought Cutting's defeat became evident when Senator James Byrnes of South Carolina, chairman of the Committee on Campaign Expenditures, launched an investigation of election spending. Byrnes instructed his investigator, a prosecuting attorney from his own state, to probe Republican expenditures in New Mexico and to overlook those of the Democratic candidates. Offering "a conservative estimate," Cutting surmised that "the Democrats were spending in New Mexico one hundred dollars to every one of ours." Cutting was awed by the "combination of the representatives of the big financial interests" aligned against him. Ordinarily, gargantuan, wealthy political machines would not alarm Cutting. Roosevelt's popularity combined with the nationwide disrepute of the Republican party, he realized, might lure even "sincere men of integrity" to his opponent.

He acknowledged the appeal of the president and the New Deal although the local Democrats were conducting a "reactionary" campaign in his estimation. Initially the Democratic platform incorporated a denunciation of excessive relief expenditures, a clause later deleted. The main plank endorsed a sales tax, which the president repudiated. A large portion of the party's effort went into disseminating a 1932 campaign statement by Herbert Hoover. According to the ex-president, Cutting and other progressive Republicans were "wild-eyed radicals engaged in undermining the foundation of the Republic."[7]

Cutting campaigned vigorously throughout the state, sometimes in places without telephone service. On October 22, Senator Joseph Robinson, with Roosevelt's blessing, announced that he and Senators Tom Connally and Morris Sheppard, both of Texas, would campaign against him in New Mexico. Touring a locale without telephone service, Cutting was unaware of this development. Upon reading the press dispatches containing the news, Hiram Johnson immediately wired a protest to James A. Farley, postmaster general and Democratic party chairman. Johnson inveighed against the "unjust and unfair" attempt "to smash a man like Cutting who rendered such invaluable service and displayed such a magnificent courage in thirty two."[8]

Other political leaders also resented the administration's failure to support Cutting. The intrusion of prominent Democrats into the New Mexico campaign lent credence to reports that the president was personally leading the charge against Cutting. Moreover, the combination of old-line Democrats and Hoover Republicans professing enthusiasm for Roosevelt and the New Deal was a source of bitterness in some quarters. Progressive leaders in both parties endorsed Cutting, placing the president and his supporters in an awkward position. The New Deal was the old party deal in New Mexico. Cutting and his supporters had the unenviable task of supporting the Republican ticket at home while criticizing its national leaders and policies. Although the New Deal made a bid for the support of progressives, it did not lend them a hand. In the New Mexico showdown, the president strove to place party above the New Deal.[9]

Aware of Roosevelt's opposition, Cutting had no option but to wage a hard campaign. He received the encouragement of many organizations and individuals. One supporter wrote Cutting, "All the good people are with you." Among the "good people," he included "Mexicans," who "are all in favor of you." He characterized Cutting "as harmless as a dove and as bold as a Lion." Only Cutting, he believed, among the Republican candidates, would win in November.[10]

Cutting personally campaigned from one corner of the state to the other. "I have driven over 900 miles in the last 48 hours," he wrote on October 28, "with six speeches and endless conferences thrown in." Fortunately, the weather was as "perfect" and the country was as beautiful as he had ever seen it. While he would not prophecy about the outcome of the "awfully tough" battle, he thought he was making "distinct progress." He was pleased with Senator Hiram Johnson's radio address in his behalf. Senator Joseph Robinson would make the closing speech of the Democratic campaign on election eve in Albuquerque, where Cutting too would deliver a major appeal.[11]

To offset Robinson, Cutting tried to lure Senator William E. Borah to New Mexico. Although busy with his own campaign in Wisconsin, Robert M. La Follette, Jr. sent a "radio record." To Cutting, he apologized, "I had to go it blind on the issues to emphasize in your campaign and hope I have not made any blunders." Echoing Cutting's wish, he wrote, "I hope that both of us are elected or both defeated." To further assist Cutting, Edward Keating, the editor of *Labor,* the weekly publication of the Railroad Brotherhoods, sent to broadcasters throughout the state a special issue endorsing his reelection. Senator Costigan had promised to speak again in New Mexico but reneged at the end of October. Edgar Puryear, managing the campaign in Santa Fe, suspected that "the national administration has persuaded him not to do so."[12]

Cutting's supporters in the national legislature included leading progressive senators and other members of Congress from both parties. The chairman of the Republican Senatorial and Congressional Committee, however, lacked the funds to assist his campaign. Collecting endorsements was the best that Cutting could manage. Without either radio play or, better still, public appearances in New Mexico, the value of peer endorsements was dubious at best.[13]

One of the hardest challenges Cutting faced in the campaign was from the American Legion. Although the executive committee promised to keep the organization out of national politics, the legion actively participated "on every platform by the opposition in an effort to discredit my veterans voting record and myself personally." Most New Mexico veterans bore a heavy grudge against the "National Legion Coordinator with his local allies." So bitter was the feeling that Cutting doubted whether the American Legion could ever be revived in New Mexico. The antipathies engendered during the senatorial campaign would not die down "in any reasonable length of time."[14]

Cutting asserted that the "heads of the Legion" hoped for his defeat. During the pension debates, he had criticized "the total inadequacy and inefficiency of their Washington office." His charges against the American Legion and his vote to override the president's pension veto added to Cutting's woes. *Forum* magazine cited his support for disabled veterans as graft on the public treasury. In a radio broadcast, its editor instructed the electorate to vote against "betraying" senators and congressmen.[15]

Although *Forum* denounced Cutting, *Colliers* praised him. Owen P. White, a journalist who had worked in New Mexico, reviewed the complex political situation and predicted that Cutting would probably win the election. White believed that the Roosevelt administration's general inattention to the campaign would assist Cutting's candidacy. Most interesting was a *Literary Digest* forecast. If Cutting won his senatorial race, the article speculated, he conceivably might become the Republican presidential nominee in 1936. Party lines meant little in the New Mexico campaign. Chavez and the Democrats appealed to conservatives; Cutting and the Republicans, to liberals.[16]

Less optimistic was Fleta Campbell Springer, a reporter for the *New Republic*. From Santa Fe, she wrote that the strong reactionary forces in New Mexico might send "an administration yes-man to the Senate and thereby lose to that body one of its most fearless, intelligent and genuinely distinguished members," Bronson Cutting. The contest was essentially between "the liberals and the reactionaries," but Cutting's opponents were "some of the most powerful money interests of the state." Their "curious underground slogan" was " 'get Cutting in 1934 and defeat Roosevelt in 1936.' "[17]

Political commentators enjoyed the rivalry between Ruth Hanna McCormick Simms and Cutting. Switching to the Democrats, she made the fight for control of New Mexico one "between the wealth of these two baronies." In the *American Mercury,* Jan Spiess explained that "the forefathers of the state of New Mexico, old guard Republicans for the most part, had absorbed the feudal attitude through long association and knowledge of the Mexican people." Embracing paternal responsibility, Cutting exploited feudalism to his own advantage. Presumably, Ruth Simms would utilize the same tactic. Spiess concluded that Cutting was so necessary in Washington "that one hopes for his reelection."[18]

On November 3, 1934, the Saturday before election day, James A. Farley prepared for the president his analysis of the various senate campaigns. In New Mexico, he declared, "Chavez has a better than even chance over Cutting. Joe Robinson's visit to New Mexico will help materially because it created the impression that he was speaking for the Administration."[19]

That same Saturday, Cutting delivered his major address in Albuquerque. Robinson had said that Cutting opposed the New Deal; Ruth Simms had gone Democratic to punish Cutting for supporting the New Deal; Dennis Chavez claimed a better friendship to the veteran than Cutting's yet accepted the endorsements of senators who were among the bitterest congressional opponents of the veterans. Cutting defended his record and criticized Chavez's. The election, he declared, was between a liberal and progressive program and "a meaningless mass of words" spoken by men who held the voters in contempt and would "not even deny the public charge that they obtained their nominations through an infamous deal."[20]

Cutting stressed his record of service in Congress. He defended the rights of the cattleman, the sheepman, the cotton grower, the petroleum producer, the home owner, the farmer, the working man, the miner, Railroad Brotherhoods and, of course, the veteran. On election eve in Santa Fe, he gave his final address to several hundred people at the Christian Brothers gymnasium. Senator Frederick Steiwer of Oregon sat on the platform but did not speak. Although hounded by doubts at the outset, Cutting had waged a hard fought, intelligent campaign. Following his initial strategy, he appealed directly to the voters in both Spanish and English. He made hay of the wealthy special interests arrayed against him and of the incongruities in their arguments.[21]

On November 7, the initial returns indicated a Democratic victory in all contests except Cutting's. No trend had emerged in his race on the basis of the more readily tabulated votes. Two days later, the *New Mexican* proudly proclaimed, "On the face of present returns, if last minute ballots do not overturn his majority and if the election is not stolen, U.S. Senator Cutting has beaten the most formidable collection of adversaries ever deployed against a candidate in New Mexico, by a moral majority of over 41,000 votes." Editor Dana Johnson's figure was considerably exaggerated. Dubbing Cutting's plurality "a moral majority" only indicated his heightened emotions and intense partisanship. The final tally was 76,245 to 74,954. Several things were clear, however. First, Cutting was the only victorious Republican, and his margin was slim. The election of 1934 gave the Democrats complete control of the state for the next two decades. Although his margin of victory was just shy of thirteen hundred votes, Cutting had turned back a veritable tidal wave of forces determined to destroy his career. He was the only major progressive, not endorsed by the New Deal, who won his race. The Roosevelt administration, for example, gave its blessing to Hiram Johnson in California. In Wisconsin, Robert M. La Follette, Jr. did not receive Roosevelt's formal approval, but neither did his Democratic opponent. In all instances when a progressive candidate was endorsed by and his Democratic opponent was opposed by the administration, the progressive won the election. Only Cutting overcame Roosevelt's resistance to his progressive candidacy.[22]

In New Mexico, Republican leaders had foreseen the doom of the ticket. Senator Cutting was their bright spot. His victory was their great consolation, worth, as one of them said, "all the time, expense and worry of the past campaign." He concluded, "Personally, I feel that we would all have been disgraced if the outcome of this contest had been otherwise."[23]

In the days following the election, the results from remote precincts trickling into party headquarters showed that Cutting's slight lead was holding. On November 13, for example, the Associated Press announced that Cutting had a lead of 1,287 votes over Chavez after all counties had reported in full and with only 471 absentee ballots still outstanding. To celebrate his marginal but impressive victory, Cutting journeyed to Taos where Mabel Dodge Luhan held a dinner for him and other Republican candidates.[24]

Cutting, however, was dissatisfied with his victory. His enemies had succeeded "to the extent of defeating our excellent state ticket running on the best platform ever adopted in New Mexico." In his opinion, the election was the first shot in a new fight for good government in New Mexico, especially now that progressives controlled the Republican party. Although Cutting lacked exuberance, his triumph elicited a congratulatory telegram from Harold Ickes, the one member of the Roosevelt administration who had long waged losing battles for the progressive cause.[25]

A week after the election, the final returns from the county canvassing boards, including the absentee ballots, had not been filed. Cutting was certain that they would record him the victor. Additional hurdles would follow. First, the state canvassing board would meet in December to review and validate the returns from the counties. Second, Chavez could demand a recount, which, Cutting said, "would in itself imply that they had meanwhile stuffed some ballot-boxes in the office of some county clerk." Finally, the Committee on Campaign Expenditures in the United States Senate would probably review the entire matter. Most New Mexicans following the tallies of the county boards deemed Cutting the victor by a small but safe majority. A tired Cutting planned a two-week escape "to some ranch or mineral springs" where he could be reached by telephone but otherwise remain generally inaccessible until the state canvassing board convened.[26]

Political analysts began to unravel facets of the election. The well-financed and bitter fight by the Republican establishment against Cutting helped to doom the Republican ticket. On the other hand, Cutting's victory was impressive. Senators Robinson and Sheppard had stated the desire of the president to elect the Democratic ticket and to defeat Cutting. In addition, approximately one-third of the voters, 115,000 people, were on federal relief; nearly 15,000 Democrats held jobs as state, county and federal employees; and the Democrats controlled the election machinery in 27 of 31 counties. Although the total vote did not differ markedly from 1932, Republican candidates who won in local elections made serious dents in the Democratic majority. Republicans primarily lost in formerly Republican counties where old guard leaders endorsed the Democratic ticket. However, they made notable gains in the Democratic counties. If anything, Cutting and the progressive Republican ticket saved New Mexico from becoming a one-party state. The election also indicated that the Republican old guard no longer influenced either party in New Mexico, but it could defeat candidates.[27] The results of the 1934 election suggested that the New Mexico Republican party, if driven by progressivism and stewarded by Cutting, could challenge the Democrats in future elections.

But before that could happen, Cutting would first have to secure his senate seat. Hiram Johnson advised him to retain the best possible lawyers and to "gird yourself for the fray and do not permit a lot of rogues to take your hard won laurels."[28] Indeed, Chavez intended to fight. Shortly after the election, he publicly declared that he had won the contest and would let no one take away his victory. Cutting's response was "that the office of U.S. Senator is not a personal perquisite belonging to him or me, but an office which belongs to the people of New Mexico and which they are entitled to fill." The people, as certified by the county canvassing boards, did not elect his opponent.

Cutting observed that the Democratic party controlled the election machinery in all but four of New Mexico's counties. In the Republican-controlled counties, Cutting either lost the election or trailed the Republican ticket. Chavez had received support from the state and national administrations and from "all the reactionary Old Guard Republican leaders." How could have election returns been twisted in his favor, he wondered. If Chavez could produce valid evidence of fraud, corruption or errors in the tabulation, Cutting would happily relinquish his claim to the senatorial seat. He was not interested enough in public office "to be the beneficiary of fraud or error."[29]

Although Cutting detected no possible grounds for challenging his election, he asked Senator Borah whether Chavez had filed charges in Washington. Since New Mexico law prohibited candidates from assuming financial obligations either by loan or donation, Chavez and his cohorts had to gather evidence of fraud at the precinct level. When he heard of possible irregularities, such as voting by aliens at Carlsbad in Eddy County, Cutting sought all the available information. He wanted to know of possible discrepancies before they were presented as formal charges against him.[30]

In Washington, Borah learned from Senator James F. Byrnes that Chavez intended to file charges relative to campaign expenditures. Borah promised Cutting that when and if charges were filed, he would immediately forward a copy. Cutting assumed that former governor Arthur Hannett was working up the charges and that "Mrs. Simms . . . will pay for the work." When Chavez and Hannett departed for Washington, Edgar Puryear followed "to keep an eye on them." Cutting informed his mother, "We are guarding the ballot boxes as well as we can." Nevertheless, he understood that if Roosevelt wanted to remove him from the Senate, he had the votes to do so.[31]

Cutting was unable to depart Santa Fe for a brief rest before the State Canvassing Board met in December. He complained, "There has been no day when a decision did not have to be made." He found the daily suspense "somewhat trying" but was adjusting to it. He received "a lot of relief from osteopathic treatments which are very soothing to the nerves."[32]

Meanwhile in Washington, Puryear was equally busy in his behalf. He spent the morning of November 26 with Senator Norris. When the president returned from Warm Springs, Norris would discuss the matter with him. The senator also agreed to collect from various colleagues statements favorable to Cutting. Norris remarked that the Democrats would not permit a disputed election, one in which Cutting would be supported by all progressives, to disrupt their agenda in the next session. Puryear also noted that Senators Joseph Robinson and Pat Harrison would visit Roosevelt at Warm Springs and that he was trying "to get Harrison to offset anything that Robinson might do." Among newspaper men and members of Congress, Puryear reported, sentiment was increasingly in his favor.[33]

Senator Costigan, a member of the Committee on Campaign Expenditures, doubted that an investigation was warranted. Costigan reported that a charge of participation in election frauds had been leveled at Cutting but that "the case presented to this committee by Senator Cutting's opponents is one of remote and insufficient insinuations." Unless Chavez built a stronger case, Costigan thought, the "Senate's attention should not be diverted from pressing public problems merely to gratify those who at the last election unsuccessfully sought to overthrow Senator Cutting's leadership in New Mexico."[34]

Senator Henry W. Keyes of New Hampshire issued a similar statement, meaning that three of the five senators on the committee did not think

New Mexico senatorial campaign expenditures merited further investigation. The termination of this committee's interest in Cutting's campaign did not preclude the Committee on Privileges and Elections, chaired by Walter F. George of Georgia, from taking up the matter. However, before acting, George would have to ask for the Senate's direction. From Puryear's sounding of Senate opinion, the answer was clear: There would be no contest.[35]

Although Cutting was pleased that the Senate Committee on Campaign Expenditures refused to entertain Chavez's charges, he was still awaiting a certificate of election by the State Canvassing Board. On December 7, when Arthur T. Hannett and Carl Hatch challenged the returns from San Miguel County, the board would not throw them out. Hannett and Hatch wanted to discount fifteen hundred votes, that, if disqualified, would have awarded the certificate to Chavez. Cutting's attorneys countered that the state canvassing board, "merely an adding machine to count the returns," had no right to throw out any votes. The three-man board, two Democrats and one Republican reached a unanimous decision not to eliminate the San Miguel County returns.

Nevertheless, the board still withheld the necessary certificate, presumably to review returns from other county canvassing boards but in fact to involve the state supreme court. Ultimately the secretary of state, Marguerite B. Baca, would issue the certificate. A Democrat and the widow of a former lieutenant governor, she was under tremendous political pressure to delay Cutting's certification. Arthur T. Hannett and the New Mexico Supreme Court eased her burden. In early December, he secured from the court a Writ of Mandamus that ordered the canvassing board either to issue Chavez a certificate of election or to show why he should not be issued the documentation.[36]

Cutting's lawyers assumed the latter responsibility. Cutting was confident that the court would ultimately decide in his favor, but he anticipated that "an unending series of technical obstacles" would be followed by a challenge in the Senate—at least six months of "petty bickering." Although the legal maneuvering distressed him, Cutting was pleased that "practically the whole of the press" and leading figures in the arts community, Witter Bynner, Andrew Dasburg, and Mabel Dodge Luhan among them, were active in his behalf. After the election, Luhan sent Cutting a photograph of Piero Della Francesca's painting of *Christ Rising from the Tomb*, "with a letter explaining its analogies to the New Mexico situation."[37]

After conferring with his lawyers to make sure his case was well presented, Cutting could only watch the maneuvering of the state supreme court. The judges, he believed, would "hardly dare do anything but the right thing."

Cutting learned that Chavez had phoned Hannett about Senator George's promising "Farley to help out in the contest." If the court decided in Cutting's favor, he expected Hannett to come forth with a new dilatory tactic.[38]

Cutting was heartened by Puryear's report of a conversation with the vice-president, John Nance Garner, who has asked Puryear to convey his best regards. Garner had served notice to several "Administration Senators" that he would not stand for interference in Cutting's election. Since he was supposed to be an impartial presiding officer, Garner did not issue a formal statement conveying his position, leaking it to several newspapermen instead.[39]

Cutting now considered Garner's aid his "strongest card," especially once he started "to work on the Robinson's and the Byrnes's." Garner's assistance would mean nothing, however, unless he received a certificate of election. On December 21, the New Mexico Supreme Court informed the State Canvassing Board that it had not reached a decision. Therefore, Cutting continued to pursue all leads relevant to graft and other malpractices within the New Deal agencies prior to the election. He concluded, after learning that both Hannett and Chavez had spent an afternoon with a member of the supreme court in his office, that the case would continue. He did not believe that the court would decide against him, but he knew that the delay would have "just as serious effects in the long run."[40]

The Christmas season found Cutting increasingly despondent. "Things are as uncertain as ever," he wrote on December 27. He was convinced that if the new state administration got underway before the court reached a decision, he would never get his certificate. With the new year, a new canvassing board would automatically come into being, "a board which could be relied on not to issue me any certificate." To add to his gloom, a friend, recently returned from Washington, confirmed Puryear's view that although newspapermen were for him, most senators were not. He refused to name all the senators he visited. But he did name Alben Barkley, Cutting's "old Russian companion," and he inferred that Key Pittman was another. One influential senator, Pat Harrison, apparently did try to intervene in his behalf with the White House. Harrison was advised that the administration was taking no part in the New Mexico fracas, a conclusion Cutting could not accept. His understanding was that James A. Farley, chairman of the Democratic National Committee, was actively involved in the case. "Enough activity of this kind," he concluded, "will be pretty effective."[41]

In a telegram on December 29, Puryear buoyed Cutting's spirits. Senator Norris had relayed the good news that Senators Joel Bennett Clark and John H. Bankhead were his outspoken supporters. Other senators were willing to issue statements but were waiting until the supreme court in Santa Fe cleared the way for the issuance of a Certificate of Election. Puryear was also arranging for pro-Cutting editorials to appear in several newspapers. While he recognized Cutting's difficulty with the court in New Mexico, Puryear nevertheless contended "that you are in splendid position here."[42]

On December 30, Cutting had still not received his certificate. If he did not have it on the following day, he concluded, "There is practically no chance of getting it at all." He was not very sanguine, "as the Supreme Court has already spent three weeks on a question which any child in high school could determine in three minutes." He could not comprehend why he should expect any better results on the morrow.[43]

During this holiday season, when Cutting could do little but await a decision of the supreme court, he drafted a new will, revoking all previous wills and codicils. Handwritten and completed on December 20, 1934, his new one was a lengthy document that would attract widespread attention when its contents became known. The finished document was duly attested by Reed Holloman of Santa Fe and Jefferson D. Atwood of Roswell, the lawyers defending his interest in the contested election. Whether Cutting had any premonition of an untimely death or of having time on his hands is unclear, but he decided to draft a new will that took into account exactly who his friends and supporters were. Aside from his lawyers, it is to be doubted whether anyone else knew what he was doing. Certainly no mention of the new will appears in his correspondence. When its contents became public, no one claimed previous knowledge of the startling document.[44]

Cutting's immediate fate was resolved at the last moment on the last day of the year. His election ordeal officially ended when Governor A. W. Hockenhull certified to the president of the United States Senate that Cutting was duly chosen by the qualified electors to represent New Mexico in that august body. On the same day, he received a congratulatory telegram from Charles McNary, minority leader in the Senate. McNary informed him of his appointment to the Committee on Committees, a key assignment that would give him a voice in selecting minority members on all senate committees.[45]

Cutting's election was approved by the County Canvassing Boards and then unanimously by the State Canvassing Board composed of a Democratic governor, a Democratic secretary of state and a Republican supreme court justice. Cutting had been unable to receive his Certificate of Election until the New Mexico Supreme Court, owing to an appeal by his opponent, reviewed the matter. Finally by a three-to-two vote at year's end, the court ruled in favor of allowing the state board to authorize the certificate of election, holding it improper to require the State Canvassing Board to go into the registration lists as part of the returns. Dennis Chavez and Arthur Hannett, his chief counsel, had been unable to substantiate before agencies dominated by Democrats evidence of fraud, undue financial expenditures or any other irregularity on the part of Cutting's supporters. Consequently, they would bring their fight into the senate chamber, despite the fact that the Senate Committee on Campaign Expenditures decided not to make an investigation. They hoped that the support of the president and a large Democratic majority in the Senate would unseat Cutting to give the Democrats complete control of all major offices in the 1934 New Mexico election. Meanwhile Cutting, upon receiving the long awaited certificate, departed for Washington and was sworn in without protest for another term on January 3, 1935.[46]

CHAPTER 24

PAYING THE PRICE

Senator Hiram Johnson spent an enjoyable evening at the White House on December 19, 1934. For a couple of hours after dinner, the president and the senator chatted intimately. Johnson had always thought that the president had "no political resentments" and could "meet people whom he knew to be against him seemingly with the same good fellowship as those who were loyal and attached to him." This evening, he learned otherwise. The president, with "vigor and earnestness," expressed his "contempt and disdain" for various members of the press and his desire to get back at them. Roosevelt's tirade explained "something of his attitude toward Cutting in the last campaign."

Johnson had the temerity to ask him about the senator from New Mexico. Apparently, Johnson wrote, Roosevelt "had forgotten" Cutting's endorsement of his candidacy in 1932. His only memory was "that Cutting had been forceful and bitter" in the "veterans" debates. Roosevelt complained that Cutting "had held him up as one who little remembered the men who had been wounded or broken by the war." Johnson clearly saw "that the Democratic activities in New Mexico against Cutting had been not only with his consent, but doubtless from his orders. . . ." Although Johnson was unsure about how the president's antipathy would affect the outcome of the election dispute, he considered his attacks "small, and ungrateful and cruel." Leaving the White House that evening, the California senator was more determined than ever "to prevent an injustice being done Cutting."[1]

Less than two months later on February 6, 1935, William E. Dodd was home on leave from his post as ambassador to Germany. Over lunch with the president, he heard another explanation of Roosevelt's attitude toward Cutting. The president mentioned that Huey Long planned to be "a candidate of the Hitler type" in 1936 and then added that Cutting too wanted the presidency and had "paid tremendous sums in order not to be defeated for the Senate last fall." In Roosevelt's eyes, Cutting's candidacy was an "ominous situation" that would divide the progressives and possibly pose a serious threat to his reelection in 1936.[2]

Roosevelt no doubt bore grudges and would have been pleased to see a Chavez victory, but little evidence indicated that he had involved himself in Cutting's election. Several progressive senators, including Cutting, cited

James A. Farley's activities as proof of Roosevelt's complicity. Progressives believed that as the chief dispenser of patronage and the chairman of the Democratic National Committee, Farley had the president's full approval to displace Cutting.

One of the closest observers of the Washington political scene doubted Roosevelt's complicity in the onslaught against Cutting. In his first column for 1935, T. R. B. wrote, "I am reliably informed that word has been conveyed to Senate leaders that Mr. Roosevelt is not interested in the Dennis Chavez contest" and that he did not endorse Farley's activities. Another Washington journalist, R. G. S., disagreed several weeks later. He argued that Farley "could not have acted without authorization from the President." All observers recognized that a "real attempt" to unseat Cutting would "kick up a thundering row" and would create more problems than it would resolve for the administration. Already, as the new Congress was about to convene, Roosevelt's "more liberal supporters" were alarmed at "the President's tendency to yield to reactionary influences." The Cutting controversy cast doubt on the president's informal alliance with the progressive wing of the Republican party.[3]

In 1936, almost a year after Cutting's death, Harold Ickes confided in his diary that he "always believed that the President was responsible for the fight on Cutting." He never discussed the matter with the president, but he went on, "According to James Farley, Chavez made the statement that he would not run for Senator against Cutting unless the President told him that was what he wanted him to do." Subsequently, after a conversation with the president, Chavez informed Farley that Roosevelt "wanted him to run for Senator." Ickes reported that Farley confirmed Chavez's candidacy with the president. Farley told Ickes "how embarrassing it was for him to be supporting La Follette in Wisconsin and Johnson in California, while opposing Cutting in New Mexico." Ickes could not fathom the president's attitude toward Cutting, writing that "in my heart I hold it against him."[4]

In January 1935, however, Cutting had little time for speculation about Roosevelt's motives. Once he received the Certificate of Election that assured him his senate seat, he would have to defend his right to it before a committee of his peers in a chamber dominated by a hostile administration. The pending battle particularly disconcerted him. For the Seventy-fourth Congress, Cutting had secured a place on the Senate Foreign Relations Committee, an assignment he dearly coveted. Instead of devoting most of his energies to public affairs, he would have to defend himself against charges that he was fraudulently elected.[5]

Cutting understood that Chavez, "spurred on by [Arthur] Hannett," would howl extravagantly about excessive expenditures and illegal voting, particularly in San Miguel County. His charges would attract newspaper coverage and might curry favor with both Roosevelt and Farley. Cutting's counterattack would have to humiliate Chavez and embarrass the Roosevelt administration. Cutting would have to gather evidence of Democratic election fraud and the illegal application of federal relief and highway funds just prior to the election.[6]

To intimate friends, Cutting occasionally betrayed his weariness with political contention. He contemplated quitting his office, leaving Washington "with all its sham and artifice" for a full-time life in Santa Fe. Jouett Elliott admonished him about surrendering in the middle of a fight. When the fight was over, he could entertain his resignation. He already had done more than his part "for the state and the people." Other close friends acknowledged that Cutting had no great political ambitions and that he preferred Santa Fe to Washington, D.C. They also understood that he was a fighter and would never strike his colors in the midst of the greatest challenge of his political career, no matter how depressing his situation.[7]

As the session got underway, constituent business took his mind from his personal plight. The state engineer brought to his attention public-works monies for the rehabilitation and construction of stations for stream gauging. According to the Roswell Chamber of Commerce, the Bankhead Act, calling for compulsory reduction of cotton production, failed to consider differences between the irrigation cotton agriculture of New Mexico, Arizona, and California and cotton agriculture in the South. Congress, the chamber said, should modify the act. From Las Vegas, the Civic Committee of the Woman's Club inquired about a possible PWA project that would enable the community to develop a municipal water system.

Conferring with Harry Hopkins, Cutting sought assurances that his political battle with the Democrats would not hold up the administration of relief in New Mexico. Although he was in favor of old-age pensions and had submitted a pension bill in the previous session, he refused to commit himself to the Old Age Revolving Pension Plan proposed by Dr. Francis Townsend. As a member of the Committee on Foreign Relations, he sponsored a joint resolution calling upon the federal government to meet a treaty obligation to Mexico. The government should fund the maintenance of the Rio Grande channel to provide its neighbor with water according to a 1906 agreement. Clearing the channel would benefit irrigation farmers and curb soil erosion, a matter of grave concern to Cutting. Plunging himself into the routine of senatorial business was an indication of Cutting's desire to function as a full, effective member of Congress.[8]

On January 17, the vice-president laid before the Senate a letter from a Washington attorney. The contents served notice to Cutting of Chavez's intention to contest his senate seat. The letter and its accompanying papers were referred to the Committee on Privileges and Elections. At the outset, the committee struck one of the provisions in the resolution attached to Chavez's letter. The item called for the impoundment of ballot boxes, a measure that would remove them from the custody of county clerks. Rather than seeking fraudulent vote tallies, Chavez and Cutting would now focus their investigations on unregistered votes by checking registration and poll lists.[9]

Chavez would have the easier task. In mid-January the new state legislature, Democrat-controlled, approved a resolution appropriating twenty-five hundred dollars to investigate the election in San Miguel County. For his part, Cutting paid two private investigators to check polling lists in other counties. In addition, his lawyers considered photographing the poll books in San Miguel County. The copies in the secretary of state's office had frequently been checked and tabulated. Any changes or alterations in them would not affect Cutting's case unless the tallies could be checked against the photographic copies. Whatever expenses Cutting incurred to prevent fraud, to accumulate evidence and to locate witnesses the federal government would reimburse, his lawyers believed.[10]

By the end of January, Chavez had filed only formal notice of his intention to contest the election, although a state legislative committee was gathering evidence in several New Mexico counties. The air crackled with rumors that the formal charges would include specifications of fraud in additional counties. Although in Washington, Cutting heard "practically nothing" about the contest. "Judging from newspaper accounts," he did not see how the kind of evidence submitted to the state legislative committee would attract much attention.[11]

The administration's effort to secure entry of the United States into the World Court put Roosevelt and Cutting on friendly terms once again. The Senate debated the issue in late January. Isolationist senators, including most progressives, sought to block the effort with crippling amendments. Cutting, who voted against reporting the resolution out of committee, was nevertheless considered doubtful in his opposition. On the morning of January 29, Cutting and three colleagues visited the president. On the final vote, they endorsed the proposal, which by seven votes lacked the two-thirds majority required for ratification.[12]

At a White House reception prior to the final vote, as Cutting went through the receiving line, the president held him for a few moments of friendly conversation. Later in the evening, they talked again. Political observers believed that the president and Cutting had restored their friendship and reconciled their differences. Among other things, Roosevelt assured Cutting that the rumors about his involvement in the New Mexico election were groundless. As Roosevelt bid Cutting good night, he expressed his appreciation for any help the senator could offer in steering through ratification the World Court proposal. At that time, Cutting was prepared to vote in favor of its passage—but, a close friend recalled, almost changed his mind.[13]

Another foreign policy matter on which Cutting was in accord with the president was the matter of copyright law. Roosevelt favored an international treaty that protected authors, but the Foreign Relations Committee, Democratic-dominated, was unwilling to act. Cutting, a minority member, had no power to protect international cultural exchange even though he had come to national attention during the Hoover administration when he successfully challenged the right of customs inspectors to censure books and art objects entering the country.[14]

Although he could not advance copyright law in the Foreign Relations Committee, he spoke out against the censorship of foreign speakers. Cutting lent his voice to a storm of protest against the threatened deportation of John Strachey, a radical British economist and author who was lecturing in the United States. The expulsion of Strachey, Cutting said, would make the "American tradition of free speech a dead letter." Conservative reactionaries, Cutting protested, were reviving the "Red menace" to divert attention from the "failure of our own government policies." Cutting inquired of the commissioner of immigration, D. W. MacCormack, what organizations had protested Strachey's admission and what courts "had decided that a philosophic advocacy of say the Marxian theory of surplus value constituted advocacy of the overthrow of the Government of the United States by force or violence." Strachey's views had been widely publicized before he entered the country. Concerned more with the imperilment of free speech than with the disposition of Strachey, Cutting deplored the harassment of radicals. The Immigration Bureau had played into the hands of the House Un-American Activities Committee, which had suppressed its findings on Fascist activities but publicized its evidence against the Communists. Strachey meant nothing to Cutting either as an individual or as a writer, but the senator was alarmed by "an obvious attempt to do away with the Bill of Rights by dragging the Red herring across the trail." Nothing came of this matter. Strachey completed his tour, and the federal government dropped the case against him.[15]

While awaiting the petition of Dennis Chavez to the Committee of Privileges and Elections, Cutting felt "perfectly useless" as a "Senator." To Phelps Putnam he complained, "The damn situation is getting no better fast." The electoral contest consumed most of his attention outside of the necessary routine. He had "no time to analyze trends or size up situations." The New Deal, he feared, was moving toward the right. His evidence was the purge of liberals from the Department of Agriculture and the creation of several NRA codes that unduly favored management. He regretted that the exposure of the rightward drift was left to Huey Long "and not to me."

Cutting was distressed that the New Mexico legislature had gone "hog-wild" and "appointed a committee of five partisan Democrats to collect evidence for Chavez." At the same time, the legislature gave the Finance Committee, appointed "by the Governor," a free hand "to spend money" on the investigation. Cutting suspected that old guard Republicans, notably Albert and Ruth Simms, had contributed funds to Chavez's war chest as well. While the state investigations had yielded no evidence incriminating him, they were bound by no time limit. Cutting sensed that "some kind of Senatorial contest seems to be on the cards."

Roosevelt's attitude was particularly disturbing. All in one day, Roosevelt would invite Cutting to the White House, calling him "Dear Bron" or "Brons," to solicit his support on a political matter, but then would urge "on my colleagues to unseat me." Miserable with the frustration, Cutting concluded that politics was "a fine life while it lasts—but surely not a useful one."[16]

Cutting's friends, however, continued to aid him both in Washington and in New Mexico. William Green, president of the American Federation of Labor, drafted a letter of protest to members of the senate. Why were they reviewing the New Mexico contest? His encouragement came from Judson King, the head of the National Popular Government League. King declared to Green, "There is no man in the Senate of wider intelligence, more fundamental integrity, and finer feeling for social justice than Cutting."[17]

In New Mexico, the legislative committee's "fishing expedition," Edgar Puryear, reported, would be of little value to Chavez. Witnesses sympathetic to Cutting had made favorable impressions. Maurice Miera, gathering evidence in Cutting's behalf, hoped to provide the committee with the financial statements of some Democratic candidates. He also was prepared to present witnesses who would testify about the alleged non registered vote in San Miguel County. Awaiting developments in Washington, Cutting was clueless about what charges Chavez intended to make. Cutting wondered how Chavez could pull together a conclusive case for his buying up the election in San Miguel County where he had finished at the bottom of the Republican ticket.[18]

Swamped with difficulties, Cutting was unprepared to debate issues on the senate floor for several weeks. On February 18, he joined the extended discussion of a joint resolution calling for several billion dollars to fund a gigantic program of emergency public employment. Cutting was disturbed by an amendment that would make men on strike ineligible for work relief. Such a disqualification would shackle "the strike weapon," the "only effective weapon which labor has had" for decades.

The proposed amendment would prevent industrial strikes and would encourage the reduction of monthly wages by unscrupulous employers to just above fifty dollars, the amount called for in the joint resolution. Striking workers would not be the only class hurt by the amendment. "Every man who for some good reason may be unable to continue in his occupation" likewise would be barred from applying for work relief. Cutting urged Congress to commit the funds to the discretion of the president. "Through his agencies," he could see that money was spent in only justifiable ways. That the Congress had confidence in the chief executive was self-evident. At the time, his colleagues were preparing to grant him the authority to spend four and a half billion dollars, the largest peacetime appropriation in the history of the nation. Cutting's defense of labor in the amendment was rejected on a voice vote.[19]

Several days later on February 25, Chavez filed his petition that contested "the purported election" of Bronson Cutting. He requested a recount "of the ballots cast" and "an investigation of the wrongful and unlawful practices" of his opponent. In eight pages, Chavez's lawyers detailed the essence of the petition under two separate headings: "Illegal Votes Counted For Bronson M. Cutting" and "Legal Votes Not Counted for Petitioner"; and "Illegal use of Money and Unlawful Expenditure of Money By Bronson M. Cutting."[20]

The day the petition was filed, Edward Keating, the editor of *Labor*, visited Cutting. The two men discussed a proposal for a quiet meeting of labor's friends in the Senate to explore "N.R.A. problems." Cutting agreed to arrange such a gathering "but pleaded that he was disturbed by the contest against him." While Cutting agreed that the Democrats could not muster enough votes to overturn his election, the case would consume much of the time that he should be devoting to his senatorial duties.

Cutting also gave Keating details about his break with the president. In the fight over veterans benefits, Roosevelt had promised to consult Cutting about changes in the measure, but he apparently forgot his "pledge" and directed the house conferees to oppose the Cutting-Steiwer amendments to the senate bill. When Congress approved the measure with these amendments, Roosevelt invited Cutting to the White House and told him that he would veto the bill but that the veterans would not suffer. He wanted Cutting to sit down with him and help him draft regulations to that end. According to Keating, Cutting said, "I couldn't resist telling him he had made a somewhat similar promise ten days before but had broken it." Roosevelt made no response but no doubt resented his attitude. The Chavez petition was the price he was paying for his independence.[21]

Those individuals in Washington and New Mexico who examined the Chavez petition generally deemed it a weak document. One Washington publication succinctly stated, "Senators who have had an opportunity to examine the Chavez petition feel that the former congressman has made a weak showing and that the document contains nothing that reflects on Cutting's integrity or seriously challenges his title to the Senate seat." E. Dana Johnson, the editor of the *New Mexican,* explained, "Chavez says he knows damn well there must have been fraud to change the result; that Cutting's relations contributed to the campaign and he didn't include his relatives' contribution as part of his personal contribution; and that he is sure the Republican organization couldnt [sic] have borrowed money unless Cutting guaranteed the loans, and doesnt [sic] the Senate think this looks suspicious and wont [sic] it please find out whether it aint [sic] illegal."

To Cutting and the pundits, the charges were vague generalizations that Chavez would have to specify. Moreover, charging fraud in San Miguel County was a double-edged sword that Cutting's investigators could use against Chavez in other counties. People familiar with New Mexico politics could have made similar charges of voter fraud, but proving Cutting's involvement was another matter that the five Republican and twelve Democratic senators, comprising the Committee on Privileges and Elections, would decide in due time. To better prepare Cutting's defense, his lawyers, Reed Holloman and Jefferson D. Atwood, came to Washington for a few days to assist Huston Thompson, his chief counsel.[22]

While lawyers on both sides of this dispute were busy developing their cases, Cutting tried to maintain some semblance of his Washington routine.

On the evening of March 3, he and his mother attended a small dinner party hosted by Senator and Mrs. Hiram Johnson. Here among familiar faces active in public affairs, Cutting was able to relax and enjoy a stimulating evening. Several days later at the Cosmos Club, he listened to the distinguished historian, Charles A. Beard, warn against policies that were dragging the nation towards war. Frustrated most of the time, he participated in the business of the Senate and kept abreast of constituent concerns. In addition, he followed the preparations by his lawyers and friends for his case and the activities of his opponents. On March 7, he reported that Chavez, Governor Clyde Tingley and others were "interviewing everybody in sight from the White House down" but seemed to have gained little ground among the Senate's sixty-eight Democrats, despite help from his New Mexico colleague, Carl Hatch.[23]

At this time, Cutting introduced a bill to regulate the value of money. The measure would create a Federal Monetary Authority to control the price of commodities and the purchasing power of money. The goal was to restore a stable and prosperous economy. A modified version of the measure that he introduced in the previous session, he recognized his bill stood no chance of winning congressional approval. However, his intention was to use his hypothetical monetary authority as a yardstick first to measure and then to amend the administration-endorsed banking bill, which the Senate would take up later in the session. While favoring the idea of a Federal Monetary Authority, he was far from insisting on all features of the bill and was open-minded to suggestions for its improvement. Since neither monetary nor banking proposals would come before the Senate for several weeks, Cutting simply dropped his proposal (S2204) into the legislative hopper. Both he and the Senate had more pressing concerns.[24]

The ongoing business of the Senate in March was still the massive work-relief measure, a provision of which Cutting had tried to amend. Now he took a much more active role in the controversy over the wage levels on public projects. Cutting and his allies wanted rates of pay for full-time work equal to and not below those prevailing elsewhere. Otherwise, many private employers would find the lower federal wage scales too attractive. The president disagreed, however. He was not convinced that private employers would lower their wages on the basis of federal pay levels. Roosevelt had taken the position that the pressure of public opinion and the admonishments of the state and federal governments would prevent employers from lowering wages. After listening to the extended debate, Cutting changed his mind and voted in favor of presidential discretion.[25]

Although Cutting yielded to the president, his amendments were intended to put as much purchasing power as possible into the hands of people on federal work relief and to prevent the deterioration of wage rates for workers in the private sector. Like the president, he considered work relief superior to direct relief, the "dole." Both the morale of the people and the infrastructure of the nation benefited from public-works projects. Cutting submitted proof in a letter delineating the various work-relief projects of the Federal Emergency Relief Administration, which would be conducted on an even larger scale once Congress acted on the measure under discussion.[26]

Taking the legislative initiative, in mid-March he offered an amendment to allocate $40 million of the $4.8 billion work-relief bill to keep open the nation's public schools. According to the federal Office of Education, many would otherwise close by April 1. Not wishing to force the president's hand with his amendment, Cutting left to his discretion how much of the $40 million he would allocate to the distressed schools. Cutting's data was culled from a survey of 32,000 school districts in 26 states by the Bureau of Education. Over 40,000 schools were on the verge of closing, jeopardizing the jobs of more than 100,000 teachers and the education of 3.5 million school children. Cutting argued that Congress should directly endorse the funding measure instead of leaving the resolution of the problem to FERA administrators.

Cutting's senate remarks focused the public spotlight on a hitherto unnoticed federal education report delineating the plight of public schools after six depression years. After generating much lively debate, his amendment handsomely carried by a 55-to-25 vote, but it did not appear in the conference report. Replacing Cutting's provision was one dealing with "educational persons," a term that he could not comprehend and that suggested an objective quite different from his. His colleagues, however, approved the new amendment by a large majority. Although he could not blame the senate conferees for the ultimate failure of his amendment, he noted, "It was the only amendment which the Senate adopted on a roll call over the opposition of those who were in charge of the joint resolution." He continued, "A majority of the conferees voted against the amendment on the floor of the Senate, just as a majority of the conferees voted against the relief measure as a whole."

Cutting's dissatisfaction got the better of him. He complained to the Senate, "While we have voted vast sums for banks, for business, for industry, for railroads, and for other private interests, we have not spent one penny which has not been appropriated directly by [an] act of Congress for the public school system." Taxpayers, who usually took care of their own schools, had suffered so terribly by the depression that they simply could not fund their schools without federal help. The conferees wanted to avoid a precedent for federal intervention in a strictly state responsibility. They utilized the term *educational persons* to reconcile the relief bill with state's rights. The education of twenty-seven million school children yielded in conference to theoretical concerns, Cutting lamented. Instead of compromising, the Senate conferees surrendered to the House—an all-too familiar story. Cutting insisted, "We cannot possibly hope to have the views of the Senate successful in conference" unless the "Senate conferees are in sympathy with the position of the Senate."

Others agreed that the system was bad. Although Cutting attached no personal blame to any conferee, he hoped that his colleagues would start "at once and try to revise our present system of getting legislative action." The Senate should not put other pieces of major legislation at risk in conference. With the public clamoring for the passage of the work-relief measure, Cutting had no intention of allowing the failure of his amendment to delay its approval. In the final roll call, he was among the sixty-six senators voting "yea."[27]

In addition, he was now beginning to probe seriously the banking and credit legislation soon to come before the Senate. Cutting was favorably impressed with Marriner Eccles, the new chairman of the Federal Reserve Board and the architect of the administration banking measure. Cutting's initial reading prompted doubts about lodging control of the Federal Reserve System in the White House. He stated that "political control of credit seems to me only a slight improvement on the present private control." But Cutting never had time to formulate a systematic critique of the bill or to prepare amendments to it. Rexford Tugwell had requested an interview with Cutting to discuss the matter. An intimate of the president, Tugwell proposed that if Cutting introduced the administration measure, the president might throw his influence against the Chavez petition.[28]

After Chavez filed his protest in late February, Cutting's lawyers gathered material to answer the charges. On March 12, they requested the Committee on Privileges and Elections to extend the deadline from March 15 to March 30. They needed additional time to gather information in New Mexico. Senator Walter George, chairman of the committee, formally acceded to the request. Although Cutting remained convinced that Chavez could "not get anywhere in the long run," he hated to have the dispute "dragged out indefinitely, as the Administration decides, so as to have something to distract one from the issues before Congress." On March 26, Cutting tried to force the issue by moving that the charges against him be dropped on grounds of insufficient evidence, but the committee literally ignored his motion and continued with its deliberations.[29]

While awaiting the formal hearing, Cutting devoted his attention to the development of New Mexico oil and natural-gas resources. In the previous session, he had introduced a bill that would extend oil- and gas-drilling permits without surrendering the primary lease rights. While the measure died in committee, Cutting and the Department of the Interior reached an agreement that extended permits to May 1, 1935. Some operators in New Mexico now wondered whether the extension to May 1 applied to drilling operations that had failed to discover either oil or gas. That concern drove some to abandon proposed drilling operations and probably prevented others from initiating new ones. The cash outlay for drilling a well could run from twenty-five to one hundred thousand dollars and on occasion to still greater amounts.

The lessee secured a permit for the privilege of bidding on a segment of the public domain. If he won, he would provide to the federal government a percentage, in most cases 12.5 percent, on his production. An act, approved in March 1931, authorized the secretary of the interior to approve plans for the development of federal oil and gas lands and for drilling operations on them. He also had to draw up plans for the conservation of the oil and gas resources of any field or pool.

On March 26, 1935, Cutting introduced a measure (S2398) authorizing extensions on oil and gas prospecting permits for not less than two nor more than three years. In that prescribed period, operators could drill both for discovery and production. A production operation, however, would have to meet the prevailing rules and regulations of the secretary of the interior. In April, Cutting introduced a clarifying measure (S2629) that would extend the time for compliance with the drilling codes attached to the oil- and gas-prospecting permits. Although his bill was only one of several to deal with the prospecting matter, it quickly gained the support of the New Mexico Oil and Gas Association. All measures were submitted to the Committee on Public Lands and Surveys, which at the end of April, had neither considered them nor scheduled hearings on them.[30]

In early April, Chavez and Cutting allies anxiously awaited the report of the Committee on Privileges and Elections. Chavez's lawyers had secured a respite until April 10 to file additional information with the committee. The interested parties expected the committee to present its findings on April 10 or shortly thereafter. Throughout these trying days, Cutting refused to submit propaganda in his behalf to the committee, unlike Chavez's lawyers who flooded it with pro-Chavez editorials and handbills. As Cutting awaited his fate, he was powerless to readjust the Republican party in New Mexico, to heal the bitter wounds of the campaign, and to enforce the progressive control of the party. Already his task was made more difficult by the severe financial difficulties of former governor Richard Dillon, a leading ally. His business ventures were on the verge of bankruptcy. Cutting recognized that Dillon would not be able to play a major role in reviving the Republican party.[31]

On April 10, the Committee on Privileges and Elections conducted open hearings from ten to twelve in the morning and from two to four in the afternoon. Counsel for both sides presented their arguments. Again calling for dismissal of the Chavez petition, Cutting's counsel argued that Chavez's evidence neither sustained the charges nor reflected guilt on Cutting in the slightest degree. On the following day, the committee overruled the motion to dismiss by a vote of 8 to 6. In another vote, the committee eliminated the charge of undue expenditures by Cutting. Only the charge of election fraud would come under consideration. Chavez was given additional time to amend his petition in light of the committee decision. Although the motion to dismiss lost by a partisan vote, Cutting was certain that he would ultimately win the case. Still paying the price for opposing the president, Cutting complained, "Farley was entirely too busy in that committee room." Although he concluded, "The game is not worth the candle," he also understood, "One can't quit in a fight."[32]

He sent a check to Maurice Miera and Ben Martinez for their ongoing investigation into Democratic voter fraud. If time allowed, he hoped "to run back to Santa Fe, if only for a couple of days." He wanted to meet with Republican leaders about raising money to strengthen the party and to continue investigations into Democratic election fraud. Meanwhile in New Mexico, political circles were buzzing with a rumor that, if true, would have ended the election contest. Miguel Antonio Otero reported that Roosevelt would soon appoint a new federal judge and that the leading candidate to fill the position was Carl Hatch, the other senator from New Mexico. His appointment would leave the way open for Governor Clyde Tingley to replace him with Chavez.[33] Although nothing would come of this rumor, its scenario offered a viable political solution if the Committee on Privileges and Elections ultimately ruled in Cutting's favor. Farley, who "had the committee hog-tied before the hearings started" according to Cutting, might recommend such a solution to the president.

In the meantime, Cutting had to check the list of twenty-eight hundred fraudulent votes that Chavez's lawyers now claimed. His investigators would have to check each name and then, Cutting said, "We shall submit a counter-list of fraudulent votes in Democratic counties." He expected that six weeks of preparation would be necessary for the next hearing.[34]

The additional examinations of voting rolls took Cutting away from his legislative concerns, particularly the hearings on banking legislation. At best, he forwarded constituent complaints to appropriate agencies. He sought adequate farm loans in the Middle Rio Grande Conservancy District, support for a soil erosion control program in eastern New Mexico and clarification on whether the grazing law precluded qualified applicants from making entries on available public lands.[35]

He removed himself from active legislative involvement, deciding to return to Santa Fe. He and Jefferson D. Atwood, his friend and legal counsel, wanted to "look on from the sidelines at a most interesting spectacle of complete breakdown of the so called Party System of Government." The two men saw only bosses, not leaders, dominating the Democratic party. Traditional factionalism was replacing the emerging pattern of responsible political leadership. They thought that they should be on hand to observe the examination of voting lists. Cutting, however, did not intend a long stay that would cause a "piling up a vast quantity of work" in Washington. Expecting Congress to be in session most of the summer, Cutting anticipated that there would be "no European interlude for me or New Mexico interlude either."[36]

On the evening of April 24, Cutting's mother saw him off at the airport and went home deeply depressed. She later noted, "I never saw him again save in his coffin."[37]

CHAPTER 25

OUT OF GAS

When he reached Santa Fe after a pleasant flight, except for the last portion through dust storms that delayed his arrival, Cutting found everyone "actively at work." His agents were accumulating evidence of Democratic vote tampering to counter Chavez's claims of Republican vote manipulation. On Monday, April 29, he told his mother that he intended to stay in New Mexico until the end of the week, "regardless of what happens in Washington" on the bonus bill. [1]

With Hiram Johnson and others, Cutting had designed a strategy to delay senate consideration of the measure. The plan succeeded to the extent that the Senate began its debate on the bonus bill, or soldiers' adjusted compensation measure, on Thursday, May 2. If he were present when the Senate convened after a weekend recess on Monday, Cutting could participate in the debate and be on hand for the final roll-call vote. By catching a late night flight on Sunday, May 5, he could be at his desk when the Senate met at noon the following day. [2]

Cutting's lawyers had until May 10 to file their briefs with the Senate Committee on Privileges and Elections. Jefferson D. Atwood, Cutting's chief counsel in New Mexico initially intended to fly to Washington with Cutting, but after reflection at the last minute, he decided to take a later flight and to utilize his time in better collating the data he and Huston Thompson would present to the committee. [3]

Sundays in Santa Fe were usually a pleasant time for Cutting. He attended the Church of the Holy Faith, where for many years he served as a vestryman, walking a distance of a bit more than a mile each way. He lunched at home with one or two friends and in the afternoon most likely read material pertaining to the bonus bill and to the disputed election contest. He also found time to play classical music on the old Steinway grand piano. In the evening, he dined with a larger group of friends and then motored to Albuquerque where he would board the plane for the return trip to Washington. [4]

Miguel Antonio Otero, who was not present and who had become embittered toward Cutting and his family, claimed that the dinner party was in effect a drunken brawl. One of the guests, H. H. Dorman, told Otero the next day, "We had a big dinner party last night at Bronson's home, and everyone present was drunk, and that when they started for Albuquerque in automobiles they were all so drunk they hardly knew where they were going and that he, Dorman, had carried Bronson to his seat in the aeroplane, and they all took a parting drink." Otero recalled this conversation in July 1937. While its veracity might be doubted, there is no doubt that Cutting and his friends drank and that Cutting might have been slightly inebriated.[5]

Transcontinental and Western Air flight number six bound for New York landed ten minutes ahead of schedule in Albuquerque giving it a twenty-five minute layover. Cutting was the only passenger to board the DC-2, joining the ten others who had boarded in Los Angeles. He was to meet Clifford McCarthy in Kansas City and together they would fly back to Washington, changing planes in Pittsburgh.

The flight took off on schedule at 9:15 P.M. but was unable to land in Kansas City because the cloud ceiling was closing in rapidly. After circling the field for an opening in the clouds, the pilot, Harvey F. Bolton, was instructed to fly toward Burlington, Iowa, the next scheduled stop, and to land at the first available field. This was located at Kirksville, Missouri, which reported better weather conditions and which also provided an opportunity to replenish the plane's dwindling fuel supply.

Weather conditions in the vicinity of Kirksville proved to be unfavorable. With the fuel gauge indicating enough fuel for nearly thirty minutes flying, not enough to reach Burlington, Bolton decided to fly under the overcast and seek out the Kirksville runway. His wheels drawn up, Bolton flew no higher than rooftop or treetop level, following a concrete highway through a rolling terrain in search of the beacon lights of the Kirksville airport. A thin mist and patches of fog obscured visibility. Bolton followed the highway into a fog shrouded draw, "one of the very few abrupt depressions marring the contour of the rolling countryside." Once in the draw, he lost visual contact and took a turn to the left. Realizing that he was below normal ground level, he skillfully picked his way between a farmhouse and a barn, but before Bolton could lift the plane again, the left wing scraped the ground and shot over the road, whereupon the aircraft ripped into an embankment and turned over. The time was approximately 3:30 in the morning. Kirksville lay sixteen miles north of the point of impact. Cutting and two others, including the copilot, were killed outright. One passenger, her back broken, died the next day. Three others suffered serious injuries. The remaining five passengers escaped with only minor leg and rib fractures. Bolton, the pilot, was thrown clear of the wreckage. When rescuers found him he explained at least three times that he had run out of gas. He died after he was carried on a door into a waiting car.[6]

All fatalities were seated in the extreme front of the craft. From the way the plane hit the ground, passengers in the right front must have been killed instantly, as was the copilot. Cutting was assigned seats 9 and 11 in the rear of the plane where no one was seriously injured. Where Cutting was sitting at the time of the accident was unclear. His younger sister, who compiled a memorandum on the accident explained, "It is practically impossible to account for the injuries sustained unless he had been sitting right behind the pilots."

Why did Cutting change his seat? In the single seat at the back sat a woman with a baby whose crying kept him awake. Thus it seems probable that Cutting moved to a vacant seat in the front of the plane in order to sleep. When the pilot light, a sign to fasten seat belts, came on shortly before the crash, Cutting did not comply, indicating that like most passengers he was probably asleep. His injuries were confirmed by a doctor at the Samaritan Hospital at Macon, Missouri, where the injured and dead were taken. Limited to his head, they indicated that death was instantaneous.[7]

Joe Breeson, one of the first persons to reach the scene, saw eight people lying on the ground. With the assistance of a couple of farmers, he pulled away the debris and entered the cabin. In the plane, there were three people one of whom was Cutting. He was dead on the floor up near the front of the cabin. His head was crushed; his body was wedged in between two seats. Only after considerable prying did rescuers finally release his body. One of the survivors believed "that Senator Cutting died without awakening or knowing what had happened," reenforcing the conclusions of the doctor who viewed his body at Samaritan Hospital.[8]

As soon as Clifford McCarthy, awaiting Cutting at Kansas City airfield, got news of the accident, he chartered a plane that landed within a few feet of the wrecked Transcontinental and Western Air flight. McCarthy talked with some of the survivors and others to find out exactly what happened. By that time, the dead and injured had been removed to the hospital at Macon, where he positively identified Cutting's body. In consultation with Mrs. Cutting in New York and Senator La Follette in Washington, McCarthy arranged to bring the senator's body to New York, arriving on the evening of May 8.[9]

News of the air crash quickly spread throughout the Capitol. When the Senate met at noon, Senator Carl Hatch, Cutting's colleague from New Mexico, made a few appropriate remarks and offered a resolution for the vice president to appoint a committee of ten senators who would superintend "the funeral of the deceased Senator." Vice-President Garner selected progressive senators and friends of Cutting. Out of respect to his memory, the Senate then adjourned until the following day. The sudden tragedy and the unexpected death plunged Washington into mourning.[10]

Hearing the news while in Cutting's office, Senator La Follette was too overcome with emotion to appear on the senate floor. With tears in his eyes, Senator Norris bitterly said to Edward Keating, "His blood is on the head of the politicians who traduced him and forced this contest on him." Norris said that the president was indirectly responsible and that he could have ended the contest with a single word. Hiram Johnson echoed his senate colleague. Harold Ickes was in the oval office when Stephen Early, assistant press secretary, brought word of Cutting's death. Speaking regretfully of the occurrence, Roosevelt admitted that he had opposed Cutting for reelection, primarily because of "the crowd that he traveled with in New Mexico." Under prodding from Ickes, Roosevelt agreed that "no one can come out of New Mexico into political life who doesn't have a bad crowd somewhere in the background, and his [Cutting's] crowd was not a bit worse than the Democratic crowd in that state."

At luncheon with the president several days later on May 9, the day before Cutting's funeral, Ickes thought that Roosevelt "felt a little conscience-stricken about the whole thing." He was distressed that Norris and others were "very bitter about Cutting's death" and were inclined to blame him. According to Ickes, Roosevelt had told Cutting that he would offer Chavez a prominent post and have him drop the charges, but Cutting "didn't want him to do that because it would have the appearance of being what in fact it would be, and [because] Cutting felt that there was no basis for the contest."[11]

Accompanied by Clifford McCarthy and his sister, the bronze, flag-draped casket was met in Grand Central Station by Mrs. Cutting, white-haired and dressed in mourning. A police honor detail escorted the casket to Mrs. Cutting's residence on East Seventy-second Street, while Clifford McCarthy and his sister rode with the weeping Mrs. Cutting. Funeral services were scheduled for the afternoon of May 10 at St. James Protestant Episcopal Church on Madison Avenue and Seventy-first Street. The senate chaplain, the Reverend Dr. Ze Barney T. Phillips, would assist the Reverend W. H. B. Donegan at the service.[12]

As "The Son of God Goes Forth To War" resounded from the roof above Cutting's casket, seldom had a church seen such a congregation. Seated in the pews were the congressional delegation and a large group from New Mexico including Hispanic friends, associates and members, past and present, of the arts community. J. P. Morgan chatted with the president's mother in the vestibule of the church. William Collins of the American Federation of Labor,

Walter Lippmann, Nicholas Murray Butler, Colonel Edwin House, British ambassador Sir Roland Lindsay, Norman Thomas, Alice Roosevelt Longworth, Mrs. August Belmont and many others represented the eastern establishment. Relatives, New Mexico residents and embittered liberals—at least two thousand mourners—attended the service at St. James. Among the group accompanying Mrs. Cutting and family members to the family vault at Greenwood Cemetery were Senators La Follette and Wagner and Mayor Fiorello H. Laguardia.[13]

Expressions of tribute, sorrow and sympathy from veterans organizations, members of Congress, Hispanic students aided by Cutting, artists and politicians in New Mexico, prominent citizens and working people poured in on his mother or appeared in the press. In Santa Fe, men, women and children from all walks of life gathered to pay tribute to their champion at a memorial service started simultaneously with the funeral in New York. The service, both in Santa Fe and New York, was a simple one requested by Cutting's mother and enhanced by the beautiful ritual of the Episcopal Church. No eulogy was delivered. Throughout New Mexico literally every community, from the few cities to the most remote hamlets, conducted a memorial service honoring a departed resident, neighbor and friend. In Albuquerque, city, county and federal offices suspended business, and banks and stores closed during the service at the University of New Mexico gymnasium. Over two thousand people heard federal judge Sam Bratton, a former Senate colleague, President James Zimmerman and several clergymen, including the Episcopal Bishop of New Mexico. Similar outpourings of grief prevailed in other communities. In addition, New Mexico women arranged for a floral blanket of red and yellow roses, bearing the state flag, to be placed on the grave in the Greenwood Cemetery.[14]

Cutting's tragic death aroused a storm of anger. His admirers lamented the needless death of one of the nation's most liberal and useful senators. Some progressive Republicans were grooming him for national leadership, and older men, like Borah, Norris, and Hiram Johnson, thought of Cutting "like a son" and expressed their personal attachment in unconcealed grief. All were outraged that the administration countenanced Chavez's challenge to Cutting's election victory. The general outrage soon intensified and spread when the public learned that Governor Clyde Tingley would appoint Chavez to Cutting's senate seat, a decision he consummated after the funeral.[15]

More disconcerting to Cutting's friends and family than the appointment of his successor was that charges leveled against him still had not been fully resolved by the Senate Committee on Privileges and Elections. The day

CHAPTER 25

following Cutting's death, Jefferson D. Atwood wrote, "Every friend of Bronson's who has discussed the matter with me has insisted that we clear his good name." He had ample data ready to file with the committee, and he was prepared to seek further affidavits pertaining to fraudulent practices in predominantly Democratic counties. Like many others, Atwood felt keenly "the horrible injustice of this whole thing" and resented bitterly "the fact that this series of attacks upon Bronson's good name which were inspired by hatred and conceived in fraud have actually brought him to an untimely end so that he was not even permitted to taste the fruits of victory which would have been his in the end."[16]

On May 21, the House of Representatives paid tribute to recently deceased members of Congress. Representative John J. Dempsey briefly eulogized Cutting. On the previous day across the Capitol in the senate chamber, Dennis Chavez was sworn in to fill Cutting's seat. In protest, Senators Johnson, Norris, Gerald Nye, La Follette and Henrick Shipstead strode silently out of the senate chamber in different directions, as the oath of office was administered to Chavez. William E. Borah absented himself from the swearing in ceremony. Their act of defiance, which broke up the clubby atmosphere of the Senate, was an expression of frustration by senators who resented the administration, the president, and particularly James A. Farley. All returned to the chamber after the ceremony concluded.[17]

By accepting the appointment without continuing the contest, Chavez could not hold Cutting's seat for the full term ending in 1940. His appointment was interim, and he would now have to seek election in 1936 for the remainder of Cutting's term. Rationalizing his position, Chavez stated, "Any effort on my part to press the contest further would place me in the attitude of attacking the title of a departed friend." Cutting's friends argued that Chavez's action indicated that he had no case.[18]

The friends of Bronson Cutting were determined to clear his name when the Committee on Privileges and Elections met two weeks later on June 4. They did not want to allow Chavez the claim that he was too magnanimous to press his contest and thus to win the seat for the full term. The committee had already cleared Cutting of the charge of unlawful expenditures. Yet to be addressed was the remaining charge of engaging in fraudulent voting practices. With Chavez safely seated in Cutting's senate seat, his lawyers expressed by telegram his desire to dismiss the election contest. Walter George, the committee chairman, learned about the motion after Cutting's chief counsel, Huston Thompson, had submitted a formal denial of Chavez's allegations. Hiram Johnson, a member of the committee, urged that "something affirmative be done to show that there has been nothing in the records presented here which reflects on the name of Bronson M. Cutting." With Cutting's mother and Senator La Follette in the audience, the committee then adjourned into executive session to consider the form of the dismissal order.[19]

The next day on the senate floor, the Chavez-Cutting battle was finally resolved. The legislative clerk read a report in which the committee unanimously agreed to a formal dismissal of the contest. The committee concluded, "No evidence has been adduced, and there is nothing in the record which, in any way, reflects, either directly or indirectly, upon the honor or integrity of the late Senator Bronson M. Cutting." The report was agreed to by the full Senate, and the disputed election contest officially came to an end.[20]

A fortnight later in Cambridge, Cutting's class at Harvard, the class of 1910, celebrated its twenty-fifth reunion during the two hundred and ninety-ninth commencement exercises of the university. The class boasted a long roster of prominent men. Besides Cutting, John Reed, buried in the Kremlin Wall, was the most prominent deceased member of the class. Among the living, Walter Lippmann and Heywood Broun were prominent journalists, Stuart Chase was an economist, John Cudahay, a diplomat, Hamilton Fish, Jr., a Congressman. In addition there were college presidents, publishers, poets (Alan Seeger and T. S. Eliot among them), artists, public officials, and many others. Cutting's absence was noted by the class. Prior to his death, he had agreed to serve as a class marshal to assist George Peabody Gardner, Jr., the chief marshal.[21]

In New Mexico and Congress, Cutting's friends vented their feelings of bitterness over his shocking end. They considered Cutting fairly and honestly elected. They were prepared to show that Chavez's charges were as false as his newly proclaimed friendship for Cutting. Referring to the charge of fraud in San Miguel County, they argued, "If he were engaged in a conspiracy to obtain his election by fraud, he certainly did a poor job for himself." Cutting had received the smallest vote in the county on the Republican ticket. Although the Senate cleared Cutting's good name, his New Mexico friends were still angry. Chavez and the Democratic party, with New Deal aid and administration support, won the election contest and henceforth would dominate politics in New Mexico, with only limited exceptions in the 1950s, until well into the 1960s.[22]

Cutting's will, executed in December 1934, was probated in New York and Santa Fe in June 1935 after the conclusion of the disputed election contest. Its contents, once known, created a sensation in New Mexico and received brief national attention. Cutting's will bequeathed more than one million dollars to friends, his office staff, humble individuals in New Mexico, and one institution, the Spanish American Normal School in El Rito, Rio Arriba County. The school received a grant of $150,000, one of Cutting's more far reaching efforts to help the people of his adopted state. Rio Arriba was one of the largest and most isolated northern counties. Its area was almost 6,000 square miles, and its population was approximately 20,000, 95 percent of whom were Hispanic. The county received little assistance from the state to establish schools or to construct roads. It had no hospital and had at best several doctors. Limping along on a meager state appropriation, the school survived only by many of the students paying their tuition with farm produce. Cutting's gift helped to stabilize the financial foundation of the normal school, which provided one of the few opportunities available to the neglected school children in northern New Mexico.[23]

The bequests in Cutting's will filled at least eight legal-sized pages. First listed were over three pages of $1,000 bequests, 91 altogether. All but one were made to New Mexicans, most of whom had Spanish surnames. Next came about two pages of $2,500 bequests. Here too, all fifty individuals were residents or former residents of New Mexico. Most had Spanish surnames. There were eighteen $5,000 bequests, all of which went to citizens of New Mexico, again chiefly with Hispanic surnames. The more generous sums were bequeathed to Cutting's close friends and associates. While many resided in New Mexico, there were fewer Hispanics among them. Each of his associates on the newspaper and on his senate staff received $25,000; his key campaign aides and associates each received $10,000. In all there were ten such bequests. Other friends received either $25,000 or $50,000. Attracting national attention were gifts of $25,000 to Philip La Follette and $50,000 to Robert M. La Follette. Bequests of $100,000 went to Herman Baca, his long time friend and American Legion associate and to Brian Boru Dunne, the manager of Cutting's personal affairs in Santa Fe, a reporter on the *New Mexican* and for a time a resident at Los Siete Burros. Jesus Baca, probably his closest and most intimate friend, received the largest bequest, $150,000 plus title to the newspaper and, though not stated in the will, to Los Siete Burros. Cutting's sisters and his niece, Iris Origo, were each to receive one-third of the residuary estate. Cutting's mother and Jesus Baca were named as executors of the estate, which had a net worth of $3,299,725.[24]

Many individuals whose names appeared in the will were indebted to the estate. Creditors of indebted individuals sought to have their bequests assigned for the amount owed them. These sums were duly deducted from the bequests. Several years later, when the estate was finally settled, Cutting's family out of the residuary estate had all of these bequests fully funded.

A few women received bequests. Callie Hull, whose name was romantically linked with Cutting's during his early days in Santa Fe, received $10,000, as did a Mrs. Mayme Benjamin. Mrs. Ed Tafoya, the widow of a political associate, received $5,000; Mrs. E. A. Perrault, a former secretary of state and a strong supporter, received $2,500. Clara True, a teacher in Española was bequeathed $2,500. The names of Clara Olsen and Jouett Fall Elliott were not included. Cutting's family later awarded Elliott a bequest of $50,000, suggesting that Cutting wished to bestow such a gift but did not to avoid unfavorable publicity. Conspicuously absent were the names of Miguel Antonio Otero, both father and son. Over the years, Otero, Sr. had been a continual recipient of Cutting's financial assistance, which often helped him meet his monthly bills and bailed him out of numerous financial difficulties. No doubt Cutting thought he had been more than generous to Otero, Jr. Cutting had paid the law-school tuition of Otero, Jr., who until the mid 1920s was one of his closest friends and associates. They had gradually drifted apart. As a state attorney general and state judge, Otero had rendered decisions that alienated Cutting. However, he remained on cordial terms with both Oteros.[25]

Clifford McCarthy, who in later years occupied a role similar to that of Miguel Antonio Otero, Jr., was bequeathed $50,000. Phelps Putnam and Frederick Manning, who became acquainted with Cutting at the time he met McCarthy, received $25,000 and $10,000 respectively. In addition, Swarthmore College where Manning taught history was the beneficiary of Cutting's record collection, while part of his sheet music library went to his niece Iris Origo and his sister, Justine. The most interesting question about Cutting's will must remain unanswered. How did he assemble it in December 1934 when he was seeking a certificate of election prior to the convening of Congress early in January?

Cutting's wealth was largely inherited and chiefly in the form of stocks and bonds. His net estate was valued at $3,299,725 exclusive of his real estate in New Mexico and Washington, D.C. Specific bequests in the will, amounting to $1,490,676, were distributed among 134 beneficiaries. An appraisal of the estate was made public in August 1937, when a copy of the will was filed in New York City to determine the amount of property held in New York and subject to the state's transfer tax.[26]

Following the appraisal of his will, the name of Bronson Cutting began to recede markedly from public view. Of course, memory of him remained alive in New Mexico and elsewhere for years to come. Among the citizens of New Mexico, few were neutral about Bronson Cutting. Consequently, his memory remains vital among a declining number of people more than a half century after his death. Since his career ended just as he was beginning to attain national stature, he has never received the scholarly attention bestowed upon other congressional progressives like Senators La Follette, Borah, Johnson and Norris. Nevertheless, as this biography has sought to demonstrate, his career is worthy of historical exploration and recognition.

CHAPTER 26

EPILOGUE

Bronson Cutting's significance as a public figure does not reside in his service as a United States senator during a critical period in the nation's history. He could not make his mark as an outstanding statesman in just a few years, although his penetrating insights and careful research on subjects that commanded his attention were beginning to have an impact. Rather his significance lies in New Mexico where he became a friend and champion of the Spanish-speaking population. First through the American Legion and then through his political leadership, he helped bring New Mexico Hispanics into the mainstream of public life.

When Cutting came on the scene in New Mexico in the early days of statehood, the intense factionalism characteristic of the late territorial period was still evident in state politics. Dominating the political life of large areas, bosses or patrones, both Anglo and Hispanic, formed coalitions and sometimes crossed party lines to secure political advantage. The basis of their power was their control of the "pobres," Spanish-speaking people who were dependent for their livelihood on the "ricos" and their political allies, the mine operators and railroad managers. Cutting, functioning as a progressive in politics, helped to break down this relationship and became a patrone himself in the process. As he assisted needy Hispanics, he won their support, loyalty and affection. In several decades, modernization in New Mexico would enable Spanish-speaking citizens become better able to provide their own leadership and find expanded economic opportunities. Increasing numbers of Hispanics would no longer be dependent on patrones of any kind. Under their own leaders, they would function on a more equitable and competitive basis throughout the state.

In his early twenties, Cutting came to New Mexico as a "lunger," literally expecting to die. His precarious health had not seriously impeded his academic performance at Groton and Harvard, nor did it make a complete invalid of him in New Mexico. His family believed that wealth entailed social responsibility. In New York City, for example, his father had played a role in fusion politics and had been active in promoting model, low-cost housing as a profitable private enterprise within the metropolitan area. More concerned with the cause of honest, efficient government, than with economic reform, Cutting's father had supported the efforts of both the Protestant Episcopal

Church and Columbia University to improve the quality of life in New York City. Theodore Roosevelt, a close family friend, had won the Cuttings's overwhelming support for his progressive programs as president and in the years thereafter.

In New Mexico, Cutting followed in his father's footsteps. He quickly aroused the ire of the established political hierarchy, remnants of the old Santa Fe Ring that had dominated politics in the late nineteenth century. The Santa Fe cultural elite—the stewards of archaeology and anthropology—were also irritated by his intervention in and criticism of their approach. (The arts colony in Santa Fe and Taos did not develop until several years later, following the arrival of Mabel Dodge in 1916 and Mary Austin in 1918.) However, his ownership of the *New Mexican* gave him a mouthpiece for advancing the progressive cause in the state. He championed the candidacy of Theodore Roosevelt in 1912 and in 1916. Progressive-minded citizens were appalled at the crass materialism and crude machinations in New Mexico politics and rallied to Cutting's campaigns. Like his father and his uncle, Robert Fulton Cutting, he was fighting the graft and corruption of boss and machine politics.

Cutting was a sophisticated, well-educated and well-traveled New Yorker who spoke several foreign languages. Like many other Anglos, he fell in love with New Mexico. He learned Spanish and quickly immersed himself in its society. His political battles with controversial individuals demonstrated to them and others that he was no "soft touch." While regaining his health, he published his newspaper, entered into the social life of Santa Fe, and participated in its public life as a vestryman, a bank-board member, and as a defendant of the freedom of the press. In his early years, Cutting became at best a prominent but essentially local figure in the state.

After World War I, the American Legion launched Cutting's public career. The national veterans organization, provided an entryway for Hispanic veterans into the political mainstream of New Mexico. They were able to control their own affairs independent of patrones or party bosses. In the state's fragmented party politics, the support of veterans could determine the outcome of an election. Legion support helped re-elect Andrieus A. Jones to a second term as a United States senator. A grateful Democratic party sought Cutting's advice and support and then awarded him a seat on the Penitentiary Board.

Cutting's initial objective was to open the political system to qualified Hispanic candidates. Government efficiency and honesty that would meliorate conditions was the essence of his reform impulse. When he sought prison reform, however, he ran into intense opposition and broke with the Democratic administration. In Washington, following his appointment by a Republican governor to the senate seat of Andrieus A. Jones, Cutting began to broaden his horizons. The Great Depression, his association with senate progressives and his investigative trip to the Soviet Union stimulated in him a wider range of reform. His initial concern was still good government: the prevention of censorship by ignorant customs inspectors; the just treatment of the veteran, particularly the disabled veteran; and the grant of independence to Philippine people.

As he watched the Hoover administration's management of the depression crisis, he became disillusioned with the president's lack of a meaningful program. Indeed, along with his fellow progressives in the Senate, he doubted whether Hoover had any program at all. Addressing the issue of good government would not resolve the economic crisis. Instead Cutting focused on the expansion of consumer purchasing power. Putting funds into the hands of potential buyers would increase consumer demand and would stimulate production. Cutting criticized Hoover for not launching a massive public-works program, for restricting Reconstruction Finance Corporation loans to large corporate enterprises, and for encouraging production at the expense of consumption. He leveled the same criticism at the New Deal programs of President Franklin D. Roosevelt. Roosevelt, Cutting thought, was only tinkering with the crisis and was interested primarily in recovery—meeting the needs of millions of increasingly desperate people—before attacking other problems.

Although Cutting voted for most New Deal legislation, he was appalled at the Economy Act. Enacted during the first hundred days of the New Deal, that cost-cutting legislation bore most heavily on veterans, particularly disabled veterans, most of whom were already in precarious circumstances. As Cutting dramatized the plight of the disabled veteran on the senate floor, he portrayed the Roosevelt administration, and by implication the president himself, as insensitive to the needs of citizens disabled by their wartime service. Sensitive to his public image, Roosevelt never forgave the New Mexico senator.

Cutting endorsed New Deal agricultural programs that expanded the purchasing power of farmers. He was pleased that the Civil Works Administration rapidly put four million people to work but was equally distressed that the government dismantled the program shortly after it started to function effectively. Although he sought to amend some provisions of the enabling legislation for what became the Works Progress Administration, he did not live to see its operations. In addition, Cutting wished to modify the banking structure to insure access to credit for all citizens. He called for the government operation of a portion of the banking system in order to establish social credit, but he knew that Congress would reject his radical proposal. He died just before the Senate took up banking reform.

The venomous partisanship in New Mexico, abetted by the Roosevelt administration, made his last months exceedingly frustrating. Dennis Chavez's challenge to his reelection in 1934 meant that he had to devote more time to preparing his defense and less to legislative business. He could not participate fully in the legislative process that would lead to the relief of a long-suffering people. He and his associates considered the Chavez petition without merit and sustained only by administration pressure. After his death, the Senate Committee on Privileges and Elections and the full Senate concurred.

In New Mexico, prior to the Great Depression, Cutting had literally been a one-man welfare agency, loaning funds to indigent veterans, impoverished Hispanics and others. The state lacked a social-welfare apparatus that could adequately meet the needs of its citizens. Cutting directly aided people in distress, advanced state education and funded the education of younger Hispanics. He encouraged the Rockefeller Foundation to establish a research museum in Santa Fe, and he supported the cultural and educational projects of Mary Austin and other members of the Taos and Santa Fe arts community. His goals in most instances were to spread purchasing power or to provide the state's youth an education, and to expose the nation to New Mexico's rich but vaguely known cultural heritage.

Through the American Legion, Cutting broadened his acquaintances and friendships and established a base for his political career. Hispanic veterans were among his closest friends. His largest bequests went to Jesus Baca and the Spanish-American School at El Rito. Cutting had the ability to maintain close friendships on diverse levels: family and school friends; Anglos associated with the arts community; associates on the *New Mexican;* and others whom he met following his arrival in Santa Fe in 1910. A good listener, he respected the views of others, and as a tubercular patient, he empathized with people suffering from conditions over which they had little to no control. He sent two of his young friends, Tony Luna and Miguel A. Otero, Jr., through law school. Later he sent Clifford McCarthy to Europe to broaden his horizons. He was a delightful companion to those who understood that his inherent modesty did not preclude a sense of humor and a love of life.

Although he was a bachelor and most of his friends and associates were men, Cutting had warm friendships with women. His sister Justine, the belles and senoritas in Santa Fe and more mature women as he grew older were among his female acquaintances. Concerned about his health in his twenties, Cutting eschewed the possibility of marriage. Some of his friendships in Santa Fe were with homosexuals, leading to rumors that Cutting was also gay. The rumors may have been true, but his true passions were playing the piano, listening to records and collecting scores of operas and sheet music. Justine became a worldwide authority on Gregorian chants, and his three closest Anglo friends were music aficionados. Cutting was not a garrulous individual. When he spoke in conversation or in a public forum, however, his remarks were effective, direct and usually devoid of mud-slinging, a difficult feat in the faction-ridden politics of New Mexico.

As in New Mexico, so in the United States Senate, Cutting immediately impressed thoughtful senate colleagues and quickly emerged as an influential member of a small progressive bloc. Robert M. La Follette, Jr. and Cutting were the youngest members of the body. Both had long histories of illness, and they were close in their political outlook. Another progressive senator, Hiram Johnson considered Cutting as another son, and Cutting returned the affection. Like La Follette, Cutting admired and respected George W. Norris, the venerable fighter for progressive causes.

In the Senate, Cutting had a chance to display his profound intellect, which was known only to a few friends. Assimilating and organizing his wide knowledge, he was able to bring it to bear upon problems and issues both great and small. Ezra Pound once remarked that Cutting had the keenest mind in the United States Senate. Other observers echoed this view.[1]

In New Mexico, his civic usefulness was a model to members of the younger generation and to his peers. He transmitted an ideal type in political life and a vision of the future. To many, Cutting had attempted the impossible in New Mexico. "Nobody," one of his admirers remarked, "had ever attempted a remedy for almost dynastic, unquestioning bossism, accepted by a whole state very much as the people accepted any other form of pestilence." Cutting, in short, was a leader to numerous idealistic individuals possessed of a more thoughtful and unselfish vision of politics. While many citizens could question Cutting's methods and expedients at times, they also recognized that he had to create his own precedents with the resources, human and material, available to him. Conservative by temperament and family background, Cutting adapted his heritage to a new environment, and by broadening his convictions, he played a role that commanded wide public respect.[2]

So unexpected an individual as Walter White, the executive secretary of the National Association for the Advancement of Colored People, testified as to

Cutting's qualities: "genuine, honest, and sincere." Cutting was a person with whom White, when discouraged, enjoyed talking. He was a friend who wanted to serve the cause of racial equality and particularly to secure anti-lynching legislation. Before leaving Santa Fe following the 1934 campaign, he had written White, "I hope my activities in the future will justify the confidence you have placed in me."[3]

Cutting's longtime friend and associate in the American Legion, Herman Baca, concluded a tribute before a veterans organization with a quotation that expressed to him the sentiment "all of us in Bronson Cutting's chosen state feel." Baca said, "'He knew neither east nor west, nor birth nor breed, nor race nor creed, nor rank nor wealth, nor any other outside mark upon the son of man.'"[4]

Mrs. Cutting kept her son's memory alive by sponsoring a series of meetings in Washington. Prominent citizens gathered to pay tribute and endorse progressive causes in which Senator Cutting had been interested. Fifteen members of the House and the Senate attended the first gathering at the Brookings Institution on May 6, 1936, a year after his death. The session featured the reading of tributes submitted by William Allan White, Mayor Fiorello H. LaGuardia of New York City, George W. Norris and others. Edwin M. Borchard of the Yale Law School led the informal discussion of the forces then frustrating representative government. Gordon Gardiner, who came over from England, delivered an address relating his thirty-year friendship with Cutting.[5]

The following year, the Bronson Cutting Memorial Lectures got underway with a generous gift from Mrs. Cutting. Richard Hogue, who had worked on legislative matters with Cutting during his last days in Congress, chaired the executive committee. On March 8, at the Rialto Theater, the series was launched before a distinguished audience that included members of the cabinet, the Supreme Court and Congress. An overflow crowd necessitated finding additional space for people to hear the prominent progressives who paid tribute to Cutting. Senator Norris made brief remarks to open the series. He was followed by Charles A. Beard and Fiorello LaGuardia both of whom lectured on the necessity of democracies to adjust to changing conditions. Later in the month at Constitution Hall before another large and enthusiastic audience, Harold J. Laski delivered two stimulating lectures on a similar theme.[6]

In 1938, the Memorial Lectures were again held at Constitution Hall. The three speakers, Bruce Bliven, Edwin M. Borchard and C. A. Dykstra, discussed how democracy related to their area of interest, respectively, public opinion, foreign policy, and education. In 1939, Adolf A. Berle delivered "Democracy and the Lima Conference." Gunnar Myrdal spoke on "Maintaining Democracy in Sweden Under the Shadow of Totalitarian States." These lectures were the last of the Cutting series. After the Daughters of the American Revolution refused the use of Constitution Hall to the distinguished black contralto, Marian Anderson, the executive committee decided not to rent the facility. No lectures were scheduled in 1940. The 1939 lectures were the last to keep the name of Bronson Cutting before a Washington audience.

Although there was no lecture series in New Mexico, Cutting's memory was recalled on various occasions throughout the remainder of the decade. In 1936 his mother and other family members endowed the Bronson Cutting Harvard National Scholarships for the benefit of students from New Mexico. Preference was given to candidates of Spanish-American descent. In 1937, on the forty-eighth anniversary of its founding, the University of New Mexico dedicated the exercises to the memory of Bronson Cutting. President James F. Zimmerman spoke on "Senator Cutting, Friend of the University," and Jefferson D. Atwood, on "Senator Cutting, Man and Statesman." The musical numbers were selections from Cutting's favorite composers. Bach's *B Minor Mass,* a composition loved by Cutting, was presented in its entirety the following evening, March 1, 1937.[7]

The next year in Santa Fe, a group of Cutting's friends and admirers decided to commission a bronze bust of the deceased senator funded by small voluntary contributions. The model had already been prepared by the sculptor, Bruce Wilder Saville. When cast and completed, the bust would be formally presented to the state of New Mexico and appropriately dedicated in appreciation of Cutting's public services, "particularly for his interest in the disabled soldiers of the World War and in the education of the sons and daughters of New Mexico's native citizens."[8]

The movement to raise funds started quietly in the summer of 1938 and quickly gained headway in various parts of the state. On the anniversary of Cutting's death in 1939, the bronze was formally presented in ceremonies on the capitol grounds. Haniel Long, a Harvard classmate and a Santa Fe resident, introduced the speakers. Featured were United States Circuit Court judge Sam G. Bratton, the ranking federal official in the state, and George Sanchez, a professor at the University of New Mexico. Sanchez delivered a crisp and unsentimental tribute in Spanish. He praised Cutting's progressive ideas and his advancement of the hopes of the Hispanic people in New Mexico.

The bust of Cutting, as Haniel Long noted in the formal presentation, was the gift of "hundreds and hundreds of men, women and children in every part of the state." Its cost was covered "entirely by small contributions, and nobody was solicited to give even a penny." The formal program of the ceremonies contained forty-one pages listing the names of contributors, chiefly those of individuals, in alphabetical order with the community following the name of each contributor. Hispanic names predominated. Those of hospitalized veterans also were noticeable. Contributors from the Spanish-American Normal School at El Rito were listed separately as were those of the members of Union Proctevia No. 1 in Santa Fe. Almost every donor was a New Mexico resident, Harold Ickes being a notable exception.[9]

The 1939 ceremonies marked the last major tribute to Cutting's memory. In later years, on the anniversary of his death, wreaths were placed at the base of the bronze memorial on the capitol grounds, and masses were celebrated in his memory. The Spanish-American Normal School at El Rito formally dedicated its Cutting Assembly Hall in 1940, and in the years following his death, the school recalled his generous gift by a moment of silence on May 6. By the war years and thereafter, public remembrance of Cutting faded, although thousands of New Mexicans would carry cherished memories for the rest of their days.[10]

The forty-six years allotted to Bronson Cutting served only as the preamble to his life and influence. Brief as it was, that preamble was inscribed by Cutting with a rare combination of moral courage, modesty and marked ability. That he could not carry his life and influence beyond its promising preface sorely disappointed his friends, who nevertheless could plumb from their recollections an understanding "that human life is something infinitely nobler and larger than sheltered comfort and swiftly passing prestige," and "that intellectual honesty combined with open-mindedness are more vital and important than inherited orthodoxy and complacent conformity." As a progressive, Cutting believed that the dictatorship of wealth and special privilege constituted "a denial of democracy and a stifling blow to human progress." His significance as a public figure rests mostly on his attempts in New Mexico to bring Spanish-speaking citizens into the mainstream of public life and to place them on an equal footing with others. In addition, it should be emphasized that Cutting won the respect, admiration and support of numerous other citizens in New Mexico: veterans; unionized workers; artists; youth; and progressive-minded individuals in all walks of life. Cutting's life was one of largely unfulfilled promise, but one remarkable in what it portended for the good of the society. It was a preamble to a career rich in promise of distinguished achievement, yet worthy of remembrance in its own right.[11]

LIST OF ABBREVIATIONS

ABF   Albert B. Fall Papers. Henry E. Huntington Library. San Marino, California.

AP   Amos Pinchot Papers. Manuscript Division. Library of Congress. Washington, D.C.

AWH   Governor A. W. Hockenhull Papers. State Records Center and Archives. Santa Fe, New Mexico.

BMC   Bronson Murray Cutting Papers. Manuscript Division. Library of Congress. Washington, D.C.

CAT   Campaign and Transition Papers. Herbert Hoover Papers. Herbert Hoover Presidential Library. West Branch, Iowa.

CF   Cassidy Family Papers. Hubert Howe Bancroft Library. University of California. Berkeley.

DC   Dennis Chavez Papers. Center for Southwest Research. Zimmerman Library. University of New Mexico. Albuquerque.

DNC   Democratic National Committee Files. Franklin D. Roosevelt Library. Hyde Park, New York.

EDJ   E. Dana Johnson Papers. History Library. Museum of New Mexico. Santa Fe.

EH   Emil Hurja Papers. Franklin D. Roosevelt Library. Hyde Park, New York.

ELH   Edgar Lee Hewett Collection. History Library. Museum of New Mexico. Santa Fe.

EK   Edward Keating Papers. University of Colorado. Boulder, Colorado.

LIST OF ABBREVIATIONS

EP   Ezra Pound Papers. Rare Book and Manuscript Library. Yale University. New Haven, Connecticut.

FCW   Francis C. Wilson Papers. New Mexico State Records Center and Archives. Santa Fe.

FDR   Franklin D. Roosevelt Papers. Franklin D. Roosevelt Library. Hyde Park, New York.

GB   George Biddle Papers. Manuscript Division. Library of Congress. Washington, D.C.

GWN   George W. Norris Papers. Manuscript Division. Library of Congress. Washington, D.C.

HAW   Henry A. Wallace Papers at the University of Iowa. Microfilm Edition. Glen Rock, N.J.: Microfilming Corporation of America, 1977.

HBF   Harvey B. Fergusson Papers. Center for Southwest Research. Zimmerman Library. University of New Mexico. Albuquerque.

HH   Harry Hopkins Papers. Franklin D. Roosevelt Library. Hyde Park, New York.

HJ   Hiram Johnson Papers. Hubert Howe Bancroft Library. University of California. Berkeley.

HLI   Harold L. Ickes Papers. Manuscript Division. Library of Congress. Washington, D.C.

HMN   Hanford MacNider Papers. Republican Service League File. Herbert Hoover Presidential Library. West Branch, Iowa.

HOB   Holm O. Bursum Papers. Center for Southwest Research. Zimmerman Library. University of New Mexico. Albuquerque.

JAF   James A. Farley Papers. Manuscript Division. Library of Congress. Washington, D.C.

KR	Kermit Roosevelt Papers. Manuscript Division. Library of Congress. Washington, D.C.
LFFC	La Follette Family Collection. Manuscript Division. Library of Congress. Washington, D.C.
LW	Leonard Wood Papers. Manuscript Division. Library of Congress. Washington, D.C.
MA	Mary Austin Papers. Henry E. Huntington Library. San Marino, California.
MA, UNM	Mary Austin Papers. Center for Southwest Research. Zimmerman Library. University of New Mexico.
MAO	Miguel Antonio Otero Papers. Center for Southwest Research. Zimmerman Library. University of New Mexico. Albuquerque.
MID	Military Intelligence Division Correspondence. Record Group 165. National Archives. Washington, D.C.
NPRL	National Progressive Republican League Papers. Manuscript Division. Library of Congress. Washington, D.C.
NWM	Nathan William MacChesnay Papers. Republican National Committee Files. Herbert Hoover Presidential Library. West Branch, Iowa.
PCFB	Professional Correspondence of Franz Boaz. Microfilm Edition. Wilmington, Delaware.
PP	Post-Presidential File. Herbert Hoover Papers. Herbert Hoover Presidential Library. West Branch, Iowa.
PSF	Presidential States File. Herbert Hoover Presidential Library. West Branch, Iowa.
RA	Rockefeller Archives. Pocantico Hills, New York.
RCD	Richard C. Dillon Papers. Center for Southwest Research. Zimmerman Library. University of New Mexico. Albuquerque.

LIST OF ABBREVIATIONS

RMLJ   Robert M. La Follette, Jr. Correspondence. La Follette Family Papers. Manuscript Division. Library of Congress. Washington, D.C.

RNC   Republican National Committee Files. Herbert Hoover Presidential Library. West Branch, Iowa.

RWH   Roy W. Howard Papers. Manuscript Division. Library of Congress. Washington, D.C.

TBC   Thomas B. Catron Papers. Center for Southwest Research. Zimmerman Library. University of New Mexico. Albuquerque.

TR   Theodore Roosevelt Papers. Microfilm Edition. Library of Congress. Washington, D.C.

WEB   William E. Borah Papers. Manuscript Division. Library of Congress. Washington, D.C.

WGM   William Gibbs McAdoo Papers. Manuscript Division. Library of Congress. Washington, D.C.

NOTES

Chapter 1

1. Mark De Wolfe Howe, *Justice Oliver Wendell Holmes, The Shaping Years, 1841–1870* (Cambridge: Harvard University Press, 1957), p. 202.

2. For a brief discussion of Gotham Court, which was demolished in 1896, see Anthony Jackson, *A Place Called Home: A History of Low-Cost Housing in Manhattan* (Cambridge: MIT Press, 1976), pp. 9–10.

3. That the ventures of William Bayard Cutting and R. Fulton Cutting were not unprofitable can be discerned in Robert W. DeForest and Lawrence Veiller, Editors, *The Tenement House Problem,* vol. 1 (New York: Macmillan, 1903), p. 364.

4. William Bayard Cutting, Jr. to Olivia Murray Cutting [hereafter OMC], March 12, March 15, March 17 and March 22, 1890, typed copies in BMC, Box 1.

5. Edward Sanford Martin, *The Life of Joseph Hodges Choate,* vol. 2 (New York: Charles Scribner's Sons, 1920), p. 166.

6. For a suggestion of William Bayard Cutting's hesitation about United States policy in the Philippines, see his Letter to the Editor of the *New York Times,* May 3, 1899.

7. For information about Westbrook and the Cutting family, I have relied heavily on two sources: a splendidly illustrated pamphlet by George Roussos, *Bayard Cutting Arboretum History* (Long Island State Park and Recreation Commission and Arboretum Trustees, 1984), and the sensitive and beautifully written chapter, "Westbrook," in the memoir of Bronson Cutting's niece, Iris Origo, *Images and Shadows* (New York: Harcourt Brace Jovanovich, Inc., 1971).

8. William Bayard Cutting, Sr. to William Bayard Cutting, Jr., October 6, 1899, BMC, Box 1. The school that Bronson attended "for a year or so" before going to Groton was managed by "two delightful ladies, Miss Eliot and Miss Miller." It was on West Forty-second Street, across the street from William Cullen Bryant Park and behind the Public Library "where the boys had recess." See the fragment of a letter to OMC dated March 21, 1939, BMC, Box 92.

Chapter 2

1. My discussion of Groton and its regimen was derived from Frank D. Ashburn, *Peabody at Groton* (New York: Coward McCann, Inc., 1944) and

relevant chapters in G. Edward White, *The Eastern Establishment and the Western Experience* (New Haven: Yale University Press, 1968); James McLachlan, *American Boarding Schools* (New York: Charles Scribner's Sons, 1970); Frank Freidel, *Franklin D. Roosevelt: The Apprenticeship* (Boston: Little, Brown and Company, 1950); and Kenneth S. Davis, *FDR: The Reckoning of Destiny, 1882–1928* (New York: G.P. Putnam's Sons, 1972). For an incisive article by a classmate of Bronson Cutting's, see George W. Martin, "Preface to A School-Master's Biography," *Harper's Magazine,* January 1944, pp. 156–62. See too the Groton Diaries of George Biddle in GB, Box 1. The diaries present a marvelous picture of Groton in the early 20th century. Biddle later became very critical of Peabody and Groton, but his diaries indicate that he found much to enjoy while a student.

2. Diary, 1906 KR, Box 1.

3. Recollections of Groton students about Cutting were derived from George Martin to Jonathan R. Cunningham, December 18, 1937; and Douglas Cochran to Cunningham, December 20, 1937. Both letters are located in BMC, Box 92. See too George Biddle, *An American Artist's Story* (Boston: Little, Brown and Company, 1939), pp. 58–59. Biddle, who was at Harvard in 1906, provided Cutting with an article for the *Grotonian* to appear in "an alumni number." BMC to Biddle, May 10, 1906, GB Box 13.

4. Groton School, Report of B. M. Cutting, VI Form, June 1906, BMC, Box 1.

5. *New York Herald,* June 24, 1906; Jonathan R. Cunningham, "Bronson Cutting: A Political Biography" (Master's thesis, University of New Mexico, 1940), appendix, p. 232.

6. The itinerary of the European vacation was excerpted by Olivia Murray Cutting after her son's death from her diary into a haphazard chronology of Bronson Murray Cutting's life. See BMC, Box 92. Apparently Bronson had a Groton friend along with him on some of his climbs. See Rogers MacVeagh to Bronson Cutting, August 1, 1906, BMC, Box 1. MacVeagh, as well as George W. Martin, whose article is noted in footnote one, was in Cutting's class at Groton.

7. E. H. Wells to W. Bayard Cutting, Jr., July 17, 1906, BMC, Box 1.

8. Samuel Eliot Morison, *Development of Harvard University* (Cambridge: Harvard University Press, 1930), p. xvi. A transcript of Cutting's grades at Harvard is available in BMC, Box 4.

9. BMC to Dear Mamma, October 1, 1906, BMC, Box 1.

10. BMC to Dear Mamma, October 1, 1906; and BMC to Dear Papa, January 10, 1907[?], BMC, Box 1.

11. Gordon Gardiner to BMC, August 6, 1908; and John Thayer Addison to BMC, June 22, 1908, BMC, Box 1.

12. B. S. Hurlbut to William Bayard Cutting, August 26, 1907; and Edwin H. Higley to BMC, BMC, Box 1.

13. For Cutting's Harvard essays, see BMC, Box 82; George Santayana to Iris Origo, March 8, 1939, BMC, Box 92. Prizes were announced in the *Harvard University Gazette,* December 17, 1909. A Deturs consisted of prize books awarded to scholars of the First Group, as were John Harvard Scholarships of which thirty-nine were awarded for the 1909–10 academic year.

14. OMC to William Bayard Cutting, Jr., February 19, 1909; Gordon Gardiner to William Bayard Cutting, Jr., n.d. [two-page fragment]; and Joan Tuckerman to BMC, June 20, 1909, BMC, Box 1.

15. William Bayard Cutting, Jr. to Joseph H. Choate, August 27, 1909, JHC, Box 12. William Bayard Cutting, Jr. relates his study and travel plans.

16. The quoted remarks from William Bayard Cutting, Jr.'s letter to his brother are included in the chapter devoted to him in the memoir by his daughter. See Iris Origo, *Images and Shadows: Part of a Life* (New York: Harcourt Brace Jovanovich, 1971), p. 79.

17. E. H. Wells to OMC, April 26, 1910 and May 3, 1910; W. R. Castle, Jr. to E. H. Wells, May 25, 1910, copy in BMC, Box 1.

Chapter 3

1. The 1910 census indicated a population of 327,301 for New Mexico, of which 19,512 were Indians. Unfortunately the census does not indicate how many Spanish-speaking people there were. The census does indicate a native white population of 281,940, and 21,948 people or parents born in Mexico. In addition, 48,697 people, or 20.2 percent of the population, were deemed illiterate in the 1910 census. Estimates place the Spanish-speaking population at 60 to 70 percent of the total. As late as 1940, they still comprised a majority. At statehood there were twenty-six counties in New Mexico.

2. BMC to Dear Papa, July 3, 1910, BMC, Box 1.

3. BMC to Dear Papa, July 7 and 10, 1910, BMC, Box 1.

4. BMC to Dear Papa, July 7 and July 10, 1910, BMC, Box 1. One of the biggest rows of the season with wide social ramifications occurred at the end of July when Mrs. Prince dismissed Edgar L. Hewett, director of the School of American Research, from her afternoon tea, remarking, "Out of the house, base viper." See BMC to Dear Papa, August 1, 1910, BMC, Box 1.

5. BMC to Dear Mamma, July 13, 1910; and BMC to Dear Papa, July 17, 1910, BMC, Box 1. By the end of July, a Kansas City architect had been contacted about the possibility of constructing a house. See Louis Curtiss to BMC, July 28, 1910, BMC, Box 1.

6. BMC to Dear Papa, July 17 and August 10, 1910; and BMC to Dear Mamma, July 21, 1910 and [n.d.] [1910], BMC, Box 1.

7. Justine Ward [hereafter JCW] to Dearest Mamma, July 20, 1910, BMC, Box 1. Bronson discussed with his father the possibility of contacting Attorney General George W. Wickersham in an effort to secure a place for Justine's husband, George Cabot Ward, then in South America, on the Territorial Supreme Court. L. Bradford Prince first suggested the idea to Justine. See BMC to Dear Papa, August 1, 1910, BMC, Box 1.

8. BMC to Dear Mamma, August 6, 1910; and BMC to Dear Papa, August 10, 1910, BMC, Box 1.

9. JCW to Dearest Mamma, August 21, September 4 and September 15, 1910, BMC, Box 1.

10. JCW to Dearest Mamma, September 19, 1910. The last four pages of this eleven-page holograph letter were written on September 20, BMC, Box 1.

11. BMC to Dear Mamma, September 23, 1910; JCW to Dearest Mamma, n.d. [September 27, 1910?], September 19 and October 2, 1910; JCW to Dear Papa, October 16, 1910; and BMC to Dear Papa, September 9, 1910 and n.d. [September 1910], BMC, Box 1. For discussion of the retrial, see *Santa Fe New Mexican* [hereafter *New Mexican*], September 18, 1910. The piano agent was sentenced to one year in jail. Upon reflection, Justine considered the entire affair "a great mistake and much better to have let the piano and him go." See JCW to Dearest Mamma, October 2, 1910, BMC, Box 1. In December 1911, the territorial Supreme Court reversed the District Court's decision. See *Territory v. Eyles,* 16 New Mexico 645.

12. Press clipping, n.d. [1910] and no paper cited, BMC, Box 1; and OMC, 1910 Entries, Notes from her Diary, pp. 9–10, BMC, Box 92.

13. BMC to Dear Papa, September 19, 1910; BMC to Dear Mamma, October 4, 1910; and holograph list of individuals and the districts they represented, n.d., BMC, Box 1.

14. JCW to Dearest Mamma, n.d. [1910]; and BMC to Dear Papa, October 10, 1910, BMC, Box 1. Among the items Justine could not secure in Santa Fe and asked her mother to send were washstand china and glass for the table. Apparently, they brought table chinaware with them. In addition, eight crates of furniture were sent to furnish the house, the cost of which was estimated by the architect at seventeen thousand dollars. With local contractors bidding against each other, Bronson believed it would be under twelve thousand dollars.

15. JCW to Dearest Mamma, n.d. [1910], BMC, Box 1.

16. OMC, Notes from her Diary, 1910 entries, pp. 10–12, BMC, Box 92.

17. JCW, "Memoir: 1910–11–13," BMC, Box 92.

18. BMC, Notes, Horoscope, BMC, Box 92.

Chapter 4

1. OMC, January and February 1911, Notes and Diary Excerpts, BMC, Box 92; OMC to Miguel Antonio Otero, April 18, [1911]; and JCW to Otero, March 7, 1911 [postcard], MAO, Box 3.

2. Sally Hull to BMC, February 25, 1911, BMC, Box 2. There is an undated letter from Lula Mae Hull to Dear Honey-Bunch, BMC, Box 2. She thanks him for "your dainty little Xmas gloves" and concludes, "Suppose you will be seeing Callie soon. . . ." Mike Otero noted that Bronson did his best to avoid "Callie's corpulent acquaintances." Miguel Antonio Otero, Jr. to BMC, February 24, 1912, BMC, Box 2.

3. BMC to Dear Mamma, March 5, March 15 and April 26, 1911; BMC to Dear Papa, March 3, March 7, April 12 and April 22, 1911, BMC, Box 2. Prince suggested to William Bayard Cutting that he knew about some question about Mythen's moral character, deficiencies of which others in the vestry were unaware. Cutting, a prominent lay leader, after some checking with church officials, could not get any substantiation for Prince's implications other than that prior to coming to Santa Fe he possibly had been indiscreet. See L. Bradford Prince to William Bayard Cutting, April 22, 1911; and William Bayard Cutting to BMC, April 28, 1911, BMC, Box 2.

4. BMC to Dear Papa, March 7 and March 31, 1911; and Herbert J. Hagerman to William Bayard Cutting, April 4, 1911, BMC, Box 2.

5. William Bayard Cutting to BMC, April 5, April 7 and April 18, 1911, BMC, Box 2.

6. BMC to Dear Papa, May 1, 1911; and William Bayard Cutting to BMC, May 16 and June 21, 1911, BMC, Box 2. JCW to Miguel Antonio Otero, May 24, 1911, MAO, Box 3. That Cutting tried to find another church for James G. Mythen is evident in Bishop N. J. Thomas to BMC, August 15, 1911. That Cutting's father contributed funds to assist Mythen in his time of troubles is evident in James G. Mythen to William Bayard Cutting, June 17, 1911, BMC, Box 2. See, too, BMC to Messrs. Sackett, Champman, Brown and Cross, August 4, 1922, BMC, Box 5. In this letter, Cutting briefly reviews Mythen's tenure as rector of the Church of the Holy Faith in Santa Fe from August 1910 to April 1911. The vestry unanimously endorsed Mythen in a letter to Bishop Thomas of Wyoming where Mythen moved after departing Santa Fe.

7. Miguel Antonio Otero, Jr. to Henry Steele Commager, July 21, 1941, BMC, Box 92.

8. Robert W. Larson, *New Mexico's Quest for Statehood, 1846–1912* (Albuquerque: University of New Mexico Press, 1968), pp. 294–97. Larson's incisive volume is the definitive study.

9. OMC, August and September 1911, Notes and Diary Excerpts, BMC, Box 92.

10. JCW to Miguel Antonio Otero, August 6, 1911, MAO, Box 3; and Miguel Antonio Otero, Jr. to BMC, September 21, 1911, BMC, Box 2.

11. OMC, September 24, 1911, Notes and Diary Entry, BMC, Box 92. She mentions Catron's strong objection to Cutting becoming a delegate. *New Mexican,* September 25, 1911.

12. OMC, September 27 through October 1, Notes and Diary Entries, BMC, Box 92.

13. Herbert J. Hagerman to BMC, September 2, 1911, BMC, Box 17. Incidentally, Albert B. Fall, William J. Mills and George Curry, the latter two former territorial governors, all prominent Republicans, were relatively recent converts to the cause, having switched parties.

14. Hagerman to BMC, September 2, 1911, BMC, Box 17.

15. Harvey B. Fergusson to William Jennings Bryan, September 15, 1911; and Fergusson to J. H. McCasland, September 21, 1911, HBF. In these letters, Fergusson, a prominent Albuquerque Democrat, indicates the progressive discontent with the political climate during the campaign.

16. Thomas B. Catron to R. Fulton Cutting, October 25, 1911, copy in BMC, Box 2. Catron was annoyed that Bronson was actively endorsing Otero, now a fusion candidate for state senator on the Democratic ticket. Cutting possibly donated funds but most obviously his automobile and chauffeur. BMC to Dear Papa, November 2, 1911, BMC, Box 2.

17. BMC to Dear Papa, November 2 and November 5, 1911; and BMC to Dear Mamma, November 21, 1911, BMC, Box 2.

18. BMC to Dear Papa, November 10, 1911, BMC, Box 2.

19. Frederic Bishop to William Bayard Cutting, November 10, 1911, BMC, Box 2.

20. William Bayard Cutting to BMC, November 10, 1911, BMC, Box 2.

21. R. H. Rose to W. L. Houser, November 25, 1911; and Charles G. Given to Robert M. La Follette, November 21, 1911, LFC, NPRL, Series J, Box 60, New Mexico. For an indication of the activities of William H. ("Bull") Andrews and his friends, see editorials in *The Raton Range,* November 17 and November 18, 1911. See, too, BMC to Dear Papa, November 16, 1911, BMC, Box 1.

22. BMC to John Addison Thayer, December 11, 1911, BMC, Box 12.

23. The quote is from R. H. Rose to Walter L. Houser, December 12, 1911, LFC, NPRL, Series J, Box 60, New Mexico. See, too, William Bayard Cutting to BMC, December 15, 1911, BMC, Box 17, for suggestions about how to play fusion politics. That the Progressives in New Mexico were unorganized is evident in R. H. Hanna to William L. Houser, January 5, 1912, LFC, NPRL, Series J, Box 60, New Mexico.

24. BMC to Theodore Roosevelt, January 9, 1912, TR, Reel 123. The education of Theodore Roosevelt, Jr. (1900–1904) and Kermit Roosevelt

(1902–1908) at Groton overlapped that of Cutting (1901–1906). For an indication that La Follette supporters were not making much headway in early 1912 and that they were waiting to see what Roosevelt would do, see R. E. Rowells to Walter L. Houser, February 13, 1912, LFC, NPRL, Series J, Box 60, New Mexico.

25. BMC to Dear Mamma, February 10, 1912; and F. A. Bishop to BMC, March 2, 1912, BMC, Box 2. See, too, Miguel Antonio Otero to OMC, December 14, 1935, MAO, Box 3. Following a dinner party, Cutting's father, Francis Wilson, Doctor Massie and Otero were enjoying "a game of auction bridge" until 11:00 P.M. when Cutting retired. Shortly thereafter he came to the door and asked for Dr. Bishop, who was playing at another table with Bronson. Otero recalled that Mr. Cutting was in "good spirits" when he boarded the private Pullman car with Dr. Bishop.

26. Frederic A. Bishop to BMC, March 2, 1912, BMC, Box 2; and Jouett Fall Elliott to OMC, July 15, 1935, BMC, Box 11.

27. BMC to Dear Mamma, n.d. [1912], BMC, Box 2.

28. BMC to My dear mother, March 2, 1912; and BMC to Dear Mamma, March 4, 1912, BMC, Box 2. See *New York Times,* March 12, 1912 for a story about William Bayard Cutting's estate.

29. BMC to Dear Mamma, March 11, March 17, March 20, March 23 and March 25, 1912, BMC, Box 2.

30. BMC to Dear Mamma, March 30, April 3, April 6, April 9, June 3 and June 9, 1912, BMC, Box 2. The senatorial election was not the only contest that depressed Cutting. In the city election in early April, all four winners of the aldermen races were owners of saloons, and Arthur Seligman, "the only good mayor they ever had," was defeated by "his own clerk." See BMC to Dear Mamma, April 3, 1912, BMC, Box 2. For an account of Mrs. Fall's hysterics, see Frederic H. Bishop to OMC, December 12, 1920, BMC, Box 5. For the broader implications of the senatorial election, see two letters: Albert B. Fall to Solomon Luna, April 9, 1912, ABF, Box 26; and Fall to H. B. Holt, April 13, 1912, ABF, Box 23; see, also, Fall to James Black, May 11, 1912, ABF, Box 14.

31. BMC to Dear Mamma, April 6 and June 9, 1912; Walter J. Hinchman to BMC, March 9, 1912; and R. B. Merriman to BMC, June 10, 1912, BMC, Box 2. Cutting sent a check for three hundred dollars to help pay Ferguson's salary. See treasurer's statement in *Reports of the President and the Treasurer of Harvard College: 1912–1913* (Cambridge: Harvard University, 1914), p. 31. In 1913, Cutting's mother bequeathed funds in her husband's name for traveling scholarships at Columbia University. See BMC to Dear Mamma, February 16, 1913, BMC, Box 2.

32. Analysis of the New Mexican Printing Company, prepared by Lyons and Johnson, n.d.; and BMC to Dear Mamma, June 13, 1912, BMC, Box 2.

The final details were worked out with the assistance of his father's secretary, Francis Bergen, who came out from New York.

33. Miguel Antonio Otero, Statement, January 22, 1922, MAO, Box 3. The announcement made on July 1, 1912 is noted in Oliver La Farge, ed., *Santa Fe: The Autobiography of a Southwestern Town* (Norman: University of Oklahoma Press, 1959), p. 207. BMC to Dear Mamma, July 3, 1912, BMC, Box 2. In this letter, Cutting requested five thousand dollars, as his account was running low. He stated, "We have to get the deal closed by Friday, in order to have control before the annual meeting next Monday."

34. BMC to Dear Mamma, July 7, July 11 and July 18, 1912, BMC, Box 2. Dunne, who was living in San Diego, agreed to return to Santa Fe. Besides his work on the paper, he also agreed to take up residence with Cutting and serve as his private secretary.

35. Frederic H. Bishop comments on Cutting's writing occasional editorials in his letter to OMC, July 25, 1912, BMC, Box 2. For indications of the gloom of the old gang, see James S. Black to Albert B. Fall, May 6, 1912, ABF, Box 14; and H. B. Holt to Fall, July 15, 1912, ABF, Box 23. See Thomas B. Catron to C. C. Catron, June 3, 1912, TBC, Box 1.

36. OMC to Theodore Roosevelt, June 14, 1912, TR, Series 1, Reel 146. Mrs. Cutting contributed two thousand dollars. BMC to Dear Mamma, July 26 and July 31, 1912, BMC, Box 2. Otero was elected state chairman of the Progressive party at a convention held in Albuquerque in late July. Cutting was not in attendance. See, too, JCW to Miguel Antonio Otero, July 28, 1912, MAO, Box 3 for an indication of how close the Roosevelt and Cutting families were. A copy of the Roosevelt telegram to Cutting can be found in BMC, Box 12.

37. Fall to H. B. Holt, July 22, 1912, ABF, Box 23. Fall was worried that Felix Martinez in San Miguel County would endorse Roosevelt. At the end of August, Cutting announced that George Armijo in Santa Fe had turned Progressive. Both Fall and Cutting knew that each man brought with him a host of supporters. See BMC to Dear Mamma, August 28, 1912, BMC, Box 2.

38. The circumstances of Luna's death were not clear. Some people thought he was murdered, possibly by his nephew and political successor, Ed Otero, but, according to Cutting, "the general opinion seems to be that Luna committed suicide." In his will, Luna deeded all of his property to Ed Otero, leaving Mrs. Luna and the rest of the family without a cent. Mrs. Luna, when Cutting commented at the end of September, was in the process of suing Otero for forging her husband's will.

39. BMC to Dear Mamma, September 1, September 14, and September 21, 1912, BMC, Box 2.

40. Ralph Henderson, recollection, May 13, 1939, BMC, Box 92.

41. BMC to Dear Mamma, September 27, October 6, October 12 and October 20, 1912, BMC, Box 2. Miguel Antonio Otero to JCW, October 29, 1912 [night letter], MAO, Box 3. Otero suggested that some of Cutting's family should be with him "to make him feel good" while he regained his strength.

42. BMC to Dear Mamma, October 6, 1912; Brian Boru Dunne to OMC, October 6 and November 2, 1912; and BMC to Dear Mamma, October 23 and October 28, 1912, BMC, Box 2. See, too, H. B. Hening, ed., *George Curry, 1861–1947: An Autobiography* (Albuquerque: University of New Mexico Press, 1958), p. 270 for a related account of the bleak outlook which mitigated sending funds to New Mexico. Frederic Bishop, the doctor who resided with Cutting, had returned to London, believing his services were no longer needed, as Cutting seemed in excellent health.

43. BMC to Dear Mamma, November 8, 1912, BMC, Box 2. See, too, Albert B. Fall to John M. Bowman, December 21, 1912, ABF, Box 14, for an indication of Fall's effort to unite Republican factions. The only offices voted upon in 1912 were the presidency and a congressional seat. No state or county offices were to be filled because the constitution at this time provided four year terms for these officials.

44. Dunne to OMC, December 23 and December 26, 1912, BMC, Box 2. JCW to OMC, January 2 and January 8, 1913, BMC, Box 2.

45. JCW to OMC, January 18, January 25, January 30 and February 8, 1913; and BMC to Dear Mamma, January 26, 1913, BMC, Box 2. BMC to Theodore Roosevelt, January 26, 1913, TR, Reel 165. See editorials in Santa Fe *New Mexican,* January 29, 1913.

46. JCW to OMC, February 17 and February 27, 1913, BMC, Box 2. In the latter letter, Justine commented again upon her brother's health, observing that "he seems to be making such good progress."

Chapter 5

1. George Chase to BMC, September 1 and November 29, 1910 and January 9, 1911, BMC, Box 13. Beatrice Chauvenet, *Hewett and Friends: A Biography of Santa Fe's Vibrant Era* (Santa Fe: Museum of New Mexico Press, 1983) is a laudatory, largely uncritical, biography by one of Hewett's admirers.

2. Franz Boas to the President and Council of the Archaeological Institute of America, December 24, 1909; and Boas to Francis M. Kelsey, December 16, 1910, copies in BMC, Box 103. In the letter to Kelsey, Boas spelled out what he meant by Hewett's failure to appreciate what constituted scientific work. Among other points, Hewett lacked thoroughness, covered too much geographical territory, and utilized an untrained person to lecture on the ethnology of a region he never worked and then let him pursue "half a dozen

subjects in one year." Hewett failed to understand the need for special training and utilized local groups without "insisting on and providing for scientific work." This last activity appeared "little short of criminal" to Boas, for archaeological remains were much safer underground where "they may await the time when competent men will save them." For evidence of friction between Boas and Hewett, see Boas to Edgar L. Hewett, November 13, 1911, copy in BMC, Box 103. In this letter, Boas mentioned Hewett's casting aspersions on him at professional gatherings. According to Boas, Hewett claimed he had proof of unethical activities by Boas. Hewett denied he had said such things, however. Boas, writing from Mexico, wanted to take Hewett to court and would have done so but for the expense involved.

3. BMC to Dear Mamma, May 21, 1912, BMC, Box 2.

4. *New Mexican,* October 9, 16, 19, 23 and 28, 1913. Almost everyday from October 3 through the entire month, some story in the paper covered this controversy.

5. Charles F. Lummis to Edgar L. Hewett, October 27, 1913; BMC to Lummis, November 10, 1913, ELH, Box 39.

6. Paul A. F. Walter to Hewett, November 6, 1913, ELH, Box 39. See the *New Mexican,* November 10, 1913 for the role of Santa Fe women's clubs in supporting Hewett. Actually, there was no danger of Hewett's operations in Santa Fe being shut down or removed from Santa Fe. On November 12, 1913, the *New Mexican* presented a profile of thirty-one managers, concluding that at best, there were only three competent archaeologists on the board. On December 18, 1913, the Executive Committee of the School of American Archaeology, meeting at the National Museum in Washington, D.C., expressed "its entire satisfaction with the existing arrangements between the people of New Mexico and the school." An extract from the minutes can be found in BMC, Box 13.

7. A story in the Santa Fe *Eagle,* dated November 19, 1913, presents the Chamber of Commerce resolutions. The *Eagle* was a weekly newspaper. Hewett to Lummis, November 27, 1913, ELH, Box 39. This seven-page letter provided Lummis with suggestions for a pamphlet that would carefully detail the support Hewett had received and would play down his critics. See too, John R. McFie to Hewett, December 22, 1913, ELH, Box 39. McFie, treasurer of the School of American Archaeology, explained that he prepared some of the telegrams, drafted some of the resolutions and wrote headings for petitions. All indicated that the people of Santa Fe "are more friendly to the school than ever before and also to yourself."

8. Franz Boas to BMC, December 9, 1913, PCFB, Reel 14. As a result of the controversy, enrollment in the School of American Archaeology, the name coming into general use, apparently was declining. See Cutting to Lummis, December 13, 1913, BMC, Box 13. By 1914, the School of Ameri-

can Archaeology, besides having at its disposal the ancient Palace of the Governors, was receiving an annual appropriation of ten thousand dollars from the legislature.

9. BMC to Boas, December 30, 1913 [telegram]; Boas et al. to BMC, January 2, 1914, PCFB, Reel 14, BMC to F. W. Shipley, two letters, n.d. [1914], BMC, Box 13. Shipley was president of the Archaeological Institute of America and a professor at Washington University. Pliny E. Goddard to BMC, January 14, 1914 and May 3, 1915, BMC, Box 13. BMC to Alfred M. Tozzer, May 16, 1915; and BMC to Dear Mamma, January 23, 1914 and April 11, 1915, BMC, Box 3. BMC to Dear Mamma, February 17, 1914, BMC, Box 2.

10. Lummis to Hewett, January 16, 1914, ELH, Box 39; Lummis to BMC, January 16, 1914, BMC, Box 13; and BMC to Dear Mamma, March 22, 1914, BMC, Box 3.

11. BMC to Dear Mamma, February 24, 1913; JCW to Dearest Mother, March 1, 1913, BMC, Box 2; and BMC to Dear Mamma, October 27, 1913, BMC, Box 2. C. J. Smith to W. J. Burns, November 29, 1913; and Francis Wilson to C. J. Smith, December 16, 1913, copy in BMC, Box 14. Smith was the Denver manager of the Burns Detective Agency. That Fall was aware of the activities of the agency is clear. His view was that Cutting endorsed Otero so that Justine could come to Washington "and keep open house, etc., for Otero, I presume bringing her husband along for a chaperon." See Albert B. Fall to Charles Springer, May 25, 1914, ABF, Box 37.

12. Brian Boru Dunne to OMC, April 8, 1913; Dunne to BMC, December 3, 1913; and Miguel Antonio Otero, Jr. to BMC, September 24, 1912 and October 26, 1913, BMC, Box 2. See too, Otero, Jr. to BMC, January 21 and February 1, 1914, BMC, Box 3.

13. BMC to Dear Mamma, July 11, July 17 and August 24, 1913, BMC, Box 2; and BMC to Theodore Roosevelt, June 30, 1913, TR, Reel 177.

14. Frederic Bishop to OMC, January 28, 1914; and BMC to Dear Mamma, January 10, January 15 and January 31, 1914 and March 8, 1914, BMC, Box 3.

15. E. Dana Johnson to BMC, February 4, 1914; and BMC to Dear Mamma, February 8 and February 23, 1914; and BMC to Dear Mamma, March 22 and March 31, 1914, BMC, Box 3.

16. BMC to Dear Mamma, April 8 and April 15, 1914, BMC, Box 4. In September, a new man, who had been in charge of a large printing plant in El Paso and who had twenty years of experience in the newspaper business, took over as business manager of the *New Mexican*. See BMC to Dear Mamma, August 24, 1914, BMC, Box 3.

17. Rufus J. Palen to BMC, March 12, 1914, BMC, Box 3.

18. BMC to Dear Mamma, June 5, June 23, July 18 and August 6, 1914; and Lytton R. Taylor to BMC, July 28, 1914, BMC, Box 3. Taylor wrote Cutting

to recommend a strong Progressive who wished to become involved in the coming campaign.

19. E. C. Burke to Miguel Antonio Otero, August 27, 1914; Otero to BMC, August 28, 1914; and George Curry to BMC, September 10, 1914, BMC, Box 3. Cutting got out of delivering the "keynote speech" as he had "a little cold" at the time. He was elected state chairman after he had gone to bed. If he had been present, he wrote, "I certainly should have declined to serve." See BMC to Dear Mamma, September 13, 1914, BMC, Box 3.

20. BMC to Dear Mamma, September 13 and September 26, 1914, BMC, Box 3.

21. J. R. Williams to BMC, September 20, 1914; and BMC to Dear Mamma, September 26, 1914, BMC, Box 3. Cutting also helped support a Las Cruces newspaper. See Orrin A. Foster to Richard H. Hanna, December 21, 1914 and May 28, 1915, BMC, Box 3.

22. H. H. Dorman to OMC, September 28, 1914; and BMC to Dear Mamma, October 3 and October 12, 1914, BMC, Box 3. The *New Mexico State Record,* edited by J. Wright Giddings, Cutting's former editor on the *New Mexican* and backed by prominent Republicans, had just started publication. It refused to print Cutting's reply to an attack on Wilson. Cutting published his rebuttal in the *New Mexican* on October 9, 1914.

23. BMC to Dear Mamma, October 20 and October 27, 1914, BMC, Box 3; and Special Report, Denver Operating #P-259, Denver Investigator #45, October 27, October 29 and October 30, 1914, BMC, Box 14.

24. BMC to Dear Mamma, November 6, 1914; and Miguel Antonio Otero, Jr. to BMC, November 5, 1914, BMC, Box 3. Otero sought to buoy Cutting's spirits by suggesting that public sentiment was becoming aroused over how the government was being administered and that his effort was worthwhile.

25. Francis C. Wilson to BMC, December 16, 1914; and E. Dana Johnson et al. to BMC, December 25, 1914 [telegram], BMC, Box 3.

26. BMC to Dear Mamma, January 18, January 26, February 10, February 24 and June 14, 1915; and Brian Boru Dunne to OMC, March 11, 1915, BMC, Box 3.

27. BMC to Dear Mamma, February 24, 1915, March 4, March 11 and March 28, August 10 and August 13, 1915, BMC, Box 3. Francis Wilson, Cutting's personal attorney, worked with the Catrons on this case. Cutting, Wilson and the *New Mexican* were involved in the suit. Both Cutting and Wilson filed demurrers to focus the libel suit on the paper and not on its publisher or legal counsel. A statement for the amount paid to Catron and Catron, dated October 2, 1915, can be found in BMC, Box 3.

28. Theodore Roosevelt to BMC, May 27, 1915; JCW to BMC, June 2, 1915; and BMC to Dear Mamma, n.d. [1915] and August 1, 1915, BMC,

Box 3. Senator Albert B. Fall was also interested in Theodore Roosevelt's playing a role in bringing the Progressives back into the Republican fold. Fall understood that "the Progressive Party is not a political factor with the people of any state, except in so far as Roosevelt is the Progressive Party." See Albert B. Fall to Ormsby McHarg, June 4, 1915, ABF, Box 26.

29. BMC to Dear Mamma, June 14, June 30, July 26, August 1 and September 5, 1915, BMC, Box 3. By December 1915, the new press was printing thirty-five hundred papers per hour.

30. BMC to Dear Mamma, October 19, 1915, BMC, Box 3; and BMC to Miguel Antonio Otero, November 20, 1915, MAO, Box 3.

31. BMC to Miguel Antonio Otero, December 12 and December 18, 1915, MAO, Box 3; Miguel Antonio Otero, Jr., to BMC, December 8, 1915; and Francis Wilson et al. to Ralph M. Henderson, December 10, 1915, BMC, Box 3. In his capacity as vice president of the New Mexican Printing Company, Wilson signed the letter to Henderson, along with Otero as treasurer and H. H. Dorman as secretary.

32. H. B. Holt to Albert B. Fall, December 31, 1915, ABF, Box 23.

Chapter 6

1. Fall to H. B. Holt, January 4, 1916, ABF, Box 23, and Fall to George Curry, January 26, 1916, ABF, Box 17. BMC to Dear Mamma, January 28, 1916; and E. R. Bujac to BMC, February 9, 1916, BMC, Box 3.

2. BMC to Dear Mamma, March 3, March 11 and March 28, 1916, BMC, Box 3.

3. BMC to Dear Mamma, March 11 and March 20, 1916, BMC, Box 3.

4. For a copy of Aero Club of America, Bulletin No. 142 [May 1916], see BMC, Box 3. A Curtiss aeroplane was shipped to the New Mexico National Guard by the end of May. See M. R. Crop to BMC, June 1, 1916, BMC, Box 3.

5. See, for example, George Curry to BMC, March 10, 1916, BMC, Box 3. Curry, a former Rough Rider, territorial governor and congressman, was concerned that Holm O. Bursum, again seeking the gubernatorial nomination on the Republican ticket, would not be censured by Roosevelt. Curry explained, "Bursum is the strongest supporter that Colonel Roosevelt has in the Old Guard and I am very anxious to see a delegation of the Republican National convention from New Mexico friendly to the Colonel."

6. BMC to Dear Mamma, March 28 and April 14, 1916; and Theodore Roosevelt to BMC, April 2 and April 22, 1916, BMC, Box 3.

7. Albert B. Fall to Holm O. Bursum, May 1, 1916, ABF, Box 15. Fall, who was not at the Republican convention, supported Bursum for the gubernatorial nomination. His letter presents his impression of the various candidates.

8. BMC to Dear Mamma, June 8, 1916, BMC, Box 3.

9. BMC to Dear Mamma, June 15, 1916; and Theodore Roosevelt to BMC, June 16, 1916, BMC, Box 3.

10. BMC to Dear Mamma, June 15 and June 25, 1916, BMC, Box 3. BMC to Dear Mamma, June 25, 1916; and Ralph C. Ely to BMC, June 26, 1916, BMC, Box 3. Ely was chairman of the Republican State Central Committee.

11. BMC to Dear Mamma, July 15, July 23 and July 30, 1916, BMC, Box 3. That Cutting's dilemma was shared by all Progressives in New Mexico is evident in Frank H. Wilcox to BMC, July 22, 1916, BMC, Box 3. Wilcox planned to vote for Wilson but believed the Progressive organization should be kept intact.

12. Albert B. Fall to George Curry, July 26, 1916, ABF, Box 17; Fall to Theodore Roosevelt, August 3, 1916, ABF, Box 34; and Fall to Holm O. Bursum, August 3, 1916, ABF, Box 15. In the letter, Fall said to Bursum that he and Roosevelt had talked for two hours about the New Mexico political scene. See, too, Roosevelt to BMC, August 8, 1916, BMC, Box 3. The letter printed in Elting E. Morison, et al., eds., *The Letters of Theodore Roosevelt*, vol. 8 (Cambridge: Harvard University Press, 1954), pp. 1097–98 does not contain the changes made by Roosevelt in the copy mailed to Cutting.

13. Brian Boru Dunne to OMC, March 9 and August 20, 1916, BMC, Box 3.

14. BMC to Dear Mamma, September 3, 1916, BMC, Box 3; Harold L. Ickes to Miguel Antonio Otero, September 8, 1916, MAO, Box 1; and BMC to Dear Mamma, September 8 and September 26, 1916, BMC, Box 3. Cutting's view of Hughes's campaign was reenforced by Andrieus A. Jones, the Democratic senatorial candidate, who told him that the president did not intend to make many speeches, as Hughes was making his campaign for him. Senator Albert Fall appeared to be the only major Republican leader in New Mexico devoting his efforts to the success of both the state and national tickets. See Fall to Frank Hitchcock, September 23, 1916, ABF, Box 23. BMC to Dear Mamma, September 16, 1916, BMC, Box 3. The Republican State Central Committee emphasized local issues, inquiring of correspondents about dissatisfaction with the operation of the county-road board system under Governor McDonald. See, for example, H. B. Hening to C. L. Parsons, September 25, 1916, TBC, PC29, 408 Box 1.

15. BMC to Dear Mamma, September 3 and September 26, 1916; Tony Luna to BMC, September 20, 1916; and Brian Boru Dunne to OMC, October 1, 1916; BMC to Dear Mamma, October 3, October 12 and October 19, 1916; and Howard Johnson to BMC, October 12, 1916, BMC, Box 3. Cutting met all the expenses incurred by Tony Luna during his final illness as well as the funeral costs, his mother being a poor widow with other children.

While in El Paso, he sent for a specialist in Fort Worth to assist the army doctors at Fort Bliss.

16. BMC to Dear Mamma, October 19, 1916, BMC, Box 3.

17. BMC to Theodore Roosevelt, October 31, 1916; and Roosevelt to Bayard Cutting, November 4, 1916, BMC, Box 3. In the heat of the campaign, Roosevelt dictated Bayard instead of Bronson as Cutting's first name. Roosevelt, of course, had known Cutting's deceased father and brother named William Bayard and Bayard, respectively.

18. E. T. Chase to BMC, November 14, 1916; and Miguel Antonio Otero to BMC, November 24, 1916, BMC, Box 3.

19. BMC to Theodore Roosevelt, November 17, 1916, BMC, Box 3.

20. Ralph C. Ely to BMC, November 20 and December 7, 1916; BMC to Ely, December 2, 1916; and BMC to E. Dana Johnson, December 2, 1916, BMC, Box 3.

21. BMC to Miguel Antonio Otero, December 7, December 9 and December 18, 1916, MAO, Box 3. Otero could not reconcile himself with either the organization of the Republican party in New Mexico or the national organization. Reformation from within seemed fruitless. He concluded that there was "an excellent chance" of securing under Wilson a "genuine Liberal or Progressive national organization." Otero also believed he could secure through election or appointment a public office under Democratic auspices. See Otero to BMC, December 27, 1916, BMC, Box 3.

Chapter 7

1. Norman L. Rosenberg, *Protecting the Best Man: An Interpretive History of the Law of Libel* (University of North Carolina Press: Chapel Hill, 1986), *passim*. An unpublished paper, "New Mexico's Dreyfus Affair: Bronson Cutting and the Freedom of the Press Cases," by Harry P. Jeffrey, facilitated my understanding of these cases. I wish to thank Professor Jeffrey at California State University, Fullerton, for making a copy of this paper, as well as other Cutting material, available to me.

2. *New Mexican,* October 11, 1916.

3. BMC to Dear Mamma, October 12, 1916; and BMC to Dear Mamma, October 19, 1916, BMC, Box 3.

4. BMC to Dear Mamma, October 27, 1916; and Brian Boru Dunne to OMC, October 27, 1916, BMC, Box 3.

5. The reports forwarded to Cutting can be found in BMC, Box 15. BMC to Dear Mamma, January 10, January 15, January 22 and January 31, 1917; and Brian Boru Dunne to OMC, January 31, 1917, BMC, Box 4. *New Mexican,* January 19, 1917.

6. H. H. Dorman to Cutting, February 8, 1917; BMC to Dear Mamma, January 10 and February 28, 1917, BMC, Box 4. Cutting chaired a citizen's committee charged by the legislature to supervise and manage a banquet honoring General Pershing and his staff on Washington's birthday at the DeVargas Hotel in Santa Fe.

7. JCW to Dearest Mother, March 3, 1917, BMC, Box 4. Phelps Dodge and Company had invested millions of dollars in New Mexico mining and railroad ventures.

8. JCW to Dearest Mother, March 7, 1917, BMC, Box 4.

9. JCW to Dearest Mother, March 9, 1917, BMC, Box 4; and "Some Salient Facts Regarding New Mexican Libel Suit," *New Mexican,* March 12, 1917.

10. B. S. Rodey to The N.M. Ptg. Co., and its friends, March 10, 1917; BMC to Dear Mamma, March 15, 1917; JCW to Dearest Mother, March 19, 1917; and Miguel Antonio Otero to BMC, April 7, 1917, BMC, Box 4. Fall's remark was reported by Otero who visited the senator prior to departing for his post in the Canal Zone.

11. JCW to Dearest Mother, March 18, 1917; BMC to Dear Mamma, March 15 and March 21, 1917; and JCW to Dearest Mother, March 18 and March 20, 1917, BMC. Box 4. See also Herbert B. Holt to Albert B. Fall, March 21, 1917, ABF, Box 23. Justine, who became "quite chummy" with Mrs. Lindsey, whose influence with her husband was "powerful," did not believe that "Bronson will ever find himself in the Penitentiary." See JCW to Dearest Mother, March 29, [1917], BMC, Box 2. This letter is misdated 1913. Its contents make abundantly clear that it should be dated 1917. A notarized affidavit by Miguel Antonio Otero, Jr., dated November 15, 1917, can be found in BMC, Box 5. At that time, Otero was an officer in the Aviation Corps of the United States Army, which was headed for France. *New Mexican,* March 30 and April 2, 1917.

12. BMC to Dear Mamma, April 9 and April 18, 1917; and General Orders No. 30, Office of the Adjutant General, Santa Fe, June 8, 1917, BMC, Box 4. JCW to Albert B. Fall, April 16, 1917, ABF, Box 42. Justine inquired about whether Fall would be in New York for the launching of the battleship, USS New Mexico. Governor Lindsey later appointed Cutting a member of the Santa Fe County Council of Defense. Cutting, about to depart for overseas service, resigned from the committee. See William E. Lindsey to BMC, July 28, 1917, BMC, Box 4. For a tiff about the battleship silver, see OMC to Mary Prince, August 25, 1917; and Prince to OMC, n.d., Prince to BMC, September 2, 1917, and BMC to Mary Prince, September 5, 1917, BMC, Box 4.

13. JCW to BMC, May 7 [telegram] and May 12, 1917; and JCW to Dearest Mother, May 16, 1917, BMC, Box 4.

14. Brian Boru Dunne to BMC, June 11, 1917, BMC, Box 4; and BMC to Herbert J. Hagerman, June 14, 1917, BMC, Box 15. Dunne kept Cutting informed of the latest gossip in Santa Fe.

15. BMC to Dear Mamma, June 19, 1917; and Sherman Miles to BMC, June 23, 1917, BMC, Box 4. The editorial appeared in *Collier's* (July 7, 1917) p. 9. JCW to BMC, July 5, 1917; JCW to Dearest Mother, July 5, 1917; and BMC to Dearest Mamma, July 8, 1917, BMC, Box 4.

16. BMC to Neill B. Field, July 10, 1917; and Field to BMC, July 17, 1917, BMC, Box 4.

17. BMC to Field, July 12, 1917, BMC, Box 4. For Mason's comments on Cutting's legal insights, see JCW to BMC, December 21, 1917, BMC, Box 15.

18. Miguel Antonio Otero, Jr. to BMC, August 6, 1917, BMC, Box 4.

19. BMC to Dear Mamma, July 15 and July 23, 1917; E. H. Wells to BMC, July 17, 1917 [telegram]; JCW to BMC, July 17, 1917; and BMC to Dear Mamma, August 9, 1917, BMC, Box 4. Francis Wilson to JCW, August 15 and October 8, 1917, BMC, Box 17; and Wilson to JCW, Sunday, n.d. [1917], BMC, Box 15.

20. The supreme court decision can be found in *25 New Mexico 102*. The memorandum regarding the contempt proceedings, presumably prepared by Herbert D. Mason, is located in BMC, Box 15.

21. Francis Wilson to BMC, August 24, 1917, EDJ, File 17, Box 418; BMC to Wilson, August 29, 1917, BMC, Box 15. A copy is also available in the papers of E. Dana Johnson. For a further insight into the tangled politics of Socorro politicians seeking to succeed Mechem as district judge, see the February 1918 deposition of E. Dana Johnson, a copy of which is located in BMC, Box 4.

22. Herbert D. Mason to JCW, August 28, 1917, BMC, Box 15; *New Mexican,* September 11, 1917. JCW to BMC, October 2, October 5 and October 13, 1917, BMC, Box 4; and Wilson to Herbert D. Mason, October 5, 1917, BMC, Box 17. An effort on the part of "Spicer, et al." to have Ralph Henderson removed as receiver "failed utterly" when considered by the supreme court. See Brian Boru Dunne to BMC, October 23, 1917, BMC, Box 4; and Ralph M. Henderson to BMC, October 27, 1917, BMC, Box 17.

23. See letters from Henderson and Dunne cited in footnote 22. See, also, JCW to BMC, December 21, 1917, BMC, Box 15, and H. H. Dorman to BMC, December 20, 1917, BMC, Box 4. JCW to BMC, January 21 and January 26, 1918; JCW to Dearest Mother, February 7 and February 23, 1918, BMC, Box 17. Cutting's approval of the sale and reorganization is noted in the "PPS" to the January 26 letter. Owing to a quirk in the Delaware legal code the company was reorganized as the Santa Fe New Mexican Printing Company.

24. JCW to BMC, February 23, 1918, BMC, Box 17. The publicity agent asked for $650 and his expenses. Justine would not reveal either the name of the agent or his firm, although she agreed to his terms. Most likely the agent was either Henry Barrett Chamberlin or an associate on the staff of *Chamberlin's* magazine, a periodical published in Chicago. Barrett was a prominent Chicago lawyer and editor. Incidentally, by April some of Cutting's associates in Santa Fe knew that Chamberlin was an agent of the Cuttings. See JCW to BMC, April 23, 1918, BMC, Box 17.

25. *Chamberlin's* April–July, 1918. Stories appear under the heading "Shall the Press Remain Free in New Mexico?" A copy of the *International News Service's* stories, dated June 11 and June 12, can be found in BMC, Box 87. See, too, the account in *Editor & Publisher* for June 15, 1918, part of a discussion of "Legal Action Comment Curbed by Court." Henry Barrett Chamberlin to Herbert D. Mason, April 18, 1918, copy in BMC, Box 4. This letter notes that *Chamberlin's* was sent to H. L. Hall, state treasurer of New Mexico. See *New Mexican,* June 9, 1918 for the story of Johnson's conviction and appeal to the supreme court, and Washington *Times,* June 20, 1918 for a further account.

26. A recollection prepared by Ralph Henderson in 1939 appears in BMC, Box 92. Francis Wilson to BMC, April 23, 1918, BMC, Box 4.

27. Will Hays to Fall, May 23, 1918, ABF, Box 36. Since Hays maintained his office as chairman of the Republican National Committee in New York City, most likely, once introduced, he and Justine occasionally conferred about the political situation in New Mexico. Herbert D. Mason to Hays, July 18, 1918, ABF, Box 36. After meeting with Hays, Mason and Justine went to Washington to see Fall, only to learn that he was in New Mexico. See Mason to OMC, July 19, 1918, BMC, Box 17. Fall to JCW, August 3, 1918, ABF, Box 36. Indicative of how vastly Fall's views had changed from those expressed in August 1918 is an undated letter in 1917 to Justine in which he wished to have a chat wherein he hoped "to persuade you that I never had been as entirely depraved as you thought." See Fall to JCW, n.d. [April or May 1917], BMC, Box 4.

28. Francis Wilson to JCW, August 15, 1918; JCW to BMC, August 31, 1918, BMC, Box 17. In the latter letter Justine explained the details pertaining to her request for Wilson's resignation.

29. Fall to Holm O. Bursum, August 22, 1918, ABF, Box 15.

30. William H. Gillenwater to Fall, August 28, 1918, ABF, Box 15; and JCW to BMC, November 2, 1918, BMC, Box 17.

31. BMC to JCW, October 17, 1918; and JCW to BMC, October 7, 1918, BMC, Box 7. Justine's letter is part of one, written over several days, that fully details her dilemma. Cutting in no way sought to direct policy, although he was clearly unhappy with Larrazolo as a candidate. The Democrats also

nominated a Spanish-American as their gubernatorial candidate. Justine considered Johnson to be something of a racial bigot, with his "*strong* anti-Latin preconceptions." She was concerned about his managing the paper during the campaign.

32. JCW to BMC, November 2, 1918, BMC, Box 17. In the last weeks of the campaign, E. Dana Johnson became a victim of the influenza epidemic and was temporarily replaced as managing editor by A. H. Lyon. Miguel Antonio Otero, who supported the Democratic ticket, agreed with Johnson that they "put up a very rotten ticket, which permitted the Republicans to go them one better." See Miguel Antonio Otero to BMC, December 10, 1918, BMC, Box 4.

33. A. H. Lyon to JCW, December 9, 1918, BMC, Box 4.

34. Mason to JCW, January 1, 1919 [telegram], BMC, Box 4. See, too, for example, Albuquerque *Morning Journal,* January 2, 1919 for a lead story and Providence *Evening Journal,* February 10, 1919 for an editorial.

35. Santa Fe *New Mexican,* October 23, 1919. This issue extensively reviewed the litigation, stressing freedom of the press.

36. F. W. Parker to Herbert Mason, December 29, 1919, copy in BMC, Box 15. Parker was a supreme court justice. See, too, Miguel Antonio Otero, to BMC, June 2, 1919, BMC, Box 5. Otero commented upon the loss of top employees at the *New Mexican* "and a ten thousand dollar verdict, all at a clip."

37. BMC to JCW, December 11, 1918, BMC, Box 17.

38. In an interview, Holm Bursum, Jr. later reported that a sum of three thousand dollars was agreed upon to settle the libel suit. Presumably Cutting was to pay Bursum, Sr. the same amount, matching the sum Bursum paid Dreyfus and thereby leading him to terminate the suit. Bursum, Jr. claimed that Cutting never followed through with the arrangement. We do know, however, that the case was terminated by Dreyfus, who received a "trifling sum" of ten thousand dollars for doing so. At this time, Cutting was still in military service, and the paper was still under the direction of his sister. The interview with Holm Bursum, Jr. is mentioned in the unpublished paper by Harry Jeffrey, "New Mexico's Dreyfus Affair: Bronson Cutting and the Freedom of the Press Cases," graciously made available to me by Professor Jeffrey.

Chapter 8

1. Andrieus A. Jones to Officials of the War Department, June 23, 1917; William E. Lindsey to Lieutenant Colonel R. H. Van Deman, July 31, 1917; Richard H. Hanna to Van Deman, July 31, 1917; and James Baca to Van Deman, August 3, 1917, BMC, Box 4. See, too, Theodore Roosevelt to Chief, Military Intelligence Division, June 20, 1917, Cutting cards in Record

Group 165 [hereafter RG 165], MID, Microfilm 912. Most of the letters stressed Cutting's fluency with languages. In addition, Senator Jones mentioned his desire to serve "in some substantial way, notwithstanding one defective eye." His bout with tuberculosis was not mentioned in any of these letters and the subject never came up in correspondence with family members and others. Moreover, Senator Jones's remark is the only one I have seen referring to a "defective eye."

2. BMC to Dear Mamma, August 8, 1917, BMC, Box 4. See, too, the Cutting cards in RG 165, MID, Microfilm 912, for notations of Cutting's orders and Order No. 60, War Department, September 4, 1917, Par. 11, copy in BMC, Box 4, and Colonel P. D. Lochridge to Colonel S. L. Slocum, September 15, 1917, copy in BMC, Box 4. Slocum, the military attaché at the London embassy, was informed that Cutting had been designated as one of his assistants.

3. BMC to Acting Director of Military Intelligence, February 3, 1919, RG 165, MID. This lengthy report, prepared shortly before Cutting left the service, provides the only statement of his military activities during the war. His available private correspondence obviously did not discuss his work and was confined to mentioning his social activities, inquiring about and commenting on affairs at home and little more. The pages discussing his work in military intelligence, unless otherwise noted, are based on this report.

4. Colonel R. H. Van Deman to Brigadier General D. E. Nolan, October 16, 1918, RG 165, MID. Van Deman, a member of the General Staff, was ordered to inquire into the organization and activities of the Military Attache's Office.

5. Edgar H. Wells to Director of Military Intelligence, January 21, 1919, RG 165, MID. In his report, Wells devoted some attention to the social aspects of the assistant military attaché's life in London, something Cutting did not mention in his report.

6. Frederic Bishop to BMC, December 3, 1917, BMC, Box 4.

7. Miguel Antonio Otero, Jr. to BMC, March 23, 1918; Sybil Cutting to BMC, January 31, 1918; and Theodore Roosevelt to BMC, August 10, 1918, BMC, Box 4.

8. Frank Hall to BMC, December 28, 1918 and March 6, 1919, BMC, Box 4. The Cutting file on microfilm in Military Intelligence Division Correspondence lists the dates of Cutting's disengagement from the service and notes the people, including William Phillips of the diplomatic service, who supported his request for a discharge.

9. John H. Dunn to BMC, February 10, 1919, BMC, Box 4. Shortly after his discharge, while in New York City at the family residence on Seventy-second Street, Cutting compiled a two page list of officers, chiefly British but including French, Italian and Serbian officers as well, who had been associ-

ated with him on a friendly basis in London, BMC, Box 12. Cutting's report, which provided the basis for my discussion in this chapter, was routed to officers and civilian employees of the Military Intelligence Division in the Office of the Chief of Staff.

Chapter 9

1. W. C. Reid, "The New Era in New Mexico," Commencement Address at the New Mexico College of Agriculture and Mechanic Arts, State College, New Mexico, June 19, 1919, copy in HOB, Box 8; and Walter V. Woehlke, "The New Day in New Mexico," *Sunset Magazine,* June 1921, pp. 21–24, 54–55.

2. *New York Times,* February 25, 1919. The letter itself was dated February 18, 1919.

3. *New York Times,* March 2, 1919. Cutting's letter was dated February 27, 1919.

4. S. L. H. Slocum to BMC, March 31, 1919, BMC, Box 4. Colonel Slocum was Cutting's superior in the Office of the Military Attache at the American embassy in London.

5. James Wilson to BMC, May 29, 1919; and E. A. Cahoon to BMC, April 18, 1919, BMC, Box 4. Colonel Wilson was superintendent of the military institute; Cahoon was its president. Cutting contributed fifteen thousand dollars to the cost of the building. At the paper, Cutting had to find a replacement for Ralph Henderson, who left for "a salary which I cannot afford to refuse" as advertising manager of the *El Paso Herald.* See Ralph M. Henderson to BMC, May 20, 1919, BMC, Box 4. In addition, difficulties emanating from the lengthy litigation involving Cutting and the *New Mexican* had to be resolved. With the assistance of Herbert Mason, these difficulties, Cutting said, were rapidly disappearing. See BMC to Dearest Mamma, July 21, 1919, BMC, Box 4.

6. BMC to Washington E. Lindsey, April 6, 1919, BMC, Box 4.

7. BMC to Dear Mamma, August 9, 1919, BMC, Box 4. Leonard Wood, August 6 and August 7, 1919, Diary, LW, Box 12.

8. William H. Llewellyn to BMC, August 23, 1919; and George R. Craig to BMC, August 16, 1919, BMC, Box 4. Cutting contributed two hundred dollars to the state committee. Wood's close association with Theodore Roosevelt added to his popularity in New Mexico.

9. M. L. Fox to Albert B. Fall, August 10, 1919, ABF, Box 13.

10. BMC to John T. King, September 4, 1919, BMC, Box 4.

11. BMC to John T. King, September 4, 1919, BMC, Box 4. King reported to Cutting that while Fall was "outspoken in his desire to see Wood nominated," he wanted "the ground looked over very thoroughly" before publicly

committing himself and before the convention instructed delegates for General Wood. In early October, Fall wrote, "I have no candidate I favor over any other at the present time. . . ." See Albert B. Fall to Price McKinney, October 7, 1919, ABF, Box 13. See too, King to BMC, September 19, 1919, BMC, Box 4. R. B. Barnes to Albert B. Fall, November 15, 1919, ABF, Box 13.

12. JCW to OMC, September 19, 1919, BMC, Box 4; and Francis Wilson to BMC, October 7, 1919, BMC, Box 15. Despite a few good months, the *New Mexican* still showed a loss of about eighty-six hundred dollars in 1919. Thus far under Cutting's direction, the paper had never had a profitable year.

13. William S. Benson to BMC, September 18, 1919, BMC, Box 4. Cutting rode in the second car of the parade welcoming the Belgian King to Albuquerque. Brian Boru Dunne to BMC, November 17, 1919 [telegram] and December 14, 1919, BMC, Box 4.

14. Dunne to BMC, December 4, 1919; Endicott Peabody to BMC, December 6, 1919; and Frederic M. Bishop to BMC, February 6, 1920, BMC, Box 4. Octaviano A. Larrazolo to Herbert J. Hagerman, January 1, 1920, copy in BMC, Box 5; and Hagerman to BMC, February 9, 1920, BMC, Box 5.

15. Hagerman to BMC, February 8, 1920, BMC, Box 5.

16. Llewellyn to BMC, March 24, 1920; and "Bibs" Chanler to BMC, two letters, n.d. [1920] one from her city residence, the other from Sweet Briar Farm, Geneseo, New York, BMC, Box 5. Cutting admitted to having a pleasant time at Geneseo. See BMC to Dear Mamma, June 14, 1920, BMC, Box 5.

17. Chanler to BMC, n.d. [1920, Geneseo, New York] BMC, Box 5.

18. Fall to Oliver M. Lee, April 14, 1920, ABF, Box 8. Incidentally, Fall, who did not expect to attend the Republican convention in Chicago in May, considered Harding "practically out of it" and thought the Republicans "absolutely at sea as to who will be their nominee" and unable to agree upon platform and issues. BMC to Dear Mamma, June 14, 1920, BMC, Box 5.

19. BMC to Dear Mamma, June 23, 1920, BMC, Box 5.

20. Thomas P. Gable to Charles Safford, July 22, 1920, ABF, Box 35; William H. Llewellyn to BMC, August 18, August 24 and August 31, 1920, BMC, Box 5. Llewellyn indicated that there was some sentiment among Republicans in Doña Ana County for presenting Cutting as a candidate for lieutenant-governor.

21. Fall to John W. Weeks, September 27, 1920, ABF, Box 42. Weeks was active in managing Harding's campaign out of National Republican Headquarters in New York City. George Curry, former territorial governor, reiterated Fall's statement about Cutting's attacks on boss rule, noting that he had been "especially bitter" in attacking Fall and Holm O. Bursum. See Curry to Fall, September 27, 1920, ABF, Box 17.

22. Fall to Will H. Hays, October 22, 1920, ABF, Box 33. Hays was

chairman of the Republican National Committee. See, too, Llewellyn to BMC, October 23, 1920, BMC, Box 5.

23. Edgar F. Puryear to BMC, n.d. [1920]; and Richard A. Hanna to BMC, November 6, 1920, BMC, Box 5. Curry to Fall, November 6, 1920, ABF, Box 17. Puryear, a Democrat, was seeking reelection as the representative from Chaves County.

24. Natalie Curtis [Mrs. Paul] Burlin to BMC, October 28, 1920, BMC, Box 5. A full discussion of this controversy can be found in Beatrice Chauvenet, *Hewett And Friends: A Biography of Santa Fe's Vibrant Era* (Santa Fe: Museum of New Mexico Press, 1983), pp. 141–46. Chauvenet published Alice Corbin Henderson's letter.

25. Cutting to Burlin, October 29, 1920, BMC, Box 5. A copy of this letter can be found in ELH, Box 8.

26. BMC to Leonard Wood, November 24, 1920, BMC, Box 5, and Clara Olsen to JCW, December 21, 1920, BMC, Box 5.

27. BMC, Notes [1920], BMC, Box 5.

28. Herbert Hoover to BMC, January 10 and January 22, 1921 [telegrams], BMC, Box 17. Hoover's goal was to raise thirty-three million dollars. A gift from John D. Rockefeller and the *Literary Digest* contributed approximately half that amount. BMC to Dear Mamma, January 13, January 24, February 11 and April 2, 1921; and Hoover to BMC, April 11, 1921, BMC, Box 5.

29. BMC to Dear Mamma, February 25, 1921, BMC, Box 5.

30. BMC to Dear Mamma, January 13, 1920 [1921], BMC, Box 5. Fall and other prominent Republicans also were aware that the party was poorly organized. Some leaders made an effort to call the Republican State Central Committee together to help carry out party pledges and to give members some say about patronage appointments, instead of leaving all major matters "to three or four leaders." See Charles Springer to Fall, January 26, 1921, ABF, Box 37. Fall to Emma Fall, February 4, 1921, ABF, Box 7; Fall to Merritt Mechem, February 12, 1921, ABF, Box 27; and Fall to Emma Fall, February 24, 1921 [telegram], ABF, Box 7.

31. Fall to Mechem, February 25, 1921, ABF, Box 27; BMC to Fall, n.d. [February 1921], BMC, Box 12.

32. Mark Thompson to Fall, March 4, 1921, ABF, Box 38; and BMC to Dear Mamma, March 10, 1921, BMC, Box 5.

33. BMC to Dear Mamma, March 22, 1921 and April 2, 1921; Octaviano Larrazolo to BMC, March 15, 1921, BMC, Box 5.

34. Thompson to Fall, August 23, 1921, ABF, Box 38; Fall to H. B. Holt, April 14, 1921, ABF, Box 23; and Larrazolo to BMC, September 1, 1921, BMC, Box 5.

35. Alvina Fall Chase to BMC, September 4 and September 12, 1921, BMC, Box 5. Mrs. Chase reminded Cutting that her family literally took

him in and consoled him at the time of his father's death in 1911. In the second letter, she explained in detail further reasons for her father's distrust of Bursum's integrity.

36. BMC to Dear Mamma, November 22, November 28, December 6, December 12 and December 17, 1921, and January 5, January 14, January 25 and February 5, 1922, BMC, Box 5.

37. Eduardo Otero to Fall, January 29, 1922, ABF, Box 30. BMC to Dear Mamma, May 3, 1922; and Felix Baca to BMC, May 22, June 14 and July 5, 1922, BMC, Box 5.

38. BMC to Carl Magee, May 18, 1922; and BMC to Dear Mamma, June 1 and June 16, 1922, BMC, Box 5. See, too, Fall to M. L. Fox, May 24, 1922, ABF, Box 13. Fox previously owned the *Albuquerque Journal* and, with Fall, had played a role in bringing Magee to New Mexico.

39. BMC to Dear Mamma, July 15, 1922, BMC, Box 5. For an indication of the increasing concern about Secretary Fall, see the article by his devoted friend, Mark Thompson, a Las Cruces lawyer, in the *El Paso Herald,* July 5, 1922. It is interesting to note that Fall, like Cutting, thought that "the women of New Mexico should be recognized in the Republican convention by the nomination for important office of one or more of their number." See Fall to Eduardo Otero, July 20, 1922, ABF, Box 30.

40. Fall to Eduardo Otero, July 20, 1922, ABF, Box 30.

41. *Albuquerque Herald,* August 22, 1922; and *New Mexican,* August 24, 1922. The *Herald* prominently featured Phillips's allegations. The *New Mexican* did the same for Cutting's response. Nine Independents, including Cutting and Larrazolo, attended the conference. Of the nine, six were Hispanic. For another story echoing Phillips's account, see the *Raton Range,* August 25, 1922.

42. Clara Olsen to Emma Fall, September 11, 1922, ABF, Box 7. The Republicans nominated Stephen B. Davis to oppose Andrieus A. Jones for the Senate and another relatively unknown candidate for governor, Dr. E. C. Hill to oppose James Hinkle, a Roswell banker. Nina Otero Warren, a member of the politically powerful Otero family, was opposed by John Morrow.

43. Julian Amador to Dear Sir, July 31, 1922, BMC, Box 5.

Chapter 10

1. American Legion, Department of New Mexico, Report of the Department Historian, April 1919 to August 1920, copy in BMC, Box 5.

2. George I. Sanchez, *Forgotten People* (Albuquerque: University of New Mexico Press, 1940), p. 26; James Baca to Newton D. Baker, October 5, 1917, copy in ABF, Box 14. Baca, New Mexico's adjutant general, commented on the lack of command of English among Hispanic soldiers.

3. BMC to Miguel Antonio Otero, Jr., May 16, 1919, BMC, Box 13. See, too, Miguel Antonio Otero, Jr., to BMC, June 2, 1919, BMC, Box 4 for a report on the progress of Donald Blevins in organizing American Legion posts. Fred B. Humphries to BMC, May 29, 1919 and Dillard Wyatt to BMC, June 10, 1919, discuss organizing efforts in Roswell and eastern New Mexico. Both letters are in BMC, Box 4. BMC to Octaviano A. Larrazolo, Jr., May 16, 1919, BMC, Box 13. Cutting served as acting chairman until October 1919 when the first state convention meeting in Albuquerque selected Herman G. Baca as commander.

4. Report of the Department Historian, April 1919 to August 1920, copy in BMC, Box 5; see Richard Seelye Jones, *A History of the American Legion* (Indianapolis: Bobbs-Merrill Company, 1946), p. 345 for a state breakdown of American Legion membership by five-year periods. A member of the Executive Committee, following the first state convention in October 1919, claimed there were 2,500 dues paying members and that "within two months we are positive that our own membership will reach 3,500 to 4,000." See Edward L. Safford to Albert B. Fall, October 28, 1919, ABF, Box 23.

5. See Herman G. Baca to BMC, February 4 and February 27, 1920, for a discussion of state affairs; Miguel Antonio Otero, Jr. to BMC, March 1, 1920 for an analysis of the Soldiers' Settlement Bill enacted by the state legislature. Both letters are in BMC, Box 5.

6. BMC to J. D. Atwood, March 17, 1920, BMC, Box 13; BMC to Wyatt, n.d. [1920], BMC, Box 5. The mayoralty post Herman G. Baca sought on a nonpartisan ticket carried no salary with it. Baca lost the race. In August 1920, Cutting, through an editorial in the Santa Fe *New Mexican,* criticized the Democrats for giving ex-service men only one place on their ticket, the lone example that I found indicating a possible legion concern in 1920. See BMC to Atwood, August 29, 1920, copy in BMC, Box 5.

7. Members of Pantalion Madrid Post No. 36, Resolutions of Condemnation, n.d., copy in BMC, Box 5; and BMC to Dear Mamma, January 24, 1921, BMC, Box 5.

8. J. W. Chapman to BMC, January 20, 1921, BMC, Box 5; Edwin K. Errett to BMC, March 27, 1920, BMC, Box 13; and BMC to Henry J. Ryan, May 6, 1921, BMC, Box 13. Errett remarked that Cutting was regarded as the "daddy of the New Mexico Legion." Ryan was the National Americanism Chairman.

9. BMC to Ryan, May 6, 1921, BMC, Box 13. That some individuals hoped to use the Legion to pursue "slackers" and draft dodgers is evident from the anonymous letter, "To the Members of the American Legion," a copy of which is located in BMC, Box 5. See, too, BMC to Natalie Curtis Burlin, October 29, 1920, BMC, Box 5.

10. Andrieus A. Jones to BMC, August 27, 1921, BMC, Box 5.

11. Copies of the letters, "A Los Exsoldados de Nuevo Mexico, Santa Fe, N.M., October 14, 1922" and "To the Ex-Service Men and Women of New Mexico, Santa Fe, N.M., October 9, 1922," can be found in BMC, Box 5. Melvin R. Chapin to BMC, October 23, 1922, BMC, Box 5. Chapin, post commander in Las Vegas, congratulated Cutting on the Healy (form) letter, which, he believed, would "do a lot of good." BMC to Dear Mamma, September 29, 1922, BMC, Box 5.

12. Puryear to BMC, October 12, 1922; BMC to Puryear, October 17, 1922; Herman Lindauer to BMC, October 21, 1922; Joseph W. Hodges to BMC, October 17, 1922; Homer Holmes to BMC, October 29, 1922; and BMC to James F. Hinkle, November 27, 1922, BMC, Box 5. Jose Ignacio Garcia to BMC, January, n.d. 1923, BMC, Box 6. A report prepared for Senator Jones after his reelection concluded that the role of ex-servicemen, supervised by Bronson Cutting, was "the most important, if not the deciding factor of the campaign." A copy of the report can be found in BMC, Box 5. See, too, BMC to Dear Mamma, n.d. [posted October 25, 1922], BMC, Box 5. Cutting explained to his mother, "I have been traveling about, and incidentally am in charge of the Jones campaign."

13. Jones received 60,969 votes to 48,721 for Stephen B. Davis, Jr. A canvass of the election returns can be found in the *New Mexico Blue Book* for 1923–1924. BMC to Dear Mamma, November 10, 1922, BMC, Box 5.

14. Bernard S. Rodey to BMC, November 14, 1922; BMC to Ed Tafoya, November 28, 1922; BMC to Thomas McGrath, November 28, 1922; BMC to Healy, December 13, 1922; Felix Baca to BMC, November 28, 1922; and George R. Quesenberry to BMC, December 8, 1922, BMC, Box 5.

15. B. Oxendine to BMC, December 10, 1922; and BMC to Oxendine, December 26, 1922, BMC, Box 5.

16. Cutting's father, William Bayard Cutting, had been a civil service commissioner in the fusion administration of William L. Strong, mayor of New York City, 1895–1899. His uncle, Robert Fulton Cutting, headed the Charity Organization Society and later the Citizens Union, which was prominent in reform politics at the turn of the century. See the discussion in Chapter 2.

17. BMC to Ed Tafoya, November 28, 1922, BMC, Box 9; BMC to Hinkle, November 27, 1922, and BMC to George H. Hunker, November 27, 1922, BMC, Box 5. Hunker was chairman of the Democratic State Central Committee. Three of the four veterans whose names Cutting brought to the attention of the governor and the party chairman were Hispanic.

Chapter 11

1. BMC to Dear Mamma, January 16, 1923; and Louis Esquibel to Cutting, January 19, 1923, BMC, Box 6.

2. BMC to Carl Magee, April 5, 1923, BMC, Box 6.

3. BMC to Miguel Antonio Otero, Jr., April 6, 1923, BMC, Box 6; BMC to Homer Holmes, April 6, 1923; BMC, Box 6; and BMC to Andrieus A. Jones, n.d. [telegram], BMC, Box 18. Cutting recognized that Senator Jones was exhausted "from several months of the 'flu' " and had neither the time nor the energy to attend to the routine of his office work.

4. Holm O. Bursum to A. E. Burkdoll, January 7, 1923, HOB, Box 8.

5. BMC to Dear Mamma, April 22, April 30, May 10, May 20, May 31 and June 10, 1923; and Frederic H. Bishop to OMC, n.d. [December 1923], BMC, Box 6.

6. BMC to Dear Mamma, July 11, 1923, BMC, Box 6.

7. *New Mexican,* July 16, 1923; and Clara Olsen to BMC, July 6, 1923, BMC, Box 6. Olsen wrote from Los Angeles where she had gone after resigning her post as secretary to the governor. BMC to Dear Mamma, July 20, 1923, BMC, Box 6. Leahy, a Republican political leader, was as vindicative and vitriolic as Magee. In attacking Leahy and his "little kingdom" in San Miguel, Magee gained considerable attention and threatened, as Cutting was unable to do in his libel and contempt cases, the already disintegrating "old gang" in the Republican party. For an extended account of this incident, see the front page story in the *St. Louis Post-Dispatch,* July 22, 1923.

8. BMC to Dear Mamma, July 20, 1923, BMC, Box 6. For an indication of the depressing economic conditions in New Mexico, see *New Mexico Tax Bulletin,* April 1924. For example, in 1921 New Mexico had 80 state banks and 47 national banks. On April 1, 1924, the figures were 44 state banks and 30 national banks. In a period of three-and-a-half years, the total resources of all banks in New Mexico decreased from $73 million to $42 million. Cutting advanced the American Legion $1,000 to continue operating and later loaned it additional sums after the bank failure. See the Report of Department Adjutant, July 15, 1924, copy in BMC, Box 13.

9. BMC to Dear Mamma, July 28, 1923; BMC to Olsen, July 29, 1923; and Joseph W. Hodges to BMC, August 4, 1923, BMC, Box 6. Hodges's letter, from Silver City in western New Mexico, suggests the impact of Magee's case in upsetting the political balance.

10. BMC to Dear Mamma, September 10, 1923, BMC, Box 6.

11. BMC to the Chester L. Thompson Post, #23, September 13, 1923, BMC, Box 13. The Chester L. Thompson Post was located at Fort Bayard.

12. Miguel Antonio Otero, Jr. to BMC, October 31, 1923, BMC, Box 6. In this letter Otero mentions a wire from Herman Baca about the Klan. Otero had run the message in the *New Mexican* and several Spanish papers. For the disputes at the American Legion convention, see the brief account in the *New York Times* for October 18, 1923.

13. Miguel Antonio Otero, Jr. to John R. Quinn, November 30, 1923,

BMC, Box 6. Incorporated as part of this letter is BMC to Alvin M. Owsley, September 25, 1923.

14. Miguel Antonio Otero, Jr. to BMC, November 26, 1923, BMC, Box 6. Apparently Cutting contemplated resigning as department commander after John R. Quinn, the national commander, made an appointment that affected the hospital at Fort Bayard and that affronted him. See, too, Herman G. Baca to BMC, November 16, 1923, BMC, Box 7.

15. BMC to Dear Mamma, January 9 and March 3, 1924; and BMC to Martin Biersmith, March 7, 1924, BMC, Box 6.

16. E. E. Young to BMC, April 12, 1924, BMC, Box 6. Young assured Cutting that he was authorized to contact him by "leaders who can deliver the goods."

17. BMC to Dear Mamma, May 21, 1924, BMC, Box 6.

18. BMC to Dear Mamma, May 21, June 11 and June 21, 1924; Juan Vigil to BMC, May 22, 1924; Juan C. Martinez to BMC, July 5, 1924; W. H. Stayton to BMC, May 22, 1924; Octaviano A. Larrazolo, Jr. to BMC, June 18, 1924; and Albert B. Fall to BMC, May 23, 1924 [telegram], BMC, Box 6.

19. BMC to Dear Mamma, June 21 and June 30, 1924, BMC, Box 6.

20. BMC to Thomas H. Barber, March 7, 1924; and William H. Llewellyn, June 21, 1924, BMC, Box 6.

21. Llewellyn to BMC, June 21, 1924; and Judson G. Osburn to BMC, July 9, 1924, BMC, Box 6. Llewellyn assured Cutting that no Republican would be elected in Doña Ana County, while Osborn said that with Cutting to head the Democratic ticket, the party, "with an aggressive campaign," could emerge victorious.

22. BMC to Dear Mamma, July 11, 1924, BMC, Box 6.

23. While precise figures are lacking, it is clear that membership both in New Mexico and the nation declined drastically during the 1920s. Only in 1930 did membership figures in both instances exceed that of 1920. According to American Legion files, the New Mexico membership was 2,557 in 1920, 1,855 in 1925 and 3,943 in 1930. National figures were respectively 843,013, 609,407 and 887,754. See Richard Seelye Jones, *A History of the American Legion* (Bobbs-Merrill: Indianapolis, 1946), p. 345. The chart on this page breaks down membership by states.

24. BMC, Notes, American Legion, n.d. [July 1924], BMC, Box 82; and Report of Miguel Antonio Otero, Jr., Department Adjutant, July 15, 1924, BMC, Box 13.

25. BMC to Dear Mamma, August 4 and August 24, 1924; and William Felter to BMC, August 25, 1924, BMC, Box 6.

26. Hanford MacNider to BMC, August 30, 1924; and Cutting to Mac-Nider, August 31, 1924. Copies of these telegrams are found in BMC,

Box 13, and in HMN, Republican Service League Files. MacNider thought Cutting was a bit hasty in his conclusions and that nothing could be done by objecting outside of "party counsels." Moreover, he resented Cutting's questioning his devotion to the "serviceman's cause." See MacNider to Cutting, September 1, 1924 in the MacNider Papers. Cutting explained his position more fully in a later letter to Theodore Roosevelt, Jr. See Cutting to Roosevelt, September 22, 1924, BMC, Box 13.

27. J. M. Luhan to BMC, September 1 and September 10, 1924; Camilo Padila to BMC, September 8, 1924; Jefferson D. Atwood to BMC, September 9, 1924; JCW to OMC, September 11 and September 15, 1924, BMC, Box 6. In Cutting's home precinct, two old, blind musicians who had played for a party at Los Siete Burros canvassed the neighborhood on his behalf, unbeknownst to any of his friends prior to the primaries.

28. JCW to OMC, September 15 and September 18, 1924; and M. R. Salazar to BMC, September 17, 1924, BMC, Box 6.

29. BMC to Dear Mamma, September 19, 1924; and Felter to BMC, September 20 and September 24, 1924, BMC, Box 6.

30. The New Mexico file of the Republican Service League in the Hanford MacNider Papers delineates its efforts during the campaign. For evidence that Progressives looked to Cutting as one of their leaders, see Aurora Lucero White to BMC, October 29, 1924, BMC, Box 6.

31. The results of the election can be examined in the *New Mexico Blue Book* for 1925–1926. Holm O. Bursum to Austin D. Crile, November 20, 1924; Bursum to James G. McNary, November 20, 1924; and Bursum to A. B. Renehan, December 26, 1924, HOB, Box 16. The brief quote is from Isabel Lancaster Eckles to Franklin D. Roosevelt, December 20, 1924, FDR, Group 11, Box 9. Eckles was the state superintendent of education.

32. Miguel Antonio Otero, Jr. to BMC, November 19, 1924, Box 6.

Chapter 12

1. Harvey Fergusson, "Out Where Bureaucracy Begins," *The Nation,* July 22, 1925, p. 112. Fergusson's article examined the role of federal agencies in New Mexico.

2. Thomas Mott Osborne, *Society and Prisons: Some Suggestions For A New Penology* (Montclair, New Jersey: Patterson Smith, 1975), *passim*. This volume, first published in 1916, presents Osborne's views clearly and concisely. See, too, Osborne to BMC, May 8, 1925, BMC, Box 6.

3. Osborne to BMC, May 8, 1925; and BMC to Dear Mamma, May 20, 1925, BMC, Box 6.

4. BMC to Dear Mamma, May 20 and June 11, 1925, BMC, Box 6. From February 13, 1926, following Justiano Baca's death, through May, the *New*

Mexican ran stories and editorials about the situation in the land office. See, for example, the issues of February 13, April 4, May 8, May 15 and May 30, 1925.

5. BMC to Dear Mamma, June 11, 1925, BMC, Box 6. With Magee blasting Cutting in his columns, a friend ironically reminded Cutting that during the 1924 nominating convention, Magee told his friends to support Cutting for governor. See J. D. Atwood to BMC, June 24, 1925, BMC, Box 6. Atwood was a Roswell attorney, a veteran, a former district commander of the American Legion in New Mexico and a prominent Democrat. He would become a close confidant to Cutting.

6. BMC to Osborne, July 1, 1925, BMC, Box 13. For a statement of Cutting's views on prisons, similar to those of Thomas Mott Osborne, see his comments on "Penal Reform," drafts of two speeches, n.d. [1925–1927], BMC, Boxes 13 and 82. Besides being familiar with Osborne's views, Cutting had examined those of Frank Tannenbaum as expressed in *Wall Shadows* (New York: G. P. Putnam's Sons, 1922). In 1929 Cutting contributed five hundred dollars to the National Society of Penal Prevention.

7. Arthur T. Hannett to BMC, July 7, 1925, BMC, Box 13. At this time, the *New Mexican* was also attacking Carl Magee as a Klan defender. See stories in the issues of July 6, July 7 and July 9, 1925. The theme of much of the *New Mexican*'s columns was "the salvation of the Democratic party from Carl Magee."

8. BMC to Hannett, July 10, 1925, BMC, Box 13. The main correspondence between Hannett and Cutting on this issue was published in the *New Mexican* on July 15, 1925. BMC to Dear Mamma, July 21, 1925, BMC, Box 6.

9. BMC to Carl C. Magee, n.d. [July 1925], BMC, Box 11. BMC to Dear Mamma, July 10, 1925, BMC, Box 6.

10. BMC to Dear Mamma, July 10, 1925, BMC, Box 6. Hannett to BMC, July 14 and July 18, 1925; and BMC to Hannett, July 16 and July 20, 1925, BMC, Box 13. On July 17, 1925, the *New Mexican* printed the entire correspondence to that time.

11. BMC to Osborne, July 21, 1925, BMC, Box 13; and BMC to Dear Mamma, July 21, 1925, BMC, Box 6.

12. BMC to Dear Mamma, July 21 and August 20, 1925, BMC, Box 6.

13. BMC to Hannett, July 22, 1925, BMC, Box 13; and BMC to Dear Mamma, August 20, 1925, BMC, Box 6.

14. BMC to Dear Mamma, July 28, 1925, BMC, Box 6. This letter was posted from Ojo Caliente, an unincorporated community along the banks of the Vallecitos River in both Taos and Rio Arriba counties. In August, he returned to Taos County "at a place called El Lano" to attend the wedding of Max Fernandez, the Republican boss of Taos. Cutting was "Padrino," which

he translated as Best Man. See BMC to Dear Mamma, August 20, 1925, BMC, Box 6.

15. BMC to Dear Mamma, August 7, 1925; and BMC to Carl Magee, August 19, 1925, BMC, Box 6. See, too, Magee's column in the *New Mexico State Tribune* for August 20, 1925. For an indication of how Magee's support of Democratic bosses was alienating longtime Democratic voters in San Miguel County, see Frank N. Page to BMC, August 22, 1925, BMC, Box 6. After leaving New Mexico for Oklahoma, Magee found both fame and fortune as the inventor and developer of the parking meter. After his departure, the name of his paper was changed from the *New Mexico State Tribune* to the *Albuquerque Tribune*.

16. BMC to Octaviano Manzanares, August 16, 1925, BMC, Box 6. Luis Martinez to Arthur Seligman, January 6, 1926, copy in BMC, Box 6; and BMC to Martinez, January 9, 1926, BMC, Box 6. Martinez edited *La Victoria,* a Spanish weekly in Raton.

17. BMC to Hannett, September 26, 1925, BMC, Box 6. In the 1980s, the prison system in New Mexico still ranked as one of the poorest in the nation.

18. Seligman to BMC, November 12, 1925; and BMC to Dear Mamma, December 28, 1925, BMC, Box 6.

19. BMC to Dear Mamma, January 18 and February 4, 1926; Frank Darrow to BMC, February 10, 1926; BMC to Darrow, February 17, 1926; and BMC to J. M. Lujan, February 28, 1926, BMC, Box 6.

20. BMC to Lujan, February 28, 1926; Dunne to OMC, March 20, 1926; and BMC to Dear Mamma, BMC, Box 6.

21. Jacob H. Crist to Mr. ———, March 30, 1925 [a form letter], copy in BMC, Box 6. Crist was a Democratic member of the 1910 Constitutional Convention.

22. H. H. Dorman to OMC, April 4, 1926, BMC, Box 6.

23. BMC to Dear Mamma, May 3, June 4, July 2, July 5, July 14, July 24 and August 22, 1926, BMC, Box 6. BMC to Darrow, September 24, 1926, BMC, Box 6; and Resolution of the Montoya y Montoya Post No. 1, November 8, 1926, BMC, Box 13.

24. BMC to U. S. Bateman, April 24, 1926; BMC to Dear Mamma, June 24 and July 5, 1926; and Seligman to Bateman, August 5, 1926, copy in BMC, Box 6.

25. John Morrow to BMC, September 8, 1926; and BMC to J. P. Maes, September 16, 1926, BMC, Box 6.

26. BMC to Maes, September 16, 1926, BMC, Box 6.

27. Seligman to BMC, September 24, 1926, BMC, Box 6. At this time, Seligman was a member of the Democratic National Committee.

28. See *Albuquerque Journal,* October 10, 1926 for an account of the independent gathering.

29. BMC to Dear Mamma, October 12, 1926; and Severino Trujillo, Jr. to BMC, October 15, 1926, BMC, Box 6.

30. Luis Martinez to BMC, October 18, 1926, BMC, Box 6. During the campaign, Cutting assisted many local and state candidates, not all of whom were Hispanic.

31. Holm Bursum to BMC, October 26, 1926, BMC, Box 6.

32. George Curry to BMC, November 4, 1926; Carl P. Dunifon to BMC, November 5, 1926; and Will Robinson to BMC, n.d. [November 1926], BMC, Box 6. *Albuquerque Tribune,* November 6, 1926. Incidentally, the *Tribune,* under Magee's direction, was losing money and attracting the attention of the publisher and owner of the Scripps-Howard chain. See Roy W. Howard to Magee, March 2, 1927, RWH, Box 12.

33. BMC to Dear Mamma, November 20, 1926, BMC, Box 6.

34. BMC to Dear Mamma, December 1 and December 8, 1926; and Bursum to BMC, December 12, 1926, BMC, Box 6. The meeting with Governor Lowden, owing to his travel plans, was never arranged. BMC to Dear Mamma, February 5, 1927, BMC, Box 7.

35. Martinez to BMC, February 18, 1927, BMC, Box 7.

36. C. A. Smith to BMC, March 19, 1927, BMC, Box 6; and A. E. White to BMC, March 23, 1927, BMC, Box 7. See, too, Ira G. Clark, *Water in New Mexico* (Albuquerque: University of New Mexico Press, 1987), pp. 209–10 for a discussion of the concern about Indian pueblos. BMC to Dear Mamma, March 30 and May 9, 1927, BMC, Box 7. See *Albuquerque Journal,* April 22, 1927, for an example of a column by former governor Hannett. *The Southwestern Dispatch,* a semiweekly published in Roswell, defended Cutting against Hannett's charges. See, for example, the issues of April 22 and June 14, 1927.

37. BMC to Dear Mamma, May 9, 1927; and Herman Baca to BMC, August 2, 1927, BMC, Box 7. It is not clear whether the figures Baca cited for 1927 were renewals of membership or new members.

38. BMC to Dear Mamma, September 4, September 13, September 21 and October 4, 1927, BMC, Box 7. For an account of the Paris convention of the American Legion, see Richard Seelye Jones, *A History of The American Legion* (Indianapolis: Bobbs-Merrill, 1946), pp. 300–302.

39. BMC to Dear Mamma, November 20, December 5 and December 12, 1927; BMC to J. D. Kavanaugh and Max Trujillo, December 23, 1927; J. S. Baca to BMC, December 14, 1927; and BMC to Dearest Mother, December 22, 1927, BMC, Box 7.

40. BMC to Dearest Mother, December 22, 1927, BMC, Box 7.

41. J. D. Atwood to Richard C. Dillon, December 24, 1927; and Dunne to OMC, December 19, 1927 [telegram], BMC, Box 7. See *New Mexican,* December 29, 1927, for Governor Dillon's statement. BMC to Atwood,

December 31, 1927, BMC, Box 7. Before departing for Washington, Cutting attended a banquet in his honor in Las Vegas. On December 30, 1927, a *Brooklyn Eagle* editorial commented on his New York background, including the fact that he was still "a director of the First National Bank of Manhattan and of several New York Corporations." The editorial also noted that in New Mexico, he had supported four Democrats and two Republicans for governor.

Chapter 13

1. Olivia Murray Cutting received letters of congratulations from, among others, Corrine Roosevelt Robinson, Colonel Edward M. House, and Anna Roosevelt Cowles. All are in BMC, Box 7.

2. "New Mexico's New Senator," *Literary Digest,* January 14, 1928, p. 11; "Cutting, of New Mexico" and "Colonel Cutting's Critics," *The Outlook,* January 11, 1928, pp. 55–56; "The Spoiled Child," by The Gentleman At the Keyhole, *Colliers,* February 18, 1928, p. 32; and J. M. Hervey to Richard C. Dillon, January 17, 1928, RCD, Box 12.

3. W. B. to David A. Reed, January 2, 1928, BMC, Box 7. Senator Reed of Pennsylvania forwarded his copy to Cutting. After the 1928 election, Cutting was located in suite 233 of the Senate Office Building.

4. Hervey to Dillon, January 7 and January 17, 1928, RCD, Box 12.

5. *Congressional Record,* 70th Congress, 1st Session, January 19, 1928, pp. 1707–8, 1710. For a comprehensive discussion, see Carroll H. Woody, *The Case of Frank L. Smith* (Chicago: University of Chicago Press, 1931). Smith resolved the entire matter by resigning his challenged seat on February 9, 1928.

6. Cutting actually introduced a resolution giving Congress the power to limit the expenditures of candidates for both the House and Senate. See BMC to Edward L. Manson, January 27, 1928, BMC, Box 7. The joint resolutions submitted by Cutting died in committee.

7. Charles G. Dawes to Dillon, January 24, 1928, copy in BMC, Box 7; Herman Baca to OMC, January 20, 1928, BMC, Box 7; and BMC to Clara Olsen, January 26, 1928, BMC, Box 36.

8. Emma Fall to BMC, January 28, 1928; Alice Massey to OMC, January 28, 1928; and BMC to Mrs. C. E. Mason, January 30, 1928, BMC, Box 7. BMC to Olsen, February 2, 1928, BMC, Box 36.

9. BMC to Olsen, February 2, 1928, BMC, Box 36; and BMC to Jose G. Rivera, February 3, 1928, BMC, Box 7.

10. George W. Martin to OMC, February 6, 1928; Martin to BMC, n.d., BMC, Box 7. The Henry (Harry) James referred to in the quote was the son of William James. He was briefly married to Cutting's younger sister, Olivia.

Walter Lippmann, who was in the same class as Cutting at Harvard, had promised to attend the gathering, but it is not clear whether he was on hand. See Herman G. Baca to BMC, February 28, 1928, BMC, Box 7.

11. Burl Noggle, *Teapot Dome: Oil and Politics in the 1920's* (Baton Rouge: Louisiana State University Press, 1962), pp. 176–99.

12. BMC to Olsen, February 13, 1928, BMC, Box 36; and John D. Rockefeller, Jr. to BMC, February 17, 1928, BMC, Box 7. Rockefeller later led the successful fight to oust Stewart from the chairmanship of the board of directors of the Standard Oil Company of Indiana. For his role in this matter, see Raymond B. Fosdick, *John D. Rockefeller, Jr.: A Portrait* (New York: Harper and Brothers, 1956), pp. 229–47. Fosdick makes the point that the Rockefellers by themselves did not have a controlling interest in Standard Oil of Indiana.

13. BMC to R. Fulton Cutting, March 21, 1928, BMC, Box 7; and *New York Times,* March 18, 1928. The *Times* listed Cutting's contribution at one thousand dollars. BMC to William E. Borah, August 20, 1928, WEB, Box 703, as noted in Noggle, *Teapot Dome,* p. 195.

14. Ira G. Clark, *Water in New Mexico* (Albuquerque: University of New Mexico Press, 1987), pp. 209–12.

15. BMC to Olsen, February 15, 1928, BMC, Box 36.

16. *Congressional Record,* 70th Congress, First Session, March 1, 1928, pp. 3850–53. Kyle S. Crichton, *Law and Order, Ltd: The Rousing Life of Elfego Baca of New Mexico* (1928; reprint New York: Arno Press, 1974), pp. 213–16. Crichton suggests that Baca, through his long-standing friendship with Senator Charles Curtis, the majority leader, was instrumental in getting Curtis to support the measure and to seek presidential approval of it.

17. See BMC to Dillon, March 6, 1928, RCD, Box 12 for an example of Cutting seeking Dillon's advice on a bill authorizing the secretary of the interior to purchase land that would be subject to state taxation for the Navajos in Arizona and New Mexico. Herman G. Baca to BMC, February 17 and February 27, 1928, BMC, Box 7.

18. BMC to Olsen, February 13, 1928, BMC, Box 36; and H. H. Dorman to BMC, February 19, 1928, BMC, Box 7. Dorman informed Cutting that Zimmerman had recently spoken at the Presbyterian Church in Santa Fe against the proposed museum on the grounds that the institutions already functioning did the same anthropological work.

19. E. Dana Johnson to BMC, February 28, 1928; Herman G. Baca to BMC, February 27, 1928, BMC, Box 7; Francis C. Wilson to Alfred V. Kidder, February 23, 1928, copy in BMC, Box 36; BMC to Olsen, March 7 and March 31, 1928, BMC, Box 36; BMC to Dear Mamma, January 7, 1929; and Kidder to BMC, January 11, 1929, BMC, Box 8. Kidder and Cutting knew one another at Harvard College. Kidder, chairman of the board of the

Museum and Laboratory of Anthropology, maintained his post in the Department of American Archaeology at Phillips Academy until the new facility was constructed.

20. *Congressional Record,* 70th Congress, First Session, March 15, 1928, pp. 4823–24. This measure, S777, was approved by Congress and became law over a presidential veto. See, too, ibid. April 8, 1928, p. 6056.

21. BMC to Miguel Antonio Otero, February 29, 1928, MAO, Box 3. Olsen to BMC, March 11, 1928; and BMC to Olsen, March 22, 1928, BMC, Box 36. Olsen to BMC, March 29, 1928, BMC, Box 7.

22. Herman G. Baca to BMC, March 30, 1928, BMC, Box 7.

23. BMC to Olsen, March 31, 1928, BMC, Box 36; and BMC to Dillon, April 5, 1928, BMC, Box 7.

24. Paul W. Garrett to BMC, April 18, 1928; Helen Keller to BMC, April 6, 1928; and BMC to E. Dana Johnson, June 8, 1928, BMC, Box 7; BMC to Charles H. Burke, April 21, 1928, BMC, Box 32.

25. Press Release, May 10, 1928, copy in BMC, Box 22. *Congressional Record,* 70th Congress, First Session, May 11, 1928, pp. 8372–73, 8375–78.

26. *Congressional Record,* 70th Congress, First Session, May 11, 1928, pp. 8374–75. Lynn Haines, the editor of *Searchlight on Congress,* advised Cutting as he prepared his bills. Haines to BMC, March 26, April 3 and April 6, 1928, BMC, Box 22.

27. Gifford Pinchot to George W. Norris, May 24, 1928, copy in RCD, Box 12; Norris to Pinchot, May 25, 1928, copy in BMC, Box 22; and John H. Gray to Norris, October 18, 1928, copy in BMC, Box 22.

28. BMC to Olsen, May 22, 1928, BMC, Box 36; and Herman G. Baca to BMC, May 22, 1928, BMC, Box 7.

29. BMC to H. H. Dorman, June 12, 1928; Severino Trujillo to BMC, June 14, 1928; and Herman G. Baca to BMC, June 13, 1928, BMC, Box 7. OMC, 1928 Calendar, BMC, Box 92.

30. Richard Hogue to Edward Keating, June 6, 1928, copy in BMC, Box 22.

31. BMC to Dear Mother, n.d., July 17 and July 31, 1928, BMC, Box 7.

32. BMC to Josephine Foster, July 7, 1928; and Herbert Hoover to BMC, June 19, 1928, BMC, Box 7.

33. BMC to Dear Mamma, July 31, 1928, BMC, Box 7. *Albuquerque Tribune,* July 28, 1928. For an indication of "Old Guard" sentiment against Cutting, see H. B. Hensley to Holm O. Bursum, August 1, 1928, HOB, Box 18.

34. Juan E. Vigil to BMC, July 22, 1928; and Edgar Puryear to Florence Dromey, July 28, 1928, BMC, Box 7.

35. BMC to Dear Mamma, August 15 and August 26, 1928, BMC, Box 7. Charles G. Dawes, *Notes as Vice President* (Boston: Little Brown and Company, 1935), p. 94.

36. BMC to Hanford MacNider, September 4, 1928; and J. H. Toulouse to MacNider, September 9, 1928, HMN, Republican Service League File, 1928, New Mexico.

37. Jouett Fall to BMC, n.d., BMC, Box 12.

38. T. M. Pepperday to BMC, September 13, 1928, BMC, Box 7. The characterization of Cutting's opponent, J. S. Vaught, is from Toulouse to MacNider, September 9, 1928, HMN, Republican Service League File, 1928, New Mexico. For another view of T. M. Pepperday and the *Albuquerque Journal,* see Kyle S. Crichton to Howard, November 18, 1928, RWH, Box 22.

39. Puryear to Dromey, September 15, 1928, BMC, Box 7; and BMC to MacNider, September 19, 1928, HMN, Republican Service League File, 1928, New Mexico.

40. Arthur J. Lovell, et al., to Chief Executives, 21 Standard Railroad Labor Organizations, September 21, 1928 [copy]; Mercer G. Johnston to Puryear, September 27, 1928; and Puryear to BMC, September 30, 1928, BMC, Box 7. Cutting claimed that he neither saw nor approved the editorials in question and that he exercised no supervision over editorials in the *New Mexican.*

41. BMC to Dear Mother, October 5, 1928, BMC, Box 7; Toulouse to MacNider, September 6, September 14 and September 21, 1928, HMN, Republican Service League File, 1928, New Mexico. The quote is from the September 14 letter; the bracketed phrase is from a September 6 letter.

42. Cutting to Dear Mother, October 5, 1928; and BMC to William E. Borah, n.d. [telegram], BMC, Box 7. Puryear to Herman G. Baca, October 6, October 16 and October 30, 1928 [all telegrams]; and J. D. Atwood, et al., to Apreciable Companero, October 25, 1928, BMC, Box 24. The last item, a letter that went to all Hispanic veterans, on its reverse side contained the same message in English.

43. An outline of his remarks at Santa Rosa on October 12, 1928 and at the American Legion Convention, n.d., is available in BMC, Box 82.

44. James A. Murray to C. J. Roberts, October 22, 1928, copy in BMC, Box 24; and Etienne de P. Bujac to Puryear, October 24, 1928, BMC, Box 24. The letter from Bujac indicated Cutting's constructive contributions to the welfare of people in New Mexico and insisted that he was "in no manner prodigal or profligate." See, too, Clinton P. Anderson to Democratic State Chairman, November 3, 1928, copy in BMC, Box 7. Anderson, the Democratic State Chairman, requested information about people in their precincts who seemed "to be working exclusively for Bronson Cutting."

45. Jouett Fall to BMC, n.d., BMC, Box 12.

46. Brian Boru Dunne to OMC, October 23, 1928; and Herbert Hoover to BMC, October 25, 1928, BMC, Box 7.

47. BMC to Dear Mamma, October 27 and November 6, 1928; and Dunne to OMC, October 23, 1928, BMC, Box 7.

48. BMC to Dear Mamma, November 10 and November 15, 1928, BMC, Box 7. Only Hoover ran better than Cutting, by about twenty-five hundred votes. Hoover missed a clean sweep of all the counties in New Mexico. He lost De Baca County by about thirty-five votes. See Cutting to Hoover, November 22, 1928, CAT, Box 19, Herbert Hoover Presidential Library. Among the other victors on the Republican ticket was Miguel Antonio Otero, Jr., elected attorney general by over eleven thousand votes. Incidentally, Cutting polled 68,070 votes to 49,913 for J. S. Vaught.

49. BMC to James E. Watson, November 22, 1928; Watson to BMC, December 1, 1928 [telegram]; BMC to George H. Moses, November 22, 1928; and BMC to Charles L. McNary, November 22, 1928, BMC, Box 24. Cutting wrote to thank McNary, a Republican senator from Oregon, for his "very generous statement of endorsement."

50. BMC to Dearest Mother, December 9 and December 28, 1928; and Manuel Gamio to BMC, December 10, 1928, BMC, Box 7. H. H. Dorman and Brian Boru Dunne accompanied Cutting to Mexico.

51. BMC to Dear Mamma, December 28 and December 30, 1928, BMC, Box 7. Larrazolo retained Cutting's staff. Severino Trujillo, Jr. reported at the end of December that although the mail was not very heavy, Cutting was receiving about twice as much as Senator Larrazolo. See Severino Trujillo, Jr. to BMC, December 19, 1928, BMC, Box 7.

Chapter 14

1. BMC to Dear Mamma, January 3, 1929, BMC, Box 8.

2. BMC to Dear Mamma, January 7, January 12 and January 16, 1929, BMC, Box 8. At this time, Cutting wrote to the president-elect, strongly endorsing the selection of "Colonel William Donovan as Attorney General." See BMC to Herbert Hoover, January 25, 1929 [telegram], CAT, Cabinet Appointments, Box 85. In addition, Cutting was concerned about the proposed abandonment of Fort Bayard as a military hospital and its use as a garrison post. See Frank T. Hines to BMC, January 26, 1929, BMC, Box 8; and Frederick Villio, et al., to BMC, February 12, 1929, BMC, Box 41.

3. BMC to Dear Mamma, February 2, 1929, BMC, Box 8; and *New Mexican,* February 13, 1929.

4. *New Mexican,* February 13, 1929. Bulletin Matter, Add Senate Santa Fe, n.d. [February 1929], EDJ, File 19, Box 418.

5. BMC to Dear Mamma, February 17, 1929, BMC, Box 8.

6. BMC to Dear Mamma, February 28, 1929, BMC, Box 8; Dan Kelley to Edward Keating, March 9, 1928 [telegram, copy], BMC, Box 8; and F. M. Chacon to BMC, March 27, 1929, BMC, Box 9. Kelley, a union official, informed Keating of Cutting's "great fight." Keating, the editor of *Labor,*

carried the news to members throughout the country. Chacon, who spoke against Cutting during the campaign, wrote to express his admiration for his "courageous stand" in "the interests of the people" and to announce his conversion to Cutting's leadership as a "true friend of the Spanish-Americans of this state." At the time of this fight, Cutting was assisting T. M. Pepperday in purchasing the *Albuquerque Journal,* thereby assuring the presence of a progressive Republican newspaper in the state's largest city. Cutting contributed twenty-five thousand dollars to assist Pepperday and agreed to furnish additional funds as needed. See J. D. Atwood to T. M. Pepperday, February 11, 1929, BMC, Box 33.

7. BMC to Dear Mamma, March 10 and March 20, 1929; and BMC to O. Ulivarri, March 20, 1929, BMC, Box 8. Hugh Russell Fraser, "Cutting In New Mexico: A Study In Courage," BMC, Box 92. This unpaginated typescript, relating aspects of Cutting's career, is informed by the comments of Cutting associates. An incomplete account, it utilizes purported conversations, but it does contain information and insights not available elsewhere [hereafter cited as Fraser-Cutting]. A slightly different version of Cutting's resignation is presented in Vorley Michael Rexroad, "The Two Administrations of Governor Richard C. Dillon," (M.A. thesis, University of New Mexico, 1947). It involves Cutting, who "had been drinking rather heavily," suggesting to Dillon at a meeting in Cutting's home that "he had a notion to resign" and then tendering his resignation through a "political henchman" who brought it to the governor. The next day the henchman inquired if Dillon intended to accept the resignation; if not, Cutting wanted it returned. At this point, a conference between the two men was arranged. Rexroad, who interviewed Dillon and several legislators at that time, does not mention the role of Clara Olsen. However, he does present an excellent discussion of the legislative situation and the pressures on Dillon to break the deadlock, pp. 112–131.

8. Herman Baca to BMC, April 10, 1929 [telegram]; Luis Martinez to BMC, April 21, 1929; BMC to Dana Johnson, April 22, 1929; and BMC to Earl Bowditch, April 18, 1929, BMC, Box 8. Arthur Seligman to Reed Smoot, et al., February 20, 1929, BMC, Box 36; and *Congressional Record,* 70th Congress, 2nd Session, January 28, 1929, p. 2311. BMC to Miguel Antonio Otero, Jr., April 24, 1929, BMC, Box 8. Cutting's staff consisted of Edgar Puryear, Mildred Dromey, Severino Trujillo, Jr. and Lola Martin. While still in Santa Fe in February, Cutting joined the National Press Club.

9. Clara H. Olsen to BMC, April 16, 1929, BMC, Box 36; BMC to Olsen, April 24 and May 22, 1929, BMC, Box 36; Camilo Padilla to BMC, May 6, 1929, BMC, Box 9; E. L. Safford to BMC, May 3 and May 20, 1929, BMC, Box 8; and Hugh H. Williams to BMC, et al., May 4, 1929, BMC, Box 8. Williams, chairman of the State Corporation Commission, was concerned

Notes to pages 157–59

about a measure introduced by Senator Carl Hayden that would allow rail carriers to avoid the long and short haul rule of the Interstate Commerce Act by using water competition as a pretext. See, too, BMC to J. Tom Dannel, June 8, 1929, BMC, Box 30 wherein Cutting suggests that he will introduce a measure providing for group life insurance for federal employees at the Indian schools.

10. See, for example, BMC to Olsen, June 4 and June 10, 1929, BMC, Box 36; and Miguel Antonio Otero, Jr. to BMC, May 22, 1929, BMC, Box 8.

11. *New Mexican,* April 24, 1929.

12. *Congressional Record,* 71st Congress, 1st Session, June 11, 1929, p. 2641; BMC to Johnson, June 12, 1929, BMC, Box 8; and BMC to Olsen, June 18, 1929, BMC, Box 36. Francis C. Wilson, a member of the New Mexico delegation to the conference held at Colorado Springs, held a more positive view of the proceedings. See Wilson to BMC, June 14, 1929, FCW.

13. OMC, 1929 Itinerary, BMC, Box 92. The itinerary provides dates of their travels and where Cutting resided.

14. BMC to Robert M. La Follette, Jr., June 4, 1929; and La Follette, Jr. to BMC, July 2, 1929, BMC, Box 8. As chairman of the Committee on Manufactures, La Follette, like his father during the Payne-Aldrich tariff debates in 1909, assigned "various important schedules in the tariff bill for study." Because he had no opportunity to ascertain Cutting's preference, he tentatively allotted him the sundries schedule for study during the recess. Incidentally, La Follette, while appreciating Cutting's invitation, decided, because of other committee business, to spend whatever free time he had resting and vacationing in Wisconsin.

15. BMC to Dear Mother, July 4, 1929, BMC, Box 8. For a discussion of Cutting's bill, S1501, see Wilson to BMC, June 20, 1929 and BMC to Wilson, October 26, 1929 [telegram]. The telegram contained the provisions of S1501 authorizing congressional approval of and appropriations for the Rio Grande Compact. The funds allocated would be for the construction of a drainage channel. The bill never got out of committee. The items are in FCW. See, too, Ira G. Clark, *Water In New Mexico* (Albuquerque: University of New Mexico Press, 1987), p. 218. Clark notes that the compact was a stopgap measure so that the parties involved could better determine the flow of the Rio Grande and consequently the best sites for drainage channels and reservoirs.

16. BMC to Dear Mother, July 12, July 13 and July 22, 1929; and Alejandro Padilla to BMC, July 8, 1929, BMC, Box 8.

17. Mary Austin to BMC, May 19, July 13 and November 3, 1928; and BMC to Austin, July 7, 1928, BMC, Box 7. Mary Austin to BMC, July 19, 1929; BMC to Austin, July 23, 1929; and BMC to Dear Mother, July 21, 1929, BMC, Box 8. See, too, Austin to BMC, August 19, 1929, BMC, Box 8; and BMC to Austin, August 28, 1929, MA, Box 7 wherein Cutting

contributed to a Spanish arts competition and also agreed to donate a thousand dollars for a drama festival. However, he insisted that he did not want his contributions publicized.

18. BMC to Dear Mother, August 22 and August 30, 1929, BMC, Box 8. Later, he spent several hours at the dying bedside of Lola Armijo, Tony Luna's mother and the daughter of a prominent Democratic politician, who, as sheriff of Santa Fe County, was assassinated in 1892. See BMC to Dear Mother, September 12, 1929, BMC, Box 8.

19. BMC to Dear Mother, August 30 and September 12, 1929 and BMC to Edgar Puryear, August 15, 1929 [telegram], BMC, Box 8; BMC to Puryear, August 14, 1929, BMC, Box 7. For further indication of Dillon's disagreement with Springer, see Herman Baca to BMC, October 5, 1929 and Miguel Antonio Otero to BMC, October 5, 1929, BMC, Box 8. Otero remarked, "The general opinion seems to be that Dillon is in with Springer and the real fight is 'Cutting vs Springer.'"

20. BMC to Miguel Antonio Otero, October 22, 1929, BMC, Box 8; and Clarence Iden to Richard C. Dillon, RCD, Box 12.

21. *Washington Post,* July 29, 1929, and *Philadelphia Public Ledger,* July 29, 1929. Witter Bynner to BMC, August 5, 1929, BMC, Box 8. Bynner's letter provides an example of the favorable response in the arts community to his statement.

22. *Congressional Record,* 71st Congress, 1st Session, October 10 and October 11, 1929, pp. 4433–39, 4445–61, and 4472 for the final vote.

23. J. E. Hardyman to BMC, October 14, 1929; BMC to Edward L. Safford, October 30, 1929; and Jesus Baca to BMC, October 31, 1929, BMC, Box 8. Jesus Baca, a close friend and associate, active in both legion affairs and Santa Fe politics, informed Cutting of recent political developments. See, too, BMC to Miguel Antonio Otero, November 5, 1929, MAO, Box 3.

24. BMC to Safford, November 5, 1929, BMC, Box 5; BMC to R. Fulton Cutting, November 8, 1929, BMC, Box 41; and BMC to Dillon, November 21, 1929 [telegram], RCD, Box 12. During these tedious tariff discussions, Cutting sent a five-hundred-dollar check to the National Society of Penal Prevention to help prepare a Handbook of Prisons and agreed to speak at a meeting of the society. See BMC to P. W. Garrett, November 5, 1929, BMC, Box 13.

25. *Congressional Record,* 71st Congress, 1st Session, November 2, 1929, pp. 5105–6. See, too, David Hodges Stratton, *Albert Fall and the Teapot Dome Affair* (University Microfilms; University of Colorado, 1955), Ph.D. diss., pp. 468–69. Heflin did not enter the Senate until December 1920.

26. BMC to Wilson, November 18, 1929 [telegram], FCW.

27. Wilson to BMC, November 20 [two letters] and November 21, 1929, FCW.

28. Mary Austin to BMC, December 9, 1929, BMC, Box 8. See, also, note 17.

29. BMC to Austin, December 16, 1929, BMC, Box 8; and BMC to Austin, February 1, 1930 [?] [telegram], MA, Box 7.

30. *Congressional Record,* 71st Congress, 2nd Session, December 6, 1929, pp. 190–91 and December 12, 1929, pp. 526–27.

31. *Congressional Record,* 71st Congress, 2nd Session, December 10, 1929, p. 344; and BMC to Miguel Antonio Otero, December 13, 1929, MAO, Box 3.

32. BMC to Dear Mother, December 30, 1929, BMC, Box 8.

33. Clyde Tingley to Franklin D. Roosevelt, November 30, 1929; and R. H. Carter to Roosevelt, December 7, 1929, FDR, Franklin D. Roosevelt-Democratic National Committee, Box 401. For additional insights into Republican squabbles, see Miguel Antonio Otero to BMC, December 3 and December 4, 1929, MAO, Box 3.

Chapter 15

1. Edgar Puryear to BMC, January 2, 1930, BMC, Box 9.

2. Puryear to BMC, January 4 and January 6, 1930, BMC, Box 9. Puryear also reported that a lady friend, a Dr. Boggs, called the office every few days inquiring about his return to the city.

3. *New Mexico Tribune,* January 9 and January 10, 1930.

4. Francis Wilson to BMC, February 27 and March 20, 1930; and BMC to Wilson, March 7, 1930, FCW.

5. *Congressional Record,* 71st Congress, 2nd Session, March 5, 1930, pp. 4794–97. Raymond Clapper suggested that Cutting's sponsorship related to the fact that his "family has for years been interested in financing the beet sugar industry in the West," which could only benefit when a tariff against threatening Philippine interests would be imposed. See Raymond Clapper, *Racketeering in Washington* (Boston: L. C. Page & Company, 1933), p. 308. Among other factors behind the Hawes-Cutting bill was the desire to curb Filipino immigration and to stop the flow of sugar and other items into the United States. Neither people nor produce were subject to restrictions as long as the Philippines remained an American dependency.

6. Garel A. Grunder and William E. Livezey, *The Philippines and the United States* (1951; reprint, Westport, Connecticut: Greenwood, 1973), pp. 190–92.

7. Mary Austin to Carey McWilliams, February 1, 1930, Mary Austin Papers, University of New Mexico, Envelope 7; and T. M. Pearce, ed., *Literary America: 1930–1934, The Mary Austin Letters* (Westport, Connecticut: Greenwood Press, 1979), pp. 167–68. Willard H. (Spud) Johnson to BMC,

March 4, 1930, BMC, Box 9. Ezra Pound, "Honor and the United States Senate," *Poetry*, 36 (June 1930), pp. 150–52.

8. *Congressional Record*, 71st Congress, 2nd Session, March 7, 1930, pp. 4893–94, March 17, 1930, p. 5415 and March 18, 1930, pp. 5487–94, 5498–501. BMC to Mrs. Richard Aldrich, April 7, 1930, BMC, Box 21.

9. BMC to Dear Mother, March 10, 1930, BMC, Box 9; and BMC to Miguel Antonio Otero, March 9, 1930, MAO, Box 3.

10. Austin to BMC, March 28, 1930, BMC, Box 9; and Austin to BMC, April 22, 1930, MA, Box 1.

11. BMC to Dear Mother, April 7 and April 13, 1930, BMC, Box 9.

12. Albert Simms to Walter Newton, April 4, 1930, RNC, New Mexico, Box 265. Miguel Antonio Otero, Jr. complained that "one is dammed lucky to get a five minute conversation with you," whereas previously they at times "had a good old undisturbed heart to heart talk." See Miguel Antonio Otero, Jr. to BMC, April 26, 1930, BMC, Box 9.

13. *Congressional Record,* 71st Congress, 2nd Session, April 24, 1930, p. 7615 and April 25, 1930, pp. 7699–700, 7708.

14. BMC to Dear Mother, April 30, 1930; and BMC to Phelps Putnam, May 9, 1930, BMC, Box 9.

15. Isabella Greenway to BMC, May 26, 1930, BMC, Box 9. Greenway, during the early New Deal, served two terms in Congress, replacing Lewis W. Douglass as a representative from Arizona.

16. Katherine Mayo, *Soldiers What Next* (Boston: Houghton-Mifflin, 1934), pp. 136–40.

17. William Starr Myers, ed., *The State Papers And Other Public Writings of Herbert Hoover*, vol. 1 (Garden City: Doubleday, Doran & Company, 1934), pp. 320–21; and BMC to Dear Mother, June 23, 1930, BMC, Box 9.

18. Myers, ed., *State Papers of Herbert Hoover*, vol. 1, 322–28 for the June 24 press statement and June 26 veto message. *Congressional Record,* 71st Congress, 2nd Session, June 23, 1930, pp. 11487, 11492 and June 26, 1930, pp. 11759–63. On July 8, all agencies dealing with veterans were consolidated into one independent agency, the Veterans Administration, with General Frank T. Hines as administrator of Veteran Affairs.

19. *Congressional Record,* 71st Congress, 2nd Session, July 1, 1930, pp. 12181–86 and July 3, 1930, pp. 12404–6. Accepting the view that a bad bill was better than no pension bill, Cutting, after amendments were accepted, voted for approval. However, the conference report deleted most of the senate amendments and Cutting voted in opposition to the final bill, which was approved by a 48-to-14 vote.

20. BMC to Herman G. Baca, July 9, 1930; BMC to Miguel Antonio Otero, Jr., July 10, 1930; and BMC to M. L. Fox, July 10, 1930, BMC, Box 9.

21. John F. Simms to BMC, July 19, 1930; and BMC to John F. Zimmer-

man, July 10, 1930, BMC, Box 9. BMC to Robert M. La Follette, Jr., August 8, 1930, RMLJ, Personal Correspondence, C8. BMC to Judson King, July 9, 1930; and Philip La Follette to BMC, July 5, 1930, BMC, Box 9.

22. BMC to Phelps Putnam, August 8, 1930, BMC, Box 9. Cutting traveled in Germany with his old friend and former doctor, Frederic Bishop. See, too, BMC to Clifford McCarthy, August 7, 1930, BMC, Box 32.

23. Burton K. Wheeler, *Yankee From the West* (Garden City: Doubleday and Company, 1962), pp. 384–85. Remarks by Ella Winter in *Pacific Weekly,* May 10, 1935. Frances Sayre, Woodrow Wilson's son-in-law, and Robert A. Taft also were on this tour.

24. Albert Rhys Williams, *The Soviets* (New York: Harcourt, Brace and Company, 1937), pp. 182–83. Williams states that the trip occurred in the summer of 1931. For a study of the cost of collectivization, see Robert Conquest, *The Harvest of Sorrow: Soviet Collectivization and the Terror-Famine* (New York: Oxford University Press, 1987).

25. BMC to Dear Mother, August 27, 1930, BMC, Box 9.

26. BMC to Mary Austin, August 27, 1930, MA, Box 7.

27. BMC to Dear Mother, August 27, 1930, BMC, Box 9. Cutting sailed for home on September 24, the day after the convention convened.

28. Herman G. Baca to BMC, August 4, 1930; and Puryear to BMC, September 4, 1930, BMC, Box 9. Baca informed Cutting about Mike Otero seeking nomination as lieutenant-governor and other political matters as well as legion affairs. Disabled legionnaires, he said, were angry over the passage of the pension bill. Simms to Newton, August 9 and September 12, 1930, PSF, New Mexico, Box 970.

29. Puryear to BMC, September 4, 1930, BMC, Box 9.

30. BMC to Dear Mother, September 16, 1930, BMC, Box 9. For an account of the Republican State Convention, see the statement by William Lloyd Harding, n.d., RNC, New Mexico, Box 265. Harding, a former governor of Iowa, spent three days in New Mexico and attended the convention.

31. Miguel Antonio Otero, Jr. to BMC, October 1, 1930; and BMC to Dear Mother, October 13, 1930, BMC, Box 9. BMC to La Follette, Jr., October 14, 1930, RMLJ, Personal Correspondence, C8.

32. BMC to Dear Mother, October 24 and November 2, 1930, BMC, Box 9.

33. Joseph Paiz, Jr. to BMC, November 6, 1930; and BMC to Dear Mother, November 12, 1930, BMC, Box 9.

34. BMC to Dear Mother, November 12, 1930, BMC, Box 9. For the views of an office seeker complaining about Cutting's neglect in forwarding endorsements for reappointment to the president, see A. M. Bergere to Lawrence Richey, November 15, 1930, PSF, New Mexico, Box 970.

35. Simms to Newton, November 17, 1930, RNC, New Mexico, Box

265. See, too, Edward Sargent to Newton, December 28, 1930, PSF, New Mexico, Box 970. Sargent, Republican National Committeeman from New Mexico, found that through the control of patronage, Cutting could build an organization "responsible to him at the expense of the nation and our state."

36. Adam Gallegos to BMC, June 27, 1930, BMC, Box 9. Gallegos represented San Miguel County in the state senate.

Chapter 16

1. See *Baltimore Sun,* February 1, 1928, for general information about Cutting, including a mention of the organizations he joined. For periodicals he subscribed to while a member of the Senate, see BMC, Box 33. See, too, the story by Douglas Gilbert, "Most Amazing Senator," *Buffalo Times,* March 1, 1931.

2. George Santayana to Iris Origo, March 8, 1939, BMC, Box 92.

3. For an indication of Cutting's charities and contributions during his years in the Senate, see the file in BMC, Box 21. Cutting's interest in cultural affairs prompted him to purchase anonymously for the Rockefeller sponsored Laboratory of Anthropology a small tract at a price of $3,392.50. See Arthur W. Packard to Thomas Debevoise, February 24, 1930 [memo], and Packard to Jesse L. Nusbaum, February 25, 1930, Office of the Messrs. Rockefeller, Cultural Interests, Laboratory of Anthropology, RA, Folder 183, Box 18.

4. Brian Boru Dunne, "Personal Recollections of a Friend," vol. 1, manuscript draft, p. 3. A copy is in BMC, Box 92.

5. Iris Origo, *Images and Shadows: Part of a Life* (New York: Harcourt Brace Jovanovich, 1971), pp. 32–35. I relied heavily on Origo's penetrating insights into her uncle's personality. The remarks of his sister, Justine, are included in Origo's discussion.

6. From remarks prepared by Gordon Gardiner and read at a gathering of friends of Bronson Cutting in Washington on May 6, 1936, the first anniversary of his death. See BMC, Box 92.

7. Extract of a letter by JCW, February 10, 1939; and Clifford McCarthy to Henry Steele Commager, October 9, 1939, BMC, Box 92. Professor Commager was contemplating, at the suggestion of Olivia Murray Cutting, a biography of Cutting.

8. Marta Weigle, *Brothers of Light, Brothers of Blood: Penitentes of the Southwest* (Albuquerque: University of New Mexico Press, 1976), p. 113; and Mary Austin to BMC, February 2, 1929 and March 28, 1930, BMC, Box 9. These letters provide a good indication of the relationship between Cutting and Mary Austin. Cutting also served with Mary Austin and others on the advisory board of the Santa Fe Art School. See Arrell Morgan Gibson, *The*

Santa Fe and Taos Colonies: Age of the Muses (Norman: University of Oklahoma Press, 1983), p. 82.

9. For insight into the role of Herman Baca, I relied on an unpublished manuscript by Hugh Russell Fraser, "Cutting in New Mexico: A Study in Courage," copy in BMC, Box 92.

10. For information about Jesus Baca, I am indebted to Professor Darlis Miller, who provided me with a copy of a paper by one of her students, James R. Silverthorn, at New Mexico State University. The paper is a personal history narrative of William Louis Baca, a son of Jesus and Julia Baca. See, too, the comments on Jesus Baca in Fraser, "Cutting in New Mexico," BMC, Box 92.

11. Eugene Manlove Rhodes to Olive Carey, n.d. [1932], W. H. Hutchinson, *A Bar Cross Man: The Life and Personal Writings of Eugene Manlove Rhodes* (Norman: University of Oklahoma Press, 1956), p. 326.

12. Mary Austin to Arthur D. Ficke, November 6, 1929, MA, UNM, Envelope 5; and James Kraft, ed., *The Works of Witter Bynner: Selected Letters* (New York: Farrar, Straus, Giroux, 1981), p. 136.

13. Kraft, ed., *The Works of Witter Bynner: Selected Letters,* pp. 125–26. See, too, BMC to Una Fairweather, February 21, 1930, BMC, Box 9. Cutting wrote, "It is hard to refuse anyone who throws himself on your mercy." And Witter Bynner, shortly after Cutting and McCarthy became acquainted, wrote that "Cliff writes of you so tenderly that I melt towards both of you," adding, "I wish I'd been on deck out there." See Witter Bynner to BMC, February 5, 1930, BMC, Box 9. See, too, the brief description of McCarthy in Fraser, "Cutting in New Mexico," BMC, Box 92.

14. BMC to Fairweather, February 21, 1930, BMC, Box 9. This letter to Fairweather apparently is the first in which he comments upon themes encompassing the relationship with his new friends.

15. Fraser, "Cutting in New Mexico," BMC, Box 92.

16. *New Mexico: A Guide To The Colorful State,* compiled by Workers, Writers Program, Work Projects Administration, State of New Mexico (New York: Hastings House, 1940), pp. 144–45. Cutting also served on the advisory board of the Art School in Santa Fe. See BMC to Ina Cassidy, November 4, 1931, CF, Box 2.

17. E. Dana Johnson to My dear wife, March 4, 1918; and Johnson to JCW, March 5, 1918, EDJ, File 5, Box 418.

18. McCarthy to BMC, March 13, 1930, BMC, Box 9.

19. McCarthy to Commager, October 9, 1939, BMC, Box 92. Only after Mrs. Cutting, who was encouraging Commager to prepare a biography, asked McCarthy, did he comment on his relationship with Cutting. Previously, he had ignored Commager's requests. Cutting's edited letters to McCarthy are available in BMC, Box 32.

20. BMC to Phelps Putnam, May 4, 1930, BMC, Box 9.

21. McCarthy's letters to Cutting, most of which are holograph and undated, appear to have been written in January and February 1930. They are filed in BMC, Box 12. In turn, Cutting's letters to McCarthy are perfunctory, detailing his activities and reiterating observations made in other letters he wrote.

22. BMC to Putnam, May 9, August 8 and December 8, 1930; and Frederick Manning to BMC, May 17, May 30, August 6 and November 12, 1930, BMC, Box 9.

23. Several undated letters from Jouett Fall Elliott to BMC can be found in BMC, Box 12. See, too, Elliott to BMC, September 9, 1928, BMC, Box 7, and Elliott to OMC, July 15, 1935, BMC, Box 11.

24. McCarthy to BMC, n.d., BMC, Box 7. Like so many of McCarthy's holograph letters, this one rambles on several topics but includes a conversation that he had with Mary Austin shortly after the PEN speech. Mary Austin to BMC, October 30, 1930, BMC, Box 9.

25. Dolly Sloan to BMC, March 23, 1931, BMC, Box 9.

26. Fulton Lewis to BMC, n.d., BMC, Box 12; and Statement dictated by Olivia Murray Cutting, January 19, 1946, BMC, Box 92.

27. Origo, *Images and Shadows,* p. 259; and Elliott to OMC, July 15, 1935, BMC, Box 11.

Chapter 17

1. Mary Austin to Arthur D. Ficke, November 17, 1930, MA, UNM, Envelope 5. Austin to BMC, November 24, 1930, BMC, Box 9. See, too, Austin to J. F. Zimmerman, November 25, 1930, copy in BMC, Box 9 and Mary Austin, "Rural Education in New Mexico," San Jose Training School, University of New Mexico Bulletin No. 205, December 1, 1931. According to the 1930 census, New Mexico ranked forty-sixth among the states in literacy in the percentage of people over ten years of age.

2. BMC to Dear Mother, November 20, 1930, BMC, Box 9. Arthur T. Hannett, Address delivered March 16, 1931 before the Young People's Democratic Club, copy in DC, Box 194. See, too, Andrea Ammann Parker, "Arthur Seligman and Bronson Cutting: Coalition Government in New Mexico, 1930–1933," (M.A. thesis, University of New Mexico, 1969). Parker's thesis follows Hannett's theme by stating, but never explicitly proving, that Cutting was the dominant figure in the Seligman administration.

3. BMC to Herman Baca, February 14, 1931, BMC, Box 36. For his part, Baca had made no suggestions to Seligman and had only been to see him when asked to do so. He agreed "that we should make few suggestions, if any, as there is plenty of criticism and would be even without suggestions." Baca

to BMC, January 30, 1931, BMC, Box 9. Jefferson D. Atwood, an independent Democrat, an associate in the American Legion and a good friend, explained in a detailed letter the problems Seligman was facing in dealing with members of his own party within his administration and in the legislature. See Atwood to BMC, February 19, 1931, BMC, Box 9.

4. Ezra Pound to BMC, December 9, 1930, EP. In a January 8, 1931 letter to Pound, Cutting reiterated that "there is no chance of accomplishing anything [with regard to Article 211] in the present Congress, and my feeling has been that we should leave it until the new Congress."

5. BMC to Clifford McCarthy, January 11, 1931, BMC, Box 32; Petition from Mescalero Indians to BMC, December 1, 1930, BMC, Box 30; H. L. Kent to BMC, December 5, 1930, BMC, Box 9; and *Congressional Record,* 71st Congress, 3rd Session, December 20, 1930, p. 1255. Cutting spoke in opposition to the nomination of George Otis Smith to a seat on the Federal Power Commission. The Senate thereafter instructed the Judiciary Committee to test in court its right to request the president to reconsider Smith's nomination. In the letter to Otero, Cutting expressed his inability to financially assist his friend, stating, "I am overdrawn in every bank where I have an account, and have got to meet an architect's bill of $12,000 in some way unknown to me." See BMC to Miguel Antonio Otero, November 25, 1930, MAO, Box 3.

6. BMC to Phelps Putnam, January 17, 1931, BMC, Box 9; and *Congressional Record,* 71st Congress, 3rd Session, January 16, 1931, pp. 2329–34.

7. BMC to "Spud Johnson," January 17, 1931, BMC, Box 22; Senate, *Hearings Before the Committee on Patents:* on HR 12549, General Revision of the Copyright Law, 71st Congress, 3rd Session, 1930–1931, pp. 151–53. See, too, BMC to Pound, January 23, 1932, EP. *Congressional Record,* 71st Congress, 3rd Session, February 28, 1931, pp. 6458–60.

8. *Congressional Record,* 71st Congress, 3rd Session, February 5, 1931, pp. 4006–7. Senator William E. Borah inserted the speech in the *Congressional Record.* A copy is available in BMC, Box 82. See, too, BMC to Pound, February 6, 1931, EP. Cutting wrote, "I used your Jefferson quotation in speaking at the National Republican Club the other day."

9. Kenneth R. Philp, *John Collier's Crusade for Indian Reform, 1920–1954* (Tucson: University of Arizona Press, 1977), pp. 103–4. Philp presents a thorough discussion of the Hagerman affair. In 1923, Hagerman was appointed commissioner for the Navajo Indians, serving as their advocate and guardian. In 1925, he was selected a member of the Pueblo Lands Board. Sitting as a judicial body to settle questions of title, the board represented the Indians no more than the settlers seeking Indian lands.

10. Miguel Antonio Otero to BMC, January 29 and January 30, 1931, MAO, Box 3; *Congressional Record,* 71st Congress, 3rd Session, February 14,

1931, pp. 4878–79. At the time that the Rattlesnake field was leased for one thousand dollars, geological reports available to Hagerman indicated little chance of finding oil there. A subsequent report by a government geologist suggested otherwise.

11. *Congressional Record,* 71st Congress, 3rd Session, February 14, 1931, pp. 4879–80. In his remarks, Cutting was seeking to balance the critical report of John Collier. He called Collier a crusader who "had done very valuable work" in behalf of Indians. But he was not alone in defending Indian rights, and his views needed to be weighed in balance with those of other friends of the Indians. A keen analysis of Collier's motives is provided in Austin to BMC, March 4, 1931, BMC, Box 9.

12. BMC to Miguel Antonio Otero, February 4, 1931, MAO, Box 3.

13. BMC to E. Dana Johnson, February 13, 1931; and BMC to Atwood, March 31, 1931, BMC, Box 9. In New Mexico, Hagerman's reputation as a friend of the Indians and as a sound businessman was not seriously impaired by the hearings. At the time, he served as president of the New Mexico Taxpayers Association. For a critical contemporary account, see Judson King, "President Lincoln's Nineteen Silver-Headed Canes," National Popular Government League, Bulletin No. 145, February 12, 1931, copy in BMC, Box 9.

14. See the story by Harry E. Shuart, *New Mexican,* February 14, 1931. Remigio Lopez *et al.* to BMC, February 17, 1931 [telegram], BMC, Box 22. Lopez and the others who sent the telegram were representatives in the state legislature.

15. *Congressional Record,* 71st Congress, 3rd Session, February 18, 1931, pp. 5369–70. For the president's views on this legislation, see William Starr Myers and Walter H. Newton, *The Hoover Administration: A Documented Narrative* (New York: Charles Scribner's Sons, 1936), pp. 66–67.

16. *Congressional Record,* 71st Congress, 3rd Session, February 27, 1931, pp. 6221–23. For the veto message, see Myers and Newton, *The Hoover Administration,* p. 68. Prior to this measure, a veteran could borrow up to 22½ percent of the value of his bonus at six percent interest. The bonus would be forfeited if the principal and interest were not repaid by 1945. With the measure approved over Hoover's veto, a veteran could now borrow up to fifty percent of the value of his policy.

17. *Congressional Record,* 71st Congress, 3rd Session, March 3, 1931, p. 6951.

18. BMC to Phelps Putnam, March 4, 1931, BMC, Box 9.

19. For Cutting's remarks, see "Proceedings of a Conference of Progressives . . ." March 11 and 12, 1931, pp. 63–69.

20. "Proceedings of a Conference of Progressives," p. 158.

21. Edmund Wilson, *The American Earthquake* (Garden City, New York: Doubleday Anchor Books, 1958), p. 275.

22. See the story on Cutting by Douglas Gilbert, *Buffalo Times,* March 1, 1931, p. 5.

23. BMC to Dear Mother, April 1 and April 13, 1931, BMC, Box 9.

24. BMC to Dear Mother, April 13, 1931, BMC, Box 9; and BMC to McCarthy, April 25 and May 5, 1931, BMC, Box 32.

25. Alice Roosevelt Longworth to BMC, April 17, 1931, BMC, Box 12; BMC to McCarthy, May 1, May 5 and May 24, 1931, BMC, Box 32; and BMC to Putnam, April 19, 1931, BMC, Box 9. For a discussion of the complex Pueblo Lands controversy, see George Fraser to BMC, April 24, 1931, BMC, Box 30. Fraser was a special assistant to the attorney general, handling the claims of settlers seeking compensation for Indian lands that they had previously purchased and that were now to be returned to the appropriate pueblo. The Pueblo Lands Act of 1924 made compensation to the Indians for lost land compulsory with certain restrictions. It left compensation to settlers optional with Congress. Cutting believed the settlers should be compensated, that their claims were valid and that the federal government should bear the burden of compensation as it was to blame for the prevailing conditions. See BMC to Fraser, April 29, 1931, BMC, Box 30.

26. BMC to Dear Mother, April 22, 1931, BMC, Box 9; and BMC to McCarthy, June 13 and June 20, 1931, BMC, Box 32. Cutting went to El Paso in response to a letter from Jouett Elliott, Fall's daughter, who reported a campaign to secure a presidential pardon for her father. See Jouett Fall Elliott to BMC, April 26, 1931; and Frances C. Wilson to Herbert Hoover, April 28, 1931, copy in BMC, Box 9. Cutting convinced Fall "that there was not the remotest chance of the President's pardoning him before election [sic], and that the only thing to do was to appeal." Fall, reversing a previous decision not to do so, took Cutting's advice, thereby keeping the case open. See Cutting to Dear Mother, May 21, 1931, BMC, Box 9. The effort was unsuccessful, and Fall entered the New Mexico State Penitentiary in Santa Fe on July 20, 1931. While in El Paso, Cutting gave Fall's daughter a check to help ease her father's financial burdens. Tears came to her eyes when he gave it to her. See Elliott to BMC, n.d.; and BMC to Putnam, April 28 and May 14, 1931, BMC, Box 9.

27. BMC to Atwood, May 17, 1931, BMC, Box 9. Editorial, "Indefensible Appointment," *New Mexican,* May 13, 1931. Besides criticizing the appointment, the editorial, commenting on the treatment extended to defendants in the recent district court term in Santa Fe, concluded that "among his many admirable qualities a judicial talent is lacking." Cutting felt sure Mike's wife, Katherine, was "responsible for the whole situation," claiming she dominated her husband and had been "trying for years to bring about a break." See BMC to Dear Mother, June 1 and June 20, 1931, BMC, Box 9.

28. BMC to Dear Mother, May 16, 1931, BMC, Box 9; and BMC to McCarthy, May 14 and May 28, 1931, BMC, Box 32.

29. BMC to Dear Mother, June 20 and July 2, 1931; and Lemar Jeffers to BMC, June 21, 1931, BMC, Box 9.

30. OMC, 1931 Journal Entries, BMC, Box 92. Olivia James [Cutting's younger sister], Note, BMC, Box 88.

31. BMC to Dear Mother, August 24, 1931, BMC, Box 9.

32. Carl Dunifon to Theodore Joslin, August 3, 1931; and Albert G. Simms to Walter Newton, September 23, 1931, RNC, New Mexico, Box 265. Simms opposed awarding Cutting patronage; and Newton, a secretary to the president, was inclined to agree. See memorandum for postmaster general, October 6, 1931, RNC, New Mexico, Box 265.

33. BMC to Dear Mother, October 11, 1931, BMC, Box 9. The *New Mexican,* on November 21 and December 18, 1931, ran editorials respectively calling for a parole and suggesting that if Fall were not paroled, his family at least should be allowed to spend time at Christmas with him. BMC to Emma Fall, December 29, 1931, BMC, Box 9.

34. BMC to Dear Mother, October 30 and November 13, 1931, BMC, Box 9; and BMC to McCarthy, October 24, 1931, BMC, Box 32. BMC to Dear Mother, November 30, 1931, BMC, Box 9; and BMC to McCarthy, November 3, 1931, BMC, Box 32.

35. Roger Baldwin to BMC, December 30, 1931, BMC, Box 30; and BMC to McCarthy, January 9, 1932, BMC, Box 32. On January 25, 1932 Cutting introduced the bill (S3275) Baldwin requested. It was sent to the Committee on Immigration and was never acted upon.

36. *Congressional Record,* 72nd Congress, 1st Session, December 22, 1931, pp. 1118–19. Cutting spoke in favor of an amendment to the effect that no agreement be made with any government, unless "in a form and manner satisfactory to the President" and that some provision calling for the reformation of the Versailles Treaty be included. The amendment by a 63-to-13 vote was defeated.

37. *Congressional Record,* 72nd Congress, 1st Session, June 8, 1932, p. 12266.

38. *Congressional Record,* 72nd Congress, 1st Session, June 13, 1932, pp. 12797–801.

39. *Congressional Record,* 72nd Congress, 1st Session, January 19, 1932, pp. 2233–35. The Finance Committee considered veterans affairs in the Senate prior to the creation of a Veterans Committee.

40. BMC to Atwood, January 21, 1932; and BMC to Dear Mother, January 21, 1932, BMC, Box 10.

41. BMC to Pound, January 23, 1932, EP; and BMC to Miguel Antonio Otero, February 4, 1932, MAO, Box 3.

42. BMC to Dear Mother, February 6 and February 22, 1932, BMC, Box 10; and BMC to Darwin Meserole, February 26, 1932, BMC, Box 37. In addition to the Costigan-La Follette measure, relief bills in the Senate were

presented by Hugo Black, Thomas J. Walsh and Robert Bulkley who sponsored one measure and Robert Wagner who presented another. See Jordan A. Schwarz, *The Interregnum of Despair* (Urbana: University of Illinois Press, 1970). Chapter six is titled "The Drive for Relief."

43. BMC to McCarthy, March 17, March 29 and March 31, 1932, BMC, Box 32. At this time, McCarthy was in Washington, working for John Collier's Indian Defense Association.

44. Frederick Manning to BMC, March 22 and April 20, 1932, BMC, Box 10. Manning purchased records and musical scores for Cutting and kept him abreast of things musical, including his efforts to master difficult pieces. He then hoped to play them with Cutting and Phelps Putnam and possibly Clifford McCarthy, all of whom played the piano and discussed and enjoyed classical music.

45. BMC to Elliott, May 8, 1932, BMC, Box 10; and BMC to Mrs. Jess J. Wright, May 21, 1932, Secretary's File, Bronson Cutting, Box 517, Herbert Hoover Presidential Library. Mrs. Wright forwarded Cutting's letter to the president.

46. Returning from the Bach Festival in Bethlehem, Pennsylvania, which he attended with Clifford McCarthy and Frederick Manning, Cutting stopped in Baltimore to have the cyst removed on May 15.

47. Statement, to accompany S4737, May 23, 1932, copy in BMC, Box 22. George Huddleston of Alabama introduced a similar measure in the House of Representatives.

48. *Congressional Record,* 72nd Congress, 1st Session, May 23, 1932, pp. 10919–23.

49. *Congressional Record,* 72nd Congress, 1st Session, May 30, 1932, pp. 11534–38. On the Santa Fe *New Mexican,* losses were mounting and all employees, none of whom were yet laid off, took a ten percent cut in wages. See J. A. McConvery to BMC, July 13, 1932, BMC, Box 10. In addition, to cut expenses, it was suggested that Cutting close his Santa Fe home, Los Siete Burros, when he was not in residence. He could save an estimated five thousand dollars. See Brian Boru Dunne to BMC, August 2, 1932, BMC, Box 10.

50. BMC to Elliott, June 3, 1932, BMC, Box 10. Cutting's mother, sitting in a senate gallery, slept through Hoover's entire address. For the president's remarks, see Myers and Newton, *The Hoover Administration,* pp. 214–16.

51. *Congressional Record,* 72nd Congress, 1st Session, June 7, 1932, pp. 12171–72.

52. *Congressional Record,* 72nd Congress, 1st Session, June 9, 1932, p. 12445. Cutting conferred with the leader of the Bonus Marchers, Walter W. Waters, prior to his remarks on the senate floor. For his views on the battling that occurred while he was ill, see BMC to Elliott, August 17, 1932, BMC,

Box 10. Cutting wrote, "The bricks were thrown only when the men realized that they had been treated in bad faith, and what little 'rioting' there was was over long before the troops appeared on the scene."

53. *Congressional Record,* 72nd Congress, 1st Session, June 15, 1932, pp. 12975–77; BMC to Dear Mother, June 14 and June 19, 1932, BMC, Box 10; and OMC, 1932 Diary Entries, BMC, Box 92.

54. BMC to Dear Mother, June 23 and June 25, 1932; and McCarthy to OMC, June 20, 1932, BMC, Box 10.

55. BMC to Frederic Bishop, July 19, 1932; and Frederic Walcott to BMC, July 23, 1932, BMC, Box 10.

56. BMC to McCarthy, August 5, 1932, BMC, Box 32; OMC, 1932 Diary Entries, BMC, Box 92; BMC to Bishop, July 19, 1932, BMC, Box 10; and Edgar Puryear to BMC, August 5, 1932, BMC, Box 10.

Chapter 18

1. Albert Simms to Walter Newton, January 26, 1932, RNC, New Mexico, Box 265.

2. Albuquerque *Journal,* February 7, 1932; and *New Mexican,* February 8, 1932.

3. BMC, to Dear Mother, March 21, 1932, BMC, Box 10; Mabel Reid to Newton, March 22, 1932, RNC, New Mexico, Box 264; Thomas Hughes to Richard C. Dillon, February 16, 1932, RCD, Box 3; and Albuquerque *Journal,* March 20, 1932.

4. *New Mexican,* March 28, 1932; and Albuquerque *Journal,* March 29, 1932. A manuscript draft of Cutting's convention speech that outlined a program for combating the depression can be found in BMC, Box 82. Hughes to Dillon, March 30, 1932, RCD, Box 3.

5. Albuquerque *Journal,* March 28, 1932.

6. *New Mexican,* April 14, 1932; BMC to Miguel Antonio Otero, May 6, 1932, MAO, Box 3; and Herman Baca to BMC, May 6, 1932, BMC, Box 10.

7. J. H. Toulouse to Newton, July 6 and July 16, 1932, RNC, New Mexico, Box 265. Toulouse reported on a meeting between T. M. Pepperday, publisher of the Albuquerque *Journal,* and Cutting. See, too, T. B. Leftwich to BMC, July 6, 1932, BMC, Box 10.

8. Miguel Antonio Otero to BMC, July 19, 1932; R. C. Miller to BMC, July 19, 1932; and George W. Armijo to BMC, July 20, 1932, BMC, Box 10. Miguel Antonio Otero to BMC, August 12, 1932, MAO, Box 3; and M. L. Fox to Newton, August 3, 1932, RNC, New Mexico, Box 265. Fox assured the president's secretary, Walter Newton, that Cutting would support the Republican ticket and would "insure the electoral vote for President Hoover." He reiterated the point several weeks later when he said that Cutting would

support the national ticket, would attack the Democrats as incapable of governing the nation and would seek a balance between his people and the old guard for state offices. See Fox to Dillon, RCD, Box 3.

9. BMC to Dear Mother, August 17, 1932, BMC, Box 10. Arthur Seligman was president of the First National Bank of Santa Fe from 1925 to 1933. Cutting was appointed a director in his early years in Santa Fe.

10. BMC to Jouett Fall Elliott, August 17, 1932; and Robert M. La Follette, Jr. to BMC, August 18, 1932, BMC, Box 10. BMC to La Follette, August 29, 1932, RMLJ, Personal Correspondence, C9. In his bid for reelection as governor of Wisconsin, Philip La Follette was defeated in the Republican primary by former governor Walter J. Kohler.

11. Francis C. Wilson to Dillon, August 22, 1932, RCD, Box 1. Wilson included with his letter a copy of the statement that he wished to deliver at the meeting of the Republican State Central Committee. He also submitted to Dillon a copy of a letter, dated August 29 and sent to Cutting, further elaborating his position while responding to an editorial in the *New Mexican* that criticized it. The original letter is in BMC, Box 10. For a more succinct statement of his position, see Wilson to Orie L. Phillips, September 12, 1932, FCW.

12. Fox to Newton, August 24, 1932, RNC, New Mexico, Box 265; and Jose Sena to Robert Lucas, August 25, 1932, NWM.

13. Carl Dunifon to Everett Sanders, August 30, 1932, RNC, New Mexico, Box 265.

14. Maurice F. Miera to BMC, September 1, 1932, BMC, Box 36.

15. Dillon to BMC, September 2, 1932, RCD, Box 5; and Dillon to Fox, September 6, 1932, RCD, Box 3.

16. Clifford McCarthy to OMC, September 11, 1932; and BMC to Dear Mother, September 13, 1932, BMC, Box 10.

17. Caswell S. Neal to Franklin D. Roosevelt, September 12, 1932, DNC, Box 403.

18. BMC to Dear Mother, September 21, 1932, BMC, Box 10.

19. See the story by Brian Boru Dunne, *New Mexican,* September 23, 1932.

20. *New Mexican,* September 24, 1932; Albuquerque *Journal,* September 24, 1932; and Dennis Chavez to John J. O'Connor, October 13, 1932, DC, 394, Box 3.

21. Ruth Hanna Simms to Laurence Richey, September 24, 1932 [memo regarding phone conversation], RNC, New Mexico, Box 265; Everett Sanders to Nathan William MacChesnay, September 24, 1932, NWM. Albert Simms was named Republican national committeeman to replace Cutting. Almost immediately thereafter he wrote the president requesting funds so that "New Mexico will be carried by a considerably better than good chance for you and for a Republican governor." See Simms to The President, September 20, 1932, RNC, New Mexico, Box 265.

22. Holm O. Bursum to Leftwich, October 16, 1932, BMC, Box 10. Leftwich, a devoted supporter, forwarded the letter to Cutting. See, too, E. L. Safford, statement for afternoon papers of October 29, 1932, copy in BMC, Box 41.

23. Report on Committee Resolutions Adopted by Torrance County Democratic Convention, September 24, 1932, copy in DC, 394, Box 3; and BMC to Dear Mother, September 21, 1932, BMC, Box 10.

24. McCarthy to OMC, September 25, 1932, BMC, Box 10; and *New York Times,* September 25 and September 28, 1932. See, particularly, the story filed by James A. Hagerty on the latter date.

25. *New York Times,* September 28, 1932; and Emma Fall to BMC, September 29 [1932], BMC, Box 8. Mrs. Fall was presenting her husband's view.

26. BMC to Dear Mother, October 5, 1932, BMC, Box 10.

27. La Follette to BMC, October 1, 1932, RMLJ, Personal Correspondence, C9.

28. BMC to Dear Mother, October 5, 1932, BMC, Box 10.

29. BMC to Dear Mother, October 10, 1932, BMC, Box 10. See, too, an undated campaign speech by Richard Dillon for an example of Republican use of the Seligman-Cutting alliance theme, RCD, Box 1. To the extent that some Cutting supporters received places on Democratic county tickets, the theme had validity.

30. BMC to Miguel Antonio Otero, October 7, 1932, MAO, Box 3; BMC to Clara True, October 15, 1932, BMC, Box 10; and BMC to McCarthy, October 11 and October 18, 1932, BMC, Box 32. For relaxation during these hectic days, Cutting sought out artist Cady Wells to play piano duets.

31. BMC to McCarthy, October 16, October 18 and October 22, 1932, BMC, Box 32; Hiram Johnson to BMC, October 18, 1932; and Frank P. Walsh to BMC, October 19, 1932, BMC, Box 10. La Follette, Johnson, Norris and Cutting were the four Republican senators who endorsed Roosevelt in 1932.

32. BMC to Dear Mother, October 21, 1932, BMC, Box 10.

33. BMC to McCarthy, October 29, 1932, BMC, Box 32; BMC to La Follette, October 29, 1932, RMLJ, Personal Correspondence, C9.

34. *New Mexican,* October 27, 1932, BMC, Box 41. The item is an extensive and detailed press clipping that I assumed to be from Cutting's newspaper. An earlier clipping from the *New Mexican* on October 21, 1932 carried an Associated Press story of a release from the National Progressive League that Cutting endorsed Roosevelt and would speak in his behalf over a national network on October 26.

35. BMC to Una Fairweather, November 1, 1932, BMC, Box 10; and BMC to McCarthy, November 6, 1932, BMC, Box 32.

36. BMC to Dear Mother, November 5, 1932, BMC, Box 10; and BMC to

McCarthy, November 6, 1932, BMC, Box 32. After the election, an official of the National Progressive League wrote that "we had more requests for copies of Senator Cutting's speeches than for any others delivered in the campaign." See Melvin Hildreth to OMC, November 8, 1932, BMC, Box 108.

37. *New York Times,* November 7, 1932, p. 14; and Adela C. Holmquist to Dillon, November 7, 1932, RCD, Box 2.

38. BMC to Dear Mother, November 11, 1932, BMC, Box 10; see Insert, "Canvas of Returns of Elections Held November 8, 1932," *New Mexico Blue Book, 1933–1934.*

39. BMC to Dear Mother, November 11, 1932, BMC, Box 10.

40. Clara Olsen to BMC, November 11, 1932; Eleanor Roosevelt to OMC, November 10, 1932; and Franklin D. Roosevelt to BMC, November 19, 1932 [telegram], BMC, Box 10. Clyde Tingley to Roosevelt, November 15, 1932, DNC, Box 403. Old guard Republicans, despite their defeat, felt that a great victory was won in purging their party of "the Cutting element." See Harry A. Wilson to Dillon, November 23, 1932, RCD, Box 5.

41. BMC to McCarthy, November 15, November 17, November 27 and November 29, 1932, BMC, Box 32; and BMC to Dear Mother, November 21, 1932, BMC, Box 10. Collier ranked his preferences for Indian commissioner at Cutting's luncheon table: Nathan Margold; Lewis Meriam or Collier himself; and lastly Harold Ickes. Cutting agreed to "feel Franklin out" on these names at Warm Springs.

42. Platform, The Progressive Party of New Mexico adopted . . . November 26, 1932, copy in BMC, Box 36; and BMC to Clara True, December 20, 1932, BMC, Box 10.

43. Miera to BMC, December 16, 1932; and BMC to Miera, December 20, 1932, BMC, Box 36.

44. *New Mexican,* November 30, 1932; story by James A. Hagerty, *New York Times,* December 5, 1932, p. 3; Boston *Globe,* December 5, 1932; and OMC, 1932 Journal Entries, BMC, Box 92.

45. Worth B. Daniels to OMC, December 20, 1932, BMC, Box 10.

46. BMC to Elliott, December 15, 1932, BMC, Box 10.

Chapter 19

1. BMC to James Murray, November 28, 1932, BMC, Box 10.

2. *Congressional Record,* 72nd Congress, 2nd Session, December 9, 1932, p. 265. The issue was compromised by allowing in fifty Philippine immigrants per year during the commonwealth period.

3. *Congressional Record,* 72nd Congress, 2nd Session, December 13, 1932, pp. 387–88. American products would enter the Philippine Islands duty free during the interim period.

4. OMC, 1932 Journal Entries, BMC, Box 92.

5. *Congressional Record,* 72nd Congress, 2nd Session, January 16, 1933, pp. 1865–67 and January 17, 1933, pp. 1911–16. Careful and well-rounded accounts of the first Philippine Independence Act can be found in Theodore Friend, *Between Two Empires: The Ordeal of the Philippines* (New Haven: Yale University Press, 1965), chap. 8; Garel A. Grunder and William E. Livezey, *The Philippines and the United States* (1951; reprint, Westport, Connecticut: Greenwood Press, 1973), chap. 12; and Grayson Kirk, *Philippine Independence* (New York: Farrar and Rinehart, 1936), chap. 5.

6. For a contemporary discussion, prepared in December 1933, of the reasons for the rejection, see "Draft Recommendations As To The Future of The Philippines," by the Committee on the Philippines. A copy is in FDR, OF 400, Box 22.

7. Clifford McCarthy to Henry Steele Commager, n.d. [1939], BMC, Box 19. McCarthy prepared a memorandum for Commager who was contemplating a biography of Cutting.

8. McCarthy to Commager, n.d., BMC, Box 19; and Huston Thompson to Meyer Jacobstein, January 9, 1933, HT, Box 3. Thompson remarked, "Both Senators Norris and Cutting are going to see the President-Elect this week . . . ."

9. BMC to Dear Mother, February 10, 1933, BMC, Box 10; Frank Freidel, *Franklin D. Roosevelt: Launching the New Deal* (Boston: Little Brown and Company, 1973), pp. 150–51. See, too, Robert M. La Follette, Jr. to Philip La Follette, January 20 and January 24, 1933, LFFP, Box A43. I am grateful to Professor Paul Glad for bringing these letters to my attention.

10. Raymond Moley, *After Seven Years* (New York: Harper and Brothers, 1939), pp. 125–26; and *New Mexican,* February 18, 1933. That Roosevelt was in earnest about working with progressive Republicans is further evidenced by his asking Senators Hiram Johnson, La Follette and Cutting to provide Moley with the names of two prominent progressives to work with him on policies he was developing for the incoming administration. See Moley, *After Seven Years,* p. 126.

11. Alford Roose to BMC, January 11, 1933, copy in HAW, Reel 18, Frame 683; BMC to Edward P. Costigan, n.d. [telegram], BMC, Box 12; and Emma Fall to BMC, n.d., BMC, Box 10. For western opposition to Walsh and support of Cutting for a cabinet post, see *The Oil News,* February 4, 1933. A copy is in FDR, DNC, Box 403; and H. Grady Gwin to Franklin D. Roosevelt, January 30, 1933, FDR, DNC, Box 403. Gwin, a Presbyterian missionary working in the Jemez Indian Pueblo, had incurred the wrath of the commissioner of Indian affairs and was facing recall by the superintendent of his church's Board of National Missions. He mentioned Cutting as one who knew of his work in the pueblo and could vouch for his character and ability.

12. *Congressional Record,* 72nd Congress, 2nd Session, February 2, 1933, p. 3163.

13. *Congressional Record,* 72nd Congress, 2nd Session, February 20, 1933, p. 4490.

14. BMC to Dear Mother, March 6 and March 10, 1933, BMC, Box 10; and BMC to McCarthy, March 8 and March 10, 1933, BMC, Box 32. The letters of March 6 and 8 were mailed from Curacao, while those of March 10 were sent from Panama City. See BMC, Box 10 for a United Press story from Colon, Panama, dated March 8, 1933, relating how Cutting delayed the *LaFayette* for half an hour.

15. BMC to McCarthy, March 20 and March 21, 1933, BMC, Box 32.

16. BMC to Harold Ickes, March 22, 1933 [telegram]; BMC to Charles Curry, March 25, 1933; and BMC to Dear Mother, March 25, 1933, BMC, Box 10. M. L. Fox to Richard C. Dillon, March 26, 1933, RCD, Box 3.

17. BMC to Dear Mother, April 8, 1933, BMC, Box 10; and Harold L. Ickes, April 13, 1933, *The Secret Diary of Harold L. Ickes: The First Thousand Days, 1933–1936* (New York: Simon and Schuster, 1953), pp. 20–21. Ickes attended a dinner party at which Cutting was a guest with several senators. They were later joined in conversation with representatives of various government departments.

18. Ickes, April 26, 1933, *The Secret Diary,* p. 27.

19. BMC to E. S. Bullock, April 28, 1933, BMC, Box 10.

20. *Congressional Record,* 73rd Congress, 1st Session, May 10, 1933, pp. 3134–39. Incidentally, Cutting's amendment was defeated by a vote of 30 yeas to 42 nays, largely along party lines.

21. BMC to Oscar K. Allen, May 11, 1933 [telegram]; and BMC to C.E. Maudlin, May 13, 1933 [telegram], BMC, Box 37. Allen was governor of Louisiana. The measure Cutting sponsored, S1596, called for an Emergency Public Works Administration, a Federal Public Works Program, Loans for Public Construction, and a Federal Industrial Stabilization Board.

22. *Congressional Record,* 73rd Congress, 1st Session, June 2, 1933, pp. 4827–32. New York *Herald Tribune,* June 2, 1933.

23. *Congressional Record,* 73rd Congress, 1st Session, June 5, 1933, pp. 4968–71.

24. *Congressional Record,* 73rd Congress, 1st Session, June 6, 1933, pp. 5089–90 and June 7, 1933, pp. 5167, 5170–73.

25. *Congressional Record,* 73rd Congress, 1st Session, June 8, 1933, pp. 5265–67.

26. *Congressional Record,* 73rd Congress, 1st Session, June 12, 1933, pp. 5731–43, 5759–60.

27. *Congressional Record,* 73rd Congress, 1st Session, June 15, 1933, pp. 6111–17; and "Glass v. Cutting," *Time,* June 26, 1933, p. 12.

28. *Congressional Record,* 73rd Congress, 1st Session, June 15, 1933, p. 6132. Although dated June 15 in the *Record,* these remarks were in fact uttered on June 16, 1933. See, too, Robert E. Burke, ed., *The Diary Letters of Hiram Johnson,* vol. 5, 1929–1933 (New York: Garland, 1983). See the second page of a letter, dated June 18, 1933, to his son and namesake. Johnson claimed to have started the fight with a May 31 speech to "protect the men shot to pieces in combat." While I have focused my concern on Cutting, James E. Sargent places his remarks in a broader context. See his *Roosevelt and The Hundred Days Struggle for the Early New Deal* (New York: Garland, 1981), pp. 250–60.

29. BMC to McCarthy, June 11, June 18 and June 19, 1933, BMC, Box 32.

30. Raymond Moley, *After Seven Years,* p. 191.

31. BMC to Jefferson D. Atwood, June 16, 1933, BMC, Box 10; and BMC to William Cowley, n.d. [June 1933] [telegram], BMC, Box 41. Cowley was national commander of the Disabled American Veterans.

32. BMC to McCarthy, June 18, 1933, BMC, Box 32; and BMC to Dear Mother, June 23, 1933, BMC, Box 10.

33. BMC to Dear Mother, June 23, 1933; and BMC to Atwood, June 16, 1933, BMC, Box 10.

34. Clara True to BMC, May 15, May 29 and July 3, 1933, BMC, Box 10.

35. BMC to Dear Mother, July 3 and July 10, 1933, BMC, Box 10.

36. Confidential Memorandum for the Secretary, July 12, 1933, EH, Box 93. Hurja was secretary of the Democratic National Committee. See, too, Arthur T. Hannett to James A. Farley, July 13, 1933, copy in DC, File 394, Box 1.

Chapter 20

1. BMC to Phelps Putnam, July 26, 1933, BMC, Box 10; and Cutting to Clifford McCarthy, July 26, 1933, BMC, Box 32.

2. BMC to Dear Mother, July 30, 1933; and Gordon Gardiner to OMC, August 13, 1933, BMC, Box 10.

3. BMC to Dear Mother, July 30 and August 14, 1933, BMC, Box 10; and BMC to McCarthy, August 8, 1933, BMC, Box 32.

4. BMC to Putnam, August 27, 1933, BMC, Box 10; and BMC to McCarthy, August 27, 1933, BMC, Box 32.

5. BMC to Dear Mother, September 3, 1933; and William S. Moore to BMC, August 28, 1933, BMC, Box 10.

6. BMC to McCarthy, September 3, 1933, BMC, Box 32; and BMC to Dear Mother, September 11, 1933, BMC, Box 10.

7. Clyde Tingley to Dennis Chavez, September 29, 1933. DC, File 394, Box 1. See, too, J. D. Atwood to Edgar Puryear, September 30, 1933, BMC, Box 37; and Albert Simms to Herbert Hoover, October 2, 1933, PP, Box 504.

8. BMC to Dear Mother, October 1, 1933, BMC, Box 10; and BMC to Frederic Bishop, January 7, 1934, BMC, Box 11. Cutting noted that among the passengers were "these celebrated Jews Bruno Walter and Emil Ludwig."

9. BMC to Putnam, October 3, 1933, BMC, Box 10.

10. BMC to Putnam, October 3, 1933, BMC, Box 10. See, too, Katherine Mayo, *Soldiers What Next* (Boston: Houghton, Mifflin, 1934), pp. 211–19 for a discussion of the president's tumultuous reception at the Chicago convention of the American Legion. For a discussion of the Gallup coal strike, see Harry R. Rubenstein, "Political Repression in New Mexico: The Destruction of the National Miners' Union in Gallup," *Labor in New Mexico,* ed. Robert Kern (Albuquerque: University of New Mexico Press, 1983), pp. 91–140. Cutting was able to induce Senator Robert Wagner, head of the National Labor Board, to send an agent to Gallup in the hope of mediating the strike. See BMC to Putnam, November 10, 1933, BMC, Box 10.

11. BMC to Dear Mother, October 11 and October 13, 1933; and BMC to Severino Trujillo, October 17, 1933, BMC, Box 10.

12. Memorandum on Public Works: Extension of Secondary Highway System in New Mexico, n.d. [October 1933], copy in BMC, Box 10. See, too, Stephen Early to BMC, August 19, 1933, FDR, OF 103, Box 1. Cutting protested the withdrawal of Public Health Service funds previously granted to local health units in New Mexico. For an excellent overall discussion of the New Deal in New Mexico, see the essay with that title by William Pickens in John Braeman, *et al.,* eds., *The New Deal,* vol. 2 (Columbus: Ohio State University Press, 1975), pp. 310–54.

13. Trujillo to BMC, October 9, 1933, BMC, Box 10. See, too, Edgar Puryear to BMC, October 24, 1933, BMC, Box 10. Puryear, Cutting's secretary, was convinced that Dennis Chavez would oppose Cutting in 1934. Chavez, he said, "seems to have only one idea, to rule the party in New Mexico, and is determined no one can remain in his path."

14. BMC to Trujillo, October 17, 1933; and BMC to Jouett Elliott, October 14, 1933, BMC, Box 10.

15. BMC to Elliott, October 14, 1933; BMC to Dear Mother, October 19, 1933; and Jose Rivera to BMC, October 19, 1933, BMC, Box 10.

16. BMC to Trujillo, October 17, 1933; Rivera to BMC, October 19, 1933; Puryear to BMC, October 24, 1933; BMC to Una Fairweather, October 27, 1933, BMC, Box 10. Rivera's letter indicates that some Hispanic veterans believed they were being persecuted by the national organization and its minions in the state.

17. BMC to Dear Mother, October 27, 1933; and Brian Boru Dunne to OMC, October 27, 1933, BMC, Box 10. BMC to Concha Ortiz y Pino, November 7, 1933, Concha Ortiz y Pino de Kleven scrapbook, University of New Mexico. Cutting thanked Ortiz y Pino for the pleasant time he had at

Galisteo and made a contribution to the industrial training school she was promoting.

18. BMC to Dear Mother, October 27, October 31, November 12 and November 24, 1933, BMC, Box 10. While Cutting was meeting with Progressives in New Mexico, he was invited by Philip La Follette to attend a meeting of progressive leaders scheduled for December in Chicago to discuss strategy and plans in opposing the New Deal. See Philip La Follette to BMC, November 7, 1933, BMC, Box 10.

19. BMC to Putnam, November 10, 1933; and BMC to Dear Mother, November 12, 1933, BMC, Box 10. See, too, Jonathan R. Cunningham, "Bronson Cutting: A Political Biography" (M.A. thesis, University of New Mexico, 1940), pp. 181–85 for a fuller discussion of the proceedings which led to the suspension of the department and to Cutting's permanent withdrawal from the American Legion.

20. BMC to Dear Mother, November 24, 1933; and Atwood to Puryear, November 27, 1933, BMC, Box 10.

21. BMC to Dear Mother, November 24, 1933, BMC, Box 10; Harold L. Ickes to BMC, November 23, 1933 [telegram], HLI, Box 249; Atwood to BMC, November 27, 1933, BMC, Box 10; and N. B. Phillips to BMC, December 19, 1933, BMC, Box 37. Phillips was treasurer of the Elephant Butte Irrigation District. See, too, BMC et al., to Ickes, November 27, 1933, FDR, OF 402, Box 1. Senators from Texas, Colorado and New Mexico endorsed the State Line Reservoir and Sump Drain as a PWA proposal, a project for which Cutting and others were unable to secure support during the Hoover administration.

22. Puryear to BMC, December 14, 1933, BMC, Box 10; Memorandum, Drought Relief in New Mexico, December 1, 1933, HH, Box 58.

23. BMC to Dear Mother, November 29, 1933; and Puryear to BMC, December 14, 1933, BMC, Box 10.

24. Puryear to BMC, December 14, 1933, BMC, Box 10; and BMC to McCarthy, December 14 and December 17, 1933, BMC, Box 32. Arrell Morgan Gibson, *The Santa Fe and Taos Colonies: Age of the Muses, 1900–1942* (Norman: University of Oklahoma Press, 1983), p. 83.

25. BMC to McCarthy, December 17, December 19 and December 21, 1933, BMC, Box 32.

26. BMC to Dear Mother, December 29, 1933, BMC, Box 10; and BMC to Puryear, December 20, 1933, BMC, Box 41. The situation regarding the New Mexico Department of the American Legion assumed a bizarre turn by year's end. Placed under suspension by the National American Legion, the department commander refused to turn over the funds and files to the receiver from Indianapolis, who was to supervise them. A law suit was initiated by Osborne Wood, the commander, and all but two posts in New Mexico

supported him. These developments indicated a long involved legal tangle and the probable expulsion of many New Mexico posts from the American Legion. See BMC to Putnam, December 29, 1933, BMC, Box 10.

27. BMC to Thomas R. Amlie, December 27, 1933, BMC, Box 21; and Clara True to BMC, December 27, 1933, BMC, Box 10.

28. BMC to Bishop, January 7, 1934, BMC, Box 11.

Chapter 21

1. M. L. Fox to Edgar Puryear, January 8, 1934, BMC, Box 25.

2. Fox to Richard Dillon, January 17, 1934, RCD, Box 3.

3. George W. Norris to Franklin D. Roosevelt, January 19, 1934; and Roosevelt to Norris, January 24, 1934, FDR, PPF 1201.

4. H. H. Bennett to BMC, January 18, 1934, and Puryear to Steve L. Villareal, January 25, 1934, BMC, Box 39; Jefferson D. Atwood to BMC, January 25, 1934, BMC, Box 29; BMC to A. W. Hockenhull, January 6, 1934 [telegram], and Hockenhull to BMC, January 24, 1934, AWH. Hockenhull was reluctant to call a special session of the legislature to enact enabling legislation for completion of many PWA loans and grants. He feared that the federal government would demand that the legislature appropriate money to match federal funds for relief and other purposes as it had done in Colorado and other states. See Atwood to BMC, January 25, 1934 [telegram], BMC, Box 37.

5. In his January 24, 1934 press conference, Roosevelt said that he had talked to Cutting about extending the time frame. An excerpt of the conference is available in Edgar B. Nixon, ed., *Franklin D. Roosevelt and Foreign Affairs,* vol. 1 (Cambridge: Harvard University Press, 1969), p. 606.

6. *Congressional Record,* 73rd Congress, 2nd Session, March 22, 1934, pp. 5160–61.

7. Phil Swing to BMC, January 16, 1934, BMC, Box 19; and New York *World Telegram,* February 4, 1934.

8. BMC to Robert M. Hutchins, December 15, 1933, BMC, Box 19; Hutchins to BMC, December 22, 1933, BMC, Box 19; and New York *World Telegram,* February 4, 1934.

9. The article, "Is Private Banking Doomed?" appeared in the March 31, 1934 issue of *Liberty Magazine.* It was also printed in the *Congressional Record,* 73rd Congress, 2nd Session, May 4, 1934, pp. 8051–53. Cutting prepared the article in "great haste" in November 1933 in Santa Fe. After its appearance he confessed "to an intense prejudice and dislike of the damn thing" and that "nothing on earth" could induce him to read it in print. Moreover, the article generated "at least 10,000 pages of unanswered correspondence on the subject." See BMC to Alfred M. Bingham, April 24, 1934, BMC, Box 19; and BMC to Phelps Putnam, April 22, 1934, BMC, Box 12.

10. BMC to Roger Baldwin, March 23, 1934, BMC, Box 19.

11. *Congressional Record,* 73rd Congress, 2nd Session, January 27, 1934, pp. 1476–77. Cutting sent a copy of these remarks to Ezra Pound. See BMC to Pound, March 8, 1934, EP.

12. *Congressional Record,* 73rd Congress, 2nd Session, February 8, 1934, pp. 2162–67.

13. Pound to BMC, February 13, 1934 and several other mostly undated letters written in 1934, BMC, Box 36; and BMC to Putnam, July 7, 1934, BMC, Box 11. See, too, E. P. Walkiewicz and Hugh Witemeyer, "Ezra Pound's Contributions to New Mexican Periodicals and His Relationship with Senator Bronson Cutting," *Paideuma* 9 (Winter 1980), 452–53.

14. Cutting's remarks are available in *Congressional Record,* 73rd Congress, 2nd Session, May 22, 1934, pp. 9225–27, 9259–61, and May 29, 1934, pp. 9795–96; and BMC to Herbert Bruce Brougham, June 8, 1934, BMC, Box 19.

15. Jouett Elliott to BMC, n.d. [February 1934]; Puryear to Atwood, February 13, 1934 [telegram]; and BMC to Dear Mother, February 12, 1934, BMC, Box 11. Brian Boru Dunne to Atwood, February 15, 1934 [telegram], BMC, Box 37; and Miguel Antonio Otero to BMC, February 21, 1934, MAO, Box 3.

16. BMC to Dear Mother, February 4 and February 23, 1934, BMC, Box 11. See, too, J. Frederick Essary, "The Unsolved Problem of Veteran Relief," *Literary Digest,* February 24, 1924, pp. 10, 46.

17. *Congressional Record,* 73rd Congress, 2nd Session, February 26, 1934, pp. 3202–10; and BMC to Putnam, April 22, 1934, BMC, Box 11.

18. Cutting expressed opposition to placing senators voting with the minority on the Conference Committee. He was also opposed to what he still considered the shabby treatment of tubercular and other nonwounded but disabled veterans. See *Congressional Record,* 73rd Congress, 2nd Session, March 26, 1934, pp. 5393–95 and March 28, 1934, pp. 5573–82. Cutting was the first senator to speak following the reading of the veto message.

19. BMC to Mrs. H. E. Luderer, March 1, 1934, BMC, Box 19; BMC to Thomas E. White, April 30, 1934, BMC, Box 19; and BMC to Pound, March 8, 1934, EP.

20. Hockenhull to BMC, March 8, 1934, AWH; Atwood to Puryear, March 9, 1934 [telegram], BMC, Box 37; E. V. Schulte to Civic Organizations in The State of Wyoming, March 14, 1934, BMC, Box 33; and Clara Olsen to BMC, March 16, 1934, BMC, Box 11.

21. BMC to Dear Mother, March 21, 1934; BMC to Putnam, March 21, 1934; and Herman Baca to BMC, March 26, 1934, BMC, Box 11. New York *Herald Tribune,* February 18, 1934; and *New York Times,* March 24, 1934.

22. BMC to Dear Mother, April 1, 1934; Herman Baca to BMC, March 26,

1934, BMC, Box 11; BMC to Miguel Antonio Otero, April 18, 1934, MAO, Box 3. See, too, Fox to BMC, May 13, 1934, copy in RCD, Box 3. Besides complimenting Cutting for his stand in overriding the president's veto, Fox expressed the hope that Cutting and the Progressives would work together in the fall. Otherwise, he thought that Cutting could win on a third ticket, despite the president's popularity.

23. Atwood to Daniel C. Roper, April 5, 1934, BMC, Box 11.

24. Miguel Antonio Otero to Carl A. Hatch, April 10, 1934, MAO, Box 2; and Otero to BMC, April 13, 1934, MAO, Box 3.

25. BMC to Miguel Antonio Otero, April 18, 1934, MAO, Box 3. For the continuing confusion in New Mexico politics with which Cutting kept abreast, see Atwood to Puryear, April 28, 1934, BMC, Box 25 and Miguel Antonio Otero to BMC, May 5, 1934, BMC, Box 11. Cutting was also aware of continuing efforts by the American Legion to cancel the charters of more than twenty posts in New Mexico after a compromise agreement ending this practice had been reached. See Atwood to Wilbur M. Alter and I. A. Jennings, May 9, 1934, BMC, Box 18.

26. BMC to Putnam, April 22, 1934, BMC, Box 12; BMC to David Warren Ryder, April 24, 1934, BMC, Box 19; BMC to William C. Whitner, May 4, 1934, BMC, Box 19; and BMC to J. Russell Smith, May 16, 1934, BMC, Box 20.

27. BMC to Pound, May 24, 1934, EP.

28. Alter to Atwood, May 19, 1934; and Edward Spafford to Edward Hayes, May 24, 1934, BMC, Box 18. Hayes was the national commander of the American Legion. He was not in office when the cancellations occurred and apparently was not in accord with them.

29. Miguel Antonio Otero to Hatch, May 21, 1934, MAO, Box 2; and Cutting to Miguel Antonio Otero, May 22, 1934, MAO, Box 3.

30. Cutting to John E. Thayer, Jr., June 7, 1934; and BMC to Putnam, May 29 and June 14, 1934, BMC, Box 11. For a discussion of the fiftieth anniversary of Groton, see Frank D. Ashburn, *Peabody of Groton* (New York: Coward McCann, 1944), pp. 352–66.

31. *Congressional Record,* 73rd Congress, 2nd Session, May 30, 1934, pp. 9958 and May 31, 1934, pp. 10084–85.

32. *Congressional Record,* 73rd Congress, 2nd Session, May 31, 1934, pp. 10085–90. Cutting's views were influenced by Lawrence Dennis, *Is Capitalism Doomed?* (New York: Harpers, 1932), which he acknowledged in the course of his remarks.

33. *Congressional Record,* 73rd Congress, 2nd Session, June 16, 1934, pp. 12051–52.

34. *Congressional Record,* 73rd Congress, 2nd Session, June 14, 1934, pp. 11453–54.

35. BMC to Putnam, June 14, 1934; and BMC to Dear Mother, June 23, 1934, BMC, Box 11.

36. BMC to Dear Mother, July 2, 1934, BMC, Box 11; and BMC to Tom W. Neal, June 29, 1934, BMC, Box 20. That elements in both parties were vying for Cutting to join them is evident in Carl Dunifon to BMC, June 22, 1934, BMC, Box 11 and in Miguel Antonio Otero to James A. Farley, June 27, 1934, MAO, Box 3. Dunifon hoped that Cutting would accept a place on the Republican ticket. Otero similarly hoped that Cutting again would affiliate with the Democratic party.

Chapter 22

1. For an indication of conditions in the West, including New Mexico, see the Report of Drought Conditions, June 1 and July 1, and Chester C. Davis, et al., to Franklin D. Roosevelt, June 4, 1934, FDR, OF 987, Box 1. See, too, Summary Data Regarding State and Local Relief Funds, New Mexico, 3110, HH, Box 58. Another source is the report prepared by Commodity Distribution Division, New Mexico Relief Administration, copy in BMC, Box 37. For an indication of what conditions were like in parts of the state, see the letter signed "Dumb Rio Arriban" in the Santa Fe *New Mexican,* July 9, 1934.

2. BMC to Phelps Putnam, July 7, 1934, BMC, Box 11.

3. BMC to Dear Mother, July 11, 1934, BMC, Box 11; and BMC to Miguel Antonio Otero, July 13, 1934, MAO, Box 3.

4. James A. Farley, Memo on Western Trip (1934), JAF, Box 37; and Albuquerque *Tribune,* July 17, 1934.

5. BMC to Frederic Bishop, July 19, 1934, BMC, Box 11; Frank S. Flynn, "Young Republicans Want 'Old Guard' Shelved," *Plain Talk,* August 1934, pp. 6–7; and G. P. Winkler to Denver Bureau Chief, July 17, 1935, EDJ, File 19, Box 418.

6. See Editorial, "Mr. Farley's Dilemma," Albuquerque *Journal,* July 17, 1934; and story by George Fitzpatrick, Albuquerque *Tribune,* July 17, 1934.

7. Jose R. Gallejos to Dennis Chavez, Jr., July 19, 1934, DC, File 394, Box 1.

8. BMC to Putnam, July 19, 1934, BMC, Box 11.

9. Santa Fe *New Mexican,* July 21, 1934. See, too, Holm Bursum to J. B. Leftwich, July 31, 1934, BMC, Box 11. Bursum denounced Cutting, saying that "ever since he came into active politics there has been intense strife and confusion." He claimed that Cutting was now "in supreme command of the so-called Republican-progressive force."

10. BMC speech, July 21, 1934, BMC, Box 11.

11. John J. Dempsey to Farley, July 23 and July 28, 1934; and Carl Hatch to Antoniette Funk, July 30, 1934; EH, Box 93.

Notes to pages 273–76

12. BMC to Dear Mother, July 24, 1934; and BMC to Putnam, July 24, 1934, BMC, Box 11. See, too, Editorial, "The Democratic Dilemma," Albuquerque *Journal,* July 24, 1934. The editorial provides a succinct review of the situation.

13. BMC to John Collier, August 1, 1934, BMC 11.

14. BMC to Dear Mother, August 11, 1934, BMC, Box 11; and BMC to Clifford McCarthy, August 7, 1934, BMC, Box 32. Several years later, McCarthy recalled Cutting's "deep terrible despair at this time." He said that Cutting was not sure, when he departed for Seattle, about whether he would accept the senatorial nomination. See McCarthy to Olivia James, December 8, 1939, BMC, Box 92. Olivia, her mother's namesake, was Cutting's younger sister.

15. BMC to Dear Mother, August 17, 1934, BMC, Box 11.

16. Jonathan R. Cunningham, "Bronson Cutting: A Political Biography" (M.A. thesis, University of New Mexico, 1940), pp. 188–89; and BMC to Fiorello LaGuardia, August 25, 1934, BMC, Box 11.

17. BMC to Dear Mother, August 24, 1934, BMC, Box 11.

18. David Chavez, Jr. to Dennis Chavez, Jr., August 17, 1934; and Joe Ramon to Dennis Chavez, Jr., August 23, 1934, DC, File 394, Box 1. Chavez was very optimistic about his chances for defeating Cutting. See Dennis Chavez to Dear Son, August 27, 1934, DC File 394, Box 2.

19. Santa Fe *New Mexican,* August 25, 1934; Cunningham, *op. cit.,* pp. 189–90; and Jefferson D. Atwood to Carl Hatch, August 27, 1934, BMC, Box 11.

20. BMC to Putnam, August 28, 1934, BMC, Box 11.

21. BMC to Dear Mother, August 31, 1934, BMC, Box 11; Edgar Puryear to Price Crume, September 5, 1934, BMC, Box 42; Statement [regarding New Mexico Gas Fields], September 7, 1934, BMC, Box 37. See, too, Brian Boru Dunne to Albuquerque *Morning Journal,* September 15, 1934 [telegram], BMC, Box 11 for protests by Cutting against actions of federal agencies affecting sheepmen and lumber companies.

22. BMC to Dear Mother, September 12 and September 15, 1934, BMC, Box 11.

23. BMC to Florence Dromey, September 17, 1934 [telegram], BMC, Box 32; BMC to Donald Richberg, September 15, 1934; and BMC to William Myers, September 15, 1934, BMC, Box 11. Both of these items are holograph drafts of telegrams. Clyde Tingley to Farley, September 17, 1934, JAF, Box 3. See, too, Harold Ickes to Franklin D. Roosevelt, September 20, 1934, FDR, OFF 300, Box 26.

24. BMC to Hiram Johnson, September 22, 1934; and BMC to Robert M. La Follette, Jr., September 22, 1934, BMC, Box 26. Johnson wrote to Harold Ickes, who forwarded a copy to the president, saying that he believed Cutting deserved the same sort of treatment accorded to him. The president endorsed

Johnson's reelection in 1934. Both Cutting and Johnson had bolted their party and endorsed Roosevelt in 1932. See Secretary of the Interior, September 19, 1934, FDR, OFF 300, Box 26.

25. A copy of Cutting's acceptance speech, delivered at the Republican State Convention in Santa Fe on September 24, 1934, can be found in BMC, Box 24.

26. "An Economic Plan for New Mexico," copy in BMC, Box 82.

27. BMC to Olivia James, September 30, 1934; and BMC to Dear Mother, September 30, 1934, BMC, Box 11.

28. BMC to Jouett Elliott, September 12 [1934?], BMC, Box 11.

Chapter 23

1. BMC to Paul Larrazolo, September 22, 1934, BMC, Box 25. See, too, BMC to Gerald P. Nye, October 9, 1934, BMC, Box 26.

2. Clifford McCarthy to Henry Steele Commager, n.d., BMC, Box 19; and BMC to Edward P. Costigan, October 13, 1934, BMC, Box 25. Early in the campaign, Costigan spoke at Raton. Cutting inquired whether he could reserve "the Friday and Saturday before election" to speak in New Mexico. Among those who endorsed Cutting for reelection were Senator Gerald P. Nye and Representative William Lemke, both of North Dakota. Lemke praised Cutting's support of the Frazier-Lemke Refinance Bill calling upon the government to assist in refinancing farm indebtedness. See Severino Trujillo, Jr. to Edgar Puryear, October 11, 1934, BMC, Box 26. Among others, Senator George W. Norris and Burton K. Wheeler also endorsed Cutting.

3. Joseph R. Gallegos to Dennis Chavez, Jr., October 1, 1934, DC, File 394, Box 1.

4. BMC to Phelps Putnam, October 13, 1934, BMC, Box 11.

5. Holm O. Bursum to Herbert Hoover, October 15, 1934, PP, Box 292.

6. BMC, Draft Speech, October 16, 1934, BMC, Box 82. See, too, L. S. Ray to BMC, October 16, 1934, BMC, Box 25. Ray, chairman of the National Legislative Committee of The Disabled Emergency Officers of the World War, specifically delineated Cutting's efforts before concluding, "A study of all beneficial legislation for disabled veterans of all wars, since you have been in the Senate, show[s] that you not only supported such legislation, but led the fight in that body."

7. BMC to Hiram Johnson, October 22, 1934, BMC, Box 26. On October 26, in San Francisco, Johnson delivered a radio address heartily endorsing Cutting's Senate record. Johnson, also seeking reelection, received the president's endorsement. Johnson, like Cutting, had supported Roosevelt in 1932. See Puryear to Johnson, October 24, 1934 [telegram], BMC, Box 26. Puryear

briefed Johnson on Cutting's voting record. See, too, *Sacramento Bee,* October 24, 1934, p. 12 for a story about a letter from Senator Johnson to New Mexico friends urging Cutting's reelection. Apparently James F. Byrnes launched the investigation without consulting other members of his committee including Edward Costigan and William Borah, both friends of Cutting. See Johnson to Puryear, October 24, 1934, BMC, Box 26.

8. Johnson to James A. Farley, October 23, 1934 [telegram], JAF, Box 3. In addition, Johnson phoned Farley to protest administration endeavors to defeat Cutting. See Johnson to Puryear, October 27, 1934, BMC, Box 26. Johnson took time from his campaign to aid Cutting. Roosevelt, learning of Johnson's concern, told Farley to call him and state that Senator Robinson was going to New Mexico because the Democratic leaders there were insisting upon it. See Private File, October 25, 1934, p. 2, JAF, Box 37. It is not clear whether Connally campaigned in New Mexico.

9. Newton Jenkins to Farley, October 27, 1934 [telegram]; and Jenkins to Harold Ickes, October 27, 1934 [telegram]. Copies are in BMC, Box 26. Jenkins, who had family in Albuquerque, was a Chicago attorney and a friend of Harold Ickes.

10. Bull Andrews to BMC, October 21 [1934], BMC, Box 12. The New Mexico State Federation of Labor actively supported Cutting. See L. M. Thompson to Peter L. Rapkoch, October 4, 1934, BMC, Box 25.

11. BMC to Dear Mother, October 28, 1934, BMC, Box 11. Both Senator and Mrs. Johnson felt very close to Cutting. Mrs. Johnson called him her adopted son. See Minnie Johnson to OMC, December 31, 1934 [telegram], BMC, Box 26.

12. BMC to Dear Mother, October 28, 1934; and Robert M. La Follette, Jr. to BMC, October 25, 1934, BMC, Box 11. Puryear to Oscar Chapman, October 31, 1934 [telegram]; and W. P. Neville to Puryear, October 24, 1934, BMC, Box 25. In early October, Senator Charles McNary of Oregon endorsed Cutting, as did William E. Borah of Idaho and Lynn Frazier of North Dakota.

13. Daniel Hastings to BMC, October 24, 1934, BMC, Box 25. Edgar Puryear tried to get Senators Patrick McCarran, Robert Wagner and George W. Norris to speak in New Mexico. He was successful in securing endorsements from Judson King of the National Popular Government League and Albert Beveridge, Jr., the son of the Indiana senator whose dilatory tactics had helped delay the admission of New Mexico and Arizona into the Union.

14. BMC to John D. Markey, November 20, 1934, BMC, Box 25. Markey was a colonel in the Maryland National Guard.

15. BMC to Henry Goddard Leach, October 3, 1934, BMC, Box 18; and *Forum,* October 1934, p. 225.

16. Owen P. White, "Cutting Free," *Collier's* October 27, 1934, pp. 24, 28

and 30; and column by "Diogenes," *Literary Digest*, November 3, 1934, p. 13.

17. *New Republic,* November 7, 1934, pp. 357–58.

18. *Literary Digest,* November 3, 1934, p. 13; Jan Spiess, "Feudalism and Senator Cutting," *American Mercury,* November 1934, pp. 371–74.

19. Farley to Franklin D. Roosevelt, November 3, 1934, JAF, Box 34.

20. Address at Albuquerque, November 3, 1934, BMC, Box 82.

21. W. A. Nicholas, President, New Mexico Petroleum Association, "Senator Cutting and Party Regularity" [speech] n.d. Nicholas delineated Cutting's assistance to the oil industry in New Mexico. Incidentally, as of November 1934 crop production in the state was about twenty percent of normal. Only one county had any possibility of producing enough to support livestock. See *Minutes of Drought Relief Service Meeting,* Kansas City, Missouri, November 3, 1934, pp. 67–74, for an examination of the situation in New Mexico. A copy is in HH, Box 69. See, too, Edward Keating, November 9, 1934, Diary, EK. Keating's special edition of *Labor* stated that "Cutting came through, largely because of labor backing." James R. O'Conner, state secretary of the Veterans Council, in a December 15, 1934 letter to the editor of the *National Tribune,* published in Lubbock, Texas, insisted that the veterans, together with the help of labor and the farmers, elected Cutting.

22. *New Mexican,* November 9 and November 21, 1934. The story on November 21 indicated Cutting's election by 1,291 votes. While Dana Johnson proclaimed Cutting's victory in the *New Mexican,* Dennis Chavez phoned his daughter, Ymelda, on November 8, advising her of his victory predicated upon the counting of two thousand absentee ballots. See Florence Dromey to Severino Trujillo, Jr., November 9, 1934 [telegram], BMC, Scrapbook 3, Box 110. Dromey said that the wire services in Washington indicated Cutting's lead was only 867 votes. Apparently, he trailed Chavez in the first returns carried by the wire services. A *Sacramento Bee* editorial on November 9, 1934 observed "that in the ranks of repudiated senators not a single Progressive, whether Republican, Democratic or Independent, is to be found. It was only the Old Guardsman who suffered repudiation at the hands of the voters." I am grateful to Professor Robert E. Burke for bringing the editorial to my attention. See, too, the Albuquerque *Journal* for November 8, 1934 that reported Marcus Alonzo Hanna's daughter, Ruth Simms, saying, "I traveled 82 miles on election day in my car, transporting Democrats to and from the polls."

23. H. E. Elliott to Peter Rapkoch, November 8, 1934, BMC, Box 25.

24. Brian Boru Dunne to OMC, November 13, 1934 [telegram and letter], BMC, Box 25. On November 9, 1934 in an Associated Press story from Albuquerque dated November 7, the *Boston Post* gave Cutting a scant lead of

654 votes in contrast to earlier returns that had him leading Chavez by 3,000 votes.

25. BMC to Judson King, November 17, 1934, BMC, Box 25; and Miguel Antonio Otero to BMC, November 9, 1934, MAO, Box 3. See, too, Johnson to BMC, November 16, 1934, BMC, Box 27.

26. BMC to Dear Mother, November 11, 1934, BMC, Box 11.

27. M. L. Fox to Henry P. Fletcher, November 12, 1934, copy in BMC, Box 26. Fox was chairman of the New Mexico Federation of Taxpayers Associations. Fletcher was chairman of the Republican National Committee.

28. BMC to A. W. Cameron, November 16, 1934, BMC, Box 25; and Johnson to BMC, November 16, 1934, BMC, Box 27.

29. BMC, Draft Statement, n.d., BMC, Box 11. In a letter to Jouett Elliott, Cutting speculated that "the Democrats must have had four or five times as much money as we did—*plus* the Federal relief agencies." See BMC to Elliott, November 21, 1934, BMC, Box 11.

30. BMC to William E. Borah, November 16, 1934; Caswell S. Neal to BMC, November 9, 1934; and BMC to Neal, November 16, 1934, BMC, Box 11. BMC to J. H. Toulouse, November 30, 1934, BMC, Box 112. Toulouse reported that detectives were engaged in manufacturing evidence, securing "perjured" testimony.

31. BMC to Dear Mother, November 17, 1934; and BMC to Elliott, November 21, 1934, BMC, Box 11.

32. BMC to Dear Mother, November 25, 1934, BMC, Box 11.

33. Puryear to BMC, November 26, 1934 [telegram], BMC, Box 27; and M. B. Smith to Ellison D. Smith, November 28, 1934, copy in BMC, Box 112. M. B. Smith, who had been living in New Mexico, commented most favorably upon Cutting's stature among the people. Smith said that New Mexicans would appreciate the South Carolina senator's assistance in the event of a senate investigation. See, too, the story in *New York Times,* November 27, 1934, reflecting Norris's remarks to Puryear.

34. Puryear to BMC, December 5, 1934 [telegram], BMC, Box 27.

35. Puryear to BMC, December 6, 1934 [telegram], BMC, Box 27. Senators James F. Byrnes and William H. Dieterich of Illinois, the remaining members of the committee did not publicly express their views. Puryear also reported that Chavez did not seem to have a congressman or senator willing to speak out for him. Nor could Puryear find a newspaperman friendly to his cause. See Puryear to BMC, December 8, 1934 [telegram], BMC, Box 27. T.R.B., *New Republic,* December 12, 1934, p. 128. The author said, "If the administration chooses to encourage the effort to unseat Cutting, it has the votes to accomplish it, but it will not, I think, be done without a damaging fight." In his broadcast on December 14, 1934, Boake Carter said that "when

one looks at the money spent in relief funds, public works and other things by the administration to put over Cutting's opponent, Chavez, the charge [of spending too much money to get reelected] gets into the realm of the pot calling the kettle black." A transcript of Carter's broadcast is in BMC, Box 11.

36. BMC to Dear Mother, December 3 and December 12, 1934; T. M. Pepperday to W. T. Kniffen, December 6, 1934 [telegram]; BMC to OMC, December 11, 1934 [telegram]; and BMC to Putnam, December 27, 1934, BMC, Box 11. Cutting did not attend any of the hearings conducted by the canvassing board. Chavez was in Washington throughout the entire period.

37. BMC to Putnam, December 14, 1934, BMC, Box 11.

38. BMC to Puryear, December 18, 1934 [telegram], BMC, Box 12; and BMC to McCarthy, December 16 and December 17, 1934, BMC, Box 32. On December 14, Chavez had a half-hour conference alone with the president. See PPF, Appointment Book, Friday, December 14, 1934, FDR. I am grateful to the late Professor David Shannon for this item.

39. Puryear to BMC, December 15, 1934 [telegram], BMC, Box 27.

40. BMC to McCarthy, December 22, 1934, BMC, Box 32; and BMC to Edward D. Tittman, December 21, 1934, BMC, Box 37.

41. BMC to McCarthy, December 22, 1934, BMC, Box 32; BMC to Putnam, December 17, 1934, BMC, Box 11; BMC to Dear Mother, December 20, 1934, BMC, Box 11; and Puryear to BMC, December 24, 1934 [telegram], BMC, Box 27.

42. Puryear to BMC, December 29, 1934, BMC, Box 27.

43. BMC to Dear Mother, December 30, 1934, BMC, Box 11.

44. The handwritten draft of Cutting's Last Will and Testament, dated December 20, 1934, can be found in BMC, Box 89.

45. A copy of the Certificate of Election can be found in BMC, Box 25; and Charles McNary to BMC, December 31, 1934, BMC, Box 26.

46. In the 1970s, the New Mexico Historical Review published a series of articles examining the 1934 senatorial campaign. Although they make important points, I have not cited them because I have covered the same material utilizing many more primary sources than were available to the authors. See William H. Pickens, "Bronson Cutting vs. Dennis Chavez: Battle of the Patrones in New Mexico, 1934," 46 (1971); T. Phillip Wolf, "Cutting vs. Chavez Re-Examined: A Commentary on Pickens' Analysis," 47 (1972); Pickens, "Cutting vs. Chavez: A Reply to Wolf's Comments," 47 (1972); and G. L. Seligman, Jr., "The Purge That Failed: The 1934 Senatorial Election in New Mexico; Yet Another View," 47 (1972). Both Seligman and Pickens, by analyzing election returns, make the point that in the predominantly Hispanic counties, Chavez ran behind Cutting, while in the east side, the "Little Texas" counties, he ran ahead of Cutting. In the predominantly mining counties, Cutting ran slightly ahead of Chavez.

Chapter 24

1. Hiram W. Johnson to Hiram W. Johnson, Jr., December 22, 1934 in Robert E. Burke, ed., *The Diary Letters of Hiram Johnson*, vol. 6, 1934–1938 (New York: Garland Publishing, Inc., 1983).

2. William E. Dodd, Jr., and Martha Dodd, eds., *Ambassador Dodd's Diary, 1933–1938* (New York: Harcourt, Brace and Company, 1941), pp. 213–14.

3. *New Republic,* January 2, 1935, p. 219; *The Nation,* January 30, 1935, p. 127. T. R. B. was the anonymous columnist for the *New Republic.* R. G. S. was Raymond Gram Swing.

4. Harold L. Ickes, February 29, 1936, Diary, Reel 1, HLI.

5. In addition to Foreign Relations, Cutting served on Irrigation and Reclamation, Manufactures, Military Affairs, Banking and Currency and Public Lands. All were key committees reflecting both his concerns and those of his constituents. Cutting's seat in the Seventy-fourth Congress was in the second row, second seat off the aisle on the diminished Republican side of the senate chamber. Twenty-seven senators were seated on the Republican side.

6. Jefferson D. Atwood to BMC, January 8, 1935, BMC, Box 27. Atwood was one of Cutting's lawyers in this contest.

7. Jouett Elliott to BMC, n.d., BMC, Box 11.

8. Thomas M. McClure to BMC, January 11, 1935, BMC, Box 33; Claude Simpson to BMC, January 14, 1935, BMC, Box 18; BMC to Clara True, January 15, 1935, BMC, Box 11; and Mrs. Edward Israel to BMC, January 16, 1935; BMC to Sam Romero, February 5, 1935, BMC, Box 37; and BMC to Mr. and Mrs. R. B. Turner, January 21, 1935, BMC, Box 34. Senate, Committee on Foreign Relations, *National Boundary Commission, United States and Mexico,* 74th Congress, 1st Session, 1934–1935, Senate Report No. 41. Harry Hopkins told Cutting that "so far as he was concerned," relief would be administered without regard to politics in New Mexico.

9. *Congressional Record,* 74th Congress, 1st Session, January 17, 1935, p. 538; and Atwood to BMC, January 18, 1935 [telegram], BMC, Box 27.

10. Clara Olsen to Herman Baca, January 18, 1935, BMC, Box 11; James Yates to Edgar Puryear, January 18, 1935; Atwood to BMC, January 18, 1935 [telegram], BMC, Box 112; and Atwood to BMC, January 21, 1935, BMC, Box 110.

11. BMC to Mrs. Albert B. Fall, February 1, 1935; BMC to M. L. Fox, February 7, 1935; Maurice Miera to BMC, February 4, 1935 [telegram], BMC, Box 112. Miera assured Cutting that "our evidence in San Miguel County completely disproved allegations." Along with Herman Baca, Miera visited several counties, anticipating investigating committee visits, to insure that nothing untoward occurred.

12. Key Pittman to Franklin D. Roosevelt, January 9, 1935 in Edgar B.

Nixon, ed., *Franklin D. Roosevelt and Foreign Affairs,* vol. 2 (Cambridge: Harvard University Press, 1969), p. 346 n. 1; Press Conference, January 23, 1935, ibid., p. 373 n. 1; and BMC to Raymond Buell, February 1, 1935, BMC, Box 87. Cutting voted for several amendments, all of which were defeated, prior to endorsing the World Court on the final vote, which was 52 to 36, seven less than the requisite two-thirds necessary for ratification.

13. Harold Brayman, "The Daily Mirror of Washington," *Philadelphia Ledger,* February 7, 1935; Notes regarding 1934–35, "The Contest, Role of F.D.R. Efforts at Reconciliation," in Clifford McCarthy to Henry Steele Commager, n.d., BMC, Box 19. See, too, William E. Borah to Ruth Simms, February 5, 1935, WEB, Box 291. Borah, an opponent, thought Cutting "had always been inclined to be in favor of the court." I am grateful to the late Professor David Shannon for this item.

14. BMC to Richard Underwood Johnson, February 7, 1935; and BMC to Thorvold Solberg, June 16, 1934, BMC, Box 22.

15. BMC to Mrs. John Strachey, n.d. [March 1935] [draft telegram]; and BMC to Elliott, April 13, 1935, BMC, Box 11. Story by Karl Schriftgiesser, *Washington Post,* March 14, 1935.

16. BMC to Phelps Putnam, February 17, 1935, BMC, Box 11.

17. Judson King to William Green, February 13, 1935, BMC, Box 112.

18. Fox to Puryear, February 17, 1935, BMC, Box 11; Miera to Puryear, February 12, 1935 [telegram], BMC, Box 112; BMC to Adam Gallejos, February 14, 1935, BMC, Box 112; BMC to Miera, February 20, 1935, BMC, Box 112; and Reed Holloman to BMC, February 21, 1935 [telegram], BMC, Box 27. Holloman, one of Cutting's lawyers, telegraphed that the committee report was "not as vitriolic as expected probably because we blew them up on everything they offered." Meanwhile, the Democratic state administration was removing officials thought to be using their agencies as "a Bronson Cutting political machine." Most notable was Margaret Reeves, state director of FERA, an outstanding administrator with a national reputation. She was replaced by a relative of Dennis Chavez.

19. *Congressional Record,* 74th Congress, 1st Session, February 18, 1935, pp. 2077, 2094–95, 2099.

20. A copy of Chavez's petition, a Senate committee print, is available in DC, 394, Box 3. Miguel Antonio Otero considered Chavez "more gullible, than I supposed, after his four years in Washington." Otero said Chavez did not seem to realize "that Farley's whole purpose, and pretended interest in *Dennis,* was solely a deep laid scheme to side-track him for the Congressional nomination, in the interest of his Tammany associate, John L. Dempsey, and to make it more binding, he had Dennis to push Dempsey's nomination." To achieve this end, Otero said that Farley had "to flatter Dennis into running for

the Senate" and would now "play his cards to the end." See Miguel Antonio Otero to BMC, February 21, 1935, MAO, Box 3.

21. Edward Keating, February 25, 1935, Diary, EK. Keating concluded his entry by noting, "Cutting is a high class gentleman and a genuine liberal."

22. The unnamed Washington publication is quoted in Editorial, "The Chavez Petition," *New Mexican,* March 4, 1935. See, too, E. Dana Johnson to Puryear, March 1, 1935; and Puryear to T. M. Pepperday, February 28, 1935 [telegram], BMC, Box 112.

23. Hiram W. Johnson to Hiram W. Johnson, Jr., March 3, 1935 in Robert E. Burke, ed., *The Diary Letters of Hiram Johnson,* vol. 6, 1934–1938; *Washington, D.C. News,* March 7, 1935; C. L. Russell, Secretary-Treasurer, San Juan Basin Livestock and Grazing Association to BMC, March 6, 1935, BMC, Box 33; Harold L. Ickes to BMC, March 8, 1935, BMC, Box 37; and BMC to Elliott, March 7, 1935, BMC, Box 11. See, too, the correspondence between Charles Chadwick and Cutting regarding the plight of farmers in the Middle Rio Grande Conservancy District. Their requests for loans did not fall within the purview of either the Federal Land Bank at Wichita, Kansas, the Land Bank Commissioner at Wichita, the Production Credit Corporation at Albuquerque or the National Banks and other banking institutions. This correspondence, occurring in March 1935, is in BMC, Box 28.

24. *Congressional Record,* 74th Congress, 1st Session, March 8, 1935, p. 3180; BMC to Edmund Platt, January 10, 1935; and BMC to Harold L. Mack, February 20, 1935, BMC, Box 20. See, too, BMC to Amos Pinchot, March 23, 1935, AP, Box 57.

25. *Congressional Record,* 74th Congress, 1st Session, March 15, 1935, pp. 3694–96, 3724. The vote on the amendment offered by Richard Russell calling for presidential discretion on wage rates was 83 to 2.

26. *Congressional Record,* 74th Congress, 1st Session, March 19, 1935, pp. 3953–55.

27. *Congressional Record,* 74th Congress, 1st Session, March 20, 1935, pp. 4062–63, 4073, March 28, 1935, pp. 4608–11, and April 5, 1935, pp. 5129, 5133–35. See, too, Richard W. Hogue, "Senator Cutting's Last Fight," *New Republic,* May 29, 1935, p. 77. An extended draft, titled "Bronson Cutting's Last Fight," is in BMC, Box 92.

28. BMC to C. P. Gardner, Jr., March 15, 1935, BMC, Box 11; BMC to Pinchot, March 23, 1935, BMC, Box 20; Notes regarding 1934–35 in McCarthy to Commager, n.d., BMC, Box 19. Cutting prepared an outline for a speech on money and banking that he never was able to deliver. See Notes, 1935, BMC, Box 21. See, too, BMC to Putnam, April 18, 1935, BMC, Box 11. In a postscript, Cutting wrote, "I was confidentially informed today that

if I would make a radio speech in favor of the administration banking bill, [the] contest would be dropped!"

29. *New Mexican,* March 13, 1935; and Cutting to Elliott, March 27, 1935, BMC, Box 11.

30. BMC to Ickes, February 21, 1935; Ickes to Robert F. Wagner, February 26, 1935; Harry Leonard to Wagner, April 20, 1935; BMC, Statement, Oil and Gas, n.d.; and E. B. Coolidge to Wagner, April 11, 1935, BMC, Box 37. Leonard was secretary of the New Mexico Oil and Gas Association. Coolidge, chairman of the Montana Oil Conservation Board, said that Cutting's bill (S2398) so "fully and fairly covers all legislation concerning Federal oil and gas prospecting permits that it is necessary or desirable [to] be enacted at this time." Wagner chaired the Senate Committee on Public Lands and Surveys.

31. Miguel Antonio Otero to BMC, March 30, 1935; and BMC to Otero, April 3, 1935, BMC, Box 11. Richard C. Dillon to BMC, April 5, 1935; and Puryear to BMC, December 17, 1934 [telegram], RCD, Box 3. BMC to Dillon, April 13, 1935, BMC, Box 28.

32. Severino Trujillo, Jr. to Herman Baca, April 11, 1935 [telegram], BMC, Box 112; BMC to Dillon, April 13, 1935, BMC, Box 28; and BMC to Elliott, April 13, 1935, BMC, Box 11. While the 8-to-6 vote was partisan, Cutting's motion to dismiss garnered support from a Democrat. There were 11 Democrats and 5 Republicans on the Privileges and Elections Committee. Cutting, who was not present at the hearing, was represented by Huston Thompson, Reed Holloman and Jefferson D. Atwood. Chavez, who was present, was represented by Arthur T. Hannett and Fred E. Wilson. The committee met again on June 4, 1935 after Cutting's death. See Senate *Hearings Before Committee on Privileges and Elections,* regarding Senator from New Mexico, April 10 and June 4, 1935, 74th Congress, 1st Session.

33. BMC to Cyrus McCormick, April 13, 1935, BMC, Box 25; and Miguel Antonio Otero to BMC, April 17, 1935, MAO, Box 3.

34. BMC to Putnam, April 18, 1935, BMC, Box 11; and BMC to J. E. Williams, April 19, 1935, BMC, Box 112. Chavez's lawyers were urging the committee to take testimony in New Mexico examining their charges of fraudulent voting. See Arthur T. Hannett and Fred E. Wilson to Walter F. George, April 16, 1935, copy in BMC, Box 11.

35. Carl Golvin to BMC, April 20, 1935, BMC, Box 28; H. H. Bennett to BMC, April 23, 1935, BMC, Box 39; and Ickes to BMC, May 2, 1935, BMC, Box 11.

36. Atwood to BMC, April 21, 1935, BMC, Box 18; and BMC to Una Fairweather [Mrs. Phelps Putnam], April 23, 1935, BMC, Box 11.

37. OMC, 1935 Itinerary, BMC, Box 92.

Chapter 25

1. BMC to Dear Mother, April 29, 1935, BMC, Box 87.

2. Hiram Johnson to BMC, April 26, 1935 [two telegrams], HJ, Part III, Box 16. See, too, the column by John Snure, Jr., "Greatest Show on Earth," *Washington Times,* May 9, 1935.

3. Jefferson D. Atwood to Edgar Puryear, May 7, 1935, BMC, Box 11. While Cutting was in Santa Fe, the president, at Farley's request, called a conference that was held on the evening of April 30 at the White House. Present were top congressional leaders and cabinet members upon whom the president occasionally relied for political advice. Among the topics discussed was the 1936 presidential election. According to Farley, Roosevelt said that "he did not fear [Huey] Long, [Francis] Townsend and the like" but that he did "have concern about Senator [George W.] Norris, Cutting, Hiram Johnson and Progressives of that type," indicating that perhaps Roosevelt had no further desire to alienate progressive Republicans by endorsing Chavez in the disputed election controversy. See Memorandum, May 1, 1935, JAF, Box 38.

4. George W. Armijo, the Speaker of the New Mexico House of Representatives in 1939 and a close friend, related this account at the dedication of a bust of Cutting on Capitol grounds in May 1939. A pamphlet, "Bronson Cutting 1888–1935," printed by the Rydal Press, contains the proceedings of the dedication program.

5. Miguel Antonio Otero to Willard T. Kniffen, July 7, 1937, MAO, Box 3. Otero was embittered because he was not included in Cutting's will and because he thought the estate should compensate him for stock his wife held in the Santa Fe *New Mexican.* H. H. Dorman, Brian Boru Dunne, Jesus Baca, Herman Baca and possibly George Armijo were among the guests at the dinner party.

6. The air crash and its manifold dimensions is carefully examined in Nick A. Komons, *The Cutting Air Crash: A Case Study in Early Federal Aviation Policy* (Washington, D.C.: U.S. Department of Transportation, Federal Aviation Administration, 1984). The accident is discussed in chapter two. See, too, *Congressional Record,* 74th Congress, 2nd Session, June 20, 1936, pp. 10349–59. The Committee on Commerce, chaired by Senator Royal S. Copeland, conducted an investigation separate from that of the Bureau of Air Commerce. These investigations revealed numerous deficiencies in federal aviation policy as conducted by the bureau. In 1938 with the enactment of the Civil Aeronautics Act, all federal aviation activities were placed in a single independent agency, the Civil Aeronautics Authority.

7. Olivia James, Memorandum in Regard to Accident of May 6, 1935, dated May 22, 1935, BMC, Box 92. Two women, who were strapped in,

were among those killed. Most of the passengers had Hollywood connections. See *Washington Daily News,* May 6, 1935, for initial accounts of the crash.

8. *St. Louis Globe Democrat,* May 7, 1935; and *Chronicle Herald* (Macon, Missouri), May 7, 1935. Both papers carried personal accounts of the crash.

9. Olivia James, Memorandum, May 22, 1935, BMC, Box 92.

10. *Congressional Record,* 74th Congress, 1st Session, May 6, 1935, p. 6999. The committee members were Senators Carl Hatch, Joseph Robinson, Charles McNary, William E. Borah, George W. Norris, Hiram Johnson, Burton K. Wheeler, Robert M. La Follette, Jr., Robert Wagner and Edward Costigan.

11. Edward Keating, May 6, 1935, Diary, EK, Hiram Johnson to Hiram Johnson, Jr., May 13, 1935 in Robert E. Burke, ed., *The Diary Letters of Hiram Johnson,* vol. 6, 1934–1938 (New York: Garland Publishing, Inc., 1983); Harold L. Ickes, *The Secret Diary of Harold L. Ickes: The First Thousand Days, 1933–1936* (New York: Simon and Schuster, 1953), pp. 358–59.

12. *Washington Post,* May 9, 1935; *New York Herald-Tribune,* May 10, 1935.

13. *New York Herald Tribune,* May 11, 1935; *Time,* May 23, 1935; *New Mexican,* May 20, 1935 for the Santa Fe residents at the funeral. Over 1,000 people attended the funeral. At least one newspaper estimated 2,000 in attendance. Fifteen New Mexicans attended the funeral: A. O. McConvery; Dana Johnson; Maurice Miera; Herman Baca; Jesus Baca; Edgar Puryear; Clifford McCarthy; T. M. Pepperday; Brian Boru Dunne; H. H. Dorman; Cyrus McCormick; William Barker; M. A. Otero; Judge M. A. Otero, Jr.; and Severino Trujillo.

14. *New Mexican,* May 8 and May 10, 1935; and Albuquerque *Journal,* May 10 and May 11, 1935. These papers carried stories of memorial services in other communities and reprinted editorials from other New Mexico newspapers. Every New Mexico newspaper carried editorials and full accounts of the local memorial service. See, too, Elias Atencio to OMC, May 9, 1935, BMC, Box 87. Cutting had paid Atencio's way through the University of New Mexico. For tributes broadcast on May 6 by Lowell Thomas and Boake Carter, see BMC, Box 90. While there was talk at the time that Cutting's remains would be transferred for burial in the Santa Fe National Cemetery, supposedly in compliance with his wishes, nothing ever came of it. Cutting remains buried alongside his entire family, with one exception, in Greenwood Cemetery. Only his sister, Justine, was able to avoid the all-encompassing embrace of Olivia Murray Cutting. See *New Mexican,* June 1, 1935.

15. William Neblett to William Gibbs McAdoo, May 11, 1935 [telegram], WGM, Box 405. Neblett informed McAdoo that everyone in New Mexico was "up in arms" over Tingley's intention to appoint Chavez. See, too, Editorial, *Nation,* May 15, 1935, p. 557 for senate reaction to Cutting's death.

I am grateful to the late Professor David Shannon for bringing these items to my attention. For senatorial tributes to Cutting, see the book, "In Memorium: Bronson Murray Cutting, May 1935," BMC, Box 90. All senators wrote a brief inscription at Mrs. Cutting's request. Hiram Johnson wrote, "Bronson was like a son to me and his passing has filled me with an infinite sorrow." The editorial, "The Chavez Appointment," in the *Albuquerque Journal* for May 13, 1935 suggests some of the outrage accompanying the appointment. It was reprinted in other newspapers.

16. Atwood to Puryear, May 7, 1935, BMC, Box 11.

17. *Congressional Record,* 74th Congress, 1st Session, May 21, 1935, pp. 7952–53; Story by Raymond Clapper, *Washington Post,* May 21, 1935. A month later Carl Hatch paid tribute to Cutting in the Senate. See *Congressional Record,* 74th Congress, 1st Session, June 26, 1935, pp. 10166–67. In November 1935, on the occasion of the presentation to the Philippine government of an oil portrait of Cutting, Harry B. Hawes, a former colleague and chief author of the Philippine independence measure that Cutting cosponsored, also eulogized Cutting. See *Congressional Record,* 74th Congress, 2nd Session, January 17, 1936, pp. 555–56.

18. *New York Herald Tribune,* May 12, 1935; and *New Mexican,* June 7, 1935.

19. Senate, *Hearings Before Committee on Privileges and Elections,* Regarding Senator from New Mexico, April 10 and June 4, 1935, 74th Congress, 1st Session, 1934–1935, p. 81ff.; *New York Sun,* June 4, 1935; and *Washington Post,* June 5, 1935. Earlier, prior to May 15, Senators Norris, Johnson and La Follette met with Huston Thompson, Cutting's chief counsel, to discuss Mrs. Cutting's desire that the contest be disposed of in a way so that it would be impossible for any criticism to be leveled at Cutting because of his record and because of allegations that might be made. She also insisted that no action derogatory to Chavez be taken. Although Hiram Johnson wished to proceed further and expose, if possible, the individuals behind the effort to unseat Cutting, all present agreed to abide by Mrs. Cutting's wishes. They were realized in June with the report of the Privileges and Elections Committee. See Johnson to OMC, May 15, 1935 and Atwood to Thompson, May 16, 1935 [telegram], BMC, Box 11.

20. *Congressional Record,* 74th Congress, 1st Session, June 5, 1935, p. 8663. No roll-call vote was taken. For the strategy Thompson intended to pursue, if opposition to dismissal of all the remaining charges arose, based on a discussion with Senator George, see Thompson to OMC, May 17, 1935, and Thompson to Walter F. George, May 18, 1935, copy in BMC, Box 11.

21. *New York Herald Tribune,* June 16, 1935.

22. See, for example, Atwood to Donovan Richardson, May 22, 1935, BMC, Box 11. Maurice Miera did most of the work gathering evidence for

Huston Thompson in preparing his briefs for presentation to the committee. See JCW to Maurice Miera, June 13, 1935, BMC, Box 11.

23. Clara Olsen to OMC, November 15, 1933, BMC, Box 11. Olsen, although discussing the critical situation at El Rito, nevertheless, suggests the significance of Cutting's bequest.

24. A copy of Cutting's will is available in RMLJ, Special Case File, C401. *New York Herald Tribune,* August 26, 1937. Jefferson D. Atwood, Cutting's lawyer and longtime friend, served as attorney for the executors. Deeds for further gifts decided upon by the executors can be found in BMC, Box 89.

25. OMC to Jouett Fall Elliott, August 16 and August 30, 1935, Jouett Fall Elliott addition to ABF. Possibly to assuage the senior Otero as "a small token of a long and close friendship," the family forwarded, as a memento from Cutting's home, four silver salt cellars that had previously belonged to Cutting's father. See Olivia James to Miguel Antonio Otero, November 22, 1925, MAO, Box 3.

26. *New York Times,* August 26, 1937; and *New York Herald Tribune,* August 26, 1937. The transfer tax was determined to be $246,899 in real estate and personal effects.

Chapter 26

1. *New Mexican,* August 5, 1935. The paper carried a column by Ezra Pound entitled "Ez Sez."

2. Clara True to BMC, n.d., BMC, Box 12.

3. Walter White to OMC, May 11, 1935, BMC, Box 89.

4. Baca's tribute to Cutting delivered on June 18, 1935 was published in *Western Labor Journal and Railway Craftsmen,* September 1935, copy in BMC, Box 89.

5. *Washington Daily News,* May 7, 1936; and *Washington Evening Star,* May 7, 1936. A copy of Gordon Gardiner's remarks can be found in BMC, Box 90.

6. For press comment on the lecture series, see *Congressional Record,* 75th Congress, 1st Session, March 31, 1937, pp. 3753–55. Senator Carl Hatch inserted the material, including Norris's remarks. See, too, Richard W. Hogue to George W. Norris, March 30, 1937, GWN, Box 360. Charles A. Beard's address was reprinted in the *Survey Graphic* for April 1937.

7. "Senator Bronson M. Cutting: A Memorial," *University of New Mexico Bulletin No. 305,* vol. 50, No. 6 (May 1, 1937).

8. *New Mexican,* July 28, 1938.

9. The full proceedings, including a listing of contributors, can be found in "Bronson Cutting 1888–1935," a pamphlet published by the Rydal Press, n.d. [1939?]. A copy is available at the University of New Mexico Library,

Department of Special Collections. See, too, Haniel Long, *Piñon Country* (New York: Duell, Sloan and Pearce, 1941), pp. 138–45 for his evaluation of Cutting.

10. *New Mexican,* May 6, 1940 noted how Cutting's memory was honored five years after his death.

11. Quotes are from "The Bronson Cutting Memorial Lectures: A Fore-word by the Executive Committee," copy in Robert M. La Follette, Jr., Special Case File, C401.

NOTE ON SOURCES

Since this biography was prepared largely from primary sources, particularly manuscripts, this essay is a selective one, citing those sources that were most useful in its preparation. Much of the available literature pertaining to Bronson Cutting does not utilize primary sources. While I have read most of this material, I have relied whenever possible on information gleaned from manuscript collections.

The basic source, 112 containers stored in the Manuscript Division of the Library of Congress, is the Bronson Murray Cutting Collection. Olivia Murray Cutting cherished her son's memory and carefully nurtured the collection so that a worthy biography could be prepared. In the late 1930s, Henry Steele Commager was asked to assume this assignment and the collection was made available to him. Others have also attempted a biography. Gustave Seligman wrote his doctoral dissertation at the University of Arizona on Bronson Cutting but did not extensively utilize the papers. While the collection is reasonably complete, it has a few gaps. Cutting did not always keep copies of his correspondence. Many of his letters, particularly family letters, were handwritten, and there is some indication that the collection was pruned, most likely by his mother. For example, Cutting's letters to Ezra Pound are not in the collection. They are available in the Ezra Pound Papers in the Beineke Library at Yale University. And Cutting's letters to Clifford McCarthy are available in the edited form provided by McCarthy. Since Cutting wrote the same thing and at times in greater detail to other friends, the letters did not prove as valuable as I initially thought. Some of the gaps in the collection can be filled in by an examination of other relevant collections.

Also available in the Manuscript Division, the papers of other public officials yielded valuable information. The La Follette Family Papers, most notably those of Robert M. La Follette, Jr., Cutting's closest friend in the Senate, helped fill in some spaces. They contained some Cutting letters unavailable in his papers. Information about Cutting at Groton can be found in diaries written by Theodore Roosevelt, Jr. and George Biddle located in their papers. Other collections that were of value are the papers of Theodore Roosevelt, James A. Farley, Harold L. Ickes, William Borah, Leonard Wood and Roy W. Howard. There are files on the New Mexico papers in the Scripps-Howard chain in this collection. At the National Archives, Record Group 165 yielded information about Cutting's wartime service with the Military Intelligence Division. Much of this material is available only on microfilm. The basic source here is Cutting's lengthy report of February 3, 1919 to the acting director of Military Intelligence. And the University Archives at Harvard contains information, including clippings from Boston papers, pertaining to Cutting and the class of 1910. Most of this material is also available in the Cutting Papers.

Two presidential libraries, those of Franklin D. Roosevelt at Hyde Park, New York, and Herbert Hoover at West Branch, Iowa, contain collections that were of great value. At Hyde Park, the New Mexico folders in the Democratic National Committee files and the president's office file (OFF) focus primarily on the political scene, as do the Emil Hurja Papers. Scattered through the president's official file (OF) are numerous items pertaining to New Mexico projects, conditions in the state and legislative issues that concerned Cutting. The president's personal file (PPF) contains a Bronson Cutting folder. In addition, folders in the Harry Hopkins Papers pertaining to New Mexico yielded information about conditions early in the New Deal.

Similarly at West Branch, the New Mexico folders in the Republican National Committee file proved invaluable. In the secretary's file is a Bronson Cutting folder. The New Mexico material in the state's file and items in the 1928 Campaign file also were of value. Also at the Hoover Library, the Hanford MacNider Papers, which include the Republican Service League file, contain information on New Mexico politics, as do the Nathan William MacChesney Papers. A published item, William Starr Myers and Walter Newton, *The Hoover Administration: A Documented Narrative* (New York: Charles Scribner's Sons, 1936) was a valuable guide allowing me to trace the president's response to legislative matters in which Cutting involved himself.

At the University of New Mexico, the papers of Miguel Antonio Otero contain correspondence unavailable in Cutting's papers. The papers of Richard C. Dillon, Dennis Chavez, Thomas B. Catron and Holm O. Bursum were examined for information pertaining to the political scene. All collections but Catron's yielded significant items, as did the Mary Austin Papers. However, the richer collection of Mary Austin's papers at the Huntington Library was of greater value in delineating Cutting's association with Austin. While I examined other collections at the University of New Mexico, I found only occasional items that bore directly on Cutting. In Santa Fe at the State Records and Archives Center, the Francis Wilson Papers, chiefly his legal files, helped illuminate aspects of their relationship. The papers of the various governors with whom Cutting had contact contain chiefly perfunctory items. More valuable were two collections at the Museum of New Mexico, those of E. Dana Johnson and Edgar Lee Hewett. A biography of Hewett by Beatrice Chauvenet (Santa Fe: Museum of New Mexico Press, 1983) is highly laudatory. But by far the most valuable collection pertaining to New Mexico for my purposes was the Albert B. Fall Collection at the Huntington Library.

Aside from the Cutting Papers, it was the most valuable collection I examined, and it is cited heavily in the text. While I have examined several more collections than those above mentioned, they yielded little material for my purposes. They are cited in the footnotes, usually once, where applicable.

As suggested, published material proved less valuable than primary sources. Newspapers, particularly Cutting's paper, the *Santa Fe New Mexican,* provide an exception and are cited with some frequency. So, too, of course, was the *Congressional Record* and relevant senate documents, notably those pertaining to the 1934 election. A series of articles in the *New Mexico Historical Review,* based primarily on published sources and unpublished graduate student theses, examine the 1934 election. William H. Pickens, "Bronson Cutting vs. Dennis Chavez: Battle of the Patrones in New Mexico, 1934" 46 (1971) and G. L. Seligman, Jr., "The Purge That Failed: The 1934 Senatorial Election in New Mexico: Yet Another View," 47 (1972) are the best of the group. Although Seligman made some use of the Cutting papers, my conclusions pertaining to the role of the Roosevelt administration differ from his. A further discussion, "A Commentary on Pickens's Analysis" by T. Phillip Wolf 47 (1972) and an extended "Cutting vs. Chavez: A Reply to Wolf's Comments" by Pickens 47 (1972) further examine the role of the Roosevelt administration in the election. While Dennis Chavez's papers were unavailable at the time these articles were written, the sources cited are largely those available at the University of New Mexico.

Among the unpublished theses and dissertations, prepared chiefly at the University of New Mexico, that pertain to Cutting, the best by far is Jonathan R. Cunningham's 1940 M.A. thesis. His "political biography" is based primarily on newspapers, but it is further informed by interviews he conducted and correspondence he engaged in with some of Cutting's Groton classmates. Andrea A. Parker's 1969 M.A. thesis, "Arthur Seligman and Bronson Cutting: Coalition Government in New Mexico, 1930–1933," presents a theme that old-line politicians in both parties insisted upon as they prepared for the 1934 election. G. L. Seligman, Jr.'s 1967 dissertation at the University of Arizona, "The Political Career of Bronson Cutting," does not make extensive use of the Cutting collection, a point that pertains to all of the available graduate student work and that consequently made them less valuable than I anticipated.

Among published items, Patricia Cadigan Armstrong, *A Portrait of Bronson Cutting Through His Papers,* Department of Government Bulletin, No. 57 (Albuquerque, 1959) presents a sampling of his letters prior to his entering the Senate. They focus on the New Mexico scene. Other Department of Government bulletins were of assistance in introducing me to the New Mexico political scene. Among them I can mention Charles Judah, "The Republican Party in New Mexico," No. 20 (1949) and also by Judah, "Governor Rich-

NOTE ON SOURCES

ard C. Dillon: A Study in New Mexico Politics," No. 19 (1948). Arthur Thomas Hannett, *Sagebrush Lawyer* (New York: Pageant Press, 1964) presents the former governor's recollection of his intense dislike of Cutting. Robert G. Thompson and Charles Judah, "Arthur T. Hannett, Governor of New Mexico," No. 36 (1950) present a more balanced view of this controversial governor. Hannett also served as Chavez's lawyer in the disputed election of 1934 and 1952. Of greater use was a file of the *New Mexico Tax Bulletins* that provides detailed information on New Mexico's economy during the years Cutting was active in the state. The New Mexico Taxpayers Association, representing the business community, was headed by Herbert Hagerman during most of these years. For an insight into the effects of the Great Depression on the state, most impressive is the essay by William H. Pickens, "The New Deal in New Mexico," in John Braeman *et al.*, eds., *The New Deal, Volume 2: The State and Local Levels* (Columbus: Ohio State University Press, 1975). A political scientist, Jack E. Holmes, *Politics in New Mexico* (Albuquerque: University of New Mexico Press, 1967), provides a good introduction to the political scene in chapters five and six during the years Cutting was active.

Two articles by E.P. Walkiewicz and Hugh Witemeyer examine the Pound-Cutting relationship: "Ezra Pound's Contributions To New Mexican Periodicals and His Relationship With Senator Bronson Cutting," *Paideuma* 9 (1980), 441–459; and "Ezra Pound, Bronson Cutting, and American Issues, 1930–1935" (forthcoming). The authors are editing the Pound-Cutting correspondence for publication.

INDEX

INDEX

INDEX

INDEX